Knowledge, Data and Computer-Assisted Decisions

NATO ASI Series

Advanced Science Institutes Series

A series presenting the results of activities sponsored by the NATO Science Committee, which aims at the dissemination of advanced scientific and technological knowledge, with a view to strengthening links between scientific communities.

The Series is published by an international board of publishers in conjunction with the NATO Scientific Affairs Division

A Life Sciences B Physics	Plenum Publishing Corporation London and New York
C Mathematical and Physical Sciences D Behavioural and Social Sciences E Applied Sciences	Kluwer Academic Publishers Dordrecht, Boston and London
F Computer and Systems Sciences G Ecological Sciences H Cell Biology	Springer-Verlag Berlin Heidelberg New York London Paris Tokyo Hong Kong Barcelona

Series F: Computer and Systems Sciences Vol. 61

Knowledge, Data and Computer-Assisted Decisions

Edited by

Martin Schader

Institut für Informatik
Universität der Bundeswehr Hamburg
D-2000 Hamburg 70, FRG

Wolfgang Gaul

Institut für Entscheidungstheorie
und Unternehmensforschung
Universität Karlsruhe (TH)
D-7500 Karlsruhe, FRG

Springer-Verlag Berlin Heidelberg New York
London Paris Tokyo Hong Kong Barcelona
Published in cooperation with NATO Scientific Affairs Division

Proceedings of the NATO Advanced Research Workshop on Data, Expert Knowledge and Decisions, held in Hamburg, FRG, September 3–5, 1989.

ISBN-13:978-3-642-84220-7 e-ISBN-13:978-3-642-84218-4
DOI: 10.1007/978-3-642-84218-4

Softcover reprint of the hardcover 1st edititon 1990

2145/3140-543210 – Printed on acid-free-paper

Preface

This volume contains revised versions of most of the papers presented at the NATO Advanced Research Workshop on Data, Expert Knowledge and Decisions. The meeting took place at the Universität der Bundeswehr Hamburg in September 1989, with local organization by the Institut für Informatik. It was the second of its kind, following a workshop held at the Universität Karlsruhe in 1987.

The workshop brought together researchers and practitioners interested in current sophisticated data analysis techniques, recent research on computer-assisted decision support, developments of knowledge-based systems, and—this was one of the main issues of the workshop—cross-disciplinary aspects of these fields. Participants in the workshop represented fifteen countries.

The meeting was organized together with

Phipps Arabie, Champaign, U.S.A.,
Alain Bultez, Bruxelles, Belgium,
Edwin Diday, Le Chesnay, France,
Franz-J. Radermacher, Ulm, Germany.

We all, gratefully, take the opportunity to acknowledge support by

NATO Scientific Affairs Division,
Gesellschaft der Freunde und Förderer der Universität der Bundeswehr Hamburg,
Universität der Bundeswehr Hamburg,
Freie und Hansestadt Hamburg,
Aachener Rückversicherungs-gesellschaft,
Hewlett Packard GmbH,
Nixdorf Computer AG,

which made it possible to stage a meeting of this international character. The volume consists of the three parts

- Symbolic Data, Concepts and Learning,
- Data Analysis and Applications,
- Computer-Assisted Decision Support: Integrating, Representing and Processing Knowledge.

A starting point for research aimed at combining data-oriented and knowledge-oriented concepts for computer-assisted decision support could be the handling of symbolic data and learning schemes. Papers in this area of research constitute part one. Part two documents continuing efforts and progress in developing and improving data analysis techniques and their applications. Part three—as the main chapter of this volume—contains various topics from knowledge-based decision support.

The arrangement of the papers into the three parts mentioned was supported by the keywords assigned to each paper by authors and referees.

We thank all authors for their contributions and the referees for their comments. Furthermore, we are indebted to Ulrich Tüshaus who organized typesetting and reproduction of figures. Finally, we would like to thank Hans Wössner from Springer-Verlag for his excellent co-operation.

Hamburg and Karlsruhe, April 1990 — M. Schader and W. Gaul

Contents

Part 1

Symbolic Data, Concepts and Learning

Pyramidal Representation of Symbolic Objects

Paula Brito and Edwin Diday
Université Paris-IX Dauphine
and
INRIA, Le Chesnay, France

Summary

The development of Symbolic Data Analysis comes from the need both to process more general data than classical techniques of Data Analysis do and to develop methods that yield easily interpretable results. In this paper we show how we may enlarge the domain of the data at the input and obtain an "explained" output of a clustering method by adopting notions of Symbolic Data Analysis. We start by recalling the definitions and properties of symbolic objects (Diday (1987b), Diday and Brito (1989)). We shall consider objects that take one and only one value per variable, objects that may present more than one value per variable, and objects such that the definition of a variable depends on the value taken by another one. We then compare notions defined on symbolic objects to similar notions present in the literature (Wille (1982), Ganter (1984), Duquenne (1986), Guénoche (1989)) and show how the former extend the latter. We then recall pyramidal clustering and the main properties of pyramids (Diday (1986)). Pyramids are halfway between hierarchies and lattices: they generalize the former by allowing the presence of non-disjoint clusters, however a pyramid does not present crossing in its graphical representation like lattices do. This intermediate situation led us to adopt pyramids to structure symbolic objects: they allow the definition of a structure on the objects representing inheritance without losing "too much" information, and they have a readable graphical representation. We present an algorithm of "symbolic pyramidal clustering". This algorithm may apply to a data set of some kind of symbolic objects considering even the case of dependence between variables. As output it yields a pyramid whose clusters are represented by symbolic objects meeting a given property. The inheritance structure between the clusters will then allow for the generation of rules.

1 Introduction

Data Analysis has mainly been developed since the sixties to answer the need to process large data sets by using the increasing performance of computing facilities. In Automatic Classification, hierarchical and non-hierarchical methods have been developed allowing to cluster large data sets where n objects in rows take values on p variables in columns.

Nowadays, data analysts are confronted with new challenges: on the one hand, they are asked to process data that go beyond the classical framework by considering both objects defined by intention and objects which are complex due to the variable structure, taking advantage of the recent advances in artificial intelligence; on the other hand, they are asked for self-explanatory outputs: the conclusions of the analysis should be expressed in terms that are understandable by the outside user.

NATO ASI Series, Vol. F 61
Knowledge, Data and Computer-Assisted Decisions
Edited by M. Schader and W. Gaul

The now classical techniques of Data Analysis are not prepared to answer these problems. New formalizations are needed, classical methods have to be extended and new criteria to be conceived. A new prespective in Data Analysis is necessary. The development of Symbolic Data Analysis arises in this context.

The need to represent objects defined by intention led to the introduction of symbolic objects (Diday (1987b), Diday and Brito (1989)) which extend the usual objects processed in classical data analysis. Generally speaking, a symbolic object is a description which is expressed by means of a conjunction of events in terms of the values taken by the variables. Symbolic objects differ from numerical objects (represented and treated as vectors of $\mathbb{R}^p$) both at the description and at the syntactic level. At the description level, the main differences come both from the fact that each variable may take a disjunction of values for a given object and that links between variable values may be present; at the syntactic level it should be stressed that symbolic objects are conceived to represent knowledge and not only single observations. As a consequence, differences arise also at the processing level: here, the focus is made on the duality intention/extension of a symbolic object and generalization/specialization techniques are widely used.

The problem of looking simultaneously for the clusters and their representation has been settled in Diday (1972), several kinds of representation have been used (see Diday and Simon (1976)), in Diday (1976) a logical representation of clusters is proposed. As regards "conceptual clustering" algorithms based on the dynamical clustering method, mention should be made to Diday, Govaert, Lechevallier and Sidi (1980), and then Michalsky, Diday and Stepp (1981). In what concerns rule generation, we may cite Quinqueton and Sallantin (1986), Ho Tu Bao, Diday and Summa (1987), H. Ralambondrainy (1987) and Guénoche (1987), Gascuel (1987); Guigues and Duquenne (1986), Ganascia (1987) in the same perspective, but using lattices and being more exhaustive; Wille (1982) for the graphical representation of "concepts" by lattices.

We shall start by recalling the main definitions of symbolic objects and show how they allow the representation of data that go beyond the framework of classical data sets. Several properties are then recalled, and a comparision is made with close notions used by other authors.

We then present an algorithm of Symbolic Pyramidal Clustering. Pyramids, introduced by Diday (1984) and further studied by Bertrand (1986) and Durand (1988), constitute an extension of hierarchical clustering, leading to overlapping classes instead of partitions. The pyramidal structure seems suitable to cluster symbolic objects. Being halfway between hierarchies and lattices, they allow for a representation of inheritance without a too important loss of information, having a readable graphical representation, since it presents no crossing. The algorithm we propose may apply to several kinds of symbolic objects and take account of background knowledge in the form of taxonomies on the variables. At the output, together with the pyramidal structure, we obtain a description of each cluster, by means of symbolic objects. The fact that clusters are represented by conjunctions of events and that there is an inheritance structure between them leads to the definition of methods to generate rules.

2 The Symbolic Objects

A symbolic object is defined as a conjunction of properties on the values taken by the variables. A variable y is, by definition, a mapping $y : \Omega \rightarrow O$, where Ω is the set of objects and O the observation set of y.

Notice that each row in the data array which characterizes an object may be expressed as a conjunction of logical propositions which we call "event". We then say that Ω is the set of "elementary objects".

A symbolic object s is said to be defined "by intention" when it is expressed under its logical form, by the symbolic expression representing it. The set of elementary objects in Ω verifying it constitutes its extension, and is denoted $|s|_\Omega$.

2.1 Different Kinds of Symbolic Objects

2.1.1 The Elementary Events

Let $y_1, \ldots, y_p$ be p variables, defined on a set Ω and taking its values in $O_1, \ldots, O_p$. Ω can be considered as a subset of $\Omega' = O_1 \times \ldots \times O_p$, the set of all possible elementary objects.

An elementary event denoted $e_i = [y_i = V_i]$ where $V_i \subset O_i$ is a predicate expressing that: "variable y_i takes its value in V_i". It follows that $[y_i = V_i]$ is the logical union of the events $[y_i = \{v_j\}]$ for all v_j in V_i. The extension of e_i is $|e_i|_\Omega = \{\omega \in \Omega \colon\ y_i(\omega) \in V_i\}$.

2.1.2 Assertion Objects

An assertion object is an event made up of a conjunction of events of the kind $[y_i = V_i]$. It is denoted $a = [y_1 = V_1] \wedge \ldots \wedge [y_q = V_q]$.

The set of objects of Ω which satisfy the event defined by the assertion object a is denoted $|a|_\Omega$ and constitutes the definition by extension of a in Ω. Hence we have:

$$|a|_\Omega = \{\omega \in \Omega \colon\ y_i(\omega) \in V_i \quad \text{for} \quad i = 1, \ldots, q\}.$$

The elementary objects are special assertion objects, induced from the elements of Ω by the mapping $\varphi\colon\ \Omega \rightarrow S : \varphi(\omega) = [y_1 = y_1(\omega)] \wedge \ldots \wedge [y_p = y_p(\omega)]$.

EXAMPLE:

Let Ω be a set of mushrooms, described by two variables: y_1 = "size of the stem" and y_2 = "color of the hat". An elementary object such that $y_1 = 1$ and $y_2 = \mathit{white}$ may be expressed by means of the following assertion object:

$$a = [y_1 = 1] \wedge [y_2 = \mathit{white}].$$

Let us now consider a set Ω reduced to the three following objects: $\omega_1 = [y_1 = 3] \wedge [y2 = \mathit{black}]$; $\omega_2 = [y_1 = 2] \wedge [y_2 = \mathit{white}]$; $\omega_3 = [y_1 = 1] \wedge [y_2 = \mathit{white}]$. The extension of the assertion object $a = [y_1 = \{2, 3\}] \wedge [y_2 = \{\mathit{white}, \mathit{black}\}]$ is $|a|_\Omega = \{\omega_1, \omega_2\}$. Formally, let $y = (y'_1, \ldots, y'_q)$ with $y'_i \in \{y_1, \ldots, y_p\}$ and $V = (V'_1, \ldots, V'_q) \subset O'_1 \times \ldots \times O'_q$, where $y'_i \colon\ \Omega \rightarrow O'_i$. An assertion object $a = [y'_1 = V'_1] \wedge \ldots \wedge [y'_q = V'_q]$ may be considered as a mapping $f_{yV} : \Omega \rightarrow \{\mathit{true}, \mathit{false}\}$ such that $f_{yV}(u) = \mathit{true}$ iff $\forall i = 1, \ldots, q$ we have $y'_i(u) \in V'_i$. Therefore, $|a|_\Omega = f^{-1}{}_{yV}(\mathit{true})$.

2.1.3 Assertion Objects in the Presence of Logical Dependencies Between Variables

Often in practice situations arise when some variables may not apply to some individuals, depending on the values taken by other variables on those individuals. Suppose we are describing computers and consider the two variables y_1 = "presence of computers" and y_2 = "type of computers". Obviously, the second variable applies iff the value for the first one is *yes*, should it be *no*, the second variable would be meaningless.

Let y_i, y_j be two variables such that y_j applies iff y_i takes values within a given set. Formally, if $y_i \colon \Omega \to O_i$ and if y_j may only apply to those $\omega \in \Omega$ for which $y_i(\omega) \in Q_i \subset O_i$, then $y_j \colon {y_i}^{-1}(Q_i) \to O_j$.

When such dependencies are present, the interpretation of an assertion object is not clear, and determining its extension is no longer straightforward. Let us go back to our example and consider the two following assertion objects

$$a_1 = [y_1 = \{yes\}] \wedge [y_2 = \{a, b\}] \quad \text{and} \quad a_2 = [y_1 = \{yes, no\}] \wedge [y_2 = \{a, b\}].$$

Clearly, $|a_1|_\Omega$ consists of all offices in Ω with computers of types a or b present, that is offices ω_i such that $(y_1, y_2)(\omega_i) \in \{(yes, a), (yes, b)\}$. What can we say in the case of a_2? Its extension is no longer given by the crossproduct of the y_1 and y_2 sets of values; for instance, the pair (no,a) is meaningless. $|a_2|_\Omega$ consists of offices either without computers or with computers of types a or b.

To formalize this case, we shall consider a new variable y_{12}, made from the previous two, and which globally describes the "computer situation", taking values in $\{no\} \cup \{yes\} \times \{computer\ types\}$.

The assertion object a_2 is now written in the form $a_2' = [y_{12} = \{no, (yes, a), (yes, b)\}]$ whose extension is not ambiguous. In general, if $y_i \colon \Omega \to O_i$, $O_i = Q_i \cup R_i$, $y_j \colon {y_i}^{-1}(Q_i) \to O_j$, the new variable y_{ij} is such that $y_{ij} \colon \Omega \to O_{ij} = R_i \cup (Q_i \times O_j)$. This approach has the two following advantages:

- It avoids the introduction—necessarily forced—of supplementary values to code the non-definition of a variable, such as "0", "$\emptyset$", etc.

- It avoids ambiguity in the definition of the extension of a symbolic object, since y_{ij} always applies and the elements of O_{ij} are mutually exclusive.

On the other hand, the two following disadvantages may be put forward:

- Non-existence of a consistent algebraic structure on O_{ij}, since it is the union of sets contained in spaces of different dimensions. Algebraic operations, when necessary, may however be defined (i) within $Q_i \times O_j$; (ii) in O_i, after projection on Q_i of the elements belonging to $Q_i \times O_j$.

- The loss of "individuality" of the variables. Notice, however, that their values may be obtained by simple projection (processing component by component) whenever it is necessary to process each variable separately.

2.2 Order, Inheritance, Union, Intersection and Lattice of Symbolic Objects

We summarize several definitions and properties which have been given in Diday (1987b); proofs of the propositions can be found in the same reference.

To simplify notation, let us suppose we are given a set of symbolic objects, S, defined on a set Ω characterized by the variables $y_i : \Omega \to O_i$. We suppose that S is the set of assertion objects. The elementary symbolic objects, induced from the elements of Ω also belong to S. In what follows we shall suppose that the extension of $\varphi(\omega)$ reduces to ω (that is, no pair of different elements of Ω may take the same value on all variables). We may then identify Ω with $\varphi(\Omega) \subset S$.

The symbolic extension of a symbolic object $s \in S$ in Ω will be denoted s' and it consists of the elementary symbolic objects $\varphi(\omega) \in S$ such that $\omega \in \Omega$ belongs to the extension of s in Ω. In other words: $s' = \{\varphi(\omega) \in \Omega : \omega \in |s|_\Omega\}$. We may now define an order on the symbolic objects. We shall adopt the following simplification rules:

1. $a \wedge [y_i = O_i]{=}a$

2. $[y_i = v_i] \wedge [y_i = V_i] = [y_i = v_i]$ if $v_i \subset V_i$.

Definition of symbolic order
$\forall s_1, s_2 \in S$, we say that $s_1 \leq s_2$ if and only if ${s_1}' \subseteq {s_2}'$. The inclusion being an order on the parts of Ω, the inequality $\leq$ just introduced is an order on the symbolic objects; the name "symbolic order" is then justified.

Definition of inheritance and generalization
$\forall s_1, s_2 \in S$, we say that s_1 inherits from s_2 and that s_2 is more general than s_1 if and only if $s_1 \leq s_2$. The symbolic objects s such that $s \geq s_1$ (resp. $s \leq s_1$) are the ascendents (resp. the descendents) of s_1.

Definition of the union and the intersection of symbolic objects
We define $s_1 \cup s_2$ (resp. $s_1 \cap s_2$) as the conjunction of all symbolic objects of S whose extension contains the set of the symbolic objects of ${s_1}'$ and ${s_2}'$ (resp. the symbolic objects belonging both to ${s_1}'$ and ${s_2}'$).

Notice that, by using simplifications we obtain an equivalent definition by replacing "symbolic object" by "elementary event". Also notice that the union and the intersection are commutative and associative. The commutativity is obvious. The associativity comes from the fact that $(s_1 \cup s_2) \cup s_3 =$ {conjunction of the elementary events whose extension contains ${s_1}' \cup {s_2}'$ and ${s_3}'$} $=$ {conjunction of the elementary events whose extension contains s'_1 and ${s_2}' \cup {s_3}'$} $= s_1 \cup (s_2 \cup s_3)$. The associativity of the intersection is proved in exactly the same way.

PROPOSITION 1:

1. The union and the intersection of symbolic objects always exist, and they are commutative and associative.

2. If $s = s_1 \cup s_2$ it doesn't necessarily follow that $s' = {s_1}' \cup {s_2}'$ but only that $s' \supseteq ({s_1}' \cup {s_2}')$. On the other hand, if $s = s_1 \cap s_2$ then $s' = ({s_1}' \cap {s_2}')$.

3. S is a lattice for the symbolic order. The upper bound of every pair of elements of S is their union, the lower bound is their intersection.

Given a symbolic object s, let $d(s)$ be the set of elementary events whose conjunction defines s. Also let $c(s)$ be the set of all elementary events whose symbolic extension contains s' and s^c the conjunction of all elements of $c(s)$.

PROPOSITION 2:

1. $d(s^c) = c(s)$ and $(s^c)' = s'$.

2. $s^c = \{\cup\varphi(\omega_i) \colon \omega_i \in |s|_\Omega\}$.

3. $s^c = \{\cap e_i \colon e_i \in c(s)\}$.

EXAMPLE:
Consider the following data:

	y_1	y_2	y_3	y_4
ω_1	1	0	0	0
ω_2	1	0	1	0
ω_3	1	1	0	1
ω_4	1	1	1	1
ω_5	0	1	0	0

The set of symbolic objects $S_1 \subset S$ is: $s_i = [y_i = 1]$ for $i = 1,4$; $s_{4+i} = \varphi(\omega_i)$ for $i = 1,5$ and $[y_i = O_i], i = 1,4$. We then have: $s_5 \leq s_1$ for $s'_5 = \{\varphi(\omega_1)\} \subset s'_1 = \{\varphi(\omega_1), \varphi(\omega_2), \varphi(\omega_3), \varphi(\omega_4)\}$. $s_1 \cup s_2 = [y_1 = O_1] \wedge [y_2 = O_2] \wedge [y_3 = O_3] \wedge [y_4 = O_4]$ and $s_1 \cap s_2 = s_1 \wedge s_2 \wedge s_4$. We also have $s_4{}^c = \varphi(\omega_3) \cup \varphi(\omega_4) = [y_1 = 1] \wedge [y_2 = 1] \wedge [y_4 = 1]$, so $d(s_4) = \{[y_4 = 1]\} \neq c(s_4) = \{s_1, s_2, s_4\}$.

2.3 Properties of Symbolic Objects

2.3.1 Refinement of a Symbolic Object

The refinement of $s \in S$ is measured by the deviation between the union of the extensions of the elementary events that define it, $\cup e_i'(s)$, and its extension $s' = \cap e_i'(s)$. It is measured by:

$$R(s) = \frac{1}{\text{card } \Omega} \text{card } (\cup e_i'(s) - \cap e_i'(s)).$$

We say that s is refined if $R(s) = 0$. Considering the above example, we have for $s = [y_1 = 1] \wedge [y_2 = 1]$, $R(s) = 1/5 \text{ card } (\Omega - \{\omega_3, \omega_4\}) = 3/5$.

2.3.2 Simplicity of a Symbolic Object

The simplicity of a symbolic object $s \in S$ is the smallest number $Si(s)$ of elementary events such that the extension of their conjunction coincides with the extension of s. An object s is said to be simple if card $d(s) = Si(s)$. In the example above, we have $Si(s) = 1$ for $s = [y_1 = 1] \wedge [y_2 = 1] \wedge [y_4 = 1]$ since $[y_4 = 1]' = s' = \{\omega_3, \omega_4\}$, so s is not simple.

2.3.3 Completeness of a Symbolic Object

If I see white dogs in my street and I state "I see dogs", my statement doesn't describe the dogs in a complete way, since I don't say that they are white. This is the idea underlying the notion of "completeness" of a symbolic object.

Formally speaking, we are led to measure the deviation between a symbolic object s and s^c, that is, between $d(s)$ and $c(s)$ (i.e., between the set of elementary events whose conjunction s consists of, and the set of all elementary events such that their conjunction has an extension containing s'). Taking the example above, we see that $s_4 = [y_4 = 1]$, $d(s_4) = \{s_4\}, c(s4) = \{s_1, s_2, s_4\}$.

How should the deviation between $d(s)$ and $c(s)$ be measured? Since $c(s)$ is always larger, the complementary of $d(s)$ in $c(s)$, denoted $c(s) - d(s)$ exists, and hence we can measure the completeness by the two following criteria: $C_1(s) = \text{card}\,(c(s)-d(s)); C_2(s) = \text{card}\,\{(\wedge e_i)' \colon\ e_i \in c(s)-d(s)\}$. In the previous example, $c(s_4)-d(s_4) = \{s_1, s_2\}$, therefore $C_1(s) = 2$ and $C_2(s) = \text{card}\,(s_1 \wedge s_2)' = 2$.

Definition of a complete symbolic object
A symbolic object s is complete if and only if $c(s) = d(s)$. More intuitively, it means that an object is complete iff the properties which characterize its extension are exactly those whose conjunction defines the object. It follows from this definition that a symbolic object s is complete if and only if $C_1(s) = 0$ (or $C_2(s) = 0$). Hence the elementary objects belonging to $\varphi(\Omega)$ are complete.

PROPOSITION 3:
$\forall s \in S, s^c$ is complete (that is $d(s^c) = c(s^c)$).

PROPOSITION 4:

1. If a symbolic object s is the union or the intersection of symbolic objects, then s is complete.

2. The set of all complete symbolic objects is a lattice for the symbolic order.

In the case of a binary data array, algorithms for the obtention of complete symbolic objects may be found in Ganter (1984) and Guénoche (1989).

It often happens that the objects being processed are not individuals but sets of individuals, treated as a whole. Take, for instance, the description of biological species, of illnesses, and so on. In these cases, each entry of the data array takes account of the variability within the set, that is, each variable may present more than one value. The data array is then no longer a data array of elementary objects, but one of assertion objects. It becomes essential to define the extension of a symbolic object on such a data array. One possible choice is:

DEFINITION:
The extension of an assertion s on a set S of assertion objects is the set of those $a \in S$ such that their extension in Ω' is included in the extension of s in Ω': $|s|_S = \{a \in S : |a|_{\Omega'} \subset |s|_{\Omega'}\}$. To define completeness in this case, we must first define $c(s)$. Let $|s|_S = \{a_j = \wedge[y_i = V_i^j]\}$. We then define $c(s) =$ set of all elementary events $[y_i = W_i]$ such that $W_i = \cup_j V_i^j$, $a_j \in |s|_S$. s is said to be complete iff $c(s) = d(s)$.

2.4 Complete Symbolic Objects and Concepts—Where They Meet and Where They Differ

The notion of "concept" is rather imprecise and even polemic. There are many definitions of what a concept is and endless discussions may take place to decide what is a concept and what isn't one. Generally authors use this term to refer both to the concept and to its representation. In Michalski (1980) we may find: "... the concepts characterizing clusters are single conjunctive statements involving relations on variables which describe the entities". Matheus (1987) starts by saying that a concept is "a knowledge structure used to represent general information", to eventually propose his own definition: "a concept is a purposeful description of a possibly fuzzy class of individuals". He himself quotes other authors: "a concept is a predicate that partitions the instance space into positive and negative subsets" (Cohen and Feigenbaum (1982)); "a concept is a classification rule that partitions a domain of instances into those which satisfy the rule and those that do not" (Utgoff (1986)); "a concept is defined as a predicate over some universe of instances, and thus characterizes some subset of the instances" (Mitchell et al. (1986)).

Wille (1982) and Ganter (1984) formalize the notion of concept. In a certain measure, the notion of complete symbolic object meets the notion of concept as defined by these authors, but it is more general, as we shall see. They define a concept as a pair (A, B) where A is a set of objects and B a set of attributes such that B is the set of attributes commonly possessed by all objects in A, and A is the set of all objects presenting all attributes in B. A is called the extent and B the intent of the concept (A, B). This is what Matheus (1987) refers to as the classical or defining features approach definition of a concept. The case of nominal variables is treated by considering each modality $m_i{}^j$ of each variable y_i as a binary attribute, and is so reduced to the former case. This definition of a concept meets the notion of complete symbolic object, when we restrict ourselves to events of the form

$$[y_i = \{m_i{}^j\}]. \tag{1}$$

Let us compare the two notions on a small example:

	y_1	y_2	y_3
ω_1	1	1	1
ω_2	2	2	3
ω_3	1	1	3
ω_4	1	2	2

Objects ω_1, ω_3 form the extent of a concept, whose intent is $B = \{[y_1 = 1], [y_2 = 1]\}$. Notice that to B corresponds the symbolic object $s = [y_1 = 1] \wedge [y_2 = 1]$. This symbolic object is complete iff we only consider events of the form (1). However, if we place ourselves in the space of assertion objects, that is, if we consider events $[y_i = V_i]$, where card V_i is not necessarily 1, then s is no longer complete, and the corresponding complete symbolic object is $s = [y_1 = 1] \wedge [y_2 = 1] \wedge [y_3 = \{1, 3\}]$. (Notice that this is the symbolic union of $\varphi(\omega_1)$ and $\varphi(\omega_3)$).

We can still go a step further, by taking account of background knowledge. It is often the case that a taxonomy is defined on the values taken by a variable. This taxonomic structure will then give a precise meaning to an event of the form $[y_i = \{m_i{}^1, \ldots, m_i{}^j\}]$ (which logically corresponds to the disjunction of the j events $[y_i = \{m_i{}^h\}], h = 1, \ldots, j$)

by replacing $\{m_i^1, \ldots, m_i^j\}$ by the value of the lowest node of the taxonomy it is contained in. This will reduce the set of complete symbolic objects, but will give a more concise interpretation of those obtained.

3 Symbolic Pyramidal Clustering

3.1 Basic Notions About Pyramids

We shall start by recalling that pyramids constitute an extension of hierarchical clustering, presenting overlapping classes instead of partitions.

DEFINITION:
Let Ω be a finite set of objects and P a set of non-empty parts of Ω (called clusters). P is a pyramid if

1. $\Omega \in P$;

2. $\forall \omega \in \Omega, \{\omega\} \in P$;

3. $\forall (p, p') \in P^2$ we have $p \cap p' = \emptyset$ or $p \cap p' \in P$;

4. There exists an order θ such that each cluster of P is an interval of θ.

The notions of successor and predecessor in a pyramid are just an extension of the corresponding notions for hierarchies: given a pyramid P, we say that $p \in P$ is a successor of $p' \in P$ if $p \subset p'$ (strictly) and there exists no $p'' \neq p, p'' \neq p'$ such that $p \subset p'' \subset p'$ (strictly). We also say that p' is a predecessor of p.

The graphic representation of the pyramid is possible because each cluster is an interval of an order θ and—as it can be shown—each element of P has at most two predecessors.

Why to choose pyramids to structure symbolic objects?

Being somehow halfway between hierarchies and lattices, pyramids allow the definition of a structure on the objects representing inheritance, without a too big loss of information, and they have a readable graphical representation, since it contains no intersecting lines.

3.2 The Method

The method we propose aims at building a pyramid P on a set of objects. Each cluster of this pyramid should fit at best the extension of a complete symbolic object. In other words, we build a pyramid bottom-up, representing each cluster by a symbolic object whose extension deviates as little as possible from the set of objects it is composed of.

The method we present in this paper differs from numerical pyramidal clustering in that it is not based upon the previous definition of a dissimilarity index between the objects. By using symbolic criteria, it allows giving a precise meaning to the clusters of the obtained pyramid.

3.2.1 The Objects

In a first approach, we shall just consider qualitative variables, $y_i: \Omega \rightarrow O_i$, where O_i is a finite set, $i = 1, \ldots, p$. As input data, we shall consider the three kinds of objects described above:

- Elementary Objects—The data consist of a $n \times p$ data array where each object (row) takes one and only one value on each variable (column).
- Assertion Objects—In this case, each line of the data array corresponds to an assertion object, and describes not a single object but a set of objects.
- Assertion Objects with Logical Dependencies Between Variables—We consider objects for which the application of some variables depends on the values taken by other variables.

Notice that the usual techniques of Data Analysis only process data of the first type, the approach we propose constitutes thus an extension towards more general data.

3.2.2 The Algorithm

Let S be the finite set of objects being clustered, $S = \{a_1, \ldots, a_n\}$. We recall the conditions that must be met at each step of the agglomerative algorithm (cf. Diday (1986)):

- Each time a cluster is formed by merging some clusters, an order on those clusters is associated;
- Two clusters cannot be merged if their union is not an interval;
- Let i and j be extreme elements of the interval of S associated to a cluster h; no cluster can be connected to a cluster included in h which does not contain either i or j.

Starting with the n singletons $\{a_i\}$, $i = 1, \ldots, n$, we aggregate, at each step, the clusters P_j verifying the aggregation conditions, such that $Q = \cup P_j$ contains the extension of a new complete symbolic object s and $D = \text{card}\,(Q - |s|_\Omega)$ is minimal.

If there exists a set of clusters $\{P_j\}$ verifying the aggregation conditions such that $Q = \cup P_j$ is the extension of a new complete symbolic object s ($D = 0$), cluster Q is formed and represented by s. If no such set exists, we form a cluster containing the extension of some new complete symbolic object s such that D is minimal; in this case the new cluster is represented by a disjunction $s \vee (s_1 \vee \ldots \vee s_h)$ where $s_1, \ldots, s_h$ account for the elements not belonging to the extension of s.

The algorithm comes to an end when $S \in P$ or, $\forall s$ such that s is a complete symbolic object $\exists Q \in P\colon\ Q \supset |s|_S$. Notice that the pyramid P obtained at the end may be such that $S \notin P$. In this case, the condition 1. of the definition of a pyramid is not met, the pyramid is said to be incomplete.

The set $\{P_j\}$ of the clusters meeting the aggregation conditions and minimizing D will be, in general, not unique. This leads us to the definition of a second criterion based on the generality degree.

DEFINITION:
Consider, as before, $y_i : \Omega \to O_i$, $i = 1, \ldots, p$. The generality degree is a mapping $G: S \to [0,1]$, such that, if $s = \wedge[y_i = V_i]$,

$$G(s) = \prod_{i=1}^{p} \frac{\text{card } V_i}{\text{card } O_i}.$$

Among the clusters minimizing D, we shall aggregate those minimizing $G(s)$, where s is the symbolic object describing the cluster. The pyramid will be indexed by $G(s)$, that is if Q is represented by s, the height of Q is $G(s)$.

EXAMPLE:
Consider the following data array

	y_1	y_2	y_3	y_4
ω_1	1	1	1	2
ω_2	1	2	1	3
ω_3	1	2	2	2
ω_4	2	1	1	2
ω_5	3	3	2	1

where $O_1 = O_2 = O_4 = \{1,2,3\}, O_3 = \{1,2\}$. The clusters of the pyramid and their representing symbolic objects are:

$$\begin{aligned}
P_1 &= \{\omega_1, \omega_4\}, s_1 = [y_1 = \{1,2\}] \wedge [y_2 = 1] \wedge [y_3 = 1] \wedge [y_4 = 2] \\
P_2 &= \{\omega_1, \omega_2\}, s_2 = [y_1 = 1] \wedge [y_2 = \{1,2\}] \wedge [y_3 = 1] \wedge [y_4 = \{2,3\}] \\
P_3 &= \{\omega_2, \omega_3\}, s_3 = [y_1 = 1] \wedge [y_2 = 2] \wedge [y_4 = \{2,3\}] \\
P_4 &= \{\omega_3, \omega_5\}, s_4 = [y_1 = \{1,3\}] \wedge [y_2 = \{2,3\}] \wedge [y_3 = 2] \wedge [y_4 = \{1,2\}] \\
P_5 &= P_1 \cup P_2, s_5 = [y_1 = \{1,2\}] \wedge [y_2 = \{1,2\}] \wedge [y_3 = 1] \wedge [y_4 = \{2,3\}] \\
P_6 &= P_2 \cup P_3, s_6 = [y_1 = 1] \wedge [y_2 = \{1,2\}] \wedge [y_4 = \{2,3\}] \\
P_7 &= P_5 \cup P_6, s_7 = [y_1 = \{1,2\}] \wedge [y_2 = \{1,2\}] \wedge [y_4 = \{2,3\}] \\
P_8 &= P_3 \cup P_4, s_8 = [y_1 = \{1,3\}] \wedge [y_2 = \{2,3\}] \\
P_9 &= P_6 \cup P_8, s_9 = [y_1 = \{1,3\}] \\
P_{10} &= P_7 \cup P_9, s_{10} = \wedge[y_i = O_i].
\end{aligned}$$

3.3 Rule Generation

The pyramidal clustering method described above induces an inheritance structure between clusters, in the sense that objects belonging to a given cluster meet the properties associated to its predecessors. This inheritance structure will then allow for the generation of rules, by two different methods.

3.3.1 Splitting Method

Let P_1, P_2, Q be clusters of the obtained pyramid, $Q = P_1 \cup P_2$ and s_1, s_2, s, respectively, the symbolic objects representing them. We can then write: $s \Rightarrow s_1 \vee s_2$.

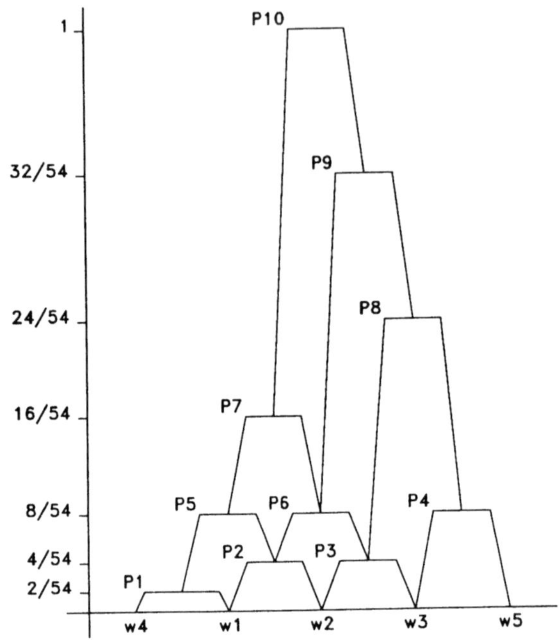

Figure 1: Graphical Representation of the Pyramid Obtained in the Example Above

EXAMPLE:
In the previous example, we have $P_5 = P_1 \cup P_2$, so $s_5 \Rightarrow s_1 \vee s_2$, namely $[y_1 = \{1,2\}] \wedge [y_2 = \{1,2\}] \wedge [y_3 = 1] \wedge [y_4 = \{2,3\}] \Rightarrow ([y_1 = \{1,2\}] \wedge [y_2 = 1] \wedge [y_3 = 1] \wedge [y_4 = 2]) \vee ([y_1 = 1] \wedge [y_2 = \{1,2\}] \wedge [y_3 = 1] \wedge [y_4 = \{2,3\}])$. Taking into account the fact that $(a \wedge b \Rightarrow a \wedge c) \Leftrightarrow (a \wedge b \Rightarrow c)$ this rule may be simplified into $s_5 \Rightarrow ([y_2 = 1] \wedge [y_4 = 2]) \vee [y_1 = 1]$.

3.3.2 Merging Method

Let $P_1, P_2 \in P$ be such that $P_{12} = P_1 \cap P_2 \neq \emptyset$, and let s_{12}, s_1, s_2, respectively, the symbolic objects representing them. Then: $s_1 \wedge s_2 \Rightarrow s_{12}$.

EXAMPLE:
Take, in the example, P_2 and P_3. We then have $P_2 \cap P_3 = \{\omega_2\}$, so $s_1 \wedge s_2 \Rightarrow \varphi(\omega_2)$: $([y_1 = 1] \wedge [y_2 = \{1,2\}] \wedge [y_3 = 1] \wedge [y_4 = \{2,3\}]) \wedge ([y_1 = 1] \wedge [y_2 = 2] \wedge [y_3 = \{1,2\}] \wedge [y_4 = \{2,3\}]) \Rightarrow [y_1 = 1] \wedge [y_2 = 2] \wedge [y_3 = 1] \wedge [y_4 = 3]$ which simplifies into $[y_1 = 1] \wedge [y_2 = 2] \wedge [y_3 = 1] \wedge [y_4 = \{2,3\}]) \Rightarrow [y_4 = 3]$.

4 Conclusion

We have shown how by the symbolic approach the framework of classical Data Analysis may be extended both at the input and at the output. At the input, we have considered data which are not processed by the classical methods of Data Analysis. As concerns the output, we aim at obtaining a clustering which contains in itself the interpretation of its clusters, an inheritance structure between clusters which allows to learn rules from the data. This led to the definition of criteria other than those of the classical methods.

The field is however far from being exhausted. Other kinds of symbolic objects may be introduced to answer practical problems—for instance, by using modal logic. On the other hand, other methods of Data Analysis may be taken into consideration.

References

BERTRAND, P. (1986), *Etude de la Représentation Pyramidale*, Thèse de 3ème cycle, Univ. Paris-IX Dauphine.

COHEN, P.R., and FEIGENBAUM, E.A. (1982), *The handbook of Artificial intelligence*, Vol. III, William Kauffman.

DIDAY, E. (1976), *Selection Typologique de Paramètres*, Rapport de Recherche 188, INRIA, Le Chesnay.

DIDAY, E. (1984), *Une Représentation Visuelle des Classes Empiétantes: Les Pyramides*, Rapport de Recherche 291, INRIA, Rocquencourt, Le Chesnay.

DIDAY, E. (1986), Orders and overlapping clusters by pyramids, in: *Multidimensional Data Analysis Proc.*, eds. J. De Leeuw et al., DSWO Press, Leiden.

DIDAY, E. (1987a), The symbolic approach in clustering and related methods of data analysis: the basic choices, in: *Classification and Related Methods of Data Analysis*, ed. H.H. Bock, North-Holland, Amsterdam, 673–684.

DIDAY, E. (1987b), Introduction à l'approche symbolique en analyse des données, in: *Actes des journées "Symboliques—Numériques" pour l'apprentissage de connaissances à partir d'observations*, eds. E. Diday and Y. Kodratoff, CEREMADE - Univ. Paris IX-Dauphine, 21–56.

DIDAY, E. (1989), Introduction à l'approche symbolique en Analyse des Données, *RAIRO, 23, 2.*

DIDAY, E., and BRITO, P. (1989), Introduction to Symbolic Data Analysis, in: *Conceptual and Numerical Analysis of Data*, ed. O. Opitz, Springer, Berlin Heidelberg New York, 45–84.

DIDAY, E., GOVAERT, G., LECHEVALLIER, Y., and SIDI, J. (1980), Clustering in pattern recognition, in: *Proc. of 5th Conf. Pattern Recognition Miami Beach FL.*, more complete in: Digital Image Processing, Proc. of the NATO Advanced Study Institute, ed. J.C. Simon.

DIDAY, E., and ROY, L. (1988), Generating rules by symbolic data analysis and application to soil feature recognition, in: *Actes des 8èmes Journées Internationales "Les systèmes experts et leurs applications"*, Avignon, 533-549.

DIDAY, E., and SIMON, J.C. (1976), Clustering Analysis, *Communication and Cybernetics 10, Digital Pattern Recognition*, ed. K.S. Fu, Springer Verlag, 47–94.

DURAND, C. (1988), *Une aproximation de Robinson inferieur maximale*, Rapport Interne, Univ. de Provence.

GANASCIA, J.G. (1987), Charade: apprentissage de bases de connaissances, in: *Actes des journées "Symboliques—Numériques" pour l'apprentissage de (1 37 44 9980) connaissances à partir d'observations*, eds. E. Diday and Y. Kodratoff, CEREMADE - Univ. Paris IX-Dauphine, 57–73.

GANASCIA, J.G. (1987), *Apprentissage de connaissance par les cubes de Hilbert*, Thèse d'Etat, Université d'Orsay.

GANTER, B. (1984), *Two basic algorithms in concept analysis*, FB4-Preprint 831, TH Darmstadt.

GASCUEL, O. (1987), *Plage, un outil pour construire des systèmes d'apprentissage*, AFCET-RFIA 6, Antibes, 863–880.

GUÉNOCHE, A. (1987), Propriétés caractéristiques d'une classe relativement à un contexte, in: *Actes des journées "Symboliques—Numériques" pour l'apprentissage de connaissances à partir d'observations*, eds. E. Diday and Y. Kodratoff, CEREMADE - Univ. Paris IX-Dauphine, 181–194.

GUÉNOCHE, A. (1989), Construction du treillis de Galois d'une relation binaire, à paraître dans: *Mathématiques et Sciences Humaines*, Paris.

GUIGUES, J.L., and DUQUENNE, V. (1986), Familles minimales d'implications informatives resultants d'un tableau binaire, *Mathématiques et Sciences Humaines, 24, 95*, 5–18.

HO TU, B., DIDAY, E., and SUMMA, M. (1987), Generating rules for expert system from observations, in: *Les systèmes experts et leurs applications*, 7ème journées internationales "Les systèmes experts et leurs applications", EC2, Nanterre, France.

MATHEUS, C. (1987), *Conceptual purpose: implications for representation and learning in machines and humans*, Report No. UIUCDCS-R-87-1370, Univ. of Illinois, Urbana.

MICHALSKI, R. (1980), Knowledge aquisition through conceptual clustering: a theoretical framework and an algorithm for partitioning data into conjunctive concepts, *Int. Journal of Policy Analysis and Information Systems, 4, 3.*

MICHALSKI, R. (1983), Automated Construction of classifications: conceptual clustering versus numerical taxonomy, *IEEE Trans. pattern analysis and Machine intelligence, PAMI-5, 4.*

MICHALSKI, R., STEPP, R.E., and DIDAY, E. (1981), Recent advances in data analysis: clustering objects into classes characterized by conjunctive concepts, *Progress in Pattern Recognition vol. 1*, eds. L. Kanal and A. Rosenfeld.

MITCHELL, T.M., KELLER, R.M., and KEDAR-CABELLI, S.T. (1986), Explanation-based generalization—a unifying view, *Machine Learning Journal, 1, 1.*

QUINQUETON, J., and SALLANTIN, J. (1986), CALM: contestation for argumentative learning machine, in: *Machine Learning, a Guide to current research*, eds. R.S. Michalski, J. Carbonnel and T.M. Mitchell, Kluwer and sons.

RALAMBONDRAINY, H. (1987), GENREG: un générateur de règles à partir de données, in: *Actes des journées "Symboliques—Numériques" pour l'apprentissage de connaissances à partir d'observations*, eds. E. Diday and Y. Kodratoff, CEREMADE - Univ. Paris IX-Dauphine, 75–82.

UTGOFF, P.E. (1986), Shift of bias for inductive concept learning, in: *Machine Learning, Vol. II*, eds. R.S. Michalski, J. Carbonnel and T.M. Mitchell, Morgan Kaufmann Publishers, 107–148.

WILLE, R. (1982), Restructuring lattice theory: an approach based on hierarchies of concepts, in: *Proceedings of the symposium on ordered sets*, ed. I. Rival, Reidel, Dordrecht Boston, 445–470.

Knowledge Representation and Symbolic Data Analysis

Edwin Diday
Université Paris-Dauphine and INRIA, Le Chesnay, France

Summary

The main aim of the symbolic approach in data analysis is to extend problems, methods and algorithms used on classical data to more complex data well adapted to represent knowledge which "unifies" instead of observations which characterize "individual things": for instance, "the customers of my shop" instead of "a customer of my shop", a "a kind of mushroom" instead of "the mushroom, that I have in my hand". In Diday (1987) we have introduced several kinds of symbolic objects ("events", "assertions", "hordes" and "synthesis objects") which describe them. We extend these to "symbolic objects of classes" whose extension are classes instead of individuals and to "modal symbolic objects" by using, as in modal logic, operators called "modes" which change the meaning of logic formula. We show that properties and qualities of symbolic objects given in Diday (1988) and Brito and Diday (1990) may be extended to these objects. As pointed out in Diday (1988), symbolic objects may be used to describe clusters obtained after a clustering or factors after a factorial analysis in a more explanatory way for the user than the usual center of gravity or a linear combination of the variables. We define a family of symbolic data analysis problems. Some general principles concerning the algorithms which yield solutions to these problems are given and illustrated by a simple example using modal symbolic assertion of classes.

1 Introduction

In his course given at the University of Freiburg im Breisgau in 1935–1936, M. Heidegger trying to answer the question "what's a thing ?" gave the definition of three kinds of things:

1. Things in the sense of being "within reach" (des Vorhandenen): a stone, a piece of wood, etc.

2. Things which "unify" things of the first kind and also resolution, reflection, action, etc.

3. Things of kind 1 or 2 and also any kind of things which are not nothing.

As clearly distinguished by Kant in the 18th century concerning "things for us" and "things by themselves", when an expert describes things of the first kind, he uses a principle of "parsimony" by describing things only by what it is useful for what he wants to do. This principle is in opposition to the tabular model of data analysis which consists

NATO ASI Series, Vol. F 61
Knowledge, Data and Computer-Assisted Decisions
Edited by M. Schader and W. Gaul

of describing all the things (rows of the data array) by the same descriptors (columns of the data array).

Already in the 17th century, to distinguish things of the first kind from things of the second kind which "unify", A. Arnault and P. Nicole (1662) (as we are reminded by V. Duquenne (1986) about "La logique de Port Royal") say that "Ideas which represent a single thing are called singular or individual, and what they represent *individuals*, and those that represent several things are called universal (...). Now for these universal ideas there are two things which are very important to clearly distinguish, *comprehension* and *extension*. We call *comprehension* of an idea those attributes which are enclosed by it and that cannot be dropped without destroying it (...). We call *extension* of the idea the subjects to which this idea is convenient (...)".

Expert knowledge mainly concerns things of the second kind and it describes them in comprehension by using the often adequate mathematical tools of predicate calculus. The tabular model of data analysis is once more in opposition to this way of description, it is for instance unable to represent a conjunction of disjunctions: first, because in data analysis we study individual observations (mainly things of the first kind) instead of expert knowledge ("mushrooms that I have in my hand" instead of "a kind of mushroom"); second, because the most adequate mathematical tools to process this kind of data are those of the numerical vectorial space $\mathbb{R}^n$ instead of those of predicate calculus. Another reason why we have to leave the tabular model is its inability to represent complex things whose description depends on relations between other things, for instance to describe a photo which contains a table and a chair: [color (chair) = white] $\wedge$ [length (table) = large] $\wedge$ [(chair) is on (table)]; to describe links between the values taken by the variables, for instance when [color = $c_1 \vee c_2$] $\wedge$ [height = $h_1 \vee h_2$] $\vee$ {if color = c_1 then height = h_2} or when some variables make sense only if other variables take some values (the description of a company will not be the same if it has computers or not).

For all those reasons the usual tabular model is inadequate to represent things. The aim of symbolic data analysis is to extend the data analysis of "individual observations" represented by rows of a data array to the data analysis of the so-called "symbolic objects" which represents mathematically things which unify (or "put together") of the second kind in Heidegger's definition. There are two kinds of such things:

- those for which their "intent" (intention, comprehension) describes all the properties valid for the individual objects of their extension and
- those for which it is not the case.

In the first case, we follow R. Wille (1981) by saying as in traditional philosophy (see H. Wagner (1973)), that these things are "concepts". In the mathematical world symbolic objects constitute a kind of representation of things from the real world. There exist at least three kinds of bijections between subsets of the set S of symbolic objects and subsets of the set of things T. Following the principle of Leibnitz (mentioned in Heidegger (1962)), saying that "two identical things do not exist in the real world" and the Plato algorithm (mentioned in P. Louis (1956)) which associates to a thing an intent by increasing the conjunction of its properties until it distinguishes this thing from all the others, we may define a first bijection: with Ω the set of individual things, this bijection, denoted φ, associates to each individual thing $\omega \in \Omega$ associated to a unique intent (chosen among

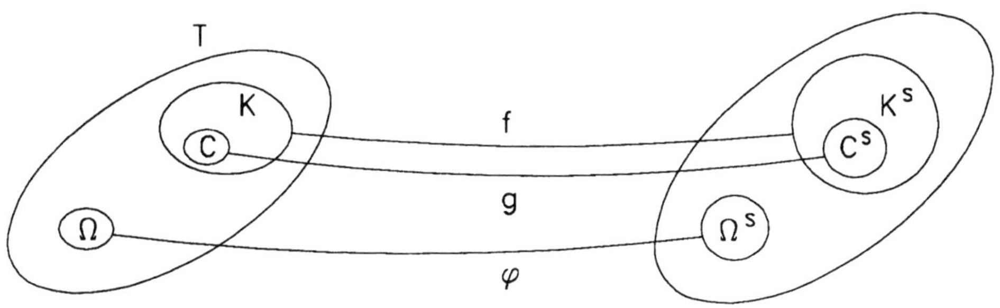

Figure 1: Three Bijections Between the Things of the Real World and the Set of Symbolic Objects

those given by the Plato algorithm) a symbolic object $\varphi(\omega) = \omega^s \in S$ which represents mathematically this intent. More explanation will be given on this mapping in section 2.

The second bijection f associates to each thing of the set K of things of the second kind, a symbolic object which expresses mathematically its intent. The third bijection g restricts f to the set of things C which are concepts. We denote $\varphi(\Omega) = \Omega^s, f(K) = K^s, g(C) = C^s$. These bijections are summarized in Fig. 1.

In this paper, after a brief recall of four kinds of symbolic objects already defined in Diday (1987), we extend them to new ones, first to symbolic objects of classes whose extension may be classes and second to modal symbolic objects where a *mode* is associated to the values taken by the descriptors (or *variables*). By introducing "modes" this work enters into the framework of three-valued or multivalued logics (Lukasievicz (1920, 1930) and Bochvar (1939)), of modal logics: for instance, *temporal logic, deontic logic, alethic logic* (see Thaysse et al. (1988) for a review), uncertainty or imprecision (Zadeh (1975), Shafer (1976) and Dubois and Prade (1984)).

As remarked by Lebbe et al. (1989), by working on things of the second kind, we use a disjunction of "variation", whereas in the case of individual things the disjunctions express only uncertainty and imprecision because variation has no sense. For instance, if we say that the customers of my shop have bought article A "or" article B it is a "or" of "variation"; if we say that a customer has bought article A "or" article B it is a "or" of "uncertainty" or "doubt" and if we say that he has paid fifty "or" fifty one it is a "or" of "imprecision".

2 From Elementary to Symbolic Objects

We consider Ω a set of individual things called "elementary objects". Now we are confronted with the following paradox: even if we know what elementary object we wish to define, we can only define it partially and so we will define it by comprehension (i.e. as a thing of the second kind even if it is a thing of the first kind). This is due to the fact to define completely an elementary object, we need an infinity of descriptor functions[1] $y_i: \Omega \rightarrow O_i$, but practically we select some of them, the most useful ("things for us")

[1] A *function* y_i is considered here as a mapping $\Omega \rightarrow O_i$ which is not necessarily defined on all the elements of Ω.

	y_1	y_2	y_3
ω_1	1		40
ω_2	2	3	
ω_3	2	5	45
ω_4	1		

Table 1: Data Array With Missing Values

which distinguish it from the others, by a "finite conjunction of properties" (using those selected descriptors) that we call a "symbolic object". Although, starting from an elementary object ω we have obtained a symbolic object $\varphi(\omega)$ where φ is a bijection $\Omega \rightarrow S$ and S is the set of all the definitions by comprehension of things of the second kind. The extension of $\varphi(\omega)$ contains all the elementary objects of Ω which satisfy the properties retained by $\varphi(\omega)$ on the selected descriptors. From this, it results that the initial elementary object ω is in the extension of $\varphi(\omega)$. By using a simple example, we illustrate these ideas by briefly recalling four kinds of symbolic objects (already defined in Diday (1987)).

EXAMPLE:
Let Ω be a set of 4 individuals described by their sex, the kind of delivery (cesarien, breech, normal, ...) and their age. These descriptors are respectively associated to the following functions: $y_1: \Omega \rightarrow O_1 = \{1,2\}$ (1 for male and 2 for female), $y_2: \Omega \rightarrow O_2 = \{1,2,\ldots,10\}$, $y_3: \Omega \rightarrow O_3 = [10,100]$. The values taken by the four individuals are given in Tab. 1.

There are two kinds of missing values; first by lack of meaning (for instance $y_2(\omega_1)$), second by indetermination (for instance $y_3(\omega_2)$). Both missing values are merged in the value X introduced in Sebag et al. (1990).

A first kind of symbolic objects are events. An event $e_i = [y_i = V_i]$ where $V_i \subset O_i$ is a function $\Omega \rightarrow \{\text{true, false}\}$ such that $e_i(\omega) = \text{true}$ iff $y_i(\omega) \in V_i$. When $y_i(\omega)$ has no sense $V_i = \emptyset$ and when it is not determined $V_i = O_i$.

In the case where $y_i(\omega)$ is not determined $e_i = [y_i = V_i]$ and $V_i \subset O_i$, $V_i \neq \emptyset$, $V_i \neq O_i$ it is not possible to know the value of $e_i(\omega)$, that is why we say that e_i is a "function" and not a "mapping" (it is also possible to define e_i as a mapping form Ω into {true, false, X} (see Sebag et al. (1990)). The extension of e_i in Ω denoted by $\text{Ext}(e_i/\Omega)$ is the set of elements $\omega \in \Omega$ such that $e_i(\omega) = \text{true}$. For instance, if $e = [y_2 = 3,5]$ then $\text{Ext}(e/\Omega) = \{w_2, w_3\}$. An assertion is a conjunction of events. For instance we have the following assertion:

$$a = [y_1 = 1,2] \wedge [y_2 = \emptyset] \wedge [y_3 = O_3]$$

we have then $\text{Ext}(a/\Omega) = \{\omega_1, \omega_4\}$.

Let us remark that it is possible to drop events as $[y_i = O_i]$ because the extension of a will not change. It is also possible to drop events as $[y_i = \emptyset]$ by making the assumption that two objects will not differ only by this event but also by another. For instance, ω_2 is not the extension of a not only because the event $[y_2 = \emptyset]$ is not satisfied but also because $[y_1 = 1]$ is not satisfied.

Any elementary object $\omega \in \Omega$ may be associated to an assertion by the mapping $\varphi: \Omega \rightarrow S$ such that $\varphi(\omega) = \bigwedge[y_i = y_i(\omega)]$. For instance, $\varphi(\omega_1) = [y_1 = 1] \wedge [y_2 = \emptyset]$

$\wedge[y_3 = 40]$. In the following we make the assumption that Ω is chosen in such a way that φ is a bijection and we denote by Ω^s the set $\varphi(\Omega)$ and ω^s the element $\varphi(\omega)$.

A horde is a symbolic object which appears for instance when we need to express relations between the parts of an object that we wish to describe. More generally a horde is a function $\Omega^p \to \{\text{true, false}\}$. For example: $h = [y_1(v_1) = 1] \wedge [y_2(v_2) = 3,5] \wedge [y_3(v_2) = [40,50]] \wedge [\text{married}(v_1, v_2) = \text{yes}]$.

In that case, h is a function $\Omega^2 \to \{\text{true, false}\}$ and the only couple in Ω which satisfies h is (ω_1, ω_2). In other words, $\text{Ext}(h/\Omega) = \{(\omega_1, \omega_2)\}$. Synthesis objects are conjunctions of hordes defined on different sets Ω_i. For instance, Ω_1 may be the individuals, Ω_2 the living place, Ω_3 the kind of job, etc.

3 Modal Symbolic Objects

3.1 Modal Assertions

In natural language we use many kinds of logic, for instance *alethic* logic or logic of possibilities: "it is possible"/"it is certain", *deontic* logic which uses the mode it is "allowed"/"forbidden", *epistemic* logic or logic of belief "Paul thinks that this wine is nice", temporal logic "always in the past"/"always in the future", etc. Our aim is to use these different logics by transforming the events $e_i = [y_i = V_i]$ in expressions of the kind $e_{ij} = M_j[y_i = V_i]$ where M_j is a mode of a given modal logic. To do so we consider that the modes $(M_1, \ldots, M_k)$ associated to a given logic satisfy the two following axioms (where e is an event):

1. $M_j e = M_k e \Rightarrow M_j = M_k$
2. $\forall i \in \{1, \ldots, k\}\ \exists j$ unique such that $M_j e = M_i \neg e$

Let us use the following modes $M = (M_1, M_2, M_3, M_4)$ and $\mathcal{M} = (m_1, m_2, m_3, m_4)$ for example where:

M_1 = necessary	m_1 = it is absolutely true
M_2 = if possible	m_2 = it is true under condition
M_3 = impossible	m_3 = it is absolutely false
M_4 = not if possible	m_4 = it is false under condition

EXAMPLE:
An advertisement says that a company is looking for people whose age is necessarily between 25 and 35 years old, if possible whose diploma must be of kind D_1 or D_2 and it is impossible to be a foreigner (i.e. not French). It may be represented by

$$a = M_1[\text{age} = [25,35]] \wedge M_2[\text{ Diploma } = D_1, D_2] \wedge M_3[\text{Nationality} = \text{foreign}].$$

An example of a candidate is described as follows: it is absolutely true that his age is 27, it is true under conditions (of equivalence) that his diploma be of kind D_2 and it is absolutely false that his nationality is French. It may be represented by $\omega^s = m_1[\text{Age} = 27] \wedge m_2[\text{Diploma} = D_2] \wedge m_3[\text{Nationality} = \text{French}]$. The problem is to know how far a candidate satisfies an advertisement. To formalize this problem, first it is easy to see that for the two sets of modes the axiom 1 is satisfied (for instance it is not possible to say

e	M_1	M_2	M_3	M_4
$\neg e$	M_3	M_4	M_1	M_2

Table 2: Negation Table of Modes M_i

e	m_1	m_2	m_3	m_4
$\neg e$	m_3	m_4	m_1	m_2

Table 3: Negation Table of Modes m_i

$M \setminus m$	m_1	m_2	m_3	m_4
M_1	L_1	L_2	L_3	L_2
M_2	L_1	L_2	L_3	L_2
M_3	L_3	L_2	L_1	L_2
M_4	L_2	L_2	L_1	L_2

Table 4: $g(M_i$, true, $m_i)$

$L \setminus L$	L_1	L_2	L_3
L_1	L_1	L_2	L_3
L_2	L_2	L_2	L_3
L_3	L_3	L_3	L_3

Table 5: $L_i \wedge L_j = L_{\max(i,j)}$

simultaneously "necessary" and "if possible" for the same event). By using Tab. 2 and 3 of negations we can see that the axiom 2 is also satisfied:

For instance, Tab. 2 of negations means that $M_1 e = M_3 \neg e$ (where e is an event), $M_2 e = M_4 \neg e$, $M_3 e = M_1 \neg e$. In fact, in practice it is sufficient to have only one of the two tables.

Secondly, we have to define connection tables as defined for instance in three-valued logic by Lukasievicz (1920, 1930), Bochvar (1939) or Kleen (1952). To do so we define an interpretation space called L in which the operator $\wedge$ takes its values in L and is commutative and associative. The aim of Tab. 4 which defines the semantic of the domain is to give a value $L_i \in L$ to each triple by using a mapping $g\colon M \times \{\text{true, false}\} \times \mathcal{M} \to L$, such that $g(M_i, p_i, m_i) = L_i$ where m_i is the mode associated to the event e_i by a given mapping $z_i\colon \Omega^s \to \mathcal{M}$ for the "elementary modal assertion" ω^s_m denoted $\omega^s_m = \bigwedge_i m_i e_i$.

M_i is the mode of the same event e_i in the definition of the assertion $a = \bigwedge_i M_i e_i$. By using the negation table it is always possible to get the same events in ω^s and a. In this case $L = \{L_1, L_2, L_3\}$ means L_1 = convenient, L_2 = may be convenient, L_3 = not convenient. As Tab. 5 is symmetric the operator $\wedge$ is commutative. Setting $L_i \wedge L_j \wedge L_k = L_n$ where $n = \max\{i, j, k\}$, it is also associative.

To illustrate these tables we can now answer the question asked in the preceding example: how far does the candidate ω^s satisfy a? First, we have by using Tab. 2 and 4: $a(\omega^s) = \bigwedge g(M_i, p_i, m_i)$ with $g(M_1, p_1, m_1) = g(M_1, \text{true}, m_1) = L_1$, $g(M_2, \text{true}, m_2) = L_2$, $g(M_3, \text{false}, m_3) = g(M_1, \text{true}, m_3) = L_3$. Now by using Tab. 5 we get $a(\omega^s) = L_1 \wedge L_2 \wedge L_2 = L_3$ and then ω^s is not convenient.

A general definition of a modal assertion may be given now. Let be given

1. three sets of modes $M, \mathcal{M}$ and L,
2. the negation table of M,
3. a mapping $M \times T \times \mathcal{M} \to L$ where $T = \{\text{true, false}\}$,
4. a mapping $z_i\colon \Omega^s \to \mathcal{M}$,
5. a binary operator $\wedge$ in L, then

Definition: A modal assertion is a function $a_{MYV\mathcal{M}}\colon \Omega^s \to L$ denoted $a = \bigwedge_i M_i[y_i = V_i]$ such that $a_{MYV\mathcal{M}}(\omega^s) = \bigwedge_i g(M_i, p_i, m_i)$ where $m_i = z_i(\omega^s)$ and p_i is a proposition which takes the value "true" iff $y_i(\varphi^{-1}(\omega^s)) \in V_i$.
Remark: ω^s may be denoted $\omega^s = \bigwedge_i m_i[y_i = V_i]$ and be considered as a modal assertion $\omega^s_{\mathcal{M}YV\mathcal{M}}$ and so on.
The modes of M and $\mathcal{M}$ may be met in many situations, for instance:

- M is a set of modes associated to elementary events of an assertion which express:
  - an advertisement for buying houses, an offer of a job,
  - the description of a concept (species of plants, illnesses),
  - a query in a data base.
- $\mathcal{M}$ is a set of modes associated to elementary events describing elementary objects of Ω, for instance:
  - a house to be sold, a candidate for a job,
  - a given plant, the illness of Paul,
  - an answer to a query in a data base.

3.2 Modal Hordes

Definition: A modal horde is a function $h_{MYV\mathcal{M}}\colon (\Omega^s)^k \to L$ denoted $h = \bigwedge_i M_i[y_i(\omega^s_i) = V_i]$ such that if $\omega^s = (\omega^s_1, \ldots, \omega^s_k)$, $h_{MYV\mathcal{M}}(\omega^s) = \bigwedge_i g(M_i, p_i, m_i)$ where p_i is a proposition which takes the value "true" iff $y_i(\varphi^{-1}(\omega^s_i)) \in V_i$ and $m_i = z_i(\omega^s_i)$.

EXAMPLE:
An observer has described three burglars that he has seen in his house by the following horde $h\colon \Omega^3 \to L$ where Ω is a set of burglars and $L_i \in L$ is a degree of suitability.

$$\begin{aligned} h &= \text{certain}[y_1(v_1) = \text{blonde, black}] \wedge \text{possible}[y_2(v_3) = \text{beard}] \\ &\quad \wedge \text{certain}[\text{height}(v_1, v_2) = \text{smaller}] \wedge \text{certain}[y_3(v_3) = \text{limp}] \end{aligned}$$

which means that he is certain that the hair of the burglar denoted v_1 is blonde or black, it is possible that the second one v_2 has a beard, that v_1 is smaller than v_2 and it is certain that v_3 limps.

Now an inspector describes several triples of possible burglars of this quarter by using the same modes for instance. Thus the problem is to know if ω^s satisfies more or less h. As before the answer requires the definition of the three tables of negation, $g(M_i, \text{true}, m_i) = L_k$ and $L_i \wedge L_j$ which define the semantics of the domain.

3.3 Modal Assertions of Classes

3.3.1 Assertions of Classes

The extension of an assertion is a set of elements of Ω that constitutes the main difference with assertions of parts for which the extension is a set of subsets of Ω. We denote $P(\Omega)$ the set of the subsets of Ω. Thus an assertion of parts is a function $a_{QYV}\colon P(\Omega) \to$

{true, false} denoted $a = \bigwedge_{i=1,q} Q_i[y_i = V_i]$ where $Q_i \in \{\forall, \exists\}$ and $a(P) = \text{true}$ iff $\forall i = 1, q$ we have $Q_i \omega \in P$, $y_i(\omega) \in V_i$. Let us remark that $\forall$ and $\exists$ are not modes as defined before because they do not satisfy the axioms 1 and 2 given in 3.1.

EXAMPLE:
We wish to describe a class of articles in a shop whose price is between 100 and 150 and the height of some of them is between 5 and 10. Thus the following assertion of classes allows their description:

$$C = \forall[\text{price} = [100, 150]] \wedge \exists[\text{height} = [5, 10]].$$

A class P or articles will satisfy C iff:

$$\forall \omega \in P, \text{price}(\omega) \in [100, 150] \text{ and } \exists \omega \in P, \text{height}(\omega) \in [5, 10].$$

3.3.2 Modal Assertion of Classes

It is an extension of assertion of parts to the case where the Q_i are replaced by modes M_j as in modal assertions. A formal definition of a modal assertion of parts may be given as follows.

Let be given

1. three sets of modes $M, \mathcal{M}, L$,
2. the negation table of M,
3. a mapping g': $M \times \{\text{true, false}\} \times \mathcal{M}' \to L$,
4. a mapping z_i': $P(\Omega^s) \to \mathcal{M}'$,
5. a binary operator $\wedge$ in L,

then:
Definition: A modal assertion of parts is a mapping $A_{MYV\mathcal{M}'} : P(\Omega^s) \to L$ denoted $A = \bigwedge_i M_i[y_i = V_i]$ such that:

$$A_{MYV\mathcal{M}'}(P^s) = g'(M_i, t_i, m_i') \text{ where } t_i = \text{true}$$
$$\text{iff } \forall \omega^s \in P^s,\ y_i(\varphi^{-1}(\omega^s)) \in V_i \text{ and } z_i'(P^s) = m_i'.$$

Remark: P^s may be denoted as a modal assertion of classes: $P^s = \bigwedge_i m_i'[y_i = V_i]$ and be considered as a mapping $P^s_{\mathcal{M}'YV\mathcal{M}''}$: $P(\Omega^s) \to L$ and so on by defining g'' and z_i''.

EXAMPLE:
An expert defines a class of articles to be sold in a shop by the following modal assertion of parts.

$$\begin{aligned} A &= \text{rather advised}[\text{price} = [100, 200]] \wedge \text{advised}[\text{make} = 1, 2] \wedge \\ &\quad \text{not advised}[\text{quality} = \text{luxurious}] \end{aligned}$$

To see if the expert has given a good advice for a class P^s of articles in a given shop during a fixed interval of time, it has been obtained:

$$P^s = \text{always}[\text{price} = [100, 200]] \wedge \text{rarely}[\text{make} = 1, 2] \wedge \text{often}[\text{quality=luxurious}].$$

e_i	M_1	M_2	M_3	M_4
$\neg e_i$	M_4	M_3	M_2	M_1

	m'_1	m'_2	m'_3	m'_4
M_1	L_1	L_2	L_3	L_4
M_2	L_2	L_1	L_3	L_3
M_3	L_3	L_3	L_1	L_2
M_4	L_4	L_3	L_2	L_1

Figure 2: Table of Negation and Table of the $g'(M_i$, true, $m_i)$

Let be M_1 = advised, M_2 = rather advised, M_3 = rather not advised, M_4 = not advised; m'_1 = always (100%), m'_2 = often ($\geq$ 75%), m'_3 = average (between 15 and 75%), m'_4 = rarely ($\leq$ 15%) and $L = (L_1, L_2, L_3, L_4)$ which means respectively that the advice was L_1 = good, L_2 = rather good, L_3 = rather bad, L_4 = bad. Thus we may for instance define the negation table and the table which gives $g'(M_i$, true, $m_i)$ as in Fig. 2.

By setting $L_i \wedge L_j = L_{\min(i,j)}$ if we wish to be kind to the expert (on the other hand by taking $L_{\max(i,j)}$), we obtain

$$\begin{aligned} A(P^s) &= g'(M_2, \text{true}, m'_1) \wedge g'(M_1, \text{true}, m'_4) \wedge g'(M_4, \text{true}, m'_2) \\ &= L_2 \wedge L_4 \wedge L_3 = L_2. \end{aligned}$$

Thus the expert was "rather good".

3.4 Generalization of Modal Assertions to the Case of Disjunctive and Conjunctive Modes

It may happen that the modes be linked to the values taken by a given variable, instead of the event concerned by this variable as done before. In such case we denote

$$a = \bigwedge_i \bigvee_j M_i^j [y_i = V_i^j] \text{ where } V_i^j \subset O_i.$$

It may also happen that V_i^j be a conjunction: $V_i^j = \bigwedge_\ell V_i^{j\ell}$ and that a mode $M_i^{j\ell}$ be linked at each $V_i^{j\ell}$. In such case we have:

$$a = \bigwedge_i \bigvee_j \bigwedge_\ell M_i^{j\ell} [y_i = V_i^{j\ell}] \text{ where } V_i^{j\ell} \subset O_i.$$

At elementary objects level, disjunction (if in doubt for instance) and conjunction may also appear; we denote

$$\omega^s = \bigwedge_i \bigvee_p \bigwedge_q m_i^{pq} [y_i = v_i^{pq}] \text{ where } v_i^{pq} \in O_i.$$

It results that the existence of a negation table is not necessary and that we need to give a table of the operator $\wedge$ in L and a mapping $z_i^{j\ell}$ to define $a(\omega^s)$ as follows.
Assume the following:

1. three sets of modes $M, \mathcal{M}$ and L,
2. a mapping $z\colon M \times T \times \mathcal{M} \to L$,
3. a mapping $z_i^{j\ell}\colon \Omega^s \to \mathcal{M}$,

4. two binary operators $\wedge$ and $\vee$ in L,

then
Definition: A modal assertion denoted $a = \bigwedge_i \bigvee_j \bigwedge_\ell M_i^{j\ell}[y_i = V_i^{j\ell}]$ is a function $a_{MYV\mathcal{M}}$: $\Omega^s \rightarrow L$ such that: $a_{MYV\mathcal{M}}(\omega^s) = \bigwedge_i \bigvee_{j,p} \bigwedge_{\ell,q} g(M_i^{j\ell}, \text{true}, m_i^{pq})$ where $m_i = z_i^{pq}(\omega^s)$ and $y_i(\varphi^{-1}(\omega^s)) = v_i^{pq} \in V_i^{j\ell}$.

Let us remark that in the case where an event has the following form: $e_i = \bigvee_j M_i^j[y_i = V_i^j]$ in a, the event associated to the same variable in ω^s is $f_i = m_i[y_i = v_i]$ and $\forall j\ v_i \cap V_i^j = \emptyset$, it is not possible to simply use the table of negation on M. In such a case, we may say that there exists $L^* \in L$ such that $L^* \equiv \{\text{incompatible}\}$ and set $g(M_i^j, \text{false}, m_i) = L^*$. In the case where $\forall j$ the M_i^j are identical in e_i, the table of negation may be used as usual.

EXAMPLE:
If we come back to the first example we may describe an advertisement looking for people for a job, as follows:

$$\begin{aligned} a &= (M_2, M_3, M_4)[\text{age} = [25, 30[, [30, 35[, [35, \infty[] \wedge \\ &\quad (M_1, (M_1, M_2))[\text{Diploma} = D_1, D_2 \wedge D_3] \wedge M_1[\text{Nationality} = \text{European}] \end{aligned}$$

where M_1, M_2, M_3, M_4 are defined as in 2.1. For instance the first event means that the age has to be if possible between 25 and 35 years and if possible it has not to be between 30 and 35 and it is impossible to be greater than 35; the second event means that it is necessary to have diploma D_1 or it is necessary to have D_2 and if possible D_3. A candidate may be described as follows:

$$\omega^s = m_1[\text{age} = 27] \wedge (m_1, m_2)[\text{Diploma} = D_2 \wedge D_3] \wedge m_3[\text{Nationality} = \text{French}].$$

Where the second event means that the candidate has for sure diploma D_2, it is true under condition that he has diploma D_3. By using the Tab. 2, 4, 5 and setting $L_i \wedge L_j = L_{\min(i,j)}$ we have $L_i \wedge L^* = L^* \wedge L_i = L^* = $ incompatible.

$$\begin{aligned} a(\omega^s) &= g(M_2, \text{true}, m_1) \wedge (g(M_1, \text{true}, m_1) \wedge g(M_2, \text{true}, m_2) \wedge g(M_1, \text{true}, m_3) \\ &= L_1 \wedge L_1 \wedge L_2 \wedge L_3 = L_3 \end{aligned}$$

If $\omega^s = m_1[age = 23] \wedge \ldots$ we have $a(\omega^s) = $ incompatible.
If $\omega^s = (m_2, m_2)[age = 29, 30] \wedge \ldots$ (we suppose that there is a doubt about the age due to the country of birth) we have

$$a(\omega^s) = (g(M_2, \text{true}, m_2) \vee g(M_3, \text{true}, m_2)) \wedge \ldots,$$

thus $a(\omega^s) = L_2 \vee L_2 \wedge \ldots = L_2 \wedge \ldots$

3.5 Generalization of Modal Assertion of Classes

It is also possible to extend the definition of modal assertions of classes, in an analogous way, as follows, if we denote

$$P_m^s = \bigwedge_i \bigvee_p \bigwedge_q m_i^{pq}[y_i = v_i^{pq}] \tag{1}$$

(at that level this is just a notation) and z_i^{pq} a mapping $P(\Omega) \rightarrow \mathcal{M}$ such that $z_i^{pq}(P^s) = m_i^{pq}$:

g'	o	a	r
o	L_1	L_2	L_3
a	L_2	L_1	L_2
r	L_3	L_2	L_1

Table 6: Table of the $g'(., true, .)$

Definition: A modal assertion of classes is a mapping $a_{MYV\mathcal{M}'}$: $P(\Omega) \rightarrow L$ denoted $A = \bigwedge_i \bigvee_j \bigwedge_\ell M_i^{j\ell}[y_i = V_i^{j\ell}]$ such that $A(P^s) = \bigwedge_i \bigvee_{j,p} \bigwedge_{\ell,q} g(M_i^{j\ell}, \text{true}, m_i^{pq})$ where $z_i^{pq} = m_i^{pq}$ and $\forall \omega^s \in P^s$, $y_i(\varphi^{-1}(\omega^s)) \in v_i^{pq} \subset V_i^{j\ell}$.

The notation (1) of P_m^s now makes sense if we define it as a modal assertion of parts.

EXAMPLE:

Experts describe kinds of branches of BNP (Banque Nationale de Paris) by modal assertions of parts which describe their typical classes of clients by using two descriptors: $y_1(\omega) =$ "Main bank of the client $\omega \in \Omega$", $y_2(\omega) =$ "Amount of loan of the client ω"; y_1 is a mapping $\Omega \rightarrow \{\text{BNP, BV, CL}\}$ where BV (Banque Verne) and CL (Crédit Lyonnais) are two other banks; y_2 is a mapping $\Omega \rightarrow \{1, 2, 3\}$ which represents three kinds of loans. Thus, an example of a branch may be described as follows (where o, a, r means often, average, rare, respectively):

$$\begin{aligned} Br_1 &= ((o,a,a),(a,o,a),(a,a,r))[y_1 = \text{BNP} \wedge \text{BV} \wedge \text{CL}, \text{BNP} \\ &\quad \wedge \text{BV} \wedge \text{CL}, \text{BNP} \wedge \text{BV} \wedge \text{CL}] \wedge (o,a,r)[y_2 = 1,2,3] \end{aligned}$$

The denotation of this modal assertion of classes may be simplified by dropping the values associated at the mode a; thus we obtain

$$Br_1 = (o,o,r)[y_1 = [\text{BNP, BV, CL}]] \wedge (o,r)[y_2 = 1,3].$$

By using Tab. 6, $L_i \wedge L_j = L_{\max(i,j)}$ and $L_i \vee L_j = L_{\min(i,j)}$ where L_1, L_2, L_3 means "suitable", "may be suitable", "is not suitable", we may compute $Br_1(P^s)$ where P^s has been obtained for instance from a survey made at a big new factory. The problem is to find how far P^s satisfies Br_1. If we have for instance:

$$\begin{aligned} P^s &= o[y_1 = \text{BNP}] \wedge (r,o)[y_2 = 1 \wedge 3] \quad \text{then} \\ Br_1(P^s) &= (g'(o,\text{true},o) \wedge g'(o,\text{true},a) \wedge g'(r,\text{true},a)) \\ &\quad \wedge ((g'(o,\text{true},r) \vee g'(r,\text{true},o)) \\ &= (L_1 \wedge L_2 \wedge L_2) \wedge (L_3 \vee L_3) = L_1 \wedge L_3 = L_3 \end{aligned}$$

Thus it is not suitable to open a branch of kind 1 near this factory.

4 Representation of Dependencies Between Variables and Between Objects

4.1 Conditional Modes to Express Dependencies Between Variables

A conditional mode M is an expression of natural language which adds a condition to an event, for instance $M =$ "save for" or $m =$ "has no sense if". We denote by N the neutral symbolic object such that $\forall s \in S$ the set of symbolic objects, we have $s \wedge N = s$.

Definition: A conditional symbolic object denoted $C = M([y_i = V_i])s$ (or if possible more simply: $C = M(V_i)s$) is a function $\Omega \to \{S, N\}$ such that if y_i is the variable associated at $V_i \subset O_i$ and $y_i(\omega) \in V_i$ then $C(\omega) = s(\omega)$ and if $y_i(\omega) \notin V_i$ then $C(\omega) = N$.

EXAMPLE:

Let be M_1 = "save for", M_2 = "has no sense if" and Loan = M_1(Paul, Jack)$a_1 \wedge M_2$ (BNP)a_2. Loan is an assertion which describes the kinds of loan which have been given to a set of clients Ω_1; a_1 and a_2 are two assertions characterizing two special kinds of loan. If y_1 is a variable such that $y_1(\omega)$ is the name of ω and y_2 is such that $y_2(\omega)$ is the list of the banks of ω, and if we set $C_1 = M_1$(Paul, Jack)a_1 and $C_2 = M_2$(BNP)a_2 we have $c_1(\omega) = a_1(\omega)$ if $y_1(\omega) \in$ {Paul, Jack} and if not $C_1(\omega) = N$. We have also $C_2(\omega) = a_2(\omega)$ if $y_2(\omega)$ = BNP and if $C_2(\omega) \neq N$. Thus, the assertion Loan describes clients' loans by using $a_1(\omega)$ save for Paul and Jack and $a_2(\omega)$ save for a client whose bank is not BNP because in that case $a_2(\omega)$ has no sense.

4.2 Multidimensional Variables to Express Dependencies Between Objects

If we wish to represent for instance an exhibition of articles for sale[2] which is composed of several displays we need to use a multidimensional variable (denoted Pos) which describes the position between the displays. An exhibition depends also on some characteristic variables denoted y_i (for instance: the kind of article exposed, the season, etc.), the number of displays (n), their position in the shop (Posinshop) and their description. If we denote E a set of exhibitions, D a set of displays, y_i a mapping $E \to O_i$, ND (Number of Displays), a mapping $E \to \mathbb{N}$, Posinshop: $D \to O_p$ (for instance Posinshop(d) = shop window), Pos: $D \times D \to O_s$ (for instance Pos(d_1, d_2) = in front means that d_1 is in front of d_2). Thus an exhibition may be represented by a horde $h: E \times D^n \to$ {true, false} such as:

$$\begin{aligned} h &= \bigwedge_i [y_i = V_i] \bigwedge [ND = n] \bigwedge_{i=1,n} [\text{Posinshop}(d_i) = p_i] \bigwedge_{i,j} [\text{Pos}(d_i, d_j) = P_{ij}] \\ &\quad \bigwedge_{i=1,n} \text{Display}(d_i). \end{aligned}$$

Here, Display is an assertion $D \to$ {true, false} such that

$$\begin{aligned} \text{Display} &= \bigwedge_i [z_i = w_i] \wedge [\text{kind of display} = \text{in bulk, ranked}] \\ &\quad \wedge M(\text{in bulk})\text{Inbulk} \wedge M(\text{ranked})\text{Ranked} \end{aligned}$$

and z_i is a variable $D \to W_i$ which characterizes displays (for instance, the kind of articles presented, the season, etc. M is the conditional mode "if". Inbulk is an assertion which is defined on a set of in bulk displays and Ranked in horde described on a set of ranked displays and depend on several ranks which are described by an assertion called Rank. We have

$$\begin{aligned} \text{Ranked} &= \bigwedge_i [z'_i = \omega'_i] \bigwedge [\text{Number of rank} = r] \\ &\quad \bigwedge_{i=1,r} \text{Rank}_i \bigwedge_{i,j} [\text{Pos}(\text{Rank}_i, \text{Rank}_j) = p_{ij}]. \end{aligned}$$

where the z'_i are variables which characterize ranked displays (for instance the name of the main criterion taken into account for ordering the ranks). Rank_i is an assertion defined on a set of ranks, which characterizes for instance the percentage of each kind of article which is presented, the ordering criterion, the kind of position of the articles in the rank.

[2]Thanks to A. Bultez who suggested this example at the workshop.

5 Qualities and Properties of Modal Symbolic Objects

5.1 Extension of a Modal Assertion

In this section we consider only the case of modal assertions but all the given definitions and properties may be extended to the other kind of objects. Let be $a\colon \Omega^s \to L$ a modal assertion.

Definition: The symbolic extension of a in S associated to the mode L_i is the set of $\omega^s \in S \subset \Omega^s$ denoted $\mathrm{Ext}(a, S, L_i)$ such that $a(\omega^s) = L_i$.

This definition allows the possibility to associate to any modal event $e_i^m = M_i[y_i = V_i]$ an elementary event e_i defined on Ω which takes the value true on Ω iff $e_i^m(\varphi(\omega)) = L_i$. In this way it is also possible to associate at any modal assertion defined on Ω^s an assertion defined on Ω.

5.2 Qualities and Properties of Modal Assertions

Thus, it is possible to extend all the definitions and qualities of symbolic objects which has been given in Diday (1988) and Brito and Diday (1990) to the modal assertions. For instance we may define a complete object as follows.

Definition: A modal assertion is a complete object for the mode L_i iff it is the conjunction of the modal elementary events whose extension contains $\mathrm{Ext}(a, \Omega^s, L_i)$.

5.3 The I-Extension

It may happen in practice, that the set Ω is unknown explicitly and so it is impossible to compute the extension of a symbolic object in Ω. For instance, it may happen that we describe several factories that we wish to compare by their symbolic representation without knowing all the factories. In that sense several kinds of extension using only the set of the given symbolic objects S, may be given by introducing the notion of I-extension.

Definition: The I-extension of a symbolic object $s \in S$ is the set of $s' \in S$ such that $\mathrm{Ext}(s, \Omega^s) I \mathrm{Ext}(s', \Omega^s)$ where I expresses a degree of intersection between both extensions.

For instance these two choices may be made: the $\cap$-extension and the $\subset$-extension which means respectively that $s' \in \mathrm{Ext}(s, \Omega^s)$ iff $\mathrm{Ext}(s', \Omega^s) \cap \mathrm{Ext}(s, \Omega^s) \neq \emptyset$ and $s' \in E(s, \Omega^s)$ iff $\mathrm{Ext}(s', \Omega^s) \subset \mathrm{Ext}(s, \Omega^s)$. In practice, if we have for instance $s = \bigwedge_i [y_i = V_i]$ and $s' = \bigwedge_i [y_i = V_i']$ we say that $s' \in \cap\!-\!\mathrm{Ext}(s, \Omega^s)$ iff $\forall i, V_i \cap V_i' \neq \emptyset$ and $s' \in \subset -\mathrm{Ext}(s, \Omega^s)$ iff $\forall i,\ V_i' \subset V_i$.

It is then possible to extend all the definitions, qualities and properties of modal symbolic objects by using the I-extension associated to a mode L_i. For instance we say that an object s is (I, L_i)-complete if it is defined by the conjunction of all the elementary events for which the I-extension for the mode L_i contains the I-extension of s for the same mode. It is possible to define an (I, L_i)-order between objects by saying that $s_1 \leq s_2$ iff $I - \mathrm{Ext}(s_1, S, L_i) \subseteq I - \mathrm{Ext}(s_2, S, L_i)$. There exists a (I, L_i)-lattice of (I, L_i)-complete objects, etc.

6 Examples of Symbolic Data Analysis Problems

The aim of this section is not to describe algorithms, but to give an idea of the complexity of symbolic data analysis by considering five kinds of problems on an extension of the example given in section 3.5.

6.1 An Example of a Symbolic Data Set

After having simplified the denotations by dropping the values associated to the mode a, we obtain the four following branches given by the experts which define S:

$$\begin{aligned} Br_1 &= (o,o,r)[y_1 = \text{BNP, BV, CL}] \wedge (o,r)[y_2 = 1,3] \\ Br_2 &= (o,r)[y_1 = \text{BNP, CL}] \wedge (r,o)[y_2 = 1,2] \\ Br_3 &= (r,o)[y_1 = \text{BNP, CL}] \wedge (o,r)[y_2 = 2,3] \\ Br_4 &= (o,r)[y_1 = \text{BV, CL}] \wedge (o,o)[y_2 = 1,2] \end{aligned}$$

It is possible to associate to each of the three banks concerned an assertion defined on the set of clients which characterizes their kind of loan ($\text{KL}: \Omega \rightarrow \{1,2,3\}$). We obtain a set of assertions denoted S_1 such as:

$$\begin{aligned} \text{BNP} &= [\text{KL} = 1,2] \wedge M([\text{KL} = 2])[\text{Ins} = 1] \\ \text{BV} &= [\text{KL} = 2,3] \wedge M([\text{KL} = 2])[\text{Ins} = 1] \\ \text{CL} &= [\text{KL} = 1,3] \wedge M([\text{KL} = 3])[\text{Ins} = 2] \end{aligned}$$

where M is the conditional mode "if". For instance, the assertion BNP takes the value "true" on a client $\omega \in \Omega$ if his loan is of kind 1 or 2 and if his kind of loan is 2, its insurance is of kind 1.

6.2 Five Kinds of Symbolic Data Analysis Problems

6.2.1 Quality of Symbolic Objects

Several kinds of qualities for symbolic objects have been defined in (Diday (1988) and Brito and Diday (1990)). For instance, if we wish to find a (I, L_i)-complete object which contains Br_1, we start with $o[y_1 = \text{BNP}]$; its (I, L_i)-extension is Br_1, Br_2, Br_3 and by merging the modes and the values taken we obtain:

$$Br^c = (o \vee r, o \vee a, o \vee r)[y_1 = \text{BNP, BV, CL}] \wedge (o \vee a \vee r, o \vee a, o \vee a \vee r)[y_2 = 1,2,3].$$

Br^c is a $(\cap, L_i)$-complete object because its $(\cap, L_i)$ extension contains Br_1, Br_2, Br_3 and not Br_4 (which doesn't satisfy at $o \vee r[y_1 = \text{BNP}]$, but at $a[y_1 = \text{BNP}]$) and it is the conjunction of the modal elementary events whose extension contains $\text{ext}(a, S, L_i)$. A branch of kind Br^c is characterized by the fact that the main bank of clients is not sometimes BNP, not rarely BV and not sometimes CL, etc., and those properties are the only ones which are satisfied by the branches of its extension.

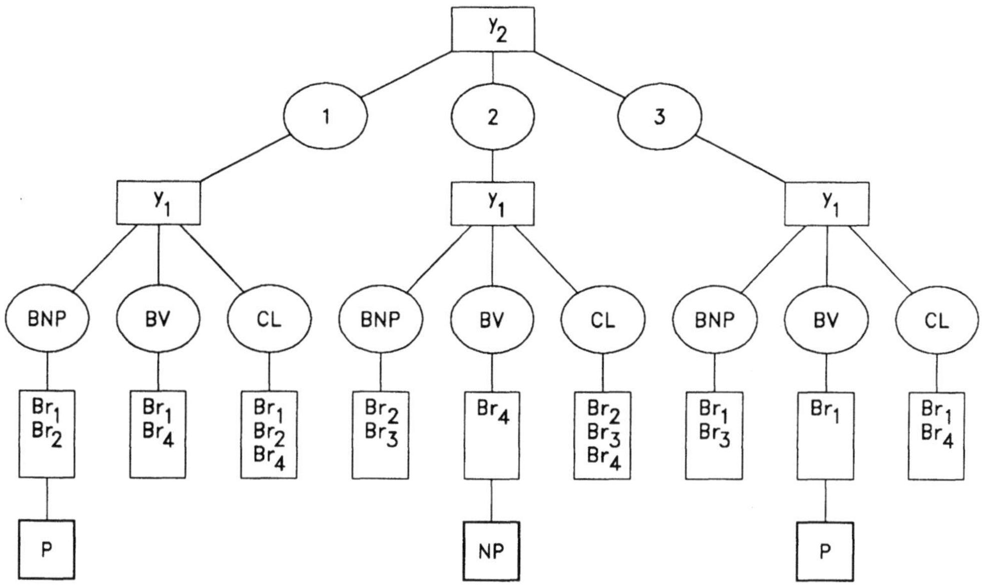

Figure 3: Decision Tree, P = Profitable Branches, NP = Non-Profitable Branches

6.2.2 Symbolic Discrimination

We suppose that Br_1 and Br_2 give profits unlike Br_3 and Br_4. We look for rules which characterize these two classes of branches. To do so we may for instance build rules by using the modalities of the variables y_1 and y_2 which are the most frequent in each class and also the modalities of the variables KL and Ins of the set S_1. We repeat the process with the branches not yet concerned by the premise of the rules already obtained and so on. By doing so we obtain, for instance, the following rule: the branches which give profits are the ones where main branches most often give for a loan of kind 2 an insurance of kind 1.

6.2.3 Decision Tree

The aim is to find a decision tree which discriminates as well as possible between the two classes of branches defined in 6.2.2. As usual the algorithm consists of looking for the variable which "explains" the best the two classes and to repeat the process on the modalities of this variable. In our example it is easy to see that y_2 explains better the classes than y_1 because one of its modalities ($y_2 = 3$) doesn't discriminate between the two classes whereas it is the case of two modes of y_1 ($y_1 =$ BV and $y_1 =$ CL). By repeating the process on each node defined by the modalities of y_1, we obtain the tree given in Fig. 3.

The example is very simple because only two variables are concerned, in practice the aim is to select the best variables among many. After having obtained the tree, it may be used to indicate the best kind of branch for a class of clients P^s (obtained for instance from a survey made at a new residential district). For instance if $P^s = (o,r)[y_1 =$ BNP, BV$] \wedge o[y_2 = 3]$, by using the decision tree it may be seen that only the branches Br_1 and Br_2 correspond to P^s. To know which one is the best for P^s, we have to compute $Br_1(P^s)$ and $Br_2(P^s)$ as has been done in section 3.5.

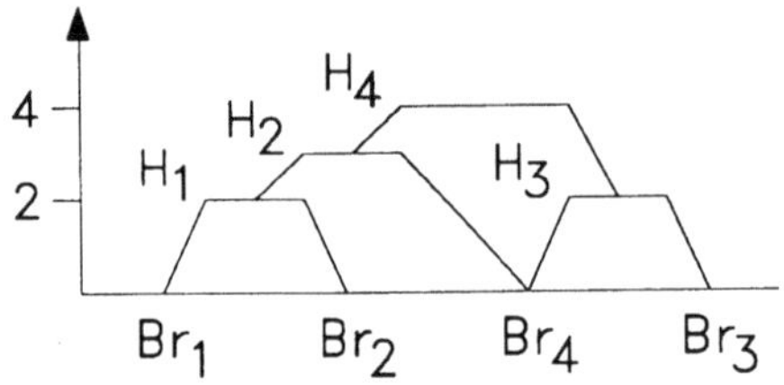

Figure 4: Symbolic Pyramidal Clustering of the Branches

6.2.4 Symbolic Clustering by Inheritance Pyramids

The aim is to obtain clusters of branches, such that each cluster is defined by a symbolic object satisfying one or several criteria associated with a given lexicographic order. By using the following criteria in a lexicographic order

1. homogenity of the modalities,

2. homogenity of the modes and

3. "simplicity" of the symbolic object which represents each cluster in such a way that its extension is as close as possible to the subset which constitutes the cluster

we obtain the pyramid (see Brito and Diday (1990)) given in Fig. 4. Each level H_i is represented by the following symbolic objects:

$$h_1 = o[y_1 = \text{BNP}], h_2 = r[y_1 = \text{CL}], h_3 = r \vee a[y_1 = \text{BNP}], h_4 = o \vee r[y_1 = \text{CL}].$$

The height of each h_i is the cardinal of its extension. It is also possible to associate to each level a complete object. By setting $r \vee a =$ "rather rare" $= rr$; $o \vee r =$ "extreme" $= ex$, $o \vee a =$ "rather often" $= ro$, we obtain by dropping the case $o \vee r \vee a$:

$$\begin{aligned} H_1 &= (o, ro, rr)[y_1 = \text{BNP, BV, CL}] \wedge (ex, ro, rr)[y_2 = 1, 2, 3] \\ H_2 &= (ro, ro, r)[y_1 = \text{BNP, BV, CL}] \wedge (ex, ro, rr)[y_2 = 1, 2, 3] \\ H_3 &= (rr, ro, ex)[y_1 = \text{BNP, BV, CL}] \wedge (ro, o, rr)[y_2 = 1, 2, 3] \\ H_4 &= \text{ex}[y_1 = \text{CL}] \wedge (ro, rr)[y_2 = 2, 3]. \end{aligned}$$

Several remarks may be made:

1. the pyramid of complete objects is a part of the lattice of complete objects;

2. it is possible to interpret the pyramid by giving rules (for instance, $h_1 \rightarrow h_2$ deduced from $H_1 \subset H_2$) and complementary symbolic objects as h_1 and h_3 because the intersection of their extension is empty;

3. it is possible to extend the pyramid by adding the elementary events to the branches and obtaining simultaneously a clustering of the branches and the events.

6.2.5 Factorial Analysis of Symbolic Objects

Depending on the kind of symbolic objects considered, it is possible to associate to each symbolic object $s \in S$ its extension in Ω^s, its I-extension or its (I, L_i)-extension in S. This may be done for each $s_i \in S$ and for each event e_i which describes each s. It is possible to associate to each extension a partition P of two classes P_1, P_2 where P_1 is the set of elements which constitute the extension and P_2 is the complementary set. It is then possible to make a contingency table of these partitions by taking as rows the partitions associated to the elementary events and as column the one associated to the symbolic objects $s \in S$ and to represent it for instance by a factorial analysis of correspondence. Another way is to make a factorial analysis on the table which cases (i, j) are defined by $Br_i(Br_j) = L_k$ or $e_i(Br_j) = L'_k$ where e_i is an elementary event.

7 Conclusion

Between the natural language in which the original symbolic data analysis problem is described and the computer language in which it will be solved, symbolic objects are a way for representing clearly and rigorously the objects on which the data analysis will be made.

Unlike most of the work carried out in expert systems, symbolic data analysis constitutes a "critic of pure reasoning" by giving less importance to the inference engine and more importance to the knowledge base. As in classical "exploratory data analysis" its main aim is to analyze, to describe, to make a synthesis, to organize, to classify and identify symbolic objects representing expert knowledge in a given domain. A wide field of research is open by extending problems, methods and algorithms of data analysis to symbolic objects.

References

ARNAULT, A., and NICOLE, P. (1665), *La logique ou l'art de penser 1662*, reprinted by Fromann, Stuttgart.

BOCHVAR, D. (1939), On three-valued logical calculus and its application to the analysis of contradictions, in: *Matematicesky Sbornik 4*.

BRITO, P., and DIDAY, E. (1990), Pyramidal representation of symbolic objects, this volume.

DIDAY, E. (1987), The symbolic approach in clustering and related methods of data analysis: The basic choices, in: *Classification and related methods of Data Analysis*, ed. H.H. Bock, North-Holland, Amsterdam, 673–684.

DIDAY, E. (1987), Introduction à l'approche symbolique en analyse des données, in: *Premières Journées Symbolique-Numérique, Université Paris-Dauphine*, ed. CEREMADE, 21–56.

DIDAY, E. (1988), Introduction à l'analyse des données symboliques: objets symboliques modaux et implicites, in: *Deuxièmes Journées Symbolique-Numérique, Université d'Orsay*, ed. LRI, 127–139.

DUBOIS, D., and PRADE, H. (1984) *Théorie des possibilités*, Masson, Paris.

DURAND, J., PAGES, J.P., BRENOT, J., and BARNY, M.H. (1990), Public opinion and conflicts. A theory and system of opinion polls, *The International Journal of public opinion research*, WAPOR Publisher.

HEIDEGGER, M. (1962), *Die Frage nach dem Ding*, Max Niemeyer Verlag, Tübingen. Editions Gallimard (1971) pour la traduction française en "Qu'est-ce qu'une chose ?".

KLEENE, S. (1952), *Introduction of metamathematics*, Van Nostrand.

LEBBE, J., VIGNE, R., and DARMONI, S. (1989), Symbolic-Numeric Approach for xs biological representation: a medical example with creation of identification graphs, in: *Data Analysis, Learning symbolic and numeric knowledge*, ed. E. Diday, Nova Science Publishers.

LOUIS, P. (1956), *Aristote, les parties des animaux*, Société d'édition "Les belles lettres".

LUKASIEVICZ, J. (1920), *On 3-values logic*, in: McCall, S., Polish logic (Oxford U.P. 1967).

LUKASIEVICZ, J. (1930), *Many-valued systems of propositional logic* in: McCall, S., Polish logic (Oxford U.P. 1967).

SEBAG, M., DIDAY, E., and SCHOENAUER, M. (1990), Incremental Learning From Symbolic Objects, this volume.

SHAFER, G. (1920), *A mathematical theory of evidence*, Princeton University Press.

THAYSSE, A. et al. (1988), *Approche logique de l'intelligence artificielle*, Dunod.

WAGNER, H. (1973), Begriff, in: *Handbuch philosophischer Grundbegriffe*, eds. H. Krings, H.M. Baumgartner and C. Wild, Kösel, München, 191–209.

WILLE, R. (1989), Knowledge acquisition by methods of formel concept analysis, in: *Data Analysis, Learning symbolic and numeric knowledge*, ed. E. Diday, Nova Science Publishers.

ZADEH, (1975), *Fuzzy logic and approximate reasoning*, Synthèse 30, 407–428.

Automated Acquisition of Production Rules by Empirical Supervised Learning Methods

Floriana Esposito
Istituto di Scienze dell'Informazione
Università degli Studi, Bari, Italy

Summary

A method of empirical and supervised learning to directly acquire knowledge from examples in form of classification rules is here proposed: the method combines a data analysis technique for linearly classifying with a conceptual method for generating disjunctive cover for each class, taking advantage of the peculiarities of both the approaches. Initial empirical results are encouraging.

1 Introduction

Knowledge engineering, that is the reduction of a large body of knowledge to a precise set of rules, is particularly critical in those fields where complex phenomena are involved and the human experts have difficulties to explain their mental processes. Techniques of inductive inference may be used to directly acquire knowledge from examples in form of classification rules organized in decision trees, usually involved in decisional processes.

The proposed methodology is definable as an empirical and supervised learning because it focuses on the classification of objects described by values of attributes, given a training set of examples belonging to given disjoint classes; it combines a data analysis method for linearly classifying (Discriminant Analysis) with a conceptual method for generating disjunctive cover for each class (INDUBI inspired to AQ algorithms), taking advantage from the peculiarities of **the parametric method** which:

- efficiently manipulates quantitative knowledge;
- works on the global characteristics of a class of objects;
- is suitable with a poor a priori knowledge;
- is synthetic;

and of **the conceptual method** which:

- uses symbolic representation of knowledge;
- works on the structure of an object;
- generates context dependent hypotheses;
- is easily understandable.

NATO ASI Series, Vol. F 61
Knowledge, Data and Computer-Assisted Decisions
Edited by M. Schader and W. Gaul

Both methods learn classification knowledge from training cases and are used sequentially in order to exploit the capability of the first one in handling continuous descriptors and its robustness as to irrelevant and noisy variables, and the better quality of the second one in formalizing the inductive generalizations as decision rules involving high level human oriented descriptions that outperform the rules obtained by interviewing an expert.

The application of Discriminant Analysis allows to obtain a new metadescriptor synthesizing the relevance, above all, of the numerical continuous descriptors in forming the classes; moreover the weight with which each initial descriptor enters to define the discriminant function may be used as a bias for the conceptual method in preferring, during the generalization process, those hypotheses involving the most discriminating descriptors.

The application of the conceptual method allows to produce a set of decision rules H, that are concept generalizations and must satisfy the completeness and the consistency conditions. The rules are structured as *Pattern* ::> *Class* where *Pattern* is an expression in a formal language and *Class* represents a concept.

Concatenating the methods works well because the discriminant function can convert its classification expertise into the form of a new feature, the metaselector, that is a suitable input for the conceptual method; the training examples, whose structure is modified by the statistical analysis, the descriptors and the inference rules, representing the background knowledge, are inputs to INDUBI. The basic weakness of this conceptual learning method consists of a poor treatment of the continuous descriptors, due to the symbolic representation language, of the dependency from the accurate choice of the examples and of the noise sensitivity: such difficulties can be overcome using the discriminant scores together with the symbolic descriptions of objects. New examples to be handled together with the old ones may be directly classified by discriminant analysis, so avoiding the trainer intervention, and new generalizations may be produced. In such a sense it is possible to increase the method performance using the knowledge acquired in the past, definable as metaknowledge, to produce new concept generalizations.

The described methodology has been implemented in the system RES capable of directly acquiring "diagnostic" production rules from classified examples: the system, which can be used in different fields being its description acquisition module "context independent" has been implemented in C/Unix. Some examples of applications in medical, agricultural and office automation environments are available.

2 Inductive Learning as a Knowledge Acquisition Tool

Knowledge acquisition and expertise transfer imply a categorization model of the expert task (Weiss and Kulikowski (1984)). According to Clancey (1984), the heuristic programs often involve classification processes and many expert systems may be defined as "diagnostic" because they allow to choose an answer in a predefined set of known solutions.

The transfer and transformation of problem-solving and classificatory expertise from some knowledge source to the program may be automated (Buchanan et al. (1983)) and the expertise may be transmitted by example: an expert may be able to transmit a skill by showing his own performance without necessarily understanding the basis of his expertise (Gaines and Boose (1988)).

Techniques of inductive learning from examples may be used to directly acquire knowledge as production rules: by a stream of facts describing some domain of application it is possible to induce general statements characterizing the domain (Dietterich and Michalski (1981); Dietterich (1986)). Induction is, basically, class formation and may be considered as the process of producing universal laws by means of generalizations based on a defined number of evidences (Mitchell (1982); Rendell (1986)). In learning from examples, to dispose of classes of objects and of characteristic examples of the classes allows to define, through an inductive generalization, what characterizes a class; the inductive method is also used in learning from observation or clustering, when a collection of facts is observed in order to develop a general description explaining the facts (Michalski and Stepp (1983)).

Parametric methods which express discriminating boundaries, firstly used in automatic systems with classification tasks, also exhibit these two kinds of learning approaches (Sklansky and Wassel (1981)). The traditional trainable classifiers, definable as devices that sort data into classes, are capable of improving their performances in response to information they receive from the environment as a function of time: learning is the measure of the effectiveness of the classifier which may work acquiring examples, already classified by a trainer (supervised learning), or directly getting observations (unsupervised learning).

The AI methods, definable as empirical learning methods since they acquire predictive knowledge from many examples, are symbolic and conceptual because concern with inducing instances of a given type of formal language in which the descriptions of the objects and of the concepts (class intention) are expressed. After the early work of Winston (1975) much work has been carried out both in the field of learning from examples and from observation. The algorithms AQ (Michalski and Chilausky (1980)), ID3 (Quinlan (1986)), CN2 (Clark and Niblett (1989)) are some of the most popular methods of supervised learning while CLUSTER/S (Stepp and Michalski (1986)), COBWEB (Fisher (1987)), UNIMEM (Lebowitz (1987)) are systems learning without teacher, based on models of concept incremental formation.

The problem of the representation language in all the AI symbolic learning approaches is fundamental: a general, formal framework for investigating learning from examples, independently from the knowledge representation scheme and from the learning techniques, has been proposed by Delgrande (1988).

Both the inductive methods of learning, the parametric or statistical approach to classification and the symbolic-conceptual approach, may be used to automatically acquire knowledge: they share implicit disjunction and exhibit important differences. An integration may be desirable, in order to realize the unification of statistical and syntactic approaches to pattern classification and recognition as suggested by Fu (1983). A first problem concerns the representation language, a second one concerns the way of combining the results of two methods which emphasize different things: the parametric methods, in fact, aim at defining the separating boundaries among the classes while the conceptual ones have the objective of finding what unifies the objects belonging to a class. In the following, after a brief description of the adopted representation language, the techniques to acquire knowledge in such a mixed approach will be presented and the results of the method application will be discussed.

3 The Representation Language

In the traditional notation a pattern, event or object can be any kind of entity, defined by its attributes, which are ascribed properties or variables: each object "o" can be identified by the vector of the observed values of the descriptive variables X

$$(X_1(o), \ldots, X_p(o)).$$

The input to trainable classifiers are data structured as vectors in the feature space; a point in this space is a feature vector and the feature vectors in a given class occupy a class region. A way of representing a class is to specify algebraic relationships among attributes of objects. The classifier assigns each feature vector to a decision region in the feature space by a set of decision hypersurfaces, that is a set of decision rules partitioning the feature space into class regions. In the symbolic approach, usual to AI, the objects are defined by a list of their properties or attributes

$$o = (V_1, V_2, \ldots, V_k),$$

where $V_j \subset D_j$ and $j = 1, 2, \ldots, k$ with $k \leq p$; that means that variables X_j take values in the power set $\mathcal{P}(D_j)$. An event E, denoted as $E = [X_i = V_i]$, where $V_i \subset D_i$ means that X_i assumes values in V_i, is a mapping $\Omega \rightarrow \{\text{true, false}\}$ such as an observed event $E(o)$ is true iff $X_i(o) \in V_i$. An assertion A is a conjunction of events: $A = [X_1 = V_1]\& \ldots \&[X_k = V_k]$ where $V_i \subset D_i, k \leq p$.

Given a universe of objects, a class is a subset of the objects, and a concept is the description of the class (intention). Partitioning a universe into subsets is induction: it implies to define an hypothesis as an assertion about objects in the universe aimed at the class formation, i.e. a candidate concept. Conceptual learning from examples means inferring plausible assertions from specific observed facts. The facts are descriptions of objects preclassified by the trainer and can be viewed as a collection of decision rules of the form

$$F = (E_{ik} ::> C_i), \quad i \in I$$

where I is a set indexing the classes C_i, E_{ik} is the event concerning the k-th object, example of the i-th concept C_i. The result of learning are rules of the form *Pattern* $::> C_i$ where *Pattern* is an expression in a formal language describing the events characterizing the given class C_i. More precisely, the result of learning is the inductive assertion H of the inductive paradigm (Michalski (1983)) expressed as a set of recognition rules of the kind

$$H = (G_i ::> C_i), \quad i \in I$$

where G_i are approximate descriptions of the i-th class or concept.

Using a complex description language means to realize multi-level class descriptions, involving attributes and measurable properties of objects, relations among them and higher level descriptors of concepts. A high level, human oriented, representation of a structured world is obtainable adopting a multi-valued version of the first order predicate calculus using typed function symbols, VL21, a subset of the complete system VL2, (Larson (1977)). The basic component of VL21 expressions is the "selector" or relational statement; it contains a function or predicate descriptor and a list of values that the descriptor may assume. It is written as

$$[L\#R], \qquad \text{where:}$$

- L, called "referee", is a function symbol with its arguments;
- R, called "reference", is a set of values of the referee's domain;
- #, is a relational operator defining the relation between the referee and the reference.

The selectors assumes a value true or false and can be seen as a test in order to state whether the predicate or the function values belong to a defined domain or not. To each variable, predicate or function symbol a domain is associated: nominal, linear, tree structured.

The selector is a powerful form to describe the characteristics of objects: attributes, relations, predicates, operators are descriptors (features) used in the observational statements and relevant to the decision classes. An event may be described as

> [on top(s_1, s_2)] [shape(s_1)=circle] & [shape(s_2)=rectangle, square] [tx(s_1)=clear] [tx(s_2)=clear]
> "There is a clear circle on a clear rectangle or on a clear square"

Each VL21 expression may be obtained from a set of selectors by applying different operators, including decision operators (::>), logic implication ($\Rightarrow$) and inference operators ($\Longrightarrow$). VL21 formulas are useful to specify the condition and the action part of a rule and it is possible to use different kinds of rules for different kinds of knowledge such as:

- decision rules to represent facts (in a decision rule the action part defines the class to which the observation belongs);
- inference rules to represent the relationships among the different descriptors (background knowledge);
- generalization rules to define the transformations applicable to facts in the hypotheses generation (selective rules, constructive rules).

Such a formalism, which has been proposed for concept learning from example, can be used to express the decision regions, which are bounded by hyperplanes or portions of hyperplanes, that are the results of the discriminant analysis (Duda and Hart (1973)).

4 The Learning Methodology

The conceptual methods of inductive learning allow:

- to express concepts in logic, as rules easily comprehensible to humans;
- to use symbolic representation of knowledge, including structural descriptions of objects, and to work on the structure treating the relations among subparts;
- to generate context dependent hypotheses, optimally using the trainer background knowledge;

while the statistical methods:

- efficiently manipulate quantitative knowledge;

- work on the global characteristics of a class of objects, showing structural relations within a class;
- are suitable when a deep a priori knowledge about the problem is not available;
- are synthetic even if barely understandable;
- are robust as to noise.

The methods are both model driven but the relevant differences consist in the

focus : symbolic methods describe concepts in the sense of what unifies a certain number of observations while the parametric methods describe boundary surfaces;

strategy: symbolic methods work sequentially (an example at a time) while data analysis works in a global way;

power of representation: conceptual methods allow to handle structural representations of facts while the statistical methods treat single-entity representations.

Integrating a statistical data analysis method for linearly classifying (Discriminant Analysis) with a conceptual learning method (hypotheses generation and testing by means of the STAR methodology) in a unique learning methodology allows to combine the advantages of both the methods. Something similar, a mixed approach, a hybrid technique that retains the characteristics of Bayesian classification while enhancing its performance, placing a symbolic learning method (IWN) in the role of teacher, has been proposed by Tan and Schlimmer (1989). However, the technique is based on concatenating instead of integrating the methods and the limits, due to IWN, in treating continuous variables remain.

The weakness in treating continuous features is common to a lot of symbolic methods, while the possibility of saving the amount of information in synthetic metadescriptors is characteristic of the parametric methods. Moreover, observational statements may contain no directly relevant descriptors: the degree at which the initial descriptors are relevant to the decision classes is a way of classifying learning techniques. Initially given descriptors may be different from the descriptors used in the final class description. The task of constructing new derived relevant descriptors may be accomplished by statistical methods which, specifying algebraic relationships among attributes of objects, allow to realize a constructive inductive learning.

The statistical method to learn by examples, namely, the Discriminant Analysis, once the classes to which the examples belong are defined, allows to calculate a general function, the form of which is known while the parameters, capable of identifying the belonging regions in the descriptors space, are unknown. A discriminant function g_i is a mapping from the set of the feature vectors to the real numbers, each value of i being associated with a single decision region: the discriminant analysis provides some decision rules partitioning the whole feature space Ω into a number of regions Ω_i, $i = 1, 2, \ldots, N$ where N is the number of classes.

$g_i(X)$ may be viewed as a macrofeature formed from the features $X_1, \ldots, X_p$. Being X the feature vector representing an object, the index of the largest of $g_i(X)$ is the classifier assignment of X to a class

$$\text{"If } g_j(X) < g_i(X) \text{ for all } j\text{"} \quad ::> X \in \Omega_i$$

The linear discriminating functions have the form $g_i(X) = w_{i1}X_1 + \cdots + w_{ip}X_p$ where w_{ik} represents the weight with which the variable X_k enters to define g_i. The functions are formed in such a way to maximize the separation of the classes: their values are similar for objects belonging to the same class, while they present the maximal differences among objects belonging to different classes.

Discriminant Analysis is used to calculate a metaselector, capable of directly classifying an object and very useful to synthesize the relevance of numerical descriptors, also quantitatively specifying their relationships in defining the hyperplanes separating the regions. Such a metaselector, together with the VL21 descriptions of the examples, is treated by the conceptual learning inductive algorithm. The conceptual method consists in the construction of a star around an example E (defined as "seed"), that is a set of descriptions covering E consistently respect to the counterexamples.

A **star of an event** E (a description of a single object) **under constraints** e, is a set of all possible alternative non-redundant descriptions of event E not violating constraints e. In this case E is an example of a concept (class) to be learned and e is a set of counterexamples of this concept. The star of the event E **against** e, denoted $G(E : e)$ is the set of the more general descriptions that are satisfied by the event E and are not satisfied by any negative event in e.

If, after generating a concept description, a new training example or event contradicts it, a new consistent concept description is created. After a consistent number of examples, the system disposes of a good description of the concept. The algorithm conducts a beam search through the space of the possible generalizations and the beam depends on the maximum order of the set of descriptions and is generally defined by the user, the width of the beam affecting the algorithm speed. A set of user-defined parameters (a Lexicographical Function measuring the fitness of alternative hypotheses with the user criterion) representing the goals and the background, context dependent knowledge guide the search in the solution space.

The results are symbolic discriminant descriptions of the concepts (classes) satisfying the completeness condition (every training example of a class must satisfy the description of the class) and the consistency condition (no training example satisfies two different concept descriptions). A generic description G of a concept, a generalization, can be thought as the left hand side (lhs) of a decision rule of the kind:

$$G ::> C$$

which may be incorporated in the knowledge base of an expert system with the task of classifying new events. Such a production rule means: "If a description of an event E matches G then E is an instance of the concept C". The descriptions G are disjunctive VL21 wff (well-formed formula): $G = \text{Or\_atom}_1 \vee \ldots \vee \text{Or\_atom}_n$ and E are conjunctive VL21 wff.

The algorithm for generating the star, using the VL21 formal language, is a modified version of INDUCE, proposed by Michalski (1980). The differences concern:

- the use of all the relational operators and not only the simple equality as in the original algorithm;

- the improvement of the new descriptors generation process using control structures, besides the simple sequence, to guide the application of the inference rules;
- a form of constructive induction using the results of the discriminant analysis (the metaselectors DISFUN);
- the possibility of storing the discriminant function coefficients in order to define a-posteriori class membership probabilities for new examples;
- a new algorithm to determine the isomorphism between two graphs representing c2_formulas in VL21;
- the use of a syntactic distance between VL21 formulas to allow flexible matching in presence of noise (Esposito and Semeraro (1989)) during the recognition phase.

As to the two last points, the VL decision rules being representable as graphs with labeled nodes and labeled directed edges, the algorithm to determine the graph isomorphism is heavily used in the system in order to decide if a formula is semantically more general and consistent than another. More in particular, the proposed algorithm aims to optimize the backtracking mechanism, sorting the VL21 descriptions. The generalized description G may be decomposed as

$$G = G1 \ \& \ G2$$

where $G1 = S_1 \ \& \ S_2 \ \& \ \ldots S_i \ \& \ \ldots \ \& \ S_n$ is a conjunction of selectors; the referee of the generic selector S_i should have at least one of the variables above not appearing in the referees of the selectors $S_1, S_2, \ldots S_{i-1}$ and $G2$ is the conjunction of the remaining selectors of G. The first sort concerns the selectors of G which are ordered so to minimize the number of selectors in $G1$. The second sort operation is on the description $G2$ that may be decomposed as

$$G2 = G2a \ \& \ G2b$$

where $G2b$ contains all the unary selectors of the kind

$$f(o) = \langle \text{reference} \rangle$$

that specify the value of an attribute for the object o. The description $G2a$ contains the remaining selectors. The selectors in $Gb2$ are sorted in order to have in the first positions the selectors containing the variable that is assigned by a selector appearing first in the description $G1$.

The third sort operation is realized once and concerns E, which is ordered in such a way that all the selectors containing the same descriptor appear consecutively. So, in order to find a match for a selector S_i of G it is not necessary to examine all the selectors in the description E, but only that concerning the descriptor in S_i. Such a technique allows to optimize the backtracking process because if the system fails in finding a match for a selector S_i of $G2$ it will consider in backtracking simply the "right" selector preceding S_i, avoiding to consider the further selectors the reassignment whose reassignment would be useless. In fact there is no sense in finding other matches for the selectors of $G2$ preceding S_i, the possibility of matching being unique for each of them. The distance is particularly useful during the recognition phase: it is based on a pure probabilistic approach and may be defined as

$$SD(G, E) = 1 - P(\text{Match } (G, E))$$

where $P(\text{Match}(G, E))$ denotes the probability that G and E unify, being G a description of a concept, expressed as a disjunctive VL21 wff and E an event expressed as a conjunctive VL21 wff. Applying such a distance in conceptual learning allows to recognize configurations of objects as corresponding to certain concepts in an approximate and context dependent way. Instead of a strict match against the prototypical description of a concept, the concept membership of an instance is defined determining the most similar concept that best matches the instance.

5 The System

The realized learning system, RES, consists of three modules:

- the description acquisition module (AC);
- the discriminant analysis module (AD);
- the conceptual learning system (INDUBI).

By the first module all the elements necessary to describe the problem are acquired: the user interfaces the system supplying the learning examples, the inference rules and the descriptors in form of strings of characters. These are syntactically and semantically analyzed and, where the analysis is successfully performed, AC decomposes each string representing a VL21 sentence into tokens. The system acquires:

- a set of learning examples of the concepts;
- a set of descriptors annotations;
- a set of inference rules;
- a set of parameters, useful to control the executions of INDUBI;
- three preference criteria used in three different moments during the concept generalization process.

In each learning example the selectors containing in the referee a continuous descriptor are chosen, with the aim of obtaining a set of n dimensioned vectors representing the set of cases which must be supplied to the statistical analysis (AD).

The Discriminant Analysis module has the task of defining n linear discriminating functions each of which best separates the vectors of a conceptual class from the vectors concerning each other class. Every discriminant function is evaluated for each learning example and when the value is > 0 a new selector DISFUN is added to the example. The output of AD is a set of new learning examples obtained from the initial ones:

- eliminating in each example the selectors involved in the statistical analysis;
- adding to each example metaselectors of the kind

  [DISFUN (function symbol = value) = real number]

where function symbol is the name of a descriptor concerning the decision part of the input examples, value is the descriptor value defining the conceptual class, while real number is the discriminant score calculated for the example.

The learning examples, whose structure is modified by the statistical analysis, the descriptors and the inference rules are the input to the conceptual learning module INDUBI which treats multiple concepts by the STAR methodology and produces a set of concept generalizations, in form of rules, that may be acquired by AC, so refining the learning process.

The output of INDUBI is a set of concept generalizations which have the form of VL21 descriptions structured as:

<c_formula> ∨ ... ∨ <c_formula> ::> <decision selector>

where ∨ is the disjunction operator and the decision selector represents the learned concept.

The user supplies the system with a set of examples of concepts, obtaining a generalized description for each concept. The basic problem of conceptual learning from examples, consisting in the careful choice of the examples so to guarantee the class separability and the significance of examples with the aim of applying the cover algorithm, is partially solved by the presence of the metaselectors resulting from the statistical analyses which supply absolutely different discriminant scores for each example. The trainer may be substituted by a program which directly acquires from the environment data and observations, on which the user-trainer intervention is only in the initial classification. New examples to handle together with the old ones may be classified by the discriminant analysis while the inference engine provides to determine a new generalization. In such a sense the system increases its performance since it uses knowledge acquired in the past, definable as metaknowledge, to produce new concept generalizations.

A simple example of application is in the following, showing the differences in using the conceptual method only or the mixed scheme. The example, due to the simplicity of the event descriptions, could be treated only with the statistical methods, being the nominal descriptors treatable by the discriminant analysis, with the only loss of rules understanding. Anyway, this is not possible when complex structured descriptions of facts are available. More consistent applications in Medicine (automatic acquisition of rules for a knowledge based system for the early diagnosis and epidemiology of the essential arterial hypertension and diabetes) and in the field of office automation (recognition of documents) are objects of two working projects.

Example

Two cultures of strawberries, Pachontas and Gorella, have been considered, observing, for each plantation, the production per year in terms of q/ha. Plantations with a low (<70 q/ha), a medium (70–100 q/ha) and a high production (>100 q/ha) have been considered. The descriptors are:

1. ph of the soil (`soil-ph`);
2. the quantity of fertilizer per ha (`q-fert`);
3. the structure of plantation, simple or coupled, (`install`);

4. the distance among the rows (d-among-rows);

5. the distance between two plants (d-on-rows);

6. time of planting (planted-on);

7. techniques of cultivation, irrigation, removal of flowers or removal of stolons (cult-tec).

Thirty examples are available as training set while 20 are available as testing set: applying only the conceptual method produces the following generalizations:

```
cult-tec(x) = none;
 v
install(x) = simple;
planted-on(x) = april            ::> low production

install(x) = coupled;
planted-on(x) = april;
 v
planted-on(x) = october;
 v
cult-tec(x) = stolon-removal;
 v
planted-on(x) = march;           ::> high production

planted-on(x) = may;
cult-tec(x) = flowers-removal;
 v
planted-on(x) = june;
cult-tec(x) = irrigation, flowers-removal;
 v
planted-on(x) = november         ::> medium production
```

Such rules allow to cover all the training cases and 70% of the testing cases. Selecting the continuous descriptors 1, 2, 4, 5, it is possible to calculate three discriminating functions, one for each class, having the form

```
9.976*soil-ph  +  0.052*q-fert  +  0.289*d-among-rows   -1.644*d-on-
rows - 38.715 > 0    ::>  low production
-.389*soil-ph  +  1.743*q-fert  -  .315*d-among-rows   +  .537*d-on-
rows + 1.941  > 0    ::>  medium production
-2.429*soil-ph -  48.459*q-fert  +  .279*d-among-rows   -  .144*d-on-
rows + 6.4    > 0    ::>  high production
```

Such functions allow to discriminate 95% of the training cases and 80% of the testing cases. The metaselectors DISFUN are substituted in the examples to the continuous descriptors. The generalizations produced by INDUBI are:

```
DISFUN(production = low) = 0.11075347 e2          ::> low production

DISFUN(production = high) = 0.19447220 e1;
cult-tec(x) = irrigation, stolon removal;         ::> high production

DISFUN(production = medium) = 0.59615600 e1;
planted-on(x) = march, april, may, october;
install(x) = simple;
cult-tec(x) = stolon removal;
 v
DISFUN(production = medium) = 0.17644542 e1;
install(x) = simple;                             ::> medium production
```

Such new generalizations allow to cover all the training cases and 80% of the testing cases. Examining these produced generalizations it is possible to notice that they are more synthetic than the first ones.

Moreover, while DISFUN is sufficient to individuate plantations with a low production, being the cultivation practices irrelevant as to the production, the discriminant analysis alone is not able to distinguish high production plantations from the others: the cultivation technique has been added to the metaselector DISFUN. As to the plantation with a medium production, both the generalizations are disjunctions of or-atoms covering some of the positive examples and none counterexample: it confirms the difficulty, common to many recognition methods, to find synthetic rules to describe intermediate situations.

6 Conclusions

The idea of combining data analysis and conceptual methods in order to reduce the amount of knowledge which is required to the trainer in the example selection and to realize a more powerful scheme of learning from examples seems attractive.
An integrated approach allows:

- to efficiently handle qualitative and quantitative features;
- to reduce the effects of noise on quantitative features;
- to efficaciously describe background knowledge;
- to accelerate the classification process and to increase the learning rate;
- to realize a form of constructive induction;
- to provide useful probabilities of class membership.

The realized system is also able to use exceptions to advantage the selective induction and to deal with uncertainty, by means of a flexible match between the graphs representing the VL formulas, in a probabilistic view. Discriminant Analysis already expresses classes in terms of belonging probabilities or degrees of belief. Extending such an approach to the conceptual method allows to realize a faster covering algorithm and more efficient learning.

References

BUCHANAN, B.G., BARSTOW, D., BECHTAL, R., BENNET, J., CLANCEY, W.J., KULIKOWSKI, C., MITCHELL, T., and WATERMAN, D.A. (1983), Constructing an expert system, in: *Building Expert Systems*, eds. F. Hayes-Roth, D.A. Waterman and D.B. Lenat. Addison-Wesley, Reading, MA.

CLANCEY, W.J. (1984), Classification problem solving, in: *AAAI-84, Proceedings of the National Conference on Artificial Intelligence*, AAAI, Los Angeles.

CLARK, P., and NIBLETT, T. (1989), The CN2 Induction Algorithm, *Machine Learning, 3.*

DELGRANDE, J.P. (1988), A formal approach to learning from examples, in: *Knowledge Acquisition for Knowledge-based Systems*, eds. B. Gaines and J. Boose, Vol. 1, Academic Press, London.

DIETTERICH, T.G., and MICHALSKI, R.S. (1981), Learning and generalization of structural descriptions evaluation criteria and comparative review of selected methods, *Artificial Intelligence J., 16, 3.*

DIETTERICH, T.G. (1986), Learning at the knowledge level, *Machine Learning, 1, 3.*

DUDA, R.O., and HART, P.E. (1973), *Pattern Classification and Scene Analysis*, Wiley, New York.

ESPOSITO, F., and SEMERARO, G. (1989), Concept Recognition through Flexible Match: the definition of a syntactic distance between structured symbolic descriptions, *Summer School on Machine Learning*, SOGESTA, Urbino.

FISHER, D.H. (1987), Knowledge Acquisition via Incremental Conceptual Clustering, *Machine Learning, 2, 3.*

FU, K.S. (1983), A step towards unification of syntactic and statistical pattern recognition, *IEEE Trans. Pattern Anal. Machine Intel., PAMI-5*, 200–205.

GAINES, B.R. (1988), An overview of knowledge acquisition and transfer, in: *Knowledge Acquisition for Knowledge Based Systems*, eds. B. Gaines and J. Boose, Academic Press, London.

LARSON, J. (1977), *Inductive Inference in the variable valued predicate logic system VL21, Ph.D. Thesis*, Dept. of Computer Science, Urbana, IL.

LEBOWITZ, M. (1987), Experiments with incremental concept formation: UNIMEM, *Machine Learning, 2, 2.*

MICHALSKI, R.S. (1980), Pattern Recognition as rule guided Inductive Inference, *IEEE Trans. Pattern Anal. Machine Intel., PAMI-2, 4*, 349–361.

MICHALSKI, R.S. (1983), A theory and methodology of inductive learning, *Artificial Intelligence, 20*, 111–161.

MICHALSKI, R.S. (1987), Learning strategies and automated knowledge acquisition, in: *Computational Models of Learning*, ed. L. Bolc, Springer Verlag, Heidelberg.

MICHALSKI, R.S., and CHILAUSKY, R.L. (1980), Knowledge acquisition by encoding expert rules versus computer induction from examples, *International Journal for Man-Machine Studies, 12*, 63–87.

MICHALSKI, R.S., and LARSON, J.B. (1978), Selection of most representative training examples and incremental generation of VL1 hypotheses, *Techn. Report UIUCDCS-R-78-867*, Dept. of Computer Science, Urbana, IL.

MICHALSKI, R.S., and STEPP, R.E. (1983), Automated construction of classifications: conceptual clustering versus numerical taxonomy, *IEEE Trans. on Pattern Anal. Machine Intel., PAMI-5, 4*, 396–410.

MITCHELL, T.M. (1982), Generalisation as search, *Artificial Intelligence, 18*, 203–226.

QUINLAN, J.R. (1986), Induction of decision trees, *Machine Learning, 1, 1.*

RENDELL, L. (1986), A general framework for induction and a study of selective induction, *Machine Learning, 1, 2.*

SKLANSKY, J., and WASSEL, G.N. (1981), *Pattern Classifiers and Trainable Machines*, Springer Verlag, New York.

STEPP, R.E., and MICHALSKI, R. (1986), Conceptual clustering: inventing goal oriented classifications of structured objects, in: *Machine Learning: an Artificial Intelligence Approach, II*, eds. R.S. Michalski, J. Carbonell and T.M. Mitchell, Morgan Kaufmann Publishers, Los Altos.

TAN, M., and SCHLIMMER, J.C. (1989), Extending a Bayes Classifier with IWN, *Proceedings of the 2nd International Workshop on Artificial Intelligence and Statistics*, Fort Lauderdale, FL.

WEISS, S.M., and KULIKOWSKI, C.A. (1984), *A practical Guide to Designing Expert systems*, Rowman & Allanhead, Totowa, NJ.

WINSTON, P.H. (1975), Learning structural descriptions from examples, in: *The Psychology of Computer Vision*, ed. P.H. Winston, McGraw-Hill, New York.

Improving Consistency Within Knowledge Bases

Guy Mineau and Jan Gecsei
Département d'Informatique et Recherche Opérationnelle
Université de Montréal, Canada
and
Robert Godin
Département de Mathématiques et d'Informatique
Université du Québec à Montréal, Canada

Summary

This paper shows how automatic symbolic classification of all knowledge objects in a knowledge base can alleviate the task of knowledge acquisition. It presents a knowledge representation structure, called knowledge space, that permits such symbolic classification. Simple and efficient algorithms which create the structure are also presented[1].

1 Introduction

Often, knowledge contained in knowledge-based systems can be divided into knowledge objects (KO)[2]. When these KOs can be grouped into different classes (according to the knowledge they embed), we could expect *set queries* to be asked. A set query concerns the description of a class as opposed to queries about individual KOs. When set query answering constitutes a major functionality of a knowledge-based system, it would be more efficient to explicitly represent the classes rather than having to recompute them when needed.

One way to represent classes of KOs is to use a frame-based knowledge representation formalism (Minsky (1975)). However, this puts the burden of creating classes solely upon knowledge acquisition, adding to the already considerable complexity of this task (Jackson (1986)). Furthermore, frames are meant to represent typical groupings of things as can be witnessed in our world. But in fact, there may be many other groupings unnatural or unfamiliar to humans not taken into account while constructing the knowledge base. For example, children may classify elephants and bears as being zoo or circus animals, depending on their personal preferences. This perspective may even change in time: adults would probably forget about that distinction unless they are veterinarians or animal trainers. Classification through such a knowledge acquisition process is thus biased according to the expected perspectives that the target users may have on the world described by the knowledge base. This consequently limits the symbolic processing of arbitrary set queries, restraining the potential scope of action of the system. Once again knowledge acquisition is pointed out as being an important bottleneck in the elaboration and applicability of knowledge-based systems.

[1]This work was supported by NSERC of Canada under grants A-9184 and A-3573.
[2]Unit containing all the knowledge about one particular thema.

NATO ASI Series, Vol. F 61
Knowledge, Data and Computer-Assisted Decisions
Edited by M. Schader and W. Gaul

In this article, we envisage the possibility of automatically building a non-subjective classification of the KOs. The role this classification will play in relieving the knowledge acquisition process will be the topic of section 4. We thus present algorithms that create such an inheritance structure which symbolically classifies the KOs of the original knowledge base. This structure is called *knowledge space* and is presented in section 2. It is a *heterarchy* of nodes, each node representing a class of KOs and containing information from which an abstracted description of that class can be generated.

In contrast to the work done with the conceptual clustering methods (Mitchell et al. (1986); Michalski et al. (1981); Stepp and Michalski (1986); Fisher and Langley (1985)), the knowledge space is not necessarily hierarchical and does not use specific domain knowledge to orient the classification process. (The potential of non-hierarchical classification is also considered by (Diday (1987)) with so called "pyramid" structures). Furthermore, our method lends itself to processing by simple and efficient algorithms for the generation and update of the structure. In effect, the memory requirements for that structure are of the same order of complexity than those of the original knowledge base, that is, $O(n)$, where n is the number of KOs. The algorithms that create the knowledge space work in time $O(n^2)$ in the worst case, because they restrict their attention to particular subsets of KOs: a complexity analysis is given in section 3. The method used to determine which subsets of KOs are relevant is also explicited in section 2.

2 The Knowledge Space

This section describes the method used to determine the relevant subsets of KOs, and to therefore construct the knowledge space accordingly. The same example will be used throughout the article in order to demonstrate the key ideas of the method.

2.1 Relevant Subsets of KOs

First of all, KOs have to be represented. In order to do so, we adopted the *conceptual graph formalism* of Sowa (1984). A KO will be defined as a conceptual graph. In this formalism, knowledge is represented by graphs in which boxes represent *concepts* and circles stand for *relations* between concepts. Fig. 1 shows a simple example of three KOs. In Fig. 1, there seems to be three classes that could be formed, based on the knowledge carried by the KOs. They are:

1. the animals located in zoos and having some color (KO1,KO2,KO3);
2. the animals who are brown (KO2,KO3);
3. the animals working in a circus (KO1,KO3).

The method we propose will extract classes from KOs, based on the *similarity* of their content. The description of each class will then be a conceptual graph that will include the largest common subgraph belonging to every KO in the class. Thus, only subsets of KOs containing identical concepts or relations become interesting. In order to avoid scanning all KOs when we wish to identify those which have some concepts or relations in common, we will use a two-dimensional table to establish correspondence between the KOs and the concepts and relations found in the original knowledge base. This table,

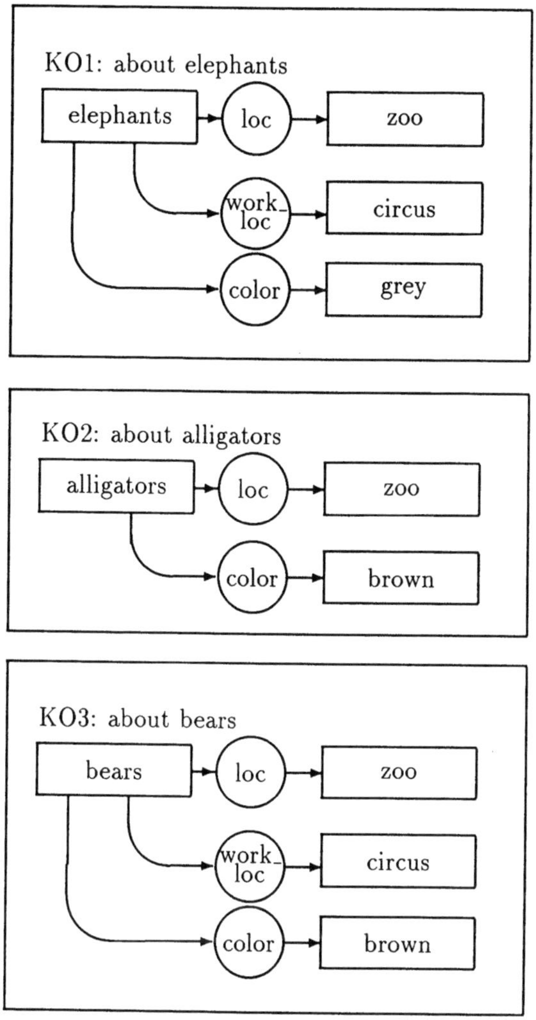

Figure 1: Three KOs Represented by Conceptual Graphs

called *intersection matrix*, will be constructed in time $O(n \log n)$ as demonstrates the following section, where n is the total number of KOs.

2.2 The Intersection Matrix

First, let us define a *triplet* as being a list of three elements, where the first and last are concepts while the second is a relation. A triplet will have the form <concept_1,relation,concept_2>. Most conceptual graphs (more precisely: those in which each concept occurs only once and in which only binary relations have been used) can be exhaustively decomposed without ambiguity into a set of triplets, where each triplet stands for a different subgraph of the conceptual graph representing the KO. Therefore, KOs can be seen as sets of such triplets; this is shown in Fig. 2. This possibility to decompose KOs into sets of uniform and simple components is one reason for choosing conceptual graphs for

KO1:
<elephants,loc,zoo>
<elephants,work_loc,circus>
<elephants,color,brown>

KO2:
<alligators,loc,zoo>
<alligators,color,brown>

KO3:
<bears,loc,zoo>
<bears,work_loc,circus>
<bears,color,brown>

Figure 2: The Same KOs Represented by Triplets

knowledge representation. Triplets can be used as descriptors of KOs, not unlikely as keywords are used to describe documents in retrieval systems. As a matter of fact, the structure proposed in this paper has its origins in the work of Godin et al. (1986), where a lattice of keyword subsets is used for classifying keyword-described documents in order to facilitate browsing.

The intersection matrix will show the occurrence of each triplet in the KOs. From Fig. 2, one can see that there are 8 different triplets (if we take all KOs altogether). The first 8 lines of the intersection matrix will each represent the occurrence of one of them in all KOs (see Fig. 3).

In this particular example, each triplet belongs to only one KO. If we consider the similarity between KOs as being the set of triplets they have in common (as often done with keywords in keywords systems), then Fig. 3 shows that there is nothing similar between any subsets of KOs: thus no classes should be formed. This seems to be in direct contradiction with the findings of the preceeding section.

To remedy this situation, we need to consider the similarity on a finer level, such as the similarity existing between *subparts* of triplets. For instance, even if KO2 and KO3 have no triplet in common, they both represent brown animals. This common property may be found by first extracting the identical subparts of the two triplets <alligators,color,brown> and <bears,color,brown>, producing <?,color,brown>, and then by finding a *common minimal supertype* for the two concepts that did not exactly match (in our example: alligators and bears). The common minimal supertype is found using a *type hierarchy* that is constructed along with the knowledge base (Sowa (1984)) and that expresses hierarchical relationships existing between concepts. In order to do this, the intersection matrix should not only show the occurrence of *complete* triplets (such as the first 8 lines), but also of all subparts of triplets. Consequently, all possible subparts of all triplets, called *generalization patterns*, must be generated and put on subsequent lines of the matrix (the remaining 31 lines). A generalization pattern (GP) is obtained from a triplet by replacing some (0 or more) of its components by the wildcard character "?". There will be 8 GPs generated

GPs:	KO1	KO2	KO3	
<elephants,loc,zoo>	x			line 1
<elephants,work_loc, circus>	x			line 2
<elephants,color,grey>	x			
<alligators,loc,zoo>		x		
<alligators,color,brown>		x		
<bears,loc,zoo>			x	
<bears,work_loc,circus>			x	line 7
<bears, color, brown>			x	line 8
<?,loc,zoo>	x	x	x	
<elephants,?,zoo>	x			
<elephants,loc,?>	x			
<?,?,zoo>	x	x	x	
<elephants,?,?>	x			
<?,loc,?>	x	x	x	
<?,?,?>	x	x	x	
<?,work_loc,circus>	x		x	line 16
<elephants,?,circus>	x			
<elephants,work_loc,?>	x			
<?,?,circus>	x		x	line 19
<?,work_loc,?>	x		x	line 20
<?,color,grey>	x			
<elephants,?,grey>	x			
<elephants,color,?>	x			
<?,?,grey>	x			
<?,color,?>	x	x	x	
<alligators,?,zoo>		x		
<alligators,loc,?>		x		
<alligators,?,?>		x		
<?,color,brown>		x	x	
<alligators,?,brown>		x		
<alligators,color,?>		x		
<?,?,brown>		x	x	
<bears,?,zoo>			x	
<bears,loc,?>			x	
<bears,?,?>			x	
<bears,?,circus>			x	
<bears,work_loc,?>			x	
<bears,?,brown>			x	
<bears,color,?>			x	line 39

Figure 3: The Intersection Matrix Associated With Fig. 2

from each triplet: the original triplet, called *complete triplet*, is also considered to be a GP. For example, the GPs of <elephants,loc,zoo> are shown in Fig. 4.

A KO will then be said to be described by the GPs generated from its set of complete triplets. Fig. 3 in complete depicts the intersection matrix where the set of triplets is the union of all possible GPs obtainable from the example of Fig. 2. Note that due to the commonality between the KOs in the example, the number of GPs is much less (39) than it would be without overlapping KOs (that is, $8 \times (2^3) = 64$). Furthermore, a partial order of generality can be defined among GPs. GP_i is said to be more general than GP_j, written $GP_i > GP_j$, iff replacing some (one or more) element of GP_j by "?" causes GP_j to be equal to GP_i. Inversely, GP_j is said to be more specific than GP_i.

<elephants,loc,zoo>
<?,loc,zoo>
<elephants,?,zoo>
<elephants,loc,?>
<?,?,zoo>
<elephants,?,?>
<?,loc,?>
<?,?,?>.

Figure 4: The Generalization Patterns of <elephants,loc,zoo>

In order to build the intersection matrix, all KOs have to be scanned only once, resulting in $O(n)$ iterations, where n is the total number of KOs. For each GP describing a particular KO, the corresponding row of the intersection matrix may already exists. It then needs to be found so x's can be appended to it. This can be done in $O(\log n)$ steps if the rows are indexed using an AVL tree and if the number of GPs describing each KO is bounded by a constant. The construction of the intersection matrix is thus bounded by $O(n \log n)$ in the worst case.

Finally, let's introduce two notions that we will use in the next section for the construction of the knowledge space: the *instantiation lists* (IL) and the *most specific sets*. Instantiation lists are added to each GP_i and represent the elements each "?" stand for in the complete triplets from which GP_i was generated. They will be needed later (section 2.4) for the descriptions of classes. There will be one IL for each KO_k that GP_i describes. The members of each IL are also lists, called *element lists* (EL). There will be as many ELs in an IL as there are complete triplets in KO_k from which GP_i can be generated. Each EL consists of as many elements as there are "?"s in GP_i. These elements are those concepts or relation that the "?"s stand for in GP_i, and are listed in the left to right order. For example, let GP_i = <?,work_loc,?> (line 20 in the intersection matrix). It would have the following two ILs (one for KO1, the other for KO3): ((elephants,circus)) and ((bears,circus)). The first of these comes from KO1: <elephants,work_loc,circus> (line 2), and the second from KO3: <bears,work_loc,circus> (line 7). In this example, each IL has *only one* EL, because *only one* complete triplet in each KO can generate GP_i[3]. If E is an arbitrary set of GPs, we will note E^+, the set obtained from E, in which the corresponding ILs have been appended to each GP.

Maximal transformations also need to be introduced. They are meant to avoid redundancy and to save space. When a certain position in *all* ELs of *all* ILs of GP_i is filled with the same concept or relation, then the corresponding "?" in GP_i can be instantiated to that concept or relation. When a "?" in GP_i is instantiated in that manner, ILs of GP_i are updated: the corresponding concept or relation can be eliminated from all ELs of all ILs. Making any number of such instantiations on GP_i generates other GPs which are said to be *transformations* of GP_i. For example, let GP_i = <?,work_loc,?> (line 20) and GP_j = <?,work_loc,circus> (line 16). Let their respective ILs be IL_i and IL_j. Then IL_i will be: ((elephants,circus)) and ((bears,circus)), and IL_j: ((elephants)) and ((bears)). One can see from GP_i, GP_j, IL_i and IL_j, that GP_j is a transformation of GP_i. In effect, the last element of both ELs in IL_i is equal to circus: thus GP_i can be transformed into

[3]Note that ILs of GPs which are complete triplets are null lists and will be omitted.

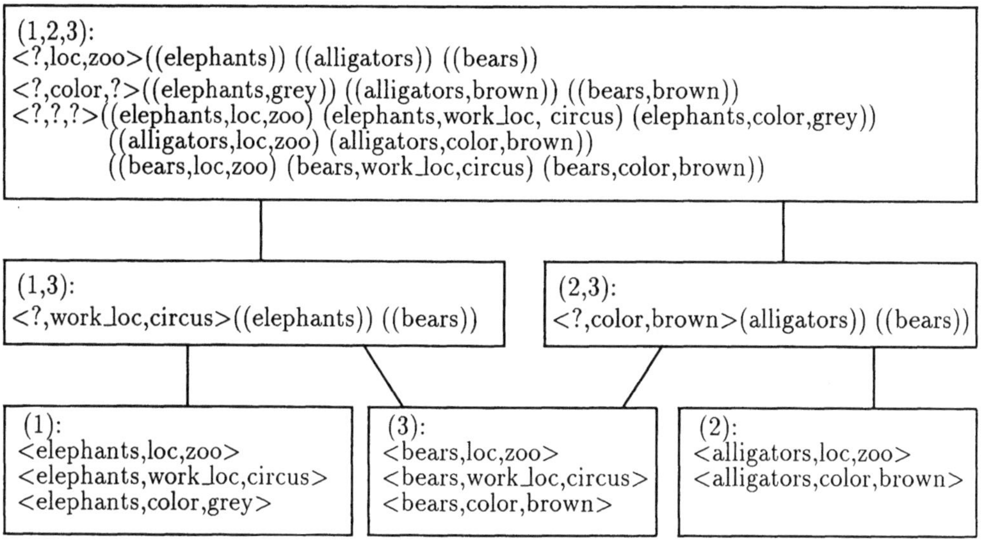

Figure 5: The Knowledge Space Generated From Fig. 3

GP_j. We will say that GP′ is a maximal transformation of GP_i iff it is a transformation of GP_i such that *all* "?" in GP_i which are instantiable in that manner have been instantiated. In the previous example, GP_j is a maximal transformation of GP_i. Also, each GP is considered to be a transformation of itself.

Finally, let $MS(E^+)$ = {maximal transformations of the GPs in E^+}. $MS(E^+)$ is said to be the *most specific set* of E^+. It can be computed by first generating the maximal transformations of all GPs in E^+, and then by eliminating duplicates. An example is given in the next subsection.

2.3 The Knowledge Space

This subsection presents the knowledge space and the algorithms which generate it from the intersection matrix. A complexity analysis follows in section 3.

As mentioned, the knowledge space is a heterarchy of nodes. Each node N corresponds to a class (subset) of knowledge objects, and contains the following information that will be needed later on to generate the description of the class (see section 2.4): (a) a *label* L consisting of the numbers of KOs represented by N, and (b) a subset C of generalization patterns, defined as follows. First, let us mention that only labels such that there exists a set of GPs which describe *all* KOs in it, *but no other* KOs, will be considered. This set of GPs will be called the *exclusive intersection set* of the KOs in L, written EI(L). Then $C = MS(EI(L)^+)$. For a given L, EI(L) may be extracted from the intersection matrix: it is the set of GPs whose corresponding lines are those which have x's *only* under the KOs in L. For example, if L = (1,3), then EI(L) will contain GPs from lines 16, 19, and 20. Further, $MS(EI(L)^+)$ will only contain <?,work_loc,circus> (line 16), and its associated ILs.

Finally, in order to connect the nodes together, we define a partial order of inclusion over the set of labels. For L_i, L_j (the labels of $node_i$ and $node_j$), $L_i < L_j$ iff the set of

KOs numbers in L_i is strictly included in the set of KOs numbers in L_j. Then node$_i$ is said to be *lower* than node$_j$ in the knowledge space, written node$_i$ < node$_j$. Also, node$_i$ is said to be the child of node$_j$ iff node$_i$ < node$_j$ and there is no node$_k$ such that node$_i$ < node$_k$ < node$_j$. Conversely, node$_j$ is said to be the *parent* of node$_i$. All nodes will be connected only to their children and parents. Note that every node (except the root) may have one or more parents: thus the knowledge space is a heterarchy.

It is possible to directly derive the nodes of the knowledge space from the intersection matrix. Examining a particular row of the intersection matrix tells exactly in which node of the knowledge space the maximal transformation of the GP should appear. Consequently, all nodes of the knowledge space may be found by scanning (only once) the rows of the intersection matrix. The process of creation of the knowledge space can be summarized by the following two algorithms. The first one creates the nodes from the intersection matrix; the second one links each node to its parents and children.

For each row of the intersection matrix:
1- the node where the GP should be placed is identified;
2- **if** (this node does not exist) **then**: -it is created;
3- **if** (the GP is a complete triplet) **then**: -it is inserted;
   else if (MS($\{GP\}^+$) = $\{GP\}^+$) and (the label of the node
      is not a one-element list)[4]
    then: -the GP is inserted with its ILs.

Finally, each node is connected to its children, based on a partial order of inclusion defined over the labels of the nodes. To do so, we first define the set of entry nodes N_0 of a set of KOs represented by label L. Let N_0 = {node$_r$ such that $L \leq L_r$, and there exists no other node$_t$ such that $L \leq L_t < L_r$, for $(t \neq r)$}. The algorithm will start by inserting the nodes which have smaller labels. This is the algorithm:

For each node to be connected (called new node):
1- the KO numbers contained in its label are identified;
2- **for** each of them:
   2.1- identify its entry nodes;
3- **for** each entry node:
   3.1- child ← entry node;{potential child}
   3.2- **if** (the label of the child is included
      into the new node's label)
    then: -findparents(child);
4- clear all markers.

where findparents(child) is the following recursive procedure:

[4]This condition states that one-member classes will be described only by complete triplets.

```
- if (the child has not yet been visited) then:
        - mark it as visited;
        - identify all its actual parents whose label
          is included into the new node's label;
        - if (this set of parents is non-empty) then:
                - for each of these nodes: -findparents(node);
        else: - connect the new node to the child.
```

2.4 Descriptions of Classes of KOs

We recall that in the knowledge space, every class is represented by a node N. Its description will be represented by the conceptual graph reconstructed from the set of triplets they all have in common (once the "?"s are instantiated). Consequently, let I(L) be the intersection of the sets of GPs that describe all, but not exclusively, the KOs in L. Also, let $G(E^+)$ be the set of GP_i belonging to E^+, where each "?" in GP_i has been instantiated to the common minimal supertype of the corresponding elements of its ILs. Then the description of class $N = G(MS(I(L)^+))$. Although $MS(I(L)^+)$ has not been explicitly stored in the knowledge space, we can regenerate it, as $MS(I(L)^+) = MS($all C sets of each node between, and including, N and its ancestors$)$. Examples of these notions are given below.

The process of generating a class description for node N has four steps: a) the content of some nodes have to be gathered (the nodes between N and the root of the knowledge space); from each node, only instantiation lists (IL) concerning the KOs in the label L of N are kept (the others being irrelevant for the present description); b) elimination of redundant GPs is done: if GP_i and GP_j have been gathered from different nodes, $GP_i > GP_j$, and $GP_i \neq$<?,?,?>, then GP_i is eliminated; c) the remaining "?"s are instantiated to the corresponding common minimal supertypes; and d) a conceptual graph can be reconstructed with the resulting triplets. As examples, we will reconstruct the conceptual graph describing each of the classes represented by nodes (2,3), (1,3), and (1,2,3). Here is the description of class (2,3).

a. Four GPs and their ILs are retrieved from the knowledge space:

GP#1: from node (1,2,3):<?,loc,zoo>	((alligators)) ((bears))
GP#2: from node (1,2,3):<?,color,?>	((alligators,brown))
	((bears,brown))
GP#3: from node (1,2,3):<?,?,?>	⇒ dropped!
GP#4: from node (2,3):<?,color,brown>	((alligators)) ((bears)).

b. GP#2 is eliminated because GP#2>GP#4, and they come from different nodes. GP#3 is dropped purely for efficiency purposes: it is untractable to try matching any GP on any other GP. Only GP#1 and GP#4 will remain.

c. Supposing the type hierarchy of Fig. 6, then the remaining "?"s are replaced by zoo_animals. The following triplets: <zoo_animals,loc,zoo> and <zoo_animals,color, brown> result.

d. The reconstructed conceptual graph is shown in Fig. 7.

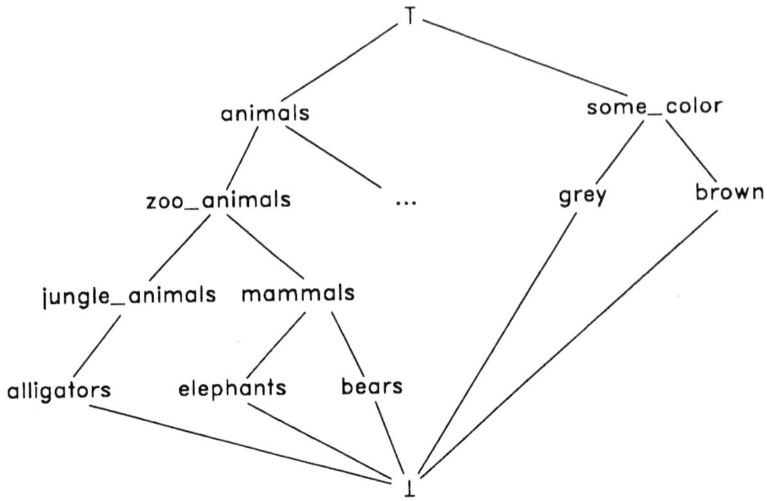

Figure 6: The Type Hierarchy Used to Find Common Minimal Supertypes

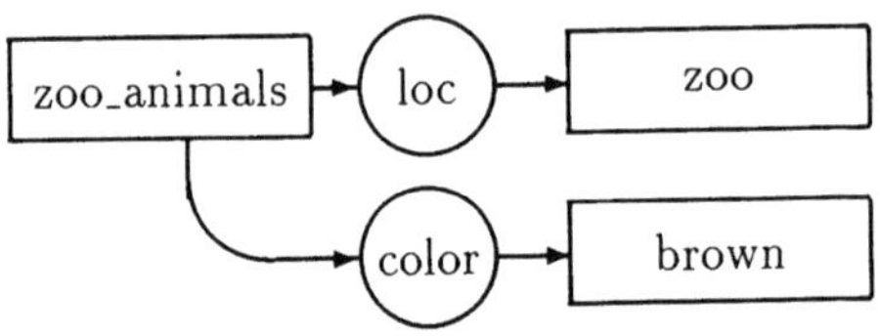

Figure 7: The Description of Class (2,3)

So class (2,3) can be described as follows: the animals located in zoos (zoo-animals) and who are brown. Similarly, we can find the description of class (1,3).

a. Four GPs and their ILs are also retrieved from the knowledge space:

GP#1: from node (1,2,3):<?,loc,zoo>	((elephants)) ((bears))
GP#2: from node (1,2,3):<?,color,?>	((elephants,grey))
	((bears,brown))
GP#3: from node (1,2,3):<?,?,?>	⇒ dropped!
GP#4: from node (1,3):<?,work_loc,circus>	((elephants)) ((bears))

b. GP#2 is not eliminated because it is not more general than any GP coming from any other node. GP#3 is dropped for efficiency purposes. Then GP#1, GP#2, and GP#4 will remain.

c. Supposing the same type hierarchy of Fig. 6, the first "?" in all GPs is replaced by mammals. The last "?" in GP#2 is replaced by some_color. The triplets: <mammals,loc,zoo>, <mammals,color,some_color>, and <mammals,work_loc,circus> result.

d. The reconstructed conceptual graph is shown in Fig. 8.

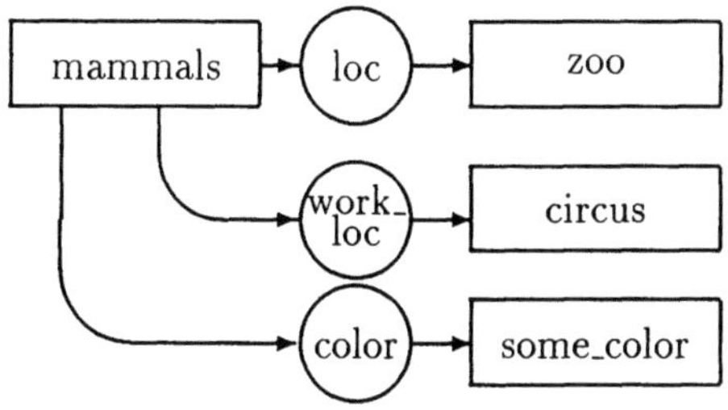

Figure 8: The Description of Class (1,3)

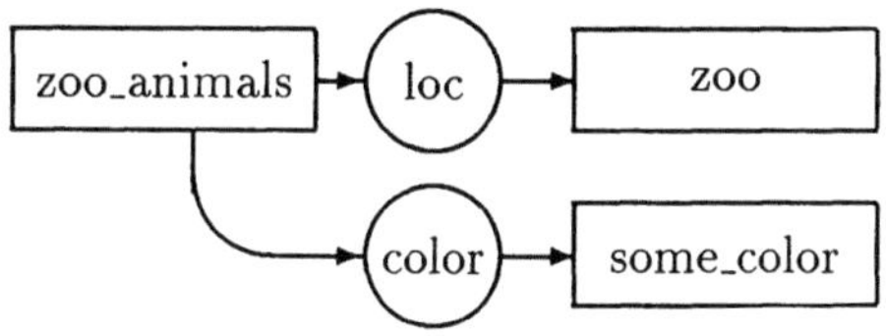

Figure 9: The Description of Class (1,2,3)

Class (1,3) defines the animals which are located in zoos, have some color, and work in a circus. We can see from the descriptions of classes (2,3) and (1,3) that they both share a common subgraph which resembles the description of class (1,2,3) as shown in Fig. 9.

a. Three GPs and their ILs are retrieved from the knowledge space:

GP#1: from node (1,2,3):<?,loc,zoo>	((elephants)) ((alligators)) ((bears))
GP#2: from node (1,2,3):<?,color,?>	((elephants,grey)) ((alligators,brown)) ((bears,brown))
GP#3: from node (1,2,3):<?,?,?>	⇒ dropped!

b. Only GP#3 is dropped; GP#1 and GP#2 remain.

c. Supposing the type hierarchy of Fig. 6, the first "?" in both GPs is replaced by "zoo_animals"; while the last "?" in GP#2 is replaced by "some_color". The triplets: <zoo_animals,loc,zoo> and <zoo_animals,color,some_color> result.

d. The corresponding conceptual graph is shown in Fig. 9.

One can see from Figures 7, 8 and 9, that the description of class (1,2,3) is not quite embedded in the descriptions of classes (2,3) and (1,3). For instance, description (1,3) concerns mammals found in zoos, while description (1,2,3) is more general and include all zoo-animals. The instantiations that are done using the type hierarchy may vary when different subsets of instantiation lists are kept, as done in step a) of the description generation process.

Precalculation of the possible instantiations of each "?" is not desired. The fundamental reason motivating this can be summarized as follows. In order for the memory requirements of the knowledge space to be of the *same order* of complexity than those of the original knowledge base, GPs needed to describe a class have to be distributed over many nodes. Thus the GPs contained in a node take part in the description of many different classes. Consequently, the "?"s can not be instantiated to any supertype in advance: they have to be stored as such. A complexity analysis of the time and memory requirements to create and store the knowledge space follows in section 3.

3 Complexity Analysis

This section gives some important results on the complexity of the knowledge space and on the complexity of the algorithms which generate it.

3.1 Memory Requirements

A fundamental question concerning the implementation of the knowledge space is the number of nodes in the heterarchy. Since there cannot be more nodes than the number of rows in the intersection matrix, obviously, the number of rows is an upper bound on the number of nodes in the worst case. Let m be the total number of complete triplets in all KOs, and p the number of nodes, then:

$$p \leq 8m$$

since every complete triplet has 8 GPs. Setting an upper bound k_{max} on the number of complete triplets for each KO, and n being the number of KOs, then:

$$p \leq 8\, k_{max}\, n$$

which is $O(n)$. However, in the average case, we could expect the number of nodes to be $O(\log n)$, referring to the well known Bradford law in information science which applies to many human processes such as the total number of words in a text or the total number of keywords in an indexed documentary database (Brookes (1977)).

Another interesting question is the complexity of the heterarchy as characterized by the number of links. Let us consider q the number of parents of a node. All ancestors of a node whose label is L, must have L contained in their labels. Any KO number in L appears in at most 8 k_{max} labels. Thus the number of ancestors of any node is bounded by 8 k_{max}, and so is the number of parents. Then:

$$q \leq 8\, k_{max} = O(1).$$

If we take the entire heterarchy, the total number of links, t, is bounded by the number of nodes multiplied by the number of parents for each node:

$$t \leq pq = O(n).$$

For the same reason as for the number of nodes, we could expect an average case of $O(\log n)$.

3.2 Worst Case Time Complexity of the Node Generation Algorithm

Scanning each row will take $8m$ iterations in the worst case for the main loop. If we use a balanced tree to index the node labels, locating the corresponding node and inserting it in the tree if absent, can be done in $O(\log m)$. Computing MS({GP}$^+$) is $O(n)$. So the generation algorithm can be done in $O(mn)$. Since m is $O(n)$, the upper bound becomes $O(n^2)$. Again we expect it to be $O((\log n)^2)$ in the average case.

3.3 Worst Case Time Complexity of the Linking Algorithm

This algorithm links the nodes in order of increasing label size. The sorting can be done by placing the nodes in buckets of same label cardinality while doing the previous node generation process. The additional cost will not change the asymptotical complexity found in section 3.2, because sorting can be done in $O(n \log n)$ steps.

The treatment of line 1 implies iterating over each KO number in each node's label, thus this will be the total number of iterations for the inner loop. Since each KO number can appear at most in 8 k_{max} labels, the total number of iterations is bounded by 8 k_{max} n. In each iteration, the ancestors of the entry nodes are tested for label inclusion until the children of the node to be linked are found. The number of entry nodes is bounded by 8 k_{max} and is thus $O(1)$. Reasoning as before, the number of ancestors of a node is $O(1)$ and so is the number of links traversed when searching for a potential child. Furthermore, because the labels can be kept sorted, the inclusion test can be done by scanning each label only once. The complexity is then bounded by the sum of the lengths of the labels. The maximum label length is n, giving a complexity of $O(n)$ for the inclusion test. Consequently the processing in line 3 is $O(n)$, and the whole algorithm is $O(n^2)$.

4 Knowledge Acquisition

This section shows how the knowledge space can intervene in knowledge acquisition. Its role will be to validate and enrich the type hierarchy, and hence, to ensure more consistency between the type hierarchy and the content of the KOs.

One of the problems knowledge acquisition is confronted with, is the creation of the type hierarchy. Normally, it is constructed using "a-kind-of" links (AKO links) which relate hierarchically the concept types together. These links are acquired in the same way as knowledge objects are: they come from the same sources of knowledge. Typically these sources are human experts or other reliable sources such as books and encyclopedias. Unfortunately, the type hierarchy of particular knowledge domains may not be as clearly defined as our representation formalisms require it to be. Consequently, even though the knowledge objects and the type hierarchy are both acquired from the same reliable sources, it is more than probable that there will be discrepancies between the contents of both.

In section 2, we discovered three classes of KOs that are of some interest, though *not explicitly* represented as such in the type hierarchy. One can deduce that these classes were willfully set aside or simply omitted. Examination of the differences existing between the

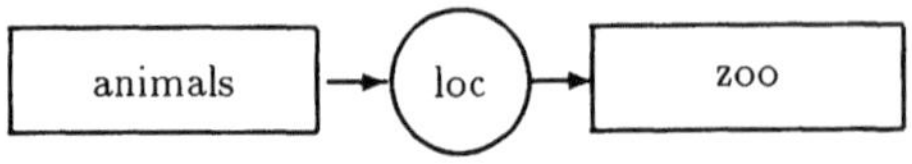

Figure 10: Type Description of zoo_animals

classes as described by Figures 7, 8 and 9, and the type hierarchy of Fig. 6, will improve the consistency of the knowledge base. For instance, we could compare the description of class (1,2,3) with the type description of zoo_animals. This latter description may be represented as a conceptual graph as suggests Sowa (1984). In our particular example, let us suppose that zoo_animals has been defined as the conceptual graph of Fig. 10.

Further, no other descriptions of concept types have been acquired, but only the hierarchical relationships existing between them. Then the triplet <zoo_animals,loc,zoo> that can be found from Fig. 9 corroborates the description of Fig. 10. However, the triplet <zoo_animals,color,some_color> is also found in Fig. 9 but not in Fig. 10. Then, the following questions arise:

a. Do we change the concept type (in the type hierarchy) to a mnemonic that would reflect more precisely the class so described? (For example, change zoo_animals to colored_zoo_animals.)

b. Do we include that aspect (color) of the description within the concept type definition? (In other words, should this be a property of the class zoo_animals instead of each individual animal?)

c. Do we ignore the color property for now, considering that it is a side-effect of incomplete knowledge, even though most KOs are acquired before the knowledge space is created?

d. Are there other concept types that have been omitted? (For example, if we discover a colored_zoo_animals class, should there be a non_colored_zoo_animals class?)

In any case, these questions, triggered by the differences which can be automatically found between the knowledge space and the type hierarchy, may prompt the system to ask for more precision on the content of the knowledge base, that is, on what this content is and what it should be. They help to refine and precise the concept types mnemonics, definitions, and relevancy; and they filter errors that could arise in KO descriptions as well. From then on, additional consistency checks can be done when new KOs are acquired. For example, if we decide to incorporate the color property to the zoo_animals description, we could verify that all subsequently acquired KOs which describe new instances of zoo_animals include the color property of that animal, forcing an early consistency check.

Furthermore, concept types may not need to be systematically changed: other concept types may be added to already existing classes. For instance, we found in section 2 that the "mammals" the system knows are animals who work in a circus (Fig. 11). We could decide to *add* a more appropriate mnemonic to this class, that is, circus_animals, creating the corresponding concept type definition.

This possibility to create new concept types corresponding to classes in the knowledge space results in an enrichment of the grammar used to describe all things in the knowledge

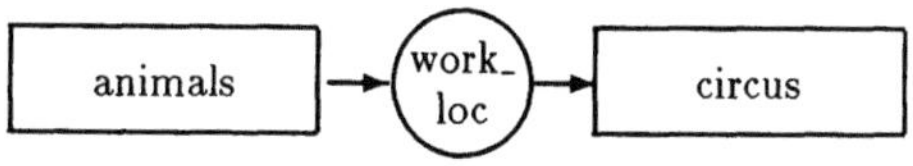

Figure 11: The New Concept Type: circus_animals

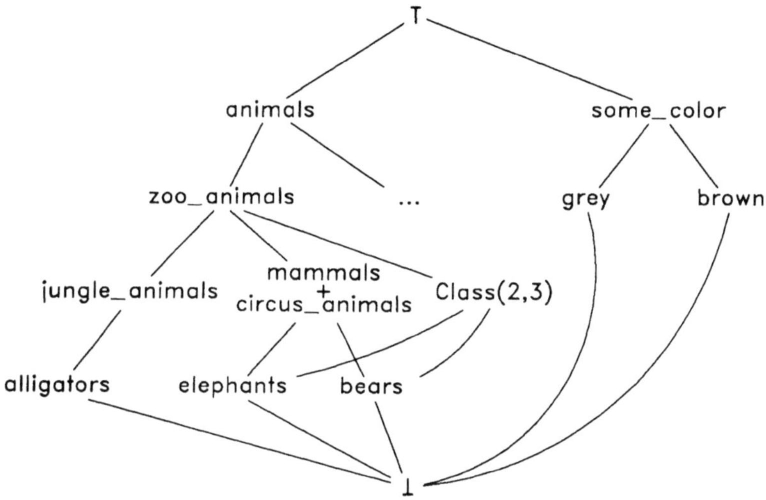

Figure 12: The Modified Type Hierarchy

base. However, not every class description need even be named: there may exist groupings of KOs for which there does not exist familiar names and for which it would then be pointless to find one. For example, the knowledge space shows a class (2,3) that is not represented in the type hierarchy: the brown zoo-animals. It would be cumbersome to try to give a different name to all different classes that could be formed with colored objects. In that case, even if such a class exists in the knowledge space, we could leave it nameless in the type hierarchy. When interacting with that precise class, we would then use the whole class description instead of its concept type.

The type hierarchy of Fig. 6 can now be slightly changed as to include the changes made while verifying consistency. The content of the modified type hierarchy (see Fig. 12) now reflects more precisely the content of the knowledge space: consistency is enforced.

5 Other Uses for the Knowledge Space

In addition to improving consistency, the knowledge space improves the capability of the system to handle different types of queries. Basically, it allows for a variety of retrieval tasks to be improved or added to the "know-how" of the system. This section summarizes them briefly.

First, with the knowledge space, much of the pattern matching normally needed when answering *simple queries* (like those processed by a Prolog system), has been done once and for all while constructing the instantiation lists. The inference engine could consequently run faster.

Secondly, because KOs are grouped into classes based on the similarity of the knowledge they embed, and because a description of each class is represented in the same formalism as is the original knowledge, queries about groups of KOs, called *set queries*, can be processed quite effectively. In effect, the knowledge space explicitly represents knowledge about groups of KOs. This knowledge is as easily available as is knowledge about one single KO, and can be as quickly retrieved.

Thirdly, the description of each class is extracted based on the similarity of the content of the KOs represented by this class. This description thus represents the similarity existing between these KOs. Consequently, a similarity inference process could be devised to abstract different levels of similarity between KOs (Mineau et al. (1989)).

Finally, the nodes of the knowledge space are linked to each other: it is possible to *browse* through the knowledge space and to explore a certain neighborhood of nodes. Naturally, closer nodes will represent more similar sets of KOs and will have more similar contents, where the differences are justified by generality levels (moving vertically in the structure). Each navigational step modifies the set of KOs under examination (represented by the label of the node), and justifies these modifications by the differences existing between the contents of the source and destination nodes. So, browsing through the knowledge space may be a self-explanatory exploration process. It allows the exploration of the *fine grain* structure of the knowledge base, in order to find alternatives for some missing or incomplete knowledge, to discover and use relationships between pieces of knowledge (e.g. to discriminate between them), and finally to correlate the browsed-through knowledge with the impact of its use on the task to be performed (e.g. to solve problems by analogy (Carbonell (1983)). The user can now *refine* his usage of the knowledge base by taking into account *not only* the knowledge as such, *but also* the links as established by the classification mechanism presented in this paper.

6 Conclusion

A knowledge representation structure, called knowledge space, has been presented (section 2). It symbolically classifies all knowledge objects based on the similarity of their content. The time and memory requirements to create and store such a structure are respectively $O(n^2)$ and $O(n)$ in the worst case, where n is the number of KOs. That is, the algorithms that create the knowledge space take $O(n^2)$ steps to extract the interesting classes that may be formed with any of the 2^n possible subsets of KOs. Furthermore, the knowledge space is of the same order of complexity than the original knowledge base from which it was constructed, that is, $O(n)$ (section 3).

Aside from other advantages concerning the processing of different types of queries (section 5), the knowledge space helps ensure that the contents of the type hierarchy and of the KOs will be consistent (section 4). It does so by automatically pinpointing the differences that arise between the two of them, that is, between the classes as defined theoretically by the type hierarchy and those formed with the contents of the actual knowledge objects. Consequently, the knowledge base may be finetuned in accordance to these differences. The knowledge space may be used as a tool that knowledge acquisition can utilize in order to achieve a higher level of consistency within the knowledge base. Thus, representing knowledge using a knowledge space can alleviate the complex and still "mystic" task of knowledge acquisition, among other things.

References

BROOKES, B.C. (1977), Theory of the Bradford Law, *Journal of Documentation, 33(3)*, 180–209.

CARBONELL, J.G. (1983), Learning by analogy: formulating and generalizing plans from past experience, in: *Machine Learning: An Artificial Intelligence Approach*, eds. R.S. Michalski, J.G. Carbonell and T.M. Mitchell, Morgan Kaufmann Publishers, Los Altos, CA, 137–161.

DIDAY, E. (1987), Orders and Overlapping Clusters by Pyramids, *Rapport de Recherche N° 730*, INRIA.

FISHER, D., and LANGLEY, P. (1985), Approaches to Conceptual Clustering, *Proceedings of IJCAI-85*, Morgan Kaufmann, Los Altos, CA, 691–697.

GODIN, R., SAUNDERS, E., and GECSEI, J. (1986), Lattice Model of Browsable Data Spaces, *Information Sciences, 40*, 89–116.

JACKSON, P. (1986), *Introduction to Expert Systems*, Addison-Wesley, New York.

MICHALSKI, R.S., STEPP, R.E., and DIDAY, E. (1981), A Recent Advance in Data Analysis: Clustering Objects into Classes Characterized by Conjunctive Concepts, in: *Progress in Pattern Recognition*, eds. L.N. Kanal and A. Rosenfeld, North-Holland, Amsterdam, 33–56.

MINEAU, G., GECSEI, J., and GODIN, R. (1989), Structuring knowledge bases using automatic learning, submitted for publication.

MINSKY, M. (1975), A Framework for Representing Knowledge, in: *The Psychology of Computer Vision*, ed. P. Winston, McGraw-Hill, New York, 211–277.

MITCHELL, T.M., CARBONELL, J.G., and MICHALSKI, R.S. (1986), *Machine Learning: A Guide to Current Research*, Kluwer Academic, New York.

SOWA, J.F. (1984), *Conceptual Structures: Information Processing in Mind and Machine*, Addison-Wesley, New York.

STEPP, R.E., and MICHALSKI, R.S. (1986), Conceptual Clustering: Inventing Goal-Oriented Classifications of Structured Objects, in: *Machine Learning: An Artificial Intelligence Approach, Vol. 2*, eds. R.S. Michalski, J.G. Carbonell and T.M. Mitchell, Morgan Kaufmann, Los Altos, CA, 471–498.

Cluster and Classify: A Conceptual Approach

Carlo Misiak
Institut für Kognitionsforschung
Universität der Bundeswehr Hamburg, Germany

Summary

From the platform of a data set that was gathered in a complex problem solving task, this paper presents preliminary results of the evaluation of the feasibility of establishing conceptual clustering schemes within the structure of an Object Oriented Programming System, namely KEE (Knowledge Engineering Environment). It is shown that both adequate data description and representation are crucial in order to successfully develop the method. The conclusion is that it is feasible to generate description primitives from the data. However, it is not quite clear yet how to evaluate the quality of potential solutions of an inductive process.

1 Introduction

Within the context of this publication it is necessary to clarify that the research presented here stems from a psychological context and thus is strongly related to issues in the fields of psychology and cognitive science, though it incorporates some ingredients of the sciences of the artificial, here especially aspects of the use of artificial intelligence methods and pattern recognition.

The questions tackled here are concerned with problems of the realization and further development of a data classification method that was, to my knowledge, introduced by Michalski (1980, 1983). This method is labeled as conceptual clustering or inductive cluster generation.

In the course of this paper, I shall first give an outline of the genesis of the data, the structure of which motivated the research. Afterwards, a short circumscription of the kernel idea of conceptual clustering will be given together with suggestions for modifications of the method. Then some implementational aspects of a prototype classifier are described and, finally, I shall give an evaluation of the research state that is reached so far.

2 A Psychological Experiment

In order to outline the motivation for trying to explore the feasibility of the development of a version of a conceptual clustering algorithm, a short description of the situation that generated the data to be analyzed is given. The data was gathered by automatically monitoring the control behavior of human problem solvers in a fully computer-driven psychological experiment. Within the experimental setting, the subjects' task was to

NATO ASI Series, Vol. F 61
Knowledge, Data and Computer-Assisted Decisions
Edited by M. Schader and W. Gaul

$$
\text{subjects}\left\{\begin{array}{l}
1\left\{\begin{array}{l}
t_1\left\{\begin{array}{llllll}
t_{c1} & t_{a1.1} & t_{a1.2} & t_{a1.3} & u_1 & x_1 \\
\vdots & & & & & \\
t_{c16} & t_{a16.1} & t_{a16.2} & t_{a16.3} & u_{16} & x_{16}
\end{array}\right. \\
\vdots \\
t_{30}\left\{\vdots\right.
\end{array}\right. \\
\vdots \\
65\left\{\begin{array}{l}
t_1\left\{\begin{array}{llllll}
t_{c1} & t_{a1.1} & t_{a1.2} & t_{a1.3} & u_1 & x_1 \\
\vdots & & & & & \\
t_{c16} & t_{a16.1} & t_{a16.2} & t_{a16.3} & u_{16} & x_{16}
\end{array}\right. \\
\vdots \\
t_{30}\left\{\vdots\right.
\end{array}\right.
\end{array}\right.
$$

Figure 1: Overview of Data-Structure

adjust the state vector x of system-variables of a dynamical linear difference system of the type defined by the equation $x_{t+1} = A(x_t + u_t)$ to a defined vector s of goal states over a period of thirty time steps t. Please note that the 16×16 system matrix A was decomposed into independent subsystems. In short, a single time step may be described by the following instructional sequence:

1. Information-retrieval: If $t \notin \{3, 6, 9, 12, \ldots, 30\}$, select up to eight system-variables in order to inspect their state-value; else automatically see a display of all state-values.

2. System-control: Construct components of input-vector u as desired within specified real-time.

Clearly, the task requires to appropriately choose components of the input vector u under restrictive conditions. Restrictions are imposed on the amount of information retrieval allowed and the time granted to make decisions. For a complete description of details of this type of experimental task see Misiak and Kluwe (1986).

The data that was obtained from 65 subjects is to be characterized as a description of different phases, degrees and styles of learning progress of humans. For each individual that took part in the experiment, the data is a set of partly interdependent data points, the structure of which is given in Fig. 1. For each subject, time step t and system-variable x_i, the data obtained were:

- if applicable, time histories of decision times leading to the selection of a system-variable for inspection (t_{ci})

- time histories of actions ($t_{ai.n}$) leading to control-input values in u

- input values, i.e. the components of u

- system-state-values, i.e. the sixteen components of vector x.

In several former studies of, among others, Kluwe, Misiak and Reimann (1984), Misiak and Kluwe (1986) and Strohschneider (1986), exorbitant variances in performance measures were found. This indicates that the exclusive employment of methods that only recur to numeric properties of the data is not feasible to reveal structures as desired. The attributes of the data, namely the interdependence structure of parts of the variables, prevented the use of methods as time series analyses as well as sorts of discriminant analyses, which otherwise might have been methods of choice.

3 Concepts and Clusters

As the type of the underlying data is made transparent, some introductory remarks on the basic ideas of the framework of conceptual clustering may be in order. Roughly, the agglomeration process can be described as the incremental transformation of a set of object attributes into a hierarchical description of object classes. It is important to note here that the attribute vectors need not necessarily be numerical.

The process is guided by a predefined set of background knowledge, namely relevant attribute descriptors together with their domain specifications. In addition to this, background knowledge may incorporate inference rules that can infer new attributes from existing ones. From single descriptors out of this background material it should be possible to generate compound descriptors by building appropriate combinations.

In theory, conceptual clustering leads to symbolic descriptions of given entities. The ultimate goal of the method is to produce results that are structurally and semantically similar to those a human expert might produce observing the same entities. The realization of this goal, though, implies knowledge of the yet unclarified reasoning process of experts.

Due to the goals envisioned by Michalski (1983), the components of these descriptions should be comprehensible as single "chunks" of information. The chunks are to be directly interpretable in natural language, and should relate quantitative and qualitative concepts in an integrated fashion. At the moment I myself do not see any chance to implement features that at least resemble what can be deduced from the description given above.

In contrast to feature oriented methods—i.e. numerical cluster analyses—, the major difference of conceptual methods, as I understand, is that concepts should be drawn from relations or combinations of attributes of the objects. This structural aspect is not yet covered by methods that cluster—or classify—by computing similarity measures of feature vector components and do not take into account inner vector relations. Thus, feature oriented methods may produce similarity within groups of structurally differentiable objects. Another problem that may not occur to conceptual methods and thus may be circumvented is that of separating overlapping clusters, which does not seem to be solved within the genre of feature oriented methods.

4 To Learn or not to Learn

A possible improvement (if any) of conceptual methods in comparison to feature oriented methods aims at the introduction of learning components into the process of data categorization. A cautious word about the definition of the term "learning" seems to be appropriate here, because common definitions of this term—and the underlying mechanisms—seem to me to be rather fuzzy. As an example of fuzzyness, I cite a definition of learning within a system that is given the attribute of being capable to learn. This definition originates from Simon (1983):

> "Learning denotes changes in the system that are adaptive in the sense that they enable the system to do the same task or tasks drawn from the same population (of tasks) more efficiently and more effectively the next time."

Simon (1983) neither gives clear definitions of whatever efficiency or effectivity may mean, nor does he give a hint what common characteristics a population of task shares. Moreover, this definition does not hold for drawbacks in performance while learning, a phenomenon that is well known in psychological research on learning processes, especially when this learning takes place as a non-monotonic process. Within this context I only want to define learning in a much simpler way:

> A classification system has learned when it is able to generate at least one compound classification scheme with the use of basic scheme constructor rules supplied to it. Furthermore, it is demanded that this same classification scheme is capable of classifying instances of other data entities derived from the same population due to the same learned rules.

5 Developmental Loop

In order to obtain classifications of different aspects of the highly time dependent learning process a multiple loop through a three step procedure seemed to be applicable.

1. The analysis and tailoring of the components of Michalski's APC (**A**nnotated **P**redicate **C**alculus) notation as the fundamental of the model to be developed.

2. The implementation and refinement of a preliminary prototype that aims at the combination of data-analyzing as well as knowledge-processing structures. This step was achieved within the environment of the LISP-based hybrid KEE (**K**nowledge **E**ngineering **E**nvironment) running on a SUN 3/60. It was undertaken in order to estimate the feasibility of the project.

3. The evaluation of preliminary partial results of the prototype construct's elements.

6 On APC

Crucial to conceptual methods is the language in which basic attribute descriptors are expressed, as it is the backbone for forming stars, that is—*all possible non redundant event descriptions under the constraint of the description language.*

The realized portion of a star, in a notation given by Shekar, Narasimha Murty and Krishna (1989) can be expressed as

$$\bigcup_{i=1}^{N} C_i \overset{c}{\Rightarrow} \bigwedge_{c\, i=1}^{N} D_i$$

where the set of objects is divided into N Clusters $C_1, C_2, C_3, \ldots, C_N$ that are described by descriptors $D_1, D_2, D_3, \ldots, D_N$, respectively. This means that the whole data set in any case implies the conjunction of all descriptors inherent to the data.

In order to demonstrate the semantic richness of APC, but also the necessity to fully automate the process of description generation, I give an example of an instance of a complicated APC expression, which is inspired by Michalski (1983), who denotes a similar expression as a "user formulated observational statement ... in terms of selected descriptors".

$$\begin{aligned}
&\exists.STEP(5), STEP(7)\& \\
&[positive(STATE.T5_{x1}, STATE.T5_{x2}, STATE.T5_{x3})]\&[negative(STATE.T5_{x4})]\& \\
&[positive(STATE.T7_{x1}, STATE.T7_{x2}, STATE.T7_{x3})]\&[negative(STATE.T7_{x4})]\& \\
&[negative(INPUT.T5_{x1}, INPUT.T5_{x2}, INPUT.T5_{x3})]\&[positive(INPUT.T5_{x4})]\& \\
&[long(OP-DECIDE.T5_{x1}, OP-DECIDE.T5_{x2}, OP-DECIDE.T5_{x3})]\& \\
&[short(OP-DECIDE.T7_{x1}, OP-DECIDE.T7_{x2}, OP-DECIDE.T7_{x3})]\& \\
&::\rangle[class = SYS1.STRUCTURE.UNDERSTOOD]
\end{aligned}$$

Though APC, as the example shows, is well suited to express static attributes of objects as well as arbitrary combinations of them under the constraints given by each descriptor's domain structure, it is not immediately clear how to express time related concepts within this notation. As the data needed descriptors of the time-related inner-data structure, this gap had to be filled in order to conveniently use parts of the formalism.

Backtracking to formal logics, it is obvious that APC can easily be augmented by adding time-related statements as defined by Sinowjew and Wessel (1975) such as $(A \uparrow B)$, which are simple statements with the meaning "event A is before event B".

6.1 Reductions of APC

In a first step to construct an inductive classifier it is not feasible to use derived or complicated logical expressions as elementary components of the description language. It is well known that all logical functions are derivatives of either Sheffe or Peirce functions (NAND and NOR). Because of this reason, only conjunction ($\wedge$), alternative ($\vee$) and negation ($\neg$) were to be used in the description language of the prototype. Possible simplifications of pseudo-complex compound statements that consist of many of the basic expressions can be achieved later by applying reduction rules.

7 An Environment and a Prototype

7.1 Some Facts on KEE

Before details of an attempt to realize the method are given, I think it is necessary to give some ideas on what is hidden behind KEE (Fikes and Kehler (1985)). As mentioned earlier, KEE, a child of UNITS (Stefik (1979)), was originally designed as a knowledge engineering tool. It combines or resembles features which are known from other systems such as AMORD, ART, BABYLON, KL-ONE, TWAICE and the like.

As a hybrid environment, KEE comprises

- a flavor-like object oriented programming structure that is strongly influenced by the frame concept established by Minsky (1975)
- an inference engine which is working on rule structures that remind of production system G by Newell (1973)
- the implementation of demons of the kind that were, to my knowledge, first introduced to the AI world within the UCI-LISP based FUZZY language.

Additionally, KEE includes a TMS (**T**ruth **M**aintenance **S**ystem (e.g., deKleer (1986)) which optionally can take care of consistency within and between labeled collections of entities called worlds. This part of the environment, to my experience, does not seem to be stable. Thus, given the presupposition of graceful environmental stability, KEE was thought of as an environment appropriate to install the necessities of a prototype of an adaptive classifier.

7.2 A Model and the Main Structure of an Algorithm

7.2.1 Clarifying the Problem

It is necessary to point out that problems encountered here are extremely difficult to handle. There are no ways to give the procedure either positive or negative examples of a concept description. Thus, it is not able to extract structural descriptions by contrasting positive and negative instances of events. Instead, the system must be supplied with a quality criterion in order to select favorable descriptions.

Please note that a quality criterion is essential in order to evaluate compound descriptions that the system generated by itself. There is no way to generate evaluation functions automatically unless there is another layer within the scheme that analyses descriptions. Even if a multiple evaluation-cluster generation process were feasible, a final intelligent quality criterion has to be supplied to stop the process.

The AI community tends to sophistically differentiate between programming as the direct implementation of knowledge and learning by the use of heuristics and by augmenting and transforming existing knowledge. It is rarely noted, though, that there is an inherent contradiction within the term heuristic programming itself: by definition, heuristics are essentially random and programs essentially algorithmic.

In other words: The more heuristic a process, the more random the outcome. With relation to the problem given this means that predefined quality criteria minimize the degree of heuristics inherent to a clustering process.

7.2.2 Input Data Representation

Now let me introduce the first step of implementation and modelling. In order to separate the data to be classified from data produced by the environment in its efforts to categorize the material, the input to the process was stored as a hash table, a LISP construct that gives easy, transparent and fast content-oriented access to data. This, as a side effect, ensures the easy exchangeability of the interface between process and data, since a hash table access mimics database retrieval operations.

7.3 UNITS of Analysis

Before any classification procedure can start, it is necessary to define the structure of the input to the process. Here, an elementary unit of analysis is the time history of a subject's actions together with the state value of the corresponding system-variable. It consists of the data sampled at a single choice-action sequence of the subjects and holds information related to time and environmental variables.

In order to make aspects of the data structure more easily accessible to the mechanism supplied by the KEE environment, random samples of the whole data set were stored in an inheritance network with a generic data-event description unit as the top node. For two important reasons, sampling is useful:

1. It is not always possible to represent large data sets as complete inheritance networks due to the constraints of the computational environment.
2. Sampling is necessary if conceptual methods are to be applied to time varying real-time processes.

As result of sampling and representational transformation a subset of the data was represented as an inheritance structure of data units. A structure of this kind is, within an object oriented programming environment, the most natural representation of an object structure to be classified.

7.4 Background Knowledge

The background knowledge is composed of descriptors and the adjunct domain constraints and was installed at appropriate places within the representational UNIT-SLOT-FACET-FACETVALUE hierarchy supplied by the KEE system. In the case of the data-set studied here, descriptors were given by the slots of UNITS holding elementary units of analysis as described above. Each descriptor-slot is holding either a measured or a derived datum as a slot-value. The domain constraints of each descriptor are defined by the values of the VALUE.CLASS facets and are essentially data-type specifications. Cardinality facets give additional control over the domain as they constrain the multiplicity of objects' attribute values.

7.5 Inferential Knowledge

The prototype structure until now does not care for generating inferential knowledge. However, propositional functions, if necessary, can be installed in and attached to slots as ACTIVE.VALUE constructs, which could take care of assertions. Another easy way of installing the option of creating new knowledge is the definition of rules of the classical production form within separate rule-trees.

7.6 First Steps Towards a Prototype

During the sampling process, the first step of the classification procedure is running those data elements that are to be taken into consideration through a filtering or recoding construct. Each one of the attribute values is evaluated by a procedure which is specified as an active value attached to the data description member slots of the generic data unit.

The result of the evaluation is stored in the own slots of the corresponding terminal data elements.

For the purpose of first evaluations, the filter simply recodes the originally continuous attribute values into a two valued scale due to a user or system supplied threshold value. If the system supplies the threshold, then it is estimated as the 50th percentile of the data from the sample. It is obvious that, in principle, the generated scale may be n valued.

After this filtering process, a terminal data unit contains the original attribute values within its member slots and the results of the evaluation in its own slots. This separation ensures the distinction necessary for potential further evaluation steps where it is necessary to separately consider original and derived data.

7.7 Logical Discriminators

Compound logical data description clauses are generated from the results of the evaluation functions. Typical description clauses have the form:

```
(AND  (A STATE.EVALUATION OF VAR.X IS LOW)
      (A INPUT.EVALUATION OF VAR.X IS LOW)
      (A SELECT.TIME.EVAL OF VAR.X IS LOW))
```

Due to the simplicity of the evaluation function, the number of possible compound combinations is intentionally limited. It may be easily increased by choosing a wider range of recode values. The generated compound statements may well be interpreted as consisting of classification rule components since they can be augmented by an `IF` precomponent and a `THEN CATEGORIZE AS CLASS?` postcomponent and then be fed into inference processes. An example is given below.

```
(IF   (AND  (A STATE.EVALUATION OF VAR.X IS LOW)
            (A INPUT.EVALUATION OF VAR.X IS LOW)
            (A SELECT.TIME.EVAL OF VAR.X IS LOW))
THEN        (ASSERT VAR.X IS IN CLASS EASY.VARS))
```

8 Evaluation

So far, it has been shown that it is possible to implement a minimal structure within the KEE environment that is capable of generating logical discriminators on the basis of random data samples.

I am well aware that at this moment a lot of questions are still open. The next question that has to be answered is how to supply the system with adequate quality criteria, as criteria should not narrow the search space too restrictively.

At the moment, two considerations for generating instances of examples and / or counter-examples for the inductive classification process seem to be adequate:

1. Supplying the system with ideal prototypes of human behavior data as rated by an expert.

2. Supplying the system with data that are generated by a problem solving system written by the author which follows well-defined *strategies* while solving the control task in question. This seems to be the preferable solution.

9 Final Remarks

Up to now, I am not able to give a definite statement about the encouragement level of the developmental status reached so far. But without exaggeration I think that it may be concluded that the approach of conceptual methods is worth to be followed by a broader group of researchers, especially within psychology, than it is done now.

References

deKLEER, J. (1986) An Assumption-Based TMS, *Artificial Intelligence, 28, 1*, 127–162.

FIKES, R.E., and KEHLER, T. (1985), The role of frame-based representation in reasoning, *Communications of the ACM, 28, 9*, 904–920.

KLUWE, R.H., MISIAK, C., and REIMANN, H. (1984), Lernvorgänge beim Umgang mit Systemen: Die Ausbildung subjektiver Ordnungsstrukturen durch Erfahrungen beim Umgang mit umfangreichen Systemen, Bericht aus dem Fachbereich Pädagogik der Hochschule der Bundeswehr, Hamburg.

MICHALSKI, R.S. (1980), Pattern Recognition as Rule-Guided Inductive Inference, *IEEE Trans. Pattern Anal. Mach. Intell., PAMI-2*, 349–361.

MICHALSKI, R.S. (1983), A Theory and Methodology of Inductive Learning, in: *Machine Learning*, eds. R.S. Michalski, J.G. Carbonell and T.M. Mitchell, Tioga, Palo Alto, 83–134.

MINSKY, M. (1975), A Framework for Representing Knowledge, in: *The Psychology of Computer Vision*, ed. P.H. Winston, McGraw-Hill, New York, 211–277.

MISIAK, C., and KLUWE, R.H. (1986), CSC - Complex System Control, Bericht aus dem Fachbereich Pädagogik der Universität der Bundeswehr, Hamburg.

NEWELL, A. (1973), Production Systems: Models of Control Structures, in: *Visual Information Processing*, ed. W.G. Chase, Academic Press, New York, 463–526.

SHEKAR, B., NARASIMHA MURTY, M., and KRISHNA, G. (1989), Structural Aspects of Semantic-Directed Clusters, *Pattern Recognition, 22, 1*, 65–74.

SIMON, H.A. (1983), Why Should Machines Learn?, in: *Machine Learning*, eds. R.S. Michalski, J.G. Carbonell and T.M. Mitchell, Tioga, Palo Alto, 25–37.

SINOWJEW, A., and WESSEL, H. (1975), *Logische Sprachregeln*, Deutscher Verlag der Wissenschaften, Berlin.

STEFIK, M. (1979), An examination of a frame-structured system, in: *Proceedings of the 6th International Joint Conference on Artificial Intelligence (Tokyo)*, International Joint Conference on Artificial Intelligence, 845–852.

STROHSCHNEIDER, S. (1986), Zur Stabilität und Validität von Handeln in komplexen Realitätsbereichen, *Sprache & Kognition, 1*, 42–48.

Incremental Learning From Symbolic Objects

Michelle Sebag
Centre de Mathématiques Appliquées,
Edwin Diday
Université Paris-IX Dauphine and INRIA, Le Chesnay, France,
and
Marc Schoenauer
Centre de Mathématiques Appliquées
Ecole Polytechnique, Palaiseau, France

Summary

This paper deals with discrimination on real-world data when examples as well as partial rules are initially available. As the learning base is both noisy and insufficiently representative, our approach is oriented towards successive approximations of a discriminant rule base; the aim is to predict conclusions according to further examples.
A 2-step iterative process is presented:

1. A sub-optimal generalization leads to an approximative rule base including redundancy (strongly overlapping, rules) and errors.
2. A change of representation called reduction transforms the refinement of the previous rule base into a new learning problem. Iteration of the generalization then defines a second rule set, refining and correcting the previous one, and so on.

First results on a well-studied learning base are detailed.

1 Introduction

We present a discriminant generalization strategy, adapted to learning rules from examples (see Mitchell (1982), Michalski (1984) and Quinlan (1986)) as well as from partial rules. The accuracy criterion is the prediction result obtained on a test set.

Previous research has stated that optimal learning was not adapted to real-world problems:

- Exact discrimination is inadequate because of the initial noise, as shown by Clark and Niblett (1987): significative rules admit exceptions, hence are not perfectly discriminant, while exact rules have a small predictive accuracy.
- Perfect conciseness is unobtainable, too, because the initial data is insufficiently representative: conciseness leads to instable and insufficient rule bases, when the initial data is not representative enough. Redundant rules, that is strongly overlapping rules, are more adapted to an incompletely known learning domain (see Cestnik, Bratko and Kononenko (1987) and Sebag and Schoenauer (1988)).

NATO ASI Series, Vol. F 61
Knowledge, Data and Computer-Assisted Decisions
Edited by M. Schader and W. Gaul

Henceforth, the learning is oriented towards successive approximations of a rule base. Two problems are then to be considered: first, what does an approximative learning mean; second, how to ensure the convergence of this approximation.

This paper focuses mainly on the second point: the proposed solution is inspired from the learning by discovery, and the works of Langley, Bradshaw and Simon (1984) and Falkenhaimer and Michalski (1986). We do not try to improve the generalization itself (by pre- or post-pruning, for instance): this paper formalizes the refinement of a rule base, approximative solution of an initial learning problem, as a new learning problem. A change of representation called *reduction* of the learning domain achieves the desired transformation from an initial to the next learning problem.

On the reduced learning problem, a second rule set is then generalized, including, for instance, rules such as:

> *IF R_1 is triggered AND R_2 is not THEN CONCLUSION is ...*
> where R_1 and R_2 are rules of the previous rule set.

These new rules behave as meta-rules controlling conflicts and exceptions among previous rules. Iteration of the process builds a sequence of rule sets, called multi-layered rule set. Three features of this approach are outlined:

1. A second layer rule is disjunctive with respect to the initial representation of the learning domain: if R_2 is given by

   R_2: *IF A true AND B true AND C true THEN CONCLUSION ...*

   then R_2 *not triggered* is equivalent to *A false OR B false OR C false.*

   Meanwhile, R_2 *not triggered* is considered as an elementary feature in the reduced learning problem. The complexity of discovered rules significantly increases (disjunctive rules are discovered) while the generalization algorithm is still looking for conjunctive rules.

2. This approach enables an incremental learning: a big learning base can be divided and rules learnt from a given subset of the initial data are gradually refined considering others subsets.

3. Whatever the logic order of the initial representation is, the propositional logic is used as soon as the first layer is reached. The optimality requirements over a first-order generalization algorithm may then be relaxed; refinements and corrections are done using a further propositional generalization.

The first section of this paper concerns the representation of data. Assertions defined by Diday (1990) and Brito and Diday (1990) are used in order to describe elementary examples together with premises of partial rules. In the second section, a bottom-up generalization is briefly reviewed (see Sebag (1990) for details); the approximation heuristics are detailed. In the third section, reduction (i.e., the transformation of the initial learning problem into a new learning problem, whose aim is to refine a solution of initial learning problem) is presented. The aim is to refine a solution of the initial learning problem (see Sebag and Schoenauer (1989b) for a detailed discussion). The iteration of the generalization-reduction process is then discussed.

Finally, first results of the *ML2* (*Multi Layered Learning*) algorithm on a well-studied learning base are detailed and compared to *AQR* from Michalski et al. (1986), *CN2* from Clark and Niblett (1987) and *Assistant 86* from Cestnik, Bratko and Kononenko (1987).

2 Representation

In some industrial domains, available data is composed of elementary examples together with partial rules. Examples and partial rules are described by attribute - (set of) values pairs. For instance, one tries to characterize the classes of soldering failures from examples and partial rules about soldering joints:

	Description				Conclusion
	Electrical intensity	Iron Reference	Presence of smoke	Soldering time	Type of Failure
Ex1	10	EF + ES	Yes	120	Fail. 0
Ru1	-	AX + ES	No	-	Fail. 1

A row represents the description of a given example, or the premise of a rule, together with the associated value of conclusion. A column represents a given descriptor (a variable in *Data Analysis* terminology or an attribute in *Machine Learning* terminology). The last column represents the conclusion to predict (the variable to explain). The aim of our approach is to express the conclusion as a logical function of the descriptors.

2.1 Completed Data Matrix

Let Ω be the learning domain. Qualitative descriptors y_j, $j = 1, \ldots, P$, are defined on (possibly not all) Ω:

$$y_j\colon\ D(y_j) \subset \Omega \rightarrow O_j.$$

After discretization of the numerical descriptors (see, for example, Lebowitz (1985) and Celeux et al. (1989)) it is possible to consider only finite spaces O_j. An element s of the learning base is then described by the assertion s', a conjunction of some elementary events $[y_i = y_i(s)]$ as defined in Diday (1990) and Brito and Diday (1990):

$$s' = \bigwedge_i [y_i = y_i(s)], \quad i \in I_s \subset [1, P].$$

The conclusion to be explained is called y_0. An element s of the learning base then encodes the rule: $s' \Rightarrow y_0(s)$.

The main difference, comparing the above table to a classical data matrix, is the high rate of missing values: not all descriptors are defined. For a given example s, the value of a descriptor y_j can be

1. irrelevant, meaning not significant (e.g., the conclusion remains unchanged whatever the age of the captain);
2. unknown (e.g., when only the fruit is seen, the color of the flower is unknown);
3. not defined (e.g., if there is no hat, then the color of the hat is not defined).

In any other case, the descriptor y_j is said to be relevant for s.

2.1.1 Not Significant Descriptors

In case 1, the example can be seen as a rule or strictly speaking: in the context given by the other descriptors values, the conclusion does not depend on the values of *not significant* descriptors (e.g., whatever the age of the captain, ...). We then introduce a set value equivalent to the set of all possible values for a descriptor y_j denoted $\{O_j\}$. y_j *not significant* is then encoded by $[y_j = \{O_j\}]$.

2.1.2 Descriptors of Unknown Value

For the problems we deal with, case 2 can be reduced to case 1: when a descriptor is unknown, this descriptor is supposed to be irrelevant; one then generalizes the examples with respect to descriptors of unknown value. This is made possible because the initial descriptors are strongly redundant: one assumes the discriminant information to subsist in an example for which "not too many" descriptors are *unknown*. As a matter of fact, as the relevant descriptors are *a priori* ignored, the experts generally give rather too much information. y_j *unknown* is then encoded by $[y_j = \{O_j\}]$.

Remark: This coding involves no falsification amongst the initial data: the lack of information is transported, not biased as it is the case when the data matrix is completed by computed values or by a specific *unknown* value, as reported by Bhatnagar and Kanal (1986).

2.1.3 Not Defined Descriptors

Let us consider now case 3 where a descriptor is not defined due, for instance, to functional dependencies among descriptors. This case would correspond to the value $\emptyset$ for a descriptor y_j, denoting the empty set of values of O_j. y_j *not defined* is then encoded by $[y_j = \emptyset]$.

From a practical point of view, the difference between case 3 and case 2 needs a complete background knowledge, i.e., the list of functional dependencies such as

$$IF \text{ [hat present = no] } THEN \text{ [hat color} = \emptyset].$$

This complete background knowledge is not likely to be available. We will then make the following assumption about the *coherence* of the learning domain: examples for which the value of a descriptor y_j is not defined are discriminated from others by at least one relevant descriptor $y_k, k \neq j$.

Hypothesis of explicit coherence

$$\begin{aligned} &\forall j \in [1, P], \quad \forall s_1, s_2 \in \Omega : y_j(s_1) = \emptyset \text{ and } y_j(s_2) \neq \emptyset \\ &\qquad \exists k \in [1, P]\colon y_k(s_1) \ \textit{relevant};\ y_k(s_2) \ \textit{relevant}, \text{ and } y_k(s_1) \neq y_k(s_2). \end{aligned}$$

Under this assumption, the values corresponding to the empty set $\emptyset$ and to the whole set $\{O_j\}$ are identified as the *any* value denoted by X. There is no loss of information: the information given by y_j *not defined* (when available) is supplied by other relevant descriptors. One defines y_j *irrelevant* for $s \Leftrightarrow y_j(s) = X$. Of course, $\forall t \in \Omega$ we have $y_j(t) \subset X$.

2.2 Formalization

The descriptors are supposed to be sufficient; the learning domain is represented by the actual descriptions

$$\Omega \equiv y_1(\Omega) \times \ldots \times y_P(\Omega)$$

where $y_j(\Omega) = \{\{v_j\} : v_j \in O_j\} \cup \{X\} \subset \mathcal{P}(O_j)$ and X is the *any* value defined above.

2.2.1 Work Space

The learning domain Ω is then embedded into the learning space Ω_s defined as

$$\Omega_s = \mathcal{P}(O_1) \times \ldots \times \mathcal{P}(O_P)$$

This learning space Ω_s includes a representation of any possible object, even those which cannot be observed; for instance, an example described by *At night, a black cat* ... is possible, but will never be observed due to the background knowledge *When the candles are out, all cats are grey.*

As the background knowledge is not completely known, we cannot characterize the learning domain Ω from the learning space Ω_s, so from now on we will only consider Ω_s. This space Ω_s is called the hypothesis space with respect to *Machine Learning* terminology: it allows to represent any assertion, that is, any premises of a conjunctive rule.

Ω_s is a lattice as it is the product of lattices $\mathcal{P}(O_i)$; this lattice is equivalent to the conceptual lattice defined by the assertions on Ω_s (see Wille (1981) and Ganascia (1987) for an overview of lattice applications to *Machine Learning*). By definition, if f and g are logical functions defined on Ω_s, f generalizes g if for any s in Ω_s, $g(s)$ *true* implies $f(s)$ *true*. It can be shown that

$$\forall s, t \in \Omega_s, \quad s \subset t \Leftrightarrow t' \textit{ generalizes } s'$$

where s' (resp. t') is the characteristic assertion associated to s (resp. t). The assertion

$$s' = \bigwedge_{i=1,\ldots,P} [y_i = y_i(s)], \quad y_i(s) \subset O_i$$

is defined on Ω_s by:

$$s' : \Omega_s \rightarrow \{\textit{true}, \textit{false}, X\}$$

$$\forall t \in \Omega_s, \; s'(t) = \begin{cases} \textit{true} & \text{if } t \subset s \\ \textit{false} & \text{if } s \cap t = \emptyset \\ X & \text{otherwise.} \end{cases}$$

2.2.2 Input and Output of the Learning Process

Examples are considered as elementary rules. The learning base denoted by A is then a set of N rules:

$$A = \{(s'_i \Rightarrow y_0(s_i)) : i = 1, \ldots, N\}$$

whose premises are assertions describing the elements s_i, and the conclusion is the diagnosis observed. The rule base B to extract fits into the same formalism :

$$B = \{(r'_j \Rightarrow y_0(r_i)) : j = 1, \ldots, M\}.$$

The theoretical optimality criterions of the learning process involves

- the compression of the information as $M \ll N$: that is, one wants less rules than initial examples.
- the extension of the information: that is, the rule base must enable prediction in further cases likely not present in the learning base.

2.3 Evaluation of a Rule Set

The practical criterion is the accuracy prediction evaluated on a test set, given within the same formalism as the learning base (training set). Given an example t or the training set and a rule base B, let $B(t)$ be the set of rules fired by t:

$$B(t) = \{(r' \Rightarrow y_0(r)) \in B : r \supset t\}$$

According to B, t is said to be

- *unknown* if $B(t)$ is empty;
- *certain* if all rules in $B(t)$ have same conclusion; the certain examples are divided into surely *well-classified* examples, and surely *bad-classified* examples, whether rules of $B(t)$ do give the right conclusion $y_0(t)$ or do not;
- *ambiguous* if $B(t)$ includes contradictory rules.

3 Generalization, Algorithm and Heuristics

From the learning base A, a rule set B is to be built; many techniques are available, such as decision trees suggested by Quinlan (1986), space versions introduced by Mitchell (1984), and the star algorithm by Michalski, Diday and Stepp (1981) and Michalski (1984).

3.1 Generalization Algorithm

Our generalization algorithm is based on a bottom-up exploration as in the star algorithm; the main difference involves the exploration of negative examples.

When a positive example s is given, the general idea is that a negative example t defines a constraint over a discriminant generalization: a rule generalizing this example must keep at least one feature of s, discriminating s from t. Those constraints are defined in a boolean space: a given descriptor does or does not discriminate a negative example t from the positive example s. A generality relation can be defined on this constraint space, and we show that only maximally general constraints should be considered, which represent maximally near-miss negative examples. (Near-miss was introduced by Winston (1975), meaning a negative example very similar to a positive example, hence providing much information; see also Kodratoff and Loisel (1984).)

A detailed description of this generalization algorithm can be found in Sebag and Schoenauer (1989a) and Sebag (1990).

3.2 Heuristics

Some heuristics are parametrized in order to deal with real data; at the moment, those parameters are supplied by the expert user.

Let $r = (r' \Rightarrow y_0(r))$ be a rule. We define:

$$\begin{aligned} Score(r) &= \text{Number of elements } s \text{ of } A\colon\ s \subset r \text{ and } y_0(r) = y_0(s) \\ Error(r) &= \text{Number of elements } s \text{ of } A\colon\ s \subset r \text{ and } y_0(r) \neq y_0(s). \end{aligned}$$

3.2.1 Noise

A perfectly discriminant rule should have a null error; this is meaningless when the initial learning base is noisy. An error threshold ϵ $(0 \leq \epsilon < 1)$ is then defined, in order to cope with false negative examples:

- negative examples are randomly taken into account with an uniform probability of $(1 - \epsilon)$;
- a rule $(r' \Rightarrow y_0(r))$ is to satisfy $Error(r)/Score(r) < \epsilon$.

To deal with false examples, we define a significance threshold α $(0 \leq \alpha < 1)$, and require $Score(r)/N \geq \alpha$, where N is the cardinality of the learning base A.

3.2.2 Insufficient Data

In a first approach, which proved to be very accurate on artificial problems, only the best rules r generalizing a given example s were retained; that is, we required:

$$Score(r) = \max\{Score(q)\colon\ s \subset q, y_0(q) = y_0(s)\}.$$

This criterion leads to a concise rule base and is not well-adapted to real problems; as few rules are extracted, the prediction results are both instable and insufficient, with a majority of *unknown* results.

If more rules are retained, the rate of *unknown* results is likely to decrease in a probabilistic way; on the other hand, the rate of *ambiguous* results is likely to increase.

Ambiguous cases are more easily handled than *unknown* cases: when no rule is fired, the problem remains; on the other hand, conflicts between rules can be solved, as discussed in the following section. Then a redundancy rate denoted by τ $(0 \leq \tau \leq 1)$ is defined, and we require:

$$Score(r) \leq \tau \cdot \max\{Score(q)\colon\ s \subset q, y_0(q) = y_0(s)\}.$$

4 Refinement of a Rule Base

In order to cope with the initial data defects, the rule base B is sub-optimal, that is, includes redundant and inexact rules. The next step is to refine B. From the discrimination point of view, the main difficulty arises from contradictory rules: what conclusion is likely when many rules of different conclusions are triggered by a given example?

4.1 Weights

A decision making process is allowed by weighted rules: let α_i be the weight of a rule $(r_i \Rightarrow y_0(r_i))$ in B.
For a given example s and for a conclusion i, let us define:

$$N(i,s) = \sum\{\alpha_j\colon\ r_j \supset s,\ y_0(r_j) = i\}.$$

We fix the conclusion of an example s to the conclusion i_0 if it exists, such that

$$N(i_0, s) > N(i,s) \quad \forall i \neq i_0.$$

Appropriate weights can be optimized using sophisticated methods; see, for instance, Lerman et al. (1989) and Perron (1989). However, this method does not solve all conflicts of a rule base. Let us consider a circular conflict: r_1, r_2 and r_3 are overlapping rules of distinct conclusion, such that:

- when r_1 and r_2 are simultaneously triggered, the conclusion of r_1 is the right one;
- when r_2 and r_3 are simultaneously triggered, the conclusion of r_2 is the right one;
- when r_1 and r_3 are simultaneously triggered, the conclusion of r_3 is the right one.

It is clear that weights give a partial order over rules r_1, r_2 and r_3, hence do not solve the circular conflict.

4.2 Iteration of Learning

Numerical methods are penalized by the logical structure of the problem. Therefore, we shall use learning techniques in order to solve conflicts arising between rules.

The first step is to formalize the new learning problem defined by the refinement of a rule base B. More details are found in Sebag and Schoenauer (1989b).

The initial learning problem is called A-problem, for which an approximated solution is given by the rule base B. The refinement of the rule base B defines a new learning problem called B-problem.

4.2.1 Reduction of the Learning Problem

Given a rule base B, a change of representation called *reduction* is defined, allowing to transform the A-problem into the B-problem:

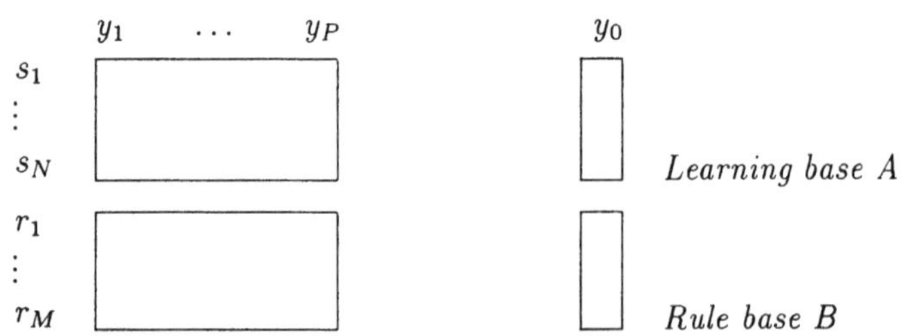

where M denotes the cardinal of rule base B.

The premises of a rule r_i are described in extension by the set of examples verifying this premises; that is, the boolean descriptor r'_i (see section 2.1) is computable on the initial learning domain (if the rule r_i is to be of any use ...), hence r'_i can be computed on the learning base A:

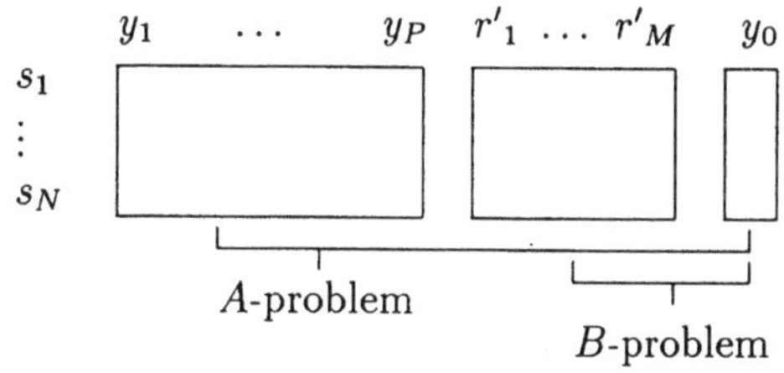

The description of s, representing an object or a set of objects within the initial representation, is transformed into a description of the behavior of B on s; it details which rules are triggered by s and which are not. Let

$$\pi_B\colon \Omega_s \to \{true,\ false,\ X\} \underbrace{\times \ldots \times}_{M \text{ times}} \{true,\ false,\ X\}$$

$$\pi_B(s) = \bigwedge_{j=1,\ldots,M} [r'_j = r'_j(s)]$$

The essential feature is that this change of representation does not affect the conclusion of an example: we have now examples of simultaneously triggered rules, together with the right conclusion. Therefore, we can learn about the behavior of rules in order to refine them and generalize their conflicts. The solutions of actual conflicts are to be given by examples, not by experts.

4.2.2 Multi-Layered Rules

The learning base A is then re-written and a reduced learning base $\Pi_B(A)$ relevant for the B-problem can be derived.

$$\Pi_B(A) = \{(\pi_B(s_i) \Rightarrow y_O(s_i))\colon i = 1, \ldots, N\}$$

This reduced learning base can be generalized[1]. This generalization applies to the reduced base $\Pi_B(A)$; new rules called second-layer rules are then generalized such as:

$$\begin{array}{lll} r_k: & \textit{IF } r_i \textit{ is triggered} & (\Leftrightarrow [r'_i = true]) \\ & \textit{AND } r_j \textit{ is not} & (\Leftrightarrow [r'_j = false]) \\ & \textit{THEN CONCLUSION is } y_O(r_k) & \end{array}$$

where r_i and r_j are 1-layer rules. 2-layer rules can be viewed as meta-rules over 1-layer rules achieving the generalization of conflicts and the detection of exceptions.

[1]Some fuzzy qualities are required from a learning base; for instance, it must include "sufficient" and coherent information. A more precise definition of such properties requires the problem to be solved. So, we suppose that the initial learning base A satisfies the right properties; we show that if the rule base B is sufficiently redundant, those properties are not affected by the reduction.

Remark: Notice that, as we mentioned earlier, those second layer rules are disjunctive with respect to the initial representation: the expression r_j *not triggered* is a disjunction while the premises of r_j are a conjunction.

The generalization-reduction process can be iterated and gives a sequence of rule set. This sequence is called a multi-layered rule set: for each layer except the first one rules achieve the control of the previous layer.

4.3 Incremental Learning

Two learning operators have been defined: the generalization operator named G learns a rule base B from a learning base A; the reduction operator Π_B gives a change of representation, transforming A-problem into B-problem. Those operators can then be composed, achieving the incrementality of the learning process.

4.3.1 Convergence of a Rule Base

The first case consider the refinement of a rule base with respect to a single learning base; section 5 shows that the iterative approximation leads to better final results than an "exact" learning approach.

Then we define two sequences of learning base and rule base, as followed:

$$\begin{array}{lllllll} A_0 & = & A; & B_1 & = & G(A_0) \\ A_1 & = & \Pi_{B_1}(A_0); & B_2 & = & G(A_1) \end{array}$$

and more generally

$$A_i = \Pi_{B_i}(A_{i-1}); \quad B_i = G(A_{i-1})$$

The iteration stops when prediction results are decreasing or stable on a test set, in order to avoid "overfitting" of the generalization—this is a classical procedure in data analysis.

4.3.2 Learning From Subsets of Examples

When a learning base is too big to be generalized as a whole, subsets are iteratively considered: an incremental learning with respect to fragments of data is then performed. Let $A_1, \ldots, A_L$ be subsets of the initial learning base with $A = A_1 \cup \cdots \cup A_L$. Those subsets are considered in cycles; we define two sequences of learning bases and rule bases as follows:

$$A_1^0 = A_1; \quad B_1 = G(A_1^0)$$

and more generally

$$A_k^i = \Pi_{B_i}(A_k^{i-1}); \quad B_i = G(A_i^{i-1})$$

5 First Results

The *ML2 (Multi Layered Learning)* program is written in C; CPU time on an Apollo DN3000 is about 2 minutes for the following problem.

ML2 has been tested on some well-studied bases from medical domains in order to compare its results to those of *AQR* by Michalski et al. (1986), *Assistant 86* by Cestnik,

Bratko and Kononenko (1987) and *CN2* by Clark and Niblett (1987). Most previous results are summed-up by Clark and Niblett, including as well those of a very simple Bayesian classifier.

The initial data set is divided into a training set (the learning base) gathering 2/3 of the population and a test set which includes the remaining examples.

The experiment described in the following (more detailed validation is given in Sebag and Schoenauer (1989b)) is related to the prognosis of breast cancer. The two classes to discriminate represent respectively 1/3 and 2/3 of the population described by 9 multi-valued attributes and 286 examples. The results are average results obtained from a learning base selected at random. Here are the results of the algorithm above:

	Test set (97 ex.)	Training set (190 ex.)
Bayes	65%	97%
AQR	72%	100%
Assistant 86	62–68%	92–95%
CN2	70–71%	76–72%

For technical reasons, the learning base considered by *ML2* has been limited to 168 examples, including the same number of examples in both classes. Here are the results obtained by *ML2*, with ϵ, α, and τ denoting respectively the error threshold, the significance threshold and the redundancy rate, and M the number of rules:

	Test set (84 ex.)	Training set (168 ex.)
Bayes	50%	64%

The best results *ML2* obtains in one layer are:

			ϵ	τ	α	M
Best 1-layer	62%	66%	.7	.3	.01	30

The best 2-layer rule set reaches the results (this best 2-layer rule set is built from a 1-layer rule set whose results are given below):

Best 2-layer	75%	93%	.2	.4	.01	32
from 1-layer	58%	79%	.5	.3	.02	35

At the third layer, best results are:

Best 3-layer	75%	97%	.1	.8	.02	13
from 2-layer	75%	88%	.2	.9	.01	31
from 1-layer	53%	77%	.5	.9	.02	38

or

Best 3-layer	76%	90%	.3	.7	.02	12
from 2-layer	60%	83%	.4	.7	.01	25
from 1-layer	46%	62%	.7	.6	.01	34

The following remarks can be made:

1. If a *n-layer* rule set gives optimal results at layer n, it is built from non-optimal previous rule sets: best 2-layers rule sets are built on 1-layer rule sets which are not the best 1-layer rule set; best 3-layers rule sets are built on 2-layers rule sets and 1-layer rule sets which are not the best ones.

2. Optimal results are reached when optimality requirements are gradually increased at each layer; in our case, more exact and more concise rules are gradually built as error threshold and redundancy rate are found to decrease.

Both previous remarks very much remind of simulated annealing and genetic algorithms (Holland et al. (1985) and Davis and Streestrup (1987)): intermediate steps must be purposely sub-optimal in order to enable further improvement and to avoid local optima; optimality requirements must gradually increase as to reach steadiness. Finally, the predictive accuracy is slightly improved by this incremental learning compared to reviewed direct learning.

6 Conclusion

We have presented a learning process as a 2-step iterative process:

- A generalization algorithm builds a rule base B from a learning base A; to cope with initial data defects, the quality requirements on the rules are lowered allowing redundant and erroneous rules.

- A change of representation called reduction transforms the initial learning problem into the problem of refining the rule base B.

Two combined features are outlined: reduction is not worthy if the generalization is not purposely sub-optimal; on the other hand, generalization of the reduced learning base allows to automatically correct defects of the rule base B.

These successive approximations of a rule base perform very well compared to the direct learning approach. Moreover, our approach uses incremental learning in order to handle large problems.

References

BHATNAGAR, R.K., and KANAL, L.N. (1986), Handling uncertain information: A review of numeric and non-numeric methods, in: *Uncertainty in Artificial Intelligence*, eds. L.N. Kanal and J.F. Lemmer, North-Holland, Amsterdam.

BRITO, P., and DIDAY, E. (1990), Pyramidal representation of symbolic objects, this volume.

CESTNIK, B., BRATKO, I., and KONONENKO, I. (1987), ASSISTANT 86: A knowledge elicitation tool for sophisticated users, in: *Progress in Machine Learning, Proceedings of EWSL 87*, eds. I. Bratko and N. Lavrac.

CLARK, P., and NIBLETT, T. (1987), Induction in noisy domains, in: *Progress in Machine Learning, Proceedings of EWSL 87*, eds. I. Bratko and N. Lavrac.

DAVIS, L, and STEENSTRUP, M. (1987), Genetic Algorithms and Simulated Annealing: An Overview, in: *Genetic Algorithms and Simulated Annealing*, ed. L. Davis, Pitman, London.

DIDAY, E. (1990), Knowledge representation and symbolic data analysis, this volume.

FALKENHAIMER, B.C., and MICHALSKI, R.S. (1986), Integrating quantitative and qualitative discovery in the ABACUS system, *Machine Learning*, April.

HOLLAND, J.H., HOLYOAK, K.J., NISBETT, R.E., and THAGARD, P.R. (1985), Classifier Systems, Q-morphisms, and Induction, in: *Genetic Algorithms and Simulated Annealing*, ed. L. Davis, Pitman, London.

KODRATOFF, Y. (1988), *Introduction to Machine Learning*, Pitman Eds.

KODRATOFF, Y., and LOISEL, R. (1984), Learning complex structural descriptions from examples, *Computer vision, graphics and image processing, 27.*

LANGLEY, P., BRADSHAW, G., and SIMON, H. (1984), Rediscovering chemistry with the BACON system, in: *Machine Learning: An Artificial Intelligence Approach*, eds. R.S. Michalski, J.G. Carbonnel and T.M. Mitchell, Palo Alto.

LEBOWITZ, M. (1985), Categorizing Numeric Information for Generalization, *Cognitive Science, 9*, 285–308.

LERMAN, I.-C., LEBBE, J., NICOLAS, J., PETER, P., and VIGNES, R. (1989), Conceptual clustering in biology: applications and perspectives, in: *Data Analysis, Learning symbolic and numeric knowledge*, ed. E. Diday, Nova Science, Antibes.

MICHALSKI, R.S. (1984), A theory and methodology for inductive learning, in: *Machine Learning: An Artificial Intelligence Approach*, eds. R.S. Michalski, J.G. Carbonnel and T.M. Mitchell, Palo Alto.

MICHALSKI, R.S., DIDAY, E., and STEPP, R.E. (1981), A recent advance in Data Analysis: clustering objects into classes characterized by conjunctive concepts, in: *Progress in Pattern Recognition*, eds. L.N. Kanal and Rosenfled, North-Holland, Amsterdam.

MICHALSKI, R.S., MOZETIC, I., HONG, J., and LAVRAC, N. (1986), *The AQ15 inductive learning system: an overview and experiments*, Proceedings of IMAL, Orsay.

MITCHELL, T.M. (1982), Generalization as Search, *Artificial Intelligence, 18.*

PERRON, M.-C. (1989), Learning differential diagnosis rules from numerical knowledge, in: *Data Analysis, Learning symbolic and numeric knowledge*, ed. E. Diday, Nova Science, Antibes.

QUINLAN, J.R. (1986), Induction of decision trees, *Machine Learning, 1*, 81–106.

SEBAG, M. (1990), *Apprentissage multi-couches: une approche symbolique numérique pour la discrimination à partir d'examples et de règles*, Thèse d'Université, Paris-IX Dauphine.

SEBAG, M., and SCHOENAUER, M. (1988), *Generation of rules with certainty and confidence factors from incomplete and incoherent learning bases*, Proceedings of EKAW 88, Bonn.

SEBAG, M., and SCHOENAUER, M. (1989a), Iterative learning and redundant generalizations, in: *Data Analysis, Learning numerical and symbolic knowledge*, ed. E. Diday, Nova Science, Antibes.

SEBAG, M., and SCHOENAUER, M. (1989b), *Learning rules and meta-rules: towards an incremental learning*, Rapport interne, Ecole Polytechnique.

WILLE, R. (1981), Restructuring lattice theory: an approach based on hierarchies of concepts, *Proceedings of the symposium on ordered sets*, ed. I. Rival.

WINSTON, P.H. (1975), Learning structural descriptions from examples, in: *The Psychology of Computer Vision*, ed. P.H. Winston, McGraw-Hill, New York.

Part 2

Data Analysis and Applications

Fitting a Quasi-Poisson Case of the GSTUN (General Stochastic Tree UNfolding) Model and Some Extensions

J. Douglas Carroll
AT&T Bell Laboratories
and Graduate School of Management, Rutgers University, New Jersey, U.S.A.
and
Geert De Soete[1]
Department of Psychology
University of Ghent, Belgium

Summary

A new family of probabilistic choice models for representing paired comparisons data from different sources (subjects or homogeneous groups of subjects) is derived and extended from a general class of stochastic tree unfolding models proposed by Carroll, DeSarbo and De Soete (1987, 1988, 1989). In this approach, both the sources and the choice objects are represented by the terminal nodes of an additive tree. The probability that source i prefers object j to object k is defined by

$$p_{i,jk} = \Phi\left(\frac{d_{ik} - d_{ij}}{\beta d_{jk}^{\alpha}}\right) \quad (0 \leq \alpha \leq 1, \ \beta > 0)$$

where d_{ij} (d_{ik}) denotes the additive tree distances between the nodes representing source i and object j (object k), and where d_{jk} denotes the additive tree distance between the nodes representing objects j and k. A mathematical programming procedure for fitting this model to three-way paired comparisons data is mentioned. The model is applied for illustrative purposes to a well-known data set gathered by Rumelhart and Greeno (1971).

1 Introduction

In some papers by Carroll, DeSarbo and De Soete (1987, 1988, 1989) a general class of stochastic choice models for paired comparisons data, called STUN (*S*tochastic *T*ree *UN*folding) models is developed. One particular special case, called SSTUN (for *S*imple or *S*pecial STUN model), which is a strong utility model (implying strong stochastic transitivity; see for instance, Luce and Suppes (1965)) was more fully developed, a procedure for fitting it described, implemented and applied to some paired comparisons data (DeSarbo, De Soete, Carroll and Ramaswamy (1988)).

Another, more general subclass of STUN models, called GSTUN (for *G*eneral STUN) models, can be shown to imply moderate stochastic transitivity, and at least in some

[1]Supported as "Bevoegdverklaard Navorser" of the Belgian N.F.W.O.

NATO ASI Series, Vol. F 61
Knowledge, Data and Computer-Assisted Decisions
Edited by M. Schader and W. Gaul

cases not to require strong stochastic transitivity (and, in fact, to explicitly violate this condition). GSTUN models, then, are moderate utility models. (Since SSTUN can itself be shown to be a special case of GSTUN, some special cases of GSTUN are strong utility models, of course.)

In this paper we shall deal first with a special class of GSTUN models which we shall call "Quasi-Poisson" GSTUN models, for reasons to be discussed below. Our "shorthand" designation for this class of GSTUN models is GSTUN-QP. We are then led to extend this subclass of models to a broader class of stochastic choice models, many of which are not special cases of GSTUN. We shall use the shorthand designation GSTUN-EQP for this class of Extended GSTUN-QP models.

First, we review the nature and motivation of GSTUN models. The basic concept underlying these models is that, in a binary forced choice situation (i.e., paired comparisons) the individual will choose the stimulus (or other object) that is momentarily closer to his/her "ideal" stimulus (or object) where closeness is defined as an inverse function of the distance between the stimulus (object) and the "ideal" stimulus (object) for that individual. In "tree unfolding" this distance is defined, not as a Euclidean (or other) distance in a continuous conceptual/perceptual space, but as distance defined on a tree structure in which both the stimuli and the "ideal" stimulus for an individual are (generally, external) nodes. The "stochastic" component in the name "Stochastic Tree Unfolding" derives from the fact that the continuous parameters on which the tree distances are based (heights, in the case of ultrametric trees, or link or branch lengths, in the case of additive or "path length" trees) are assumed not to be fixed values, but to be random variables, subject to momentary fluctuation from choice to choice. Largely for reasons of mathematical tractability, these random variables are assumed to be jointly multivariate normally distributed, with certain constraints on the structure of the covariance matrix leading to various special cases of interest. As will be argued below, this assumption of multivariate normality may not be too critical to an important subclass of GSTUN (excluding SSTUN) models, because the central limit theorem implies asymptotic normality as the number of stimuli grows large, irrespective of the joint distribution of the individual parameters (in particular, link or branch lengths). Individual differences in choice probabilities are accommodated in this class of models by assuming that different individuals have different ideal stimuli (as in the case of the spatial unfolding models; Coombs (1964)). As in the spatial unfolding models (and other multidimensional models for individual differences in preferential choice behavior) a common structure is assumed to underlie the actual stimuli or other objects about which choices are made. In GSTUN (and all STUN) models, this underlying structure is a tree structure, rather than a multidimensional space of some fixed dimensionality. We shall now develop these "intuitive" notions underlying GSTUN models in a more explicit mathematical way.

2 The GSTUN Models

Given a fixed tree (hierarchical in the ultrametric case, or a rootless, nonhierarchical tree, or "free tree" in the path length case), we can define a matrix associated with that tree which we call the "Path Matrix" denoted **P**. We call it that since, in the case of a path length (or additive) metric the matrix can be viewed as defining the unique path connecting every pair of terminal nodes i and j. In the case of an ultrametric it does *not* define a path, but instead designates the "least common ancestor" (l.c.a) node for every pair i and j. This l.c.a node can be viewed as specifying the "path" between the two (if one views the pair as interconnecting directly via this l.c.a node).

In the case of a path length or additive metric $\mathbf{P}$ is a matrix whose rows correspond to pairs of terminal nodes i and j, where i corresponds to a subject and j to a stimulus. The columns of $\mathbf{P}$ correspond to links or branches in the tree. The general entry in $\mathbf{P}$, which we shall designate as $p_{(ij)q}$ (for the entry in the row corresponding to node pair (i,j) and to branch q) will be 1 if and only if branch q is included in the path connecting i to j, and 0 otherwise. Thus, this matrix is a binary "indicator" matrix indicating which branches are involved in the path interconnecting a pair of nodes i and j.

Given a set of branch lengths $h_1, h_2, \ldots, h_Q$ which we may represent as a Q-dimensional (column) vector $\mathbf{h}$, the distances g_{ij} $(i = 1, \ldots, I,\ j = 1, \ldots, J)$, which can be "packed" into another column vector of $I \times J$ components, $\mathbf{g}$, can be defined via the matrix equation

$$\mathbf{g} = \mathbf{P}\mathbf{h}. \tag{1}$$

Now, let us suppose that $\mathbf{h}$, rather than being a fixed vector of branch lengths, is a random variable. Furthermore, let us assume that, for individual i the distribution of $\mathbf{h}$ is

$$\mathbf{h}_i \sim N(\boldsymbol{\mu}_i, \boldsymbol{\Sigma}_i) \tag{2}$$

then, on a particular paired comparisons trial in which subject i is presented stimuli j and k and forced to choose one, we have:

$$p_{i,jk} \equiv P_i(j \succ k) = P(g_{ij} < g_{ik}) = P(s_{i,jk} > 0), \tag{3}$$

where $s_{i,jk} = g_{ik} - g_{ij}$. Under the assumptions we have made in the GSTUN models the distribution of $s_{i,jk}$ is:

$$s_{i,jk} \sim N(d_{ik} - d_{ij}, \delta^2_{(ij)(ik)}) \tag{4}$$

where

$$d_{ij} = \mathbf{p}_{(ij)}\boldsymbol{\mu}_i \qquad \text{and} \qquad d_{ik} = \mathbf{p}_{(ik)}\boldsymbol{\mu}_i, \tag{5}$$

while

$$\delta^2_{(ij)(ik)} = (\mathbf{p}_{(ij)} - \mathbf{p}_{(ik)})\boldsymbol{\Sigma}_i(\mathbf{p}_{(ij)} - \mathbf{p}_{(ik)})', \tag{6}$$

where $\mathbf{p}_{(ij)}$ and $\mathbf{p}_{(ik)}$ are the row vectors corresponding to the (i,j) and (i,k) rows of the Path Matrix $\mathbf{P}$, respectively. Since $\boldsymbol{\Sigma}_i$ is a covariance matrix, it is positive definite (or semidefinite). This implies that $\delta^2_{(ij)(ik)}$ is the squared *generalized* Euclidean distance between rows (i,j) and (i,k) of $\mathbf{P}$ in the metric of $\boldsymbol{\Sigma}_i$. Thus, we have:

$$p_{i,jk} = \Phi\left(\frac{d_{ik} - d_{ij}}{\delta_{(ij)(ik)}}\right), \tag{7}$$

where Φ denotes the standard normal distribution function. Since δ is a (Euclidean) metric, model (7) is a moderate utility model (see Halff (1976)).

Exactly the same development holds for the ultrametric case, except that the rows of the Path Matrix $\mathbf{P}$ correspond to Q internal nodes (rather than Q branches) with $p_{(ij)q}$ being 1 if and only if node q is the l.c.a of i and j. For reasons discussed below, however, we do not find this ultrametric case of GSTUN of great interest, and shall focus primarily on the path length or additive tree case.

It is clear, however, if one considers the structure of the path matrix, $\mathbf{P}$, that the distribution of the choice probabilities for subject i are dependent only on the distribution of those components of $\mathbf{h}$ that affect the distances from the node for subject i to the stimulus nodes. Those distributional parameters for subject i involving components of $\mathbf{h}$ not affecting these distances are indeterminate without further constraints.

3 Special Cases of GSTUN Models

While the completely general GSTUN model with $\boldsymbol{\mu}_i$ and $\boldsymbol{\Sigma}_i$ unconstrained is of some theoretical interest, it is much too general for practical application to real data. In some cases some of the parameters are intrinsically undefined. In all cases the unconstrained GSTUN model has more parameters than observed data values, and thus cannot be uniquely fitted. Like Thurstone's (1927) general Law of Comparative Judgment model, the general, unconstrained GSTUN model should be taken as providing only a broad theoretical framework from which a large number of interesting special cases can be derived by imposing suitable constraints, rather than as a tractable statistical model per se. We now consider some restricted cases of particular interest. Most importantly, we assume $\boldsymbol{\mu}_i = \boldsymbol{\mu}$ and $\boldsymbol{\Sigma}_i = \boldsymbol{\Sigma}$, for all i. Imposing these constraints is the simplest way to avoid the intrinsic indeterminacies discussed above. These constraints on the $\boldsymbol{\mu}_i$'s and $\boldsymbol{\Sigma}_i$'s will, therefore, be assumed from this point on.

Now, consider two constraints of interest on $\boldsymbol{\Sigma}$ (now assumed common over subjects).

1. $\boldsymbol{\Sigma}$ diagonal (i.e., the h_q's are independently normally distributed, but with different variances). In this case $\boldsymbol{\Sigma} \equiv \text{diag}(\sigma_q^2)$ so that $\delta_{(ij)(ik)}$ is the weighted Euclidean metric with weights σ_q^2. I.e.,

$$\delta_{(ij)(ik)}^2 = \sum_{q=1}^{Q} \sigma_q^2 (p_{(ij)q} - p_{(ik)q})^2. \tag{8}$$

2. $\boldsymbol{\Sigma} = \sigma^2\mathbf{I}$. This is the case first above, with the variances of the h_q's all equal. Since an arbitrary scale constant can be absorbed into the definition of $\boldsymbol{\mu}$, we can without loss of generality set the common variance equal to one, thus making $\boldsymbol{\Sigma} = \mathbf{I}$. In this case, of course, $\delta_{(ij)(ik)}$ is the ordinary Euclidean distance between $\mathbf{p}_{(ij)}$ and $\mathbf{p}_{(ik)}$; i.e.:

$$\delta_{(ij)(ik)}^2 = \sum_{q=1}^{Q} (p_{(ij)q} - p_{(ik)q})^2. \tag{9}$$

It might be noted that all GSTUN models can be viewed as special cases of the wandering vector model (WVM) (Carroll (1980); De Soete and Carroll (1983)) but with a *different* dimensional stimulus space defined for each subject (corresponding to the submatrix of $\mathbf{P}$ associated with the distances from that subject's node to the J stimulus nodes), with centroid vector $\boldsymbol{\mu}_i$, covariance matrix $\boldsymbol{\Sigma}_i$ for that subject (assuming here, for the moment, the most general form of GSTUN). This means that GSTUN "inherits" many important properties of the WVM.

One notable feature of the GSTUN model in the ultrametric case, which we call GSTUN(u), is that (regardless of the definition of $\mathbf{\Sigma}$) the variance term $\delta^2_{(ij)(ik)}$ will be identically zero for any pair of pairs (i,j) and (i,k) sharing the same l.c.a nodes. This is because the rows $\mathbf{p}_{(ij)}$ and $\mathbf{p}_{(ik)}$ must be identical in such cases, and thus the distance between those rows (however, defined) will be zero. However, since we have already assumed that, for the i, j and k under consideration, subject i meets both stimuli j and k at the same internal node, it follows that, in this ultrametric case, $d_{ij} = d_{ik}$. Consequently $d_{ik} - d_{ij}$ is zero, and $p_{i,jk} = \Phi(0/0)$. Thus $p_{i,jk}$ is undefined, but could be defined by fiat as equal to 1/2. It should be further noted, however, that since ultrametric distances can, as discussed earlier, be obtained as a special case of the path length metric, this makes it possible to fit the latter model but with constraints on the $\boldsymbol{\mu}$'s that make the *expected* values of the distances d_{ij} conform to the ultrametric conditions. For the case of the GSTUN model with an ultrametric, GSTUN(u) with $\mathbf{\Sigma} = \sigma^2\mathbf{I}$ will be exactly equivalent (in terms of the predicted choice probabilities) to SSTUN(u), (SSTUN with an ultrametric) if we resolve the indeterminacy mentioned earlier "by fiat," by defining $p_{i,jk} = 1/2$ in the case in which (subject) i meets (stimuli) j and k both at the same internal node. The choice probabilities predicted by GSTUN(u) in this case will then be identically the same as those predicted by SSTUN(u)! Thus, in fact GSTUN(u) (with a scalar covariance matrix) is indistinguishable from SSTUN(u). (Of course, GSTUN(u) is still more general, since it need not be restricted to a scalar covariance matrix, in which case its properties are distinctly different from SSTUN—even if SSTUN is generalized to allow different variances or a general covariance matrix.)

GSTUN with a path length or additive metric, which we call GSTUN(pl), is by far the more general model, and thus, we feel, is to be favored over GSTUN(u) on theoretical grounds. As discussed earlier, it is possible to fit GSTUN(pl) with constraints making the expected distances ultrametric, which we call GSTUN(pl|u), so we do not feel that this theoretical argument favoring GSTUN(pl) necessarily rules out what is essentially an ultrametric model (in its "central tendency"). In fact, even SSTUN(u) can be generated as a special case of GSTUN(pl), with ultrametric constraints on $E(\mathbf{g})$ (which implies certain constraints on $\boldsymbol{\mu}$), but with a separate covariance matrix, $\mathbf{\Sigma}_i$, for each subject, and with certain constraints on $\mathbf{\Sigma}_i$ (see Carroll et al. (1987, 1989)).

4 Quasi-Poisson Case of GSTUN

Recently, the first author has noticed that in the case of $\mathbf{\Sigma}$ diagonal and for path length or additive trees, $\delta^2_{(ij)(ik)}$ is itself a tree metric, of the same type (path length, or additive) as the d_{ij}'s. In this case, $\delta^2_{(ij)(ik)}$ is a path length or additive distance defined on the same tree, and, furthermore, is independent of i! It is, in fact, of the form

$$\delta^2_{(ij)(ik)} = d^*_{jk} \tag{10}$$

where d^*_{jk} is the (path length/additive) metric defined when the parameter σ^2_q is the branch length for branch q. Only nonnegativity of these parameters is required—which necessarily holds since the σ^2_q's are variances.

Since the ultrametric case (as distinguishing from the GSTUN(pl|u) case; i.e., the path length case, but with constraints on the link lengths that force the ultrametric condition to hold) appears, for reasons already stated, to be of very little (other than a mild theoretical) interest, we shall concentrate henceforth only on the path length or additive metric case. We first prove the result asserted above. In the case of $\boldsymbol{\Sigma}$ diagonal $\delta^2_{(ij)(ik)}$ is of the form:

$$\delta^2_{(ij)(ik)} = \sum_{q=1}^{Q} \sigma_q^2 \left(p_{(ij)q} - p_{(ik)q}\right)^2 . \tag{11}$$

Now $p_{(ik)q}$ is the q-th element in an indicator vector that has a 1 in precisely those cells corresponding to the links in the unique path in the tree leading from (subject) node i to (stimulus) node j. Similarly for $p_{(ik)q}$. Let $A^{[i]}_{[jk]}$ be the "least common ancestor" node in the hierarchical tree induced by rooting the initial (unrooted tree) at the node corresponding to subject i. It is easy to see that $p_{(ij)q} = 1$ for all links in the tree leading from i to $A^{[i]}_{[jk]}$ *and* in those leading from $A^{[i]}_{[jk]}$ to j, and $p_{(ij)q} = 0$ for all other links in the tree. On the other hand $p_{(ik)q} = 1$ *also* for all links leading from i to $A^{[i]}_{[jk]}$, and then for those leading from $A^{[i]}_{[jk]}$ to k. Thus $(p_{(ij)q} - p_{(ik)q}) = 0$ for those links leading from i to $A^{[i]}_{[jk]}$ (since both $p_{(ij)q}$ and $p_{(ik)q}$ equal one for these links) *and* for any links in the tree not involved in either of these paths. Consequently,

$$|p_{(ij)q} - p_{(ik)q}| = \left(p_{(ij)q} - p_{(ik)q}\right)^2 = 1 \tag{12}$$

for those links (and only those links) leading from j to $A^{[i]}_{[jk]}$, and those leading from $A^{[i]}_{[jk]}$ to k; ergo, in those links in the *unique* path leading from j to k (through $A^{[i]}_{[jk]}$).

Since the weight for link q in defining $\delta^2_{(ij)(ik)}$ is either 0 (if $|p_{(ij)q} - p_{(ik)q}| = 0$) or σ_q^2 (if $|p_{(ij)q} - p_{(ik)q}| = 1$) it follows that $\delta^2_{(ij)(ik)}$ is precisely the path length distance, d^*_{jk}, between j and k in the original tree, but with weights σ_q^2 instead of μ_q. In particular $\delta^2_{(ij)(ik)} = d^*_{jk}$ is *independent* of i. (This condition—of independence of $\delta^2_{(ij)(ik)}$ of i, *and* of that quantity being a tree metric, does *not* hold in general in the case where the underlying structural model is an ultrametric tree, with continuous [distributional] parameters associated with "heights" of internal nodes—seems to be another reason for dismissing this class of structural models underlying GSTUN models as being inherently of less interest.)

We now consider an even more special case, which we dub the "Quasi-Poisson" case, which we shall abbreviate, simply, as GSTUN-QP (keeping in mind that we are now restricting ourselves to the case of path length or additive metric). In the Quasi-Poisson case we assume $\sigma_q^2 = \mu_q$, as is the case for the Poisson distribution. We call it "Quasi-Poisson" because we are assuming, in GSTUN models, normally distributed h's. In the Quasi-Poisson case we merely assume that, in these normal distributions $\sigma_q^2 = \mu_q$, mimicking the Poisson in their first two moments, but (obviously) not in higher moments. (Of course, the Poisson distribution entails a random variable which takes on only non-negative values, while the normal allows negative as well as positive values, which seems unreasonable for variables which are defined to be lengths of links in a tree). In fact, the Quasi-Poisson case approximates very closely the situation in which these distributions are *exactly* Poisson. This is because, in the path length case, the individual "scale values" g_{ij} and g_{ik} (the *perturbed* distances) and their differences $g_{ik} - g_{ij}$ are all sums of independent (Poisson) distributions. For this reason, the variable $g_{ik} - g_{ij}$, whose distribution determines $p_{i,jk}$, will be *approximately* normal in any case, due to operation of the central limit theorem. Thus GSTUN-QP can be thought of as a reasonably close approximation to the theoretically more elegant GSTUN with Poisson assumptions.

In the Quasi-Poisson case, since $\sigma_q^2 = \mu_q$, we have $d_{jk}^* = d_{jk}$, in which case the choice probabilities take on the particularly simple form

$$p_{i,jk} = \Phi\left(\frac{d_{ik} - d_{ij}}{\sqrt{d_{jk}}}\right). \tag{13}$$

At first this seems a bit strange, given that the *square root* of d_{jk}, rather than d_{jk} itself, is in the denominator. However, this does not appear so strange when we realize that, if d_{jk} is a metric, so is any power of d_{jk} between 0 and 1. In particular $\sqrt{d_{jk}}$ is also a metric (which we also knew from the fact that $\sqrt{d_{jk}} = \delta_{(ij)(ik)}$, which we have seen to be, in fact, a *Euclidean* metric). This, however, suggests a generalization, or extension, of GSTUN-QP, replacing the $\sqrt{d_{jk}}$ in the denominator with d_{jk}^{α} for $0 \leq \alpha \leq 1$. This leads to a model which we shall call, simply GSTUN-EQP(α, β) , for which the choice probabilities are of the form:

$$p_{i,jk} = \Phi\left(\frac{d_{ik} - d_{ij}}{d_{jk}^{\alpha}}\right).$$

The cases of most interest of GSTUN-EQP(α) are $\alpha = 0$, $1/2$ and 1 respectively. For $\alpha = 0$ we have

$$p_{i,jk} = \Phi\left(d_{ik} - d_{ij}\right) \tag{14}$$

which is exactly the form of the SSTUN model (DeSarbo et al. (1988)). $\alpha = 1/2$, of course, corresponds to GSTUN-QP. Finally, for $\alpha = 1$ we have

$$p_{i,jk} = \Phi\left(\frac{d_{ik} - d_{ij}}{d_{jk}}\right) \tag{15}$$

which has a particularly simple form, and which bears some general resemblance to the PRETREE (PREference TREE) model of Tversky and Sattath (1979) (although this resemblance may be more superficial than real on closer examination).

Finally, as a further extension of this class of models we might weaken the "Quasi-Poisson" assumption that $\sigma_q^2 = \mu_q$ to the more general and flexible assumption (which holds at least approximately for many plausible distributions, such as the log normal) that $\sigma_q^2 = \beta\mu_q$ $(\beta > 0)$. This leads to $d_{jk}^* = \beta d_{jk}$, with β a positive scale parameter. Combining this with the exponent α discussed above leads, finally, to the most general class of models we consider here, which we call GSTUN-EQP(α, β), with choice probabilities of the general form:

$$p_{i,jk} = \Phi\left(\frac{d_{ik} - d_{ij}}{\beta d_{jk}^{\alpha}}\right). \tag{16}$$

α and β can be viewed as *parameters* to be fitted, together with the d_{jk}'s (satisfying the four-point condition necessary for additive or path length distances defined on a tree), or as *fixed* values. (Or, alternatively, α could be fixed at one of the three values, $\alpha = 0$, $1/2$ or 1 discussed earlier, while β can be allowed to be a parameter to be fitted).

5 Fitting the GSTUN-EQP(α, β) Model

Maximum likelihood estimates of the additive tree distances $\mathbf{D} = \{d_{ij}\}$ can be obtained by maximizing the following log-likelihood function

$$\log L(\mathbf{D}, \alpha, \beta) = \sum_i \sum_{j<k} \left[r_{i,jk} \log p_{i,jk} + (R_{i,jk} - r_{i,jk}) \log(1 - p_{i,jk}) \right], \tag{17}$$

subject to the constraints that the elements in $\mathbf{D}$ are non-negative

$$d_{ij} \geq 0, \tag{18}$$

and satisfy the additive inequality (or four point condition)

$$d_{ij} + d_{kl} \leq \max(d_{ik} + d_{jl}, d_{il} + d_{jk}) \tag{19}$$

and the triangle inequality

$$d_{ij} \leq d_{ik} + d_{jk}. \tag{20}$$

In equation (17), $R_{i,jk}$ denotes the number of times the stimulus pair (j, k) was presented to subject i, while $r_{i,jk}$ indicates the number of times out of $R_{i,jk}$ stimulus j was preferred to stimulus k by subject i. If α and β are considered as parameters rather than as fixed values, the additional constraints

$$0 \leq \alpha \leq 1, \tag{21}$$

and

$$\beta > 0 \tag{22}$$

need to be imposed. This constrained nonlinear optimization problem can be solved by a sequential unconstrained optimization technique similar to the one utilized by De Soete (1983) for fitting additive trees to similarity data by minimizing a least squares criterion. In this approach, penalty functions are used to impose constraints (18)–(20), and optionally (21)–(22) (depending on whether α and β are fixed values or parameters to be solved for).

To illustrate the algorithm, the GSTUN-EQP(1/2,1) model was fit to some data collected by Rumelhart and Greeno (1971). The data consist of pairwise preference judgments from 234 undergraduates about nine celebrities. Of these nine celebrities three were politicians (L.B. Johnson, Harold Wilson, Charles De Gaulle), three were athletes (A.J. Foyt, Johnny Unitas, Carl Yastrzemski), and three were movie stars (Brigitte Bardot, Sophia Loren, Elizabeth Talyor). The subjects were treated as replications of each other, so that a tree with ten terminal nodes was fit to the data, nine nodes representing the stimuli and one node representing the subjects. The tree obtained by fitting the GSTUN-EQP(1/2,1) model to these data by means of our mathematical programming procedure, is shown in Fig. 1. As can be seen from the figure, the three politicians are clustered together and were clearly more popular than the movie stars and the athletes. The most preferred celebrity by these subjects appears to be L.B. Johnson. Somewhat surprisingly, Brigitte Bardot is grouped together with the athletes, rather than with the movie stars. Of course, any judgment about the appropriateness of this clustering depends on the particular definition of athletics that one adopts!

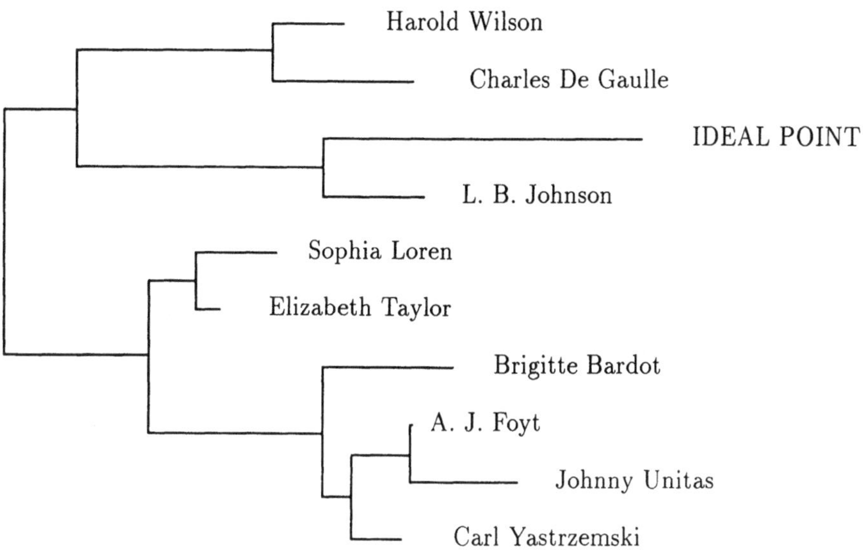

Figure 1: Representation of the Rumelhart and Greeno (1971) Data According to the GSTUN-EQP(1/2,1) Model

References

CARROLL, J.D. (1980), Models and Methods for Multidimensional Analysis of Preferential Choice (or Other Dominance) Data, in: *Similarity and Choice*, eds. E.D. Lantermann and H. Feger, Huber, Bern, 234-289.

CARROLL, J.D., DeSARBO, W.S., and DE SOETE, G. (1987), Stochastic Tree Unfolding (STUN) Models, *Communication & Cognition, 20*, 63–76.

CARROLL, J.D., DeSARBO, W.S., and DE SOETE, G. (1988), Stochastic Tree Unfolding (STUN) Models: Theory and application, in: *Classification and Related Methods of Data Analysis*, ed. H.H. Bock, North-Holland, Amsterdam, 421–430.

CARROLL, J.D., DeSARBO, W.S., and DE SOETE, G. (1989), Two Classes of Stochastic Unfolding Models, in: *New Developments in Psychological Choice Modeling*, eds. G. De Soete, H. Feger and K.C. Klauer, North-Holland, Amsterdam, 161–176.

COOMBS, C.H. (1964), *A Theory of Data*, Wiley, New York.

DeSARBO, W.S., DE SOETE, G., CARROLL, J.D., and RAMASWAMY, V. (1988), A New Stochastic Ultrametric Tree Unfolding Methodology for Assessing Competitive Market Structure and Deriving Market Segments, *Applied Stochastic Models and Data Analysis, 4*, 185–204.

DE SOETE, G. (1983), A Least Squares Algorithm for Fitting Additive Trees to Proximity Data, *Psychometrika, 48*, 621–626.

DE SOETE, G., and CARROLL, J.D. (1983), A Maximum Likelihood Method for Fitting the Wandering Vector Model, *Psychometrika, 48*, 621–626.

HALFF, H.M. (1976), Choice Theories for Differentially Comparable Alternatives, *Journal of Mathematical Psychology, 14*, 244–246.

LUCE, R.D., and SUPPES, P. (1965), Preference, Utility, and Subjective Probability, in: *Handbook of Mathematical Psychology, Vol. 3*, eds. R.D. Luce, R.R. Bush and E. Galanter, Wiley, New York, 249–410.

RUMELHART, D.L., and GREENO, J.G. (1971), Similarity Between Stimuli: An Experimental Test of the Luce and Restle Choice Models, *Journal of Mathematical Psychology, 8*, 370–381.

THURSTONE, L.L. (1927), A Law of Comparative Judgment, *Psychological Review, 34*, 273–286.

TVERSKY, A., and SATTATH, S. (1979), Preference Trees, *Psychological Review, 86*, 542–573.

A Latent Class Approach to Modeling Pairwise Preferential Choice Data

Geert De Soete[1]
Department of Psychology
University of Ghent, Belgium

Summary

Several probabilistic models have been proposed for representing two-way and three-way replicated paired comparisons data. Such data are usually obtained by having N subjects judge all $n(n-1)/2$ possible pairs of n stimuli. If the N subjects are grouped into T ($T \ll N$) homogeneous groups, an $n \times n \times T$ replicated paired comparisons data array is obtained. Examples of models for representing such three-way paired comparisons data are the wandering vector model and the wandering ideal point model. These models predict a different $n(n-1)/2$-variate Bernoulli distribution for each level t ($1 \leq t \leq T$) of the third way of the data array. By applying a latent class approach, the a priori grouping of the N subjects into T groups can be avoided. This is especially useful when one wants to estimate market segments from the preferential choice data. In the latent class formulation, a different multivariate Bernoulli distribution is predicted for each class and the data of an individual subject are assumed to be sampled from a finite mixture of these multivariate Bernoulli distributions. An EM algorithm for simultaneously estimating the mixture parameters and the choice model parameters is developed. The algorithm as well as a Monte Carlo significance test for the number of latent classes are illustrated on some real data.

1 Introduction

The data of concern in this paper are obtained by presenting all $\binom{n}{2}$ different pairs of n stimuli to N subjects by means of the method of paired comparisons (David (1988)). Each subject i ($1 \leq i \leq N$) is presented every pair of stimuli (j,k) ($1 \leq k < j \leq n$) once and only once. For each pair of stimuli the subject has to indicate which of the two he or she prefers. The data obtained in this way can be coded by means of binary variables as follows:

$$y_{ijk} = \begin{cases} 1 & \textit{iff} \text{ subject } i \text{ prefers stimulus } j \text{ to stimulus } k, \\ 0 & \textit{iff} \text{ subject } i \text{ prefers stimulus } k \text{ to stimulus } j. \end{cases}$$

The data of subject i will be denoted by the $n(n-1)/2$-component column vector $\mathbf{y}_i = (y_{i21}, y_{i31}, y_{i32}, \ldots, y_{in(n-1)})'$ and the total data set will be denoted by the matrix $\mathbf{Y} = (\mathbf{y}_1, \ldots, \mathbf{y}_N)'$.

A choice model defines the probability that a subject i prefers a stimulus j to a stimulus k as a function of a vector of model parameters $\boldsymbol{\theta}_i$. It is commonly assumed that, for a

[1]Supported as "Bevoegdverklaard Navorser" of the Belgian N.F.W.O.

NATO ASI Series, Vol. F 61
Knowledge, Data and Computer-Assisted Decisions
Edited by M. Schader and W. Gaul

particular subject i, the data for the $n(n-1)/2$ pairs of stimuli are independent of each other. Consequently, $\mathbf{y}_i$, the data of subject i, are distributed according to a multivariate Bernoulli distribution

$$f(\mathbf{y}_i|\boldsymbol{\theta}_i) = \prod_{j=2}^{n}\prod_{k=1}^{j-1} p_{jk}(\boldsymbol{\theta}_i)^{y_{ijk}}\left[1 - p_{jk}(\boldsymbol{\theta}_i)^{1-y_{ijk}}\right], \tag{1}$$

where $p_{jk}(\boldsymbol{\theta}_i)$ denotes the probability that subject i prefers j to k.

A data set $\mathbf{Y}$ consisting of unreplicated paired comparisons data from N subjects is usually analyzed in one of the following three ways: (i) the N subjects are treated as replications of each other and a two-way replicated paired comparisons matrix is derived from $\mathbf{Y}$; (ii) the subjects are considered to be all different and individual parameters are estimated per subject; and (iii) $\mathbf{Y}$ is reduced to a three-way replicated $n \times n \times T$ paired comparisons array by grouping the N subjects into T ($T \ll N$) homogeneous groups.

In the first case, the data are treated as *replicated* paired comparisons data from a single subject, so that

$$\boldsymbol{\theta}_1 = \boldsymbol{\theta}_2 = \ldots = \boldsymbol{\theta}_N \equiv \boldsymbol{\theta}. \tag{2}$$

This amounts to collapsing $\mathbf{Y}$ into a two-way $n \times n$ paired comparisons matrix with as general entry n_{jk}, the number of subjects that preferred j to k. Maximum likelihood estimates of the model parameters $\boldsymbol{\theta}$ are obtained by maximizing the log-likelihood function

$$\begin{aligned}\log L_1(\boldsymbol{\theta}|\mathbf{Y}) &= \sum_{i=1}^{N} \log f(\mathbf{y}_i|\boldsymbol{\theta}) \\ &= \sum_{j=2}^{n}\sum_{k=1}^{j-1} \{n_{jk}\log p_{jk}(\boldsymbol{\theta}) + (N - n_{jk})\log\left[1 - p_{jk}(\boldsymbol{\theta})\right]\}. \end{aligned} \tag{3}$$

An example of this approach would be to analyze $\mathbf{Y}$ by means of Thurstone's (1927) Law of Comparative Judgment Case V. If the subjects can indeed be considered to be replications of each other, this approach leads to a very parsimonious representation of $\mathbf{Y}$. However, if there are some systematic inter-individual differences, then the assumption on which (1) is based will be violated and any analysis based on (1) will give a rather incomplete, if not totally distorted, account of the data.

In the second approach, one explicitly allows for differences among the subjects by adopting a choice model that incorporates some distinct parameters per subject. Examples of such models are presented in DeSarbo, Oliver and De Soete (1986), DeSarbo, De Soete and Eliashberg (1987) and DeSarbo, De Soete, Carroll and Ramaswamy (1988). Since individual subject parameters are allowed for and since there are no replications within a single subject, these models tend to have a number of parameters that is rather large relative to the amount of data available. This limits the complexity of the structural part of such models. For instance, the models by De Sarbo et al. referred to above are all strong utility models. It is not straightforward, and probable not feasible from a parameter estimation point of view, to extend these models to allow for violations of the strong transitivity condition while still modeling unreplicated individual subject data.

An approach that is intermediary between treating all subjects as replications of each other and assuming that all subjects differ from each other, is to assume that the N subjects belong to T ($T \ll N$) homogeneous groups. Subjects within the same group are treated as replications of each other, but the choice model incorporates parameters to account for systematic differences among the T groups. In this approach the raw data $\mathbf{Y}$ are collapsed into an $n \times n \times T$ three-way replicated paired comparison array with general entry n_{jkt}, the number of subjects in group t that preferred stimulus j to k. Maximum likelihood estimates of the model parameters $\boldsymbol{\theta}_1, \ldots, \boldsymbol{\theta}_T$, can be obtained by maximizing

$$\log L_2(\boldsymbol{\theta}_1, \ldots, \boldsymbol{\theta}_T|\mathbf{Y}) = \sum_{t=1}^{T}\sum_{j=2}^{n}\sum_{k=1}^{j-1} \{n_{jkt} \log p_{jk}(\boldsymbol{\theta}_t) + (N_t - n_{jkt}) \log [1 - p_{jk}(\boldsymbol{\theta}_t)]\}, \quad (4)$$

where N_t ($N_t > 1$) denotes the number of subjects in group t. Examples of choice models that can be used for analyzing such a three-way replicated paired comparison array are the wandering vector model (De Soete and Carroll (1983)) and the wandering ideal point model (De Soete, Carroll and DeSarbo (1986)). Although intuitively this approach seems attractive, it has not been adopted very often in practical applications, mainly because it is usually very difficult to group the N subjects *a priori* into T homogeneous groups. For instance in marketing research, one would like to model the differences in preference structure among different market segments, but it is very hard to assign the N subjects to T market segments on an a priori basis. Rather, one would like a procedure that, on the basis of the choice data $\mathbf{Y}$, *simultaneously* groups the subjects into T groups *and* models the preference structures of these groups. Such an approach is developed in this paper using a latent class formulation (Lazarsfeld and Henry (1968)).

2 A Latent Class Formulation

Suppose there exist T latent classes. Each subject i belongs to one and only one latent class t ($1 \leq t \leq T$), but we do not know in advance to which specific class a particular subject belongs. In addition to a set of parameters τ that are common for the T classes, the choice model now incorporates for each class t a set of class specific parameters ζ_t. Thus, $\boldsymbol{\theta}$, the vector of all parameters in the choice model, comprises all elements in

$$\tau \cup \bigcup_{t=1}^{T} \zeta_t.$$

Because of the class specific parameters, the choice probabilities that are predicted by the model can be different for different latent classes. The probability that a particular subject i belongs to latent class t is λ_t, with of course

$$\sum_{t=1}^{T} \lambda_t = 1. \quad (5)$$

The vector $\boldsymbol{\lambda}$ is defined as $(\lambda_1, \ldots, \lambda_T)'$. Hence, the distribution of the data of subject i is a finite mixture of multivariate Bernoulli distributions:

$$g(\mathbf{y}_i|\boldsymbol{\theta}, \boldsymbol{\lambda}) = \sum_{t=1}^{T} \lambda_t f(\mathbf{y}_i|\tau, \zeta_t) \quad (6)$$

with

$$f(\mathbf{y}_i|\tau, \zeta_t) = \prod_{j=2}^{n}\prod_{k=2}^{j-1} p_{jkt}^{y_{ijk}} (1 - p_{jkt})^{(1-y_{ijk})}, \quad (7)$$

where

$$p_{jkt} \equiv p_{jk}(\tau, \zeta_t). \tag{8}$$

A simple example of a latent class choice model is a Thurstone (1927) Case V model where separate stimulus utilities are estimated for each latent class. In this case, the probability that stimulus j is preferred to stimulus k in latent class t is defined as

$$p_{jkt} = \Phi\left(x_{jt} - x_{kt}\right),$$

where Φ is the standard normal cumulative distribution function and where x_{jt} denotes the utility of stimulus j in latent class t. Thus, the parameter sets τ and ζ_t are here defined as

$$\tau = \emptyset \qquad \text{and} \qquad \zeta_t = \{x_{1t}, \ldots, x_{nt}\}.$$

More complex latent class choice models are for instance based on the wandering vector model (De Soete and Carroll (1983)) and the wandering ideal point model (De Soete et al. (1986)). In a latent class choice model based on the wandering vector model, the n stimuli are represented as points $\mathbf{x}_1, \ldots, \mathbf{x}_n$ in a multidimensional Euclidean space. Each latent class t is represented by means of a vector in the same space, emanating from the origin. The endpoint of this vector is assumed to follow a multivariate normal distribution with mean $\boldsymbol{\mu}_t$ and variance $\boldsymbol{\Sigma}_t$. Whenever a subject belonging to latent class t is presented a pair of stimuli (j, k), a point is sampled from that multivariate normal distribution. The stimulus with the largest orthogonal projection on the vector from the origin to the sampled point is preferred. It can be shown that this model predicts the following choice probabilities

$$p_{jkt} = \Phi\left(\frac{(\mathbf{x}_j - \mathbf{x}_k)'\boldsymbol{\mu}_t}{\delta_{jkt}}\right)$$

with

$$\delta^2_{jkt} = (\mathbf{x}_j - \mathbf{x}_k)'\boldsymbol{\Sigma}_t(\mathbf{x}_j - \mathbf{x}_k).$$

In this case, τ and ζ_t are defined as

$$\tau = \{\mathbf{x}_1, \ldots, \mathbf{x}_n\} \qquad \text{and} \qquad \zeta_t = \{\boldsymbol{\mu}_t, \boldsymbol{\Sigma}_t\}.$$

In a latent class choice model based on the wandering ideal point model, each stimulus j is also represented as a point $\mathbf{x}_j$ in a multidimensional space. However, a latent class is no longer represented by a vector, but by a point in the same space. This point is assumed to be multivariate normally distributed with mean $\boldsymbol{\mu}_t$ and variance $\boldsymbol{\Sigma}_t$. Each time a pair of stimuli is presented, a point is sampled from this distribution and the stimulus that is the closest to the sampled point is chosen. The choice probability predicted by this model then becomes

$$p_{jkt} = \Phi\left(\frac{(\mathbf{x}_k'\mathbf{x}_k - \mathbf{x}_j'\mathbf{x}_j) - 2(\mathbf{x}_k - \mathbf{x}_j)'\boldsymbol{\mu}_t}{2\delta_{jkt}}\right)$$

where δ_{jkt} is defined as before. The parameter sets τ and ζ_t consist of the same elements as in the latent class choice model based on the wandering vector model.

As a final example, a latent class choice model that is based on the stochastic additive tree unfolding model elaborated by Carroll and De Soete (1990) can be mentioned. In this model, both the stimuli and the latent classes are represented by the terminal nodes of an additive tree. The probability that a subject belonging to class t prefers stimulus j to k is

$$p_{jkt} = \Phi\left(\frac{d_{kt} - d_{jt}}{\alpha d_{jk}^{\beta}}\right) \quad (\alpha > 0,\ \beta \in \{1/2, 1\})$$

where d_{kt} denotes the additive tree distance between the node representing stimulus k and the node representing latent class t, while d_{jk} denotes the additive tree distance between the nodes representing stimuli j and k. Here, the parameter sets τ and ζ_t are

$$\tau = \{d_{jk} \mid 1 \leq k < j \leq n\} \qquad \text{and} \qquad \zeta_t = \{d_{1t}, \ldots, d_{nt}\}.$$

If one wants to apply one of these latent class choice models, the parameter vectors $\boldsymbol{\theta}$ and $\boldsymbol{\lambda}$ need to be estimated on the basis of the observed data $\mathbf{Y}$. Once parameter estimates are obtained, the *a posteriori* probability that a subject i belongs to latent class t can be calculated by means of Bayes' theorem. This a posteriori probability, written as $h_{it}(\boldsymbol{\theta}, \boldsymbol{\lambda})$, is

$$\begin{aligned} h_{it}(\boldsymbol{\theta}, \boldsymbol{\lambda}) &= \text{Prob}(t \mid \mathbf{y}_i, \boldsymbol{\theta}, \boldsymbol{\lambda}) = \frac{\text{Prob}(t) \times \text{Prob}(\mathbf{y}_i|t)}{\text{Prob}(\mathbf{y}_i)} \\ &= \frac{\lambda_t f(\mathbf{y}_i|\tau, \zeta_t)}{g(\mathbf{y}_i|\boldsymbol{\theta}, \boldsymbol{\lambda})}. \end{aligned} \tag{9}$$

A subject can then be assigned to the class for which the a posteriori membership probability is the largest. Maximum likelihood estimates of the parameters $\boldsymbol{\theta}$ and $\boldsymbol{\lambda}$ can be obtained by maximizing the likelihood function

$$\log L_3(\boldsymbol{\theta}, \boldsymbol{\lambda}|\mathbf{Y}) = \prod_{i=1}^{N} g(\mathbf{y}_i|\boldsymbol{\theta}, \boldsymbol{\lambda}) \tag{10}$$

with respect to $\boldsymbol{\theta}$ and $\boldsymbol{\lambda}$. This amounts to solving the following constrained optimization problem

$$\left.\begin{array}{l} \max\limits_{\boldsymbol{\theta}, \boldsymbol{\lambda}} \log L_3(\boldsymbol{\theta}, \boldsymbol{\lambda}|\mathbf{Y}) \\ \text{such that} \sum\limits_{t=1}^{T} \lambda_t = 1 \end{array}\right\}. \tag{11}$$

In the next section we present an EM algorithm for solving (11).

3 EM Algorithm

Like most estimation problems with finite mixture models (cf. McLachlan and Basford (1988)), (11) is most easily solved by means of an EM algorithm (Dempster, Laird and Rubin (1977)). In order to enable an EM algorithm formulation, some non-observed data are introduced:

$$z_{it} = \begin{cases} 1 & \textit{iff} \text{ subject } i \text{ belongs to latent class } t, \\ 0 & \text{otherwise.} \end{cases}$$

The column vector $\mathbf{z}_i$ is defined as $(z_{i1}, \ldots, z_{iT})'$ and the matrix $\mathbf{Z}$ as $(\mathbf{z}_1, \ldots, \mathbf{z}_N)'$. We assume that the non-observed data $\mathbf{z}_i$ are independently and identically multinomially distributed with probabilities $\boldsymbol{\lambda}$, i.e.,

$$(\mathbf{z}_i|\boldsymbol{\lambda}) \sim \prod_{t=1}^{T} \lambda_t^{y_{it}}. \tag{12}$$

The distribution of $\mathbf{y}_i$ given $\mathbf{z}_i$ is

$$\begin{aligned}(\mathbf{y}_i|\mathbf{z}_i,\boldsymbol{\theta}) &\sim \sum_{t=1}^{T} z_{it} f(\mathbf{y}_i|\tau,\zeta_t) \\ &\sim \prod_{t=1}^{T} f(\mathbf{y}_i|\tau,\zeta_t)^{z_{it}}.\end{aligned} \tag{13}$$

When $\mathbf{Z}$ is considered as missing data, the total likelihood function becomes

$$\log L_T(\boldsymbol{\theta},\boldsymbol{\lambda}|\mathbf{Y},\mathbf{Z}) = \sum_{i=1}^{N}\sum_{t=1}^{T} z_{it} \log f(\mathbf{y}_i|\tau,\zeta_t) + \sum_{i=1}^{N}\sum_{t=1}^{T} z_{it} \log \lambda_t. \tag{14}$$

An EM algorithm amounts to iteratively alternating between two steps: a so-called E-step (expectation step) and a so-called M-step (model step).

In the E-step the expectation of $\log L_T$ needs to be calculated over the conditional distribution of the non-observed data $\mathbf{Z}$, given the observed data $\mathbf{Y}$ and provisional estimates $\boldsymbol{\theta}^{(0)}$, $\boldsymbol{\lambda}^{(0)}$ of the parameters $\boldsymbol{\theta}$ and $\boldsymbol{\lambda}$. This expectation is

$$\begin{aligned}Q(\boldsymbol{\theta},\boldsymbol{\lambda},\boldsymbol{\theta}^{(0)},\boldsymbol{\lambda}^{(0)}) &= \sum_{i=1}^{N}\sum_{t=1}^{T} E(z_{it}|\mathbf{Y},\boldsymbol{\theta}^{(0)},\boldsymbol{\lambda}^{(0)}) \log f(\mathbf{y}_i|\tau,\zeta_t) \\ &+\sum_{i=1}^{N}\sum_{t=1}^{T} E(z_{it}|\mathbf{Y},\boldsymbol{\theta}^{(0)},\boldsymbol{\lambda}^{(0)}) \log \lambda_t.\end{aligned} \tag{15}$$

By using Bayes' theorem, one can derive from (12) and (13) the conditional distribution of $\mathbf{z}_i$:

$$(\mathbf{z}_i|\mathbf{y}_i,\boldsymbol{\theta},\boldsymbol{\lambda}) \sim \prod_{t=1}^{T} [\lambda_t f(\mathbf{y}_i|\tau,\zeta_t)]^{z_{it}}. \tag{16}$$

This implies

$$E(z_{it}|\mathbf{Y},\boldsymbol{\theta},\boldsymbol{\lambda}) = \frac{\lambda_t f(\mathbf{y}_i|\tau,\zeta_t)}{\sum_{s=1}^{T} \lambda_s f(\mathbf{y}_i|\tau,\zeta_s)}, \tag{17}$$

which is identical to the a posteriori probability $h_{it}(\boldsymbol{\theta},\boldsymbol{\lambda})$. Consequently,

$$E(z_{it}|\mathbf{Y},\boldsymbol{\theta}^{(0)},\boldsymbol{\lambda}^{(0)}) = h_{it}(\boldsymbol{\theta}^{(0)},\boldsymbol{\lambda}^{(0)}). \tag{18}$$

Thus, in the E-step, the non-observed discrete data $\mathbf{Z}$ are replaced by the a posteriori probabilities calculated on the basis of the provisional estimates $\boldsymbol{\theta}^{(0)},\boldsymbol{\lambda}^{(0)}$. If we write (18) as $z_{it}^{(0)}$, then (15) becomes

$$Q(\boldsymbol{\theta},\boldsymbol{\lambda},\boldsymbol{\theta}^{(0)},\boldsymbol{\lambda}^{(0)}) = \sum_{i=1}^{N}\sum_{t=1}^{T} z_{it}^{(0)} \log f(\mathbf{y}_i|\tau,\zeta_t) + \sum_{i=1}^{N}\sum_{t=1}^{T} z_{it}^{(0)} \log \lambda_t. \tag{19}$$

In the M-step of the EM algorithm, $Q(\boldsymbol{\theta}, \boldsymbol{\lambda}, \boldsymbol{\theta}^{(0)}, \boldsymbol{\lambda}^{(0)})$ needs to be maximized with respect to $\boldsymbol{\theta}$ and $\boldsymbol{\lambda}$ in order to obtain new provisional parameter estimates. These new estimates are then used in the next E-step to compute new estimates of the non-observed data $\mathbf{Z}$. These new estimates of z_{it} are subsequently used in the next M-step to arrive at new estimates of $\boldsymbol{\theta}$ and $\boldsymbol{\lambda}$, etc. These E- and M-steps are successively applied until no further improvement in the likelihood function is possible.

In order to maximize $Q(\boldsymbol{\theta}, \boldsymbol{\lambda}, \boldsymbol{\theta}^{(0)}, \boldsymbol{\lambda}^{(0)})$ with respect to $\boldsymbol{\theta}$ in the M-step, it suffices to solve the following optimization problem:

$$\max_{\boldsymbol{\theta}} \left\{ q_1(\boldsymbol{\theta}|\boldsymbol{\theta}^{(0)}, \boldsymbol{\lambda}^{(0)}) = \sum_{i=1}^{N} \sum_{t=1}^{T} h_{it}(\boldsymbol{\theta}^{(0)}, \boldsymbol{\lambda}^{(0)}) \log f(\mathbf{y}_i|\tau, \zeta_t) \right\}. \tag{20}$$

The function $q_1(\boldsymbol{\theta}|\boldsymbol{\theta}^{(0)}, \boldsymbol{\lambda}^{(0)})$ can be rewritten as follows

$$\begin{aligned} q_1(\boldsymbol{\theta}|\boldsymbol{\theta}^{(0)}, \boldsymbol{\lambda}^{(0)}) &= \sum_{i=1}^{N} \sum_{t=1}^{T} z_{it}^{(0)} \sum_{j=2}^{n} \sum_{k=1}^{j-1} [y_{ijk} \log p_{jkt} + (1 - y_{ijk}) \log(1 - p_{jkt})] \\ &= \sum_{t=1}^{T} \sum_{j=2}^{n} \sum_{k=1}^{j-1} \left\{ \left[\sum_{i=1}^{N} z_{it}^{(0)} y_{ijk} \right] \log p_{jkt} \right. \\ &\quad \left. + \left[\sum_{i=1}^{N} z_{it}^{(0)} (1 - y_{ijk}) \right] \log(1 - p_{jkt}) \right\} \\ &= \sum_{t=1}^{T} \sum_{j=2}^{n} \sum_{k=1}^{j-1} [f_{jkt} \log p_{jkt} + (F_t - f_{jkt}) \log(1 - p_{jkt})], \end{aligned} \tag{21}$$

with

$$f_{jkt} = \sum_{i=1}^{N} z_{it}^{(0)} y_{ijk} \quad \text{and} \quad F_t = \sum_{i=1}^{N} z_{it}^{(0)}. \tag{22}$$

Thus, the parameters $\boldsymbol{\theta}$ can be estimated on the basis of $\{f_{jkt}, F_t \mid 1 \le t \le T,\ 1 \le k < j \le n\}$. For the latent class choice models discussed in the previous section, $q_1(\boldsymbol{\theta}|\boldsymbol{\theta}^{(0)}, \boldsymbol{\lambda}^{(0)})$ cannot be maximized analytically because it involves a non-linear optimization problem. Therefore, an iterative procedure must be applied in the M-step. For the latent class models based on Thurstone's Case V model, the wandering vector model and the wandering ideal point model, a generalized Fisher scoring method can be used, while for the latent class model based on the stochastic additive tree unfolding model a conjugate gradient technique can be used. Note that (21) is very similar to (4). The only difference between (4) and (21) is that in (4) n_{jkt} and N_t are integers, while in (21) f_{jkt} and F_t are sums of of (a posteriori) probabilities and can therefore assume non-integer values. Nevertheless, existing maximum likelihood estimation algorithms for fitting the wandering vector model (cf. De Soete and Carroll (1983)), wandering ideal point model (cf. De Soete et al. (1986)) and the stochastic additive tree unfolding model (cf. Carroll and De Soete (1990)) can be utilized in the M-step.

In order to maximize $Q(\boldsymbol{\theta}, \boldsymbol{\lambda}, \boldsymbol{\theta}^{(0)}, \boldsymbol{\lambda}^{(0)})$ with respect to $\boldsymbol{\lambda}$ subject to restriction (5), it suffices to maximize the augmented function $q_2^*(\boldsymbol{\lambda}|\boldsymbol{\theta}^{(0)}, \boldsymbol{\lambda}^{(0)})$

$$q_2^*(\boldsymbol{\lambda}|\boldsymbol{\theta}^{(0)}, \boldsymbol{\lambda}^{(0)}) = \sum_{i=1}^{N} \sum_{t=1}^{T} z_{it}^{(0)} \log \lambda_t - \mu \left(\sum_{t=1}^{T} \lambda_t - 1 \right), \tag{23}$$

where μ denotes a Lagrange multiplier. It can easily be shown that (23) is maximized by

$$\lambda_t = \frac{\sum_{i=1}^{N} z_{it}^{(0)}}{N}. \qquad (24)$$

Schematically, the EM algorithm can be described as follows:

(i) Initialize iteration index h: $h \leftarrow 0$.
Determine initial estimates $\boldsymbol{\theta}^{(0)}$ and $\boldsymbol{\lambda}^{(0)}$ of $\boldsymbol{\theta}$ and $\boldsymbol{\lambda}$.

(ii) Compute $\mathbf{Z}^{(h)} = ((z_{it}^{(h)}))$: $z_{it}^{(h)} = h_{it}(\boldsymbol{\theta}^{(h)}, \boldsymbol{\lambda}^{(h)})$.

(iii) Compute a new estimate $\boldsymbol{\theta}^{(h+1)}$ of $\boldsymbol{\theta}$ by maximizing $q_1(\boldsymbol{\theta}|\boldsymbol{\theta}^{(h)}, \boldsymbol{\lambda}^{(h)})$ using a non-linear programming method starting from $\boldsymbol{\theta}^{(h)}$.

(iv) Compute a new estimate $\boldsymbol{\lambda}^{(h+1)}$ of $\boldsymbol{\lambda}$:

$$\lambda_t^{(h+1)} = \frac{1}{N} \sum_{t=1}^{T} h_{it}(\boldsymbol{\theta}^{(h)}, \boldsymbol{\lambda}^{(h)}).$$

(v) Convergence test: if

$$\log L(\boldsymbol{\theta}^{(h+1)}, \boldsymbol{\lambda}^{(h+1)}|\mathbf{Y}) - \log L(\boldsymbol{\theta}^{(h)}, \boldsymbol{\lambda}^{(h)}|\mathbf{Y}) < \epsilon$$

where ϵ is a small positive constant, stop.

(vi) Increment h: $h \leftarrow h + 1$.
Go back to step (ii).

4 Significance Testing

When applying latent class choice models to real data, one would like to find out how many latent classes (or market segments) are required for adequately representing the data. The usual way for making such a decision amounts to testing whether a solution with $T+1$ latent classes gives a significantly better fit than a solution with T latent classes. If a solution with $T+1$ latent classes does not significantly improve the T-class solution, T classes suffice to describe the data adequately. Unfortunately, like in most mixture distribution problems, the asymptotic likelihood ratio statistic for testing T versus $T+1$ latent classes

$$U = -2 \log \left(\frac{\hat{L}^{(T)}}{\hat{L}^{(T+1)}} \right), \qquad (25)$$

where $\hat{L}^{(T)}$ denotes the maximum obtained for the likelihood function with T latent classes, is *not* asymptotically distributed as a chi-square with known degrees of freedom (McLachlan and Basford (1988)).

As an alternative, one can resort to a—computationally rather intensive—Monte Carlo significance testing procedure due to Hope (1968). This procedure has first been used in the context of mixture distribution problems by Aitkin, Anderson and Hinde (1981) and can be considered as a *parametric* bootstrap method (cf. McLachlan (1987)).

Let $\hat{\boldsymbol{\theta}}^{(T)}$ and $\hat{\boldsymbol{\lambda}}^{(T)}$ denote the maximum likelihood estimates of $\boldsymbol{\theta}$ and $\boldsymbol{\lambda}$ for the T-class model. From the T-class population with parameters $\hat{\boldsymbol{\theta}}^{(T)}$ and $\hat{\boldsymbol{\lambda}}^{(T)}$, $(K-1)$ random Monte Carlo samples $\tilde{\mathbf{Y}}$ of size N are generated. The latent class choice model is fitted to each of the generated data sets $\tilde{\mathbf{Y}}$ with T and $T+1$ latent classes and the likelihood ratio statistic U is computed. The null hypothesis that a T-class solution gives an equally good account of the observed data $\mathbf{Y}$ as a $(T+1)$-class solution is rejected, if the value of U for $\mathbf{Y}$ exceeds $K(1-\alpha)$ of the values of U obtained for the Monte Carlo samples $\tilde{\mathbf{Y}}$. A minimal value of K when using a significance level of $\alpha = 0.05$ is 20. Hope (1968) showed that the larger K, the more power the Monte Carlo significance test procedure has. The use of this Monte Carlo test is illustrated on a real data set in the next section.

5 Illustrative Application

In this section, a latent class choice model is applied to pairwise preferences from 80 first-year university students for 16 family compositions. Each family was characterized by the number of sons (0, 1, 2, or 3) and the number of daughters (0, 1, 2, or 3) in the family. Similar data have been analyzed in the past by Coxon (1974) and Delbeke (1968, 1980). The particular latent class model that was used here was based on a probabilistic additive conjoint measurement model described by De Soete (1982). In this model, the probability that a subject in latent class t will prefer a family with a sons and q daughters to a family with b sons and r daughters is defined as

$$p^{(t)}_{aq,br} = \Phi(u_{at} + v_{qt} - u_{bt} - v_{rt}), \tag{26}$$

where u_{at} denotes the utility in class t of having a sons, and where v_{qt} denotes the utility in class t of having q daughters. Using the Monte Carlo significance testing procedure (with $\alpha = 0.05$ and $K = 20$) described in the previous section, it was decided that a 3-class solution gave a good account of the data. The maximum likelihood estimates of the utility parameters are displayed in Fig. 1. As one would expect, all utility functions are single-peaked. The subjects in latent class 1 have a clear preference for two sons and two daughters. The subjects in latent class 2 mostly prefer two sons but only one daughter, while the subjects in latent class 3 prefer one son and one daughter. All three classes are about equally large. The maximum likelihood estimate of $\boldsymbol{\lambda}$ is $(0.36, 0.35, 0.29)'$. This application illustrates how one can simultaneously cluster the subjects into a number of homogeneous groups *and* model the preference structures of these groups by using a latent class choice model.

References

AITKIN, M., ANDERSON, D., and HINDE, J. (1981), Statistical Modelling of Data on Teaching Styles, *Journal of the Royal Statistical Society, Series A, 144*, 419–461.

CARROLL, J.D., and DE SOETE, G. (1990), Fitting A Quasi-Poisson Case of the GSTUN (General Stochastic Tree Unfolding) Model and Some Extensions, this volume.

COXON, A.P.M. (1974), The Mapping of Family Composition Preferences: A Scaling Analysis, *Social Science Research, 3*, 191–210.

DAVID, H.A. (1988), *The Method of Paired Comparisons*, 2nd. Rev. Ed., Griffin, London.

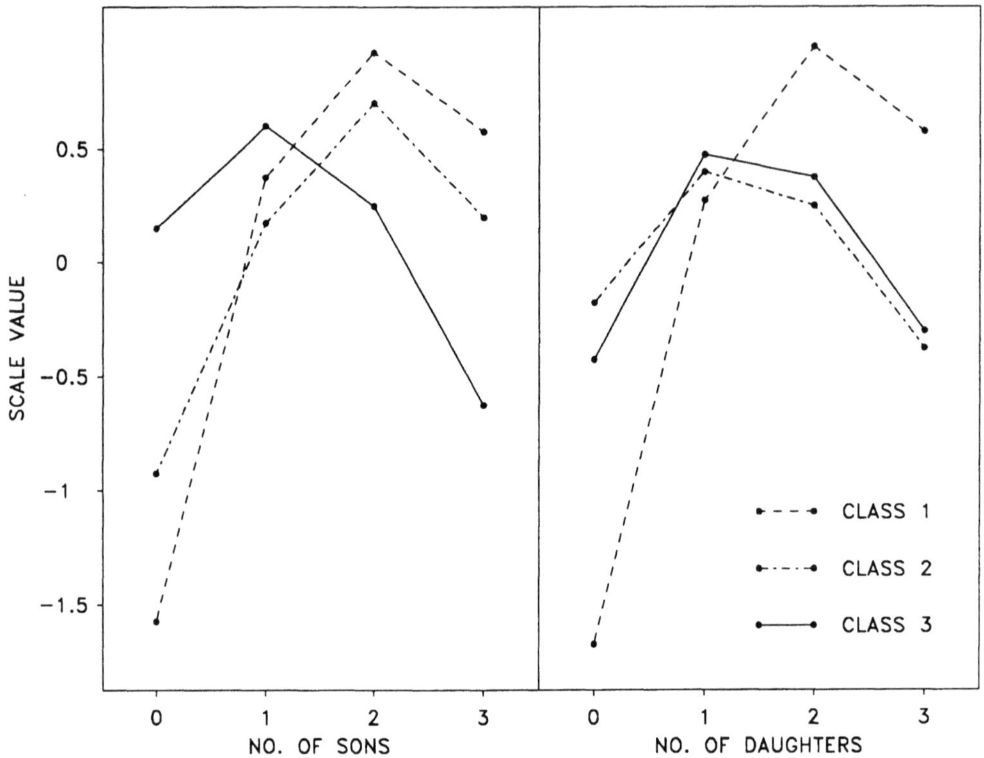

Figure 1: Utility Estimates for the 3-Class Representation of Preferences for Family Compositions Data

DELBEKE, L. (1968), *Construction of Preference Spaces*, Leuven University Press, Leuven.

DELBEKE, L. (1980), Voorkeuroordelen voor Gezinssamenstellingen, Geanalyseerd en Geinterpreteerd in het Kader van een Algemene Theorie over het Keuzegedrag, in: *Gedrag, Dynamische Relatie en Betekeniswereld. Liber Amicorum Prof. J. R. Nuttin*, Leuven University Press, Leuven, 285–302.

DEMPSTER, A.P., LAIRD, N.M., and RUBIN, D.B. (1977), Maximum Likelihood from Incomplete Data via the EM Algorithm, *Journal of the Royal Statistical Society, Series B, 39*, 1–38.

DeSARBO, W.S., DE SOETE, G., CARROLL, J.D., and RAMASWAMY, V. (1988), A New Stochastic Ultrametric Tree Unfolding Methodology for Assessing Competitive Market Structure and Deriving Market Segments, *Applied Stochastic Models and Data Analysis, 4*, 185–204.

DeSARBO, W.S., DE SOETE, G., and ELIASHBERG, J. (1987), A New Stochastic Multidimensional Unfolding Model for the Investigation of Paired Comparison Consumer Preference/Choice Data, *Journal of Economic Psychology, 8*, 357–384.

DeSARBO, W.S., OLIVER, R.L., and DE SOETE, G. (1986), A Probabilistic Multidimensional Scaling Vector Model, *Applied Psychological Measurement, 10*, 78–98.

DE SOETE, G. (1982), A Thurstonian Approach to Probabilistic Conjoint Measurement, *Archiv für Psychologie, 134*, 59–71.

DE SOETE, G., and CARROLL, J. D. (1983), A Maximum Likelihood Method for Fitting the Wandering Vector Model, *Psychometrika, 48*, 621–626.

DE SOETE, G., CARROLL, J. D., and DeSARBO, W. S. (1986), The Wandering Ideal Point Model: A Probabilistic Multidimensional Unfolding Model for Paired Comparisons Data, *Journal of Mathematical Psychology, 30*, 28–41.

HOPE, A.C. (1968), A Simplified Monte Carlo Significance Test Procedure, *Journal of the Royal Statistical Society, Series B, 30*, 582–598.

LAZARSFELD, P.F., and HENRY, N.W. (1968), *Latent Structure Analysis*, Houghton Mifflin, New York.

McLACHLAN, G.J. (1987), On Bootstrapping the Likelihood Ratio Test Statistic for the Number of Components in a Normal Mixture, *Applied Statistics, 36*, 318–324.

McLACHLAN, G.J., and BASFORD, K.E. (1988), *Mixture Models*, Marcel Dekker, New York.

THURSTONE, L.L. (1927), A Law of Comparative Judgment, *Psychological Review, 34*, 273–286.

Dual Scaling of Designed Experiments

Shizuhiko Nishisato
The Ontario Institute for Studies in Education (OISE)
and University of Toronto, Canada

Summary

Quantification of categorical data, with external criteria, is considered. The focal point of the study is to propose and discuss a graphical method to elucidate structure of data which involve experimental designs. Two examples are presented to illustrate some advantages of the method over the traditional joint row/column display.

1 Introduction

Data collection is often carried out with a special experimental design in mind, be it a simple one-way design with subjects as units or a more complex multi-way design. When collected data are categorical or qualitative, the object of analysis is typically to quantify the data in such a way that a particular structure, specified by the design, be captured most distinctly. Such an idea can be traced back to studies by Fisher (1948) in which non-numerical data were quantified for the one-way analysis of variance, by Hayashi and his associates (Hayashi, Higuchi and Komazawa (1970), Iwatsubo (1987) and Komazawa (1984)) in Hayashi's quantification theory and by Nishisato (1971, 1972) in which categorical data were scaled in terms of a multiway crossed design, and to recent studies by Sabatier, Lebreton and Chessel (1989) and Takane and Shibayama (1989).

The basic problem can be explained as follows: Suppose that data were collected from N subjects answering n multiple-choice questions. Let F be the $N \times m$ data matrix, consisting of 1's (responses) and 0's, where m is the total number of options of the n questions. Suppose that N subjects were sampled in terms of a two-way factorial design, and that A is the design matrix for the N subjects. Then, we wish to quantify m options in such a way that a particular design effect be a maximum. Let us indicate by y the $n \times 1$ vector of weighted linear combinations of responses, that is, $y = Fx$, where x is an $m \times 1$ vector of weights. The analysis of variance of y can be carried out as follows:

$$\begin{aligned} y &= Fx = A\beta + e = KL\beta + e \\ &= K\theta + e, \end{aligned} \tag{1}$$

where θ is an estimable vector of functions of parameters β_j, that is, $L\beta$, and K is a basis matrix. Assuming that the errors are independently and identically distributed, the best linear unbiased estimate of θ is given by

$$\hat{\theta} = (K'K)^{-1}K'y = (K'K)^{-1}K'Fx \tag{2}$$

NATO ASI Series, Vol. F 61
Knowledge, Data and Computer-Assisted Decisions
Edited by M. Schader and W. Gaul

If one wishes to maximize the sum of squares of $\hat{\theta}$ in terms of x under an appropriate constraint on x, the problem can be stated as

$$\begin{aligned}\max_x\{SS(\hat{\theta})\} &= \max_x\{x'F'K(K'K)^{-1}K'Fx\} \\ &= \max_x\{x'F'PFx\},\end{aligned} \tag{3}$$

subject to a constraint on x, where $P = K(K'K)^{-1}K'$ and is a projector. Or, more directly, in terms of orthogonal projectors,

$$\begin{aligned}y = Fx &= P_\mu y + P_\alpha y + P_\beta y + P_{\alpha\beta}y + P_e y \\ &= [P_\mu + P_\alpha + P_{\alpha\beta}]y + P_e y \\ &= Py + (I - P)y,\end{aligned} \tag{4}$$

where $P = P_\mu + P_\alpha + P_\beta + P_{\alpha\beta}$ and $P_e = I - P$. Thus, to maximize the design effect, we may determine x, under an appropriate constraint, so as to maximize

$$y'Py = x'F'PFx. \tag{5}$$

It follows from the above discussion that maximizing the effect of α, for example, can be stated as the problem of

$$\max_x\{x'F'P_\alpha Fx\}, \text{subject to a constraint on } x. \tag{6}$$

Noting that $F'P_\alpha'P_\alpha F = F'P_\alpha F$, the above problem can be stated as the problem of dual scaling of a modified matrix, that is, $P_\alpha F$ in the example.

As a general form of a modified matrix, Nishisato (1976) proposed the form $A_r'FA_c$, where A_r and A_c are matrices to capture designs for rows and columns, respectively. A_r and A_c may be familiar design matrices used in the analysis of variance, basis matrices or projection operators (see Nishisato (1971, 1972, 1975, 1980, 1982), Poon (1977) and Nishisato and Lawrence (1981, 1982, 1984, 1989)). Takane and Shibayama (1988) proposed a more specific decomposition of F than the previous studies, namel

$$F = P_rFP_c + P_rFQ_c + Q_rFP_c + Q_rFQ_c, \tag{7}$$

where P_r and P_c are orthogonal projectors for row and column subspaces, respectively, $Q_r = I - P_r$ and $Q_c = I - P_c$. Nishisato and Lawrence (1989) proposed a more general decomposition of F than (7),

$$F = (\sum_i P_{ri})F(\sum_j P_{cj}), \tag{8}$$

where P_{ri} and P_{cj} are projectors for rows and column subspaces, respectively, satisfying $\sum_i P_{ri} = I$ and $\sum_j P_{cj} = I$. For instance, suppose that the subjects (rows of F) are sampled by a two-way crossed design, and that the objects (columns) have a one-way design, then,

$$\sum P_{ri} = P_\mu + P_\alpha + P_\beta + P_{\alpha\beta} + P_e, \qquad \text{and}$$

$$\sum P_{cj} = P_\alpha^* + P_e^* = P_\alpha^* + (I - P_\alpha^*) \qquad \text{so that}$$

$$\begin{aligned}F &= (\sum P_{ri})F(\sum P_{cj}) = (P_\mu + P_\alpha + P_{\alpha\beta} + P_e)F(P_\alpha^* + (I - P_\alpha^*)) \\ &= P_\mu FP_\alpha^* + P_\mu F(I - P_\alpha^*) + P_\alpha FP_\alpha^* + P_\alpha F(I - P_\alpha^*) + P_\beta FP_\alpha^* + P_\beta F(I - P_\alpha^*) \\ &\quad + P_{\alpha\beta}FP_\alpha^* + P_{\alpha\beta}F(I - P_\alpha^*) + P_eFP_\alpha^* + P_eF(I - P_\alpha^*)\end{aligned}$$

2 Dual Scaling of Modified Data Matrices

Once the design for rows and columns of data matrix F is specified, the next step is to quantify the data so as to represent the design structure as clearly as possible. This optimization should be supplemented by an appropriate way of presenting the outcome. In other words, optimization effects should be described, revealed, or captured in a maximally communicable manner. To this end, graphical display of the outcome will be used in the present study.

Suppose that the subjects were randomly sampled from three professions, and that the investigator wishes to quantify the subjects' responses to a set of multiple-choice questions by determining weights for the choice alternatives (options) of the questions. If no other designs are considered for rows, or columns, or both, it is a case of the one-way design for the rows of the subjects-by-options response pattern (incidence) matrix, F. The design matrix, A, can be expressed as

$$A = \begin{bmatrix} 1 & 0 & 0 \\ 1 & 0 & 0 \\ \vdots & \vdots & \vdots \\ 1 & 0 & 0 \\ 0 & 1 & 0 \\ \vdots & \vdots & \vdots \\ 0 & 1 & 0 \\ 0 & 0 & 1 \\ \vdots & \vdots & \vdots \\ 0 & 0 & 1 \end{bmatrix} \begin{matrix} \\ \\ n_1 \\ \\ \\ n_2 \\ \\ \\ n_3 \\ \\ \end{matrix}$$

where n_j is the number of subjects in group j. The projection operator of our interest is given by

$$P_a = A(A'A)^{-1}A' - 1(1'1)^{-1}1' = H_a - H_m, \qquad \text{say}$$

It is the widely used practice that when dual scaling of data matrix F is carried out the sum of the weighted responses is set equal to zero, that is, $1'Fx = 0$, where x is a vector of weights for the options of the questions. Using the same condition, one can numerically demonstrate that dual scaling of P_aF provides the same optimal vector, x, with dual scaling of any of the following matrices, $A'F$, H_aF and $[F, kA]$ with a large value of k, that is, forced classification (Nishisato (1984)). Out of the four possible matrices, however, P_aF seems to be the only form which is applicable to a more general case such as maximizing the effect of interaction $\alpha\beta$ in a multiway factorial design.

In using the projection operators, however, there may be two practical problems. The first one lies in the fact that a projector for the rows of an $N \times m$ matrix is $N \times N$, which may be too large to handle in practice. This concern, however, is at least partly solved by Takane and Shibayama (1988), who proposed an algorithm for simplifying the computation. Note that in our example of three groups with N subjects the $N \times N$ projector is only of rank two $r(P) = 2$, meaning many redundant computations when P_j is used. The second concern is that orthogonal projectors have many negative elements. In other words, unlike data matrix F in which marginals provide numbers of responses in rows and columns, the marginals of the modified matrix are in general not equal to the numbers of responses in rows and columns. If P_a is examined, the key structure of P_a is H_a because H_m is simply to adjust the centroid of projections to the origin. Thus, the knowledge of the structure of H_aF tells us exactly how many responses are involved in rows and columns of P_aF. From H_aF, one knows that the column marginals of H_aF are the same as those of F, and that the first n_1 row marginals of H_aF are identical and equal to the average of the first n_1 marginals of F, where n_1 is the number of subjects in group 1. Thus, if there are p groups, the number of distinct row marginals is at most p, and those distinct numbers are repeated as many times as there are subjects in the corresponding groups. In the case of multiple-choice data, the data matrix is often partitioned into n incidence matrices for n questions, that is,

$$F = [F_1, F_2, \ldots, F_n],$$

and the condition that $F_j 1 = 1$ is imposed on each submatrix. In other words, each subject chooses one option per question, and there are no missing responses. Under this usual condition, the row marginals of F are identical, leading to the relation that numbers of responses for rows and columns of P_aF are the same as row marginals and column marginals of F, respectively. Alternatively, one can use H_a, instead of P_a, since dual scaling adjusts the sum of the quantified responses to zero. This means that dual scaling of H_aF provides identical results with dual scaling of P_aF. Similarly, if we wish to scale $[P_a + P_b]F$, we may analyze $[H_a + H_b]F$.

3 Graphical Display

There have been controversies over graphical display of quantified responses. Some investigators, in particular, Greenacre (1984), Lebart, Morineau and Warwick (1984) and Nishisato (1988), stress the inappropriateness of attempting to obtain precise information from a joint plot of row variates and column variates. Nevertheless, it is the French tradition to use a visual display of correspondence analysis results for interpretation. As Lebart, Morineau and Warwick (1984) would suggest, the French statisticians must know very well the precaution they should exercise in handling such a joint graph. One should also admit that joint display is almost indispensable for interpretation of results from correspondence analysis and dual scaling. Thus, the general situation is that we continue to use inaccurate information, displayed in a joint graph, to get useful clues for interpreting the quantified results. Under these circumstances, Nishisato (1988) presented an attempt to assess the quality of joint graphical display.

The heart of the controversies lies in the dual relations or substitution formulas,

$$y = {D_N}^{-1}Fx/\rho \quad , \quad x = D^{-1}F'y/\rho, \tag{9}$$

where D_N and D are diagonal matrices of row marginals and column marginals of F, respectively, and ρ is a singular value or the product-moment correlation between responses weighted by y and those weighted by x, that is,

$$\rho = y'Fx/\{[y'D_Ny][x'Dx]\}^{1/2}. \tag{10}$$

From (9), it is obvious that averages of responses weighted by x are not y, but ρy. Similarly, averages of responses weighted by y are not x, but ρx. This is a typical case of regression. Thus, the two spaces, one for row variates and the other for column variates, coincide if and only if $\rho = 1$, an improbable case in practice, or, even if probable, a case of little interest from the quantification point of view.

Recent studies by Carroll, Green and Schaffer (1986, 1987) propose plotting only column variates of a partitioned incidence matrix $F = [F_1, F_2]$ which constitute row variates and column variates of a contingency table, say C, for $C = F_1'F_2$. But, it is one of the well known aspects of quantification that column weights of F are identical, except for their singular values, to the row weights and the column weights of C (see de Leeuw (1973) and Nishisato (1980)). The important point of this equivalent relation is the fact that changing from quantification of C to that of F does not alter the regression effects mentioned above. It seems that the proposal by Carroll, Green and Schaffer is in essence the same as the French practice. Greenacre (1989) objects to the CGS (Carroll-Green-Schaffer) scaling for other reasons. See also a rebuttal from Carroll, Green and Schaffer (1989) to Greenacre (1989).

The present study offers an alternative to the joint display. The proposed graphical method is completely free from the regression effect and is perhaps the most natural way of displaying the data structure. It still looks after the investigator's interests in both row variates and column variates. It is based on the following considerations:

i) The graphical display of quantification of modified data PF should in principle be presented in the p-dimensional space, where p is the rank of P, the dimensionality of the subspace where principal axes are sought.

ii) The position of each row variable (i.e., subject) should be plotted in the p-dimensional space and the position should be labelled by the response pattern of that row.

iii) The positions of the group centroids should be plotted in the p-dimensional space, and the group boundaries should be determined in such a way that the total number of misclassifications be minimal.

iv) Clustering of individual data points should be carried out by identifying a subset of responses which are common among closely located data points, that is, by checking response patterns which are used to label data points.

v) One should also plot how subjects are distributed with respect to a particular item. For instance, in medical data where subjects are classified into several groups of illnesses, it would be useful to know how the patients with abnormal EKG are distributed in the space that maximally distinguishes among the groups. If the item 1 is whether or not they have abnormal EKG, the above analysis is to identify the cluster characterized by $(1{*}{*}\cdots{*})$, where option 1 of item 1 refers to the presence of abnormal EKG and $*$ in the k-th place indicates an unspecified response to item k.

The proposed method offers two interesting ways of looking at the data structure, namely, partitioning the p-dimensional subspace into minimally overlapping regions of data points, and making use of response patterns to identify characteristics of clusters, which may or may not coincide with the minimally overlapping regions. The use of response patterns is free from the regression effects among variables (items), hence no distortion is introduced into graphical display. To illustrate this point, consider three items of three options per item. Instead of using $(1,0)$ response patterns, consisting of nine elements, let us indicate response patterns in terms of chosen option numbers such as (312), in lieu of $(0,0,1,1,0,0,0,1,0)$. Suppose that ten subjects answered these three questions. In the traditional joint display, ten row points (subjects) and nine column points (options) are plotted in the same graph. In contrast, only ten row points are plotted, each point being labelled by the response pattern. If three subjects, having response patterns (122), (132) and (112), are closely located, they are characterized by pattern $(1 * 2)$, where "$*$" indicates that the responses to this item (i.e., item 2) are not shared by them. Here, the combination of two responses $(1*2)$ plays an important role for the cluster. However, this does not necessarily imply that these three subjects are positioned closely to the options 1 and 2 of items 1 and 3, respectively, the type of inference one tends to draw from joint graphical display. As dual relations between row and column weights show, the weight for option 1 of item 1, for example, is proportional to the mean of the scores of the subjects who chose that option. Therefore, in the above example, if there exists another cluster $(13*)$, lying far away from the cluster $(1 * 2)$, the position of option 1 of item 1 is likely located somewhere between and away from the two clusters.

4 Examples

[EXAMPLE 1]: Data were collected from subjects during a workshop in Singapore by asking the following questions:

Q.1: "How old are you?"
(1) 20–29; (2) 30–39; (3) 40 or over
Q.2: "Children today are not as disciplined as I was as a child"
(1) agree; (2) disagree; (3) I can't tell
Q.3: "Children today are not as fortunate as I was as a child"
(1) agree; (2) disagree; (3) I can't tell
Q.4: "Religions should be taught at school"
(1) agree; (2) disagree; (3) indifferent

Question 4 was used as the external criterion. In other words, dual scaling of modified data matrix P_4F was carried out, where $P_4 = F_4({F_4}'F_4)^{-1}{F_4}'$ and $F = [F_1, F_2, F_3]$. Note that $r(P_4) = 2$, indicating a two-dimensional graph for describing the results of analysis. Fig. 1 shows twenty-three positions of the subjects, with the corresponding response patterns over question 1, 2 and 3, and group centroids (i.e., the positions of categories of the criterion variable). Note that response patterns are very informative about the distribution of the subjects. The proposed graphical display is not to plot row weights (subjects) and column weights (options), but to refer row weights directly to the input data themselves, a very useful practice in interpreting the quantification results. Tab. 1 shows match-mismatch frequencies based on minimally overlapping segmentation and clusters of subjects obtained from common response patterns in Fig. 2. In this example, there exists a complete match between categories of the criterion variable and age groups.

[EXAMPLE 2]: Data are from Komazawa (1978). Fifty-two subjects, who were classified into four groups (the criterion variable), (a) cerebral hemorrhage, (b) brain infarction, (c) miocardial infarction and (d) angina pectoris, provided categorical/categorized data on the following variables:

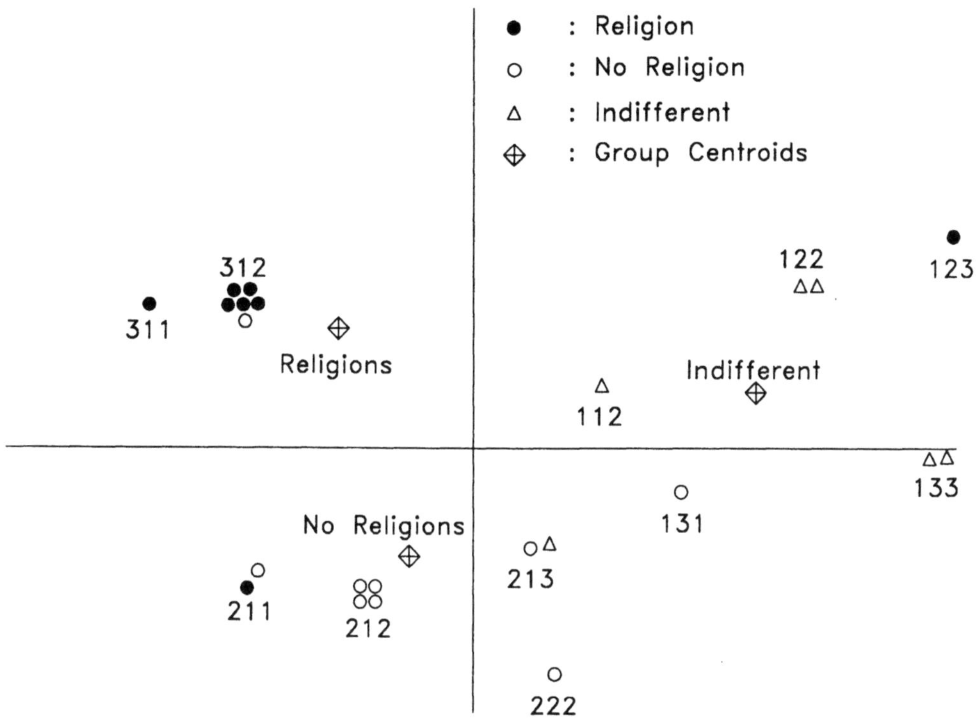

Figure 1: The Positions of the Subjects With Corresponding Response Patterns and Group Centroids

Criterion Response Options	Classified into R	NR	I
Religions (R)	**6**	1	1
No Religions (NR)	1	**8**	0
Indifferent (I)	1	0	**5**

Table 1: Match-Mismatch Frequencies Based on Minimally Overlapping Segmentation (Those in Boldface are Frequencies of Matched Classification)

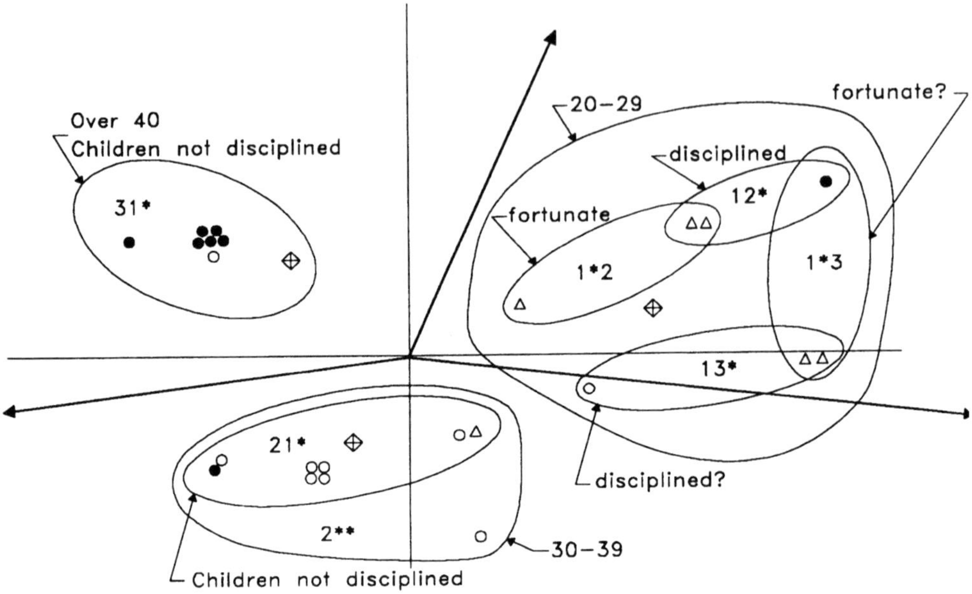

Figure 2: Clusters of Subjects Obtained From Common Response Patterns

Q.1: Age (1) 49–50; (2) 55–59
Q.2: Intraocular pressure (1) normal; (2) abnormal
Q.3: EKG (1) normal; (2) abnormal
Q.4: Maximal blood pressure (1) below 139; (2) 140–170; (3) over 170
Q.5: Minimal blood pressure (1) below 84; (2) 85–95; (4) over 95
Q.6: Pulse rate (1) below 7.4; (2) 7.5–8.5; (3) over 8.5
Q.7: Cholesterol level (1) below 169; (2) 170–210; (2) over 210

Given the criterion matrix, F_8, of the four-class variates and data matrix F, where $F = [F_1, F_2, F_3, F_4, F_5, F_6, F_7]$, modified matrix P_8F was subjected to dual scaling. Although $r(P_8) = 3$, the first two dimensions account for 89% of the variance, hence for simplicity of graphical display only the first two dimensions will be examined. Fig. 3 shows minimally overlapping segmentation of the four criterion groups. Since response patterns are too long to label all the fifty-three points, the labels are omitted in Fig. 3. Tab. 2 presents match-mismatch frequencies.

Criterion Response Options	Classified into C	B	M	A
Cerebral Hemorrhage (C)	**12**	1	0	1
Brain Infarction (B)	4	**9**	1	1
Miocardial Infarction (M)	3	1	**8**	0
Angina Pectoris (A)	1	0	2	**8**

Table 2: Match-Mismatch Frequencies

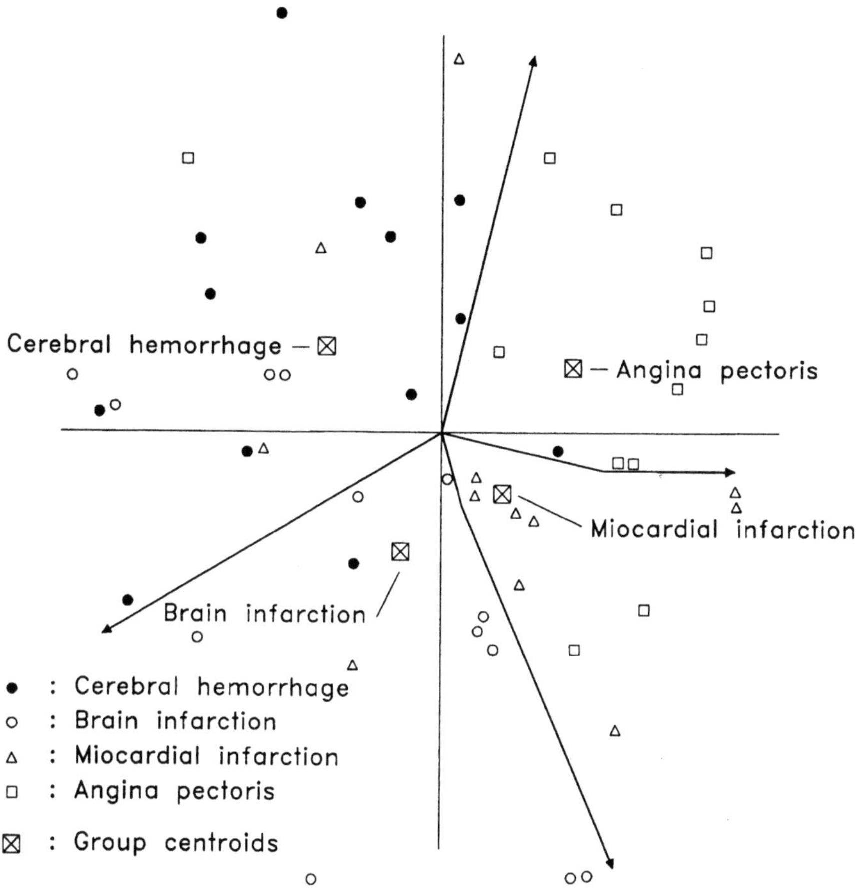

Figure 3: Minimally Overlapping Segmentation of the Four Criterion Groups

One may wish to have a match-mismatch table which has the same marginals as the data matrix. Tab. 3 is an example, obtained under the restriction of identical marginals.

Criteria	C	B	M	A	Total
C	**10**	2	1	1	14
B	3	**10**	2	0	15
M	0	2	**8**	2	12
A	1	1	1	**8**	11
Total	14	15	12	11	

Table 3: Match-Mismatch Frequencies Under the Restriction of Identical Marginals

Clusters sharing only one response are principal plane associated with the subspace spanned by the rows of P_8F. Imagine what interpretations one may come up with if

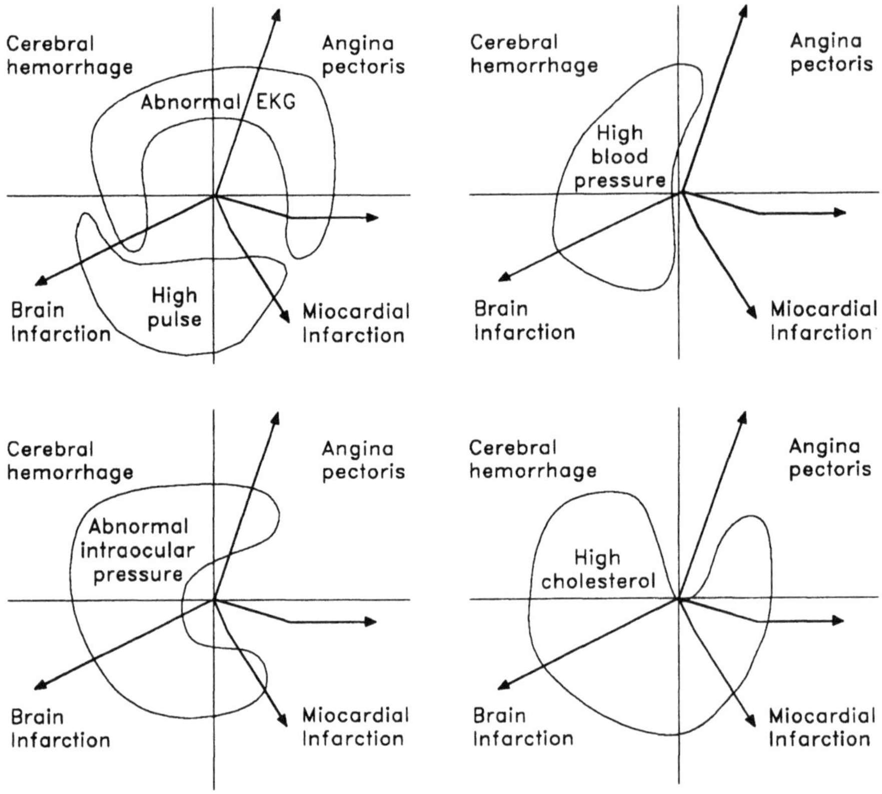

Figure 4: The Data Points Represented in the Two-Dimensional Principal Plain

each cluster of responses is represented by its centroid, a practice which is essentially the same as used in the joint graphical display of rows and columns (except for being free from the regression effect, mentioned earlier). As these examples show, classification of data points in the $r(P)$-dimensional space presents a clearer picture of data structure than $r(P)$ linear plots of projections. Furthermore, the use of shared response patterns for segmentation makes sense because being free from the regression effect it does not distort the data configuration, and because it reflects the main source of data structure, that is, the input data themselves.

References

CARROLL, J.D., GREEN, P.E., and SCHAFFER, C.M. (1986), Interpoint Distance Comparison in Correspondence Analysis, *Journal of Marketing Research*, 23, 271–280.

CARROLL, J.D., GREEN, P.E., and SCHAFFER, C.M. (1987), Comparing Interpoint Distances in Correspondence Analysis: A clarification, *Journal of Marketing Research*, 24, 445–450.

CARROLL, J.D., GREEN, P.E., and SCHAFFER, C.M. (1989), Reply to Greenacre's Commentary on the Carroll-Green-Schaffer Scaling of Two-way Correspondence Analysis Solutions, *Journal of Marketing Research* , 26, 366–368.

FISHER, R.A. (1948), *Statistical Methods for Research Workers*, 10th ed., Academic Press, Inc., London.

GREENACRE, M.J. (1984), *Theory and Applications of Correspondence Analysis*, Academic Press, London.

GREENACRE, M.J. (1989), The Carroll-Green-Schaffer Scaling in Correspondence Analysis: A Theoretical and Empirical Appraisal, *Journal of Marketing Research*, 26, 358–365.

HAYASHI, C., HIGUCHI, I., and KOMAZAWA, T. (1970), *Joho shori to Tokei Suri*, Sangyo Tosho, Tokyo. (in Japanese).

IWATSUBO, S. (1987), *Suryokahoh no Kiso*, Asakura Shoten, Tokyo. (in Japanese).

KOMAZAWA, T. (1982), *Surjoka Riron to Data Shori*, Asakura Shoten, Tokyo. (in Japanese).

LEBART, L., MORINEAU, A., and WARWICK, K.M. (1984), *Multivariate Descriptive Statistical Analysis*, Wiley, New York.

NISHISATO, S. (1971), Analysis of Variance Through Optimal Scaling. *Proceedings of the First Canadian Conference on Applied Statistics*, Sir George Williams University Press, Montreal, 306–316.

NISHISATO, S. (1972), Analysis of Variance of Categorical Data Through Selective Scaling, *Proceedings of the 20th International Congress of Psychology*, Tokyo, 279.

NISHISATO, S. (1980), *Analysis of Categorical Data: Dual Scaling and Its Applications*, University of Toronto Press, Toronto.

NISHISATO, S. (1982), *Shitsuteki Data no Suryoka*, Asakura Shoten, Tokyo. (in Japanese).

NISHISATO, S. (1984), Forced Classification: A Simple Application of a Quantification Method, *Psychometrika, 49*, 25–36.

NISHISATO, S. (1988), Assessing Quality of Joint Graphical Display in Correspondence Analysis and Dual Scaling, in: *Data Analysis and Informatics, V*, eds. E. Diday et al., North-Holland, Amsterdam.

NISHISATO, S., and LAWRENCE, D.R. (1981), Dual Scaling of Multidimensional Tables, A Comparative Study, Paper presented at the Psychometric Society Meeting.

NISHISATO, S., and LAWRENCE, D.R. (1982), Dual Scaling of Multidimensional Tables: Proportional and Non-orthogonal Cases, Paper presented at the Psychometric Society Meeting.

NISHISATO, S., and LAWRENCE, D.R. (1984), Dual Scaling of Multidimensional Tables: Further Results, Paper presented at the Psychometric Society Meeting.

NISHISATO, S., and LAWRENCE, D.R. (1989), Dual Scaling of Multiway Data Matrices: Several Variants, in: *Analysis of Multiway Data Matrices*, eds. R. Coppi and S. Bolasco, Elsevier Science Publishers B.V., Amsterdam, 317–326.

POON, W. (1977), Transformations of Data Matrices in Optimal Scaling, unpublished M.A. Thesis, University of Toronto.

SABATIER, R., LEBRETON, J.D., and CHESSEL, D. (1989), Principal Component Analysis with Instrumental Variables as a Tool for Modelling Composition Data, in: *Analysis of Multiway Data Matrices*, eds. R. Coppi et al., North-Holland, Amsterdam, 341–352.

TAKANE, Y. (1988), (Personal communication).

TAKANE, Y., and SHIBAYAMA, T. (1988), Dual Scaling with External Criteria Reconsidered, Paper presented at the Annual Meeting of the Japanese Behaviormetric Society.

TAKANE, Y., and SHIBAYAMA, T. (1989), Principal Component Analysis with External Information, Paper presented at the Annual Meeting of the Psychometric Society, University of California at Los Angeles.

A Generalization of Asymmetric Multidimensional Scaling

Akinori Okada
Department of Industrial Relations
Rikkyo (St. Paul's) University, Tokyo, Japan

Summary

An asymmetric multidimensional scaling model, which is derived by generalizing the predecessor, and the nonmetric algorithm to fit the present model to an asymmetric proximity matrix is presented. In the present model asymmetries in proximities are accounted for not only by the term related with stimuli or with dimensions but by the term related with stimuli and dimensions. Geometrically each stimulus is represented as a point and an ellipse (ellipsoid, hyperellipsoid) in a multidimensional Euclidean space. The present model is applied to car switching data among 12 car segments. The obtained two-dimensional solution is compatible with the previous analyses. And it seems that the length of the semiaxes of the ellipse might represent the relative dominance or attractiveness on the two dimensions respectively.

1 Introduction

Various kinds of multidimensional scaling procedures have been introduced to analyze asymmetric proximities (Chino (1978), Constantine and Gower (1978), Cunningham (1978), Gower (1977), Harshman (1978, 1981), Harshman, Green, Wind and Lundy (1982), Okada and Imaizumi (1987), Tobler (1977, 1979), Weeks and Bentler (1982) and Young (1975, 1987)). There have been important developments in applying these asymmetric multidimensional scaling procedures along with theoretical considerations on asymmetries in proximities (Krumhansl (1978), Rosch (1975) and Tversky (1977)). The asymmetric multidimensional scaling procedures have been applied to analyze international trade (Chino (1978)), car switching (Harshman et al. (1982) and Okada (1988a)), occupational mobility (Okada (1988d)), telephone calls (Harshman and Lundy (1984) and Okada (1988c)), sociometry (Collins (1987)), and so on.

Particularly the car switching data was analyzed by two different asymmetric multidimensional scaling procedures (Harshman et al. (1982) and Okada (1988a)). Harshman et al. (1982) accounts for asymmetries in proximities by a matrix representing the asymmetric relationship among factors or dimensions. On the other hand, Okada (1988a) accounts for asymmetries in proximities by the term related with stimuli. The model used in Harshman et al. (1982) seems to originate from factor analysis, while the model used in Okada (1988a) seems to originate from multidimensional scaling. The result obtained in the former is four-dimensional, and result obtained in the latter is three-dimensional. And only two dimensions of the latter are required to accommodate the four factors which were disclosed in the former. Although the model used in these two analyses are completely

NATO ASI Series, Vol. F 61
Knowledge, Data and Computer-Assisted Decisions
Edited by M. Schader and W. Gaul

different and the dimensionality of the two results differs, the two results are compatible each other in the interpretation (Okada (1988a) and Okada and Imaizumi (1987)).

It would be fruitful if we can ascribe the asymmetries in proximities not simply to stimuli or to dimensions but to stimuli and dimensions. The purpose of the present paper is to introduce a model and an accompanying procedure of asymmetric multidimensional scaling which accounts for asymmetries in proximities by the term related with stimuli and dimensions of the space wherein the stimuli are embedded. The multidimensional scaling model which accounts for asymmetries in proximities by the term related with stimuli and dimensions seems to be adequate to analyze the occupational mobility, telephone calls, and migration. In analyzing intergenerational occupational mobility (Okada (1986, 1988d)) two dimensions were extracted. One dimension was interpreted as representing the discrimination between manual and non manual occupational categories, and the other was interpreted as representing the average annual income of each occupational category. It appears to be interesting to account for the asymmetries in intergenerational occupational mobility not simply by the term related with stimuli but by the term related with stimuli and dimensions. The analyses of telephone calls among 16 areas of Japan (Okada (1988c)) and migration among 47 prefectures in Japan (Okada (1988b)) also suggest the necessity of accounting for asymmetries in the data by the term related with stimuli and dimensions.

2 Model

The model of the present asymmetric multidimensional scaling is a generalization of the predecessor (Okada (1988a) and Okada and Imaizumi (1987)), which was briefly discussed in Okada and Imaizumi (1984). Let s_{jk} be the proximity of stimulus j to k. It is assumed that s_{jk} is monotonically increasingly related with m_{jk} (when s_{jk} is similarity) or is monotonically decreasingly related with m_{jk} (when s_{jk} is dissimilarity). Then m_{jk} is defined as

$$m_{jk} = d_{jk}(1 - v_{jk} + v_{kj}). \tag{1}$$

The term d_{jk} of Equation (1) is the Euclidean distance between stimulus j and k which is defined as

$$d_{jk} = \left[\sum_{t=1}^{p}(x_{jt} - x_{kt})^2\right]^{1/2}, \tag{2}$$

where x_{jt} is the t-th coordinate of the point representing stimulus j in a p-dimensional Euclidean space. The second term in the parentheses of Equation (1) is defined as

$$v_{jk} = \left\{\sum_{t=1}^{p}\left[(x_{jt} - x_{kt})/r_{jt}\right]^2\right\}^{-1/2}. \tag{3}$$

The third term in the parentheses of Equation (1) is defined simply by interchanging j and k in Equation (3). r_{jt} which is related with stimulus j and dimension t is introduced to account for skew symmetries in s_{jk}.

Equation (1) is very similar to the definition of m_{jk} of Okada and Imaizumi (1987). In fact, if r_{jt} in Equation (3) is equal to r_j, then $v_{jk} = r_j/d_{jk}$ and $v_{kj} = r_k/d_{kj}$. Thus Equation (1) becomes

$$m_{jk} = d_{jk} - r_j + r_k, \tag{4}$$

which is the definition of m_{jk} in Okada and Imaizumi (1987). Therefore the present model is the generalization of that of the predecessor. Like r_j of the predecessor the interpretation of the meaning of r_{jt} does not depend on whether similarities or dissimilarities are analyzed.

The relationship of the present model and the predecessor would be more clearly be shown if the two models are represented geometrically. As shown elsewhere (Okada (1988a) and Okada and Imaizumi (1987)) in case of the predecessor (less general model) each stimulus is represented as a point and a circle (sphere, hypersphere) in a Euclidean space. On the other hand in case of the present model (general model) each stimulus is represented as a point and an ellipse (ellipsoid, hyperellipsoid) in a Euclidean space. Hereafter the less general model is called circle model, and the present general model is called ellipse model. Specifically in the two-dimensional case, stimulus j is represented as a point and a circle with radius r_j centered at the point in the circle model, while the stimulus j is represented as a point and an ellipse with the semiaxes of length r_{j1} and r_{j2} respectively centered at the point in the ellipse model. The two-dimensional model is represented in Fig. 1. Here to center an ellipse at a point means that the intersection of axes of the ellipse is at the point as shown in Fig. 1.

In Fig. 1 r_{j1} is shown as the length of the semiaxis parallel with dimension 1 of the ellipse representing stimulus j, and r_{j2} is shown as the length of the semiaxis parallel with dimension 2 of the ellipse. The length of the arrow in the upper panel shows m_{jk}, and the length of the arrow in the lower panel shows m_{kj}. The length of the dashed line inside the ellipse representing stimulus j in the upper panel shows $d_{jk}v_{jk}$. And the length of the dashed line inside the ellipse representing stimulus k in the lower panel shows $d_{jk}v_{kj}$. The introduction of the ellipse to represent the stimulus is benefitted in getting inherently unique orientation of axes of the stimulus configuration. More precisely, the orientation of the axes is determined up to the reflections and permutations of the axes. Because r_{jt} is defined parallel with the axes of the stimulus configuration, m_{jk} defined by Equation (1) depends on the orientation of the axes of the stimulus configuration. This could increase the possibility that the obtained axes correspond to the fundamental processes which govern the asymmetric proximity relationship among stimuli (Arabie, Carroll and DeSarbo (1987)). It seems that this property makes the ellipse model more advantageous over the circle model which has the rotationally invariant axes.

3 Algorithm

The nonmetric algorithm to fit the ellipse model to an asymmetric proximity matrix is very similar to the one which was developed to fit the circle model (Okada and Imaizumi (1987)). Like the algorithm for the circle model, the present algorithm was derived by adapting Kruskal's nonmetric multidimensional scaling (Kruskal (1964a, 1964b), Lingoes and Roskam (1973), Okada and Imaizumi (1984)). The algorithm consists of three phases:

a. construct an initial stimulus configuration and initial values of the length of the semiaxes (r_{jt}) of the ellipse,

b. improve the configuration (stimulus configuration and r_{jt}) iteratively, and

c. stop the iteration when no further improvement of the configuration is possible.

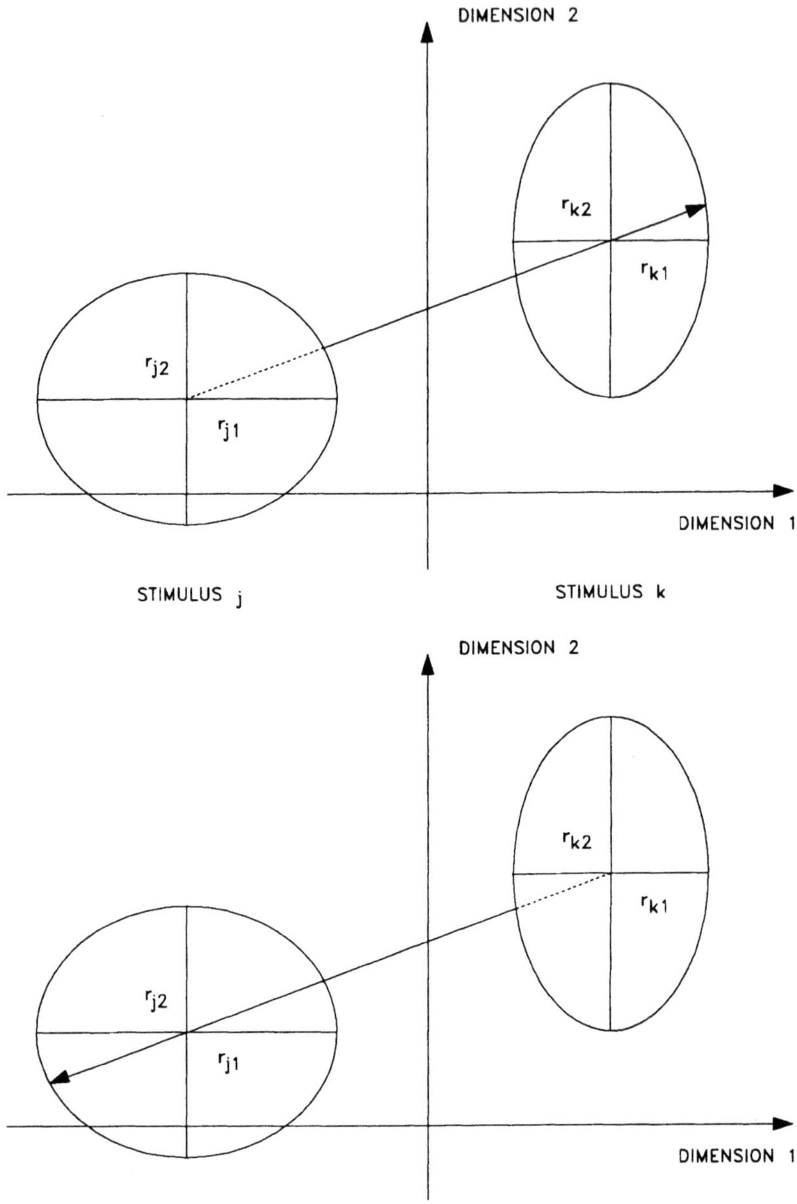

Figure 1: Geometric Representation of the Model in a Two-Dimensional Space

The measure of goodness of fit of m_{jk} to the monotone relationship with s_{jk} is defined as

$$S = \sum_{j=1}^{n} \sum_{\substack{k=1 \\ k \neq j}}^{n} (m_{jk} - \widehat{m}_{jk})^2 \Big/ \sum_{j=1}^{n} \sum_{\substack{k=1 \\ k \neq j}}^{n} (m_{jk} - \overline{m})^{1/2}, \tag{5}$$

where n is the number of stimuli, $\widehat{m}_{jk}$ is the disparity defined by Kruskal's monotonicity principle, and $\overline{m}$ is the mean of m_{jk}. S defined by Equation (5) is the same as the goodness of fit measure for the circle model except that S defined above includes differently defined m_{jk} and $\widehat{m}_{jk}$ compared with the algorithm for the circle model. The configuration which minimizes S is derived by the steepest descent method for a given dimensionality. The close relationship between the ellipse model and the circle model has been kept in the relationship between the algorithms for these two models. The two algorithms are parallel except that the present algorithm is adapted for deriving r_{jt} instead of r_j.

The initial stimulus configuration is derived exactly the same procedure adopted in the algorithm for the circle model. And the initial value of r_{jt} is also derived by the same procedure adopted in the former one. Thus the length of semiaxes of the ellipse is set to be equal when the iteration starts. Namely each stimulus is represented as a point and a circle (not an ellipse) initially when the iteration begins. The step size algorithm is exactly the same as that of the former one except for the gradient. Partial derivatives of S with respect to x_{lq} and r_{lq} are described in the following. Let y represent either x_{lq} or r_{lq}.

$$\frac{\partial S}{\partial y} = \sum_{j=1}^{n} \sum_{\substack{k=1 \\ k \neq j}}^{n} \left[\frac{S}{S^*}(m_{jk} - \widehat{m}_{jk}) \frac{S}{T^*}(m_{jk} - \overline{m}) \right] \frac{\partial m_{jk}}{\partial y}, \tag{6}$$

where

$$S^* = \sum_{j=1}^{n} \sum_{\substack{k=1 \\ k \neq j}}^{n} (m_{jk} - \widehat{m}_{jk})^2 \quad \text{and} \quad T^* = \sum_{j=1}^{n} \sum_{\substack{k=1 \\ k \neq j}}^{n} (m_{jk} - \overline{m})^2. \tag{7}$$

$\frac{\partial m_{jk}}{\partial x_{lq}}$ and $\frac{\partial m_{jk}}{\partial r_{lq}}$ in Equation (6) are given in Equations (8) and (11).

$$\frac{\partial m_{jk}}{\partial x_{lq}} = \frac{\partial d_{jk}}{\partial x_{lq}}(1 - v_{jk} + v_{kj}) + (\frac{\partial v_{kj}}{\partial x_{lq}} - \frac{\partial v_{jk}}{\partial x_{lq}}) d_{jk} \tag{8}$$

where

$$\frac{\partial d_{jk}}{\partial x_{lq}} = (x_{js} - x_{ks})(D^{jl} D^{sq} - D^{kl} D^{sq}) / d_{jk}, \tag{9}$$

and

$$\frac{\partial v_{jk}}{\partial x_{lq}} = -v_{jk}{}^{-3/2}(D^{jl} D^{sq} - D^{kl} D^{sq})(x_{js} - x_{ks}) / r_{js}{}^2. \tag{10}$$

D_{jk} is Kronecker's delta. And

$$\frac{\partial m_{jk}}{\partial r_{lq}} = \left(-\frac{\partial v_{jk}}{\partial r_{lq}} + \frac{\partial v_{kj}}{\partial r_{lq}} \right) d_{jk}, \text{ where } \frac{\partial v_{jk}}{\partial r_{lq}} = v_{jk}{}^{3/2} D^{jl} D^{sq} (x_{js} - x_{ks})^2 / r_{js}{}^3. \tag{11}$$

The stimulus configuration is normalized such that its centroid is at the origin and the sum of squares of distances from the origin to the points is equal to n. The length of semiaxes of the ellipse is adjusted by proportionally stretching or shrinking to the stimulus configuration.

4 Application

The car switching data was analyzed by fitting the ellipse model. The characteristics of the car switching data has been relatively well known to us through the previous analyses

(Harshman et al. (1982), Okada (1988a) and Okada and Imaizumi (1987)) compared with other data. This is the reason why the car switching data was chosen here to be analyzed by the present generalized asymmetric multidimensional scaling. The previous analysis by fitting the circle model (Okada (1988a) and Okada and Imaizumi (1987)) resulted in the three-dimensional configurations. The first dimension was called size or price dimension. The second dimension was called imports–captive imports–domestic dimension. And the third dimension was called specialty dimension.

In the present analysis four car segments of specialty cars (SMALL SPECIALTY DOMESTIC, SMALL SPECIALTY CAPTIVE IMPORTS, SMALL SPECIALTY IMPORTS, and MIDSIZE SPECIALTY) were eliminated. The intention of eliminating them are threefold. One reason is that by eliminating the four car segments which constitute the specialty dimension in the previous analyses it seems that we can obtain a two-dimensional solution which is very easily represented graphically than a three dimensional solution. The three-dimensional configuration of the ellipse model seems to be extremely complicated to be graphically represented. And this might cause the difficulty in interpreting the configuration. The second reason is that while three of the four segments have large positive coordinates on the specialty dimension, SMALL SPECIALTY CAPTIVE IMPORTS failed to have a large positive coordinate on the this dimension (Okada (1988a) and Okada and Imaizumi (1987)). The third reason is that eliminating the four car segments makes the remaining 12 car segments be completely in accord with the traditional way of categorizing the auto market (Urban and Hauser (1980)). The 12 car segments used in the present analysis are SUBCOMPACT DOMESTIC, SUBCOMPACT CAPTIVE IMPORTS, SUBCOMPACT IMPORTS, LOW PRICE COMPACT, MEDIUM PRICE COMPACT, IMPORT COMPACT, MIDSIZE DOMESTIC, MIDSIZE IMPORTS, LOW PRICE STANDARD, MEDIUM PRICE STANDARD, LUXURY DOMESTIC, and LUXURY IMPORT. These 12 car segments are expected to be embedded in a two-dimensional space which is spanned by the price or size dimension and the imports–captive imports–domestic dimension.

The car switching data matrix among 12 car segments was rescaled to remove the size difference in market share of each car segment. The rescaling was done by multiplying the rescaling constant to each row and column of the original car switching data matrix such that the row plus column sum (including diagonal elements) in the rescaled matrix becomes to be equal to a constant for all the 12 car segments. As the constant the mean row plus column sum across 12 car segments in the original car switching data matrix was chosen. The detail of the rescaling is described elsewhere (Okada (1988a)).

The rescaled car switching data matrix was analyzed by the asymmetric multidimensional scaling described above from five- through uni-dimensional spaces. The obtained minimized S values are 0.131, 0.155, 0.197, 0.240, and 0.475 respectively. The elbow criterion suggests that the two-dimensional configuration should be chosen as a solution. The interpretation of the configuration seems to strongly suggest to choose the two-dimensional configuration as a solution as well. The stimulus configuration and ellipses are geometrically shown in Fig. 2.

The two dimensions can be substantively interpreted without any rotation as expected. The horizontal dimension seems to represent size or price, and the vertical dimension seems to represent the difference among imports, captive imports, and domestic. These dimensions are identical with the first two dimensions obtained in the previous analyses (Okada

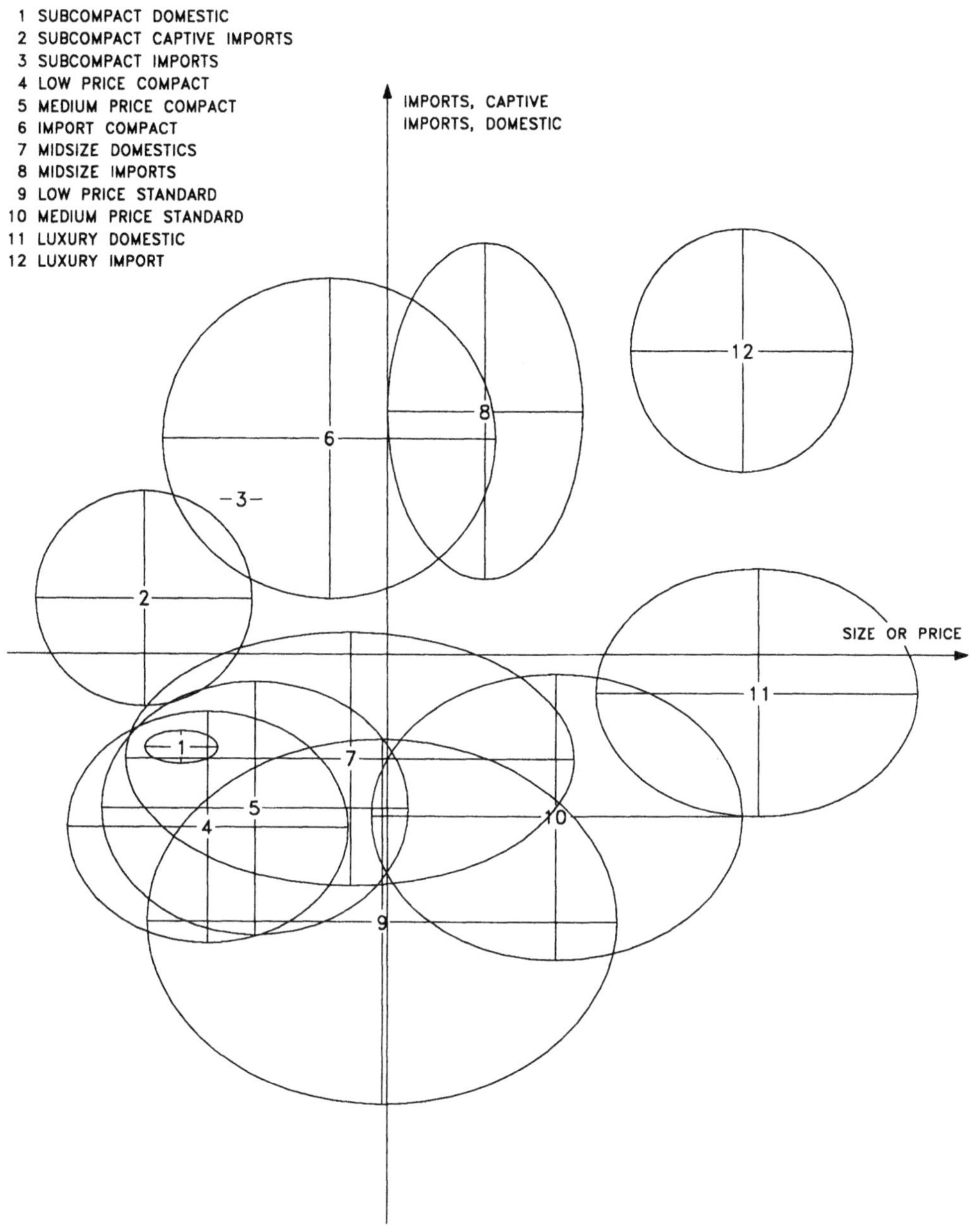

Figure 2: Two-Dimensional Representation of the Configuration

(1988a) and Okada and Imaizumi (1987)). It should be emphasized that no rotation or transformation was needed to obtain the two dimensions in the present analysis, while the rotation of axes was needed to obtain the dimensions in the previous analyses. This shows the advantageous aspect of the ellipse model over the circle model.

As for the length of semiaxes, SUBCOMPACT IMPORTS has the smallest value on the horizontal dimension as well as on the vertical dimension. SUBCOMPACT DOMESTIC has the second smallest value on each of the two dimensions. These two car segments

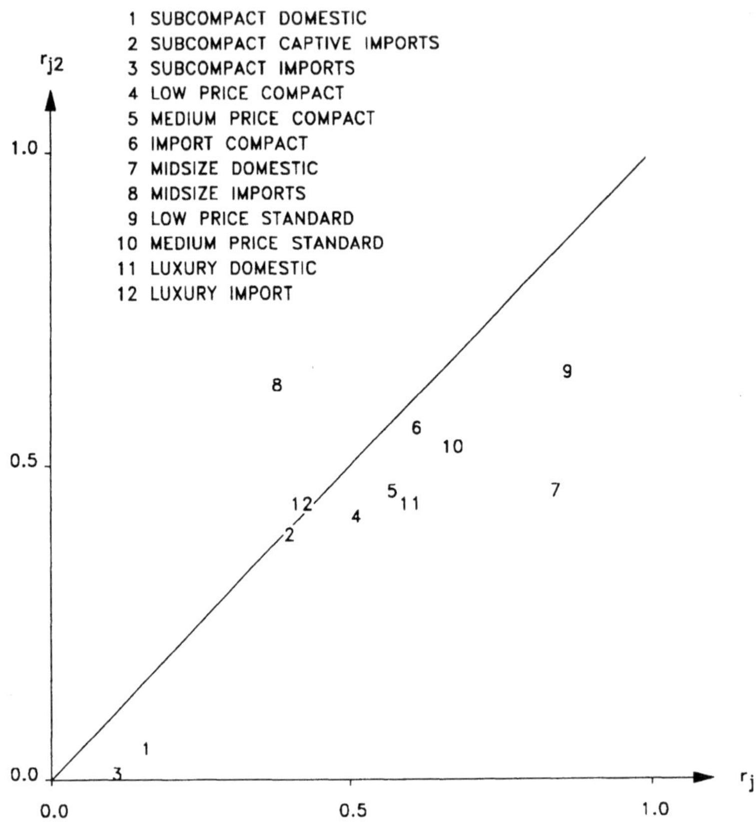

Figure 3: Semiaxes of Dimension 1 (r_{j1}) and Dimension 2 (r_{j2})

have extremely small values of r_{jt} on both of the dimensions. LOW PRICE STANDARD has the largest values of r_{jt} on both of the dimensions. The features of r_{jt} are clearly represented in Fig. 3.

In Fig. 3 the horizontal axis represents r_{j1}, and the vertical axis represents r_{j2}. The diagonal line represents the line defined by the equation $r_{j1} = r_{j2}$. In Fig. 3 the points representing MIDSIZE IMPORTS and LUXURY IMPORT are above the diagonal line, while the other 10 points are below the diagonal line. Thus r_{j1} is smaller than r_{j2} in case of MIDSIZE IMPORTS and LUXURY IMPORT. In case of the other 10 car segments r_{j1} is larger than r_{j2}. It seems that r_{j1} and r_{j2} correlate highly positively.

In the previous studies using the circle model the radius of each car segment is regarded to represent the relative dominance or attractiveness of the car segment which governs the asymmetries in the car switching. A parallel consideration suggests that r_{j1} might represent the relative dominance or attractiveness of the car segment on the size or price dimension and that r_{j2} might represent the relative dominance on the imports–captive imports–domestic dimension.

The meaning of r_{j1} was examined in the manner described in the following. First, the 12 car segments were divided into four categories [(subcompact, compact); (midsize);

(standard); (luxury)]. (The result of the cluster analysis (Okada (1988a)) seems to suggest subcompact car and compact segments are very close. And thus they are merged into one category.) Second, for car segment j the sum of elements (k, j) of the rescaled car switching data matrix, where car segment k belongs to the different car category with car segment j, was calculated. The sum is called car segment j's 'between column sum of dimension 1'. Third, car segment j's between row sum of dimension 1 was calculated in the similar manner. Fourth, between column sum and between row sum were calculated for each of the 12 car segments, and the between row sum was subtracted from the between column sum for each category. The obtained number (called between column sum minus row sum of dimension 1) of car segment j shows the net increase of car segment j between the car segments which belong to the different car category with car segment j. Finally, the correlation coefficient between r_{j1} and these numbers was calculated. The obtained correlation coefficient was -0.90. Then to examine the meaning of r_{j2}, the 12 car segments were divided into two categories [(domestic, captive imports); (imports)]. (The cluster analysis seems to suggest captive import car segment is closely related to domestic car segments than to import car segments.) The parallel calculation yielded the correlation coefficient of -0.85.

These two correlation coefficients seem to suggest that r_{j1} might represent the relative dominance or attractiveness of car segment j against car segments which belong to different size or price categories with car segment j, and that r_{j2} might represent the relative dominance or attractiveness of car segment j against car segments which belong to different domestic/captive imports or imports category with car segment j. Although the correlation coefficients themselves seem to be satisfactorily high to suggest the interpretation of r_{jt} just mentioned above, the between column sum minus row sum of dimension 1 correlates highly negatively with r_{j2} (-0.80) and the between column sum minus row sum of dimension 2 correlates highly negatively with r_{j1} (-0.74). This is probably due to the highly positive correlation between r_{j1} and r_{j2} (0.79), but undermines the interpretation.

5 Discussion

A model of asymmetric multidimensional scaling and the accompanying algorithm to analyze asymmetric proximities were described. The model (ellipse model), which is a generalization of the circle model, accounts for the asymmetries by the term related with stimuli and dimensions. Geometrically each stimulus is represented as a point and an ellipse centered at the point in a Euclidean space.

Some of the asymmetric multidimensional scaling models account for asymmetries in proximities by the term related with stimuli (Chino (1978), Okada and Imaizumi (1987), Tobler (1979) and Weeks and Bentler (1982)), and some account for by the term related with dimensions (Harshman et al. (1982)). When the asymmetries are accounted for by the term related only with stimuli, the asymmetries have no relationship with the space or the dimensions of the space where the stimuli are embedded. And when the asymmetries are accounted for by the term related only with dimensions, the direct effect of stimuli onto the asymmetries are not made clear.

The asymmetries in proximities are accounted for by the term related with stimuli and dimensions in Young (1975, 1987). In his model each stimulus requires its own stimulus configuration which is derived by stretching or shrinking the axes of the common stimulus configuration. Therefore it seems to be difficult to interpret these configurations derived from the common stimulus configuration. On the other hand, the ellipse model represents all information in one configuration, and thus can easily be interpreted. The ellipse model has a significant characteristic, which the circle model does not have, that the orientation of the axes of the stimulus configuration is determined uniquely up to the reflections and the permutations of axes. But when the ratio r_{jq}/r_{jp} is constant over all stimuli ($j = 1, \ldots, n$), the orientation of the axes q and p is indeterminate within the plane formed by the two axes. This is equivalent with the indeterminate of the orientation of axes in INDSCAL model (Carroll and Chang (1970)).

Like the circle model, the square of the denominator of S of Equation (1) can be divided into two terms, where one term is connected with the symmetric component of a configuration and the other term is connected with the skew symmetric component of a configuration, as

$$\begin{aligned}&(\text{square of the denominator of } S)\\&= n(n-1)\ \mathrm{var}[d_{jk}] + n(n-1)\ \mathrm{var}[(m_{jk} - m_{kj})/2]\end{aligned} \qquad (12)$$

The first term of Equation (12) is equal to the first term of Equation (5) of Okada (1988a). The relative weights of the two terms to the sum of them seem to have important effects on uniquely determining the orientation of the axes of the stimulus configuration. In the present application the relative weights of the first and second terms are 0.805 and 0.195 respectively.

In the application to the car switching data among 12 car segments, the resulting stimulus configuration was satisfactorily explained by the two dimensions as expected. The two dimensions were derived directly from the analysis and look like to correspond to the properties which are anticipated from the previous studies. As for the interpretation of r_{jt}, r_{j1} seems to suggest to represents the relative dominance or attractiveness of car segment j on the size or price dimension and r_{j2} seems to suggest to represent the relative dominance or attractiveness on the imports–captive imports–domestic dimension. Although features of the ellipse model does not seem to be fully represented in the application, the ellipse model seems to develop new scopes in investigating asymmetries in proximities which will be pointers to future researches.

Acknowledgements

The present research is supported by a grant from the Rikkyo (St. Paul's) University Research Fund.

References

ARABIE, P., CARROLL, J.D., and DESARBO, W.S. (1987), *Three-way Scaling and Clustering*, Sage Publications, Newbury Park, CA.

CARROLL, J.D., and CHANG, J.J. (1970), Analysis of Individual Differences in Multidimensional scaling via an N-way Generalization of "Eckart-Young Decomposition", *Psychometrika, 35*, 283–319.

CHINO, N. (1978), A Graphical Technique for Representing the Asymmetric Relationships between N objects, *Behaviormetrika 5*, 23–40.

COLLINS, L.M. (1987), Deriving Sociograms via Asymmetric Multidimensional Scaling, in: *Multidimensional Scaling: History, Theory, and Applications*, ed. R.M. Hamer, Lawrence Erlbaum Associates, Hillsdale, 179–196.

CONSTANTINE, A.G., and GOWER, J.C. (1978), Graphical Representation of Asymmetric Matrices, *Applied Statistics, 27*, 297–304.

CUNNINGHAM, J.P. (1978), Free Trees and Bidirectional Trees as Representations of Psychological Distance, *Journal of Mathematical Psychology, 17*, 165–188.

GOWER, J.C. (1977), The Analysis of Asymmetry and Orthogonality, in: *Recent Developments in Statistics*, eds. J.R. Barra, F. Brodeau, F.G. Romier and B. van Cutsem, North Holland, Amsterdam, 109–123.

HARSHMAN, R.A. (1978), *Models for Analysis of Asymmetrical Relationships among N Objects or Stimuli*, Paper presented at the First Joint Meeting of the Psychometric Society and the Society for Mathematical Psychology at McMaster University, Hamilton, Ontario.

HARSHMAN, R.A. (1981), *DEDICOM Multidimensional Analysis of Skew-Symmetric Data*, Technical Memorandum, Bell Telephone Laboratories.

HARSHMAN, R.A., GREEN, P.E., WIND, Y., and LUNDY, M.E. (1982), A Model for the Analysis of Asymmetric Data in Marketing Research, *Marketing Science, 1*, 205–242.

HARSHMAN, R.A., and LUNDY, M.E. (1984), The PARAFAC Model for Three-Way Factor Analysis and Multidimensional Scaling, in: *Research Methods for Multimode Data Analysis*, eds. L.G. Law, C.W. Snyder, J.A. Hattie and R.P. McDonald, Praeger, New York, 122–215.

KRUMHANSL, C.L. (1978), Concerning the Applicability of Geometric Models to Similarity Data: The Interrelationship between Similarity and Spatial Density, *Psychological Review, 85*, 445–463.

KRUSKAL, J.B. (1964a), Multidimensional Scaling by Optimizing Goodness of Fit to a Nonmetric Hypothesis, *Psychometrika, 29*, 1–27.

KRUSKAL, J.B. (1964b), Nonmetric Multidimensional Scaling: A Numerical Method, *Psychometrika, 29*, 115–129.

LINGOES, J.C., and ROSKAM, E.E. (1973), A Mathematical and Empirical Analysis of Two Multidimensional Scaling Algorithms, *Psychometrika Monograph Supplement 19*.

OKADA, A. (1986), Asymmetric Multidimensional Scaling of Intergenerational Occupational Mobility, *Proceedings of the Second Japan-China Symposium on Statistic at Kyushu University*, Fukuoka, Japan, 197–200.

OKADA, A. (1988a), Asymmetric Multidimensional Scaling of Car Switching Data, in: *Data, Expert Knowledge and Decisions*, eds. W. Gaul and M. Schader, Springer-Verlag, 279–290.

OKADA, A. (1988b), Asymmetric Multidimensional Scaling and Internal Migration, in: *Proceedings of the 6th Biannual Meeting of the Japanese Association for Mathematical Sociology at Tohoku Gakuin University*, Sendai, 17–18.

OKADA, A. (1988c), Asymmetric Multidimensional Scaling, *bit, 20*, 444–445.

OKADA, A. (1988d), An Analysis of Intergenerational Mobility by Asymmetric Multidimensional Scaling, in: *The Many Faces of Multivariate Analysis*, eds. M.G.H. Jansen and W.H. Schuur, RION, Groningen, 1–15.

OKADA, A. and IMAIZUMI, T. (1984), *Geometric Models for Asymmetric Similarity Data*, Research Report, Rikkyo (St. Paul's) University.

OKADA, A., and IMAIZUMI, T. (1987), Nonmetric Multidimensional Scaling of Asymmetric Proximities, *Behaviormetrika, 21*, 81–96.

ROSCH, E. (1975), Cognitive Reference Points, *Cognitive Psychology, 7*, 532–547.

TOBLER, W.R. (1977), Spatial Interaction Patterns, *Journal of Environmental Systems, 6*, 271–301.

TOBLER, W.R. (1979), Estimation of Attractivities from Interactions, *Environment and Planning, A, 11*, 121–127.

TVERSKY, A. (1977), Features of Similarity, *Psychological Review, 84*, 327–352.

URBAN, G.L., and HAUSER, J.R. (1980), *Design and Marketing of New Products*, Prentice Hall, Englewood Cliffs.

WEEKS, D.G., and BENTLER, P.M. (1982), Restricted Multidimensional Scaling Models for Asymmetric Proximities, *Psychometrika, 47*, 201–208.

YOUNG, F.W. (1975), An Asymmetric Euclidean Model for Multi-process Asymmetric Data, in: *Proceedings of the US-Japan Seminar on the Theory, Methods and Applications of Multidimensional Scaling and Related Techniques at the University of California San Diego*, La Jolla, California, 79–88.

YOUNG, F.W. (1987), *Multidimensional Scaling: History, Theory, and Applications*, Lawrence Erlbaum Associates, Hillsdale.

Some Algorithms for "Bond Energy" Data Analysis, Including Simulated Annealing

Sylvia Schleutermann, Phipps Arabie, Lawrence J. Hubert and François Bronsard
Department of Psychology
University of Illinois at Champaign, U.S.A.

Summary

The applicability of Simulated Annealing (SA) (Kirkpatrick et al. (1983)) is studied in the context of the data analysis scheme of the "bond energy algorithm" originally proposed by McCormick et al. (1972) for permuting rows and columns of data matrices into visually interpretable forms. To evaluate the performance of three variations of SA, they were compared to two deterministic, heuristic methods known to perform well for the particular type of data analysis task chosen: (1) the streamlined implementation of the Bond Energy Algorithm (BEA) of Arabie et al. (1988) and Schleutermann (1989) that improves upon the original version of McCormick et al. (1972), and (2) the well-known Lin and Kernighan Algorithm (LK) (1973) for the Traveling Salesman Problem (TSP). Contrary to earlier findings (e.g., De Soete et al. (1988a, 1988b)), a version of simulated annealing was developed that performs well in a time complexity comparable to that of our implementation of Lin and Kernighan's algorithm. From the empirical results, it appears that suitable implementation of a simulated annealing algorithm can outperform good deterministic algorithms in some data analysis applications. For speeding up execution of the SA algorithm, the focus here is on the use of a state transition scheme less randomized than others often suggested in the literature on SA.

1 Introduction

The "bond energy" data analysis task was originally proposed by McCormick, Schweitzer and White (1972) and further investigated by Arabie, Schleutermann, Daws and Hubert (1988). For additional details, see Arabie et al. (1989) and Arabie and Hubert (1989). The objective is to group numerically large entries of an input data matrix close together to render the data interpretable by visual inspection, and to simplify such subsequent analysis tasks as the formation of clusters. The corresponding objective function (the Bond Energy (BE) function) suggested by McCormick et al. (1972) attempts to maximize the value of

$$BE = \sum_{i=1}^{N} \sum_{j=1}^{M} a_{i,j}(a_{i,j-1} + a_{i,j+1} + a_{i-1,j} + a_{i+1,j}),$$

over all permutations on the rows and columns of one or more input data matrices. Optimizing the above expression is equivalent to solving two traveling salesman problems (Lenstra (1974)), and thus, the problem type belongs to the class that can only be solved in time exponential in the size of the input data.

Heuristic (polynomial) algorithms investigated here are:

NATO ASI Series, Vol. F 61
Knowledge, Data and Computer-Assisted Decisions
Edited by M. Schader and W. Gaul

1. the Bond Energy Algorithm (BEA) originally proposed by McCormick et al. (1972), implemented by Spaeth (1980), and substantially improved by Arabie et al. (1988);

2. the Lin and Kernighan Algorithm (LK) for solving the traveling salesman problem; see Lin (1965), Lin and Kernighan (1973), Lawler et al. (1985) and Schleutermann (1989, 37–40, 57) for details for this particular implementation;

3. Simulated Annealing (SA), first suggested by Kirkpatrick et al. (1983) and Černy (1985) for solving large combinatorial optimization problems. (Three different implementations of SA were tested; details are presented below.)

To evaluate the performance of the algorithms, they were subjected to a set of experiments. Standard measures together with the utility test in Golden and Stewart (1985) were used to determine whether one algorithm's performance was superior to the others.

2 Simulated Annealing Implementation

Simulated annealing is a general-purpose technique for finding optima in (combinatorial) optimization problems. The algorithm was proposed independently by Kirkpatrick et al. (1983) and Černy (1985) for solving large NP-complete problems involving many parameters, and whose objective functions may have multiple local extrema. In contrast to iterative improvement algorithms and other problem-specific heuristic methods, SA allegedly can avoid getting trapped in non-global extrema, by randomly accepting deteriorations of the objective function. For a generic outline of SA, see Tab. 1.

When implementing SA for a particular application, explicit specifications must be made for:

1. the *temperature schedule*, comprised of an initial temperature, a final temperature, the rule for decreasing the temperature, and the amount of time that the process is to spend at each temperature (since the SA process can be modeled by Markov chains, the last term is often referred to as the *Markov chain length*),

2. the *state transition scheme*, which provides the mechanism for generating a new state given the current one, and

3. the *termination condition*, which can be a final temperature, a certain time limit for the execution of SA, or some other criterion.

Since the basic form of SA is rather simple, it can be used for solving problems even when they are not well understood (in the sense of the unavailability of efficient heuristics specifically designed for the structure of the given problem). Since its first publication, SA has been applied to numerous optimization problems. For those relevant to combinatorial data analysis, see for example, De Soete et al. (1988a, 1988b) and Burkhard and Rendl (1984).

The response to SA from researchers has been mixed, with the most common complaint being that SA often requires an almost prohibitively large amount of computational effort. SA's alleged capability of avoiding non-global extrema is also viewed with skepticism (see De Soete et al. (1988a, 1988b)). In their extensive empirical study of SA's performance, Johnson et al. (in press-a, in press-b) express doubts that SA (as a derivative of local improvement strategies) can be competitive with sophisticated constructive algorithms tailored to a specific problem type. In particular, Johnson et al. have practical reservations about SA's mathematically derived property of terminating in an optimum state with probability equal to 1, since the infinite execution times assumed obviously are impossible to implement in any actual application.

Much research has focused on shortening the run-times of SA while maintaining high probability of terminating the SA process with a solution that is globally optimal or satisfactorily close. The emphasis from theoretical research has been on designing optimum temperature schedules with the most prominent being those from Hajek (1988) and van Laarhoven and Aarts (1987), which have been tested here. For details on the implementation of the two schedules for this project, see Tables 2 and 3. Limitations of space preclude giving full-length explanations concerning the derivation of parameters, but for further information see Schleutermann (1989, 19–20, 43–47).

To shorten further the execution time of SA, we have experimented with a different approach to designing the state transition scheme. If the state of a particular problem can be represented by a vector, then the literature often suggests randomly applying simple transformations like interchanges, rotations, inversions, and insertions. Research on improving the state transition scheme has been done by White (1984) and by Greene and Supowit (1986). State transition schemes that operate with a high degree of randomness often result in long run-times of the algorithm to achieve a result sufficiently close to the optimum solution. At first, when the temperatures are high, almost all negative state transitions are accepted and cause the SA process to remain at states having mediocre values of the objective function. SA then requires long run-times to reach better states. When the temperatures are low, the system is likely to be in a locally optimum state. Especially for TSP-like problems, local optima share a significant amount of local structure with the global optimum, so that a specific set of transformations is needed to reach the global optimum state without destroying the local structures. A state transition scheme that operates too randomly is unlikely to produce such transformations. If negative state transitions are required, they are unlikely to be accepted because of low temperatures, so that long run-times are in turn required to escape local optima and reach a global one. Our own empirical results have confirmed that such randomized state transition schemes result in extremely long run times of SA, and therefore, we decided to experiment with an approach suggested by Lundy and Mees (1986) of using a state transition scheme that produces good results in a deterministic heuristic algorithm.

Since the 2-opt and 3-opt moves of Lin (1965) have already been shown quite effective when used in heuristic algorithms and are computationally not too expensive, we chose them as a basis for our state transition scheme, which is a variation of 3-opt moves that exploits a nearest-neighbor strategy. The advantage of such a scheme is that the algorithm improves the current *BE* value for the configuration quickly. The time complexity for generating a state from a given one is on the order of $O((7N+1)/2)$ for the columns and $O((7M+1)/2)$ the rows. (An outline of the state transition scheme in a pseudo-programming language is in Tab. 5.)

To improve further the performance of SA, a number of variations, extensions and modifications of its basic form have been considered. One promising variation has been suggested by Lundy and Mees (1986): at the termination of the SA process, deterministic measures are applied to search for any possible moves that could improve the value of the objective function. Only moves that result in cost improvements are accepted. This procedure is called "quenching" and is an analogue to rapidly lowering the temperature of physical systems to freeze them.

Any reasonably quick, heuristic measure could be used for finding possible improvements. The state transition scheme of the annealing algorithm is often chosen to produce all possible neighbor states of the final solution until none yields an improvement in the final solution, so that it is indeed a local (and hopefully) global optimum with respect to the given state transition scheme. We have implemented such an approach by using the state transition scheme detailed in Tab. 5 to generate all possible neighbors of the current best solution. The neighboring states are produced by setting the starting column s successively to $1, 2, \ldots, N$, instead of selecting it randomly as in Step 2 of the state transition scheme. Any transformation that improves the objective function is immediately accepted and the solution is updated accordingly. Quenching is then applied repeatedly to the new solution until no further improvements can be found. A detailed outline of the quenching procedure is given in Tab. 4.

The three different implementations of SA can be characterized and denoted as

SAH : an implementation of SA with Hajek's (1988) temperature schedule and corresponding setup of parameters as presented in Tab. 2. See Schleutermann (1989, 19, 43–45) for additional information.

SAQ : the same implementation of SAH, but with additional quenching performed at the termination of the annealing process.

SAL : an implementation of SA employing van Laarhoven and Aarts's (1987) temperature schedule and quenching at the termination of the annealing process. See Schleutermann (1989, 20, 45–47) for additional information.

In algorithms SAQ and SAL where quenching is performed, we first apply the chosen implementation of SA to some initial state. When SA has terminated, the state having the best value of the objective function found thus far is passed to the quenching routine to find any possible local improvements. Typically, the larger the size of the input data matrix, the higher the likelihood that the quenching routine indeed finds local improvements to the state returned by SA.

3 Empirical Results

In our study, three versions of simulated annealing were tested against BEA and LK by observing their respective performances on the nine data sets summarized below:

BLOCK1 : the 10×10 artificial binary data set from Breiger, Boorman and Arabie (1975).

BLOCK2 : the same data set as above, but the *type* of analysis to be performed is slightly different. Instead of seeking a permutation on both the rows and columns, we instead compute the locally best permutation on the columns and then apply it to the rows as well.

SOFTBASS : the soft drink switching matrix of data collected by Bass, Pessemier and Lehmann (1972).

SOFTN : the above data set normalized by DeSarbo (1982).

McCORMICK : the data set on airport facility layout of McCormick et al. (1972).

PARTS : the parts by machine data set of Garcia and Proth (1987).

SALANCIK : Salancik's (1986) table on cross-citations among journals relevant to organizational behavior.

WIRING : Roethlisberger and Dickson's (1939) Bank Wiring Room data set.

SAMPSON : Sampson's (1968) Monastery data set.

For each data set and each algorithm, 25 different random initial permutations were generated so that a total of 1125 analyses were performed. To evaluate the performance of the algorithms, the final BE value of each analysis is used along with the execution time in CPU seconds on an IBM PC/AT running MS-DOS on an Intel 80286 processor.

Tab. 6 displays the following (standard) measures and statistics: first, for each data set, the best BE determined by all algorithms over all 25 random initial permutations. This value is placed immediately below the name identifying a particular data set. The second column (#Ties) counts the number of times an algorithm obtained this best BE value over the 25 random initial permutations. The third and fourth columns (Max and Min) contain the maximum and minimum values for BE that an algorithm obtained over the 25 random initial permutations. The columns labeled $\overline{BE}$ and SD_{BE} are respectively the average value for BE and the standard deviation of BE that an algorithm achieved over the 25 random initial permutations. Finally, column $\overline{Ratio}$ displays the average ratio of the final BE values an algorithm achieved for a dataset and the best BE value for a data set.

Tab. 7 concerns the time that any particular algorithm needed for finding a solution. Columns $\bar{t}$ and SD_t display respectively the average time and standard deviation in CPU seconds an algorithm required to obtain a solution for a data set. For the SA algorithms, we also examine the time that the algorithm needs for *first* establishing the final solution. The average value per SA algorithm and per data set is recorded in column $\overline{Ft}$ and the standard deviation in column SD_{Ft}.

The information in Tab. 6 can be used to rank the algorithms according to various criteria to gain an (admittedly intuitive) overview of the algorithms' performances. The objective is to find algorithms that have a high probability of generating a solution that is optimal or sufficiently close, and a low probability of generating a particularly bad solution. Furthermore, the final solutions of an algorithm for a given data set should not vary extensively, so that a small number of trials would be sufficient to produce satisfactory results with confidence.

Tab. 8 displays the results of ranking the algorithms. Although this table has been constructed using rather ad hoc measures, several observations can be drawn that are nevertheless significant. Algorithm SAQ is consistently in first place or tied for it, whereas BEA is consistently at the bottom or tied for it. Algorithm LK is on the average in second place, so that one might conclude that SAQ is the best algorithm, followed by LK.

Considering the time required by each algorithm, it is obvious that LK needs the least; however, the elapsed time (in CPU seconds) required by the SA algorithms to reach the final *BE* value is comparable to the total amount of time used by LK. For example, the time required by SAQ varies from a factor between 1.0 and 4.5 of LK's time, with an average of about 2.5. The corresponding average factors for SAH and SAL are 5.9 and 4.3. Nevertheless, the execution times required by SAQ and LK are quite comparable, and the difference could be reduced further by improving the code for SAQ that has been written to allow easy modifications and alterations, rather than for maximal efficiency.

De Soete (personal communication) pointed out that the Lin and Kernighan algorithm can be speeded up significantly by using additional heuristics and procedures suggested in Lin and Kernighan (1973) and elsewhere. This observation holds for our implementation of LK, since we have refrained from using measures that are tailored to rather large input data sets. Our implementation of SA, however, has much more potential for optimization for speed by improving the algorithm design and providing more efficient coding. When testing the performance of SA against a tailored heuristic, one must remember that SA is really an approach rather than an algorithm, so that the evaluation is only for a particular set of SA implementations.

Finally, we have used the utility test of Golden and Stewart (1985) that assigns high values to algorithms that perform well on the average and rarely do poorly. The expected utility values for each algorithm are displayed in Tab. 9. Again, it is significant that algorithm BEA consistently has the lowest utility value. The best values are shared by SAH and SAQ, with SAH taking the highest utility values when the parameter t indicates a high degree of sensitivity to the downside risk of the algorithm, and SAQ being prominent when the parameter t corresponds to less sensitivity to the downside risk. Considering the previous comparisons of the algorithms' performances, the prominence of SAH in this table seems surprising, especially because SAQ is an extension of SAH and should perform no worse than SAH, given the same experimental conditions. But in our study, SAH has been allowed a much longer run-time than SAQ and thus has been able to produce results with lower variance, which is an important criterion for the utility test.

4 Conclusion

The objective of this project has not been to provide an "ultimately" superior version of SA for solving a particular type of combinatorial optimization problem. Instead, the goal was to demonstrate that the resources of SA have not been exhausted by defining optimal temperature schedules and that the performance of the approach is to a large degree dependent on the topology of the problem and the distribution of the objective function's values over the states. More (theoretical) research is needed in those areas that could ultimately yield versions of SA competitive to good, tailored, heuristic algorithms. For the chosen data analysis task here, we have demonstrated that SA, when carefully implemented, is a viable competitor to very successful heuristic strategies. We expect that these results can be extended to other areas and types of problems as well.

Acknowledgements

This research was supported by AT & T Information Systems' Industrial Affiliates Program at the University of Illinois and was begun while the second author was Fulbright Visiting Professor of Computer

Science at University College Dublin, Republic of Ireland and completed while the first author was visiting at the Zentralarchiv für Empirische Sozialforschung, Universität zu Köln, Federal Republic of Germany. We gratefully acknowledge the hospitality of these institutions. For helpful comments on this research we are indebted to Professor Geert De Soete.

References

ARABIE, P., and HUBERT, L.J. (1989), The bond energy algorithm reconsidered, *IEEE Transactions on System, Man and Cybernetics.*

ARABIE, P., HUBERT, L.J., and SCHLEUTERMANN, S. (1989), Blockmodels from the bond energy algorithm, Submitted to: *Social Networks.*

ARABIE, P., SCHLEUTERMANN, S., DAWS, J., and HUBERT, L.J. (1988), Marketing applications of sequencing and partitioning of nonsymmetric and/or two mode matrices, in: *Data, Expert Knowledge and Decisions*, eds. W. Gaul and M. Schader, Springer Verlag, Berlin, 215–224.

BASS, F., PESSEMIER, E., and LEHMANN, D. (1972), An experimental study of relationships between attitudes, brand preference, and choice, *Behavioral Science 17*, 532–541.

BREIGER, R., BOORMAN, S., and ARABIE, P. (1975), An algorithm for clustering relational data with applications to social network analysis and comparison with multidimensional scaling, *Journal of Mathematical Psychology, 12, 3*, 328–383.

ČERNY, V. (1985), A thermodynamical approach to the traveling salesman problem: an efficient simulation algorithm, *Journal of Optimization Theory and Application, 45*, 41–51.

DE SOETE, G., HUBERT, L., and ARABIE, P. (1988a), The comparative performance of simulated annealing on two problems of combinatorial data analysis, in: *Data Analysis and Informatics V*, ed. E. Diday, North-Holland, Amsterdam, 489–496.

DE SOETE, G., HUBERT, L., and ARABIE, P. (1988b), On the use of simulated annealing for combinatorial data analysis, in: *Data, Expert Knowledge and Decisions*, eds. W. Gaul and M. Schader, Springer Verlag, Berlin, 329–340.

DESARBO, W.S. (1982), GENNCLUS: New models for general nonhierarchical clustering analysis, *Psychometrika, 47*, 449–475.

GARCIA, H., and PROTH, J.M. (1987), The short horizon planning level-generalized issue, in: *Data Analysis: the Ins and Outs of Solving Real Problems*, eds. J. Janssen, F. Marcotorchino and J. Proth, Plenum Press, New York, 273–282.

GOLDEN, B.L., and STEWART, W.R. (1985), Empirical analysis of heuristics, in: *Traveling Salesman Problem: A Guided Tour of Combinatorial Optimization*, eds. E.L. Lawler, J.K. Lenstra, A.H.G. Rinnooy Kan and D.B. Shmoys, Wiley, Chichester, England, 207–249.

GREENE, J.W., and SUPOWIT, K.J. (1986), Simulated annealing without rejected moves, *IEEE Transactions on Computer-Aided Design 5*, 221–228.

HAJEK, B. (1988), Cooling schedules for optimal annealing, *Mathematics of Operations Research, 13, 2*, 311–329.

JOHNSON, D., ARAGON, C., MCGEOCH, L., and SCHEVON, C. (in press a), Optimization by simulated annealing: an experimental evaluation (part i), *Operations Research.*

JOHNSON, D., ARAGON, C., MCGEOCH, L., and SCHEVON, C. (in press b), Optimization by simulated annealing: an experimental evaluation (part ii), *Operations Research.*

KIRKPATRICK, S., C.D.GELATT, J., and VECCHI, M.P. (1983), Optimization by simulated annealing, *Science, 220*, 671–680.

LAWLER, E.L., LENSTRA, J.K., RINNOOY KAN, A.H.G., and SHMOYS, D.B. (1985), *Traveling Salesman Problem: A Guided Tour of Combinatorial Optimization*, Wiley, Chichester, England.

LENSTRA, J. (1974), Clustering a data array and the traveling-salesman problem, *Operations Research, 22*, 413–414.

LIN, S. (1965), Computer solutions of the traveling salesman problem, *Bell System Technical Journal, 44*, 2245–2269.

LIN, S., and KERNIGHAN, B. (1973), An effective heuristic algorithm for the traveling-salesman problem, *Operations Research, 21*, 498–516.

LUNDY, M., and MEES, A. (1986), Convergence of the annealing algorithm, *Mathematical Programming, 34*, 111–124.

MCCORMICK, JR., W.T., SCHWEITZER, P.J., and WHITE, T.W. (1972), Problem decomposition and data reorganization by a clustering technique, *Operations Research, 20*, 993–1009.

ROETHLISBERGER, F., and DICKSON, W. (1939), *Management and the Worker*, Harvard University Press, Cambridge, MA.

SALANCIK, G. (1986), An index of subgroup influence in dependency networks, *Administrative Science Quarterly, 31*, 194–211.

SAMPSON, S. (1968), *A novitiate in a period of change: An experimental and case study of social relationships*, PhD Thesis, Cornell University.

SCHLEUTERMANN, S.E. (1989), *Pattern Recognition with Simulated Annealing*, Master's thesis, University of Illinois, Urbana.

SPAETH, H. (1988), *Cluster analysis algorithms*, Ellis Horwood (Original work published 1977), Chichester, England.

VAN LAARHOVEN, P., and AARTS, E. (1987), *Simulated Annealing: Theory and Applications*, Reidel, Dordrecht, The Netherlands.

WHITE, S.R. (1984), Concepts of scale in simulated annealing, in: *Proceedings of the IEEE International Conference on Computer-Aided Design*, 646–651.

```
initialize σ to an initial state ∈ S
choose initial temperature T
while (termination condition not satisfied)
    while (inner loop criterion not satisfied)
        generate a state σ*
        ΔBE = BE(σ) − BE(σ*)
        if (ΔBE ≤ 0) σ → σ*
        else
                set σ → σ* with probability exp(−ΔBE/T)
    decrement T
return σ
```

Table 1: Generic Outline of the Simulated Annealing Approach

Basic Form	$T_k = C/\log(k+1), \quad k = 1, 2, \ldots$
Initial Temperature	$T_1 = C/\log(2)$, or user-defined
Decrement Rule	$T_k = C/\log(k + k_{off} + 1)$, where $k_{off} = \max\{0, \exp(\frac{C}{T_1}) - 1\}$
Markov Chain Length	10
Stopping Criterion	user-defined time limit
Parameters	$C = M_1 + M_2 + M_3 - m_1 - m_2 - m_3$, where M_1, M_2, M_3 are the three strongest links, and m_1, m_2, m_3 are the three weakest links.

This table displays the most important characteristics of Hajek's (1988) temperature schedule, which was originally a one-step schedule, i.e., the temperature is to be decremented after each time a state has been generated and its acceptance determined. In our implementation, we have chosen 10 instead of 1 for the number of steps to be executed before the temperature is decremented. For explanations see Schleutermann (1989, 44). In the computation of the constant C, the three "strongest" links are given by the three maximum BE values between any pair of columns/rows, and the three "weakest" links are given by the three smallest BE values between any pair of columns/rows.

Table 2: Hajek's Temperature Schedule

Basic Form	$T_{k+1} = T_k/(1+\alpha_k T_k)$, $k = 0, 1, \ldots$ (The value of α_k that we have used is given in the Decrement Rule below.)
Initial Temperature	$T_0 = \lvert(\Delta C)_2\rvert / \ln(n_2/(n_2 \cdot \chi - n_1(1-\chi)))$ where n_1 (respectively n_2) is the number of transitions causing an increase (respectively decrease) in the value of the objective function, and $\lvert(\Delta C)_2\rvert$ is the absolute value of the average decrease of the objective function over the n_2 negative transitions.
Decrement Rule	$T_{k+1} = T_k/(1 + \alpha_k T_k)$ where $\alpha_k = \ln(1+\delta)/3(Sdk)$. Here $\delta = 0.1$ and (Sdk) is the standard deviation of the objective function values obtained at temperature T_k.
Markov Chain Length	N for the rows, M for the columns
Stopping Criterion	The algorithm is terminated when the average objective function values $\overline{\mu}(T)$ fails to change significantly: $(T_k/\mu_1)\frac{\partial\overline{\mu}}{\partial T}(T_k) < \epsilon$ where $\mu_1 = \overline{\mu}(T_0)$.
Parameters	$\delta = 0.1, \chi = 0.95, \epsilon = 0.001$. These are default values; the user can enter different values for these parameters.

This schedule is an equilibrium schedule, in which the equilibrium distribution is to be approximated for each temperature. The future temperature values depend on the behavior of the SA process at the current temperature. For details of this implementation see Schleutermann (1989, 45–47).

Table 3: Van Laarhoven and Aarts' Temperature Schedule

quench(σ, N)
Parameters: σ is the state, i.e., a permutation of the first N integers.
Variables: $s, i, B, B', \sigma', \pi$.
$\pi = \sigma, s = 1, B = \sum_{i=1}^{N-1} BE(\sigma(i), \sigma(i+1))$
while $(s \leq N)$
    $\sigma' =$ **generate** (π, N, s)
    $B' = \sum_{i=1}^{N-1} BE(\sigma'(i), \sigma'(i+1))$
    if $(B' > B)$ $(\pi = \sigma', B = B', s = 1)$
    else $s = s + 1$
return π

Above is the outline of the quenching routine **quench**(σ, N). It is invoked after the annealing process has been terminated. The argument σ is set to the state of best value of the objective function found by the annealing routine. **quench** calls the state transition function **generate** detailed in Table 5. $BE(\sigma(i), \sigma(j))$ is the bond energy value between columns $\sigma(i)$ and $\sigma(j)$. **quench** returns a permutation π of the integers between 1 and N.

Table 4: Outline of the Quenching Algorithm

generate (σ, N, s')

Parameters: σ is the current state, i.e., a permutation of the first N integers. The third argument s' is used to determine whether the new state is generated deterministically or with a certain degree of randomness.

Variables: $s, t, t'_{max}, i, i_{max}, b_1, b_2, G_1, G_2, G_{max}$.

1. $G_{max} = 0.0$
2. **if** $(s' \in \{1, \ldots, N\})$ $s = s'$
   else set $s \in \{1, \ldots, N\}$ randomly
3. set t such that $BE(\sigma(s), \sigma(t)) = \max_j BE(\sigma(s), j)$
   (Columns s and t will be adjacent in the new state.)
4. **if** $(s < t)$ $b_1 = 1, b_2 = t - 1$
   else
   $b_1 = t + 1, b_2 = N$
5. $i = b_1$
   while $(i \leq b_2)$
   if $(i \leq s)$

$$G_1 = BE(\sigma(s),\sigma(t)) + BE(\sigma(i),\sigma(t-1)) - BE(\sigma(t-1),\sigma(t)) + BE(\sigma(i-1),\sigma(s+1)) - BE(\sigma(i-1),\sigma(i)) - BE(\sigma(s),\sigma(s+1))$$

$$G_2 = BE(\sigma(s),\sigma(t)) + BE(\sigma(i),\sigma(t+1)) - BE(\sigma(t),\sigma(t+1)) + BE(\sigma(i-1),\sigma(s+1)) - BE(\sigma(i-1),\sigma(i)) - BE(\sigma(s),\sigma(s+1))$$

   if $(i > s)$

$$G_1 = BE(\sigma(s),\sigma(t)) + BE(\sigma(i),\sigma(t-1)) - BE(\sigma(t-1),\sigma(t)) + BE(\sigma(s-1),\sigma(i+1)) - BE(\sigma(s-1),\sigma(s)) - BE(\sigma(i),\sigma(i+1))$$

$$G_2 = BE(\sigma(s),\sigma(t)) + BE(\sigma(i),\sigma(t+1)) - BE(\sigma(t),\sigma(t+1)) + BE(\sigma(s-1),\sigma(i+1)) - BE(\sigma(s-1),\sigma(s)) - BE(\sigma(i),\sigma(i+1))$$

   if $(G_1 > G_{max})$ $G_{max} = G_1, t'_{max} = t - 1, i_{max} = i$
   if $(G_2 > G_{max})$ $G_{max} = G_2, t'_{max} = t + 1, i_{max} = i$
   $i = i + 1$
6. Move the block of columns between i_{max} and s between the columns t'_{max} and t, so that s is adjacent to t and i_{max} is adjacent to t'_{max}. For example, if $t'_{max} = t - 1$ and $i = i_{max} < s < t - 1$, then we have the following transition:
   $\sigma = (\sigma(1) \ldots \sigma(i-1), \sigma(i) \ldots \sigma(s), \sigma(s+1) \ldots \sigma(t-1), \sigma(t) \ldots \sigma(N))$
   $\sigma' = (\sigma(1) \ldots \sigma(i-1), \sigma(s+1) \ldots \sigma(t-1), \sigma(i) \ldots \sigma(s), \sigma(t) \ldots \sigma(N))$
7. **return** σ'

This outline is the function **generate**(σ, N, s') that produces a new state from the given one according to the state transition scheme. A new state is a permutation of the first N integers. In the outline above, $BE(\sigma(i), \sigma(j))$ is the bond energy value between the columns $\sigma(i)$ and $\sigma(j)$. Not all cases relevant to the computation of the internal variables G_1 and G_2 have been detailed here. Special attention is needed when any two of s, i, t are adjacent, on the margins of the data matrix, or adjacent to the borders of the data matrix.

Table 5: The Function **generate** *Representing the State Transition Scheme*

Data Set Best *BE*	Algorithm	#Ties	Max	Min	$\overline{BE}$	SD_{BE}	$\overline{Ratio}$
BLOCK1	BEA	22	84	80	83.68	0.92	0.99
	LK	23	84	82	83.84	0.54	0.99
	SAH	25	84	84	84.00	0.00	1.00
84	SAQ	25	84	84	84.00	0.00	1.00
	SAL	25	84	84	84.00	0.00	1.00
BLOCK2	BEA	8	72	68	69.28	1.86	0.96
	LK	5	72	68	68.80	1.60	0.95
	SAH	11	72	68	69.76	1.98	0.96
72	SAQ	10	72	68	69.60	1.95	0.96
	SAL	7	72	68	69.12	1.79	0.96
SOFTBASS	BEA	0	4363994	4313902	4351325.76	17536.39	0.99
	LK	1	4379278	4284300	4340440.08	23612.39	0.99
	SAH	17	4379278	4370454	4376759.12	3737.17	0.99
4379278	SAQ	20	4379278	4370454	4377513.20	3529.60	0.99
	SAL	7	4379278	4281954	4354122.88	30249.44	0.99
SOFTN	BEA	25	1740934	1740934	1740934.00	0.00	1.00
	LK	25	1740934	1740934	1740934.00	0.00	1.00
	SAH	20	1740934	1734286	1739719.84	2482.59	0.99
1740934	SAQ	19	1740934	1734286	1739338.48	2839.24	0.99
	SAL	14	1740934	1715692	1736274.40	7404.69	0.99
McCORMICK	BEA	1	2320	2160	2234.24	49.84	0.96
	LK	0	2312	2248	2288.96	17.46	0.98
	SAH	1	2320	2284	2303.52	6.91	0.99
2320	SAQ	5	2320	2300	2305.76	7.33	0.99
	SAL	1	2320	2276	2302.56	7.49	0.99
PARTS	BEA	1	438	426	431.20	2.46	0.98
	LK	12	438	432	436.08	2.07	0.99
	SAH	0	434	428	430.96	1.39	0.98
438	SAQ	0	436	428	432.72	2.18	0.98
	SAL	1	438	430	432.88	2.19	0.98
SALANCIK	BEA	0	4033632	3985050	4014733.36	12913.26	0.99
	LK	0	4030840	3999186	4015870.56	8245.16	0.99
	SAH	0	4017084	3982220	3999191.52	8304.65	0.99
4033732	SAQ	0	4023458	3984870	4009084.16	11323.46	0.99
	SAL	1	4033732	3997662	4024679.44	6912.96	0.99
WIRING	BEA	3	366	350	360.72	4.99	0.98
	LK	9	366	356	362.72	3.29	0.99
	SAH	23	366	364	365.84	0.54	0.99
366	SAQ	23	366	364	365.84	0.54	0.99
	SAL	14	366	356	364.32	2.50	0.99
SAMPSON	BEA	0	2726	2610	2678.88	40.02	0.97
	LK	0	2754	2680	2725.12	18.87	0.98
	SAH	1	2756	2730	2746.48	6.40	0.99
2756	SAQ	0	2754	2734	2745.76	5.69	0.99
	SAL	1	2756	2680	2744.88	15.52	0.99

Table 6: Comparison of Algorithms

Data Set	Algorithm	$\bar{t}$	SD_t	$\overline{Ft}$	SD_{Ft}
BLOCK1	BEA	0.33	0.01		
	LK	0.57	0.09		
	SAH	1.53	0.03	0.38	0.13
	SAQ	1.89	0.03	0.58	0.09
	SAL	2.13	0.37	0.35	0.12
BLOCK2	BEA	0.17	0.01		
	LK	0.28	0.08		
	SAH	0.77	0.02	0.19	0.07
	SAQ	0.95	0.02	0.30	0.08
	SAL	1.13	0.29	0.23	0.10
SOFTBASS	BEA	0.19	0.02		
	LK	0.48	0.10		
	SAH	11.75	3.29	4.73	3.41
	SAQ	8.87	0.06	1.74	1.16
	SAL	1.41	0.20	0.32	0.17
SOFTN	BEA	0.22	0.04		
	LK	0.43	0.10		
	SAH	55.92	0.12	10.88	9.43
	SAQ	8.51	0.05	1.30	1.00
	SAL	4.42	1.56	1.25	1.42
McCORMICK	BEA	3.65	0.92		
	LK	5.71	0.94		
	SAH	67.32	0.40	18.46	9.67
	SAQ	23.45	0.27	11.26	5.64
	SAL	69.96	23.55	18.55	12.47
PARTS	BEA	31.13	6.70		
	LK	48.33	11.65		
	SAH	127.20	0.57	44.94	23.09
	SAQ	131.42	1.29	44.50	23.47
	SAL	486.99	250.05	245.75	200.84
SALANCIK	BEA	5.57	0.56		
	LK	21.39	3.22		
	SAH	130.76	0.30	74.45	25.31
	SAQ	89.20	0.58	47.57	13.22
	SAL	364.66	41.89	283.87	65.32
WIRING	BEA	1.04	0.16		
	LK	2.24	0.55		
	SAH	15.58	0.13	4.60	1.79
	SAQ	15.83	0.14	4.61	1.80
	SAL	13.16	4.59	3.88	2.96
SAMPSON	BEA	2.13	0.32		
	LK	5.15	1.31		
	SAH	50.01	0.28	24.73	8.17
	SAQ	50.55	0.25	23.15	9.80
	SAL	100.14	26.93	45.17	25.20

This table contains the statistics for the execution time of the algorithms. The average CPU time is given in seconds along with the corresponding standard deviation. For the SA$*$ algorithms, the average time in seconds is also given for first determining the final BE, along with the corresponding standard deviation. The values are entered in blocks, one for each data set. The averages in the blocks are over the 25 random initial permutations of the objects.

Table 7: Time Analysis

Criterion	1	2	3	4	5
Ties	SAQ (102)	SAH (98)	LK (75)	SAL (71)	BEA (60)
worst Max	SAQ (0)	SAL (0)	LK (1)	BEA (2)	SAH (2)
worst Min	SAQ (0)	LK (0)	SAH (1)	SAL (2)	BEA (5)
best Min	SAQ (5)	SAH (3)	LK (3)	BEA (1)	SAL (1)
worst $\overline{BE}$	SAQ (0)	LK (1)	SAH (2)	SAL (2)	BEA (4)
best $\overline{BE}$	SAH (4)	SAQ (4)	LK (2)	SAL (2)	BEA (1)
worst $\overline{Ratio}$	SAQ (0)	SAL (1)	LK (2)	SAH (2)	BEA (4)
best $\overline{Ratio}$	SAH (4)	SAQ (4)	LK (2)	SAL (2)	BEA (1)

The algorithms are ranked according to various criteria concerning the final *BE* values. The position indicates the rank order, with 1 being the best and 5 the worst. The number of times the algorithm satisfies a positive or negative criterion is entered in parentheses behind the name of the algorithm. It should be obvious which criteria are considered positive and which ones are negative. When algorithms share the same count for a criterion, their order is arbitrary.

Table 8: Ranking the Algorithms

	BEA	LK	SAH	SAQ	SAL
$\bar{x}$	1.63	1.08	0.75	0.70	0.87
SD	1.94	1.56	1.35	1.37	1.48
$\hat{b}$	2.29	2.25	2.41	2.68	2.54
$\hat{c}$	0.71	0.48	0.31	0.26	0.34
$1/\hat{b}$	0.43	0.44	0.41	0.37	0.39
	Expected Utility for each Algorithm				
t	$\alpha - \beta(1 - \hat{b}t)^{-\hat{c}}$				
0.34	203.93(-)	298.76	328.59(+)	310.20	301.42
0.32	241.66(-)	315.13	340.96(+)	332.85	322.01
0.3	269.59(-)	327.99	350.28(+)	346.48	336.16
0.28	291.21(-)	338.44	357.67(+)	356.00	346.73
0.26	308.53(-)	347.16	363.73(+)	363.21	355.04
0.24	322.75(-)	354.57	368.84	368.95(+)	361.83
0.22	334.68(-)	360.98	373.23	373.69(+)	367.53
0.2	344.84(-)	366.59	377.06	377.70(+)	372.40
0.18	353.62(-)	371.55	380.45	381.16(+)	376.64
0.16	361.30(-)	375.99	383.48	384.19(+)	380.37

This table illustrates the expected utility for each algorithm over different values of the parameter t of the utility test. High values of t indicate greater sensitivity of the utility measure to the downside risk of an algorithm. The choices for the other parameters are $\alpha = 500, \beta = 100$. For each value of t, the algorithm with the highest value for the utility is marked with $(+)$, and the the one of lowest with $(-)$.

Table 9: Comparing Accuracy of the Algorithms With the Utility Function

Part 3

Computer-Assisted Decision Support: Integrating, Representing and Processing Knowledge

Building an Expert Decision Support System: The Integration of Artificial Intelligence and Operations Research Methods

Pedro Barahona and Rita Ribeiro
Departamento de Informática
Universidade Nova de Lisboa, Monte da Caparica, Portugal

Summary

The concept of Expert Decision Support Systems is based on the integration of Decision Support Systems and Expert Systems, providing the decision maker with features from both types of systems (e.g. simulation, explanations, control of reasoning). Constraint logic programming languages, such as CLP(R) or CHIP, achieve this integration by merging logic programming, a paradigm of Artificial Intelligence and Expert Systems, with constraint solving techniques similar to those used in Operations Research and Decision Support Systems. Their embedded constraint solver extends the expressive power of logic programming languages, most notably on the domain of numerical expressions. The paper illustrates how constraint logic programming may be used in EDSS development by presenting a small classroom scheduling problem developed with CLP(R), and compares this approach to more traditional Operations Research techniques.

1 Introduction

The concept of Expert Decision Support Systems (EDSS) introduced by Sen and Biswas (1985) (or Intelligent Decision Support Systems in Jelassi and Ozernay (1988) terminology) is based on the integration of features from both Decision Support Systems (DSS) and Expert Systems (ES). EDSSs thus provide the decision maker with the capabilities of both types of systems such as simulation (what–if questions), and explanations about the reasoning process (why and how questions). These are some of the demands that are put on (increasingly) complex information systems, where the decision maker requires not more information, but more intelligent information. In particular, the ability to combine numerical and qualitative aspects is becoming essential to support multiple criteria decisions in today's complex organizations environment.

Logic programming (e.g. Prolog) is able to achieve some of the required EDSS features. In particular, it allows the handling of both logical and numerical information, the incorporation of qualitative and quantitative reasoning, and meta-level facilities for the manipulation of data and models in the same formalism. For these reasons, it has been advocated as a paradigm for several types of applications. For example, Minch (1989) advocates its use in financial modeling.

Nevertheless, Prolog is able to handle numerical information only in a limited way, and to be of practical use in EDSS development, it must be integrated, in general, with

NATO ASI Series, Vol. F 61
Knowledge, Data and Computer-Assisted Decisions
Edited by M. Schader and W. Gaul

efficient numerical modeling extensions. So far, ES and DSS integration has mostly been achieved by coupling independent systems, either by having an ES supporting a DSS or a DSS supporting an ES[1]. Prolog programs might therefore be considered as ES tools to be coupled with DSS tools that solve efficiently numerical models. For example, one might build with Prolog (the ES component) a set of scenarios from which decisions and choices have to be made. However, some numerical parameters of these scenarios would not be evaluated in Prolog, but rather by some DSS component coupled with the former. This simple coupling of tools is, however, insufficient in many cases to override the specific limitations and disadvantages of these technologies. In particular, many scenarios proposed for evaluation could be simply eliminated by a tighter coupling of the ES and DSS component (see the following section).

A deeper integration of Artificial Intelligence/Expert Systems and Operations Research/Decision Support Systems is achieved by constraint logic programming languages (or simply CLP languages), such as CLP(R), Prolog III or CHIP, recently proposed by Jaffar and Michaylov (1987), Colmerauer (1988) and Dincbas et al. (1988), respectively[2]. These languages allow for an easier incorporation of logic extensions (more powerful explanations, semantic knowledge and reasoning) into quantitative models, increasing the sophistication of the solutions by the synergy effect achieved, as proposed by Bennet (1983).

In this paper we investigate the development of EDSSs by means of these new languages. In the following section we briefly overview the main features of constraint logic programming languages. In section 3, we present a small classroom scheduling problem, to illustrate how qualitative and quantitative aspects are specified and their integration achieved. Finally, section 4 presents the main conclusions.

2 Constraint Logic Programming Languages: CLP(R)

Logic Programming languages such as Prolog, possess a declarative reading, which means that programs written in them are (to a certain extent) executable specifications. The user only has to specify what the relationships and constraints between the variables of the problem domain should be. Prolog is able to execute these specifications, and through its backtracking feature, search alternative solutions that satisfy the constraints.

In spite of its expressing power, Prolog is not adequate for many applications, in particular those dealing with numerical variables, for it may not handle numerical expressions (involving operations and relations), unless all variables appearing in these expressions are instantiated. This problem with Prolog is alleviated with CLP languages.

Constraint Solving implemented in these languages, extends the parameter passing mechanism of Prolog, unification. In general, unification is a very powerful feature that allows parameters to be used either as input or output. For example, a predicate `scenario(V1,V2)` could, in principle, be used in many different modes, namely

a. check whether there is a scenario with given values `V1` and `V2`;

[1]See Turban (1988) and Ribeiro and Barahona (1989) for a more complete account.

[2]In this paper, and unless explicitly mentioned, we will focus on CLP(R) features, which are largely shared with the other CLP languages.

b. search all values V2 (or V1) for scenarios that have a given V1 (or V2);

c. find all possible scenarios with arbitrary V1 - V2 pairs.

However, if the predicate definition is

```
scenario(V1, V2) :- V1 + V2 = 5, V1 - V2 = 1.
```

unification is only able to cope with the first mode above (in fact, Prolog requires the use of its assignment operator — `is`). The second mode could be used after some program transformation (e.g. `V2 = 5 - V1`, `V2 = V1 - 1` or `V1 = 5 - V2`, `V1 = V2 + 1`). The third mode could not be handled at all by unification. In contrast, the constraint solving mechanism can solve sets of linear constraints and therefore cope with all modes, directly.

Furthermore, CLP(R) can solve more general sets of constraints, also containing inequalities, as soon as they become linear (either at the time of the call or whenever sufficient variables become ground so that the expressions become linear). Hence, many constraints can be combined together and produce simpler constraints. Take for example the following program

```
test&generate(W,X,Y,Z) :-
   W*X+Y+Z<5, X+Y>3, c1(W), c2(Z), generate(X,Y,Z).
```

Solving constraints `W * X + Y + Z < 5` and `X + Y > 3` is delayed until `W` is instantiated to a constant value. Assuming that `c1` makes `W = 1` the above two constraints can now be combined (they are both linear now) to enforce `Z < 2`. If predicate `c2` forces `Z > 5`, the goals become unsatisfiable. Upon finding this, CLP(R) will immediately backtrack before ever instantiate variables `X`, `Y` and `Z`.

Since Prolog can only deal with numerical relations whose arguments are ground (i.e. the variables have assigned values) the above predicate **test&generate**, would have to be replaced in Prolog by predicate **generate&test** below, since only after generating the values for `X`, `Y`, `Z` and `W` can the inequalities be tested.

```
generate&test(W,X,Y,Z) :-
   c1(W), generate(X,Y,Z), W*X+Y+Z<5, X+Y>3, c2(Z).
```

In general, CLP(R) test_and_generate paradigm is more efficient than Prolog's generate_and_test, because the handling of constraints reduce the domain of the variables and leads to less backtracking. This tight integration, achieved by CLP languages, of logic programming (the AI-ES side) and constraint solving techniques (the OR-DSS side) justifies in our view the use of these languages to implement EDSSs. This type of integration can achieve results not possible by a more loose coupling alone. In the example above, even if some function, taking the values of variables `W`, `X`, `Y` and `Z` as input, could be more efficiently implemented by means of an external call to a DSS package, the simple coupling of the package to Prolog would not avoid the backtracking inefficiency explained above.

3 Building an Expert Decision Support System

Until now many articles and journals addressed the problem of timetabling. Some authors defend a more quantitative approach, while others follow a more qualitative approach, or even a combination of heuristics and mathematics[3]. Anyway, our main objective is not to propose a new approach to timetabling but rather to show how a simple timetable problem, that requires both numerical and qualitative decision factors, can be easily developed with CLP languages, using the EDSS perspective of model integration.

Our development strategy includes five steps — specification of requirements, definition of a solution strategy, selection of tools and techniques, solving the problem and evaluation of results. These steps are included in the traditional development phases of any decision making process presented in Turban (1988), with the following correspondence:

a. intelligent phase (first step),

b. design phase (second and third steps),

c. choice (fourth and fifth steps).

Of course, our deliberate choice of CLP(R) as the tool to develop this example, somehow changes the time order in which the steps were performed. Hence, we will only mention very briefly the third step, selection of tools and techniques, and present the others assuming a CLP(R) implementation.

3.1 First Step: Specification of Requirements

The Computer Science Department of the Universidade Nova de Lisboa (UNL) is responsible for planning the schedule of the computer practice classes to be held in the computer laboratories. It is a policy of the university that the general schedule of the university, which is the responsibility of the registration and planning department, is almost static and any change on it implies superior authorization. Hence, the scheduling of the computer practice classes can only be executed after obtaining the general university timetable, in order to avoid redundancies or collisions between different courses and computer theoretical and practice classes. The small timetabling problem that we present meets these rules although the problem itself has only demonstration purposes.

The Computer Science Department offers 5 courses with practice classes to be held in two laboratories. These labs can only be occupied with classes 2 mornings per week (Tuesdays and Saturdays), since it is policy of the university to offer the maximum possible available time (at the labs) for all university students to execute their assignments and self-training. Some requirements of the courses, namely its duration, are pre-defined by the administrative services and the Computer Science Department. The lecturers of the courses also have their own preferences namely the days and labs in which their courses should be taught. Finally, there are costs associated to each class to cover the depreciation of the computers and some extra payment due to Saturday's lectures. These are the goals and constraints of the problem which are now described in more detail.

[3]See de Werra (1985) and Bettin (1985) for examples.

3.1.1 Resources Availability

The resources availability, representing the frontiers of our system, are the number of hours per week a course is taught, and the teaching time available at the computer laboratories. The total number of hours per week for each course is respectively 3, 4, 4, 2 and 3 hours. Additionally, both computer labs are available for teaching 4 hours each Tuesday and Saturday morning[4]. In CLP(R), these constraints can be specified similarly to linear programming, with predicates `lab_resources` and `course_resources`. Variables `Xijk` in the predicate's body represent the duration of a class of course `i` (in the range 1...5) being taught in lab `j` (in range 1...2) on weekday `k` (either `s` for Saturday or `t` for Tuesday).

```
lab_resources(Xijk_List) :-
    X11s + X12s + X11t + X12t = 3,
    X21s + X22s + X21t + X22t = 4,
    X31s + X32s + X31t + X32t = 4,
    X41s + X42s + X41t + X42t = 2,
    X51s + X52s + X51t + X52t = 3.

course_resources(Xijk_List) :-
    X11s + X21s + X31s + X41s + X51s <= 4,
    X12s + X22s + X32s + X42s + X52s <= 4,
    X11t + X21t + X31t + X41t + X51t <= 4,
    X12t + X22t + X32t + X42t + X52t <= 4.
```

3.1.2 Course Demands

Based on past experience, some courses put some extra demands pre-defined by the administrative services of the computer science department. The directives are

a. in general, no class should exceed 3 hours;

b. in particular, Course 2 and Course 4 classes must be 2 hours each;

c. Course 5 should only have one class per week of 3 hours.

The CLP(R) predicates below, include all these pre-defined course demands in terms of class duration per course. For reasons explained later, `conj_course_demands` and `disj_course_demands` group together course demands for which there are and there are not, respectively, logical disjunctions (i.e. backtracking choice points).

```
conj_course_demands(Xijk_List):-
    X <= 3 forall X in X1jk_List,
    X <= 3 forall X in X3jk_List,
disj_course_demands(Xijk_List):-
    two_or_zero(X) forall X in X2jk_List,
    two_or_zero(X) forall X in X4jk_List,
    three_and_zero(X5jk_List).
```

[4] In this small problem, we do not take into account the beginning time of each class.

```
Cx forall X in [].
Cx forall X in [H,T] :-
   assert(prov(X,Cx)),  % this predicate creates a detached
   retract(prov(H,Ch)), % copy H, Ch of condition X, Cx
   call(Ch),
   Cx forall X in T.

two_or_zero(0).
two_or_zero(2).

three_and_zero([H|T]):- H = 3, X = 0 forall X in T.
three_and_zero([H|T]):- H = 0, three_and_zero(T).
```

Predicate `forall` is used both to specify the general condition (i.e. to be less or equal to 3) to all classes `X1jk` and `X3jk` of courses 1 and 3, and, together with predicate `two_or_zero`, to specify condition (b) above to courses 2 and 4 classes. Incidently, predicate `forall` shows how CLP(R) shares features of logic programming such as improved readability and meta-level programming. The declaration of predicates `forall` and `in` as operators allows its specification in the form — `Condition forall X in List` — much clearer than its equivalent form `forall(Condition, in(X, List))`. Furthermore, notice that the `Condition` which is passed as a parameter is itself a predicate. This meta-level programming facility allows higher-level programming with great generality (the higher-level predicate `forall` is instantiated with proper (first-order) predicates `<=` and `two_or_zero`).

Finally, predicate `three_and_zero` imposes that one and only one of the variables for course 5 has value three, while the others have value 0. We have used this predicate (instead of the simpler disjunction `X51s = 3`; `X52s = 3`; `X51t = 3`; `X52t = 3` which has the same effect combined with the previous constraint `X51s + X52s + X51t + X52t = 3`) to keep the specifications modular.

3.1.3 Lecturer Preferences

The preferences of the lecturers are expressed in terms of the days and laboratories they prefer for their courses. These preferences, annually expressed by the faculty members, are analyzed and classified as approved (meaning that they are mandatory) or optional. In our example we have the following preferences:

1. Lecturer of course 2 requires to use LAB-2 because he is using a CASE software that needs 2 MB RAM memory. LAB-1 only has 5 computers with the 2 MB while LAB-2 has 10 PCs with 2 MB;

2. Lecturer of course 4 does not wish to have classes on Tuesdays because it is the day of his department weekly meeting and any change will involve all other professors of his own department;

3. Lecturer of course 1 prefers most of his scheduled time (i.e. at least two hours) to be in LAB-1 on Tuesdays, because he has office hours in the room next door to the lab;

4. Lecturer of course 4 prefers to have all his classes in Lab-2 because its computers are faster;

5. Lecturer of course 5 prefers not to have classes on Saturdays since he usually goes out for the weekend;

6. Lecturer of Course 3 whishes to teach in the LAB-2 on Tuesdays because its computers are newer. Predicates pref1 to pref6, shown below, specify the above preferences, the first two preferences being considered mandatory, while the others are simple optional decision factors.

```
pref1(Xijk_List):- X21s = 0, X21t = 0.
pref2(Xijk_List):- X41t = 0, X42t = 0.
pref3(Xijk_List):- X11t >= 2.
pref4(Xijk_List):- X41s = 0, X41t = 0.
pref5(Xijk_List):- X51s = 0, X52s = 0.
pref6(Xijk_List):- X32t > 0.
```

3.1.4 Costs

The (approximate) cost of occupation of the labs depends on three factors,

a. type of computer (computers with 640KB or 2MB main memory);

b. number of students enrolled in each course (each computer has a cost/hour for depreciation+amortization);

c. days of the week of the classes (on Saturdays there is an extra cost that the university must pay to the lecturers).

The numerical formulation of the objective function is specified with predicate cost, shown below. All courses on Saturdays have an extra cost of 5 compared with their Tuesdays counterparts. LAB-2 costs are always greater than LAB-1's because of its better equipment. Course 2 has higher costs than the others because it has more students.

```
cost(Xijk_List, Cost) :- Cost =
   35 * X11s + 50 * X12s + 30 * X11t + 45 * X12t +
   65 * X21s + 95 * X22s + 60 * X21t + 90 * X22t +
   45 * X31s + 65 * X32s + 40 * X31t + 60 * X32t +
   41 * X41s + 59 * X42s + 36 * X41t + 54 * X42t +
   49 * X51s + 71 * X52s + 44 * X51t + 66 * X52t .
```

3.2 Second Step: Definition of a Solution Strategy Model

As other multiple criteria problems, this problem could be modeled and solved by means of conventional O.R. techniques such as (Integer) Linear Programming. The objective function would be a linear weighted combination of the different goals (in our case, cost and optional preferences), reflecting the importance of each of them to the overall quality of the solution.

This conventional approach oversimplifies in many ways the user's intentions. In general, the user has to estimate (based on his/her past experience) the value of the coefficients used in the objective function to weight the criteria. These estimates very often prove not to be adequate (in particular when applied to multiple criteria problems in which some criteria are largely qualitative), and the tuning of these weighting factors might become elusive. Hence, the meaning and usefulness of an optimal solution (referred to such objective function) becomes quite debatable. In fact, the user might end up preferring a "non-optimal" solution, meeting a pattern of preferences not anticipated when the weighting factors were assigned.

Our solution strategy clearly has to take into account the minimization of the overall cost. Nevertheless, this is not the only goal to be taken into account for various reasons. One such reason is the fact that the cost function is just an approximation of the real costs involved, since other costs (e.g. building depreciation, cleaning costs, etc.) involved were not considered or were simply estimated for the assigning values to the coefficients of the cost function. Furthermore, there should be a trade off between the minimization of costs and the satisfaction of other hidden and ill-defined factors. For example, if lecturers' preferences are not met, it is expected that their absentism increases, and the quality of teaching decreases. Since these hidden costs are difficult to quantify, instead of attempting to minimize the costs, costs are used as a guide to a good solution.

Hence, rather than focusing on the optimization of an objective function, our strategy will aim at computing several possible solutions with acceptable costs, such that the decision maker might choose between them, based on his/her expert knowledge (e.g. the expected behavior of lecturers whose preferences are not met). Of course some qualitative aspects are already considered in the computation of the solutions. Others can be included later in a refinement of the model incorporating more expert and qualitative knowledge.

In the context of CLP(R) implementation, and given its ability to prune scenarios with its test_and_generate paradigm, a convenient solution for our problem is the inclusion of all mandatory and optional constraints into an integrated model (of course, if the mandatory constraints alone could not be met the problem would have to be redefined). Then a satisfaction process, or a minimization process if the problem size is not too large, takes place to provide the decision maker with the acceptable solutions (with respect to their cost) that satisfy the constraints. If no acceptable solutions are found, or if the decision maker does not accept the solutions found, the optional constraints are relaxed, taking into account qualitative criteria specified by the decision maker, and the process is iterated.

3.3 Third Step: Selection of the Tools and Techniques

For the reasons explained in the beginning of the section, we have used CLP(R) to solve this timetabling problem. Other components are nevertheless required for the development of a complete EDSS, namely the interface/dialog and data subsystems. This paper does not address these topics, although they show the need for integrating CLP(R) in powerful programming environments[5].

[5]The demo version 2.0 of CLP(R) developed by Heintze et al. (1987), that we have used, already provides a set of UNIX interface primitives, that enable its integration with common UNIX tools such as windowing systems, graphic packages, databases, etc.

3.4 Fourth Step: Solving the Problem

The solution strategy explained in section 3.2 is implemented by means of the CLP(R) predicate `problem`, shown below (in fact, the predicate does not check whether the mandatory constraints are satisfiable). This predicate returns `Solutions` whose cost does not exceed a certain `Threshold`. Solutions are provided with a certain time order that reflects a qualitative appreciation of the preferences, specified by the decision maker (see below).

Operationally, predicate `problem` creates a list of (nonnegative) `Xijk` variables, and sets scenarios meeting the `lab_resources`, `course_resources`, `conj_course_demands` and `mandatory_preferences` (i.e. `pref1` and `pref2`). These scenarios are then further restricted by means of predicate `satisfy`, which is input the list of already constrained `Xijk` variables and a list with `OtherConstraints`. These include the `disj_course_demands` and a set of `OptionalPreferences`, chosen by predicate `choose_preferences` among lecturers' preferences 3 to 6. Predicate `satisfy` will thus return all the `Solutions` that satisfy the previously set constraints, and whose cost does not exceed the `Threshold` input to the predicate.

```
problem(Threshold, Solutions) :-
   variables_Xijk(Xijk_List), X>=0 forall X in Xijk_List,
   lab_resources(Xijk_List),
   course_resources(Xijk_List).
   conj_course_demands(Xijk_List),
   pref1(Xijk_List), pref2(Xijk_List),
   choose_preferences(Xijk_List, OptionalPreferences),
   OtherConstraints =
      [disj_course_demands(Xijk_List)| OptionalPreferences],
   satisfy(Threshold, Xijk_List, OtherConstraints,Solutions).
```

Notice how the constraints were organized in the body of predicate `problem`. Some of them are directly coded in the body of the predicate whereas others (`OtherConstraints`) are passed as parameters to goal satisfy. Since all mandatory constraints that do not include backtracking points (i.e. disjunctions), have to be considered in the solutions, it is more efficient to set these constraints once and for all, and restrict all backtracking to goals `choose_preferences` and `satisfy`. Backtracking of goal `choose_preferences` implements the relaxation of the optional preferences of our solution strategy, supplying sets of `OptionalPreferences` in some intended order of relevance, specified by the user. Backtracking of goal `satisfy` returns acceptable scenarios. This predicate is defined as follows:

```
satisfy(Threshold, Xijk_List, OtherConstraints, Solutions):-
   assert(so_far([])),
   impose(OtherConstraints),
   instantiate(Xijk_List),
   cost(Xijk_List, Cost),
   check(Threshold, Cost,Xijk_List),
   fail.
satisfy (Threshold, Xijk_List, _, Solutions):-
   retractall(so_far(Solutions)).
```

```
check(Threshold, Cost, Xijk_List) :-
   Cost < Threshold,
   so_far(Solutions),
   append(Xijk_ist), Solutions, NewSolutions),
   retractall(so_far(_)),
   assert(so_far(NewSolutions)).
```

The execution of goal satisfy imposes the satisfaction of OtherConstraints (by recursive use of meta-predicate call, not shown) and computes the Cost of all scenarios meeting the constraints (using values in the range 0..3 for variables Xijk not yet instantiated by the constraints). These scenarios are then checked for its cost and those that do not exceed the Threshold are accumulated as Solutions (by means of assertions and retractions of predicate so_far, initialized with the empty list). The first satisfy clause is forced to backtrack and the solutions are collected by the second clause.

Predicate choose_preferences supplies, through backtracking, sets of preferences in an order defined by the user. Without going into details, this is achieved by means of a combination of extra-logical features, namely

a. a repeat-cut combination to control backtracking,

b. an assert-retract combination to memorize the summed weight of the last selected set of preferences. When this weight is zero (i.e. the relaxation is maximum and no preferences were selected) the cut prevents further backtracking.

```
choose_preferences(Xijk_List, Selected):-
   Options =
      [pref5(Xijk_List) ww 8, pref4(Xijk_List) ww 4,
       pref6(Xijk_List) ww 2, pref3(Xijk_List) ww 1],
   assert(weight(100)),
   repeat,
   retract(weight(MaxWeight)),
   select(Options, 0, MaxWeight, Selected, NewWeight),
   (NewWeight = 0, !  ; assert(weight(NewWeight))).

select([First ww W|OtherPrefs], SoFar, Max, Selected, New):-
   W + SoFar >= Max,
   select(OtherPrefs, SoFar, Max, Selected, New).
select([First ww W|OtherPrefs], SoFar, Max,[First|Other],New):-
   W + SoFar < Max,
   select(OtherPrefs, W + WeightSoFar, Max, Other,New).
select([], SoFar, Max, [], SoFar).
```

Notice again the use of the meta-level facilities of CLP(R) that allow the reasoning about models (higher level concepts) in a similar way to object variables. We assume that the user can rank the optional preferences according to some qualitative criteria and weight them by means of the user-defined operator ww (pref5 is the most relevant with weight 8 and pref3 is the least with weight 1). Hence, meta-level programming allows the reasoning about preferences (higher level concepts that encapsulate models of object-level variables) with the same formalisms used with the object variables themselves.

Selection of preferences for each backtracking execution of `choose_preferences` is performed by goal `select`. This recursively defined predicate returns a list of preferences with a certain summed weight (the last two parameters) given a list of preferences still available, the summed weight of preferences already made (initially zero) and a value that the summed weight of the whole preferences may not reach (the first 3 parameters). Recursion of the goal terminates when it traverses the whole list of `OptionalPreferences`.

The code shown implements an eager selection strategy. If the weight of the highest not yet considered preference summed up to those of the already selected preferences does not reach the maximum allowed, the preference is immediately selected. In general, this eager selection is only complete (it produces all possible combinations of preferences) if the weight of each preference is greater than the sum of the weights of all less relevant preferences. In our case the weights 8, 4, 2, 1 meet this requirement (see next section for more details). In more complex problems, the exponential number of combinations forced by a complete strategy might be not usable. In any case, by adjusting the weights of the preferences the decision maker might implement some intended heuristics for the selection of the preferences.

Of course, still other strategies for preference selection could have been used. For example, a more formalized implementation of preferences has been proposed by Borning et al. (1989), that is able to build constraint hierarchies by assigning labels (such as strong_prefer and weak_prefer) to preferences and provide a set of methods (globally-better, locally-better, worst-case-better, etc.) to judge the quality of solutions. In other problems the modeling of qualitative aspects by means of ranking the preferences might not be convenient. In particular, a more interactive approach could ask the user which optional preferences should be enforced. Here again, the extensions of logic programming provided by CLP(R) can be very useful. Some of the object-level `Xijk` variables might be already constrained, and this fact can be used by the decision maker to help in the selection of scenarios. For example, if the combination of mandatory and already selected optional constraints enforce that a variable `X` is greater than 2, the user is shown this constraint as `X > 2` (or in a more convenient way with a sophisticated interface/dialog subsystem), and eliminate from consideration preferences that violate this constraint.

3.5 Fifth Step: Evaluation of Results

The purpose of this evaluation step is twofold. On the one hand, we briefly report on the results obtained with the small EDSS prototype presented in the previous subsections. On the other hand, these results are compared with those that could be obtained following other alternative approaches.

To begin with, a `Threshold = 925` was fixed as the maximum cost of an acceptable solution. This fixed threshold could have been imposed as a mandatory constraint of the application. More generally, it can be estimated possibly by use of other software tools. In our case, we have firstly used a simplified version of the problem, that could be input (all constraints were conjunctions and no preferences were used) to the software package QSB (Quantitative Systems for Business) developed by Chang and Sullivan (1986). Using the integer linear programming facilities of this tool, we have obtained a minimum cost of 919. The value of 925 was then used allowing some margin for the preferences that we had further to include[6]. Of course, other approaches could be used relying solely on CLP(R). For example, the threshold could be initialized to a large number and change dynamically as more cost effective solutions are found.

As to the relaxation of the preferences, weights of 8, 4, 2 and 1 were used for preferences 5, 4, 6 and 3, respectively (lecturer of course 5 will very likely fail to teach on Saturdays — `pref5`, whereas lecturer of course 1 seemed only vaguely interested in having most of his classes on LAB-1 on Tuesdays — `pref3`). As mentioned earlier, all preferences are imposed initially (summed weight, `SW = 8 + 4 + 2 + 1 = 15`). The relaxation of preferences that follows tries next preferences 5, 4 and 3 (`SW = 14`), then 5, 4 and 3 (`SW = 13`), then 5 and 4 (`SW = 12`), etc. Given the small size of the problem and its illustrative purposes we have decided to use this weighting scheme which is complete.

When we first run the problem with all the optional preferences imposed (`SW = 15`), no solution was produced within the specified cost threshold. Two solutions, both with the same cost (925) were obtained when the preferences were relaxed and preference 3 was dropped (`SW = 14`). Since, we hoped to obtained better costs, the preferences were relaxed further but no solutions were obtained dropping preference 6 alone (`SW = 13`). When both preferences 3 and 6 were dropped afterwards (`SW = 12`), three solutions were obtained, the previous 2 solutions when preference 3 was dropped alone, plus a new and cheaper one costing 920 (that we denote by solution A). When we proceeded further, we have verified that dropping preference 4 alone would produce no solution. Then dropping preferences 4 and 3 (`SW = 10`) we have obtained several solutions, one having cost 919 (denoted as solution B). We could have stopped here, since we knew that this was a minimum, from our previous use of QSB. Nevertheless, we proceeded the relaxation process, and imposing preference 5 alone (`SW = 8`) a different solution (solution C) with cost 919 was obtained. Other distinct solutions obtained with lower `SW`s did not have such low cost.

At this point we notice an important difference between our approach and approaches used by conventional packages, namely those aiming at optimizing objective functions. Whereas our prototype was able to find two minimum cost solutions, QSB was only able to provide one. The existence of conflicting goals in multiple criteria problems, makes the provision of alternative solutions an important asset.

For example, comparing solutions A and B, with almost equal costs (920 vs. 919), the decision maker might prefer a slightly more expensive solution (A) that nevertheless satisfies a more important preference (preference 4 vs. preference 6). On the other hand, between solutions B and C, with equal cost, one is likely to prefer solution B since it satisfies all the optional preferences that solution C satisfies (preference 5), and still satisfies an additional one (preference 6). Even so, a closer inspection of the solutions show that, though none of the solutions satisfies preference 3 (that course 1 has 2 hours of class in LAB-1 on Tuesdays), solution C nevertheless assigns 2 hours of class on Tuesdays (though in LAB-2), whereas solution B only assigns one hour. Although partially satisfied preferences were not considered in our system, the decision maker might, for these and other reasons, end up preferring solution C.

The lesson to take from this example is that our EDSS approach provides a rich and

[6]Though we have not integrated CLP with the QSB package, we think that, notwithstanding the limitations explained in section 2, a loose coupling can be useful.

flexible and adaptive model, lending itself to an easy interaction with the decision maker that must, in the end, make the decisions. The subtleties involved even in a small problem such as the one we have been using, illustrate the difficulty of specifying complete and accurately all the intentions of the decision maker. Hence, the ability of constraint logic programming languages to supply the decision maker with alternative solutions, sieved from the enormous amount of potential scenarios by means of constraint specifications, is an important asset of our approach.

Of course, efficiency is also an important aspect decision maker are concerned with. At this stage we feel that comparisons between the absolute speed (CPU time or similar measure) between CLP(R) systems and more conventional ones are not fair, since our CLP(R) demo version is just that -- a demo version. Newer releases of CLP(R) due for the end of this year (Jaffar, personal communication) might allow a fairer comparison.

An important aspect regarding efficiency is the handling of disjunctions. The ability to express disjunctions in a natural way is an important asset of constraint logic programming. Iteration of traditional tools with alternative values might, of course, be performed and results obtained with different executions of the tools collected. Nevertheless, we think that the incremental character of constraint solving techniques embedded in CLP languages[7], combined with a careful ordering of the constraints (as illustrated in the previous subsection) is a very powerful feature of these languages to be used in EDSS implementation.

4 Conclusion

This paper discussed the integration of DSS and ES features for the implementation of EDSS systems. In particular it focussed EDSS development by means of constraint logic programming languages, combining paradigms of AI-ES (logic programming) and DSS-OR (constraint satisfaction). We discussed the merits of this deeper integration, compared with the simple coupling of existing programs and tools that implement each of the paradigms alone. Our example of a classroom allocation problem illustrates some of the advantages of this approach.

Other points were not addressed and deserve further study, most noticeably, efficiency. The constraint solver used by the constraint logic programming is a key factor for efficiency. Although only general purpose constraint solvers have been studied in the context of constraint logic programming, specialized and more efficient constraint solvers might have to be developed to be used with CLP languages, either implicitly or explicitly called by the user.

Acknowledgements

We wish to thank the members of the Logic Programming and Artificial Intelligence Group (GPLIA) of Universidade Nova de Lisboa for all the support given. This research was supported by the Gabinete de Filosofia do Conhecimento.

---

[7]See Jaffar and Michaylov (1987) for a thorough discussion.

References

BENNET, J.L. (1983), *Building Decision Support Systems*, Addison-Wesley, Reading, MA.

BETTIN, M. (1985), *A Heuristic Algorithm For Constructing University Timetables On Microcomputers*, Conference on O.R. Models in Microcomputers, Lisbon.

BORNING, A., MAHER, M., MARTINDALE, A., and WILSON, M. (1989), *Constraint Hierarchies and Logic Programming*, Sixth International Conference of Logic Programming, Lisbon, MIT Press.

CHANG, Y.-L., and SULLIVAN, R.S. (1986), *Quantitative Systems for Business*, Prentice-Hall, Englewood Cliffs, NJ.

COLMERAUER, A. (1987), Opening the PROLOG III Universe, *BYTE magazine, Special Issue on Logic Programming, August*.

DE WERRA, D. (1985), An Introduction to Timetabling, *European Journal of Operational Research, 19*, North-Holland, Amsterdam.

DINCBAS, M., VAN HENTENRYNCK, P., SIMONIS, H., AGGOUN, A., GRAF, T., and BERTHIER, F. (1988), *The Constraint Logic Programming Language CHIP*, Proc. of the FGCS '88 Conference, Tokio, Japan.

HEINTZE, N., JAFFAR, J., MICHAYLOV, S., STUCKEY, P., and YAP, R. (1987), *The CLP(R) Programmer's Manual*, Department of Computer Science, Monash University, Australia.

JAFFAR, J., and MICHAYLOV, S. (1987), *Methodology and Implementation of a CLP System*, Fourth International Conference of Logic Programming, Melbourne, MIT Press.

JELASSI, T.M., and OZERNAY, V.M. (1988), *A Framework for Building an Expert System for MCDM Models Selection*, Eight International Conference on Multiple Criteria Decision Making, Manchester, England.

MINCH, R.P. (1989), Logic Programming as a Paradigm for Financial Modeling, *MIS Quarterly, March*.

RIBEIRO, R., and BARAHONA, P. (1989), *Constraints in Logic Programming or Logic in Constraint Programming?*, presented at the Euro-Summer Institute, Funchal, Portugal.

SEN, A., and BISWAS, G. (1985), Decision Support Systems: an Expert System Approach, *Decision Support Systems, 1*, North-Holland.

TURBAN, E. (1988), *Decision Support and Expert Systems*, MacMillan Publishing Company, New York.

Space Management Support Systems: From SH.A.R.P. to M.E.S.s?[1]

Alain Bultez
Catholic University of Mons (FUCAM)
and
European Institute for Advanced Studies in Management
Brussels, Belgium

Summary

During the eighties, the number of new package goods introduced per year on the market increased tenfold, while the store space available to display them remained virtually flat. "The race for space is the new frontier of marketing" (Hapoienu (1989)). Consequently and as predicted by basic economics, space is regarded as a rare commodity, rented by retailers at a raising price. "Slotting allowances" and "stocking fees" are getting charged by the store keepers to the suppliers who want to have their products stocked on the outlet shelves. Hence supermarkets are caricatured as the "pile it high, sell it cheap" (Ashby (1989)) landlords of the distribution channels (Flanagan (1989)).

This recent trend combined with the possibility of gathering check-out data through UPC scanning systems has stimulated the management scientists' interest for designing intelligent space-management decision support tools. The SH.A.R.P. model, recently developed and tested by Bultez et al. (1988, 1989), is extended here to encompass shoppers' hierarchically structured product-choice behavior. Normative implications are explored and expressed in situation-action merchandising rules.

1 Introduction

Commenting upon a recently published article, co-authored by Bultez and Naert (1988), Curry (1989) states: "Market basket models are being developed so that retailers can manage store space intelligently ... The trend is to adopt a demand framework incorporating direct- and cross-elasticities, in order to model share within and across logical product divisions as well as to model overall volume".

Building upon the work of Anderson and Amato (1974), Anderson (1979), and Corstjens and Doyle (1981), Bultez et al. (1988 and 1989) have indeed studied how a retailer seeking to maximize the total profit, flowing from one of the merchandise lines he carries, should allocate the display area available, S. Their approach concentrates on the items' sales responses to their own, as well as to their substitutes', visibility on the store shelves. Thus they tackle explicitly the cannibalism resulting from the depth of retail assortments.

[1]SH.A.R.P.: SHelf Allocation for Retailers's Profit. M.E.S.s.: Merchandising Expert Systems. Using the abbreviation M.E.S.s. is not meant to offend (true) expert-system experts but reflects the exact self-evaluation of my own (incapacity-driven) biases. It is also intended to evoke the puzzling questions and doubts that available commercial merchandising packages elicit in a skeptical mind.

NATO ASI Series, Vol. F 61
Knowledge, Data and Computer-Assisted Decisions
Edited by M. Schader and W. Gaul

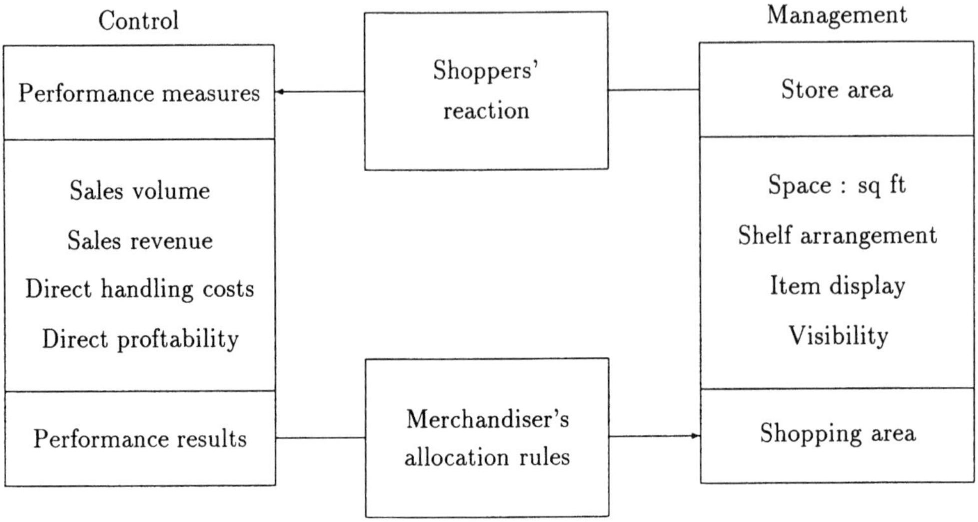

Figure 1: Merchandising and the Jobber

The merchandiser's job can be viewed as in Fig. 1.

It consists in a systematic tracking of sales volumes, revenues and DPC leading to frequent reallocations which in turn result in performance variations. With more than 26,000 items listed in a typical supermarket, this can hardly be done without computers and adequate software. But despite the celebrated revolution of retail audit, facilitated by UPC scanning and the concept of single-source reports (Little (1988)), the most sophisticated space-management commercial packages simply overlook sales responses. They just help merchandisers in the passive control of performance (measurement) and in visualizing the impact of reallocations on the store configuration and shelf arrangement: "Management can trade space on-screen between sections, can identify problem areas that exhibit slow movement, low profit, or frequent out-of-stocks, and can reallocate space according to one of several available criteria (e.g., profit-to-space ratios or direct product profitability)", notes Curry (1989). But no explicit shopping feedback relates space reallocations to performance forecasts or observations.

Academics, however, have precisely addressed the modelling and measurement of that feedback; furthermore, they have devised allocation rules consistent with optimization objectives. Without recourse to restrictive assumptions regarding the shoppers' behavior, Bultez and Naert (1988) consider that any item's—identified hereafter by the (b, v, d)-triple subscript—sales volume, q_{bvd}, does not only depend on its own visibility, hence on the space allocated to itself, s_{bvd}, but may also depend on any other item's display. Defining an item's contribution to profit as the difference between the margin generated by its sales, $g_{bvd}q_{bvd}$, and the cost, C_{bvd}, that its handling entails, they prove that the optimal repartition of the space available for the display of the merchandise line must satisfy,

$$\sigma_{bvd} = s_{bvd}/S = (\gamma_{bvd}\, c_{bvd} + \overline{\eta}_{bvd})/(G + \bar{N}) \tag{1}$$

for all b's, v's and d's, and where:

σ_{bvd} is the share of the display area to be allocated to the (b,v,d)-th item;

$c_{bvd} = C_{bvd}/\Pi$ is the ratio of the replenishment cost resulting from carrying the item to the assortment overall profitability (Π differs from the actual profit in that the marginal handling cost gets substituted for its average);

γ_{bvd} stands for the absolute value of the partial elasticity of the item's handling cost w.r.t. the space allocated to it (at a constant sales volume);

$\overline{\eta}_{bvd} = \sum_i \sum_j \sum_k r_{ijk}\, \eta(q_{ijk}, s_{bvd})$ is the weighted mean of all item's sales elasticities, $\eta(q_{ijk}, s_{bvd})$, w.r.t. the space allocated to the (b,v,d)-th item, with $r_{ijk} = \pi_{ijk}/\Pi$, the relative contribution of the (i,j,k)-th item to the assortment profitability;

$\bar{N} = \sum_i \sum_j \sum_k \overline{\eta}_{ijk}$ and $G = \sum_i \sum_j \sum_k \gamma_{ijk}\, c_{ijk}$ are the normalizing terms.

The replenishment cost is assumed to be an increasing function of the sales-to-space ratio,

$$C_{bvd} = f_{bvd}(q_{bvd}/s_{bvd}), \tag{2}$$

with a non-negative first-derivative w.r.t. the ratio: $f'_{bvd} \geq 0$.

Although those optimality conditions may apply to a variety of merchandise lines, Bultez et al. have exclusively worked on lines of substitute items, meeting basically the same consumer needs. Hence the explicit specifications of the sales response functions used to model demand interactions (cross-elasticities) either assume perfectly symmetric patterns of substitution, or limit the sources of asymmetries to a single one.

Here we integrate into Bultez et al.'s approach a shopping model which generalizes those tested so far. The extension suggested allows the analysis of merchandise lines which are perceived hierarchically nested by the shoppers. Previously derived optimization formula are then revised accordingly.

Capitalizing on this generalization and results previously obtained, a set of practical space-management rules are inferred from the theoretical framework developed.

2 Shopping Model Specification

Many facets of the consumer's behavior—especially taste preferences, variety seeking, quantity consumption habits, brand loyalty, multi-attribute comparative evaluation of alternatives, etc.—concur in the perceptual differentiation of the substitutes making up a product category. All together they shape the substitution patterns and inflect the degree of cannibalism within (and sometimes across) the merchandise lines carried by retailers.

Three dimensions generally suffice to identify specifically each of the items constituting an assortment: e.g., each "stock-keeping unit" (hereafter, sku) can be defined unambiguously by its packaging (form and/or size), its variety type and its brand name[2]. Therefore, the item selection operation, conducted by a shopper facing the shelf on which the assortment is displayed, can be described as a three-step hierarchically structured process. The purchaser refers first to the attribute perceived as the most salient dimension

[2]In the retailers' jargon, the sku is the lowest level of identification of a merchandise for inventory management purpose.

along which the assortment may be partitioned into various broad classes: $d \in D$ where $D = \{1, 2, \ldots, n\}$. Focusing next on the class of items opted for at the first stage (say d, for small package size), the shopper subdivides it into clusters according to the second dimension (attribute) which retains her/his attention: $v \in V_d$ where $V_d = \{1, 2, \ldots, n_d\}$. Once a specific cluster has been chosen at the second stage (say vd, for the v-th variety in small package size), the shopper picks one of the skus among those belonging to that same cluster: $b \in B_{vd}$ where $B_{vd} = \{1, 2, \ldots, n_{vd}\}$, which are distinguished from one another by the third dimension (say the brand attribute).

Aggregating shoppers' purchases, the sales volume of the (b, v, d)-th sku can be determined by

$$q_{bvd} = Q\, m_{bvd},$$

where Q stands for the merchandise-line total volume,

$$Q = \sum_b \sum_v \sum_d q_{bvd};$$

and m_{bvd} denotes the share of the (b, v, d)-th sku in the line total sales volume. In parallel to the shopper's stepwise selection of an sku, this share can be decomposed into three factors,

$$m_{bvd} = M_d\, \mu_{v|d}\, \mu_{b|vd} \tag{3}$$

defined respectively as follows,

$\mu_{b|vd}$: Share of the sales volume accounted for by the b-th sku, calculated in relation to the cluster of skus determined at the 3rd choice-level by the v-th and d-th alternatives on the attributes scanned by the consumer at the 2nd and 1st choice-levels, respectively; i.e., $\mu_{b|vd} = q_{bvd}/Q_{.vd}$, with $Q_{.vd} = \sum_i q_{ivd}$.

$\mu_{v|d}$: Share of the sales volume accounted for by the v-th cluster of skus, calculated in relation to the class of items determined at the 2nd choice-level by the d-th alternative on the attribute considered by the consumer at the 1st choice-level; i.e., $\mu_{v|d} = Q_{.vd}/Q_{..d}$, with $Q_{..d} = \sum_j Q_{.jd}$.

M_d: Overall share of the assortment total sales volume captured by all items belonging to the d-th alternative class resulting from the partition of the product-category according to the 1st attribute reviewed by the consumer; i.e., $M_d = Q_{..d}/Q$, with $Q = \sum_k Q_{..k}$.

Thus, while the m's and M's denote marginal shares of the total sales volume, the μ's represent conditional shares of clusters' subtotals.

Of course, the display of the items on the supermarket shelves may differentially influence the shopper's choice at the various stages of the selection process he works through. The more substitutable the skus are perceived to be, the more sensitive the consumer is to their visibility. Hence it seems natural to introduce the response to product visibility primarily at the 3rd stage of the choice process: first, within the most homogeneous clusters of skus. But the specification of the competitive interactions at work here requires logically consistent formulations (see Weverbergh, Naert and Bultez (1981)), i.e. satisfying the following constraints:

$$0 \leq \{\mu_{b|vd}, \mu_{v|d}, M_d, m_{bvd}\} \leq 1$$

and

$$\sum_b \mu_{b|vd} = \sum_v \mu_{v|d} = \sum_d M_d = \sum_b \sum_v \sum_d m_{bvd} = 1.$$

The market-share attraction model[3] reveals to be the appropriately robust kernel. Transposed at the 3rd choice-level it can be expressed as

$$\mu_{b|vd} = a_{bvd} \Big/ \sum_{i \in B_{vd}} a_{ivd}, \tag{4}$$

where the attraction of the (b, v, d)-th sku is given by

$$a_{bvd} = \alpha_{bvd}\, s_{bvd}^{\beta}, \tag{5}$$

with

> s_{bvd}: the sku's visibility,
>
> $\alpha_{bvd} \geq 0$, the parameters reflecting the consumer's relative preferences for the various substitutable skus;
>
> $\beta \geq 0$, the parameter modulating the incidence of the skus' visibility on the shopper's choice and thereby determining the ferocity of cannibalism within clusters.

Following the sequential dependence pattern determined by the assumed choice process and illustrated in Fig. 2, the sales repartition between clusters can be also derived from the same core-function, i.e.

$$\mu_{v|d} = \varphi_{vd}\, A_{.vd}^{(1-\theta_2)} \Big/ \sum_{j \in V_d} \varphi_{jd}\, A_{.jd}^{(1-\theta_2)}, \tag{6}$$

with $A_{.vd} = \sum_{b \in B_{vd}} a_{bvd}$, the total attraction exerted by the (v, d)-th cluster on the shopper's attention; and $0 \leq \theta_2 \leq 1$, the parameter governing the degree of substitutability across clusters. Analogously, at the 1st choice-level the sales distribution between product classes can be modelled by

$$M_d = \phi_d A_{..d}^{(1-\theta_1)} \Big/ \sum_{k \in D} \phi_k A_{..k}^{(1-\theta_1)}, \tag{7}$$

where $A_{..d} = \sum_{v \in V_d} \varphi_{vd}\, A_{.vd}^{(1-\theta_2)}$ represents the overall attraction exerted by all the items constituting the d-th product class. Integrating (4) to (7) in the definition of the (b, v, d)-th sku's sales share (3), the suggested model sums up to

$$m_{bvd} = \frac{\phi_d\, A_{..d}^{(1-\theta_1)}}{\sum_{k \in D} \phi_k\, A_{..k}^{(1-\theta_1)}} \times \frac{\varphi_{vd}\, A_{.vd}^{(1-\theta_2)}}{\sum_{j \in V_d} \varphi_{jd}\, A_{.jd}^{(1-\theta_2)}} \times \frac{\alpha_{bvd}\, s_{bvd}^{\beta}}{\sum_{i \in B_{vd}} \alpha_{ivd}\, s_{ivd}^{\beta}}, \tag{8}$$

a formulation which can in fact be related to the multinomial nested logit. Given the definitions of $A_{.vd}$ and $A_{..d}$, it can be simplified to

$$m_{bvd} = \left[(\alpha_{bvd}\, \varphi_{vd}\, \phi_d)\, s_{bvd}^{\beta}\, A_{.vd}^{-\theta_2}\, A_{..d}^{-\theta_1} \right] \Big/ \sum_{k \in D} \phi_k\, A_{..k}^{(1-\theta_1)}, \tag{9}$$

[3]Named after Bultez and Naert (1975), Little et al. (1975) and Bultez (1978), but also known as the MCI (Multiple Competitive Interactions) model according to Nakanishi and Cooper (1974).

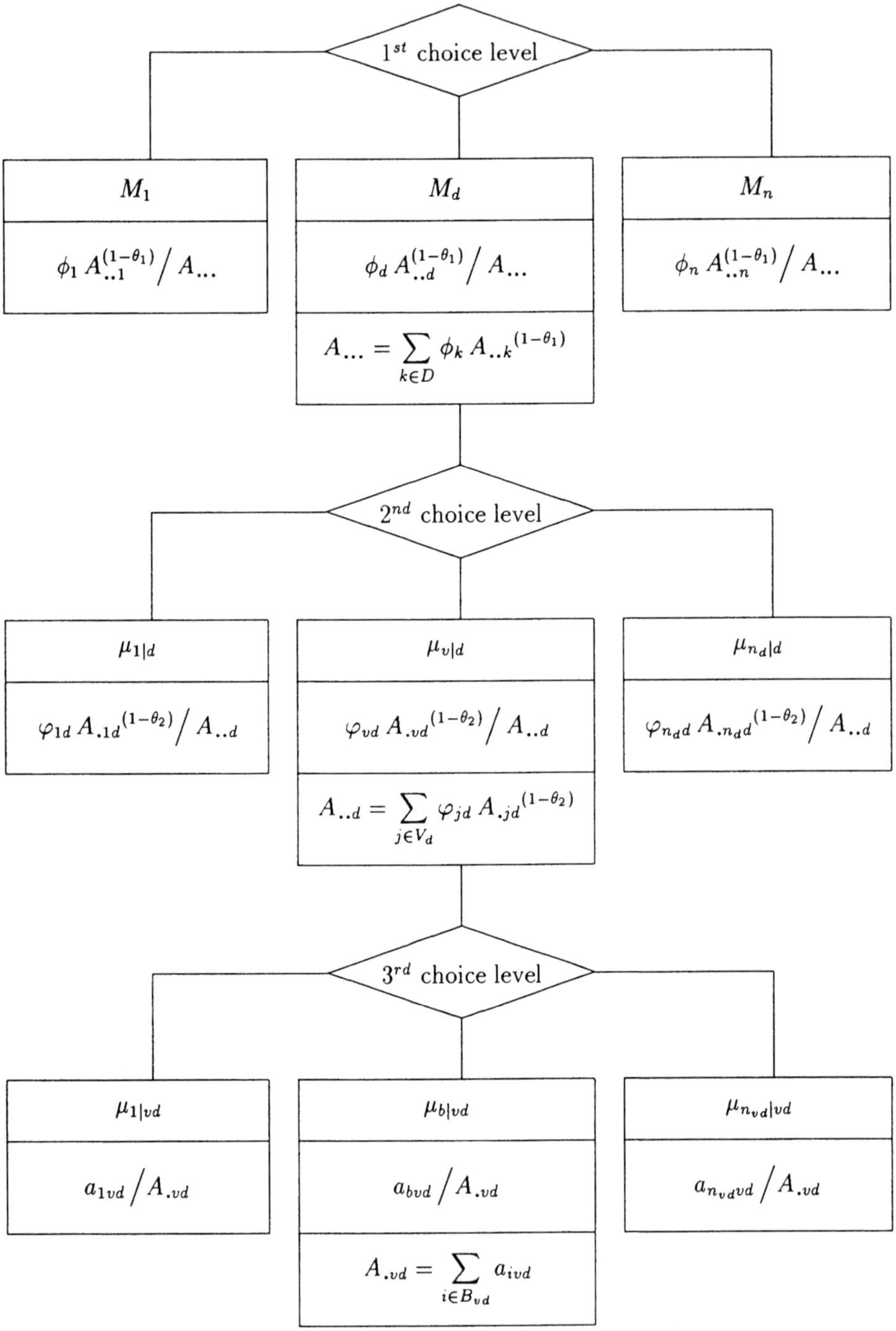

Figure 2: Model Tree-Structure Based on the Hierarchical Consumer Choice

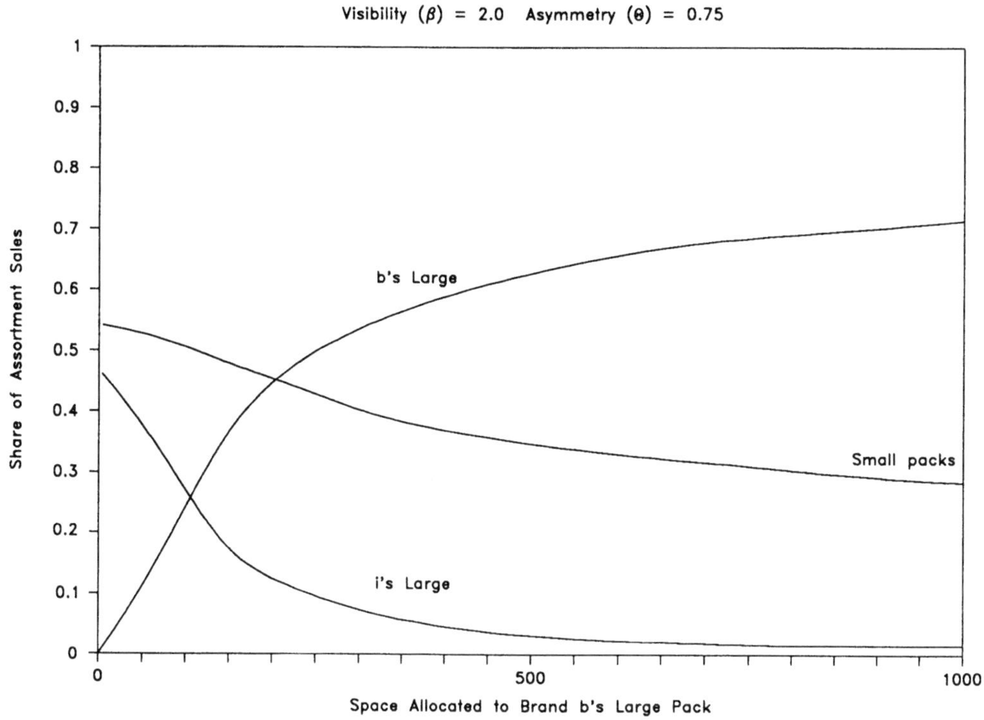

Figure 3: Sales Distribution

an extended variant of the asymmetric specification proposed by Bultez et al. (1989). It is obvious that it reduces to the simple attraction model when $\theta_1 = \theta_2 = 0$,

$$m_{bvd}(\theta_1 = \theta_2 = 0) = \alpha^*_{bvd}\, s^{\beta}_{bvd} \Big/ \sum_k \sum_j \sum_i \alpha^*_{ijk}\, s^{\beta}_{ijk} \tag{10}$$

where: $\alpha^*_{bvd} = \phi_d\, \varphi_{vd}\, \alpha_{bvd}$. At the other extreme, when $\theta_1 = \theta_2 = 1$, model (8) becomes

$$m_{bvd}(\theta_1 = \theta_2 = 1) = \phi^*_d\, \varphi^*_{vd}\, \alpha_{bvd}\, s^{\beta}_{bvd} \Big/ \sum_i \alpha_{ivd}\, s^{\beta}_{ivd} \tag{11}$$

where: ϕ^*_d and φ^*_{vd} are the normalized values of ϕ_d and φ_{vd}, respectively. Although looking very much alike, (10) and (11) have totally opposite meanings: (10) expresses that skus' sales are fully interdependent (only the consumer's intrinsic preferences, reflected in the α^*_{bvd}'s, can limit their substitutability), while (11) indicates that the cannibalism, that space reallocations foster, is strictly restricted to each cluster's boundaries. Those implications should come as no great surprise since the introduction of the θ's in the specification is intended to modulate the degree of cannibalism across clusters and subclasses within a given retail assortment.

Fig. 3 illustrates the incidence of the asymmetry parameters, θ_1 and θ_2, on the substitutability of items within the assortment. The graphs are obtained for a 2-level choice process; thus, only two dimensions mould the shoppers' perceptions: first, the package size (large vs. small packs) and second, the brand (i vs. b). Brand b's large pack is assumed to become more and more visible, while the display of the other items in the merchandise-line considered remains unchanged. Due to the primary clustering of items according to the package size attribute, the resulting increase in the sales of brand b's large pack comes more at the expense of brand i's large pack than at the expense of brand b's and i's small packs.

3 Optimal Space Allocation

Applying (1) postulates the definition of the sales direct- and cross-elasticities, which enter in the determination of the $\overline{\eta}_{bvd}$-terms.

3.1 Underlying Cross-Elasticities

Applying the logarithmic transformation to (3) gives

$$\ln m_{ijk} = \ln \mu_{i|jk} + \ln \mu_{j|k} + \ln M_k$$

and differentiating yields,

$$\frac{1}{m_{ijk}} \frac{\partial m_{ijk}}{\partial s_{bvd}} = \frac{1}{\mu_{i|jk}} \frac{\partial \mu_{i|jk}}{\partial s_{bvd}} + \frac{1}{\mu_{j|k}} \frac{\partial \mu_{j|k}}{\partial s_{bvd}} + \frac{1}{M_k} \frac{\partial M_k}{\partial s_{bvd}}.$$

Multiplying all through by s_{bvd}, one establishes the additivity of the sales-shares elasticities across the various hierarchical choice-levels, i.e.

$$\eta(m_{ijk}, s_{bvd}) = \eta(\mu_{i|jk}, s_{bvd}) + \eta(\mu_{j|k}, s_{bvd}) + \eta(M_k, s_{bvd}).$$

Working backwards (bottom-up) let us examine the interactions prevailing among the most conditional options first, i.e.

$$\eta(\mu_{i|jk}, s_{bvd}) = s_{bvd} \frac{\partial \ln \mu_{i|jk}}{\partial s_{bvd}} = s_{bvd} \frac{\partial}{\partial s_{bvd}} \left(\ln a_{ijk} - \ln A_{.jk} \right)$$

We realize that[4]

$$\frac{\partial \ln a_{ijk}}{\partial s_{bvd}} = \delta_{ib}\, \delta_{jv}\, \delta_{kd}\, (\beta / a_{bvd})(\alpha_{bvd}\, s_{bvd}^{\beta-1}) = \delta_{ib}\, \delta_{jv}\, \delta_{kd}\, (\beta / s_{bvd})$$

and

$$\frac{\partial \ln A_{.jk}}{\partial s_{bvd}} = \frac{1}{A_{.jk}} \sum_i \frac{\partial a_{ijk}}{\partial s_{bvd}} = \frac{\delta_{jv}\, \delta_{kd}\, \beta}{A_{.jk}\, s_{bvd}} \sum_i \delta_{ib}\, a_{ijk},$$

or

$$\frac{\partial \ln A_{.jk}}{\partial s_{bvd}} = \delta_{jv}\, \delta_{kd} \frac{\beta}{s_{bvd}} \frac{a_{bjk}}{A_{.jk}} = \delta_{jv}\, \delta_{kd}\, (\beta / s_{bvd})\, \mu_{b|jk},$$

which can also be rewritten

$$\frac{\partial \ln A_{.jk}}{\partial s_{bvd}} = \delta_{jv}\, \delta_{kd}\, \mu_{b|vd}\, (\beta / s_{bvd}). \tag{12}$$

[4]The δ's are the usual Kronecker's binary variables.

Hence we obtain

$$\eta(\mu_{i|jk}, s_{bvd}) = \delta_{jv}\, \delta_{kd}\, \beta\, (\delta_{ib} - \mu_{b|vd}). \tag{13}$$

Turning to the 2nd choice-level, we observe analogously that

$$\eta(\mu_{i|jk}, s_{bvd}) = s_{bvd} \frac{\partial}{\partial s_{bvd}} \left(\ln \varphi_{jk} + (1-\theta_2) \ln A_{.jk} - \ln A_{..k} \right), \tag{14}$$

and

$$\begin{aligned} \frac{\partial \ln A_{..k}}{\partial s_{bvd}} &= \frac{1}{A_{..k}} \sum_j \varphi_{jk} \frac{\partial A_{.jk}^{(1-\theta_2)}}{\partial s_{bvd}} = \frac{(1-\theta_2)}{A_{..k}} \sum_j \varphi_{jk}\, A_{.jk}^{-\theta_2} \frac{\partial A_{.jk}}{\partial s_{bvd}} \\ &= (1-\theta_2) \sum_j \frac{\varphi_{jk}\, A_{.jk}^{(1-\theta_2)}}{A_{..k}} \left(\frac{1}{A_{.jk}} \frac{\partial A_{.jk}}{\partial s_{bvd}} \right) \\ &= (1-\theta_2) \sum_j \mu_{j|k} \left(\frac{\partial \ln A_{.jk}}{\partial s_{bvd}} \right). \end{aligned}$$

Using (12), we get

$$\begin{aligned} \frac{\partial \ln A_{..k}}{\partial s_{bvd}} &= (1-\theta_2)\, \delta_{kd}\, \mu_{b|vd}\, (\beta / s_{bvd}) \sum_j \delta_{jv}\, \mu_{j|k} \\ &= \delta_{kd}\, (1-\theta_2)\, \mu_{b|vd}\, \mu_{v|d}\, (\beta / s_{bvd}). \end{aligned} \tag{15}$$

Substituting (12) and (15) into (14), the general expression for the cross-elasticities relevant to the 2nd choice-level becomes

$$\eta(\mu_{j|k}, s_{bvd}) = \delta_{kd}\, (1-\theta_2)\, \beta\, \mu_{b|vd}\, (\delta_{jv} - \mu_{v|d}). \tag{16}$$

Finally, at the 1st choice-level, we consider

$$\eta(M_k, s_{bvd}) = s_{bvd} \frac{\partial}{\partial s_{bvd}} (\ln \phi_k + (1-\theta_1) \ln A_{..k} - \ln A_{...}) \tag{17}$$

and similarly to hereabove,

$$\begin{aligned} \frac{\partial \ln A_{...}}{\partial s_{bvd}} &= \frac{1}{A_{...}} \sum_k \phi_k \frac{\partial A_{..k}^{(1-\theta_1)}}{\partial s_{bvd}} = \frac{(1-\theta_1)}{A_{...}} \sum_k \phi_k A_{..k}^{-\theta_1} \frac{\partial A_{..k}}{\partial s_{bvd}} \\ &= (1-\theta_1) \sum_k M_k \left(\frac{1}{A_{..k}} \frac{\partial A_{..k}}{\partial s_{bvd}} \right) \\ &= (1-\theta_1) \sum_k M_k \left(\frac{\partial \ln A_{..k}}{\partial s_{bvd}} \right) \end{aligned}$$

Referring to (15), we see that

$$\begin{aligned} \frac{\partial \ln A_{...}}{\partial s_{bvd}} &= (1-\theta_1)(1-\theta_2)\, \mu_{b|vd}\, \mu_{v|d}\, (\beta / s_{bvd}) \sum_k \delta_{kd} M_k \\ &= (1-\theta_1)(1-\theta_2)\, \mu_{b|vd}\, \mu_{v|d}\, (\beta / s_{bvd}) M_d \end{aligned} \tag{18}$$

Substituting the latter result and (15) in (17), we ultimately obtain,

$$\eta(M_k, s_{bvd}) = (1-\theta_1)(1-\theta_2)\,\beta\,\mu_{b|vd}\,\mu_{v|d}\,(\delta_{kd} - M_d) \tag{19}$$

Summing up (13), (16) and (19), the cross-elasticities reflecting the cannibalism at the bottom choice-level can be deduced,

$$\begin{aligned} \eta(m_{ijk}, s_{bvd}) &= \beta\Big\{\delta_{kd}\,\delta_{jv}(\delta_{ib} - \mu_{b|vd}) \\ &\quad + (1-\theta_2)\,\mu_{b|vd}\Big[\delta_{kd}(\delta_{jv} - \mu_{v|d}) + (1-\theta_1)\mu_{v|d}(\delta_{kd} - M_d)\Big]\Big\} \end{aligned} \tag{20}$$

Expanding this expression,

$$\begin{aligned} \eta(m_{ijk}, s_{bvd}) &= \beta\Big\{\delta_{kd}\,\delta_{jv}\,\delta_{ib} - \delta_{kd}\,\delta_{jv}\,\mu_{b|vd} + \mu_{b|vd}\,\delta_{kd}\,\delta_{jv} \\ &\quad - \mu_{b|vd}\,\delta_{kd}\,\mu_{v|d} - \theta_2\,\delta_{kd}\,\delta_{jv}\,\mu_{b|vd} + \theta_2\,\mu_{b|vd}\,\delta_{kd}\,\mu_{v|d} \\ &\quad + (1-\theta_2)(1-\theta_1)\mu_{b|vd}\,\mu_{v|d}\,\delta_{kd} - (1-\theta_1)(1-\theta_2)\mu_{b|vd}\,\mu_{v|d}\,M_d\Big\} \end{aligned}$$

simplifying and regrouping terms,

$$\begin{aligned} \eta(m_{ijk}, s_{bvd}) &= \beta\Big\{\delta_{kd}\,\delta_{jv}\,\delta_{ib} - (1-\theta_1)(1-\theta_2)\,m_{bvd} \\ &\quad - \delta_{kd}\,\mu_{b|vd}\,\mu_{v|d}\,[1-\theta_2 - (1-\theta_2)(1-\theta_1)] - \theta_2\,\delta_{kd}\,\delta_{jv}\,\mu_{b|vd}\Big\}, \end{aligned}$$

and since $\mu_{b|vd}\,\mu_{v|d} = m_{bvd}/M_d$,

$$\begin{aligned} \eta(m_{ijk}, s_{bvd}) &= \beta\Big\{\delta_{kd}\,\delta_{jv}\,\delta_{ib} - (1-\theta_1)(1-\theta_2)\,m_{bvd} \\ &\quad - \theta_1(1-\theta_2)\,\delta_{kd}(m_{bvd}/M_d) - \theta_2\,\delta_{kd}\,\delta_{jv}\,\mu_{b|vd}\Big\}, \end{aligned}$$

or,

$$\begin{aligned} \eta(m_{ijk}, s_{bvd}) &= \beta\Big\{\delta_{kd}\,\delta_{jv}\,\delta_{ib} - (1-\theta_2)\,m_{bvd}\,[(1-\theta_1) + \theta_1(\delta_{kd}/M_d)] \\ &\quad - \theta_2\,\delta_{kd}\,\delta_{jv}\,\mu_{b|vd}\Big\}, \end{aligned}$$

and we ultimately arrive at the following essential result,

$$\begin{aligned} \eta(m_{ijk}, s_{bvd}) &= \beta\left\{\delta_{kd}\,\delta_{jv}\,\delta_{ib} - (1-\theta_2)\,m_{bvd}\left[1 + \theta_1\left(\frac{\delta_{kd} - M_d}{M_d}\right)\right]\right. \\ &\quad \left. - \theta_2\,\delta_{kd}\,\delta_{jv}\,\mu_{b|vd}\right\}. \end{aligned} \tag{21}$$

3.2 Optimization Rule

The weighted mean of all sales-elasticities with respect to the visibility of the (b, v, d)-th sku can be directly computed from (21), i.e.

$$\begin{aligned} \overline{\eta}_{bvd} &= \epsilon_{bvd} + \beta\left\{\sum_i\sum_j\sum_k r_{ijk}\,\delta_{kd}\,\delta_{jv}\,\delta_{iv} - (1-\theta_2)\,m_{bvd}\sum_i\sum_j\sum_k r_{ijk}\right. \\ &\quad - \theta_1(1-\theta_2)(m_{bvd}/M_d)\left[\sum_k \delta_{kd}\sum_i\sum_j r_{ijk} - M_d\sum_i\sum_j\sum_k r_{ijk}\right] \\ &\quad \left. - \theta_2\,\mu_{b|vd}\sum_k \delta_{kd}\sum_j \delta_{jv}\sum_i r_{ijk}\right\}, \end{aligned}$$

where: $\epsilon_{bvd} = (\partial Q/\partial s_{bvd})(s_{bvd}/Q) \geq 0$, measures the overall shopping-traffic attraction capacity of the sku.
As $\sum_i \sum_j \sum_k r_{ijk} = 1$ and letting: $R_k = \sum_i \sum_j r_{ijk}$ and $R_{.jk} = \sum_i r_{ijk}$, we get

$$\begin{aligned}\overline{\eta}_{bvd} &= \epsilon_{bvd} + \beta \Big[r_{bvd} - (1-\theta_2)m_{bvd} \\ &\quad - \theta_1(1-\theta_2)(m_{bvd}/M_d)(R_d - M_d) - \theta_2\, \mu_{b|vd}\, R_{.vd}\Big]\end{aligned}$$

or,

$$\begin{aligned}\overline{\eta}_{bvd} &= \epsilon_{bvd} + \beta \Big[(r_{bvd} - m_{bvd}) - \theta_1(1-\theta_2)(m_{bvd}/M_d)(R_d - M_d) \\ &\quad + \theta_2(m_{bvd} - \mu_{b|vd} R_{.vd})\Big]\end{aligned}$$

and substituting $m_{bvd}/M_{.vd}$ for $\mu_{b|vd}$,

$$\begin{aligned}\overline{\eta}_{bvd} &= \epsilon_{bvd} + \beta \left\{(r_{bvd} - m_{bvd}) - m_{bvd} \left[\theta_1(1-\theta_2)\left(\frac{R_d - M_d}{M_d}\right)\right.\right. \\ &\quad \left.\left. + \theta_2 \left(\frac{R_{.vd} - M_{.vd}}{M_{.vd}}\right)\right]\right\} \end{aligned} \tag{22}$$

The sum of those weighted means gives

$$\begin{aligned}\bar{N} = \sum_b \sum_v \sum_d \overline{\eta}_{bvd} &= E + \beta \left\{(1-1) - \theta_1(1-\theta_2)\sum_d \left(\frac{R_d - M_d}{M_d}\right) \sum_b \sum_v m_{bvd}\right. \\ &\quad \left. - \theta_2 \sum_v \sum_d \left(\frac{R_{.vd} - M_{.vd}}{M_{.vd}}\right) \sum_b m_{bvd}\right\},\end{aligned}$$

with: $E = \sum_b \sum_v \sum_d \epsilon_{bvd}$.
But since $\sum_b m_{bvd} = M_{.vd}$ and $\sum_b \sum_v m_{bvd} = M_d$, this sum reduces to

$$\bar{N} = E - \beta \left\{\theta_1(1-\theta_2)\sum_d (R_d - M_d) + \theta_2 \sum_v \sum_d (R_{.vd} - M_{.vd})\right\} = E.$$

From (22) and since $\bar{N} = E$, the space share to be allocated to the (b,v,d)-th sku is determined by (1),

$$\begin{aligned}\sigma_{bvd} &= c^*_{bvd} + \epsilon^*_{bvd} + \beta^* \left\{(r_{bvd} - m_{bvd}) - m_{bvd} \left[\theta_1(1-\theta_2)\left(\frac{R_d - M_d}{M_d}\right)\right.\right. \\ &\quad \left.\left. + \theta_2 \left(\frac{R_{.vd} - M_{.vd}}{M_{.vd}}\right)\right]\right\}, \end{aligned} \tag{23}$$

with $c^*_{bvd} = \gamma_{bvd} C_{bvd}/(G+E)$, $\epsilon^*_{bvd} = \epsilon_{bvd}/(G+E)$ and $\beta^* = \beta/(G+E)$.

3.3 Economic Interpretation

The general formula (23), regulating the repartition of the display area, appears quite complex at first sight. Yet its meaning can be clarified first by reviewing a few special cases.

Case I: **Full substitutability**. Setting $\theta_1 = \theta_2 = 0$ amounts to assuming that a unique pattern of interactions channels the cannibalism among skus: whatever the cluster in which they are classified, they are fully interdependent. Then in that case, (23) reduces to,

$$\sigma^{I}_{bvd} = c^{*}_{bvd} + \epsilon^{*}_{bvd} + \beta^{*}(r_{bvd} - m_{bvd}), \tag{24}$$

which is the result derived by Bultez and Naert (1988). It simply proves that all distinctions between classes and clusters can safely be ignored: the consumer's choice process comes down to a one-shot unidimensional comparative evaluation.

Case II: **Bidimensional hierarchical choice**. If the skus are clustered according to the modalities of a single product-attribute, then $\theta_2 = 0$ and (23) reads

$$\sigma^{II}_{bvd} = c^{*}_{bvd} + \epsilon^{*}_{bvd} + \beta^{*}\left\{(r_{bvd} - m_{bvd}) - \theta\, \mu_{bv|d}(R_d - M_d)\right\}, \tag{25}$$

with: $\theta = \theta_1$ and $\mu_{bv|d} = m_{bvd}/M_d$, which is the rule recommended by Bultez et al. (1989).

Case III: **Strictly restricted cannibalism**. Should the substitutability of skus to one another be limited only to the frontiers of their respective clusters, then: $\theta_1 = \theta_2 = 1$ and (23) becomes

$$\sigma^{III}_{bvd} = c^{*}_{bvd} + \epsilon^{*}_{bvd} + \beta^{*}\left\{r_{bvd} - m_{bvd}\left(1 + \frac{R_{.vd} - M_{.vd}}{M_{.vd}}\right)\right\},$$

or

$$\sigma^{III}_{bvd} = c^{*}_{bvd} + \epsilon^{*}_{bvd} + \beta^{*}_{vd}(\rho_{b|vd} - \mu_{b|vd}) \tag{26}$$

where: $\rho_{b|vd} = r_{bvd}/R_{.vd}$ and $\beta^{*}_{vd} = \beta^{*} R_{.vd}$.

Comparing (26) with (24), one realizes that when the cannibalism does not extend beyond the clusters' barriers, then the allocation should be guided essentially by within-clusters considerations[5].

More light can be shed on (23) by considering the allocation at a more aggregate level, i.e. the portions of the gondola to be saved for entire groups of items. For the (v,d)-th cluster, we get

$$\begin{aligned} S_{.vd} &= \sum_b \sigma_{bvd} = C^{*}_{.vd} + E^{*}_{.vd} + \beta^{*}\left\{(R_{.vd} - M_{.vd})\right. \\ &\quad \left. - \theta_1(1-\theta_2)(R_d - M_d)(M_{.vd}/M_d) - \theta_2(R_{.vd} - M_{.vd})\right\}, \end{aligned}$$

or

$$S_{.vd} = C^{*}_{.vd} + E^{*}_{.vd} + \beta^{*}(1-\theta_2)\left\{(R_{.vd} - M_{.vd}) - \theta_1\, \mu_{v|d}\,(R_d - M_d)\right\}, \tag{27}$$

with $C^{*}_{.vd} = \sum_b c^{*}_{bvd}$ and $E^{*}_{.vd} = \sum_b \epsilon^{*}_{bvd}$. Actually, (27) reveals to be the aggregate variant of (25) and can therefore be interpreted similarly. For the d-th class, we observe that

$$S_{..d} = \sum_v S_{.vd} = C^{*}_{..d} + E^{*}_{..d} + \beta^{*}(1-\theta_1)(1-\theta_2)(R_d - M_d) \tag{28}$$

with $C^{*}_{..d} = \sum_v C^{*}_{.vd}$ and $E^{*}_{..d} = \sum_v E^{*}_{.vd}$; then the rule transforms into the aggregate variant of (24).

[5]Beyond the impact on the assortment total sales volume reflected in ϵ^{*}_{bvd}, across-cluster links subsist because the space-availability constraint binds the entire assortment and also because different segments may have different preferences ($\alpha_{bvd} \neq \alpha_{bjk}$).

The close connections established hereabove between the generalized optimization formula (23) and those previously developed demonstrate that (23) effectively captures the essence and features of the allocation plans determined by less sophisticated models of cannibalism in retail assortments[6].

Thus its economic interpretation does not differ much from that already presented by Bultez et al. (1989). Rather than restating it here we use (23) in the next section to infer a series of space-management rules which in fact can be regarded as the theory-rooted knowledge base of a Merchandising Expert System (M.E.S., hereafter).

4 Knowledge Base for a M.E.S.

Formula (23) enables us to deduce a set of retail situation–action rules for the merchandising of an assortment of substitutable skus. Some of those are listed and justified hereafter.

R.0. If *shoppers have strong (weak) preferences for specific classes* and *clusters of items* and *specifically plan their purchases (buy on impulse),* then *the incidence of the skus' visibility on their behavior is insignificant (significant).*

RATIONALE: Purchase planning opposes to impulse buying which in our model can be reflected by very distinct values of the α_{bvd}, φ_{vd} and ϕ_d's but also in values of θ_1 and θ_2 close to unity. Then the impact of β, the parameter which accounts for the sensitivity to product visibility, is relatively small in (23). Moreover, the ϵ^*_{bvd}'s are also negligible in this case.

R.1.1. If *the incidence of the skus' visibility on the shoppers' choice is not significant,* then *only the handling costs should be taken into consideration in designing the shelf-allocation plan.*

RATIONALE: Obvious, since weak effects of product display on substitutability result in a negligible value for β. Then (23) reduces to

$$\sigma_{bvd} \cong c^*_{bvd}$$

with: $c^*_{bvd} = \gamma_{bvd} C_{bvd}/G$ since: $E \cong 0$.

R.1.2. If *handling costs dominate other considerations,* then *the sku's stock-turnover must be the key determinant of the space allocated to it.*

RATIONALE: Given that the incidence of visibility on the line's sales (re)distribution is negligible, an increase in a sku's sales-to-space ratio diminishes its DPP, since it results in higher handling costs: unless one is willing to accept out-of-stocks, the shelf must be replenished more often when the stock-turnover accelerates. Therefore allocating more space to the sku considered would maintain the sales-to-space ratio stable, hence its profitability. The c^*_{bvd}-term in (23) actually regulates this mechanism. Assuming linear costs ($\gamma_{bvd} = 1$),

$$C_{bvd} = u_{bvd}(q_{bvd}/s_{bvd}),$$

where u_{bvd} stands for the handling cost per replenishment operation, then

$$c^*_{bvd} = (u_{bvd}\, m_{bvd}/s_{bvd}) \Big/ \sum_i \sum_j \sum_k (u_{ijk}\, m_{ijk}/s_{ijk}) \ ,$$

[6]It should also be noted that it can be straightforwardly related to the pioneering contributions of Anderson and Amato (1974) and Anderson (1979).

which can be approximated by reference to the space equi-distribution case ($s_{bvd} \cong s_{ijk}$),

$$c^*_{bvd} \cong w_{bvd}\, m_{bvd},$$

with: $w_{bvd} = u_{bvd}/\overline{u}$ and $\overline{u} = \sum_i \sum_j \sum_k m_{ijk}\, u_{ijk}$.

R.2.1. If *the skus' visibility exclusively influences the shoppers' selection process*[7] and if *merchandise handling costs do not differ much among items of the same class,* then *the space share to be allocated to each class must be a combination (weighted average) of on the one hand, its relative contribution to the line's profitability and on the other, its relative share of the line's total sales volume.*

RATIONALE: Since product visibility does not influence the assortment total sales volume, $E = E^*_{..d} = 0$. When costs do not vary much within a class of items, then $u_{bvd} \cong u_d$ and

$$w_{bvd} \cong u_d \Big/ \sum_k u_k M_k = w_d\,.$$

As a result, $c^*_{bvd} \cong w_d\, m_{bvd}$ and $C^*_{..d} \cong w_d\, M_d$, hence (28) implies

$$S_{..d} \cong \omega^1_d M_d + \omega^2_d R_d,$$

where: $\omega^1_d = w_d - \beta^*(1-\theta_1)(1-\theta_2)$ and $\omega^2_d = w_d - \omega^1_d$.

Furthermore, when cost differences between classes of items are small, $w_d \cong 1$ and

$$S_{..d} \cong \omega M_d + (1-\omega) R_d.$$

R.2.2. If *the skus' visibility exclusively influences the shoppers' selection process,* but if *the cannibalism that product display stimulates remains restricted within the boundaries of each cluster* and if *merchandise handling costs do not vary much among skus of the same cluster,* then *the space share to be allocated to each sku must also be a combination (weighted average) of on the one hand, its relative contribution to the cluster's profitability and on the other, its relative share of the cluster's total sales volume.*

RATIONALE: As discussed in the previous section (case III), restricted cannibalism implies $\theta_1 = \theta_2 = 1$; thus from (26) and using the cost approximation introduced for R.1.2.,

$$\sigma_{bvd} \cong (w_{bvd} M_{.vd} - \beta^* R_{.vd})\mu_{b|vd} + (\beta^* R_{.vd})\, \rho_{b|vd}$$

and because differences in handling costs are small within the cluster, $w_{bvd} \cong w_{vd}$,

$$\omega_{bvd} \cong \lambda^1_{vd}\, \mu_{b|vd} + \lambda^2_{vd}\, \rho_{b|vd},$$

with: $\lambda^1_{vd} = (w_{vd} M_{.vd} - \beta^* R_{.vd})$ and $\lambda^2_{vd} = \beta^* R_{.vd}$.

5 Conclusion

Far from exhausting the rules which could be drawn from (23), the above sample illustrates how a system of complex non-linear optimality conditions can be disentangled into a set of *If-then* logical propositions which can be discussed with, and possibly qualified by,

[7] That is, it has no impact on the assortment total sales volume.

merchandisers. Those rules should of course be supplemented by an adhoc base of facts- which retailers and/or manufacturers could supply about the shoppers' behavior (e.g., consumers' perceptions of the merchandise line's structure, extent of purchase planning vs. impulse buying, etc.) and about direct distribution costs (DPC) or which could be collected through experimental tests.

Should quantitative and reliable data be available to calibrate the model parameters, (23) can of course be used as a heuristic. Simple iterative numerical procedures can be imagined: starting from an initial solution of space-equirepartition, (23) can be applied recursively to revise the allocation (see Bultez et al. (1989)).

But given the width and depth of stores' assortments only mixed decision support systems will really be efficient: logical rules being applied to lines for which an experimentation is difficult or has not been conducted yet.

References

ANDERSON, E.E. (1979), An Analysis of Retail Display Space: Theory and Methods, *Journal of Business, 52*, 103–118.

ANDERSON, E.E., and AMATO, H.N. (1974), A Mathematical Model for Simultaneously Determining the Optimal Brand Collection and Display Area Allocation, *Operations Research, 22*, 13–21.

ASHBY, J. (1989), U.S. Retail Environment Stifles Creativity, *Marketing News, January 16, 10.*

BULTEZ, A. (1978), Econometric Specification and Estimation of Market-Share Models: The State of the Art, in: *Marketing: Neue Ergebnisse aus Forschung und Praxis*, ed. E. Topritzhofer, Gabler Verlag, Wiesbaden, 239–263.

BULTEZ, A., GIJSBRECHTS, E., NAERT, P., and VANDEN ABEELE, P. (1989), Asymmetric Cannibalism in Retail Assortments, *Journal of Retailing, 65*, 153–192.

BULTEZ, A., and NAERT, P. (1975), Consistent Sum-Constrained Models, *Journal of the American Statistical Association, 70*, 529–535.

BULTEZ, A., and NAERT, P. (1988), SH.A.R.P.: SHelf Allocation for Retailers' Profit, *Marketing Science, 7*, 211–231.

CORSTJENS, M., and DOYLE, P. (1981), A Model for Optimizing Retail Space Allocations, *Management Science, 27*, 822–833.

CORSTJENS, M., and DOYLE, P. (1989), Evaluating Alternative Retail Positioning, *Marketing Science, 8*, 170–180.

CURRY, D.J. (1989), Single-Source Systems: Retail Management Present and Future, *Journal of Retailing, 65*, 1–20.

FLANAGAN, J.P. (1989), Two Trends Propelling New Retail Partnerships, *Marketing News, January 16, 12.*

HAPOIENU, S.L. (1989), Product Glut Sparks Struggle for Shelf Space, *Marketing News, January 16, 2.*

LITTLE, J.D.C. (1988), Finding the News in Scanner Data, unpublished paper, presented at the Marketing Decision Support Systems Workshop, *European Institute for Advanced Studies in Management*, Brussels.

LITTLE, J.D.C., BELL, D.E., and KEENEY, R.L. (1975), A Market Share Theorem, *Journal of Marketing Research, 12*, 136–141.

NAKANISHI, M., and COOPER, L.G. (1974), Parameter Estimation for a Multiplicative Competitive Interaction Model-Least Squares Approach, *Journal of Marketing Research, 11*, 303–311.

WEVERBERGH, M., NAERT, P., and BULTEZ, A. (1981), Logically Consistent Market Share Models Revisited, *Revue Belge de Statistique, d'Informatique et de Recherche Opérationnelle, 21, 1*, 3–27.

Decision Making: A Computational Approach

Abhijit Chaudhury and Andrew B. Whinston
Department of Management Science and Information Systems
University of Texas at Austin, U.S.A.

Summary

The objective of our research is to incorporate into a computerized environment the intrinsic capabilities of an intelligent decision-maker to function and decide in an environment characterized by a lack of information, inconsistency and ambiguity. There is much (though not all) that decision-makers do in realistic situations that is sound and reasonable, in view of all the constraints to which they are subject. Our perspective draws upon research in cognitive psychology as to how people construct and revise beliefs. We show how such a perspective leads us to a model of an artificially intelligent (A.I.) decision-making system that can reason with incomplete knowledge, make revisions in beliefs due to new evidence, and modify the reasoning model itself when it is so warranted. Such a capability is achieved by a synergistic combination of several metaphors of reasoning and learning. In particular, the model integrates three previously unrelated themes developed in the A.I. field: explanation based learning, truth maintenance systems and analogical reasoning.

1 Introduction: Why a New Model?

The major objective of this research is to furnish a detailed and a plausible computational model of how decision-makers generate, maintain and revise beliefs about a decision situation, particularly in the context of incomplete and imprecise information. In the paper, we argue for a computational model that is based on ideas in cognitive psychology. The model is also normative in nature because it incorporates the best abilities of humans to function in ambiguous situations. In a time constrained world—such as in a battle field or in a business world—where limitations of computational resources and time are critical constraints, computational systems that incorporate human abilities can play a very useful role.

In the classical framework of decision theory, the focus is how to make the best decisions when existing beliefs and relationships concerning the environment are known and can be quantified. However, in realistic situations, it rarely happens that such precise knowledge exists. Our approach, in contrast to the classical one, is to focus on how these beliefs arise, how they are used for decision-making, and how they are modified in light of new evidence. We begin with a short review of the three approaches to decision theory currently in vogue: normative, descriptive and prescriptive. We show the limitation of existing research in decision-making to explain in a plausible fashion how managers develop or modify beliefs on the basis of which they make their decisions. In the next section, we

NATO ASI Series, Vol. F 61
Knowledge, Data and Computer-Assisted Decisions
Edited by M. Schader and W. Gaul

describe our model. In the subsequent sections (3–5), we describe in detail the individual components of the model, and their underlying computational paradigms.

1.1 Normative Approach

Developments in decision theory began with the *normative* perspective which focuses on what a rational decision maker ought to do, based on formal definitions derived from Bayesian statistical decision theory and game theory. Following such a perspective, operations researchers and economists have concentrated on rational procedures for decision makers (i.e., how people should make decisions based on a certain idea of optimality).

The definition of optimality in these models is a very restrictive one; namely "*decisions or judgements that maximize or minimize some explicit and measurable criterion conditional on certain environmental assumptions and a specified time horizon*" (Einhorn and Hogarth (1981)). Simon (1979) points out that because of the complexity of the environment, a decision-maker has but two alternatives: either to build optimal models by simplifying the assumptions, or to build heuristic models that maintain greater realism. Einhorn and Hogarth (1981) question the reasonableness of the normative models because of these simplifying assumptions. This leaves us, they argue, "in the horns of dilemma. Given the complexity of the environment, it is uncertain whether human responses or optimal models are more appropriate".

1.2 Behavioral Approach

Kahneman and Tversky (1981) observe that the descriptive validity of the normative models has been repeatedly challenged. Direct violation of the axioms and failures of the utility theory (on which the normative models are based) to predict have been reported. This research has led to the development of a *behavioral* decision theory which, in turn, has produced a wide range of literature concerning the way people actually evaluate information and decide on a course of action. Such a theory concerns itself with the ways to describe and quantify issues in the process of decision making and show the kind of errors to which normal human judgement could lead. The focus is on how well people perform instead of the earlier focus on what constitutes the best performance. This observation has been corroborated in the empirical research literature. Biggs, Mock and Watkins (1988) observe about the decision processes adopted by auditors that the "result of this study showed *no evidence that the auditors were using probabilistic reasoning process*".

1.3 Prescriptive Approach

An even more recent development in decision theory has been the introduction of ideas and models of decision making from the area of artificial intelligence. The focus of this research is on how people make decisions. The focus is on the process of decision making and not on the quality of performance which is the focus of behavioral decision theory. Such an orientation may be characterized as *prescriptive*, in contrast to the normative approach of decision theory and the descriptive approach of behavioral decision theory. The prescriptive approach is a constructive or an engineering approach (Klienmutz et al. (1988)). Given a decision problem it attempts to construct a computational system that would perform (i.e., make decisions). The emphasis here is on building, in a computerized environment, models and techniques that work in practice.

Prescriptive decision theory has been based on the famous Newell and Simon (1972) model of decision-making. For the past two decades their information processing metaphor has guided research in decision theory and cognitive sciences. However, the results of this research leave a lot to be desired in terms of understanding how decision-makers form beliefs and revise their beliefs in a realistic environment characterized by missing information, imprecise knowledge, and ambiguity. None of the models are precise enough so that a unique computational model can be derived. Einhorn and Hogarth (1981) observe that in the research into human decision-making behavior "the most important results in the period under review have shown the sensitivity to judgements and choice to seemingly minor changes to task". There is little in the human processing models used in current research that explains such sensitivity of human choice to task definition. Moreover, there is little guidance as to how one may relate these various human characteristics in a single integrated framework.

2 Methodology and Model

There are several advantages in computational modeling (Thagard (1988)), i.e., modeling a decision-making system as a computer program:

- A.I. and computer science provide a systematic vocabulary for describing an informational and decision-making structure;
- the implementation of ideas in a running program provides a test of internal coherence; and
- running the program is a test of the foreseen and unforeseen consequences of a hypothesis.

We use the computational paradigm of A.I. to construct our model. The model depicts the process of reasoning as a synergistic combination of several paradigms and computational metaphors in the area of artificial intelligence. These A.I. models focus on different aspects of common sense reasoning and learning. This paper discusses how these metaphors can be integrated to provide a more unified and comprehensive treatment of the problem of computationally modeling the process of belief creation and maintenance in realistic settings. The utility and generality of the approach are demonstrated in a unified framework which integrates three previously unrelated systems in A.I.:

- truth maintenance system,
- explanation based learning (EBL), and
- analogical reasoning.

In the next few paragraphs we will discuss the role played by each of the three systems. The basic representation of our model is a 2-level system (refer to Fig. 1). The lower level consists of two modules:

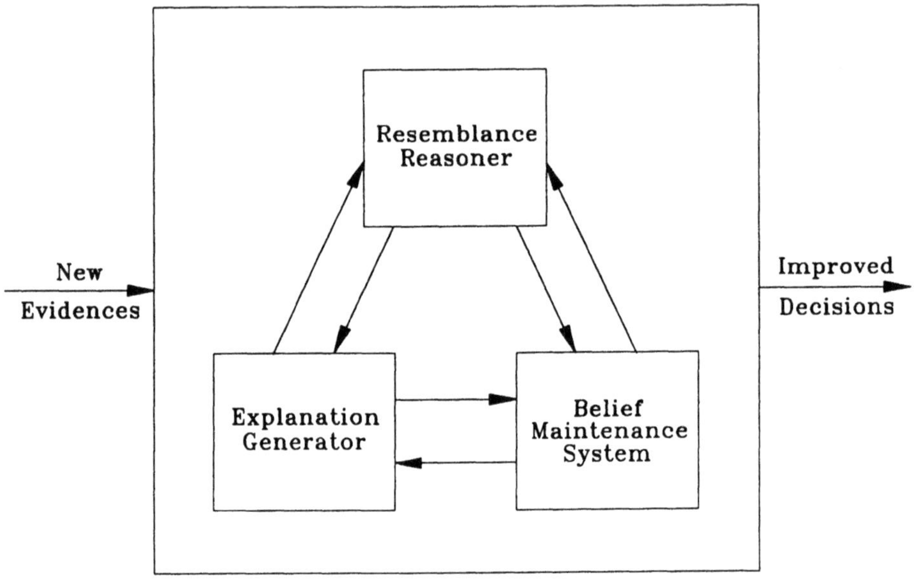

Figure 1: A Model of an Artificial Decision-Making System

- the assumption based belief maintenance system, and
- the explanation generator.

At the top level, we have the resemblance reasoner.

2.1 Belief Maintenance System (BMS)

At level one, the BMS can be viewed as a collection of expert systems or causal structure for each kind of problem that is of interest to the decision maker. Like an expert system, each system in a BMS is a collection of inter-related symptom-hypothesis rules. Given certain data for a problem, the relevant belief system is accessed and inference is carried out to give a solution. The solution could be in the nature of a plan or an explanation or a prediction. Unlike an expert system a belief system in a BMS allows non-monotonic reasoning. This becomes useful when not all data about a problem is available and the system makes the most plausible assumptions relating to the missing data. At any point in time, the BMS represents the current state of beliefs about propositions known to be true, about default assumptions made, and what can be derived from these belief systems by forward propagation.

The BMS constitutes, for an artificial decision making system, its knowledge base and its manipulation capabilities, i.e., its inference engine. Frensch and Sterberg (1989) describe human expertise in a similar fashion as the

a. "size of the knowledge base,

b. the abstract nature of the knowledge, and

c. the procedural nature of the problem solutions".

The BMS is, therefore, the mental model of an expert decision maker. However, such expertise is generally accompanied by inflexibility and brittleness on the part of the expert. Frensch and Sterberg (1989), in describing relationships between flexibility and expertise, observe that "three major characteristics of expertise (indicated earlier) ... cause inflexible thinking". In situations that are new to the expert, his/her performance can degrade to that of a non-expert. This is where the second module, the explanation generator plays an important role by providing the ability to modify expertise encapsulated in the BMS as the environment changes. Our model, therefore, describes a *super-expert* or a flexible problem solver in a changing environment.

A single belief system in a BMS is essentially a truth maintenance system that can reason with default relationships and assumptions. Recently, truth maintenance systems—A.I. systems that model common sense reasoning under uncertainty—have been the object of study by researchers in decision theory literature. Biggs, Mock and Watkins (1988) while discussing the applicability of probabilistic reasoning versus truth maintenance systems (TMS) of Doyle (1979) have observed that "there is support in the protocols for the alternative approaches", where the alternative approaches refer to Doyle's TMS. The functions of the BMS can be summarized as follows:

- It maintains the database of belief structures.
- For a given problem situation it provides the inference mechanism to derive new beliefs.
- It checks for consistency between derived beliefs and evidence. If found contradictory, default assumptions are manipulated to regain consistency. This is similar to the hypothesis generation and evaluation phase in diagnostic systems. It is represented by steps (4), (5) and (6) in Fig. 2.
- When such a process for consistency recovery fails, it informs the explanation generator module of the necessity for generating a new belief system. The interaction between the BMS and the explanation generator is represented by the cycle of steps (4)-(5)-(6)-(7)-(8)-(4) in Fig. 2.

(We discuss in more detail the computational paradigm of the truth maintenance system in Section 3.)

As is well known, however, expert systems are brittle in nature, and so are the belief systems. This is not unlike human experts, who also lose flexibility with increased acquisition of expertise. An explanation generator helps to analyze the reasons the module failed. Failure is characterized by a wrong prediction, a plan that did not work, or an explanation that is erroneous.

2.2 Explanation Generator Module

The BMS interacts with the explanation generator module, where new belief systems are created, when existing modules fail to perform. This module creates new explanations according to new evidence, when the existing BMS fails. If the predictions from the existing system are inconsistent with the observations and this cannot be resolved by manipulation of the default assumptions, then the BMS needs to be revised.

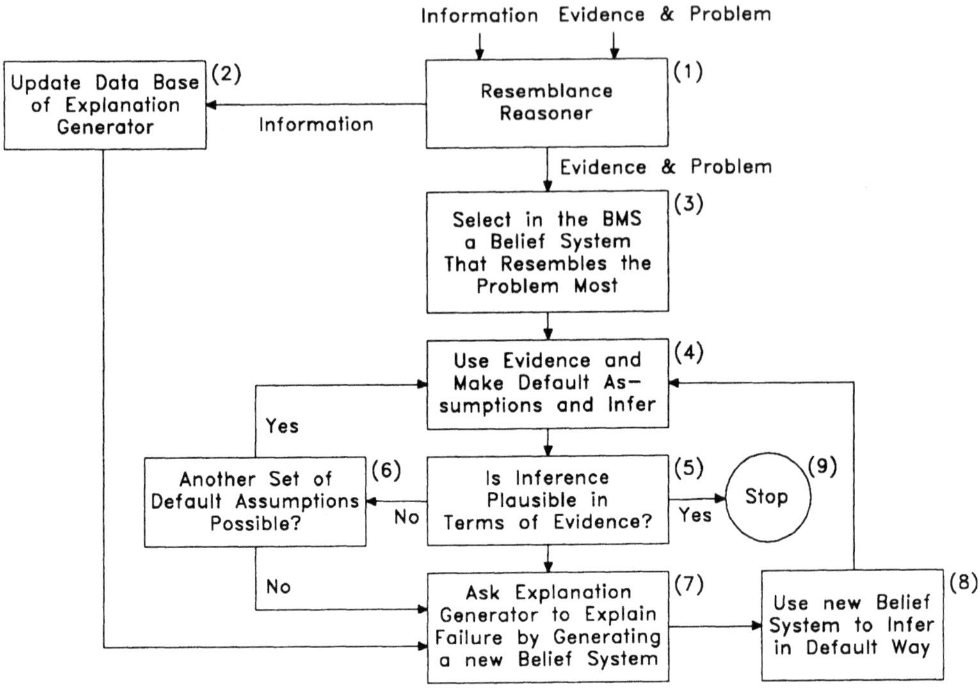

Figure 2: The Decision-Making Cycle

The explanation generator is able to revise a belief system in a BMS by the use of its own knowledge base. In contrast to the knowledge base of the BMS, the knowledge available with the explanation generator consists of the deep and detailed knowledge about the causal relationships among the concepts that appear in the BMS. A single belief system in a BMS can be viewed as in a chunked or compiled form of the knowledge that is available with the explanation generator. This compilation or chunking helps to make efficient the process of inference that the BMS conducts. The revision of a belief system by the explanation generator occurs in the following steps: (i) contradiction detection, (ii) informational search and manipulation of defaults to resolve contradictions, and finally, (iii) revision of the structure of the BMS itself when manipulation of default assumptions fails to produce a state that is consistent with the observations (refer to Fig. 3).

How are belief systems revised or new systems created? This is done by a process called abduction. Abduction can be defined as jumping to a hypothesis that explains a puzzling situation. The purpose of abduction is to explain. People generally try to explain events or phenomena when they are out of the ordinary. Abduction is a pervasive phenomenon that people utilize constantly in their daily lives and the study of which is becoming increasingly popular in A.I. (Pope (1977), Charniak and McDermott (1985)).

There are various ways that abduction can be carried out. The explanation generator module is a mechanism that carries out abduction based on a domain theory relevant to the subject at hand, and which provides the causal or probabilistic relationships between concepts that constitute the theory. The explanations generated by this module are in the form of belief systems which are then incorporated into the database of belief systems maintained in the BMS. Explanation based learning (EBL), a paradigm in A.I., can create an explanation that explains a puzzling phenomenon. By use of the fundamental knowledge present in the domain theory, an EBL system creates a new belief system to be incorporated in the BMS and that can now apply to a novel situation that the reasoner has come across for the first time. In this manner, the explanation generator mitigates the brittleness and limitations of the BMS module. (We discuss in more detail the computational paradigm of EBL in Section 4.)

Pennington and Hastie (1988) provide experimental evidence that EBL is a plausible account of the way jurors do their reasoning given their tasks in a law suit. They (1986) comment that "a central question in decision making research concerns how people evaluate available evidence. We have argued that evidence evaluation in complex diagnostic situation is *explanation based*" (italics by the original authors). Also in philosophy of science, Thagard (1988, page 73) notes that "abduction—formation of explanatory hypothesis—is the primary means for introducing new theories. Active rules in a problem solving system whose explananda are goals can suggest hypothesis that suggest them". The functions of the explanation generator module are summarized below:

- It is the repository of the deep knowledge that underlies the concepts and the knowledge base of the BMS.
- It generates new belief structures when the existing belief systems in the BMS fail to remove inconsistency among derived beliefs and evidence.
- It integrates existing belief systems into a larger, but consistent belief system.
- It oversees the successes and failures of belief systems to explain situations and purges those belief structures in a BMS that perform poorly.

2.3 Resemblance Reasoner

At the top is the resemblance reasoner, which oversees the performance of the explanation generator and the BMS module and improves them over time. The resemblance reasoner performs several vital tasks. A primary task is to interact with the world outside on behalf of the BMS and the explanation generator. During such interaction it has to infer that two things or events are causally related from the fact that they resemble each other (analogy) or to infer that two things or two events are causally related because of the frequency of their joint appearances (inductive). The knowledge that it gathers from the world outside may also be tentative in nature, i.e., it is not evaluated to be true or false immediately on receipt or observation but only when it is required to be used (Gilbert (1989)). With such inductive and analogical knowledge it helps the explanation generator to do abductive reasoning in terms of analogies to previous problems.

Resemblance thinking is not a mere creation of A.I. or cognitive psychologists. The first piece of evidence that it is a very natural general method of thinking is found in Tversky and Kahneman (1974). They maintain that people often make judgements about the relation of classes and events using a "representative heuristic", which represents their judgement of the degree of resemblance. Given a certain situation, the resemblance reasoner determines the context and the applicable belief structure in a BMS that most resembles the situation. The way the resemblance reasoner reads the present context determines which belief system is going to be retrieved from level one and used for reasoning.

Determination of a context is a vital first step in reasoning. This is illustrated by Hanson (1958): "There are as many causes of x as there are explanations of x. Consider how the death might have been set out by the physician as 'multiple haemorrhage', by the barrister as 'negligence on the part of the driver', and by a carriage builder as 'a defect in the construction' ". In an insightful article, Tversky (1977) analyzed the psychological basis of similarity judgement, and in doing so emphasized the importance of context and biased selection in judgemental processes. Einhorn and Hogarth (1986) concluded that "the idea of a causal field is central to determining causal relevance". By causal field the authors imply the context in which the reasoning is going to take place. The sensitivity to context and task description and previous experience are brought about in our model by the resemblance reasoner which acts as a filter to all the interactions that the BMS or the explanation generator module undergo with the real world. Our model, thus, in a natural fashion integrates three modes of reasoning: non-monotonic deductive (BMS), abductive (explanation generator), and the inductive/analogical reasoning (resemblance reasoner).

The incorporation of the different paradigms from A.I. into our model helps to mitigate the failure of the current information-theoretic approach research to find plausible models of choice and decision-making. This has been largely due to the excessive focus on the logicist-deductive view of reasoning as a process or a process based on a sound theory like the Bayesian theory or a first order logic. As Harman (1986) points out, reasoning as a human enterprise is not synonymous with inferencing. Reasoning is a human activity that can only be inadequately captured by a logicist-deductive or the Bayesian paradigm. Our model captures better the human attributes of a belief generation, maintenance, and revision process. The functions of the Resemblance reasoner can be summarized as follows:

- This is the only module that interacts with the world outside. It acts as a filter to all that goes on between the BMS, the explanation generator, and the real world outside.
- For all observations it selects the most plausible (or closest in similarity) belief structure available in the BMS, and this belief structure then does the reasoning.
- The reasoner also observes relationships between different types of evidence and checks to see if the current domain theory in the explanation generator is consistent with them.
- The inductive and analogical relationship between different evidence is observed by the resemblance reasoner and is used to assist the explanation generator in its process of abduction.
- Finally, an important role that it also plays is that of the supervisory relationship with the modules at the lower level. This helps it to translate the experience it gathers over time by repeated interactions with the world into more efficient performance by the BMS and the explanation generator.

The rest of the paper is organized as follows: **Section 3:** Truth Maintenance Systems; **Section 4:** Explanation Based Reasoning, and **Section 5:** Conclusion.

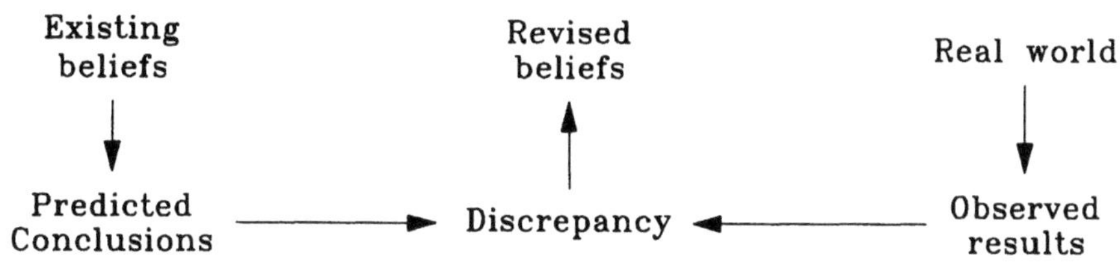

Figure 3: Schema for Belief Revision

3 Truth Maintenance Systems

How do people make choices in an environment characterized by time constraints and ambiguous information? Do they follow Bayesian principles? Even more importantly, can they follow Bayesian principles if they wish? Experiments in behavioral decision theory have confirmed that people do not exhibit Bayesian behavior. In a realistic environment where one does not have either the prior values, or their distributions, and the problem suffers from an exponential nature of computations, it is unrealistic to expect them to behave in a Bayesian fashion. As Harman (1986) remarks, "doing extensive updating by conditionalization ... would be too complicated in practice. Therefore one must follow other principles in revising one's views". In a time constrained decision-making situation—such as in a battle field—it is unrealistic to expect computational systems to behave likewise.

Most situations of daily decision making are characterized by propositions which are nearly true or nearly false, i.e., their truth values are very close to one or zero. However, the number of such propositions is generally large, and while individually their uncertainty can be neglected, the cumulative effects of such uncertainty are significant. How then do people actually decide in such situations?

An ubiquitous feature of daily common sense reasoning is people's readiness to "jump to conclusion" so as to be able to act on imperfect information. People adopt tentative beliefs about the world and use them as if they were true, and then retract them as new information is received. The aim of the belief revision model is to give a symbolic, nonnumeric account of the dynamics of this belief commitment process. This process of belief revision can be figuratively described as shown in Fig. 3.

Doyle's (1979) truth maintenance system was the first attempt to model human reasoning behavior in natural circumstances where a lot of vital information is not readily observable. Since then it has been a very active area of research in A.I. The latest models of such systems include de Kleer (1986). A truth maintenance system is a computational tool to support an approach to the belief revision problem, i.e., to the problem of appropriately revising the totality of beliefs held by a problem solver when facing a situation where new information is provided. The need for a belief revision system arises in several situations, some of which are highlighted below (Reinfrank (1986)):

- *Dynamic World:* In a dynamic world such as the one we live in, some facts that hold true at one instant do not hold in some others. Any reasoning system about such a world should be able to update its internal model with respect to changes occurring in the world. This problem is also known as the frame problem: how to efficiently identify and update only those beliefs affected by change.

- *Varying Input:* Input to a certain inference system may change due to changes in assumptions. Derived beliefs sometimes have to be abandoned due to such changes, preferably without necessarily withdrawing too many beliefs, e.g., derivations based on other than the retracted input.

- *Non-monotonic inference:* In many cases, especially problem solving in real world situations, the knowledge is sufficient to formulate general rules of thumb that usually apply, but that also allow exceptions. The usual AI-approach towards this problem is known as the qualification problem and advocates jumping to a tentative conclusion unless there is contradictory evidence, by means of rules such as these:

  if *you want to go to the market*
  then *use your car*
  unless *something is evidently wrong with your car*

  The conclusion adopted by this rule in the absence of any information about something being wrong clearly can be invalidated by the added information that the car is yet to be repaired by the mechanic. This kind of reasoning is called non-monotonic. Additionally, this translation of "unless something is evidently wrong" will often be replaced by "unless you can prove".

  This implies that previously made inferences can be invalidated by some further inferential steps without assimilating new information from outside. Thus, a non-monotonic reasoning system may result also when reasoning from a fixed premise set.

- *Contradiction:* In inferencing on the basis of assumptions and assumed relationships, there is always the possibility of deriving a proposition and its negation, due to inconsistent assumptions or relationships. In such cases, the system should be able to identify the source of conflict, and to withdraw any belief depending on conflicting assumptions or inconsistent data.

4 Explanation Based Reasoning

When do people look or try to construct an explanation? Weiner (1985) states that "there is reasonable consensus in the reviewed research that search is elicited by an unexpected event—a loss by a favored team, much less profit than expected"; that is when the existing belief system turns out conclusions that are contradictory to the evidence at hand.

What is an explanation? Gardenfors (1988, page 167) says that "according to a well known tradition, an explanation is understood as some kind of inferential relation between the sentences included in the explanans and the explanandum". Hempel (1965) views both deductive and inductive-statistical explanations in this way. He describes the general structure of an explanation as follows:

$C_1, C_2, ..., C_r$	: Statements of the antecedent conditions
$L_1, L_2, ..., L_k$	: General laws
E	: Description of the phenomenon E to be explained.

Here the empirical phenomenon E is explained by showing that it follows from the antecedent conditions and the general laws. C's are called the explanans and E is called the explanandum.

How are explanations created? Thagard (1988) describes the process as follows: "The link between facts and explanandum come through a form of reasoning that Pierce called abduction". Like induction or generalization, abduction is not a fool-proof process and can be often erroneous. There are several ways that abduction can be performed such as (1) backward inference, (2) existential inference, and (3) analogy. In backward inference if we are trying to explain P, and we have a rule $Q \rightarrow P$, one can evaluate the truth of the antecedent as a hypothesis Q to explain P. In existential abduction we postulate the existence of an object previously unobserved. Pasteur's investigation of diseases led him to postulate the existence of undetected infectious agents, much later identified as germs. In general, if one is trying to explain P, and one is aware of a rule that links a relationship $R(Q, P)$ to P via implication such as $R(Q, P) \rightarrow P$, then one can hypothesize the existence of Q. In analogical inference if one is trying to explain P, and one is aware of a rule $Q' \rightarrow P'$, where Q' and P' are analogical to Q and P respectively, then one generates the hypothesis Q' as an explanation of P.

The process of abduction plays a major role in the A.I. learning paradigm called explanation based learning (EBL). Since EBL employs the same mechanism (abduction) for the same purpose (building a proof structure), we will review the method of EBL as is currently being developed in A.I. Recent research into learning has focussed on learning concepts on the basis of a single example in contrast to data intensive procedures of statistical learning or learning by induction. These methods analyze a single example along with a deductive justification of the generalization in terms of the system's knowledge of the domain. By relying on the knowledge of the domain and the example under study, the explanation based method is able to provide a justification as to why the single example it produced is an instance of the concept (Mooney (1988)). The basic insight that underlies the success of the explanation based method is that it is possible to form a justified generalization of a single positive example provided the learning system incorporates sufficient explanatory capabilities. Some EBL models use backward inference as a method of induction. In Branting (1989), exemplars and inference mechanisms are used to reason in a legal domain. The exemplars are the previous cases and judgements, and the system GREBE tries to capture the understanding from existing exemplars and extend it to new cases. This power can obviously be extended to situations where the exemplars are Harvard style business cases, and the knowledge and judgement encapsulated in these cases can be used to guide managers in analogous situations.

5 Conclusion

In summary, this paper presents an integrated model of a decision making process in a realistic environment characterized by incomplete and imprecise knowledge. We have shown in a computational framework, how beliefs about the problem situation arise, how they are amended, and how new belief systems are created for the managers to cope with novel situations.

This is achieved by a synergistic combination of several metaphors of reasoning and learning in A.I. In particular, the decision-making model integrates three previously unrelated systems: explanation based learning, truth maintenance system and analogical reasoning system.

References

BIGGS, S.F., MOCK, T.J., and WATKINS, P.R. (1988), Auditors use of analytical review in audit program design, *The Accounting Review, LXIII, 1*, 148–161.

BRANTING, L.K. (1989), Integrating Generalization with Exemplar-based Reasoning, to appear in: *Proceedings of the 11th Annual Conference of the Cognitive Science Society*, Ann Arbor.

CHARNIAK, E., and McDERMOTT, D. (1985), *Introduction to Artificial Intelligence*, Addison-Wesley, Reading.

DE KLEER, J. (1986), An assumption based TMS, *Artificial Intelligence, 28*, 127–162.

DOYLE, J. (1979), A truth maintenance system, *Artificial Intelligence, 12*, 231–272.

EINHORN, H.J., and HOGARTH, R. (1981), Behavioral decision theory: Processes of judgement and choice, *Journal of Accounting Research, 19, 1*, 1–31.

EINHORN, H.J., and HOGARTH, R. (1986), Judging Probable Cause, *Psychological Bulletin, 19, 1*, 3–19.

FRENSCH, P.A., and STERBERG, R.A. (1989), Expertise and Intelligent Thinking: When is it worse to know better, in: *Advances in Psychology of human intelligence*, ed. R.J. Sterberg.

GARDENFORS, P. (1988), *Knowledge in Flux*, The MIT Press, Cambridge, MA.

GILBERT, D.T. (1989), *How mental systems believe*, A private document, Department of Psychology, University of Texas, Austin.

HARMAN, G. (1986), *Change of view: Principles of reasoning*, The MIT Press, Cambridge, MA.

HANSON, M.R. (1958), *Pattern of Discovery: An enquiry into conceptual foundation of science*, Cambridge University Press.

HEMPEL, C.G. (1965), *Aspects of Scientific Explanation*, The Free Press.

KAHNEMAN, D., and TVERSKY, A. (1981), The framing of decisions and the psychology of choice, *Science*.

KLIENMUTZ, D., ASHTON, R., SULLIVAN, J.R., and TOMASSINI, L.A. (1988), Audit Decision Making, in: *Research Opportunities in Auditing: The second decade*, eds. A.R. Abdel-Khalil and Ira Solomon, American Association of Accountants, Audit Section, Florida.

MOONEY, R.J. (1988), *A general explanation based learning mechanism and its application to narrative understanding*, Technical Report: AITR 88-66, Artificial Intelligence Laboratory, University of Texas, Austin.

NEWELL, A., and SIMON, H.A. (1972), *Human Problem Solving*, Prentice Hall, Englewood Cliffs.

PENNINGTON, N., and HASTIE, R. (1986), Evidence evaluation in complex decision making, *Journal of Personality and Social Psychology, 5*, 242–258.

PENNINGTON, N., and HASTIE, R. (1988), Explanation-based decision-making: Effects of memory structure on judgement, *Journal of Experimental Psychology Learning, Memory, and Cognition, 14, 3*, 521–533.

POPLE, H. (1977), The formation of composite hypothesis in diagnostic problem solving, in: *Proceedings of the Fifth International Joint Conference on A.I.*, Morgan Kaufmann, San Francisco, 1030–1037.

REINFRANK, M. (1986), *Reason Maintenance System*, Unpublished document, Department of Computer Science, Linköping University, Sweden.

SIMON, H.A. (1979), Rational Decision Making in Business Organizations, *American Economic Review*, *69*, 493–511.

THAGARD, P. (1988), *Computational philosophy of science*, The MIT Press, Cambridge, MA.

TVERSKY, A. (1977), Features of similarity, *Psychological Review*, *84*, 327–352.

TVERSKY, A., and KAHNEMAN, D. (1974), Judgement under uncertainty: Heuristics and Biases, *Science*.

TVERSKY, A., and KAHNEMAN, D. (1981), The framing of decisions and psychology of choice, *Science*.

WEINER, B. (1985), Spontaneous causal thinking, *Psychological Bulletin*, *97*, 74–84.

Artificial Intelligence Methods in Data Analysis and Interpretation

Shamsul Chowdhury and Ove Wigertz
Department of Medical Informatics,
Department of Computer and Information Science,
Linköping University, Sweden
and
Bo Sundgren
Statistics Sweden and Stockholm School of Economics, Sweden

Summary

Knowledge-based interfaces to existing statistical software are one way of applying artificial intelligence methods in data analysis and interpretation. In this paper we discuss our experiences from the implementations of knowledge-based systems for time series analyses, in particular for eliminating seasonal variations in statistical studies of industry and trade, and for multivariate tabular analysis. We further discuss the problems of realizing knowledge-based systems in a production environment and present an integrated conceptual model for knowledge-based data analysis and interpretation.

1 Introduction

Statistical packages are generally employed for analysis and interpretation of data because they not only provide statistical analyses of different kinds but also other facilities for the users which are essential for these tasks, e.g. editing, aggregation, tabulation, etc. The available statistical packages (like MINITAB, SPSS, SAS, etc.) may easily be used by statistically inexperienced users to produce as much statistics as the user wants, without him understanding the relevance of the results. This seeming easiness of use of statistics has encouraged overuse and misuse.

The existing statistical packages, although rather powerful concerning their computational capabilities, are often weak about the statistical aspect of a computation. They have a number of deficiencies. They are meant for statisticians and are not provided with statistical expertise. The packages rely on the user possessing that skill. The risk of inappropriate use of these packages by statistically ignorant users is apparent. A statistically naive user needs to be guided in all the phases of data analysis and interpretation. These phases are broadly:

a. selecting an appropriate statistical technique;

b. applying the selected technique in a proper way;

c. interpreting the results and presenting them in an understandable way to the users.

The guidance needed could possibly be provided as a knowledge-based interface to the existing statistical software.

NATO ASI Series, Vol. F 61
Knowledge, Data and Computer-Assisted Decisions
Edited by M. Schader and W. Gaul

1.1 A Knowledge-Based Architecture for Statistical Analysis

In an integrated system for statistics production, statistical packages could be used as an Operator Base (OB) which is a part of a time-dependent triple in a so called Production Base (PB), as discussed by Sundgren (1985a):

$$PB^{(t)} = < DB^{(t)}, OB^{(t)}, PE^{(t)} >,$$

where $DB^{(t)}$ is the database and $PE^{(t)}$ is the production environment at time t. The production environment provides the users with the assistance needed in using the other components of the production base. The CONDUCTOR is described elsewhere by Nordbäck (1984), Sundgren (1985b) and is a working system at Statistics Sweden for this purpose.

These knowledge-based interfaces comprising statistical expertise, henceforth termed as Statistical Expert Systems (SES), could either be integrated with the statistical package in use or reside as a fourth component in the PB:

$$PB^{(t)} = < DB^{(t)}, OB^{(t)}, PE^{(t)}, SES^{(t)} > .$$

A gross architecture of the production base may be seen in Fig. 1, where the individual packages like SAS, MINITAB, BOS (Base Operators Systems) could very well play the role of Operator Base (OB). A general description of Base Operators is given in Sundgren (1985a).

2 Statistical Applications of AI

2.1 Statistics Production

Statistics production and interpretation is the subject matter of a statistical data processing system which is a major subsystem of a statistical information system. Statistical data processing systems deal with the methodology of collecting and analyzing data. Data are collected and analyzed for different types of investigation. One common issue which leads to an investigation is the identification of a problem which one wants to solve.

Statistical data processing can be divided into four different phases as discussed in Wallgren and Wallgren (1983):

1. problem formulation and planning of a statistical investigation,

2. data gathering,

3. data analysis and interpretation,

4. documentation and presentation.

SES could very well be constructed for all the major parts of statistics production. In this paper we shall discuss data analysis and interpretation to help statistically inexperienced consumers of statistics in using data in a better way. Moreover this category of users would outnumber the available statistical consultants, so an SES would be helpful for them.

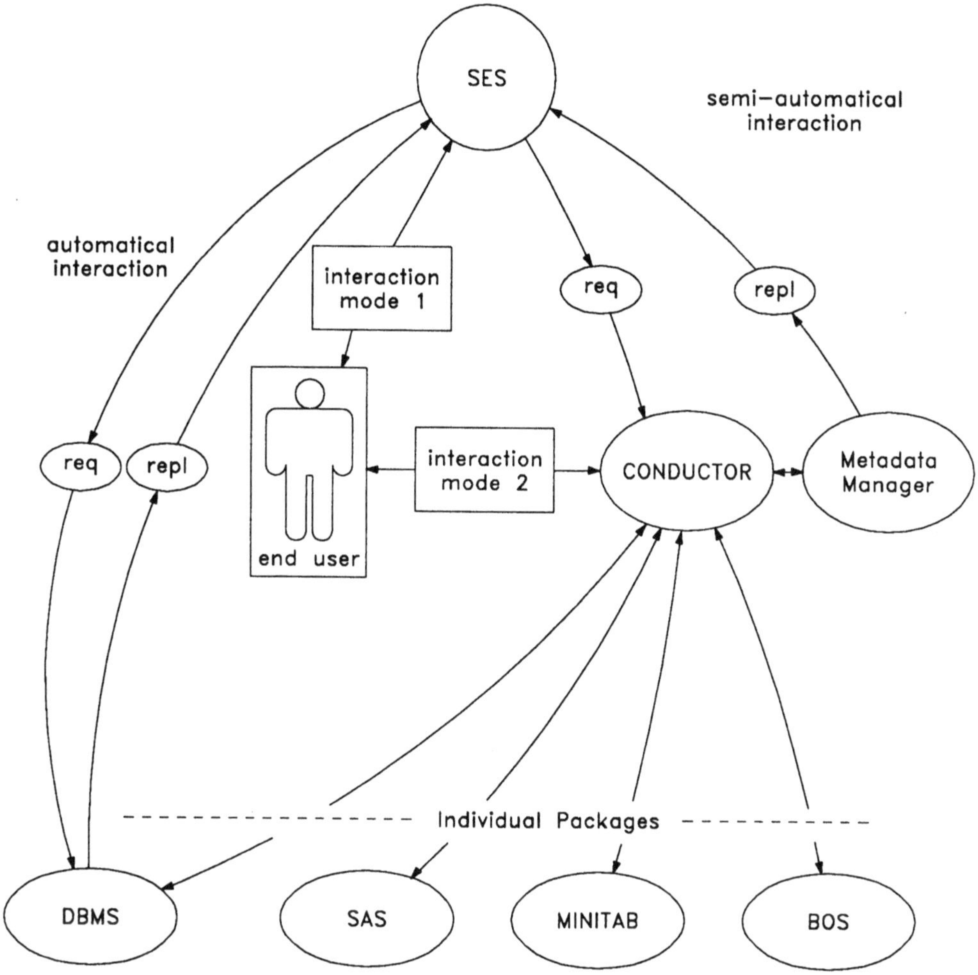

Figure 1: Architecture of the Production Base

2.1.1 Data Analysis and Interpretation

Statistical analysis of data is a common requirement in many areas of business and science. From the analysis point of view data can be classified broadly into two major classes:

- **Time-series data:** representing a behavior measured in the Universe of Discourse for different time periods.

- **Cross-section data:** representing the same or maximally two time periods.

These two classes of data require different methods of analysis even though the analysis is based on the same basic principle. In the analysis of time-series data chronological order is important. Information about chronological order is lost if it is presented against variables other than time. Analysis of cross-section data generally involve a large number of interrelated variables. The task is complex and requires special education and training.

2.2 Statistical Expert Systems: What, for Whom, and Why?

While designing a statistical expert system one has to take into consideration *what* the system would do and *for whom*? The purpose of a SES would be to provide guidance in different phases of a statistical investigation and as regards the *for whom* part we can briefly mention that our objective is to mainly provide help for the statistically inexperienced consumers of statistics in the tasks. We also aim at the professional statisticians in the sense that systems of this category would not only help them to improve and compare their skills, but would also provide them with the opportunity to concentrate on more challenging tasks.

As to *why* statistical expert systems, we would like to quote Mainland (1982): "When I look through the (medical journal) articles and when I see the recent eager acceptance by medical investigators of statistical cookbook recipes I wonder if conditions are much better than in 1950 when the experimental biologist Lancelot Hogben affirmed that 'less than 1% of research workers clearly apprehend the rationale of the statistical techniques they commonly invoke' ".

2.3 Similarities and Differences Between SES and ES in Other Areas

Earliest successful ES were implemented in the field of medicine. However, there are interesting similarities and differences between expert software applications to medicine and data analysis and are described in Chambers (1981), Hahn (1985). In both cases, the software's role is consultative. The users consult the software, but it is up to them to make the actual decision. The basic differences are:

- **The degree of problem definition**. Problems in medical advice and automobiles that need reparation start with well-defined symptoms resulting in a specific diagnosis. A statistician's client has often an ill structured problem according to Simon (1973). Consultant statisticians could help to structure the problem.

- **The end result**. Expert systems in medicine and automobile reparation end up with specific, recommended courses of action. In statistics the nature of information is directive, most data analyses provide input for a recommended action but are not generally equivalent to the recommendation. That is, data analysis is a more heterogeneous, quantitative and iterative process. Each of these iterations are refinements towards more specific goals.

- **Control information**. In SES the choice process of a statistical technique is controlled by two sources of information, one is the users objectives and the other one is the data themselves.

- **Alternative strategies**. Data analysis is an iterative and heterogeneous process. In the process of analysis different strategies might evolve. SES would have a choice of such evolving strategies explaining what strategy is good for a particular choice and why.

- **Common terminology and domain knowledge**. In medicine, the client and expert share a common terminology and medical knowledge. In data analysis the need is to communicate across very different areas of specialization, i.e., economics, medicine, sociology, etc., because statistics is an autonomous discipline on the one hand, and an integral part and tool of other branches of science on the other.

- **Explanation facilities—why and why not?** In statistics *why not* explanation is equally important as *why* because the naive user might wonder *why not* a different method of his familiarity has been adopted.

These differences have the consequences that, although the general approach may be common, the emphasis might be different.

3 Implementations

3.1 Systems for Seasonal Adjustment

Periodic behavior in a time series whose period is exactly a year is termed as seasonal variation. It may be caused by some phenomenon related to the annual calendar. Seasonal adjustments are necessary to understand the behavior of the time series. Adjusted series are probably more reliable and useful for many purposes than an unadjusted series.

There exists a number of computerized techniques for seasonal adjustments. It is not very clear for a statistically naive user to choose the appropriate one. The choice depends on the type of model, purpose of the analysis, and other statistical knowledge. Systems aiding a user in choosing a statistical technique are termed as front end systems by Hand (1986). Possible program structures for the realization of systems of this type and their advantages and disadvantages have been discussed by Hand (1985). In order to guide a naive user in this task a prototype system ADJUST was first developed on a PC employing the expert system shell SAGE (1985). ADJUST described in Block (1986) is a consultation system, based on a pure production system approach, which considers the above facts while interactively guiding a user in selecting an appropriate technique for eliminating seasonal variations in statistical studies of industry and trade.

This was later converted to an AI workstation employing the expert system shell KEE to understand the system behavior in a structured environment. We propose that the best way to achieve this is to employ a hybrid AI tool which integrates the facilities offered by traditional AI systems. ADJUST was converted to TIME-SERIES described in Chowdhury (1987) in the KEE system giving structures to the problem domain. KEE stands for Knowledge Engineering Environment and is a hybrid AI tool for developing expert systems (Intellicorp (1985)). The TIME-SERIES implementation in the KEE on XEROX 1108 machines with multiple window facilities is helpful in selecting the appropriate technique with an understanding of the problem domain, because of the structural representation of the same. Moreover it allows the domain expert to edit and restructure the knowledge base very conveniently through graphic interaction.

3.1.1 Comparative Remarks

Our experiments to develop the front end systems ADJUST, TIME-SERIES are very initial. The knowledge and experience gained would be helpful in the development of a full fledged system for estimating not only the seasonal components but also the other components that together might affect a time-series.

A comparative evaluation of the expert system development tools SAGE and KEE citing examples from implemented prototypes is reported by Chowdhury (1987). The system development tool KEE provides a much better environment in developing expert systems. Structural representations and other facilities make it possible to represent a domain in such a way that the transparency and understandability of the domain become obvious even to a novice end-user.

There are several other elements notable in the implementations. In the hybrid system, the application includes only 12 objects with approximately 4 attributes per object. In addition, the rule-based part of the system includes 27 decision rules, independent of the conceptual hierarchy, but are attached to objects they describe and are distributed throughout the hierarchy. In the pure rule-based system the same structure has been described with 58 conceptual objects, a redundant number of attributes and rules.

3.2 The MAXITAB System for Data Analysis and Interpretation

We will explain the ideas behind MAXITAB by a simple example. The statistical task consists of analyzing and reporting salaries and other conditions for bank clerks. The data set consists of four-dimensional observations. The following variables have been recorded:

SALARY	monthly salary (in $)
SEX	
POSITION	high or low position in the bank
AGE	years, grouped in a number of age-classes

A data set of this kind is generally described by a number of tables. However, multivariate tabular analysis is a rather complicated task—the analysis consists of many steps and each step depends of earlier steps. The problem is to find those tables which describe the data set in a meaningful way and the tables should be as simple and easy to read as possible. For our simple example we could produce at least 124 different tables—many of these are complicated, confusing and rather meaningless. There are two reasons why statistical tables should be as simple as possible:

- A three- or fourway table is difficult to read and understand;
- A table with many cells will contain empty cells or cells with only a few observations.

To ease the difficulties encountered in conducting a multivariate tabular analysis employing a statistical package, for example MINITAB, a program called MAXITAB was developed incorporating the statistical expertise needed for conducting the analysis. A MAXITAB-session with the bank data has the following structure: The answers given during the analysis are within " ".

I. Scales of measurement

Variable	*Scale?*
SALARY	"quantitative"
SEX	"nominal"
POSITION	"ordinal"
AGE	"ordinal"

Comment: The scale determines the type of table which can be done.

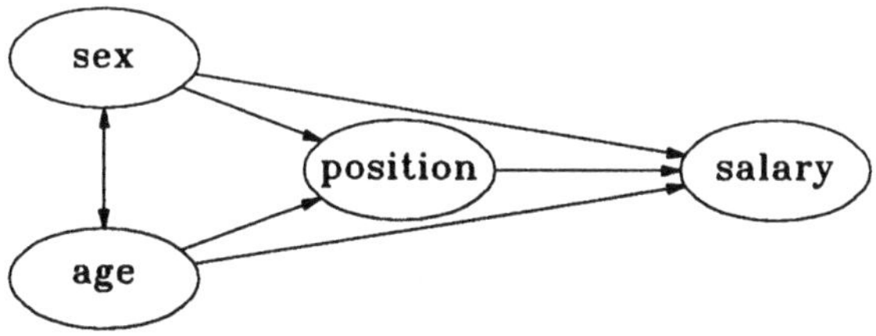

Figure 2: The Data Model Showing the Casual Ordering Between the Variables and Determines the Step of the Analysis

II. Causal structure

VARIABLE	*causal relation with*	*VARIABLE*
SALARY	" <—— "	SEX
SALARY	" <—— "	POSITION
SALARY	" <—— "	AGE
SEX	" ——> "	POSITION
SEX	" <—> "	AGE
POSITION	" <—— "	AGE

With this information MAXITAB will build the model depicted in Fig. 2.

MAXITAB interactively helps the users to define the (hypothesized) causal structure of the data. As soon as the causal structure is defined and accepted by the users MAXITAB goes on with the analysis step by step by presenting tables with the help of MINITAB. At each step of the analysis the users have to approve or disapprove the causality between a pair of variables. The next step of the analysis is very much dependent on the previous step and the system has the ability to select the appropriate variables to investigate as well as to control for during the analysis. The strategies in MAXITAB are based on Wallgren and Wallgren (1983) and Hellevik (1984).

In MAXITAB, there are ways to save tables with comments, etc. These tables can later be interpreted and presented employing traditional methods. Interpretation requires knowledge of statistical techniques as well as knowledge of the discipline (ground domain) to which the technique is applied.

4 Problems in Realizing SES in a Production Environment

Research in AI and development of knowledge-based expert systems has spread recently in widely diverse fields. Still, the estimated number of expert systems that are in regular use are very low. This is mainly because the development is generally carried out in an environment which is very different from the target or production environment. A successful *migration* of the system developed in the former to the latter is necessary before it can be put to use. However, this migration process is not problem free and has been studied within one of our group by Sandhal et al. (1985). The study includes the process of migration of an expert system prototype called A^3, described by Sandhal

(1983), and was developed using the INTERLISP-based expert system development tool EMYCIN (Melle (1981)) on a DECsystem 20. The target environment uses MUMPS (Bowie et al. (1976)), a DBMS suitable for medical applications on a VAX computer.

The A^3 system is intended for use by a laboratory technician seeking guidance in the choice process between 13 different analysis techniques in the initial step of identification of irregular antibodies in blood samples. The choice process here is identical (in a lesser complexity) to the choice process described in our systems for seasonal adjustments reported by Chowdhury (1987). The problems and possible solutions investigated in the study are applicable in migrating SES from development to the target environment with the exceptions that SES should be able to communicate with a large number of software systems including graphical packages, databases, etc., which might be available on different type of machines.

Our development environment includes PCs, INTERLISP-D based AI workstations, a DECsystem 20 and a number of statistical and graphical software packages. The development environment is significantly different from the target environment for our work which is located at Statistics Sweden. A schematic model of the target environment was given in Fig. 1. The hardware resource is an IBM mainframe. The CONDUCTOR would provide the communication facilities and it is already a working system. The facilities of the CONDUCTOR needs to be extended in order to encompass the SES into the environment, and before that, SES has to be converted into a suitable module to fit in the environment.

5 Design Specification for an Integrated SES

The desirable characteristics with an integrated knowledge-based system for data analysis and interpretation have been discussed by Chowdhury (1987). A schematical representation of the interrelated modules necessary to achieve the functionalities that have been demonstrated in the scenario is given in Fig. 3. The representation shows calls from one module to the other with arrows.

The *selection, analysis and interpretation* modules together would comprise the kernel of the integrated SES based on a single *inference engine*. We would prefer a hybrid AI tool like, KEE or EPITOOL (Epitec (1986)) for the implementation of STATEX (STATistical EXpertise). The inference engine for STATEX could also be modeled after REX reported by Gale (1986), which was modeled after CENTAUR described by Aikins (1983). Each of the modules is connected to two submodules below: *frames* and *rules*. For example, table analysis frames or table analysis rules. They are in fact modules with rules and frames applicable to different applications, like multivariate table analysis, regression analysis, etc. They comprise the knowledge base but are not part of the inference engine. They are in fact the data structures that the inference engine operates on. So are the modules, selection, analysis and interpretation. But they contain knowledge of more general character about selecting a technique, guidance in the application of a selected technique and interpreting the results.

They would also provide *control* and *consistency* to the submodules (frames, rules). The knowledge in frames and rules is more specific for a particular application. By *domain knowledge* we do not mean any specific domain but SES would include capabilities to manage a particular domain knowledge within itself.

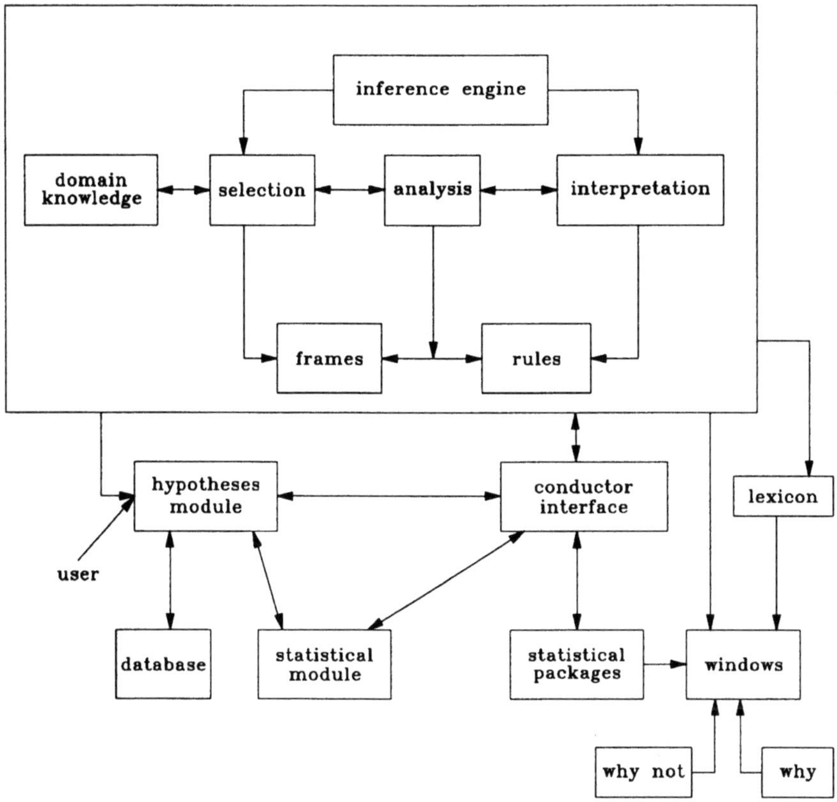

Figure 3: Conceptualization of a Future SES—the STATEX System—Consisting of Interrelated Modules

The *domain knowledge* and the *analysis* to be performed on the data would provide sufficient information to the *hypotheses* module to generate plausible hypotheses by direct use of the *data base*. Users would also have possibilities to feed in hypotheses for further analysis. The *statistical* module converts the hypotheses into a *statistical study* and controls the mode of analysis. The *windows* module manages the display of information and query. The *CONDUCTOR interface* manages calls to statistical packages and provides communication facilities with other parts of the system whenever necessary. The *lexicon* module provides on-line definitions of the statistical vocabulary and concepts. As we claim that a SES would be able to include capabilities to manage a particular domain, we also claim that the lexicon module should be cross-linked with the domain related vocabulary and concepts. The *why* and *why not* modules provide explanations to queries.

6 Concluding Remarks

Our work with the systems for seasonal adjustment can be placed in the first phase of data analysis and interpretation, namely, "selection of a technique". The system MAXITAB includes all the three phases of data analysis and interpretation. The emphasis is on the "application of a technique".

References

AIKINS, J.S. (1983), Prototypical knowledge for expert systems, *Artificial intelligence, 120*, 163–210.

BLOCK, H. (1986), *ADJUST*, Internal report, Statistics Sweden, Sweden.

BOWIE, J., and BARNETT, G.O. (1976), MUMPS—An Economical and Efficient Time-Sharing System for Information Management, *Computers Programs in Biomedicine, 6*, 11–22.

CHAMBERS, J.M. (1981), *Some thoughts on expert software*, Proceedings of the 13th Symposium on the Interface of Computer Science and Statistics, Springer Verlag, New York, 36–40.

CHOWDHURY, S.I. (1987), *Statistical Expert Systems—A Special Application Area for Knowledge-based Computer Methodology*, Linköping Studies in Science and Technology, Thesis No 104., Department of Computer and Information Science, University of Linköping, Sweden.

EPITEC (1986), *Epitool development environment reference manual*, Epitec AB, Linköping, Sweden.

GALE, W.A. (1986), REX review, in: *Artificial Intelligence and Statistics*, eds. W.A. Gale, Addison-Wesley, Reading, Massachusetts, 173–225.

HAHN, G.J. (1985), More intelligent statistical software and statistical expert systems: Future directions, *The American Statistician, 39, 1*.

HAND, D.J. (1985), *Choice of Statistical Technique*, Institute of Psychiatry, De Crespigny Park, England.

HAND, D.J. (1986), Patterns in statistical strategy, in: *Artificial Intelligence and Statistics*, eds. W.A. Gale, Addison-Wesley, Reading, Massachusetts, 335–376.

HELLEVIK, O. (1984), *Introduction to Causal Analysis*, George Allen & Unwin, London.

INTELLICORP (1985), *KEE Technical Manuals*.

MAINLAND, D.V. (1982), Medical Statistics—Thinking vs. Arithmetic, *Journal of Chronic Diseases, 35*, 413–417.

MELLE, V.W. (1981), *Systems Aids in Constructing Consultation Programs*, UMI Research Press.

NORDBÄCK, L. (1984), *The Conductor*, Statistics Sweden.

SANDAHL, K. (1983), *An Experimental Evaluation of EMYCIN as a Tool for Implementation of Expert Systems*, Report LiTH-IDA-EX-83-01.

SANDAHL, K., HÄGGLUND,S., HILDEN, J-O., REHMNERT, R., and RESHAGEN, L. (1985), *The Antibody Analysis Advisor and its Migration into a Production Environment*, Proc. of the 1st Int. Conf. on Expert Systems, London.

SIMON, H.A. (1973), The structure of Ill-structured problems, *Artificial Intelligence, 4*, 181–201.

SPL (1985), *SAGE—An expert system generator and environment*, Systems Programming Ltd. Svenska AB.

SUNDGREN, B. (1985a), *Outline of an algebra of base operators for production of statistics*, Statistics Sweden.

SUNDGREN, B. (1985b), *A session with the CONDUCTOR*, SCB, Statistics Sweden.

WALLGREN, A., and WALLGREN, B. (1983), *Undersökningar och statistik*, Natur och kultur, Stockholm, (in Swedish).

Market-Share Analysis: A Core Technology for Learning About Markets and Competition

Lee G. Cooper
Anderson Graduate School of Management
UCLA, Los Angeles, U.S.A.
and
Masao Nakanishi
School of Business Administration
Kwansei Gakuin University, Nishinomiya-shi, Japan

Summary

The current state of market-share analysis is summarized according to the five-stage model described in Cooper and Nakanishi (1988). Consideration of what is needed to help managers learn about markets and competition leads to a discussion of CHAINs (Combined Human- and Artificial-Intelligence Networks)—open systems in which growth of the *knowledge base* is the primary concern.

1 Introduction

The salient characteristics of the contemporary marketing environment are that the data resources are vast and growing, and that expertise, while substantial, is disjoint and incomplete. The data resources are best represented by the enormous scanner databases reflecting a complete record of retail transactions at the store level (as well as the promotional environment in which these transactions occur) and reflecting the over-time purchases of members of huge consumer panels. The consumer panels are now providing records of television-viewing behavior—a micro record of advertising exposures which can be linked directly to purchases in the relevant categories.

The new challenge these data create concerns what it means to manage in an information-rich environment. What should managers do with the millions of new and relevant numbers which become available each week? The expertise available to confront this task is disjoint in that the methodological expertise for dealing with these vast data is being developed predominantly by marketing academics and the modeling staffs of the syndicated data sources such as A.C. Nielsen, Information Resources Inc., and SAMI/Burke, while the existing brand-management expertise and the knowledge of each product domain is held by the brand-management groups of various manufacturers, and knowledge of the retail environment is shared by brand managers and managers in the channels of distribution. The expertise is incomplete in that academics and practitioners are still very early on the experience curve. There is much left to learn.

But with marketing academics becoming intrigued by the challenges of these new data, and with marketing professionals turning toward technology to help them cope with an

NATO ASI Series, Vol. F 61
Knowledge, Data and Computer-Assisted Decisions
Edited by M. Schader and W. Gaul

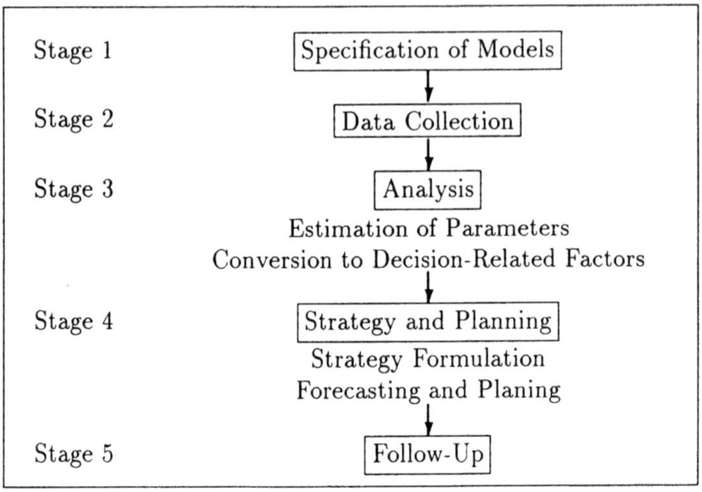

Figure 1: The Five Stages of Market-Share Analysis

information-rich environment, there has evolved a rare alignment of agendas between the academic and professional communities. Sensing the early, but obvious signs of this alignment, we decided to write *Market-Share Analysis: Evaluating Competitive Marketing Effectiveness.* This book started with a shared vision of the future role of technology in management (which some of our colleagues have called "The Starship Enterprise"), and how technology could aid managers trying to learn about the competitive environment. The goal of this chapter is to describe the process of learning we call *market-share analysis.* In section 2 the five-stage model for market-share analysis is described. Section 3 summarizes three new developments that help make market-share analysis a more practical and broadly applicable approach to learning about markets and competition. And, since the most wonderful aspect of our time is the speed at which technology overtakes our fantasies, we relate in Section 4 a vision of how future technology can be adapted to our tasks.

2 The Process of Market-Share Analysis

The three key characteristics are that market-share analysis is *competitive, descriptive* as well as predictive, and *profit-oriented. Competitive* implies that the effect of one's actions must be analyzed in conjunction with the market positions and actions of competitors. We must differentiate the forces which affect one's product/brand from the more general factors which affect the whole industry. To be *descriptive* as well as predictive indicates we are not satisfied with a forecast unless it tells us how our marketing actions and those of our competitors affect outcomes. Such diagnostic information is essential for brand planning. Being *profit-oriented* means that we must consider the costs and revenues associated with marketing actions, not just the market-share response. With these characteristics in mind, market-share analysis can be thought of as the five-stage process shown in Fig. 1.

The first stage involves specification of models. While this stage is indispensable since the choice of model determines the data requirements in the data-collection stage, a more fundamental purpose is being served here. Model specification requires management to come to a common understanding of the variables that affect performance in a competitive environment and how those variables relate to each other. This common understanding can be very helpful in getting organization members to interpret and value market outcomes from the same point of view. The perspective offered most dominantly in the book is that the set of measures should be as comprehensive as possible and that all the measured aspects interact to form the attractiveness of an offering in the marketplace. A second fundamental perspective is that while the raw level of marketing activities affects the total volume of sales for all brands in the category, it is the distinctiveness of marketing actions which counts in determining market shares.

The second stage involves data collection and review. While many organizations are well equipped to track information on their own activities, the fundamental *competitiveness* of market-share analysis urges organizations to measure on the competitors whatever they track for their own brands. The scanner databases have been the biggest boon in making available the kind of competitive information which is otherwise often too difficult to obtain.

The third stage involves both the estimation of model parameters and the conversion to decision-related factors. Regarding parameter estimation the book describes methods for calibrating MCI (Multiplicative Competitive-Interaction) Models and MNL (Multinominal Logic) Models. Simple-effects versions of these models reflect a world in which each brand can have its own level of loyal consumers, but all brands share a common sensitivity to changes in the levels of each marketing variable. The attraction function and the relation of attraction to market share are summarized as follows:

$$\mathcal{A}_i = \exp(\alpha_i + \epsilon_i) \prod_{k=1}^{K} f_k(X_{ki})^{\beta_k} \tag{1}$$

$$s_i = \mathcal{A}_i / \sum_{j=1}^{m} \mathcal{A}_j \tag{2}$$

where parameters α_i $(i = 1, 2, \ldots, m)$ are constant, brand-specific effects representing the marketing effectiveness of the respective brands, ϵ_i reflects specification error, X_{ki} are the marketing instruments $(k = 1, 2, \ldots, K)$ for brand i $(i, j = 1, 2, \ldots, m)$, $f_k(\cdot)$ is a positive, monotone function[1], and β_k is a parameter for the sensitivity of all brands to changes in variable k. Equation (2) shows how attraction translates into market share s_i for brand i.

The inclusion of the α's in attraction models, however, does not fully account for differential effectiveness among brands. The differential effectiveness may be specific to each marketing instrument, such as a brand which has a particularly effective pricing policy or an effective advertising campaign. The α_i's do not appear in the elasticity formulas for a particular marketing instrument, X_k (namely, $e_{s_i} = \beta_k(1 - s_i)$ for MCI models and $e_{s_i} = \beta_k X_{ki}(1 - s_i)$ for MNL models). The *marketing-effectiveness* parameters may reflect differences in the *brand franchise* or *brand loyalty*. Literally, they are the constant component of each brand's attraction, but they have nothing to do with elasticities. As a result, elasticity formulas for simple attraction models do not reflect differential effectiveness.

[1]If $f_k(\cdot)$ is the exponential transformation Equation (1) specifies a MNL Model. If $f_k(\cdot)$ is the identity transformation Equation (1) specifies an MCI Model. $f_k(\cdot)$ may also be used to reflect how the raw marketing instruments are transformed to reflect the distinctiveness of marketing activities—using *z-scores* in the MNL Model or *zeta-scores* in the MCI Model.

If we wish to reflect a world in which brands are differentially effective in implementing their marketing programs, this may be achieved in only one way, that is, by specifying parameters β_k's in such a manner that each brand has a special parameter, β_{ki}, for variable X_k. The attraction component of the differential-effect market share model is represented as follows:

$$\mathcal{A}_i = \exp(\alpha_i + \epsilon_i) \prod_{k=1}^{K} f_k(X_{ki})^{\beta_{ki}} \tag{3}$$

Cross-competitive-effects (asymmetric) versions of these models allow further that brands can be differentially sensitive to the actions of particular competitors.

$$\mathcal{A}_i = \exp(\alpha_i + \epsilon_i) \prod_{k=1}^{K} \prod_{j=1}^{m} f_k(X_{kj})^{\beta_{kij}} \tag{4}$$

where β_{kij} is the parameter for the cross-competitive effect of variable X_{kj} on brand i.

Equation (4) is called an attraction model with differential cross-competitive effects or a *fully extended* attraction model to distinguish it from a differential-effect attraction model (3). The most important feature of the fully extended model is that the attraction for brand i is now a function not only of the firm's own actions (variables X_{ki}'s, $k = 1, 2, \ldots, K$), but also of all other brands' actions (variables X_{kj}'s, $k = 1, 2, \ldots, K; j = 1, 2, \ldots, m$). The β_{kij}'s for which i is different from j are the *cross-competitive effect* parameters. The β_{kij}'s for which j equals i (i.e., β_{kii}) are *direct-effect* parameters and are equivalent to the β_{ki}'s in the differential-effect model (3). This notation is cumbersome, but it is necessary to keep track of who is influencing whom. Note that the fully extended model has many more parameters (with $m \times m \times K$ β_{kij}'s and m α_i's) than the original attraction model (with $K + m$ parameters) and the differential-effect model (with $m \times K + m$ parameters).

When there are sufficient degrees of freedom to estimate all these cross-effect parameters, model calibration is straightforward[2]. But for the cases in which one expects many of the cross-effect parameters to be insignificant, a statistical expert system (SES) has been developed to estimate the parameters of these models. There are 15 steps which have been integrated into a SAS[(R)] program (called MACRO MCI) to perform the analytical tasks in estimating asymmetric market-share models.

1. Form the flat file containing variables [Sales plus Marketing Instruments] and observations [Brands × Stores × Weeks].

2. Choose the model form (MCI or MNL) and the transformations of variables (zeta-scores, exp(z-scores), or raw scores).

3. Form the differential-effects file containing the expanded set of variables [Sales + (Instruments + 1) × Brands] for the same observations.

4. Form the differential-effects covariance matrix and store.

5. Estimate the differential-effects model.

[2]We have known for a long time (Nakanishi and Cooper (1974)) that these nonlinear market-share models can be linearized by log centering (dividing each sides of the market-share equation by its geometric mean and then taking the log of each side).

6. Find the brand intercept nearest zero and delete.
7. Re-estimate the differential-effects model.
8. Compute the residuals and sort by brand.
9. Cross correlate each brand's residuals with the marketing instruments of every competitor.
10. Tally the significant cross correlations.
11. Form the differential cross-effect variables.
12. Compute and store complete covariances (differential effects and cross-competitive effects).
13. Simultaneously re-estimate the parameters for all the effects in the calibration data.
14. Estimate WLS or GLS weights and re-estimate parameters.
15. Cross validate on fresh data.

This macro program makes it practical to estimate the parameters of large-scale market-share models. The first step in converting model results to decision-related factors is the computation of elasticities. But in using more and more realistic market-share models we find that elasticities change with market conditions. Constant-elasticity models reflect far too simplistic a view of markets and competition. To represent the elasticities which characterize market behavior we discuss a second step involving both competitive maps and models which can locate ideal points or vectors in those maps. We have a brand × brand array of cross elasticities for each time period and/or store. The systematic structures underlying this three-mode array can be revealed using a special case of three-mode factor analysis (Tucker (1969), Cooper (1988)). There are two kinds of graphic outputs. The first summarizes the competitive structure over time and/or stores. Given what is known about the competitive activity at each place and time, this display helps identify what produces the major shifts in competitive structure. We can then create the second graphic display—¡a brand map—corresponding to each of these major shifts in competitive structure. The brand-to-brand competition represented in brand maps recognizes that two basic patterns need to be reflected. First there is a pattern of how each brand exerts influence over all the brands in the market. Similar positions in this pattern indicates that two brands exert similar kinds of influence over all other brands. And second there is the pattern of how brands are influenced by marketplace forces. Similar positions in this pattern indicate that two brands are influenced by the same basic forces in the marketplace. Brands can differ in their clout (i.e. their ability to exert influence) and they may differ in the vulnerability (i.e. their ability to be influenced by other brands or their receptivity to their own marketing actions). The brand map represents these two sides of the influencing process by a joint space. Each brand appears twice—once to reflect its clout and once to reflect its vulnerability. The length of the clout vector reflects the overall clout of a brand, just as the length of a vulnerability vector reflects the overall vulnerability of a brand. The angle between brand A's clout vector and brand B's vulnerability vector reflects the cross-competitive pressure A exerts on B.

The ability to imbed ideal points or preference vectors into a competitive map is merely an additional device to aid in interpretation of the spatial relations. The decision-support software CASPER was designed to help with Stage 4: Strategy and Planning. CASPER was designed with three principles in mind. First, managers must be able to learn from history. Thus a year worth of historical data, covering nine coffee brands and three grocery chains, was incorporated into CASPER along with the graphing utilities to be able to summarize each brand's performance over time or the performance of all competitors in a single time period. Second, managers must be able to simulate the consequences of any competitive scenario in terms of sales, costs, and revenues for all competitors in the marketplace. Thus the asymmetric market-share model and category-volume model developed in Chapter 5 of the book were incorporated into CASPER's simulator, along with the basics of financial analysis—allowing managers readily to assess the impact of a plan on costs and revenues. The simulator is an *inference engine* in the planning system. It describes how each of the marketing actions of each brand translates into sales. We do not understand how data are useful for planning without an *inference engine* of this sort. And third, managers must be able to test out a proposed plan in a dynamic, competitive environment. And thus a dynamic simulator was created in the form of a promotion-analysis game with three game periods of nine weeks each. Brand managers and store managers can compete against each other and against the results obtained by the real brands and stores in the corresponding time periods.

Stage 5 involves follow up. It is critically important that the analyst reviews the performance of a firm's product/brand after the marketing plans are put into effect. Discrepancies between forecasts and performance might be due to errors in forecasting industry sales, errors in forecasting market shares or that marketing activities were not carried out as planned by the firms or competitors' activities were not as anticipated. The sources of errors must be isolated so that the proper remedial actions are undertaken for the next planning cycle.

3 New Developments

There are three new areas explored in the book that make market-share analysis more broadly applicable. These deal with time-series issues, issues in collinearity, and estimation of the fully extended (cross-competitive effects) models.

3.1 Time-Series Issues

One of the most fundamental properties of attraction models has been that they produce logically consistent estimates of market shares (i.e. market shares are non-negative and sum to one over all competitors in a time period and/or region). It has been believed that this very desirable property was lost if lagged dependent variables were incorporated into the attraction specification. The book demonstrates (Sections 3.9 and 3.10) that lagged dependent and/or independent variables can be incorporated into MCI or MNL models without losing the logical-consistency property as long as the specification is done with log-centered variables.

3.2 Issues in Collinearity

The primary objection to log centering as a way of linearizing the market-share equation was that in differential-effects models or cross-competitive-effects models log centering somehow induced high collinearity even if the original variables were only modestly correlated (Bultez and Naert (1975), Naert and Weverbergh (1981)). Section 5.6 demonstrates three important results. First, the high collinearity observed in differential-effects models or cross-competitive-effects models is not due to log centering. It is present in linear, multiplicative and attraction specifications of market-share models if the explanatory variables are expressed in either raw or share form. Second, using distinctiveness coefficients such as either exp(z-scores) or zeta-scores effectively controls the collinearity in these equations. Third, when viewed as a numerical-analysis problem, collinearity becomes serious when the cross-products matrix can not be inverted. But the special structure of the cross-products matrix from a differential-effects attraction model makes it robust against high correlations induced by the model's structure. It should be invertible when the original variables themselves are not extremely correlated.

3.3 Estimation of the Fully Extended Model

The fully extended model has a parameter for every cross-competitive effect of each brand's full complement of marketing instruments on each other competitor. Thus with K marketing instruments on each of m brands the model would estimate a total of $(m + K \times m^2)$ parameters. When sufficient degrees of freedom are available to estimate this many parameters a very simple multivariate regression model can be used. Section 5.8 points out that OLS procedures produce the best linear-unbiased estimates (BLUE) of the parameters. It is not necessary to resort to GLS procedures to obtain minimum-variance estimates of this model.

4 A Look to the Future

Chapter 8 in the book briefly delineates a research agenda dealing with estimation problems, integration of panel data and store-level data, market-basket models, and issues in decision support.

The agenda concerning estimation problems involves dealing with missing data, developing constrained parameter estimates, and determining the long-run effects of marketing actions. Missing data are a concern in estimation of the category-volume model and the fully extended attraction model. We want to use all the data that are available, but want the missing elements in each observation have as little influence on the parameter estimates as possible. Cooper, de Leeuw and Sogomonian (1989) have recently developed an algorithm to impute the missing values in this way. Regarding constrained parameters we note that managers (dealing with FPBGs) expect all price parameters to have a negative sign and all promotion parameters to have a positive sign. This can be achieved through constrained parameter estimation. But these procedures should be thoroughly investigated before a well-reasoned decision on parameter-estimation methods is made. Regarding long-run effects Hanssens (1987) shows that no permanent effects of marketing action could be found in 106 tests on scanner data relating to instant coffee. But further study is needed to detect if differences in the brand-specific intercepts could be related to differences in national advertising or other variables which are typically not included in scanner data sets.

The book relies predominantly on store-level data for market-share analysis, while many market modelers have followed the path of Guadagni and Little (1983) in developing models based on scanner panels. The integration of these data sources is now a reality, but the methods to use both data in analyzing market response require much further development. Moore and Wine (1987) report the only published research in this important domain.

Many of the issues of interest to retailers center on purchases across product categories (e.g. shelf-space allocation). The ultimate extension of the ideas in the book will be to create a system of hierarchically organized category-volume and market-share models which collectively reflect the competitive interplay among all the items in a market basket.

The issues in decision support focus on needed developments in game theory and extensions of expert systems. Generalizing game theory to reflect all the competitive influences described in the book will be a difficult task, but realistic scenarios are needed if policy implications usually stemming from game-theoretic analyses are to be useful for management in information-rich environments. Regarding traditional expert systems it is important to note that they are not learning systems. Yet learning is what is so clearly called for at this stage of development. The following section deals with the creation of learning systems.

4.1 From CASPER to CHAINs

A **CHAIN** is a Combined **H**uman- and **A**rtificial-**I**ntelligence **N**etwork. Explicitly considering the role of human intelligence in a management system encourages us to take a broader, open-systems view of the process. Open systems have semi-permeable boundaries with the environment. Such systems actively regulate the flow of information and other resources across their boundaries in a purposeful effort to achieve system goals. Opens systems can learn from their interaction with the environment. A traditional expert system, on the other hand, is a closed system once the knowledge engineering has taken place. The human role is merely to provide input to the closed expert system, and to receive the answer. There is no learning on the part of the expert system.

Consider a manager/management scientist sitting at a microcomputer with CASPER as the two central links in a CHAIN. What more is needed to facilitate learning? Having helped a few generations of students through this learning process, we see the need for several developments. Fig. 2 summarizes the key functions and relations. As stated earlier, a manager must be able to learn from history. The raw data in a *fact base* are of very limited use until they are visualized using graphics generators and/or report generators. The increasing importance of graphics in summarizing vast amounts of information and driving the interactions between humans and computers is why we refer to visualization stations rather than workstations. So we need to plan for graphic information as well as numeric and textual information in a *fact base*. CASPER's standard graphic libraries begin this process by summarizing within-brand performance over time and across-brand performance within a time period. CASPER currently summarizes history in spreadsheets reflecting store-level sales. This will have to evolve so that CASPER links to CD-ROM databases with both store-level data and scanner-panel data included. Textual databases

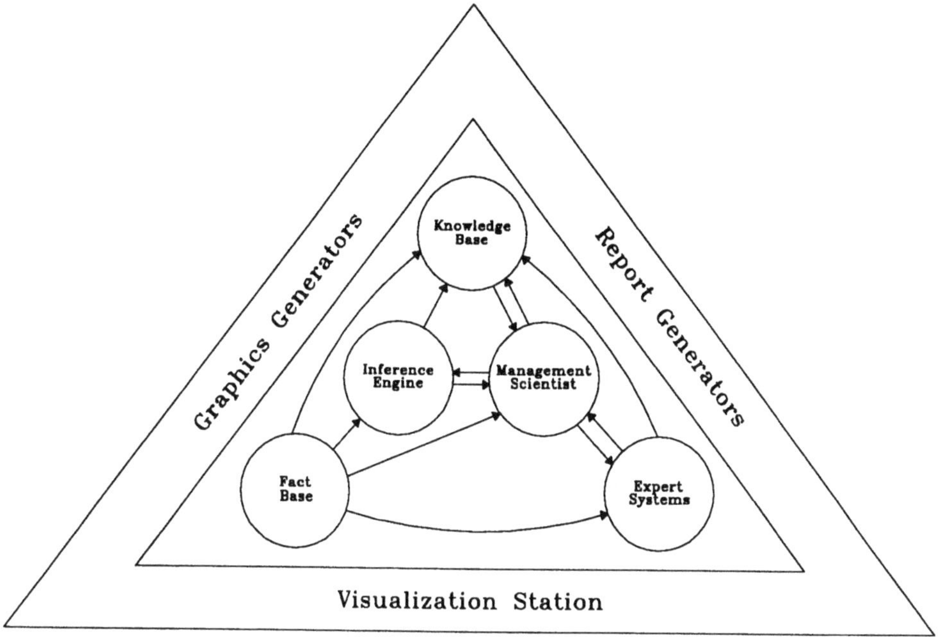

Figure 2: An Open-Systems Model for Learning About Markets and Competition

will also have to be integrated.

The *knowledge base* at any point in time is considered to be open and partial. The emphasis in the open system is on growth in the knowledge base. While facts themselves are best considered as separate from the *knowledge base*, the linkages between entities in the *fact base* are part of the *knowledge base*. The process of inquiry of MBA students and managers typically begins by reviewing the past performances of brands (both over time and across different retail outlets), looking for patterns. Their inquiry could be more systematic if they could create hypertext linkages to written notes concerning store policies and interactions between brands, hypermedia linkages to all graphs relating to particular issues or linkages between notes and graphs. Searches could be made for all notes referring to a brand or a topic or to all graphs mentioned in some set of notes. A permanent record of the preliminary inquiry process—reflecting both the insights and the blind alleys, could help others to move more rapidly along the experience curve.

The most basic function of CASPER is as an *inference engine* allowing a manager/management scientist to translate hypothetical market conditions into forecasts of market response. Imbedding even a complex market-response model in a spreadsheet is a trivial task, but making it useful as an *inference engine* requires far greater functionality. A manager needs to be able to visualize the results of simulations. Numeric and graphic databases will have to be created from the results of CASPER simulations. Hypertext or hypermedia linkages again have a very important role in organizing the *knowledge base* to be useful for inquiry. Also the manager/management scientist must be able to evaluate the *model base* (a component in the *knowledge base*) periodically to assess if the inference engine requires recalibration. This opportunity arises each time the *fact base* is refreshed with new market data. CASPER currently has functions which will run a new mass of data through the *inference engine* to help assess if the model is still a good predictor.

A naive approach to the use of the *inference engine* is to manipulate all the major variables for all the major brands. Testing the influence of newspaper features, in-store displays, store coupons at just five price levels for the three major brands in the coffee-market example in CASPER would require 64,000 iterations. It is obvious that thoughtful consideration is needed in selecting the market scenarios to run through the *inference engine*. Competitive maps should be linked into the *knowledge base* so that they have a more integral role in choosing which scenarios to simulate. But to use these complex maps more readily we need to develop real-time animation. Motion and choice of orientation are very useful techniques for aiding the visual understanding of these high-dimensional information spaces. To be able to rotate these maps and look at the competitive patterns from each brand's point of view would be very helpful.

We also need the ability to bring a auxiliary information (e.g. prices and promotions) from the *fact base* into the competitive-structure graphs to help managers interpret what causes shifts in the structure of the market. The competitive-structure graph is analogous to the *person space* in a multivariate individual-differences analysis (here the individuals are stores or store-weeks). After the millions of machine cycles needed to create such maps, the interpretation is still dependent on an analyst detecting a pattern when simple (often demographic) variables are used to label the points in the space. Given this dependency, we need less cumbersome procedures for using auxiliary information to label points in 3-dimensional space, and some artificial-intelligence algorithms to keep these labels from colliding as these spaces are rotated.

Expert systems have roles both in summarizing existing knowledge (i.e. the *received view* of knowledge in a domain) and in shaping the learning process. Instead of leading a manager/management scientist through a series of descriptive questions about the promotional environment in the formulation of an *expert* promotional plan, the systems could suggest the most informative simulations to run or the graphic summaries which might be most relevant to review Artificial-intelligence algorithms for exception reporting could be used to detect unusual patterns in the *fact base* or in the accumulating results of simulations. Artificial-intelligence algorithms have begun to be used in marketing to help investigators learn about the choice processes of individuals in scanner panels (Currim, Meyer and Le, (1988)). Similar *rule-learning algorithms* (cf. Michalski, (1983)) can be used to *learn* about aggregate market-response. These kinds of applications are worthwhile extensions of current uses. What is more problematic and challenging is the need for ways for the manager/management scientist to interact with the *rule base*—adding rules and reclassifying rules—without, on the one hand, compromising the integrity of the *expert system*, or, on the other hand, requiring managers to become knowledge engineers. Classification of rules into either *received view* or *evolving view* could allow the management scientist to evaluate a *rule base* in a manner similar to the evaluation of a *model base*. The important step is in the opening up of traditionally closed *expert systems*, and allowing of them to grow as knowledge expands.

So the *knowledge base* contains the hypertext or hypermedia linkages among entities in the *fact base* and the results of simulations, as well as the *model base* and the *rule base*. This makes a CHAIN seem like a hypermedia application, which it almost is. But current industry thinking about hypermedia is missing the crucial understanding of the human's (user's) role in building the hypermedia application.

The basic components of hypermedia systems are typically represented to include a video monitor, video-disk player, microcomputer and screen, CD-ROM drives and multimedia software. But this choice stems from a conceptualization of manufacturers as providers of all knowledge and users as recipients of knowledge. A CHAIN recognizes that the human subsystem is an active developer of knowledge which needs to be passed on. Thus CD-ROM should be replaced by or augmented with WORM (write once read many) drives or erasable optical disks. The emphasis is not on erasability, rather it is on writability or creatability. The quality of the creation should be at least as high as that of the received knowledge. Similarly, the video-disk player should be replaced by or augmented with hardware and software related to digital video-tape (DVT) and digital audio-tape (DAT) technologies. Stored knowledge, both methodological and managerial are both needed, but these are not the only ingredients. There must be a way for knowledge to grow and for that growth of knowledge to accumulate—becoming as integral to the system as the *received knowledge*.

There are serious barriers to the development of hypermedia applications. A recent survey of academics conducted by a field-study team at UCLA cited in order of importance: the time required to develop multimedia applications, technical support costs, data acquisition costs, lack of expertise regarding multimedia, lack of preconstructed multimedia databases in a particular subject area, and lack of financial resources. Academics do not in general believe that software developers can create multimedia databases for their specialities. Underlying this is, we believe, a realization that high-tech manufacturers are oriented to providing finished solutions which only require users. Whereas the concept of a CHAIN is that no part of a network should be so encapsulated that a multi-way linkage cannot be established of equivalent quality.

It is the multi-way linkages potentially going throughout the network which makes a CHAIN overcome the old saw that a chain is only as strong as its weakest link. In this sense a CHAIN is more like chain mail, than it is like the single-linkage versions.

References

BULTEZ, A.V., and NAERT, P.A. (1975), Consistent Sum-Constrained Models, *Journal of the American Statistical Association, 70, 351*, 529–535.

COOPER, L.G. (1988), Competitive Maps: The Structure Underlying Asymmetric Cross Elasticities, *Management Science, 34, 6*, 707–723.

COOPER, L.G., DE LEEUW, J., and SOGOMONIAN, A.G. (1989), An Imputation Method for Dealing with Missing Data in Regression, *UCLA Statistics Series 38*.

COOPER, L.G., and NAKANISHI, M. (1988), *Market-Share Analysis: Evaluating Competitive Marketing Effectiveness*, Kluwer Academic Publishers, Boston.

CURRIM, I.S., MEYER, R.J., and LE, N.T. (1988), Disaggregate Tree-Structured Modeling of Consumer Choice Data, *Journal of Marketing Research, 25*, 253–265.

GUADAGNI, P.M., and LITTLE, J.D.C. (1983), A Logit Model of Brand Choice Calibrated on Scanner Data, *Marketing Science, 2, 3*, 203–238.

HANSSENS, D.M. (1987), Marketing and the Long Run, *Center for Marketing Studies Working Paper 164*, Anderson Graduate School of Management, UCLA.

MICHALSKI, R.S. (1983), A Theory and Methodology of Inductive Learning, in: *Machine Learning: An Artificial Intelligence Approach*, eds. R.S. Michalski, J.G. Carbonell and T.M. Mitchell, Tioga Publishing, Palo Alto, CA, 83–134.

MOORE, W.L., and WINER, R.S. (1987), A Panel-Data Based Method for Merging Joint Space and Market Response Function Estimation, *Marketing Science, 6, 1*, 25–42.

NAERT, P.A., and WEVERBERGH, M. (1981), On the Prediction Power of Market Share Attraction Models, *Journal of Marketing Research, 18*, 146–153.

NAKANISHI, M., and COOPER, L.G. (1974), Parameter Estimation for a Multiplicative Competitive Interaction Model—Least Squares Approach, *Journal of Marketing Research, 11*, 303–311.

TUCKER, L.R. (1969), *Some Relations Between Multi-Mode Factor Analysis and Linear Models for Individual Differences in Choice, Judgmental and Performance Data*, Paper presented to the Psychometric Society Symposium, Multi-Mode Factor Analysis and Models for Individual Differences in Psychological Phenomena, April 18.

A Tentative Approach to Integrate AI Techniques to Improve a Heuristic-Based OR Model for Rural Telephone Network Planning

João P. Costa
Faculdade de Economia
and
João N. Clímaco, José F. Craveirinha
Faculdade de Ciências e Tecnologia
Universidade de Coimbra, Portugal

Summary

The mathematical modeling of many real-world problems is a complex and perhaps an impracticable task when it leads to an explosion of the computational calculations. OR has attempted to obtain satisfactory results for this type of problems by resorting to heuristic models. However, the attempts to integrate AI techniques in OR heuristics suggest the possibility of obtaining solutions of better quality. In this paper we present a knowledge-based system that enables the DM (Decision Maker) to define and/or change rules which support a post-optimal analysis of results obtained from traditional heuristic procedures. The characteristics of the referred system enable the DM to incorporate in the system the acquired experience. Results of the application of the system to a problem of rural telephone network planning will be presented.

1 Introduction

In the first part of this contribution we stress the importance of the knowledge about the approximations included in the model that the DM is using. We also present an attempt to explain these aspects in the context of a telecommunication planning model. In the second section we present a model for rural telecommunication network planning and its approximations. In the third section we present in detail some of the more relevant features of a system for evaluating the solutions produced by the model described in the second section. In the fourth section we present an example of how the evaluating system works and in the 5th section the results of the tests carried out with the model are presented. In the appendices we present technical details which are not essential for understanding the system presented here but which are important for people interested in getting a deeper knowledge of its characteristics. We had no space to explain further the details in the appendices.

1.1 DSS Approach

A DSS (Decision Support System) is intended for real world problems. Ideally, a DSS should give the DM a measure of its closeness to the real world problem. This is not

NATO ASI Series, Vol. F 61
Knowledge, Data and Computer-Assisted Decisions
Edited by M. Schader and W. Gaul

possible because it would imply that the system should possess a representation ('the system should know') of the existing differences between itself and the reality. On the one hand this representation should itself be somehow distant from the reality of the true existing differences. On the other hand if that representation was possible it would have to incorporate the represented differences in the model initially implemented in the DSS.

Nevertheless, a DSS must facilitate the knowledge of its 'distance' from reality thereby enabling the DM to carry out, 'a posteriori', the adaptation of the modeled 'vision' of the world (implemented in the DSS), to reality. The work here presented was organized according to this perspective. We have previously implemented a DSS for dynamic rural telecommunication network planning. We used an algorithmic model presented by Costa, Antunes, Clímaco and Craveirinha (1989), where reality is presented with some approximations namely by linearizing the transmission equipment costs and by considering only the fixed switching costs in some phases of the system. We now try to supply the DSS with features which enable the DM to evaluate the proximity between the model and the reality, that is enabling the DM to recognize in which circumstances the DSS has 'both feet on the ground'. In our opinion only a DSS with this feature may claim to be effective and usable in decision support on real world problems.

1.2 Solution Evaluation: DSS for Rural Telecommunication Network Planning

A subsystem for evaluating the solutions supplied by a module for static planning of rural telecommunication network, described by Costa et al. (1989), was implemented. Note that the referred solutions are not optimal solutions. The method used in this module is of heuristic nature and contains various sources of error. Therefore we only may reach admissible solutions the quality of which is supposed to be 'good'. With the evaluator the DM may act directly on the solutions by changing the parameters considered convenient and then the DM may evaluate the effect of those changes by recalculating their real cost. An evaluator of this type assumes that the interface between the computational representation of the solutions and the user is implemented in such a way that it enables the DM to evaluate correctly the given solutions thereby grasping their 'optimality', that is in what measure they are approximations to the optimal solution of the real problem. In the present case the interface is a graphical one and compresses the topological representation of the network and easy access to detailed (numerical) information about the network plan. This evaluator integrates a knowledge-base and an inference engine (IE).

Knowledge is stored in the base in the form of production rules, i.e., of condition-action type. It is the user who has to insert the rules in the base by using a rule editor. These rules may be (within certain limits, described later) changed, replaced or suppressed according to the DM's wish. These facts make the rule-base interactive and the knowledge that it contains adaptable to different types of situations. On the other hand the base works as a 'register' of the experience accumulated by the DM in the process of solution evaluation. The subsystem includes tools (a 'debugger' and a 'tracer') for maintaining the consistence of the knowledge registered in the base both at the syntactic and semantic level.

As for the inference engine (IE), it evaluates the rules contained in the base and

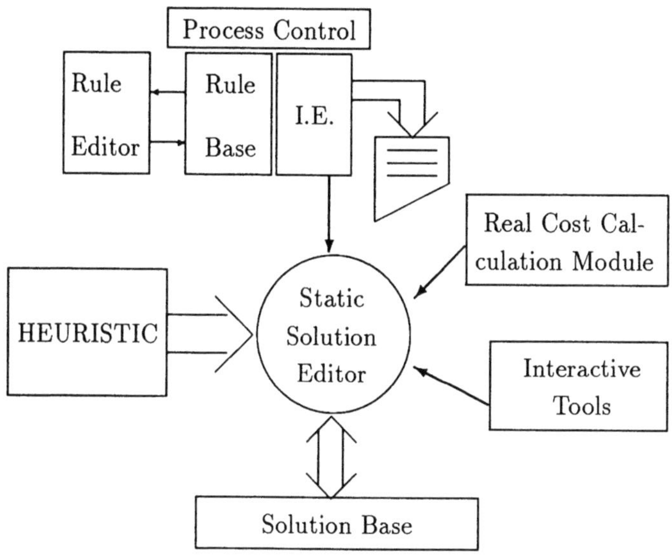

Figure 1: Block Diagram of the Sub-System

determines the moment of their application. In essence its task consists in going through the whole rule-base and select the rule(s) the condition part of which is currently fulfilled. Then it proceeds to the execution of the action part of the rule. The conditions of the rules are dependent on the solution to be evaluated and/or on the control variables of the process. These variables characterize the present state of the process of evaluation of a solution. It is the DM who declares—through the rule editor—the process variables and their type.

The user may opt for the IE to generate reports on the application of rules in the base to the solution being evaluated. The IE may also keep (by option of the DM) the register of the evolution of the solutions in the course of the application of the rules. The tools for acting on the network, the module for real cost calculations and the rule editor may be considered as a knowledge acquisition subsystem. The rules that the DM inserts in the rule base, through the rule editor, result from the DM's experimentation with the network for the year-horizon of the planning period. The validity of these rules is tested by applying them to problems which appear before the DM and they may be modified whenever necessary.

2 Static Planning of Rural Telecommunication Networks

2.1 The Model Used

The definition used of rural telecommunication network as well as the generic presentation of the rural telecommunication network planning problem (r.t.n.p.p.) may be found in Costa et al. (1989). The objectives and global strategies of the model are also described in that reference. In synthesis we may say that the model is dynamic, with a predefined

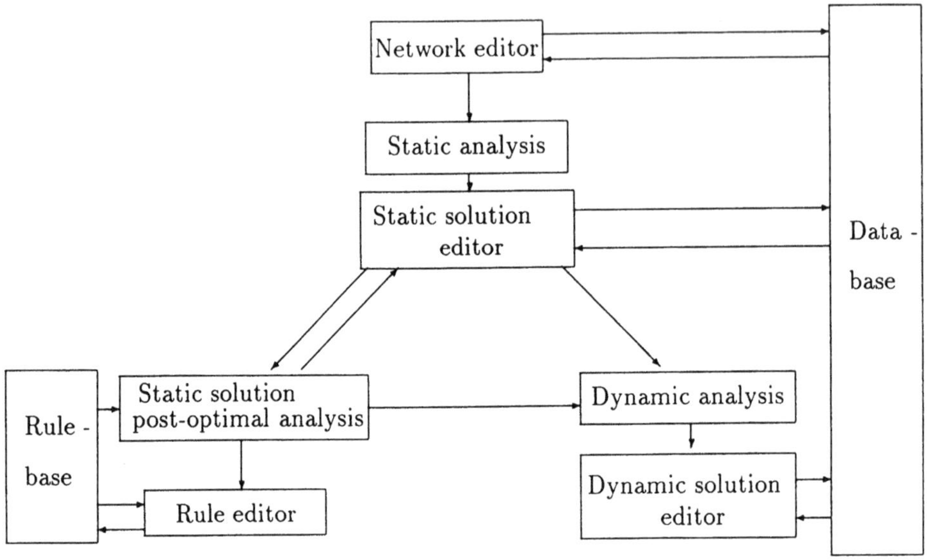

Figure 2: Block Diagram of the Model

planning period; it is interactive; it takes into account the existing network and it is based on heuristic algorithms, including sub-problems solved by exact methods. The model has three phases. In the first phase the user characterizes the local network under study and the planning period. In the second phase the static planning is carried out. Finally in the third phase the 'k-best' expansion strategies (in terms of topological evolution and cable capacity expansions) are determined-dynamic planning. The block diagram of the global system including the static solution evaluating module, is presented in Fig. 2.

The solutions of the second phase (static planning) are questioned by the evaluator sub-system. The static planning aims at determining the 'k-best' network plans (in terms of number of exchanges and their location and service areas) for the year-horizon of the planning period, which minimize the costs and satisfy the new subscribers foreseen for the whole period. The mathematical programming formulation used in the model is described in Costa et al. (1989).

2.2 Approximation of the Model to Reality

The parameters which more significantly decrease the closeness of the model to reality are summarized in the following paragraphs.

i) The r.t.n.p.p. is a combinatorial problem of great complexity and it was approached by dividing the problem into three distinct phases. This division is not found in the real problem and it merely represents an attempt to reduce the problem to a number of sub-problems of lower dimension and complexity. Some of the problem parameters are only taken into account in the phases where most of their influence may be felt. However they also affect the other phases (where they are not taken into account) although in a less strong manner.

ii) The junction network (which interconnects the local exchanges and these to the upper level switching center) is not taken into consideration, that is, the local r.t.n.p.p. is carried out ignoring the fact that the exchanges are interconnected through the junction network. If the cost of this network was taken into account in the optimization process it could affect the number and location of the local exchanges.

iii) The main source of error in the static planning model used (which is presented in third place by reasons of specificity grading) is the way in which the switching and transmission costs are considered. The model used assumes the transmission costs (conduits, cables, interconnections) are linear. In reality these costs have two non-linear features: on the one hand the cable cost varies according to a step-wise function in the number of subscribers (for example only cables for 8, 14, 28, 56, ... subscribers are used); on the other hand there is a fixed cost per unit of length associated with the cable installation. The adopted method consists in linearizing the transmission costs as indicated in Costa et al. (1989). The switching costs have also two components. One component is the fixed cost associated with the installation of an exchange (building, common equipment, etc.) and the second component varies in a modular manner with respect to the number of subscribers served by the exchange (the exchanges are composed of modules each of them having n switching elements). If the variable part of the switching cost is linearized it becomes constant for a given telecommunication network whichever plan is considered. That cost then ceases to be an influent parameter for the decision process and may be disregarded. Therefore only the fixed part of the switching costs was considered. Note that the linearization of costs also implies that the transmission equipment installed at year 0 of the planning period is disregarded.

iv) The aggregation of subscribers into distribution points ('DPs') and the aggregation of DPs into centers of demand was carried out in the first phase of the model without taking into account the costs of the DPs and the costs of the centers of demand. It is necessary to refer that the main implication of the static plan in the global system results from the limitation imposed on the number of possible locations for the exchanges. Note that the evaluation of the solutions from the 2nd phase (static planning) only enables the effects mentioned in items ii) and iii) to be attenuated.

3 The Knowledge Based System

3.1 The Rules

As mentioned in section 1.2 the knowledge is formalized in the base in the form of rules of 'condition/action' type. The condition of a rule is obtained from the logical 'and' and from the logical 'or' of conditions which we will consider as basic. A boolean function (which outputs a value 'true' or 'false') is made to correspond to each of these conditions. These functions are implemented in the system in Pascal. The conditions may refer to the state of the process variables and/or to the network (static solution) being evaluated. The basic conditions relative to the network test certain characteristics of the solution and may output, beyond the value 'true' or 'false', some additional information about the network. We tried to supply the system with the exhaustive implementation of the possible basic conditions which may become condition of a rule. Of course this objective was not attained and at the moment only some basic conditions are implemented.

The action of a rule (similarly to the one of a condition) consists in a sequence of punctual actions incident on the network under evaluation and on the process variables. A procedure implemented in the system corresponds to each of these punctual actions. These actions are implemented in a given solution (static plan) only if that entails an improvement in the network cost. On the other hand those actions have actual effect over the process variables whenever it becomes necessary to change the state of the process. As well as for the conditions, we tried to implement all the basic actions which may become necessary. It should be noted that the exhaustive implementation of actions and conditions is a very important factor in increasing the flexibility of the knowledge base. Since each action or condition requires the corresponding computational implementation (in Pascal) the user is confined to the implemented actions and conditions. This means that there may only exist rules in the base which are composed of such actions and conditions, thereby reducing the variation introduced by the user in the base.

3.2 Rule Editor

As previously referred the user may change the knowledge-base by changing the rules which compose the base. The rules are represented computationally in the form of 'strings', these being later interpreted by the IE. The user has access to these 'strings' and may change, in this way, the corresponding rules. Of course these changes must respect the syntax consistency of the rules, a debugger existing in the editor which helps the user in this task. On the other hand the user is limited to the basic conditions and punctual actions implemented in the system. Finally the user must keep the semantic consistency of the base. The IE has 'devices' which permit the DM to control the application of the rules thereby enabling the verification of the semantic consistency of the knowledge-base. The 'strings' which constitute the rules are kept on hard-disk in the form of files. These are loaded in the system at the user's request whenever their application becomes necessary. In this way we enable the existence of several consistent and independent sets of rules applicable to distinct situations and/or when the user wants to use them.

3.3 Process Variables

The task of changing the network plan (which results from the 2nd phase of the model) into a network of lower cost is carried out step by step that is by application not only of one rule but of a sequence of chained rules. There is a 'correct' occasion for applying each rule and this implies the knowledge of the state of the cost improvement process. In order to characterize this state we use the so called process variables. If by hypothesis we were in a phase of relocation of exchanges then there may exist a logical variable (i.e., 'location') with the function of indicating that only location rules may be applied. If the network for the year-horizon is the solution to be post-optimized (hence defining the work memory), the set composed of the network and the process variables constitutes the work environment. This work environment determines the best occasion for applying (i.e., for 'waking up') the rules in the base. The IE compares ('matching') the condition of each rule with the work environment and thereby selects those which should be applied. The process variables as well as the rules, are declared through the rule editor and they may be defined as logical, integer or real.

3.4 The Inference Engine

The IE's main task is to select the rules to be applied at each moment. Whenever there is more than one applicable rule (in a given context) the IE presents the rules to the DM and asks him to decide upon the rules which must be applied and the order of application. If by chance there are inconsistencies in the base, i.e., several rules are applicable at the same occasion, then they will be signaled and eliminated in this manner. The IE, at the user request, may generate a report presenting the sequence of applied rules and the changes carried out in the work memory by application of those rules. This report is—beyond a written document created by the system, usable for documentation of the planning process of a given local network—a control tool for application of the rules in the base. The IE may also maintain, at the user's request, a register (on hard-disk) of the different solutions resulting from the post-optimal process. Those solutions may be later visualized in the static solution editor.

4 Example of Working With the System

Next we will present an example of the use of the knowledge base. The rules used in this example are enunciated in Appendix I. The characteristics of the local network under analysis are indicated in Appendix II. In Appendix III we present the detailed features of a solution obtained from the 2nd phase of the model (static analysis) when the maximum number of exchanges is 3 and '5-best' solutions are being considered. Finally in Appendix IV we present the detailed features of the post-optimal analysis of the solution in Appendix III.

The initial network topology for the year-horizon of the planning period (obtained from the static analysis phase) is presented in Fig. 3. The corresponding cost is 229 691.616 cost units. If we ask the system to analyze this situation, supported in the knowledge-base, it begins by applying some of the rules. When the last rule is applied it gives origin to a slight network topology variation and the corresponding cost is 227 204.898 c.u. The solution is improved by 1.07%. The IE proceeds to select rules and applies one rule which gives origin to a new solution with the cost of 227 012.786 c.u. (0.08% improvement). Afterwards the IE proceeds with its action, the improved solution cost being 226 742.965 c.u. (0.12%). In this case the location of one exchange was modified. If the IE continues working it gives origin to a solution with the cost of 172 937.639 (23.73%). Note that an exchange was eliminated in this step. Finally, a message appears: "There are no more applicable rules in the rule-base." and the IE stops the execution. The execution time in this example was approximately 5 minutes; however, a great part of this time was consumed in the printing of the report generated by the system.

5 Results of the Tests With the Evaluating System

The tests were carried out with the set of rules indicated in App. I. It does not make sense to test the static solution evaluator by using networks randomly generated (and so obtaining statistical parameters for the system performance) because the networks which in practice the DM has to evaluate are not 'random' but follow some typical patterns. So we preferred to choose two typical networks, one with 10 nodes and the other with 20 nodes. In the network with 10 nodes firstly we considered 15 arcs representing the possible connections and we performed the static analysis of the network by considering a maximum of 3 exchanges and '5-best' solutions (heuristically calculated). The results obtained are indicated in Tab. 1. Next we performed the static analysis for a maximum of 4 exchanges and the same number of 'best' solutions. The results obtained are in Tab. 2. We increased the number of possible connections between the nodes from 15 to 20 and we performed the static analysis of the resulting network for a maximum of 4 exchanges and '5-best' solutions. The results obtained are presented in Tab. 3. Finally we considered the network of 20 nodes with 25 possible connections and we carried out the static analysis for a maximum of 4 exchanges and '5-best' solutions. The results obtained are indicated in Tab. 4.

One of the factors which determines such a high percental improvement in the cost is the fact that the set of rules used takes into account the whole problem (assignment and location). Since the objective of the 2nd phase of the global heuristic model is only to reduce the number of possible exchange locations, more emphasis is given to the location of the exchanges. On the other hand the number of exchanges in the solutions resulting from the static analysis is normally higher than the optimal number. As shown in the example of section 4 the highest relative improvement in the cost is obtained when the number of exchanges is changed (decreased). If we started with solutions the number of exchanges of which was optimal then the improvement would be 4% at the most. However we opted for presenting these results because the typical solutions from the static analysis are 'inflated' in terms of optimal number of exchanges. From the point of view of the system global perspective the post-optimal analysis of solutions has interest only if the quality of the set of possible exchange locations is improved.

The execution times obtained in the present tests vary from 4 to 5 minutes, strongly depending on the number of times the solution under analysis is changed. For each alteration the system includes in the generated report the new network obtained by the process described thereby consuming a lot of execution time.

References

BUTLER, C.W., HODIL, E.D., and RICHARDSON, G.L. (1988), Building Knowledge-Based Systems with Procedural Languages, *IEEE Expert*.

COSTA, J.P., ANTUNES, C.H., CLÍMACO, J.C., and CRAVEIRINHA, J.F. (1989), *A Dynamic Interactive Model for Rural Telephone Network Planning*, presented at EURO X, Beograd, submitted for publication.

FRANCIONI, J.M., and KANDEL, A. (1988), A Software Engineering Tool for Expert System Design, *IEEE Expert, Spring 1988*.

Appendix I — A Set of Rules

*The file of linear costs may not correspond to the file of non-linear costs and the approximation may not be a linear regression. This leads to rules of improvement of any solution and not only specific rules based on the disregarded (by the model) parameters. Different sets of rules may be used in different cases.

*We can only think of changing the number of local exchanges after obtaining the best possible assignment for the present configuration.

*If the switching cost is greater than the distribution cost a local exchange has to be eliminated.

*In case of the elimination of one exchange, the one to be eliminated is the one which serves the area the subscribers of which could be connected to another exchange through the arc the cost of which is less than the cost of one exchange installation.

*Whenever the order of magnitude of cost of one arc is the same as the cost of installation of one exchange (with the necessary number of modules of commutation) a new exchange must be installed.

*In case of installation of a new exchange this has to be located at the root of the subtree supported by the arc to be eliminated. The next step is to relocate the local exchanges in their service areas.

*The cost of the switching modules is generally greater than the fixed cost of installation of one exchange— The heuristic generally gives more exchanges than the optimum number because it does not consider the cost of the switching modules.

*If the total switching capacity is greater than the total number of subscribers served by the local network, by an amount of two or more modules, and the exchanges have only one switching module, then it is necessary to eliminate local exchanges.

*If the total number of switching elements installed in the exchanges, subtracted from the total number of subscribers of the local network area, is greater than the number of elements of one switching module and there are exchanges with more than one switching module, then it is necessary to rebalance the service areas.

*The 'balance' of the service areas is obtained with 'intelligent' changes (trying to use installed and not used switching capacity and eliminating nodes from the service areas with more than one switching module) of the nodes in the periphery of the service areas.

*If a subtree connected to one exchange has more subscribers than those served by the exchange subtracted from the number of subscribers of that subtree, then the exchange must be moved to the subtree root. If the solution under evaluation process is of good quality, it is sufficient to verify the subtrees in the neighborhood of the exchange.

*The assignment of nodes to exchanges is evaluated arc by arc.

*If arc i is the only possible physic connection to one node then it remains untouched.

*If arc i has installed and not used capacity then it must serve more subscribers.

*If arc i serves node j the number of subscribers of which puts the arc cost one step down then the node j, must be served by another arc.

*If arc i serves only one or two nodes then those nodes must be served by another installed arcs because of the fixed installation costs.

Appendix II — Network and Planning Period

The local area telecommunication network serves: 135 existing subscribers at the year 'zero', 187 probable new subscribers for the final year of a 20 year planning period. The subscribers are aggregated in distribution points (DP's) and these in centers of demand. The centers of demand constitute the nodes of the network. The network has 44 Distribution points, 10 Centers of demand, 15 Arcs. The planning period is 20 years and the discount rate is 15%. The local exchanges are characterized by Fixed cost: 1 950.000, Service time: 20 years, Capacity of one switching module: 200, Cost of one module: 24 722.000, Costs of operation and maintenance: 20% of the total cost, per year. The cables are characterized by Fixed cost/km: 230.000, Service time: 20 years, Costs of operation and maintenance: 20% of the total cost, per year. The variable costs of the cables are in Tab. 5 C).

Heuristic cost	Initial real cost	Final real cost	Δ cost	Δ cost %
17 423.800	226 742.965	172 937.639	53 805.326	23.73
17 607.550	226 742.965	172 937.639	53 805.326	32.73
17 688.400	226 796.929	173 088.738	53 708.191	23.68
17 872.150	226 796.929	173 088.738	53 708.191	23.68
18 109.800	229 681.616	172 937.639	56 743.977	24.71

Table 1: Network With 10 Nodes/15 Arcs. Static Analysis Carried out for a Maximum of 3 Exchanges and Considering '5-best' Solutions

16 073.650	284 653.001	173 179.830	111 473.171	39.16
16 201.050	284 680.631	172 937.639	111 742.992	39.25
16 257.400	284 653.001	173 179.830	111 473.171	39.16
16 299.050	283 366.722	177 765.638	105 601.084	37.27
16 384.800	284 680.631	230 875.305	53 805.326	18.90

Table 2: Network With 10 Nodes/15 Arcs. Static Analysis Carried out of a Maximum of 4 Exchanges and Considering '5-best' Solutions

16 073.650	284 653.001	173 179.830	111 473.171	39.16
16 201.050	284 680.631	172 937.639	111 742.992	39.25
16 257.400	284 653.001	173 179.830	111 473.171	39.16
16 299.050	283 366.722	173 088.738	110 277.984	38.92
16 384.800	284 680.631	172 937.639	111 742.992	39.25

Table 3: Network With 10 Nodes/15 Arcs. Static Analysis Carried out of a Maximum of 4 Exchanges and Considering '5-best' Solutions

35 705.500	441 617.878	385 532.863	56 085.015	12.70
35 989.700	441 671.842	385 532.863	56 138.979	12.71
35 999.500	441 715.013	385 532.863	56 182.150	12.72
36 283.700	441 768.978	385 532.863	56 236.115	12.73
36 460.100	439 056.976	387 164.082	51 892.894	11.82

Table 4: Network With 20 Nodes/25 Arcs. Static Analysis Carried out of a Maximum of 4 Exchanges and Considering '5-best' Solutions

A

N.	weight	prob. weight
1	20	0
2	43	10
3	40	21
4	23	23
5	31	31
6	14	14
7	32	11
8	47	19
9	35	35
10	37	23

B

Arc	Node	Node	Length [km]
1	4	1	10.0
2	1	3	10.0
3	5	3	15.0
4	4	5	2.0
5	5	8	12.5
6	8	7	15.0
7	7	2	20.0
8	2	6	10.0
9	6	9	7.5
10	7	10	7.5
11	3	2	10.0
12	7	6	15.0
13	10	9	30.0
14	8	10	20.0
15	1	2	30.0

C

Pair	Cost
8	4.870
14	6.410
28	9.290
56	15.050
112	26.300
224	46.550
448	102.000
896	223.500
1792	468.500

Table 5: A) Centers of Demand B) Arcs C) Variable Costs of the Cables

Appendix III — Heuristic Solution for the Network of App. II

Arc	Capacity	Cost
1	28	5 739.15
3	56	8 815.95
4	56	1 175.46
5	56	7 346.62
8	56	5 877.30
9	56	4 407.97
10	56	4 407.97
Total		37 770.42

Distribution

Node	Capacity	Cost
5	200	63 970.3
6	200	63 970.3
10	200	63 970.3
Total		191 910.9

Switching

Appendix IV — Solution for the Network of the App. III, After the Post-optimal Analysis of the App. IV Solution

Arc	Capacity	Cost
1	28	5 739.15
4	56	1 175.46
5	224	8 291.00
6	112	9 220.68
8	56	5 877.30
9	56	4 407.97
10	56	4 407.97
11	56	5 877.30
Total		44 996.83

Distribution

Node	Capacity	Cost
5	200	63 970.3
2	200	63 970.3
Total		127 940.6

Switching

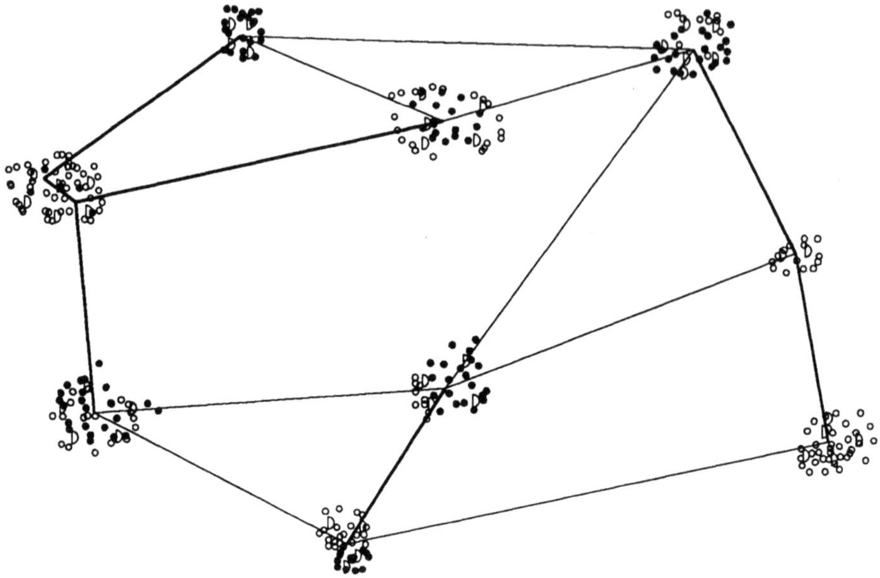

Figure 3: The Initial Topology Used in the Example of Section 4

A Knowledge-Based Multimedia Distributed System Model

Danco Davcev, Dusan Cakmakov and Vanco Cabukovski
Faculty of Electrical Engineering and Computer Science
University of Skopje, Yugoslavia

Summary

The next generation of information retrieval technology will essentially be distributed multimedia systems. The main objective of these systems is to integrate multiple databases in order to provide efficient multimedia information retrieval and transparent services for the end user. In the paper we show that the integration of multimedia and knowledge-based systems increases the retrieval possibilities of the system. Actually, we are going to develop a cognitive-based retrieval system.

1 Introduction

The next generation of database technology will essentially be distributed multimedia (MM) database systems. These systems will include office information systems, CAD/ CAM systems, documents, medical, military and bibliographic retrieval systems, etc. (Egloff and Scheller (1988), Croft and Stemple (1987), Hudson and King (1987), Krawczak et al. (1987), Kemper et al. (1987)). The main objective of these systems is to integrate multiple databases in order to provide efficient MM information retrieval and transparent services for the end user.

Due to the diversified nature of users and information, a very important problem is how to represent, store, and fetch such information. An efficient method is the object-oriented approach in which each information token is treated as an object (Black et al. (1987), Almes and Holman (1987), Tag et al. (1988), Hudson and King (1987)). This approach has been studied in the literature but an efficient distributed architecture to support such models has not been addressed (Ghafoor (1988)).

We propose a new methodology to manipulate a multimedia object in a distributed multimedia database system. Some elements of a general object-oriented multimedia data model have been described by Davcev and Dimitrova (1989). The model has to integrate multiple data streams in order to build the multimedia object as requested by the user. In this paper, we show that the integration of multimedia and knowledge-based systems increases the retrieval possibilities of the system. Actually, we are going to develop a multimedia cognitive-based information retrieval system (AMCIRS).

The paper is organized as follows. In section 2, a global knowledge-based multimedia distributed system model will be presented, section 3 gives the representation of text, images and pictures data and in section 4, a cognitive network is presented. Section 5 introduces some MM operations and in section 6, a conclusion is given.

NATO ASI Series, Vol. F 61
Knowledge, Data and Computer-Assisted Decisions
Edited by M. Schader and W. Gaul

2 A Global Knowledge-Based Distributed System Model

The system consists of m servers and n client processes. Each client process initiates a corresponding CB (cognitive-based) process which is responsible for access plan generation. We assume the existence of client stubs as described in Gibbons (1987), Davcev et al. (1988). The communication network interconnects geographically dispersed servers and clients with broadband multimegabit services. At each node in the system, a local catalog is assumed together with a copy of the catalog directory. The number of servers and clients is dynamic and can be changed according to the actual needs (Davcev et al. (1988)).

A UFI (User Friendly Interface) is designed to enable easy interaction with the resources to the end users. It can provide a powerful abstraction enabling a system of databases in a heterogenous multimedia environment to be viewed as an organized collection of objects and tools which use these objects. The UFI module enables processing of users' queries, their transfer to the CB process, capturing and displaying of results and interfacing of users to the catalog. We shall discuss the UFI module from several points of view.

- Firstly, user interfaces have to provide insulation of the end users from an underlying heterogeneous environment. The interaction with all resources is handled by the client and server stubs (Davcev et al. (1988)).
- Secondly, a UFI module in a multimedia environment will display multiple data to the user in the desired format. For example, a conversion from digital to analog form, different forms of image data, etc., may be required. The UFI has to provide editing and browsing functions for objects of different media. For that purpose, the technique of boxes and glue can be used (Woo et al. (1985)), where an appropriate type of box and editor is invoked for the desired type of media.
- Finally, we would like to design a multimedia object-oriented query language suitable for all types of databases in a multimedia environment. In this way, the structure of the multimedia objects is visible only indirectly via the object operators. The heart of our query language are predicates which enable filtering of MM objects and MM objects definition via MM view (Davcev and Dimitrova (1989)).

To provide the desired level of abstraction, we introduce our cognitive network to realize some conceptual predicates. In our model, the cognitive network is represented by a connected graph. The nodes of the graph represent the concept objects which can be represented as text, image or other type of objects. The arcs determine the concept objects' hierarchy and the degree of relevance between the nodes. The cognitive network is a basis for the cognitive predicates' implementation.

As can be seen from Fig. 1, the client process is represented by a UFI or I/O process, a CB process is conducted by the AMCIRS SUBSYSTEM and servers are responsible for database manipulations. The inference machine is responsible for communication with UFI and servers using and manipulating the information from the conceptual network and catalog. The definition of multimedia objects is made by object-oriented multimedia view (Davcev and Dimitrova (1989)).

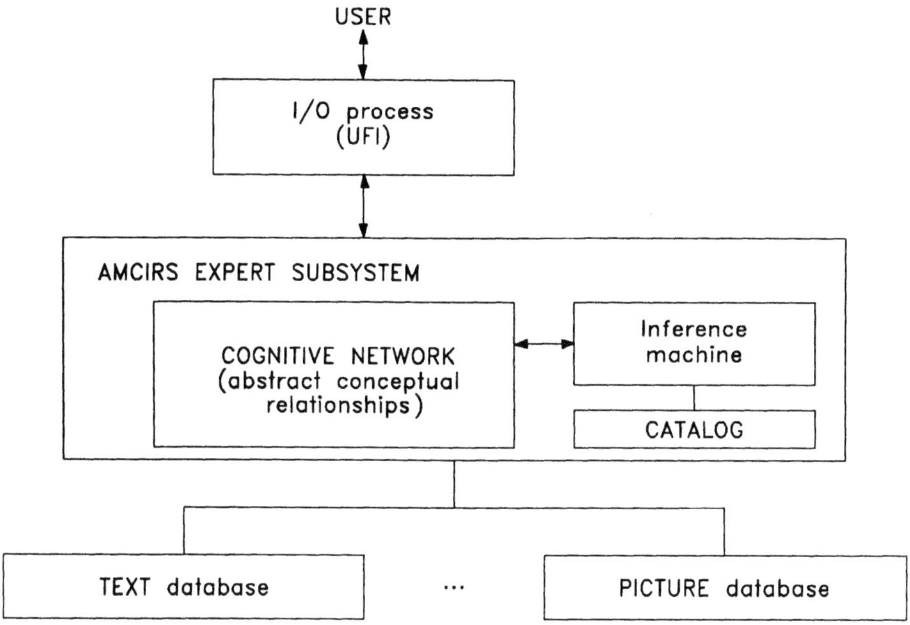

Figure 1: A Global System Model

3 Representation of Text and Image Data

The server is a source of diverse databases which can be used for many multimedia applications. It can be envisioned as a LAN interconnecting local databases and providing transparent services to the user with respect to the heterogeneous databases. The CB process will integrate multiple data from the servers in order to build the multimedia object as requested by the client process.

In addition, the server must provide the management of multimedia databases locally available on that server such as file and schema management for formatted data, concurrency control, synchronization, integrity control, etc. The server stub is also assumed to operate as described in Davcev et al. (1988). We will now describe some techniques for diverse database representation and retrieval operations.

3.1 Text Data

A number of data models in this area have strong similarities with models of multimedia databases. The object-oriented approach has been shown to be useful in applications oriented to text databases (Croft and Stemple (1987)). The text databases contain the following basic classes of objects:

- Symbol object class (font, type);
- Word object class (length, symbol object);
- Phrase object class (description, word object);

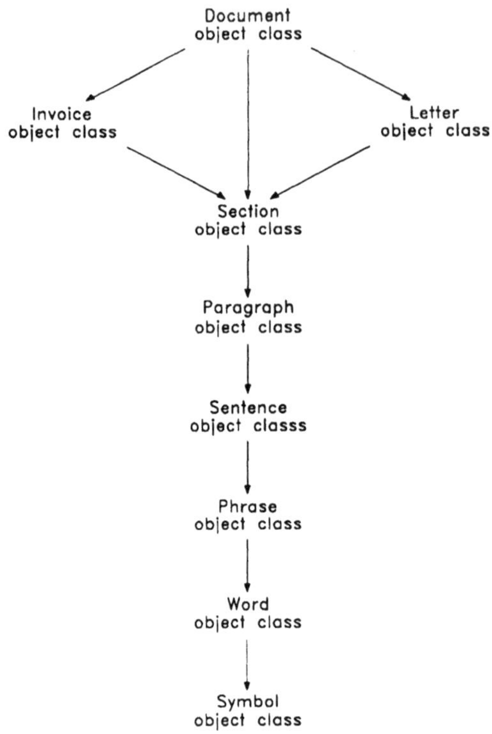

Figure 2: An Example of Text Object Classes

- Sentence object class (description, phrase object, word object, endmark);
- Paragraph object class (description, sentence object);
- Section object class (description, title, paragraph object)
- Document object class (description, title, authors, section object);

Every object will be defined via previously defined objects of a lower hierarchical level.

Our model allows the dynamic definition of new object classes by: adding or deleting new variables in an object class description (enrichment or generalization), adding or deleting new rules in an object class definition (derivation or generalization), restricting or augmenting variable and rule domains and aggregating object classes (Croft and Stemple (1987), Nierstrasz (1985)).

For example, the letter object class is defined by adding the variables for sender and receiver and rule "number of authors is 1" to the definition of the document object class. As a second example, let us define an invoice object class. It can be made by adding account number and expiration date to the description variables in the document object class.

The previous basic text object classes extended by the letter and invoice object classes are illustrated in Fig. 2. Links among them denote the object class subtype/supertype hierarchy.

3.2 Images and Pictures Data

Image and picture data consist of a collection of objects, relationships, object types and subtypes. The following "graphical" objects are especially of interest:

- small objects such as points and pixels;
- medium objects (geometrical shapes such as line segment, region, boxes, circles, cubes, spheres, etc.; natural shapes such as clouds, leaves, trees, faces, rivers, etc.);
- large objects which are more complex collections of small objects and/or medium objects.

Medium and large objects are built recursively via relationships which define the existing logical connections between the objects. A picture or image is represented by a collection of small, medium and large objects.

Technical pictures such as pictures in architecture or mechanical engineering are collections of simple geometrical objects with a hierarchical structure description in the sense of small, medium and large objects. But, in general, any arbitrary picture or image is composed by many natural objects (clouds, trees, rivers, faces, etc.) and a description with geometrical objects in this case is not possible. For example, faces are not ellipses and clouds are not spheres. Fractal geometry provides an efficient way for natural objects' description (Mandelbrot (1977), Mandelbrot (1982)). We need a rich database of natural shapes or subshapes which are fractals. This database will contain relatively compact sets of numbers called iterated function system (IFS) codes, which will reproduce the corresponding fractals (Barnsley (1988), Barnsley and Demko (1985), Barnsley et al. (1986)).

In consequence of the previous discussion, we propose the following basic object classes according to the object class hierarchy:

- Point object class (position, color);
- Line object class (line-type, start-position, length, width, color);
- Fractal object class (description, initial data, set of recursive formulas or analytical relations, set of rules about formulas execution);
- Geometrical object class (description, points, lines, set of interconnection rules);
- Natural object class (description, initial data, fractal objects, geometrical objects, set of interconnection rules);
- Image object class (description (start-position, scale-horizontal, scale-vertical, orientation, etc.), natural objects, geometrical objects, set of interconnection rules).

In our model, any spatial entity which has a defined shape (natural or geometrical) can be represented as an individual "graphical" object. This object representation captures the inherent structure of the image and picture data.

The objects can be created at various levels of spatial resolution and the information about the hierarchical links between objects are stored along with the objects themselves.

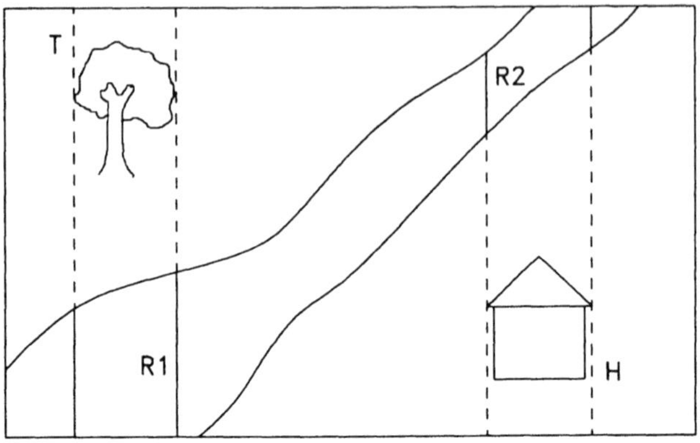

Figure 3: An Example of 2-D String Creation

Natural, geometrical and image objects in our model are defined as a composite objects containing information about subobject class interconnections.

The interconnections are realized by "component-of" and "comprised-of" attributes (Mohan and Kashyap (1988)). For example, if "NO" is a natural object from an image "I" which is a collection of fractal objects "FO1", "FO2" and "FO3", then its description will contain the following information:

> Object class: NATURAL Name: NO Component-of: I Comprised-of: FO1, FO2, FO3

Our model will provide more intelligent image spatial reasoning by adding a 2-D string description (Chang et al. (1988)) to the image object class-description. This string determines position relationships between objects in the image (east, west, north,..., between, surrounded-by). It enables specification of queries and image objects filtering in a natural way. Abstraction and specialization are possible on any object level. This representation provides a clean method for any form of conceptual abstraction.

To illustrate the above discussion let us suppose that we have the image "I" (see Fig. 3) which consists of the objects: tree, house and road between them. There are two natural objects (tree T and road R) and one geometrical object (house H). Natural objects T and R consist of fractal objects: TF1, TF2, ..., TFn and RF1, RF2, ..., RFn. Geometrical object H is a collection of two geometrical objects: a triangle HG1 and a square HG2. The image representation is given in Fig. 4. The description of the image "I" contains the 2-D string "R1 T $<$ H R2" which describes the spatial position relationship of the objects. This string description gives the following information: "R1 is on the south of T", "H is on the south of R2", "R1 is on the west of H", "T is on the west of R2", "R1 is on the southwest of R2", and "R is between T and H".

4 Representing Information in a Cognitive Network

A cognitive network (CN) enables efficient objects retrieval by specifying information relevant to the object content. The user will have some idea of the content of the objects

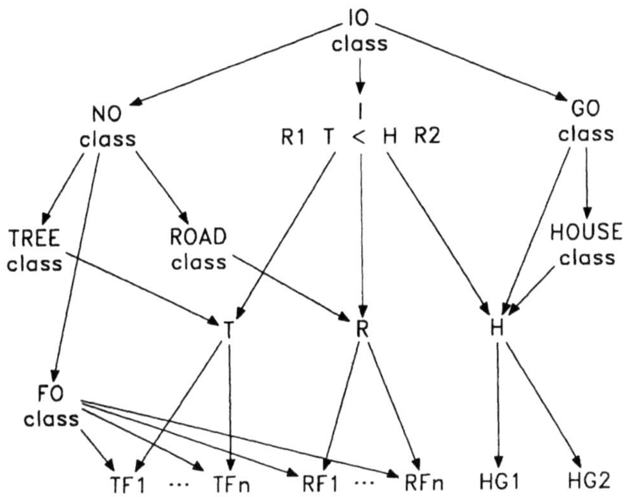

Figure 4: An Image Object Description

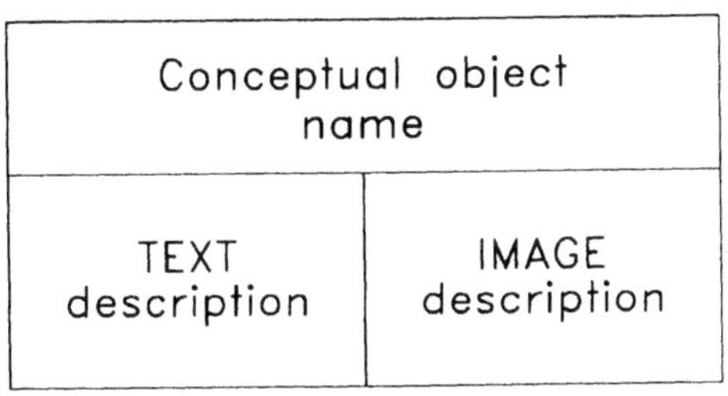

Figure 5: CN Node Information

that he wants to see, and he will specify this information in the query. As a result, all relevant objects will be returned to him by the system.

A CN is represented by a connected graph as a concept object class. The nodes of the graph represent concept objects such as: entities, attributes, states, events, etc. Concept objects have text and image descriptions. A text description includes text objects (text expressions) which are synonymously used in the process of text database retrieval. The image description includes features (conceptual properties) as a basis for image database retrieval. Fig. 5 shows the cognitive network node information.

Similary, as in AI applications, we divide concept objects into concrete and abstract ones. In our approach, every concept object has its text materialization, but only a concrete concept object has an image materialization.

Unoriented arcs represent the degree of relevance and oriented arcs determine the subtype/supertype hierarchy between concept objects. We find that the degree of relevançe between concept objects is an essential relationship for MM object conceptual retrievals. This relationship is natural for the user, it is easy for implementation and can be established between any couple of concept objects. This relationship reflects dependencies in the real world. The hierarchy between concept objects is introduced to enable the processing of queries when the user reasons in a hierarchical way.

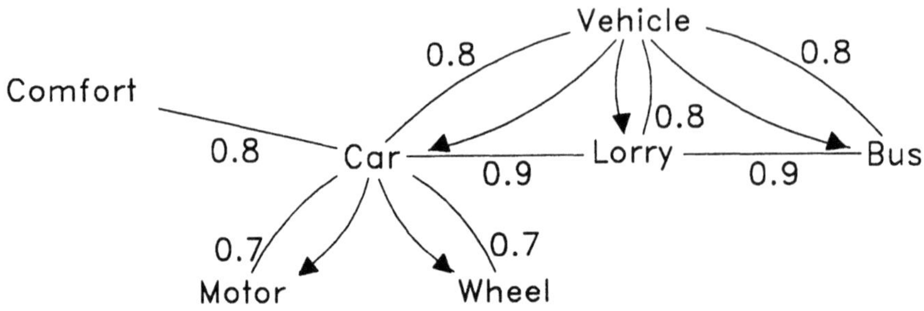

Figure 6: An Example of a CN

Fig. 6 shows a simple example of a CN. 'Comfort' is an abstract concept object and it will have no image representation. Numbers in the [0, 1] interval, which represent the degree of relevance are associated to the unoriented arcs. For example, the degree of relevance between concept objects 'Comfort' and 'Car' is 0.8, between 'Lorry' and 'Bus' is 0.9, etc.

It is natural that the degree of relevance decreases when the distance between concept objects increases. If n is the number of different paths between nodes C_p and C_q, and m_i is the number of arcs on path_i between C_p and C_q, the following function can be used to determine the degree of relevence between them:

$$\text{Rel}(C_p, C_q) = \frac{1}{n} \sum_{i=1}^{n} \text{path}_i, \quad \text{where } \text{path}_i = \prod_{j=1}^{m_i} \text{Rel}_j.$$

For example: Rel('Lorry', 'Comfort') $= \frac{1}{2}(0.9 \times 0.8 + 0.8 \times 0.8 \times 0.8) = 0.615$.

The above function will provide important features of the system. Every new user will contribute (by her/his view of the world) to increase the cognition of the real world by the system. The concept objects hierarchy is represented by oriented arcs: for example, 'Lorry' < 'Vehicle', 'Motor' < 'Car', etc.

We found that the level of abstraction provided by a CN is more important than the time lost in the CN retrieval process. As a CN gives many synonyms for objects retrieval, the image retrieval process through image databases becomes critical. We would like to avoid general pattern recognition problems associated with images retrieval. In many cases, converting image recognition to text recognition using some specific conditions on the image text part or defining similarity conditions over image objects provides us with satisfying alternatives (Cristodoulakis (1985)).

Image description with predefined similarity functions is used for image objects filtering. These functions are based on image property weights. In our approach, the contour has highest weight, the size and position have lower and color has lowest weight. All image objects which have such weighted properties with a predefined tolerance distance, will be returned to the user.

Finding all concepts with a predefined degree of relevance or subconcepts/superconcepts for a given concept object is a transitive closure (recursive traversal) operation on the CN.

5 Operations

Data model operations are divided into operations which are definitional in nature and operations for manipulating instances.

Our discussion will be focussed on predicates which are the heart of any query language for object instance manipulation. We want to develop precidates according to the desired type of media. Our intention is to standardize text and image predicates. The text and image data filtering and MM views definition are performed using these predicates.

5.1 Text Retrieval Operations

The abstraction of the problem of text retrieval means moving from the lexical to a semantically based approach (Krawczak et al. (1987) and Tong et al. (1987)). In many cases, simple keyword based retrieval system have shown inadequate results. Of particular interest are those systems that derive from the efforts in natural language understanding and which advocate a conceptually oriented approach. We intend to develop predicates according to the text data retrieval requests. The predicate descriptions presented below use the following meta-symbols and meanings:

<x> non-terminal symbol x,
[x] zero or one instance of x,
{x} zero or more instances of x,
| alternatively.

Firstly, we will describe some lexically based predicates.

[NOT] EXIST <object> { AND | OR <object>} [IN <object class>].

This predicate will filter text objects which contain (or do not contain) the objects satisfying the EXIST condition. The second part of the predicate '[IN <object class>]' is used for testing if the objects in the EXIST condition occur within the same sentence, paragraph or other higher-level object class.

[NOT] EXIST <object class> LIKE <object description>.

The non-terminal <object description> denotes descriptions of the text object such as: words, phrases and sentences where their unknown parts are represented by predefined symbols.

DISTANCE BETWEEN <object> AND <object>
<compare operator> <num. value>.

This predicate will give the distance between pair of text objects. The distance is expressed in lower-level text objects. For example, the distance between word and sentence is expressed in number of words, the distance between sentence and section in number of sentences, etc.

LOCATION OF <object> <compare operator> <num. value>.

This predicate will search for the location of some lower-level text object (word, phrase or sentence) in higher-level text objects such as a paragraph, section or document.

<object> [NOT] PRECEDES <object>.

This predicate will test whether one text object occurs (or does not occur) before another.

Conceptually based predicates will increase the cognitive compatibility between the system and the end user by allowing the interaction at a more natural, semantic oriented level. They focus the user's attention on the essential objects and relationships while hiding unimportant details. We use two conceptual relationships to realize conceptual based predicates. They are denoted as "degree of relevance" and "subtype/supertype hierarchy" These relationships are defined in the CN.

The following predicate illustrates how the subtype/supertype hierarchy relationship can be used.

EXISTS CONCEPT <compare operator> <concept object>.

In this predicate, <compare operator> reflects a relationship between concepts. The text descriptions from all concept objects satisfying the specified <compare operator> in a hierarchical sense, will be used as synonyms in text data retrieval.

The next predicate illustrates how the degree of relevance relationship is used.

EXISTS CONCEPT <concept object><compare operator><relevance>.

In this predicate, the <relevance> reflects the degree of relevance between the concept objects. The text descriptions from all concept objects satisfying the specified <relevance> will be used as synonyms in text data retrieval. We can have a powerful method of text retrieving using logical connections of lexical and conceptual predicates described.

5.2 Image Retrieval Operations

Image object manipulation operations are especially of interest (Roussopoulos et al. (1988), Joseph and Cardenos (1988)). We will introduce some predicates for image objects retrieval. We propose the following algorithm for image objects retrieval via image and conceptual object names:

```
/* <object> is the name of an object or concept object
 <object class> is the name of an object class */
INPUT: <object>, <object class>
OUTPUT: image objects
DO CASE
 CASE <object> exists in CN
  begin
  TAKE <object> description
  FIND image objects from Image data base (IDB)
  end
 CASE <object> exists as a name of object in IDB
  begin
  FIND image objects from IDB
  end
 OTHER CASE
  begin
```

```
  GET <object> description from the user
  end
 ENDCASE
 END
```

We will now introduce the modified versions of text retrieval predicates according to the image retrieval requirements.

[NOT] EXIST <object> { AND | OR <object> } [IN <object class>],

where <object> is the name of the image object or concept object, and <object class> is the name of the object class.

This predicate will filter the image objects which contains (or does not contain) the objects satisfying the EXIST condition. The second part of the predicate "[IN <object class>]" is used for testing if the objects in the EXIST condition occur within the same natural object, geometrical object, image or some other object class.

[NOT] EXIST <object class> LIKE <object>
[BASED ON <property> { AND | OR <property>}],

where <property> can be AREA, CONTOUR, SIZE, etc.

This predicate filters image objects from object classes which are similar to the object in the LIKE option. As a basis of similarity determination the following elements are used: area, contour, size, etc. If a BASED ON option does not exist, the predefined object weights properties are used.

DISTANCE BETWEEN <object> AND <object><compare operator>
<num. value> [ANGLE <compare operator><num. value>].

This predicate gives the distance between a pair of image objects. The position of the object is specified by the angle. The angle will take values from an interval of $[0, 360]$. If an ANGLE option does not exist, any couple of the image objects must satisfy the distance condition. The distance is expressed in number of pixels.

LOCATION OF <object> IN (<num. value>,<num. value>,<num. value>).

This predicate locates the specified object in a square given by specified numerical values. The starting position of the square is defined by the first two numerical values. The third numerical value determines the length of the square edge. This predicate is applicable only to image object classes. However, the <object> can belong to any object class. The EXIST CONCEPT predicates can be used in the image retrieval in the same way as was described in section 5.1.

6 Conclusion

In the paper, a distributed MM model and some operations in an object-oriented multimedia system are described. It is shown that the integration of MM and knowledge-based system increases the retrieval possibilities of the system. Furthermore, we are going to develop a cognitive-based retrieval system. We are continuing our research in a number of directions:

- development of a more general object-oriented multimedia data model suitable for all types of information,
- development of our cognitive network and AMCIRS subsystem in a formal way,
- efficient organization and manipulation of object-oriented multimedia views,
- efficient techniques and algorithms for operations support,
- development of fault-tolerant models to provide the possibility of user cognition correction using a CN.

References

ALMES, G.T., and HOLMAN, C.L. (1987), Edemas: An Object-Oriented Locally Distributed Mail System, *IEEE Trans. on Software Eng., SE-13, 9*, 1001–1009.

BARNSLEY, M.F. (1988), *Fractals Everywhere*, Academic Press, Inc., San Diego.

BARNSLEY, M.F., and DEMKO, S. (1985), Iterated function systems and the global construction of fractals, *Proc. R. Soc., Lond. A399*, 243–275.

BARNSLEY, M.F., ERWIN, V., HARDIN, D., and LANCASTER, J. (1986), Solution of an inverse problem for fractals and other sets, *Proc. Nat. Acad. Sci. U.S.A., 83*, 1975–1977.

BLACK, A., HUTCHINSON, N., JUL, E., LEVY, H., and CARTER, L. (19897), Distribution and Abstract Types in: *Emerald, IEEE Trans. on Software Eng., SE-13, 1*, 65–76.

CHANG, S.K., YAN, C.W., DIMITROFF, D.C., and ARNDT, T. (1988), An Intelligent Image Database System, *IEEE Trans. on Soft. Eng., SE-14, 5*, 681–688.

CRISTODOULAKIS, S. (1985), Office Filing, in: *Office Automation*, Springer-Verlag, Berlin, 67–89.

CROFT, W.B., and STEMPLE, D.W. (1987), Supporting Office Document Architectures with constrained Types, *Proc. of the ACM SIG of Management of Data*, San Francisco, May 27–29, 504–509.

DAVCEV, D., and DIMITROVA, N. (1989), A Model of Multimedia Object-Oriented System, *Proc. of Convention UNIX 89*, Paris.

DAVCEV, D., DIMITROVA, N., and CAKMAKOV, D. (1988), Relational Fault-Tolerant Interface to Heterogeneous Distributed Databases, *Proc. of Workshop on future trends of DCS in 1990s*, 14–16 Sept., Hong Kong, 470–476.

EGLOFF, P., and SCHELLER, A. (1988), Multi-Media Documents in Broadband ISDN: Development of a Generalized Telecommunication Model in BERKOM, *Proc. of Workshop on the future trends of Distributed Computing Systems in the 1990s*, 14–16 Sept., Hong Kong, 103–110.

GHAFOOR, A. (1988), A Distributed Multimedia Database System, *Proc. of Workshop on future trends of DCS in 1990s*, 14–16 Sept., Hong Kong, 461–469.

GIBBONS, P.B. (1987), A Stub Generator for Multilanguage RPC in Heterogeneous Environments, *IEEE Trans. on Software Eng., SE-13, No.1*, 77–87.

HUDSON, S.E., and KING, R. (1987), Object-Oriented Database Support for Software Environments, *Proc. of the ACM SIG of Management of Data*, San Francisco, May 27–29, 491–503.

JOSEPH, T., and CARDENOS, A.F. (1988), PICQUERY: A High Level Query Language for Pictorial Database Management, *IEEE Trans. on Soft. Eng., SE- 14, 5*, 630–638.

KEMPER, A., LOCKEMANN, P.C., and WALLRATH, M. (1987), An Object-Oriented Dastabase System for Engineering Applications, *Proc. of the ACM SIG of Management of Data*, San Francisco, May 27–29, 299–310.

KRAWCZAK, D., SMITH, P.J., and SHUTE, S.J. (1987), EP-X: A Demonstration of semantically based search of bibliographic databases, *Proc. of the 10th Ann. Int. ACMSIGIR Conference on Research and Develop. in Information Retrieval*, New Orleans, June 3–5, 263–271.

MANDELBROT, B. (1977), *FRACTALS: Form, chance and dimension*, W.H.Freeman and Co., San Francisco.

MANDELBROT, B. (1982), *The Fractal Geometry of Nature*, W.H.Freeman and Co., San Francisco.

MOHAN, L., and KASHYAP, R.L. (1988), An Object-Oriented Knowledge Representation for Spatial Information, *IEEE Trans. on Soft. Eng., SE-14, 5*, 675–681.

NIERSTRASZ, O.M. (1985), An Object-Oriented System, in: *Office Automation*, Springer-Verlag, Berlin, 167–189.

ROUSSOPOULOS, N., FALOUTSOS, C., and SELLIS, T. (1988), An Efficient Pictorial Database System for PSQL, *IEEE Trans. on Soft. Eng., SE-14, 5*, 639–650.

TAG, M.A., BENKIRAN, A., DURAND, G., and WILSON, N.J. (1988), Design of an object-oriented Distributed System: Experience with CSA, *Proc. of Workshop on the future trends of DCS in the 1990s*, 14–16 Sept., Hong Kong, 192–201.

TONG, M.R., APPELBAUM, L.A., ASKMAN, V.N., and CUNNINGHAM, J.F. (1987), Conceptual Information retrieval using RUBRIC, *Proc. of the 10th Ann. Int. ASMSIGIR Conference on Research and Develop. in Information Retrieval*, New Orleans, June 3–5,. 263–271.

WOO, C.C., LOCHOVSKY, F.H., and LEE, A. (1985), Document Management System, in: *Office Automation*, Springer-Verlag, Berlin, 21–40.

Knowledge Representation and Search Methods for Decision Support Systems

Agoston E. Eiben and Kees M. van Hee
Department of Mathematics and Computing Science
Eindhoven University of Technology, The Netherlands

Summary

Decision support systems (DSS) are often very inflexible in the sense that they cannot be adapted to environmental changes or new wishes of the decision makers. Therefore they become quickly outdated. In this paper we analyze this problem and propose a new approach to the development of DSS's: a DSS should be a system or shell with parameters that can be specified in a high level declarative language. These parameters express the specific knowledge about the environment, constraints and criteria of the decision maker. We elaborate this idea for a special class of problems called resource constrained project scheduling.

1 A Summary of Decision Support Systems

Through this article the term 'decision problem' is meant for a situation where we have a system to control. The name 'decision' is used for the unit of information that is sent to the controlled system. A decision might be a simple control action that influences the controlled system for a short period of time, or it may be a set or sequence of such actions (a production plan for instance). It also may be a function that assigns actions to observed behavior of the controlled system so that one decision can control the system for an arbitrary long period of time.

We consider a DSS as an automated information system that assists users in making decisions to control another system by:

- performing data management functions,
- evaluating the effects of a proposed decision,
- generating decisions that satisfy some user given criteria.

The evaluation facility can be split into two parts: one to check whether a user-defined decision is allowed or not, and one to assign a quality measure to allowable decisions. These requirements restrict the class of information systems that could be called a DSS more then other authors do, cf. Keen and Scott Morton (1978).

In an incremental way of DSS-development it is natural to start with a data management module, then to add a facility for checking, and afterwards to extend this to a full evaluation facility. Finally one develops a generation engine. Other facilities to assist

NATO ASI Series, Vol. F 61
Knowledge, Data and Computer-Assisted Decisions
Edited by M. Schader and W. Gaul

decision makers are for instance multicriteria analysis in situations with several conflicting criteria, and sensitivity analysis concerning influences of non-decision variables. One of the main problems of DSS's is the lack of adaptivity: it is difficult to adapt them to structural environmental changes and to new constraints imposed by the user (decision maker). For example, a DSS based on linear constraints cannot handle non-linear ones. Designing a DSS one often makes assumptions that turn out to be wrong after some time. In particular, if a DSS is based on a sophisticated optimization algorithm then we encounter inflexibility because sophisticated algorithms exploit structural properties of the problem type, properties that might not hold for long.

In van Hee and Lapinski (1989) we have presented an abstract model that could be easily adapted to several kinds of structural changes. In van Hee, Somers and Voorhoeve (1989) we have sketched another approach based on a flexible modeling environment in which one may develop a simulation model of the controlled system and, within the same framework, one may develop a prototype of the DSS rather quickly. This is a raw version, with low computing performance and no user-friendliness. Nevertheless, such a prototype helps to determine the structural properties of the problem type by experiments with the potential users. Later on one may design a full DSS exploiting as much as possible of the discovered structural properties.

The aim of this paper is to present an approach that can lead to an easy-to-adapt DSS. The basic paradigm is that of high parameterization. We establish parameters to express the typical knowledge about the circumstances in which the DSS should be used. Then it is the user who will specify these parameters. Therefore the parameters should have a quite natural meaning and should be expressed in a very high level language. This saves the technicalities for the user. After all, the DSS should be a shell that contains

- an interpreter for the language in which the parameters are expressed,
- problem solving algorithms, partly hard-coded, partly parameterized.

The language presented in section 3 for knowledge representation is a functional language. Such a language is too difficult for the average end-user. Therefore we advocate the role of a DSS expert as a mediator between the end-user and the designer of the system. This expert should be able to translate the knowledge of the user in the language of the DSS. He would be active at the introduction of the DSS in the decision environment and would return periodically for updating.

To illustrate these concepts we have chosen a specific problem type, namely resource constrained project scheduling (RCPS). In Antonisse, van Hee and Lenstra (1988) we argue that this problem type is very suitable to demonstrate the typical problems of DSS-design. Problems of this type have three features that makes them good for illustration:

- RCPS problem occur frequently in practice at the level of operation management,
- they are too complex to handle them with a nice polynomial algorithm, thus the need for some heuristics and/or user interaction is great,
- an RCPS problem can evolve in many ways, requiring new constraints and criteria, hence it requires a flexible system to handle it.

In section 2 we define what RCPS problems are, in section 3 we consider the knowledge representation language, and in section 4 we discuss the algorithmic aspects: we present a general search method that can be instantiated to particular problem solving algorithms.

2 Resource Constrained Project Scheduling

As we have mentioned before RCPS problems are very suitable to illustrate our concepts. In this section we define this problem class.

In common parlance we can characterize RCPS problems by having resources (machines) to work with, each of them possessing some abilities, tasks to be done each of which requires some abilities. A machine can do only one task at a time. A task t can have predecessors, that is other tasks that must be completed before we can begin t. A schedule is an assignment of the tasks to the machines and begin-times in such a way that the assigned machine can perform the task. The goal is to have all that tasks completed. For the details turn to Antonisse et al. (1988). The mathematical description of an RCPS problem is the following.

a) **Kernel parameters**

- T is a set of tasks, $T \subseteq \mathcal{T}$, $\mathcal{T}$ is the set of all possible tasks,
- M is a set of machines, $M \subseteq \mathcal{M}$, $\mathcal{M}$ is the set of all possible machines,
- A is a set of abilities, $A \subseteq \mathcal{A}$, $\mathcal{A}$ is the set of all possible abilities,
- $F \in T \rightarrow A$ is a function that assigns to each task a required ability,
- $G \in M \rightarrow \mathcal{P}(A)$ is a function to indicate the abilities a machine possesses,
- $P \subseteq T \times T$ is a predecessor relation on the set of tasks,
- $D \in M \times A \rightarrow \mathbb{R}$ is a function that assigns to each resource and each possible ability a process speed: $< m, a > \in dom(D) \Leftrightarrow m \in M \wedge a \in G(m)$,
- $C \in T \rightarrow \mathbb{R}$ is a function that assigns to each task a required processing capacity,
- $H \in M \rightarrow \mathcal{P}(I)$ is a function that assigns to each resource a set of time intervals where the given resource is not available, such that $\forall x, y \in H(m)\ [x \neq y \Rightarrow x \cap y = \emptyset]$. ($I$ denotes the set of all intervals of $\mathbb{R}$.)

b) **Partial schedules**

We define the set of partial schedules as $S \subset T \rightarrow M \times \mathbb{R} \times \mathbb{R}$. For $s \in S$ and $t \in dom(s)$, $s_i(t)$ denotes the projection of $s(t)$ to its i-th component. Here $s_1(t)$ is the resource to which the task is assigned, $s_2(t)$ is the start time of processing t, $s_3(t) = s_2(t) + C(t)/D(m, a)$ is the end time, where $m = s_1(t), a = F(t)$. Notice that the notation is redundant because $s_3(t)$ can be computed from $s_2(t)$ and the kernel parameters. A pair $< t, s(t) >$ is called an operation, thus a schedule can be understood as a set of operations.

c) **Kernel constraints**

Obviously not any possible set of operation makes sense as a schedule. Constraints are to express feasibility of the partial schedules.

- R_1 requires that each task is assigned to a machine that possesses the ability needed for that task:
  $R_1(s) \Leftrightarrow \forall t \in dom(s) : F(t) \in G(s_1(t))$.

- R_2 requires that the operation falls in an available time interval: $R_2(s) \Leftrightarrow \forall t \in dom(s)\, \forall x \in H(t) : [s_2(t), s_3(t)] \cap x = \emptyset$.
- R_3 requires that all predecessors of a scheduled task are already processed: $R_3(s) \Leftrightarrow \forall t \in dom(s)\, \forall \tau \in T : < \tau, t > \in P \Rightarrow \tau \in dom(s) \wedge s_3(\tau) \leq s_2(t)$.
- R_4 requires that no two tasks on the same resource have overlapping process-intervals $R_4(s) \Leftrightarrow \forall t, \tau \in dom(s) : t \neq \tau \wedge s_1(t) = s_1(\tau) \Rightarrow [s_2(t), s_3(t)] \cap [s_2(\tau), s_3(\tau)] = \emptyset$.

Let R be the kernel feasibility constraint: $R(s) \Leftrightarrow R_1(s) \wedge R_2(s) \wedge R_3(s) \wedge R_4(s)$. Next we define the kernel search graph, $< N, E >$, where $N = \{s \in S \mid R(s)\}$ is the set of all feasible partial schedules and $E = (N \times N) \backslash \{< s, s > \mid s \in S\}$ is the set of edges. Each edge represents a possible step in a scheduling process. We exclude steps that do not change a partial schedule. This graph $< N, E >$ embodies the entire search space; the problem solving algorithm is traversing $< N, E >$ to find a solution. Notice that the role of R_3 is not crucial during the search process, we could easily drop it and only require it for the final solution. The rationale to incorporate it in R is that we want that also partial schedules are executable.

d) **User defined constraints and criteria**

In a scheduling session there can be always schedules that make sense, (are feasible) but for some reason the user wants to exclude them as possible solutions. To provide the decision-maker with such an opportunity we introduce the set UB below. The set of user-fined constraints is a set of Boolean valued functions: $UB \subset S \rightarrow B$. The user defined constraints reduce the search space by cutting the number of acceptable solutions. To express preferences among the solutions the user can define criteria, that is a set of real valued functions: $UR \subset S \rightarrow \mathbb{R}$. Notice that the function in UB and in UR may depend on the kernel parameters. On UR we can define weight-functions in the form $w \in UR \rightarrow \mathbb{R}$. By such a weight function w we can enforce the influence of certain criteria, i.e. we can make a new criterion as a linear combination of the old ones: $v_w(s) = \sum_{u \in UR} w(u) \times u(s)$.

In the search method we shall consider subsets of E to define neighborhoods of a partial schedule. An example is: $E_k = \{< s, s' > \in E \mid \#(s \Delta s') \leq k\}, k \in N$. ($\#$ denotes the cardinality of a set, $X \Delta Y$ is the symmetric difference of the sets X, Y.) For $k = 1$, E_1 characterizes the search methods where an atomic action means that only one task is deleted, added or changed. If $\tilde{E} \subseteq E$ then we define the neighborhood function $\tilde{N} \in S \rightarrow \mathcal{P}(S)$ induced by $\tilde{E}$ as $\tilde{N}(s) = \{s' \in S \mid < s, s' > \in \tilde{E}\}$.

3 Knowledge Representation

In the second section we used an informal mathematical notation to define kernel parameters, schedules, user constraints and criteria. In a DSS, however, this knowledge should be expressed in a formal language that can be interpreted by the system. This formal language could be a third generation programming language, such as Pascal, but it would have inconvenient consequences: to express user-defined constraints and criteria the user should be a programmer! As an alternative we suggest the "shell principle". According to this, the DSS is created as a shell that contains the facility to interpret a high level formal language. This formalism should have three important features:

a. it has to be powerful enough to express all the necessary knowledge,

b. it has to be a high level one, such that its usage does not require programming skills from the user,

c. it has to be 'interpretable', that is it has to be supported by a computer implementation.

Such a DSS shell is considered as a system with high level parameters which should be set by the user.

There are many ways to carry out the above idea and express knowledge at a high niveau. What we have chosen is a typed λ-calculus, or functional programming language. There are several good examples of such a language, for instance Milner's SML, cf. Harper, Milner and Tofte (1988). We base our treatment on the functional part of the language Exspect, cf. van Hee, Somers and Voorhoeve (1988, 1989). A very important feature of Exspect is that it is constructive and allows static type checking. We need to specify a many sorted algebra made from types and functions: types denote sets, functions are mappings from one or more set(s) to another set. Type expressions are formed from type identifiers and type constructors. A type variable is a type identifier used to define so called polymorphic functions that work on more different types. The function that inserts an object (of an arbitrary type τ) into a set (of type τ) to obtain a new set (of type τ) has a domain $\tau \times \mathcal{P}(\tau)$ and a range $\mathcal{P}(\tau)$, where τ is a type variable. Constant primitive types are for instance: *Num, String, Bool*, representing the real numbers, character strings and the Boolean truth values respectively. Once we have some types in hand, we can create new ones by defining subtypes of them and by the type constructors. These type constructors are $\times, \rightarrow, \mathcal{P}$ standing for Carthesian product, (finite domain) function space and (finite) power set. $A \times B, A \rightarrow B, \mathcal{P}(A)$ are examples of constructed types. Function expressions are constructed by the standard mechanisms of λ-calculus (cf. Stoy (1977)): abstraction, application and by recursive definition. For instance $f[x : T] := h(g(x), k(x)) : S$ is a function with domain type T and range type S, built up from the functions g, h, k. The language based on the λ-calculus is not too complicated, 16 primitive functions are enough to compose all the computable functions. As an illustration let us consider the construction of a (polymorphic) function '*dom*', that assigns the corresponding domain to a mapping.

$dom[x : \tau \rightarrow \sigma] := \textit{if } x = \textit{empty then empty else } ins(\pi_1(pick(x)), dom(rest(x)))$, where *if-then-else*, $=$, *ins*, π_i, *pick* and *rest* are basic functions the formal definition of which is omitted here. *if-then-else*, $=$ and π_i (for the i-th projection) are self-evident. *ins* inserts an element into a set, *pick* is an arbitrary selection function that assigns to each set an element of that set, $rest(x)$ is the set that remains from the set x after deleting $pick(x)$ from it.

We do not have room here to give all the necessary definitions, nor it is the goal of this paper. For reference turn to van Hee et al. (1988). Nevertheless, we give an illustration of how the knowledge of an RCPS problem looks in the language Exspect. We start with some type expressions:

$$Task := String,\ Mach := String,\ Abil := String$$

In an unsugared form the constant T could be *ins('task1', ins('task2', ins('task3', empty)))*. With a more familiar notation it would be { *'task1', 'task2', 'task3'*}. Now we are able to define the kernel parameters, they are constants of their types. These types are the following:

$$T : \mathcal{P}(Task),\ M : \mathcal{P}(Mach),\ A : \mathcal{P}(Abil),\ F : Task \to Abil,$$
$$G : Mach \to \mathcal{P}(Abil),\ P : Task \times Task \to Bool$$

The type of partial schedules is $S : Task \to Mach \times (Num \times Num)$. This type is, however, too broad. There are syntactically correct expressions that are in fact meaningless, that is they do not belong to any schedule. Notice that in a schedule s, $dom(s)$ should be a subset of the given T, and that the first component of the range values must be from M. To express this we make up an extra constraint:

$$R_0[s : S] := (dom(s) \subset T) \wedge \forall[x : dom(s) | \pi_1(s.x) \in M].$$

The symbols $\subset, \wedge, \forall, \in$, are defined in Exspect and have their common meaning. The other kernel restrictions are defined similarly, R_4, for instance, is written as

$$\begin{aligned} &R_4[s : S] := \\ &\quad \forall[t : dom(s) \mid \forall[t' : dom(s) \mid \\ &\qquad t \neq t' \wedge \pi_1(s.t) = \pi_1(s.t') \\ &\qquad\quad \Rightarrow \pi_1(\pi_2(s.t)) > \pi_2(\pi_2(s.t')) \vee \pi_1(\pi_2(s.t')) > \pi_2(\pi_2(s.t))]] \end{aligned}$$

The symbols $\neq, =, ., \Rightarrow, >, \vee$ are all defined functions in Exspect. To the user defined constraints we can use the same approach. Suppose that the user wants to express that each resource is a set of component resources and that no component can be shared by two resources at the same time. First of all the user has to add a new type to represent components and a new constant (of a functional type) to tell which components are used in a resource. Formally it is as follows. Let $Comp : String$ be a type and K be a constant of the type $Mach \to \mathcal{P}(Comp)$. With these we can define a new constraint '*clashfree*':

$$\begin{aligned} &clashfree[s : S] := \\ &\quad \forall[x : rng(s) \mid \forall[y : rng(s) \mid \\ &\qquad (\pi_1(x) = \pi_1(y) \wedge K(\pi_1(x)) \cap K(\pi_1(y)) \neq empty) \\ &\qquad\quad \Rightarrow \pi_1(\pi_2(x)) > \pi_2(\pi_2(y)) \vee \pi_1(\pi_2(y)) > \pi_2(\pi_2(x))]] \end{aligned}$$

The function *rng* can be defined similary to the function *dom*, *rng* stands for the range of mappings. In the same way we can express user-defined criteria. Let us suppose we want to express the *makespan* of a schedule s, that is the moment the latest task of s becomes completed. The corresponding function is: $makespan[s : S] := max[x : dom(s) | \pi_2(\pi_2(x))]$, where *max* is another standard Exspect function with its usual meaning.

A second example of a user-defined criterion is the total waiting time of the scheduled tasks in a schedule s. We say that a task is waiting if all of its predecessors are completed and the task itself in not being processed.

$$\begin{aligned} &wait[s : S] := \\ &\quad \sum[t : dom(s) \mid \pi_1(\pi_2(s.t)) - max[t' : (\$[x : dom(s) \mid P(x, t)]) \mid \pi_2(\pi_2(s.t'))]]. \end{aligned}$$

The functions $\sum$ and \$ are defined in Exspect again, where $\sum$ is the usual summation, \$ is the set restriction. Although the notations are not always as convenient as the informal mathematical notation, it is easy to read it after some exercise. Of course only well-trained users are able to add complex knowledge to a DSS-shell.

There are alternatives for functional languages to provide the formalism for the knowledge representation shell. An important and well-known branch is logic programming (LP), see Lloyd (1988). LP is but a restricted version of the classic first order logic. Its basic notion is 'relation' while in Exspect, and the functional languages in general, the functions form the basis. There are several versions of logic programming, most of which differs from the other ones in the execution method. Although theory permits other possibilities, almost all logic programming languages work with clauses of the form: $A \leftarrow L_1 \wedge \ldots \wedge L_n$, where A is a single predicate, L_i is a literal (either a predicate or a negated form of a predicate). The practical side of LP is the family of PROLOG languages. In Europe they are more popular and spread out then the functional based LISP-like languages, whilst the opposite holds for the U.S. Without going into details let us outline the major points of LP w.r.t. our shell:

- LP is suited for defining relations, Boolean functions, thus it handles *UB* easily,
- it is not so easy to specify mappings and functions with it, while it is very easy to do it in a functional language,
- syntactically correct logic programs can be 'unsafe', that is lead to a non-terminating computation,
- LP is implemented, many commercial PROLOG versions are available with good user support.

4 Search Methods

The search methods we consider here belong to the class of local search methods, cf. Papadimitriou and Steiglitz (1982). The idea is that we set up a general algorithm as a frame that can be instantiated to several different algorithms by specifying its parameters.

4.1 General Algorithm

Our search methods have the following scheme.

1. **Initialization**
   Start with an $Y \in \mathcal{P}(S)$ and three pairs $< u, I_u >$, $< v, I_v >$, $< w, I_w >$, where $u, v, w \in UR$, are user criteria belonging respectively to the Selection, Evaluation and the Reduction step (see further). The second element of the pair $< u, I_u >$ ($< v, I_v >$, $< w, I_w >$) is an interval of $\mathbb{R}$. Here we understand an interval in the broad sense, that is (r, ∞) and $(-\infty, r)$ are also considered as intervals. Notice that any criterion $\alpha \in S \rightarrow \mathbb{R}$ naturally generates a partial ordering on S, and hence on Y. If this a is an injection from S to then it determines a linear ordering.

2. **Selection**
   Take the pair $< u, I_u >$ and choose a subset $sel(Y, u, I_u) \subseteq Y$, where sel: $\mathcal{P}(S) \times UR \times I \rightarrow \mathcal{P}(S)$ is the selection function, such that $sel(Z, f, I_f) \subseteq Z$ for any $(Z, f, I_f) \in dom(sel)$. Although the notation does not indicate it we assume that the function *sel* does not look 'inside' the schedules. Our idea is that the decision made by *sel* is based only on the u-value (and the identifier) of the schedules. It is easy to extend the domain of *sel* by an extra argument of the type *Num* that could be set at each iteration with a new value. With this changing value we can employ a random influence on the search process. Let X be $sel(Y, u, I_u)$.

3. **Generation**
   Generate for each $s \in X$ the set of all neighbors $\tilde{N}(s)$, delete all the neighbors that do not satisfy the user-defined constraints of *UB*, and delete also the ones that occur in X already. Let X' be the set of the remaining new schedules.

4. **Evaluation**
   Compute the value of the evaluation criterion $v(s)$ for every $s \in X'$. If $v(s) \in I_v$ then accept s as a solution, otherwise continue by Step 4. Notice that I_v is a user defined domain of acceptance.

5. **Reduction**
   Choose a new element $red(X' \cup Y, w, I_w)$ from $\mathcal{P}(S)$, where *red* is the reduction function with the signature $red : \mathcal{P}(S) \times UR \times I \rightarrow \mathcal{P}(S)$. Obviously we require that $red(Z, f, I_f) \subseteq Z$ for any $(Z, f, I_f) \in dom(red)$. Here again, we assume that the function *red* only makes use of the identifiers and the w-values of the schedules. The function *red* can be augmented by an extra parameter like the function *sel*. Let Y' be $red(X' \cup Y, w, I_w)$.

6. **Iteration**
   If Y' is not empty then set $Y := Y'$ and return to Step 1.

Observe that the search method depends only on the following parameters: $\tilde{N}$, *UB*, *UR*, *sel*, *red*, u, v, w, I_u, I_v, I_w. Since $\tilde{N}$ heavily determines the algorithm we assume it to be specific for a search shell. The other parameters, however, can be set by the user.

Next we shall consider some implementational issues. Notice that the size of a neighborhood should not be too large because the whole $\tilde{N}(s)$ is generated in Step 2. There is an obvious need for some good neighborhood structure that is simple but still complete, i.e. the whole search space can be reached through the neighborhoods. Depending on the neighborhood function (whether extension by one operation yields a neighbor) and on the sets *UB* and *UR*, the constraints and the criteria can be computed inductively in certain cases, that is

$$u(s') = f(u(s), g(t, m, b, e)) \text{ for } s' \in \tilde{N}(s),\ s' = s \cup \{< t, < m, b, e >>\}, \qquad (\star)$$

where u is either a constraint or a criterion. Such an 'additivity' saves computation time. To save storage space one needs to invent a smart representation of schedules. A possibility is to have two tables for all the schedules of Y. One with attribute set {*sid, fsid, t, m, b, e*} where *sid* is the schedule identifier, *fsid* is the identification of the father-schedule, (i.e. the schedule from which *sid* is derived), and t, m, b, e define the operation that makes *sid* different from *fsid*. The second table has $\{sid, rank\}$ as attribute set and it represents the order of schedules in Y'. It can be handy to augment the first table with attributes representing the values of the criterion functions of the given schedules. By these implementational considerations we wanted to show that the search methods are not necessarily expensive in computing time or memory space.

4.2 Instances of the General Algorithm

Here we present three instances of the general algorithm given above. For all the three we fix the same neighborhood function $\tilde{N}$ defined by:

1. $\forall s' \in \tilde{N}(s) : s \subset s'$ and $\#(s' \backslash s) = 1$,
2. if $s' \in \tilde{N}(s)$ and the operation $< t, < m, b, e >> \in s' \backslash s$ then there are no other $b', e' \in \mathbb{R}$ such that $b' < b$ and $s \cup \{< t, < m, b', e' >>\}$ is feasible (R evaluates to true), that is we require that t is scheduled on m at the earliest possible time w.r.t. the other operations of s.

Observe that this neighborhood function is not symmetric: $s' \in \tilde{N}(s) \Rightarrow s \in \tilde{N}(s')$ does not hold, what more $s' \in \tilde{N}(s) \Rightarrow s \notin \tilde{N}(s')$ does. An advantage of this neighborhood function is that the generation of all neighbors is very easy.

4.2.1 Greedy Search

The basic idea here is that Y contains only one schedule all the time. Hence, the selection function *sel* is the identity here. Since the neighborhood function gives neighbors containing one operation more, the search process continues until all tasks are scheduled (if possible). To control the process we may choose several criteria. For instance, if we are looking for a schedule with a small makespan, i.e. an early final time, then we can aim at a low value of $u_1(s) = max\{s_3(t) \mid t \in dom(s)\}$. If we prefer tasks with short processing time first then we may choose $u_2(s) = \sum\{s_3(t) - s_2(t) \mid t \in dom(s)\}$ and try to keep its value down.

A yet other preference is to consider the schedule s better than the schedule s' if the total restwork of s is smaller than that of s'. The (worst case based) approximation of the total restwork is

$$u_3(s) = \sum\{max\{C(t)/D(m) \mid m \in M \wedge F(t) \in G(m)\} \mid t \in T \backslash dom(s)\}.$$

These criteria are to be used in the Reduction step, i.e. the function *red* can be based on them. It could be for instance: $x \in red(Z, u_i, [0, a_i]) \Leftrightarrow x \in Z \wedge u_i(x) \in [0, a_i]$. Notice that all these criterion functions can be defined inductively in the sense discussed in 4.1. The function f in the formula $(\star)$ then must be maximum, addition and subtraction respectively.

4.2.2 Random Search

This method differs from the standard simulated annealing (cf. Aarts and Korst (1989)) in an important feature. Namely, irreducibility is lost in the sense that not every schedule can be reached from any schedule. This is due to the chosen neighborhood function, since it allows only neighbors with one element more. Nevertheless, if we keep the empty schedule in Y, then all the elements of S remain reachable from every state of the search (i.e. from every Y). So we can regain irreducibility w.r.t. the actual set of schedules. Besides the empty one we want to keep the best schedule seen before and a set of randomly chosen ones in Y. The selection function selects the whole Y, the criterion functions have no restrictions. The reduction function always chooses the empty schedule, the best schedule and a fixed number of other schedules from the set $Y \cup X'$. This choice is affected by a random mechanism that assigns higher probabilities to schedules with a higher w-value. Eventually these probabilities may tend to a degenerated distribution that only gives positive probabilities to the best schedules. This solution resembles the way the cooling parameter works in simulated annealing. As a whole, however, the random search defined here falls rather in the class of genetic algorithms, cf. Aarts, Eiben and van Hee (1989).

4.2.3 Depth-first Search

We define u as $u(s) = \#(dom(s))$, so that the best schedule is the one with the most operations. The method will not only store schedules, but it also keeps track on the trace from the empty schedule up to the one in question. We start with $Y = [\textit{empty-schedule}]$, and expand Y by choosing the best element of the actual Y, and replacing it by a subset of its neighbors. The process continues until a schedule is accepted as a solution, or it turns out that no schedule can be reached from the chosen element of the actual Y. In the first case the search process terminates, in the second case a backtrack step is performed. The function *sel* is simple, it always chooses the best element. The reduction function deletes the chosen element and the 'hopeless' elements of the newly generated neighborhood (i.e. the ones which do not fall in the acceptance interval) and adds the remaining schedules to the end of Y. To illustrate the criteria used in the function *red* let us consider the following example.

For the estimation of the rest processing time we define

$$u_4(s) = max[min\{C(t)/D(m) \mid m \in M \wedge F(t) \in G(m)\},\ t \in T \backslash dom(s)].$$

Then we take $w(s) = u_1(s) + u_4(s)$, which is an estimation for the total processing time. Now we can set an acceptance interval $I_w = [0, a]$ and say that a schedule x is hopeful, $x \in red(Z, w, I_w)$ iff $w(x) \in I_w$.

We do not advocate any of these search methods, nor do we claim that they are very original. They are presented to demonstrate the easy way of programming such a search shell.

5 Conclusions and Further Work

The main issue of this paper is how to help the inflexibility of the DSS's. Our proposal is the following: make your DSS a shell with lower performance on wide range of application, rather then a system fine tuned on a narrow domain. The notion of a shell—although never defined precisely—is well-known. A shell is a skeleton-system where only the frame of the whole architecture is fixed, many important factors are unspecified. These unspecified factors are called parameters, they have to be set to get a complete system. Of course, not any system that has parameters is a shell yet (think of a program with an input value), a shell has high level parameters, such as expressions in a high level language. In such a case the influence of the parameters is more crucial, and for the user it is easier to understand and set them. A high level language permits a new extent of flexibility too: besides **setting** parameters the user can **make up** some new elements of the system without being a programmer himself.

We distinguished two components in a system: one for storing, and one for using knowledge, that is a knowledge representation side and an algorithmic side of a DSS. We applied the shell-principle for both, leaving free parameters at the problem specification as well as in the problem solving module. The result was satisfactory: after fixing a problem class as application domain we could define the components of the shell. The design is summarized below:

- The necessary domain knowledge is carried by the kernel parameters, kernel constraints, the user defined constraints and criteria.
- The necessary executive core is embodied by the general search algorithm, that relies on the domain knowledge but also has free parameters for its own, like the function *sel, red, u, v, w*.
- The above entities can be expressed—thus defined—in a high level functional language.
- Correctly specified functions of the chosen language are computable, that is the program produced is executable.

In the future we are going to implement these ideas by a prototype using Exspect. Experience will show the limits of our approach, and the points where further investigation has to be carried out.

References

AARTS, E.H.L., EIBEN, A.E., and HEE, K.M. van (1989), *A general theory of genetic algorithms*, Computing Science Note, Eindhoven University of Technology.

AARTS, E.H.L., and KORST, J. (1989), *Simulated annealing and Boltzmann machines: a stochastic approach to combinatorial optimization and neural computing*, Wiley, New York.

ANTONISSE, J.M., HEE, K.M. van, and LENSTRA, J.K. (1988), Resource-Constrained Project Scheduling: an International Exercise in DSS Development, *Decision Support Systems 4*, 249–257.

HARPER, R., MILNER, R., and TOFTE, M. (1988), *The definition of standard ML: version 2*, Report ECS-LFC-88-62, Laboratory of Foundations of Computer Science, Edinburgh.

HEE, K.M. van, and LAPINSKI, A. (1989), OR and AI approaches to decision support, *Decision Support Systems 4*, 447–459.

HEE, K.M. van, SOMERS, L.J., and VOORHOEVE, M. (1989a), *A formal framework for simulation of discrete event systems*, Proceedings of 3rd ESC Conference, to appear.

HEE, K.M. van, SOMERS, L.J., and VOORHOEVE, M. (1989b), *Executable specifications for distributed information systems*, Proceedings of IFIP WG8.1 Working Conference, to appear.

KEEN, P.G.W., and SCOTT MORTON, M.S. (1978), *Decision support systems: an organized perspective*, Addison-Wesley, Reading, MA.

LAARHOVEN, J.M. van, AARTS, E.H.L., and LENSTRA, J.K. (1988), *Job shop scheduling by simulated annealing*, Technical Report, Center for Mathematics and Computer Science, Amsterdam.

LLOYD, J.W. (1987), *Foundations of logic programming*, Springer-Verlag, New York.

PAPADIMITRIOU, C.H., and STEIGLITZ, K. (1982), *Combinatorial optimization: algorithms and complexity*, Prentice-Hall, Englewood Cliffs.

STOY, J. (1977), *Denotational semantics*, MIT Press, Cambridge, MA.

Knowledge-Oriented Support for Data Analysis Applications to Marketing

Wolfgang Gaul
Institut für Entscheidungstheorie und Unternehmensforschung
Universität Karlsruhe,
Martin Schader
Institut für Informatik
Universität der Bundeswehr Hamburg
and
Martin Both
Dornier GmbH, Friedrichshafen, Germany

Summary

Efforts undertaken to develop software tools for knowledge-oriented support usable in marketing applications are reported. Possibilities of extensions of an existing prototype which—in the current implementation stage—consists of knowledge-oriented support for some market research and data analysis applications are discussed. An example demonstrates how new software is incorporated in the prototype and how new applications can be handled in the extended environment.

1 Introduction

Attempts to discuss computer-assisted decision support—for whatever application area—should start with calling to mind at least part of the large amount of literature already present for this topic. To mention just two of our own publications with reference lists which, hopefully, give good overviews about existing literature we refer to Gaul and Schader (1989) for a recent paper on data analysis and decision support and Gaul and Both (1989) for a book on computer-assisted marketing. From Fig. 1 it can be seen that the discussion of aspects of computer-assisted decision support for marketing problems has some history; here, we combined elements of different contributions from the sixties and seventies which pictured their specific view of the structure of a computer-based decision support system in quite similar ways. We recognize that between the marketing manager on the one hand and the environment with its competitors looking for profits on the other, a decision support system is visualized. The system's main components are a data-oriented part, a model-oriented part, a methods (mainly statistics)-oriented part and an input/output- or display-component. Some (sequences of) arrows between different parts explain how communication between these components should be organized but, of course, in the beginning of the discussion of computer-assisted decision support the possibilities depicted here were rather what one was wishing that decision support systems should be able to perform, and not reality. One part which is receiving increasing interest in today's discussion—the knowledge-oriented part—is still missing in Fig. 1. This recent research direction aims at combining expert knowledge with existing decision support approaches

NATO ASI Series, Vol. F 61
Knowledge, Data and Computer-Assisted Decisions
Edited by M. Schader and W. Gaul

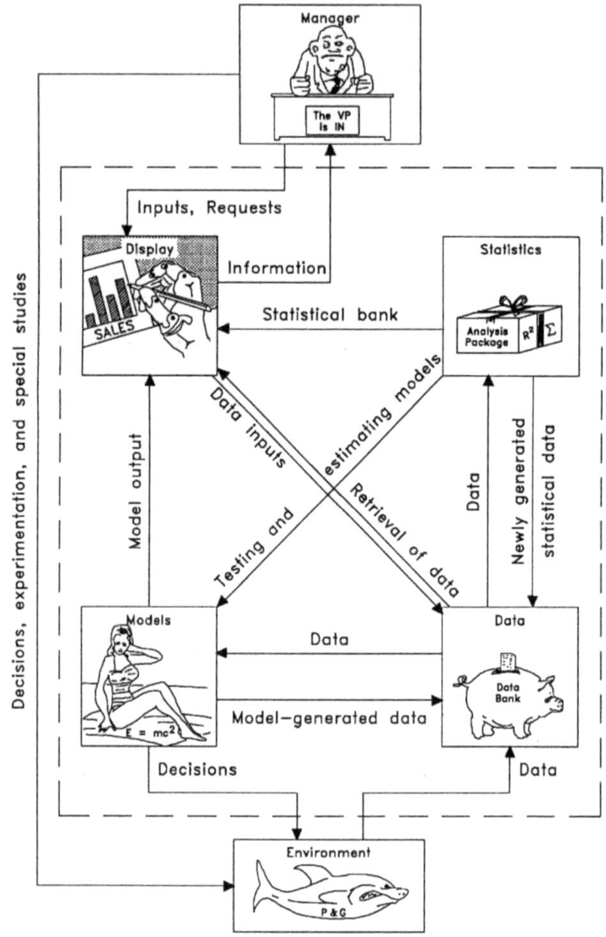

Figure 1: Computer-Assisted but not yet Knowledge-Oriented Decision Support (see Montgomery and Urban (1969) and Little (1979))

and at incorporating knowledge into new software. Together with interdisciplinary efforts to link up attempts from different research areas and to emphasize the knowledge-oriented part within the interplay of all parts of a decision support system it constitutes one of the main goals of the contributions in the present proceedings volume and its predecessor (Gaul and Schader (eds.) (1988b)).

Thus, in section 2 of this paper, we would like to start the discussion of our recent work on knowledge-oriented decision support by, first of all, mentioning briefly important characteristics of decision situations in general, and, secondly, outlining different concepts of computer-assisted decision support, namely information-oriented, model-oriented, and knowledge-oriented support. In the next section we describe possible extensions of our own prototype which in the current implementation stage consists in knowledge-oriented support for some market research and data analysis applications (see Baier, Böckenholt, Both, Decker, Espejo, Gaul, Hantelmann, Kiel, Marx, Müller, Schader, Schaer and Tüshaus in the list of references for contributions which—in different ways—influenced the

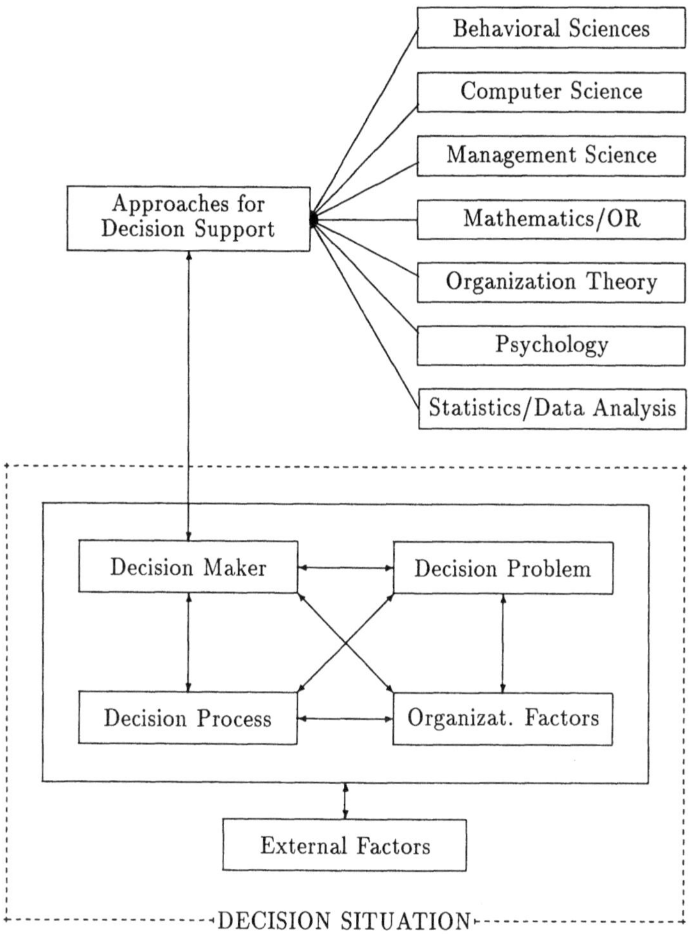

Figure 2: Description of the Decision Situation

building of this prototype). In section 4, we demonstrate how new software is incorporated in the prototype and how new applications can be handled in the extended environment.

2 Characteristics of Decision Situations and Concepts for Computer-Assisted Decision Support

When discussing decision support, one should first have a look at the underlying decision situation and clarify the meaning of the term support. In general, decision situations can be characterized by at least the following five features: decision maker, decision problem, decision process, organizational factors, and external factors. This is depicted in Fig. 2.

Characteristics of decision makers and the ways they got used to when tackling questions of decision support have been the object of research for quite a long time. In this context, psychological types of decision makers concerning perception and judgement were identified and integrated in frameworks of decision support (see, e.g., Mason and Mitroff

(1973)). Furthermore, cognitive styles of decision makers (see, e.g., the critical review of Huber (1983) and the survey by Liang (1986)) and ways how to take into account individual differences when designing DSS (Decision Support Systems) were discussed. While in most contributions the decision maker was viewed as a "single person" research efforts which aim at supporting group decision making (see, e.g., De Sanctis and Gallupe (1987)) are receiving increasing attention.

Taxonomies of decision problems were already proposed in the sixties (see, e.g., Simon (1960) and Anthony (1965)) and later on included in the DSS-discussion (see, e.g., Keen and Scott Morton (1978)). In addition to general characteristics such as structural type, level of managerial activity or complexity, specific aspects of the underlying application area of the decision problem have to be studied (see, e.g., Lilien and Kotler (1983) who outline marketing-specific problems a decision maker is faced with). In this context, questions of modeling the phenomena of the application area arise.

Research on decision processes aims at structuring the process of decision making by separating several phases which are distinguished by specific activities (see, e.g., Mintzberg, Raisinghani and Théorêt (1976) for a comprehensive model of the decision process). Possible phases are, e.g., problem identification, diagnosis, design, analysis, selection of alternatives and evaluation, and—of course—depending on the phases a specific system is mainly designated to support various requirements will have to be fulfilled.

Organizational factors comprise mechanisms for co-ordinating decision making activities as well as control mechanisms in order to trace the decision outcomes. Here, one has also to take into account situation-dependent factors important for both the process of decision making and the implementation of the decision.

Finally, *external factors* which are not under the control of decision makers or cannot be influenced directly within the organizational context have to be considered. They might be more of a short-term type, such as actions of competitors in marketing decision situations, or more of a long-term type, such as technological and economic developments.

Therefore, on one side we have a rather complex decision situation which could only be sketched in the preceding argumentation; on the other, the need for supporting decision makers is widely recognized. It has initiated various approaches for decision support which have to take into consideration interdisciplinary research efforts regarding reference disciplines, such as Behavioral Sciences, Computer Science, Management Science, Mathematics/Operations Research, Organization Theory, Psychology and Statistics/Data Analysis (in alphabetical order) and the like.

Surely, one question of importance is whether there are different types of decision support approaches which support different aspects within decision situations, which are based upon different reference disciplines, which use different models and methods, and so on. Instead of discussing different taxonomies for structuring various ways of providing support known from the literature (see, e.g., Keen (1986) who—in an abstract way—distinguishes passive support, traditional support, normative support and extended support, or Young (1983), who discusses left-brained and right-brained support thus alluding to functions performed by the human brain) we will briefly describe our individual taxonomy (see Gaul and Both (1989)) consisting of three kinds of support for decision makers: information-oriented concepts, model-oriented concepts, and knowledge-oriented concepts, see Tab. 1 for an overview.

Information-Oriented Concepts	Model-Oriented Concepts	Knowledge-Oriented Concepts
	History	
◇ Development of MIS (Management Information Systems) and MAIS (MArketing Information Systems) in the sixties ◇ Reporting systems ⟶ information retrieval systems	◇ Long tradition of modeling marketing phenomena ◇ Problems regarding acceptance / usage of complex tools ◇ Decision calculus; *Little (1970)* ◇ DSS research ⟶ implementation aspects	◇ Offspring of AI (Artificial Intelligence) research ◇ Change of paradigm: general problem solver ⟶ expert systems ◇ Applications originally of more technical nature ◇ Mainly prototype developments in marketing
	Computer Science Technology	
◇ Report generators ◇ Data base systems ◇ Query languages ◇ High degree of diffusion ◇ Mature techniques	◇ DSS Generators; *Sprague and Carlson (1982)* ◇ Model management	◇ Specific tools and shells ◇ AI – workstations ◇ Specific programming languages; *Tello (1985), Harmon and King (1985)*
	Support	
◇ Provide access to internal and external data ◇ Perform "status reporting" in various ways ◇ Facilitate the application of "Management by Exception"-principle	◇ Structure important parts of the decision situation ◇ Make explicit assumptions, objectives, restrictions ◇ Make proposals of optimal/satisfactory alternatives ◇ Perform "response reporting" ◇ What-if-scenarios, ad hoc-analysis	◇ Make available expert knowledge for problem solving ◇ Give advice on problems hardly amenable to quantitative approaches ◇ Explain solutions proposed by the system ◇ Make transparent the way experts perform their tasks
	Means	
◇ Aggregation of information due to hierarchical rank ◇ Elementary operations to generate summaries and statistics ◇ Selecting and combining specific pieces of information	◇ Mathematics/OR/Statistics ◇ Substantive theory of consumer behavior ◇ Approaches for integrating subjective judgement	◇ Knowledge engineering techniques; *Boose (1986)* ◇ Various ways of representation & manipulation ◇ Reasoning mechanisms; *Baldwin, Kasper (1986)* ◇ Mainly rule-based approaches
	Type of Problem	
◇ Structuring of information flows	◇ "Semi-structured" problems which can't be fully automated; *Keen and Scott Morton (1978)*	◇ Criteria for selecting appropriate domains; *Prerau (1985)* ◇ Problem-specific criteria
	Integration	
◇ Build on internal transaction processing systems ◇ Provide basis for model- and knowledge-oriented concepts ◇ Facilitate co-ordination and control	◇ Usage often voluntary ◇ Personal instrument ◇ Local data base with access to global data	◇ Often stand-alone developments ◇ Usage voluntary ◇ High degree of authority with the system
	Recent Developments	
◇ New kinds of information sources: Scanner data, targetable TV, electronic data bases, telecommunication, portable PC	◇ Provision of model-oriented concepts by means of spreadsheets; *Lilien (1986), Clarke (1987)*	◇ See, e.g., most of the papers in this volume

Table 1: Concepts for Computer-Assisted Decision Support

Obviously, the borderlines between these concepts are rather fuzzy but with regard to history, computer science technology, support provided, means, type of problem, integration and recent developments one can distinguish between the different objectives of research; the contents of Tab. 1 just gives some examples. Efforts to combine aspects from the three concepts and attempts to include an integrated concept in recently developed software have started, see, e.g., the DANEX (Data ANalysis EXpert) prototype described in Böckenholt, Both and Gaul (1988, 1989) and Gaul and Both (1989). In the next section we will discuss how possible extensions of existing computer-assisted software can incorporate such interdisciplinary aspects.

3 Extension of Existing Knowledge-Oriented Decision Support Software

Considering what has been elaborated on decision situations and concepts for decision support in the preceding section, now, questions arise how far existing decision support software has coped with corresponding necessities and wishes, and to which extent existing and new approaches incorporate aspects of the concepts mentioned above.

Since an answer to this question would justify a survey in its own right this paper restricts the discussion to our own software, and—even more restrictive—to a knowledge-oriented system called WIMDAS (WIssensorientiertes Marketing Daten Analyse System) the successor of the DANEX prototype already referred to. In Fig. 3 the structure of the current WIMDAS version is presented.

WIMDAS is the synonym for a joint project which research groups in Hamburg (M. Schader) and Karlsruhe (W. Gaul) have initiated. WIMDAS just as DANEX combines aspects from information-oriented as well as from model-oriented and knowledge-oriented concepts. As a starting point of the WIMDAS project the DANEX prototype—which aimed at supporting data analysis situations which frequently occur in market research—was transformed from PCs to workstations. More precisely, the following tasks were tackled up to now:

(1) Exchange of hardware and software;

(2) Incorporation of additional commercial software;

(3) Extensions of the method base; and

(4) Extensions of the knowledge base.

(1): Limitations of the PC version of DANEX and conceptions of what the software within the WIMDAS project should be able to perform caused us to prefer a workstation environment. When transferring DANEX from PCs to workstations we also replaced Turbo Prolog by IF/Prolog.

(2): In the very first attempt to link together what became the DANEX version our own stand alone programs for dedicated data analysis problems—which all had their own input/output and display facilities—were integrated into a knowledge-oriented environment. Although a data management component, common to all programs, was added to DANEX, we felt that for the WIMDAS-project commercial software for data management and graphical display had to be incorporated. We decided for Oracle as data base system and GKS (Graphical Kernel System) as graphical subsystem. In addition to Fortran and

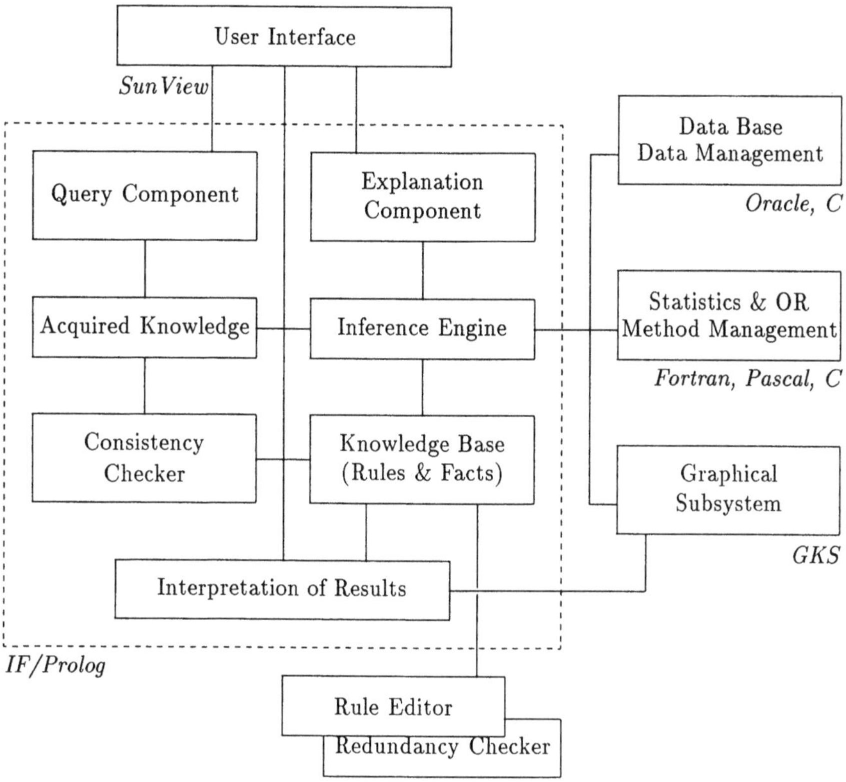

Figure 3: Structure of the Current Knowledge-Oriented WIMDAS Version

Pascal used for the earlier implementations of data analysis algorithms, now, the interfaces between the different system components and all newly developed methods are programmed in C.

(3): In the beginning the method base of DANEX contained standard algorithms of cluster analysis and multidimensional scaling. Meanwhile, a lot of research has been done by members of the WIMDAS-project which could lead to extensions of the DANEX method base. For all of these research efforts suitable software is already available. Also, a multitude of new research contributions within the data analysis area (see, e.g., Bock (ed.) (1988) and Gaul and Schader (eds.) (1986) for recent proceedings volumes within this field) could be checked for possible incorporation into a method base for data analysis problems applicable in the fields of market research and marketing. In the next section an example is used to show how clustering of relations, two-mode clustering and pyramidal clustering (for pyramids see, e.g., Diday and Bertrand (1986), Diday (1987) and Brito and Diday (1990)) can be combined to support the interpretation of suitable data by two-mode pyramidal clustering.

(4): When new algorithms are added to those already included in the existing method base one also has to change the knowledge base (KB). Thus, extensions of the KB due to new algorithms or other exchanges/improvements of system components have to be carried out rather automatically using the system's rule editor—and, afterwards, the redundancy checker in order to prevent augmentation of the KB by subsumed rules and facts, unfireable rules, etc. (These program-dependent modifications in the KB were, of course, not possible within the PC/Turbo Prolog version.)

One of the topics of future research is how the KB can be improved from a marketing point of view and to which extent additional knowledge about the correct way to handle specific data analysis situations can be incorporated (see, e.g., Baier and Gaul (1989) for a concept to combine knowledge-, data- and method-bases).

Another research area of interest aims at allowing WIMDAS users to run all the system components on any machine in their network and control them all from one dedicated terminal (provided that a Unix network with a transparent windowing system such as, e.g., X11 or NeWS is available). To reach that goal the user interface will be rewritten for X11 and the graphical subsystem will be ported to PHIGS & PEX. At the moment method management can be executed on Convex, Targon or Sun hardware and will transmit its results via socket based inter process communication.

4 Example

For a demonstration of part of the WIMDAS possibilities let us suppose that the following data from a marketing research experiment are at hand: Individual paired comparisons matrices of 69 participants who had to judge 10 print ads of French cognac in a paired comparisons experiment make up one part of the available data. Additionally, the participants were asked to associate attributes like "credible", "precious", "stimulating", ... and the like to the print ads. Thus, 69 association matrices (print ads $\times$ attributes) and 69 paired comparisons matrices (print ads $\times$ print ads) form the basic information for which WIMDAS has to suggest appropriate data analysis techniques and—after the choice of the technique desired by the user—provide corresponding solutions. Starting with the paired comparisons data WIMDAS in its present version suggests, e.g.,

Aggregation to Central Relation;
Clusterwise Aggregation of Relations;
Transformation to One-mode Data.

Selecting the CAR (Clusterwise Aggregation of Relations)-algorithm (Gaul and Schader (1988a)), WIMDAS suggests to choose two classes of participants and two different rankings of the print ads. The first class consists of 43 participants with the following ranking (ranking 1)

MARTELL 1 < MARTELL 2 < COURVOISIER 1 < COURVOISIER 2
< REMY 1 < HENNESSY 2 < REMY 2 < BISQUIT 1 < HENNESSY 1
< BISQUIT 2

while the second class contains the remaining 26 participants with the ranking (ranking 2)

BISQUIT 2 < BISQUIT 1 < MARTELL 1 < REMY 1 < MARTELL 2
< COURVOISIER 1 < COURVOISIER 2 < HENNESSY 2 < REMY 2
< HENNESSY 1.

(Here, "<" stands for "is preferred to".) Now, of course, questions such as "Why are there two different rankings?", "Why do participants of the first class put the MARTELL ads in the first positions of ranking 1 while in ranking 2 the BISQUIT ads are in the lead?",

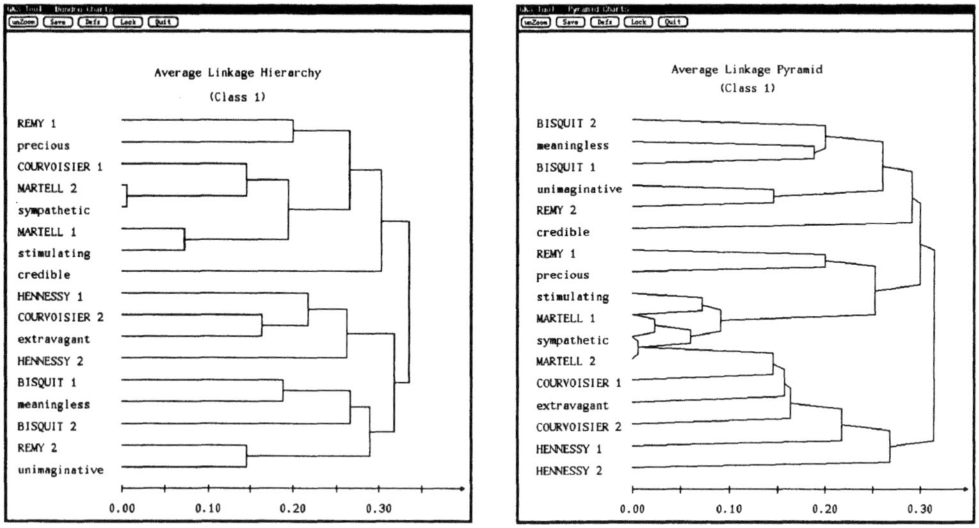

Figure 4: Two-Mode Hierarchical and Pyramidal Clustering Results for Class 1

etc., arise. Remember that rankings 1 and 2 resulted from applying the CAR-algorithm to the paired comparisons data and that, additionally, association data are at hand.

If the association matrices are rearranged according to the two classes proposed in the first consultation step and then, using the data management part, are aggregated in such a way that two-mode data analysis is applicable then, e.g.,

Individual Differences MDS;
INDTREE;
Two-mode Hierarchical Clustering;
Two-mode Pyramidal Clustering

are recommended. Now, if we choose two-mode hierarchical clustering as well as two-mode pyramidal clustering for both classes WIMDAS provides the outputs depicted in Figs. 4 and 5.

A comparison of the different rankings and two-mode hierarchical and pyramidal results reveals the following:
The MARTELL ads together with COURVOISIER 1 (and—to some extent—together with REMY 1) constitute the beginning of ranking 1. They are associated with attributes like "sympathetic", "stimulating" and "precious" in the two-mode hierarchy, and in the corresponding pyramid as well (see Fig. 4). In class 2, again, the attributes "sympathetic" and "precious" are associated with the ads at the front—which are the BISQUIT ads in this case (see Fig. 5).

On the other side, the BISQUIT ads which together with REMY 2 hold positions at the end of ranking 1 are associated with "meaningless" and "unimaginative". In class 2 these attributes are combined with MARTELL 2 and REMY 2 although in ranking 2 only REMY 2 holds a position at the end.

For ads in the center of both rankings we do not find the same pronounced association of attributes to ads in terms of hierarchical or pyramidal clustering structures. This

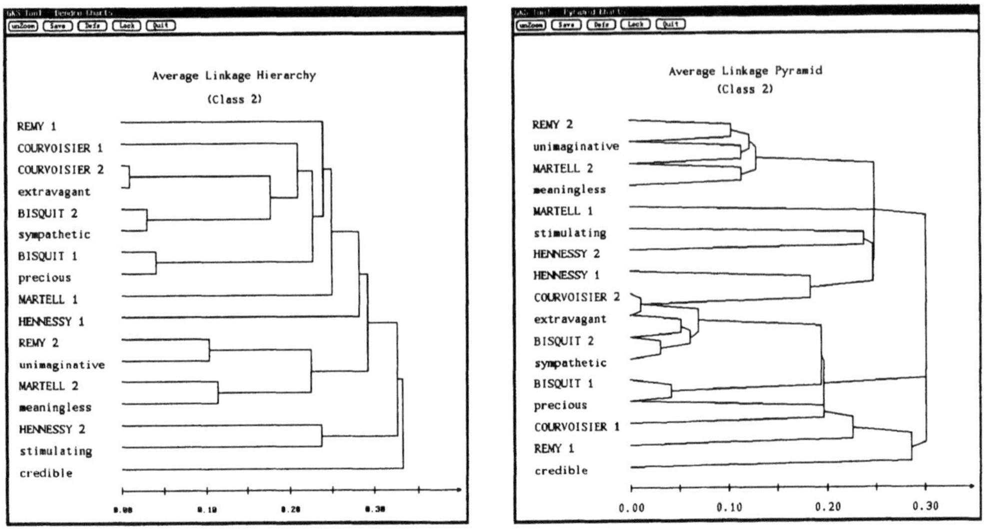

Figure 5: Two-Mode Hierarchical and Pyramidal Clustering Results for Class 2

supports the impression that the first and last positions in a ranking are more important for the judging participants. They are willing to—conformably for both classes—assign attributes to these positions rather than to those in the center.

The hierarchical and pyramidal clustering results reveal structures which are in good accordance and indicate that for illustrating structures pyramids could be better suited than dendrograms. (Here, further research has already started which compares dendrograms and pyramids for different data sets.) All in all, the CAR-results and the class-specific two-mode analyses by hierarchical and pyramidal clustering allow a good interpretation of the choice behavior of the participants under study.

Although class-specific reactions to advertising messages of print ads are revealed by the CAR-algorithm on the basis of paired comparisons data, for both classes attributes like "sympathetic" and "precious" or "meaningless" and "unimaginative" are class-independently associated with print ads which hold positions at the front or at the end of the rankings. Together with the pictorial representation of the print ads this is part of what a knowledge-oriented decision support system like WIMDAS could make available for (re-)designing advertising campaigns.

5 Conclusions

In this paper we have briefly discussed some characteristics of decision situations and how computer-assisted decision support can be complemented by incorporating knowledge-oriented approaches. Additionally, extensions of our own knowledge-oriented decision support software for data analysis applications to marketing—the WIMDAS system—have been mentioned. Finally, an example from the marketing area demonstrates part of the support available at the current implementation stage.

References

ANTHONY, R.N. (1965), *Planning and Control Systems: A Framework for Analysis*, Harvard University, Graduate School of Business Administration.

BAIER, D., and GAUL, W. (1989), Entscheidungsunterstützung bei der Auswertung von Primärforschungsdaten — Ein Konzept zur Verbindung von Wissensbasis, Datenbank und Methoden, in: *Operations Research Proceedings 1989*, Springer, Berlin Heidelberg New York.

BALDWIN, D., and KASPER, G.M. (1986), Towards Representing Management-Domain Knowledge, *Decision Support Systems, 2*, 159–172.

BOCK, H.H. (ed.) (1988), *Classification and Related Methods of Data Analysis*, North Holland, Amsterdam.

BÖCKENHOLT, I., BOTH, M., and GAUL, W. (1988), PROLOG-Based Decision Support for Data Analysis in Marketing, in: *Data, Expert Knowledge and Decisions*, eds. W. Gaul and M. Schader, Springer, Berlin Heidelberg New York, 19–34.

BÖCKENHOLT, I., BOTH, M., and GAUL, W. (1989), A Knowledge-Based System for Supporting Data Analysis Problems, *Decision Support Systems, 5*, 345–354.

BÖCKENHOLT, I., and GAUL, W. (1984), A Multidimensional Analysis of Consumer Preference Judgements Related to Print Ads, in: *Methodological Advances in Marketing Research in Theory and Practice*, EMAC/ESOMAR Symposion, Copenhagen, 83–105.

BÖCKENHOLT, I., and GAUL, W. (1985), Zur mehrdimensionalen Analyse von Bildinformationen in Anzeigen für Imagery-Produkte, *Viertel-Jahreshefte für Mediaplanung, 4*, 20–29.

BÖCKENHOLT, I., and GAUL, W. (1989), Generalized Latent Class Analysis: A New Methodology for Market Structure Analysis, in: *Conceptual and Numerical Analysis of Data*, ed. O. Opitz, Springer, Berlin Heidelberg New York, 367–376.

BOOSE, J.H. (1986), *Expertise Transfer for Expert System Design*, North-Holland, Amsterdam.

BOTH, M., and GAUL, W. (1987), Ein Vergleich zweimodaler Clusteranalyseverfahren, *Methods of Operations Research, 57*, 593–605.

BRITO, P., and DIDAY, E. (1990), *Pyramidal Representation of Symbolic Objects*, this volume.

CLARKE, D.G. (1987), *Marketing Analysis and Decision Making*, Scientific Press, Redwood City, CA.

DECKER, R., and GAUL, W. (1989a), Classification and Selection of Consumer Purchase Behaviour Models, in: *Conceptual and Numerical Analysis of Data*, ed. O. Opitz, Springer, Berlin Heidelberg New York, 389–398.

DECKER, R., and GAUL, W. (1989b), Einige Bemerkungen über Expertensysteme für Marketing und Marktforschung, to appear.

DE SANCTIS, G., and GALLUPE, R.B. (1987), A Foundation for the Study of Group Decision Support Systems, *Management Science, 33*, 589–609.

DIDAY, E. (1987), *Orders and Overlapping Clusters by Pyramids*, Rapports de Recherche, No. 730, Institut National de Recherche en Informatique et en Automatique (INRIA), Octobre 1987.

DIDAY, E., and BERTRAND, P. (1986), An Extension of Hierarchical Clustering: The Pyramidal Presentation, in: *Pattern Recognition in Practice II*, eds. E.S. Gelsema and L.N. Kanal, North-Holland, Amsterdam, 411–424.

ESPEJO, E., and GAUL, W. (1987), Two-Mode Hierarchical Clustering as an Instrument for Marketing Research, in: *Classification as a Tool of Research*, eds. W. Gaul and M. Schader, North Holland, Amsterdam, 121–128.

GAUL, W. (1984), Datenanalyse auf der Basis von Ordinalurteilen, *Studien zur Klassifikation, 15*, 142–152.

GAUL, W., BÖCKENHOLT, I., and BAIER, D. (1990), *MARK²MAN: MARKtforschung & MARKeting MANagement*, in preparation.

GAUL, W., and BOTH, M. (1989), *Computergestütztes Marketing*, Springer, Berlin Heidelberg New York, in press.

GAUL, W., and SCHADER, M. (eds.) (1986), *Classification as a Tool of Research*, North-Holland, Amsterdam.

GAUL, W., and SCHADER, M. (1988a), Clusterwise Aggregation of Relations, *Applied Stochastic Models and Data Analysis, 4*, 273–282.

GAUL, W., and SCHADER, M. (eds.) (1988b), *Data, Expert Knowledge and Decisions: An Interdisciplinary Approach with Emphasis on Marketing Applications*, Springer, Berlin Heidelberg New York.

GAUL, W., and SCHADER, M. (1989), Data Analysis and Decision Support, *Applied Stochastic Models and Data Analysis, 5*, 341–356.

GAUL, W., and SCHAER, M. (1988), A PROLOG-Based PC-Implementation for New Product Introduction, in: *Data, Expert Knowledge and Decisions*, eds. W. Gaul and M. Schader, Springer, Berlin Heidelberg New York, 42–53.

HANTELMANN, F. (1989a), Normendschungel: Grafikstandards unter Unix, *ix 6*, 96–101.

HANTELMANN, F. (1989b), Grafische Präsentation statistischer Daten unter UNIX: Ein Konzept zur Gestaltung von Graphiksubsystemen für KI-Umgebungen, to appear in: *Operations Research Proceedings 1989*, Springer, Berlin Heidelberg New York.

HARMON, P., and KING, D. (1985), *Expert Systems*, Wiley, New York.

HUBER, G.P. (1983), Cognitive Style as a Basis for MIS and DSS Designs: Much Ado about Nothing, *Management Science, 29*, 567–582.

KEEN, P.G.W. (1986), Decision Support Systems: The Next Decade, in: *Decision Support Systems — A Decade in Perspective*, eds. E.R. Mclean and H.G. Sol, North-Holland, Amsterdam, 221–237.

KEEN, P.G.W., and SCOTT MORTON, M.S. (1978), *Decision Support Systems: An Organizational Perspective*, Addison-Wesley, Reading, MA.

KIEL, R., and SCHADER, M. (1990), A lint-type Tool for Validating Prolog Programs, to appear.

LIANG, T.P. (1986), Critical Success Factors of Decision Support Systems: An Experimental Study, *Data Base, 18*, 3–15.

LILIEN, G.L. (1986), *Marketing Mix Analysis with LOTUS 1-2-3*, Scientific Press, Redwood City, CA.

LILIEN, G.L., and KOTLER, P. (1983), *Marketing Decision Making: A Model Building Approach*, Harper and Row, New York.

LITTLE, J.D.C. (1970), Models and Managers: The Concept of a Decision Calculus, *Management Science, 16*, 466–485.

LITTLE, J.D.C. (1979), Decision Support Systems for Marketing Managers, *Journal of Marketing, 43*, 9–26.

MARX, S., MÜLLER, H., and SCHADER, M. (1990), On an Interface Between a Knowledge Base and a Data Base System, to appear.

MASON, R.O., and MITROFF, I.I. (1973), A Program for Research on Management Information Systems, *Management Science, 19*, 475–485.

MINTZBERG, H., RAISINGHANI, D., and THEORET, A. (1976), The Structure of Unstructered Decision Processes, *Administrative Science Quarterly, 21*, 246–275.

MONTGOMERY, G.B., and URBAN, G.L. (1969), *Management Science in Marketing*, Prentice-Hall, Englewood Cliffs, NJ.

NISHISATO, S., and GAUL, W. (1988), Marketing Data Analysis by Dual Scaling, *International Journal of Research in Marketing, 5*, 151–170.

NISHISATO, S., and GAUL, W. (1990), An Approach to Marketing Data Analysis: The Forced Classification Procedure of Dual Scaling, to appear in: *Journal of Marketing Research*.

PRERAU, D.S. (1985), Selection of an Appropriate Domain for an Expert System, *AI Magazine, 6*, 26–30.

SCHADER, M. (1989), Inference Techniques in Decision Support Systems—Comparison and Example From Data Analysis, in: *Conceptual and Numerical Analysis of Data*, ed. O. Opitz, Springer, Berlin Heidelberg New York, 441–449.

SCHADER, M., and TÜSHAUS, U. (1986), Subgradient Methods for Analyzing Qualitative Data, in: *Classification as a Tool of Research*, eds. W. Gaul and M. Schader, North Holland, Amsterdam, 397–403.

SCHADER, M., and TÜSHAUS, U. (1988), Analysis of Qualitative Data—A Heuristic for Finding a Complete Preorder, in: *Classification and Related Methods of Data Analysis*, ed. H.H. Bock, North Holland, Amsterdam, 341–346.

SIMON, H.A. (1960), *The New Science of Management Decision*, Harper and Row, New York.

SPRAGUE, R.H., and CARLSON, E.D. (1982), *Building Effective Decision Support Systems*, Prentice-Hall, Englewood Cliffs, NJ.

TELLO, E. (1985), Knowledge Systems for the IBM PC, Part 1, *Computer Language, July*, 71–83, Part 2, *Computer Language, August*, 87–102.

TÜSHAUS, U. (1989a), On the Interpretation of Median Relations, in: *Conceptual and Numerical Analysis of Data*, ed. O. Opitz, Springer, Berlin Heidelberg New York, 222–229.

TÜSHAUS, U. (1989b), Entscheidungsunterstützung bei der Datenaufbereitung, in: *Operations Research Proceedings 1988*, eds. D. Preßmar et al., Springer, Berlin Heidelberg New York, 412–417.

YOUNG, L.F. (1983), Computer Support for Creative Decision Making: Right-Brained DSS, in: *Processes and Tools for Decision Support*, ed. H.G. Sol, North-Holland, Amsterdam, 47–64.

Expert Systems as Support in Economic Planning

Björn Grönquist
Cap Sesa Innovation
Meylan, France

Summary

In the first part of this paper will discuss how expert system techniques are evolving and how they can be applied to new types of problem. They are changing in their functionalities. The integration of domain knowledge with knowledge of methods is the major change from which decision support systems will profit.

In the second part of this paper an application of expert systems techniques to economic planning is presented. Sapho2 is an economic planning system for water resources, based on the expert system approach. It supports user in the analysis of problems and in finding possible solutions. These solutions are afterwards compared according to different economic and political criteria. The system is built on the paradigm of problem finding and problem solving and offers facilities for interactive simulation.

1 General Considerations About Expert Systems Techniques

1.1 Expert Systems and Operational Research

Expert systems currently furnish support to users in different manners. We can distinguish between two main uses of expert systems in planning: in addition to existing tools or in replacement of existing tools. The first approach furnishes methodical support, the second approach is a method for problem solving.

The enhancement of existing tools is done by encapsulation of them. The results are intelligent interfaces proposing graphical facilities based on advanced windowing techniques. This 'front–end' tool supports the user first by reducing the need of additional information by generating it automatically from given macro instructions. This permits by using classical tools, the simulation of different possible situations and the testing of their consequences. A second kind of support is direct methodical help. Advice for configuring models and explanations of results are the major support given by this approach.

Presently a third type of applications integrating both methods for solving problems and methodical support is appearing. This 'integrated' approach becomes more powerful by tightly mixing methodical support with the way to solve the problem. This enables structuring of knowledge at different levels of abstraction and integrates them naturally in one model. Often this approach integrates both heuristic and non heuristic knowledge working together in the resolution mechanism. Different kinds of knowledge are expressed by domain specific rules, model specific rules, heuristic rules and method specific rules.

NATO ASI Series, Vol. F 61
Knowledge, Data and Computer-Assisted Decisions
Edited by M. Schader and W. Gaul

1.2 Second Generation of Expert Systems

Currently expert systems solve complex problems in several domains. Their 'reasoning' is mainly based on direct observable data. The major motivation of the expert system approach is to derive problem solving methods from human behavior in problem solving. This approach is innovative in comparison to classical operational research which looks for formal methods. So far the expert system approach can be an attractive alternative for problems which have not yet been solved by OR. In particular some combinatoric problems, too complex for general models, might find solutions with expert system techniques if expertise is present.

The first generation of expert systems was based on experimental knowledge. They have now been solving specific problems for a while. In most cases these expert systems are hard wired to particular situations and they lack generality. One of the well known limitations of this approach is the restricted application domain dependent on a specific environment. This 'narrow' approach to problem solving used by expert systems of the first generation has now been overcome. Second generation expert systems are more general and no longer bound to specific contexts. In early stages of expert system technique people simply reproduced the behavior of the human expert. In well defined contexts and stable situations this approach is sufficient. The second generation expert systems are more general and solve classes of problems independently of their contexts. Such an approach is much more ambitious and requires better understanding of problems. Understanding depends on underlying theory and the corresponding model. So far the second generation expert systems tackle problems in a similar way to OR. The difference between the two approaches is that expert systems model problems by rules and objects using backward chaining, forward chaining and inheritance instead of mathematical models. They take inspiration for their method from human behavior in problem solving. Observation and direct transcription of behavior into rules and objects is not sufficient. The knowledge engineer has to analyze the problem and extract the general principles of the underlying model able to support the whole process. This goes far beyond the extraction of deep knowledge from 'surface' knowledge, which was the main problem of the first generation expert systems. An underlying theory improves quality of expertise by systematically eliminating 'forgotten cases'. At the same time it supports explanation by structuring reasons. The use of general models in combination with heuristic knowledge of the experts generates powerful tools.

1.3 Expert Systems for Decision Support

Expert systems are mainly used for reproducing expert knowledge with little user interaction. These systems are destined for naive users, replacing experts in their task of consultants. Specific knowledge is structured in the data base. These systems are made for taking over the consultant role of experts. The aim of such systems is clearly to make decisions for the user and not to support decision making.

Presently, expert systems are also used for assisting the expert in his tasks of problem solving. For difficult problems, however, specifically in planning, where strategic choices are important, it is not possible to replace the expert. It is, however, still possible to assist him in his task of expertise by taking over a part of the problem solving. Such systems are characterized by their great interaction with the user. The user not only has to respond to questions about facts but also about the way of solving problems.

The aim of these systems is not to replace the decision maker but to support him in his activity of decision making. They focus specifically on explanation facilities and methodical advices.

Expert systems used for decision support should integrate model knowledge, domain knowledge, knowledge about methods and choice structures. It should support understanding of the problem, design of solving strategies and choice procedures. Methodical assistance and suggestions for possible actions would be of great help. In order to cope with ill structured and complex problems a procedural approach is preferred to a substantive approach (in terms of DSS). The decision is not a static process but a dynamic process of evolution towards a solution. This kind of decision process can be supported by a system using expert system techniques progressively integrating constraints and objectives.

2 Application of EXPERT System Techniques for a Water Resource Planning System

2.1 Use of Expert System Techniques to Support Economic Planning

Expert systems propose a solution to these problems. Expert system techniques make it possible to reason 'automatically' on qualitative facts. It even makes an integration of qualitative and quantitative data possible. Local information can easily be integrated to the model.

The policy analysis works on a basis of "what happens if" instead of "which is the best solution" as used in micro-economic models. This process is supported by the possibility of specifying its own criteria and constraints. Different types of knowledge have to be taken into account: knowledge of economic functions, knowledge about model behavior and knowledge about environmental conditions. Expert systems can be used for representing economic models of this type.

In the absence of precise quantitative data it is natural to perform qualitative reasoning with economic models. However it is extremely difficult to reason with already moderately complex qualitative models. Assistance for checking coherency with theory would be of great help to the economist. There is not enough use of qualitative criterias in economic models, they almost have to be expressed in numerical form. Most existing methods are not adapted to treat problems formulated in a qualitative manner.

Another use of expert systems in economic planning is to automatically generate data for specific economic situations. The economist will have to specify his criteria and constraints as a function of a particular situation. At present there is a great need for assistance in simulation with economic models. Planning not only deals with quantitative but also with significant qualitative data. The classical economic models do not take into account such kind of information.

2.2 Problem of Economic Water Resource Planning

Water resource planning is a complex process with many interactions in differents sectors (departments). Technological solutions are not easy to find and they are difficult to evaluate. Separation of tasks between technicians preparing proposals and politicians making decisions, complicates the process.

The essential characteristic of economic problems is the lack of coordination between social factors, specifically between different levels of responsibility and different sectors. The intervention of several social actors from different levels of decision making: local, regional and national segregates the different interventions. In organizations almost nobody knows who is doing what and what are the possible consequences of a decision taken at an other level or in another sector for the problem. There is clearly a need of support for intelligent access to information and a need for help in finding solutions previously ignored by the particular decision maker. Communication between different services and information provided by the decision maker, about other possible or necessary actions to solve the problem, should be supported. Often such investigations are simply not possible because of lack of resources and time. Solutions are in these cases simply a result from local decisions without greater research.

The solving process of water resource planning contains two types of actions: diagnosis and planning. When a problem has been identified, one must determine causes of the problem. This means that one must look for dependent problems. The problem space can be seen as a graph of dependent problems, solving one of them will have consequences on the others. It is important to determine the size of the problem space to consider the whole problem and solve it correctly. Once analysis of the problem is done, the next step is to look for possible solutions, then starts planning. A solution is always composed of different actions which have to be coordinated in space and in time. Afterwards economic evaluation is done by comparing the different solutions under different aspects. The economic criterion is only one among others determining the choice.

2.3 Sapho2: A Water Resource Planning (Expert) System

Sapho2 is a decision support system for planning of water resources and related problems based on expert system techniques. It was developed in order to help solve water resource problems in Algeria.

Sapho2 is based on expert system techniques firstly for diagnosis and secondly for planning.

The system assists the user in analyzing the problem and finding possible technical solutions taking into account the constraints of the concrete situation. Then different economic-political choices are simulated in relation to wishes of the decision maker and the consequences are presented to him. The aim is to evaluate the different technical solutions (finite or infinite) by different criteria.

The system is divided into three steps:

1. In the beginning it helps to analyze the problem. This means search of the problem space, causes of the problem and identifying involved actors.

2. Afterwards search of technical possibilities is supported and partial almost satisfactory solutions are proposed. They are constructed interactively with the help of the user. The expert enters data about the exact situation.

3. Finally the choice procedure is supported taking into account different criteria specified by the decision maker. He simulates different policies of economics and he studies the consequences.

Sapho2 supports the decision maker by:

- finding the problem size,
- giving explanations about interdependencies of problems,
- analyzing the problem and generating different possible solutions,
- generating economic scenarios as a function of the decision maker's criteria and preferences.

The main advantage of Sapho2 is the integration of technical and political aspects of the system. The system tackles the whole process from the beginning to the end. The system can explain the interrelations between technical problems and economic choices.

The expert system integrates an economic model. This makes an automatic 'economic' evaluation of the technical solutions possible. Facilities of explanation are well structured in relation to the economic model.

3 Conclusion

Recent evolution in expert system techniques makes new applications possible. Integration of underlying models and methodical knowledge with domain knowledge makes expert systems much more powerful. Such systems are no longer built for unexperienced users but for expert users. They do not replace the decision maker but they assist him in solving problems.

The new type of problems tackled by this approach is characterized by greater complexity. Strategic decisions have to be taken by the expert in order to guide the systems. The combinatorics of these problems is to big for automatic resolution. The expert system supports the expert by heuristic search but it still needs some information about how to orient the problem solving.

References

ARRUS, R., GRÖNQUIST, B., LELIS, D., OLLIVIER, M., and TARI, Z. (1988), *Considerations on the use of an expert system to support economic and social planning*, 1st International conference in social science, Köln.

BERDSEN, R.J., and DANIELS, H.A.M. (1989), Application of constraint propagation in monetary economics, in: *Systèmes Experts*, Avignon, France.

BOURGINE, P., and RAIMAN, O. (1986), Economics as reasoning on qualitative model, in: *IFAC Economics and Artificial Intelligence*, Aix-en-Provence, France.

DENNA, E., McCARTHY, and W.E. (1987), An event accounting foundation for DSS implementation, in: *Decision support systems: Theory and Applications*, Springer Verlag, New York.

FARLEY, A.M. (1986), Qualitative modelling of economic systems, in: *IFAC Economics and Artificial Intelligence*, Aix-en-Provence, France.

KUIPERS, B. (1986), Qualitative simulation, *Artificial Intelligence, 29.*

STEELS, L. (1985), Second generation expert systems, in: *Future Computer Systems*, North-Holland, Amsterdam.

Emergent Themes in Statistical Expert Systems

David J. Hand
Statistics Department
The Open University, Milton Keynes, United Kingdom

Summary

Research into statistical expert systems is relatively young, but old enough so that one can examine the progress that has been made. In this paper I compare achievements with requirements stated a few years ago. Certain themes are apparent in today's work and some of these are explored in detail. In particular the following are addressed:

- strategy: formalising the choices, actions, and decisions to be made in a statistical analysis
- hypertext: a nonlinear high level knowledge representation which has been used in several systems
- metadata: computer manipulable information supplementing the data.

1 Introduction

In the first half of this decade research into statistical expert systems was just beginning. In parallel with other areas of artificial intelligence research it was characterised by optimism and papers of the kind "my system will solve all these problems—when I've built it". Since then progress has been made: there are fewer papers containing such fantasies and more of the kind "my system is intended to do this. It's not much but it does it successfully". This represents a realistic lowering of sights.

In addition to this more realistic approach to what might be accomplished in the near future, the field has now matured to the stage at which one might attempt to establish what has been achieved and what directions will prove most fruitful for future research. To structure my approach, I shall begin in the next section by referring to a description, published in 1985, of the necessary attributes for statistical expert systems. I shall then focus on certain themes which seem to be becoming increasingly dominant, and develop them in detail. In particular, I shall address notions of strategy (formalising the choices, actions, and decisions to be made in a statistical analysis), hypertext (a nonlinear high level knowledge representation which has been used in several recent systems), and metadata (computer manipulable information supplementing the data).

Statistical knowledge consists of a complex structure of interrelated ideas and concepts. These range from low level arithmetic and algebraic notions (such as how best to invert a particular kind of matrix or the structure of a least squares solution) through intermediate level concepts (such as what a variance or a principal component analysis is and how to interpret them) to issues of how one should go about performing an analysis, what parts of

NATO ASI Series, Vol. F 61
Knowledge, Data and Computer-Assisted Decisions
Edited by M. Schader and W. Gaul

the data one should look at first, how data structure influences choice of techniques, how earlier results affect later methods, and so on. These last issues are the subject matter of statistical strategy.

Traditionally teaching has focussed on the lower levels, leaving the high level strategic issues to be discovered by the statistician in practical application after formal education has finished. It is clear, however, that if one hopes to develop a statistical expert system which can offer guidance at a strategic level then study and formalization of these ideas is vital.

Turning from questions of what to represent to how to represent it, it is now widely recognized that different problems require different kinds of software architectures. Thus, for example, while rule-based approaches are very powerful and flexible, with attractive properties such as modularity, they are not a universal solution. Forcing a problem which does not naturally fit into a rule representation will neither be particular easy nor will it produce attractive and effective software. It is in fact necessary to match the structure of the software to the structure of the problem. This poses particular problems for statistical expert systems because of the wide range of different kinds of knowledge which has to be represented.

Examples of different kinds of knowledge representations are those implemented in TESS (Lubinsky and Pregibon (1987)), DINDE (Oldford (1986)), SAS (O'Keefe (1985)), and KENS (Hand (1987)). The last of these is a step towards the use of hypertext, which represents the statistical knowledge as a collection of small text chunks linked by a dense collection of cross-references which can be immediately traced by the computer. The claim is that this produces a very flexible knowledge base which can be accessed in an unlimited number of different ways.

Statistical knowledge is only one half of the knowledge necessary for successful statistical consultancy. The other half is world knowledge—knowledge about the particular area or discipline to which the statistical expertise must be applied. Most expert systems work to data has assumed that this knowledge will come from the user of the system, and it is certainly correct to assume that the user must have some of this information. In many cases, however, there will be things the user does not know about the data—and this is especially true if the analyst and the data compiler are different people (as with official statistics). The concept of metadata has been introduced as a way of tackling this problem. This is extra information, obtained and recorded along with the data, which can later be accessed by the analyst to direct and mediate the course of the analysis. This is expanded on below.

2 Five Years on

In 1985 (Hand (1985a)) I published a paper with the title "Statistical expert systems: necessary attributes" in which I posed two questions about statistical expert systems and described 13 features which I considered to be necessary for such systems. How well has recent work answered those questions and conformed to those features?

Q1: For what will the system be used?

Here I distinguished choices of designs or methods from analysis, suggesting that the classical rule-based approach might be suitable for the first but that a more structured algorithmic approach might be better for the second. I did not predict the large number of very small systems which would be built (for regression, canonical correlations analysis, principal components analysis, etc.). Although systems for both sides have been developed, a majority have focussed on analysis—correct application of technique.

Q2: Who will use the system?

This was a reference to the statistically naive/expert continuum. A major motivation for work in this area has been to protect the statistically naive—and most (but not all) systems assume a naive user. However, it seems to be the case that the most effective systems are those aimed at the expert, with little evidence that systems for the naive succeed. The last point is an important one, for it is undoubtedly the case that more evaluation and critical assessment is needed and it might simply be that no proper evaluations of systems for the naive have been made. On the other hand, such systems must inevitably be large, shifting from abstract statistical knowledge to substantive expertise for their consulting area. To achieve a workable system in reasonable time, I would recommend focussing on a system for experts—providing a "second opinion".

F1: Systems must be structured for easy modifiability.

This was an obvious requirement in view of the dynamic change which statistics as a discipline is experiencing. Questions, however, arise as to the best way to achieve this. Does one require the user (at best a statistician) to be able to write Lisp or Prolog code. Or does one go to the other extreme (e.g. Darius (1989)) and write the whole system in SAS? Easy updating also implies a potential for easy corruption.

F2: Ability to explain actions.

This is often taken to be one of the defining characteristics of expert systems. However, many existing systems do not succeed: simple rule mapping is insufficient and a simple list of rules is not enough. Bell (1989) has described how one might select the most important rule antecedents in explanations, rather than giving them all. Certainly much more extensive work is needed on explanation facilities.

F3: Explain technical terms.

This will be necessary for the expert (as a reminder, perhaps) as well as the naive. Most existing systems are rudimentary. One or two have adopted a hypertext approach which looks promising. More work is needed in this area, with the explanation being better integrated, rather than an appended afterthought.

F4: Able to give more than one answer.

F5: Able to do full analysis.

F6: Able to adapt dynamically as analysis proceeds.

These attributes reflect the fact that clients typically have multiple objectives and need systems which can assist (or guide) in a complete analysis. One implication is that systems focussed on a very narrow area will be of limited value. They will also be extremely difficult to assess because the client base will be small.

F7: Able to examine the data critically.

Statistical expert systems take information from two sources: the client and the data. Most effort to date has been on the former, perhaps in recognition that this is the tougher.

F8: Handle user error.

Some kind of backtracking facility or blackboard architecture is needed. Some existing systems do this very clumsily and improvement is needed. It might also be desirable to permit the user (if an expert) to explore options—"What would happen if I say yes, and what if I say no?"

F9: Freeze session, to be continued later.

A common complaint amongst human statisticians is that the client collects the data before seeking advice. It would be nice if this facility could encourage early consultation—which was stored to inform the later analysis consultations.

F10: Identify best solution, not merely an adequate one.

This was in reference to, for example, choosing the most powerful available test, rather than a general one which was less powerful. To date there has been too little evaluation to comment on this.

F11: Focus user interaction.

Since rules are common, focus seems adequate—but again there has been too little or no critical assessment.

F12: Didactic role.

The potential here seems to be becoming of growing importance, especially for the naive. It is important to recognize this potential from the start—and tie it in with designs for the explanation facilities.

F13: The system should be self-contained.

Meaning that only a rudimentary manual should be necessary, with the system guiding the client in its use. Few systems have reached this stage of exploitation.

3 Theme 1: Strategy

A statistical strategy is a formal description of the choices, actions, and decisions, to be made while using statistical methods in the course of a study. There are a few references predating work on expert systems, but by far the most important motivation for the study of strategy has been statistical expert systems. The aims of studying strategy parallel those of statistical expert systems in general: to help researchers choose and use methods and to protect researchers from misusing methods.

Study of strategy has implications beyond this, however. Formalization of effective strategies will help to protect the discipline of statistics (from misunderstandings which result in the discipline being criticised rather than misapplication or other misuse). Formalization will help in statistical education: we can send out students who know how to perform complete analysis, rather than merely how to apply distinct tools. It will also aid in methodological research—serving to identify gaps in the available techniques. And finally, outline strategies will improve a consultant's performance: despite available computer packages, it is still too easy to overlook aspects of the data which have relevance to the analysis.

Pregibon (1985) stresses the value of low level strategies, while Hand (1985) describes a high level strategy. There is a place for both. The former will lead to something working quickly, albeit for a narrow area, while the latter will lead to a global overview. Development of strategies involves the analysis of many data sets and the recording of the steps taken. It also requires the development of some way of comparing strategies so that one can recognize good and bad ones.

In general, it will only be to the benefit of statistics if more explicit thought is given to strategy. The power of modern software packages has given us the freedom to focus attention at this high level, just as earlier generation software permitted us to move up from considerations of arithmetic.

4 Theme 2: Hypertext

The most common internal architecture for expert systems has been rule-based. Such an architecture is ideal for certain kinds of problems—for example, diagnostic problems—but may not be perfect for others. In particular, I would suggest that rule-based approaches are not ideal for the situation where the client may have any one of a large number of different types of questions, or may not have a well-formulated question in mind at all. Suppose the client might come in wanting to know (Coombs and Alty (1984); Hand (1987))

What would happen if X?
or Why would X happen?
or How could X be prevented?
or What are the critical factors in X?
or How do I do X?
or How can I compare X and Y?
or Is there a relationship between X and Y?
or Is this formulation complete?
or What is this?
or Tell me about X?
etc.

If one could guarantee that the clients would always have a particular type of question then no doubt an efficient architecture for that type (perhaps rule-based) could be adopted. But if one does not know a priori the type of question then flexibility is of the essence. Thus we need a very general kind of knowledge representation. One or two systems have adopted hypertext as such a general representation (Hand (1989); Clayden and Croft (1989)).

Hypertext systems come in many shapes and sizes but they all have at their core a graph representation, with the nodes being small text chunks and the edges links between them, leading from identified regions (buttons) such as words or phrases to new chunks expanding these phrases. More generally, clicking a mouse on a button can lead to some action, such as a computation being carried out, and the text chunks might be graphical displays. Their history can be traced back at least 40 years, but it is only recently, with the advent of powerful computing facilities, that such systems have become practically realizable. There are now several hypertext "shells" commercially available.

I have coined the term "knowledge enhancement systems" to describe hypertext based systems, in contrast to "expert systems". The practical distinction lies in the emphasis on flexibility and on dialogue between the user and the system: instead of providing an expert in a box, the aim is to provide material which can supplement and enhance the user's native intelligence and knowledge.

Our first attempt to build such a system resulted in KENS (described in detail in Hand (1987)), a knowledge enhancement system for nonparametric statistics. Emphasis in KENS was on matching the client's description of their interests via a similarity coefficient rather than on the use of the hypertext links. KENS became available in the spring of 1987 and has been used by over 50 research groups, who have sent back comments. These latter have been very valuable for directing our later work. Some of the comments related to aesthetics: we deliberately restricted KENS not to use windows, mice, etc. for reasons of portability. It runs on an IBM-PC under MS-DOS with 512K of RAM. Others related to inadequacies of the knowledge base. Such things can be improved, but never perfected. A discussion of KEN's strengths and weaknesses is given in Hand (1989).

Following from KENS, we have been working on NONPAREIL (Hand (1989)), a system for nonparametric statistics which is explicitly hypertext based and runs on an Apple Macintosh under HyperCard, and LMG, a system for guiding in the analysis of linear models (Lunneborg et al. (1989)), which uses a hypertext system built in the statistical language ISP.

5 Theme 3: Metadata

Existing statistical packages require the user to know

(a) their research questions

(b) details of the origins of the data, its measurement scale, etc.

(c) what these imply in terms of the analysis.

Of these, (c) is the sort of statistical expertise that people are currently struggling to build into systems, (a) still lies firmly in the human domain, and (b) represents information which supplements the data and which can be made use of by the expertise of (c). Since we are concerned with putting the (c) expertise into programs, it goes without saying that the supplementary information of (b) must be computer accessible and manipulable.

As with any novel ideas, several researchers produced it at the same time. The European Statistical Office, EUROSTAT, have adopted it as one of the bases of their DOSES project on statistical expert systems. Lawson (1989) described the "semantics of data", referring to the same thing. Oldford (1987) has used object oriented programming to achieve the same result. Lubinsky (1989) has produced similar ideas from a different perspective. Computer database researchers sometimes refer to metadata, to mean the same thing, and this is the terminology we shall adopt.

Metadata may be used in each of the two ways that the statistical expert systems have been perceived as being useful: to guide the user and guard the user, as outlined above. We illustrate below, but first some examples of metadata:

- in a randomised clinical trial of anorexia one of the variables may be weight. The metadata will indicate that it is measured in Kg, that it is strictly positive, that it has an upper bound etc.
- metadata may indicate that a zero is structural (e.g. the number of men in a population who have had a hysterectomy).
- metadata may indicate how data is missing: is it missing at random, completely at random, or what?
- metadata may indicate that two groups of scores are matched.

In each of these examples the information provided by the metadata mediates in some way in controlling the analysis which may be performed. In the first example, automatic data checking is obvious. Less obvious is the fact that since only positive values are allowed it might be worth considering logarithmic transformations—this is a commonly applied statistical heuristic. Given that one knows the unit of measurement, one can relate it to other units of measurement. In the second example, one can take the known pattern of structural zeros into account when fitting a log-linear model. In the third example, knowledge of the missing data mechanism will help one choose an appropriate way of tackling it.

There seem to be two main origins for the concern about metadata. One is to facilitate the construction of interfaces to existing packages. Another is to permit the accurate use of data by analysts other than those who collected it. This raises what may be a problem since it makes the implicit assumption that it can be foreseen at the time of data collection what will be the relevant aspects of the data during the analysis.

For example, the metadata may say this variable is human height, it is measured in meters, it is on a ratio scale, it is strictly positive. And the metadata may also contain the information that:

- height in m = (height in cm)/100.
- body mass index = weight (Kg)/height^2 (m^2).
- adult height is bounded by .5m and 3m.
- height is related to age.
- certain diseases cause height decrease, etc.

So where does one stop? And how does the data compiler know where to stop? The use of metadata to prevent misuse is fairly obvious. The ideas have been developed extensively for the parallel task of data imputation in surveys (see, for example, Fellegi and Holt (1976)). Perhaps less obvious is the fact that the combination of metadata with some

common statistical heuristics can be immensely powerful. As an example, suppose we wish to find a relationship between two physical variables. We take the example of the pressure and the volume of a gas at constant temperature to illustrate.
We might begin by trying

$$p(x) + v(x) = c_1 \tag{1}$$

The metadata tell us that the pressure, p, and the volume, v, are each measured on a ratio scale, so that similarity transformations are permissible. Thus

$$\begin{aligned} ap(x) + bv(x) &= c_2 \\ \text{i.e., } ac_1 + (b-a)v &= c_2 \end{aligned}$$

which is false, so that (1) is rejected as a possible relationship. The metadata also tell us that pressure and volume are strictly positive. A common statistical heuristic (mentioned above) says that for strictly positive variables log transforms are often useful. We therefore try

$$\log p(x) + \log v(x) = c_1 \tag{2}$$

Applying similarity transforms, this reduces to

$$\log a + \log b + c_1 = c_2$$

so that (2) is a legitimate possible relationship. Note that (2) can be rewritten as

$$pv = \text{constant}$$

which is Boyle's law.

6 Conclusion

There are general conclusions which may be drawn from work to date on statistical expert systems. One is doubt about the practical feasibility of systems aimed at the statistically naive. It seems likely that such systems will need to have an internal understanding of statistics and of the substantive area in which they are being applied. Either that, or they must be very highly constrained systems.

There are some striking parallels here with natural language translation systems. It has been found that simple mapping followed by rules to handle idioms is not enough, and some deeper understanding of meaning is required (so that the input language is mapped to an internal representation and then back out into the target tongue). In translation, also, an alternative is to apply it to a restricted domain of discourse.

Thus one might recommend that researchers should concentrate on systems which they themselves would find valuable—to provide support and "second opinions".

A minor general point is that many current systems adopt tedious question/answer series, and this must be avoided.

To date many small systems have been built "to explore the feasibility of developing a statistical expert system" for some domain. They have generally partially succeeded. However, it is pointless to go on doing this ad infinitum. We have now reached the stage where, before embarking on such a project, some hard questions must be asked about the contribution the effort will make to the sub-discipline. A key observation arising from recent work is that critical evaluation is needed. Where did the system succeed? Where did it fail, and why? A PhD project to build such a system should not be awarded the degree without such an assessment.

The literature on statistical expert systems is now quite extensive. It is scattered, which makes it difficult to find, but before embarking on research in this area it must be read. The name "statistical expert systems" has also recently been criticised. In view of the above comments "consultations systems" or for the systems we have been developing "knowledge enhancement systems" might be better.

Finally, some themes are becoming apparent as the area matures. Amongst these are the ones briefly described above: strategy, hypertext, and metadata.

References

BELL, E. (1989), Private communication.

CLAYDEN, D., and CROFT, M. (1989), Statistical consultation — who's the expert, to appear in: *Annals of Mathematics and Artificial Intelligence.*

COOMBS, M.J., and ALTY, J. (1984), Expert systems: an alternative paradigm, in: *Developments in statistical expert systems.*, ed. M.J. Coombs, Academic Press.

DARIUS, P. (1989), A toolbox for adding knowledge based modules to existing statistical software, to appear in: *Annals of Mathematics and Artificial Intelligence.*

FELLEGI, I.P., and HOLT, D. (1976), A systematic approach to automatic edit and imputation, *JASA, 71*, 17–35.

HAND, D.J. (1985a), Statistical expert systems: necessary attributes, *J. Appl. Stats, 12*, 19–27.

HAND, D.J. (1985b), Patterns in statistical strategy, in: *Artificial intelligence and statistics*, ed. W.A. Gale, Addison-Wesley.

HAND, D.J. (1987), A statistical knowledge enhancement system, *JRSS, Series A, 150*, 334–345.

HAND, D.J. (1989), Practical experience in developing statistical knowledge enhancement systems, to appear in: *Annals of Mathematics and Artificial Intelligence.*

LAWSON, (1989), *A semantic modelling approach to knowledge-based statistical software*, Ph.D. Thesis, University of Aston, UK.

LUBINSKY, D. (1989), Integrating statistical theory with statistical databases, to appear in: *Annals of Mathematics and Artificial Intelligence.*

LUBINSKY, D., and PREGIBON, D. (1987), Data analysis as search, in: *Interactions in artificial intelligence and statistical methods.*, ed. B. Phelps, Gower Technical Press.

LUNNEBORG, C.E., HAND, D.J., HITCHCOCK, S.E., and EDWARDS, J. (1989), *LMG: data analysis knowledge enhancement in an MS-DOS statistical computing environment*, to be presented at the ISI meeting, Paris.

O'KEEFE, R.A. (1985), *Logic and lattices for a statistics advisor*, Ph.D. Thesis, University of Edinburgh, UK.

OLDFORD, R.W. (1987), *Object-oriented software representations for statistical data*, University of Waterloo Technical Report: STAT–87–18.

OLDFORD, R.W., and PETERS, S.C. (1986), Data analysis networks and DINDE, *Proc. ASA Stat. Computing section*, 19–24.

PREGIBON, D. (1985), A DIY guide to statistical strategy, in: *Artificial intelligence and statistics*, ed. W.A. Gale, Addison-Wesley, Reading, MA.

Business Forecasts Using a Forecasting Expert System

Karl-Werner Hansmann and Wolfgang Zetsche
Institut für Industriebetriebsforschung
Universität der Bundeswehr Hamburg, Germany

Summary

The paper will present the architecture of the Expert System FOCA. It will introduce the forecasting methods and forecasting programming language used by the Expert and will give details of how the Expert produces knowledge about a given problem. The way the Expert interacts with the user will be demonstrated, as well as the opportunity of the user to propose solutions. The Expert System will then be applied to empirical data taken from industry. It will be described how a suitable model is developed.

1 Introduction

The general idea of the Expert System is to achieve two major goals:

- to relieve the user from statistical and mathematical details,
- to propose solutions and to suggest appropriate steps for improvement.

Consequently, a user can concentrate on how to solve his economic problem rather then being confronted with too many statistical details. The Expert facilitates work on forecasting problems. It takes control of all necessary computation and estimation and checks all parameters for suitability. The expert acts as an experienced advisor expanding the user's knowledge on the statistical side of the problem. The final conclusion is still left to the user with reliable guideline when methods, estimation, interpretation is concerned.

2 Architecture of the System

The Expert System consists of 4 main components (see Fig. 1 below):

- editor for time series, model frames and programming language,
- high level programming language,
- method database and
- knowledge-based expert.

The editor (called BINEDI) enables the user to set-up new time series or update old ones. It displays values in tabular form on screen or shows them graphically. It facilitates handling of large time series databases.

NATO ASI Series, Vol. F 61
Knowledge, Data and Computer-Assisted Decisions
Edited by M. Schader and W. Gaul

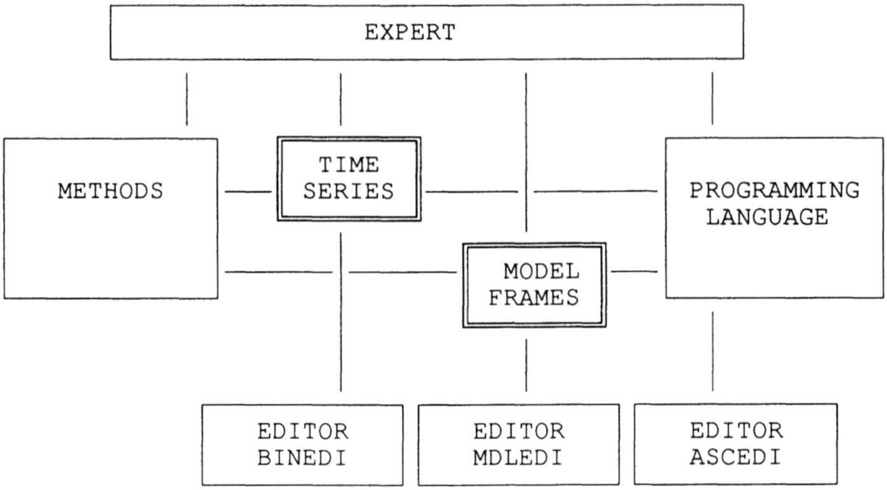

Figure 1: Main Components of the System

The available methods consist of:

- methods based on exponential smoothing;
- seasonal methods (with parameter optimization);
- spectral and cross spectral analysis;
- saturation and growth models (with exogenous variables);
- BOX-Jenkins ARIMA modelling;
- adaptive filtering;
- multiple regression analysis.

They allow univariate as well as multivariate approaches for a long, medium or short forecasting horizon. The programming language gives the system the necessary flexibility to be applicable to the wide range of different types of forecasting problems. It contains commands specialized on processing time series. Single statements allow complex calculations with any set of series.

A program is set-up by the editor (called ASCEDI) which enables the user to work on text files containing ASCII-characters. A special feature of this editor is to change into a compiler if the extension '.PRG' is encountered. Once a program has been developed, it is compiled forming an executable macro with extension '.MCR'.

The Expert uses these three components in order to find a solution. Fig. 2 shows the way the Expert is implemented in FOCA and how it interacts with the other components.

The Expert chooses a macro from the list of preset programs, alters it according to the given problem and passes this new macro on to be executed. During execution the new facts are stored in two databases. One contains the facts about the problem, the other

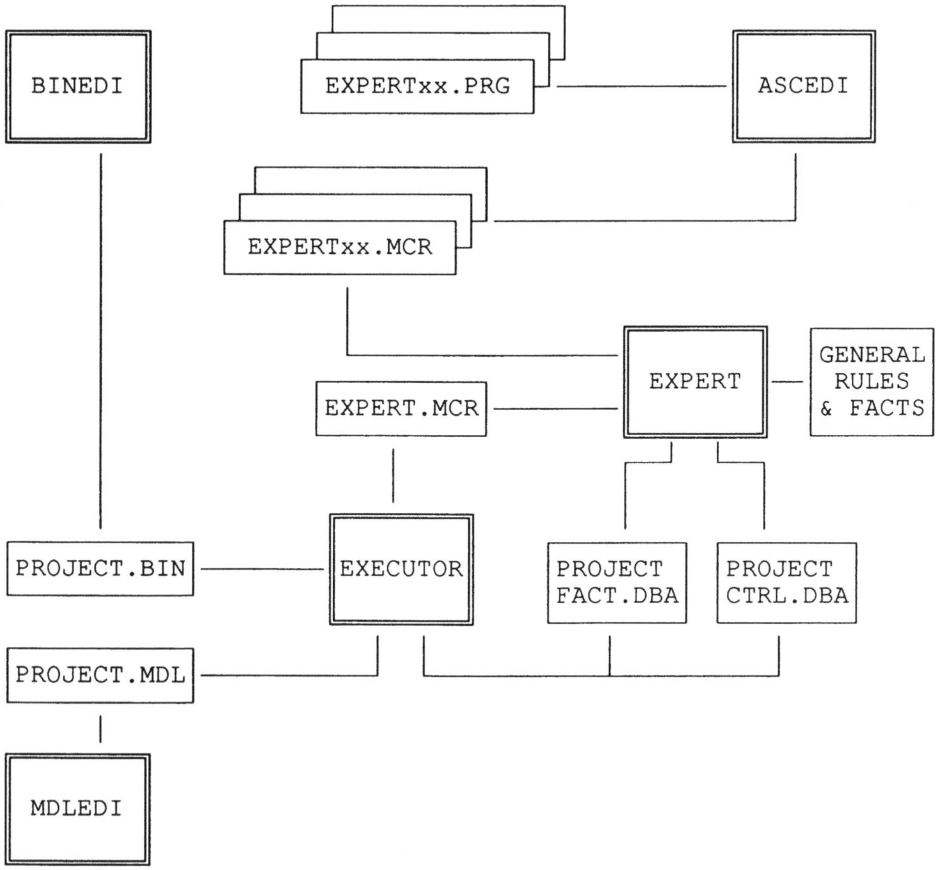

Figure 2: Implementation of the Expert in FOCA

about the progress made so far. Both databases are consulted by the Expert. They are taken into consideration for deriving further actions. The result of the Expert's analysis is a more or less suitable forecasting model. This model is determined by the

- path, file and name of the endogenous series,
- path, file and name of all exogenous series,
- intervals and horizon,
- forecasting method,
- estimated parameters,
- quality measurements, etc.

and is stored in a model database. The user can access the database via model-editor (called MDLEDI). He is able to alter existing models or add new models. The Expert can read complete models from the database and include it into its analysis on the given problem. The outstanding advantages of this architecture are:

- The executive and expert-module can use the available memory (DOS: 640 KB) for their specific purposes. Sharing the memory is not necessary and thus each module can be more capable and can run on any ordinary PC.
- The number of macros usable by the Expert is unlimited. This allows the system to be steadily enhanced by further methods, estimation procedures or other complex computation on the data.
- The system is rather flexible and can easily be adjusted to recent developments.
- Since the programming language as well as the rule database is available the user is able to control the Expert's behavior in general or in certain situations. The system can be regarded as an Expert SHELL for forecasting purposes.

After having gained a better understanding about the principal concept of the system we now can concentrate on the Expert itself.

3 The Expert's Approach to Solve a Problem

A sequence of steps generally taken to solve a forecasting problem is given in the following Tab. 1:

step	0	:	enter data, including exogenous and endogenous variables
step	1	:	run EXPERT
	1.1	:	answer questions
	1.2	:	let Expert produce facts
	1.3	:	gain a (so far) best model
	1.4	:	answer final questions
step	2	:	introduce new data, if possible, continue with step 1
step	3	:	try to improve proposed model by applying methods manually
step	4	:	run EXPERT again and let it judge new models
step	5	:	implement the best model as a turn-key application using the programming language.
step	6	:	pass the programmed application on to users in other departments

Table 1: Steps to Solve a Forecasting Problem

The most important step is the first. Therefore we should have a closer look at it.

3.1 Step 1.1: Answer Question

Beside the pure time series data there is additional information concerning the economic background of the problem. This information often requires certain properties of the forecasting model and therefore restricts the model chosen to meet these requirements. A simple example shall illustrate this. In order to have enough time to manufacture the sales forecasted, it is essential to be ahead more than just one time unit with the forecast. Subsequently only those models or methods are applicable which at least cover

```
--------------------------- Dialog Window ---------------------------

 Statement: After the Expert presented the quality of the
            model, you have to judge whether it is economical
            suitable.

 Question:  Is the chosen model economically suitable ?

 Note:      When you enter NO, the model will be deleted.

                                     MENU
                                     yes
                                     no
```

Figure 3: User Dialog

this forecasting horizon. All others (simple moving average or exponential smoothing) have to be rejected because they are economically unsuitable.

The economic background information can be gathered from the user who is familiar with all details, by asking questions. Some of the questions asked by the Expert are listed in Tab. 2 below. Questions generally consist of 4 components:

1. **statement**, where the situation is described in which the question is asked (reasons)
2. **question**, which is the text of the question to be asked
3. **note**, where hints for the user can be given
4. **prompt**, where the prompt to the user and the type of the expected answer is specified. If the type of answer is 'menu', then the list of menu items is stored here.

The 4 components of a question are identified by a number. For each question exists a corresponding fact describing the question and the numbers. Consequently statements, notes or prompts can be used with different questions.

The answers to the question are of different types. The majority ask the user to select from a menu. Others require single integer or real values or prompt the user to give a list of values or to enter character strings. All answers are stored in the fact-database and are valid until the user answers them again or starts right at the beginning again. That enables the user to always continue on the stage which has been achieved during previous sessions. He may interrupt his search for a suitable model at any time and return to it if convenient. An example how questions appear on screen is given in Fig. 3.

In order to understand how different answers influence the Expert's behavior we want to have a closer look at two questions. One of the first questions asked is:

```
"What is the objective of applying FOCA ?"
```

The user can choose between the answers:

```
1 - "Estimate future development"
2 - "Recognize influencing factors"
3 - "Recognize changes in trend"
```

No.		Description
1	Question:	Is it ESPECIALLY important to avoid great deviations?
5	Question:	What kind of values does the series contain
6	Question:	Would you consider the past development to be following a trend?
7	Question:	How many values would you like to forecast in the future?
8	Question:	Are there any other explaining factors?
9	Question:	Which series number has the explaining series and in which file can it be found?
10	Question:	Which series number contains the series to be analysed?
12	Question:	Shall the expert produce information?
13	Question:	Would you consider the past development to be seasonal?
14	Question:	Has data already been stored in the project file?
15	Question:	Does the data tend to a saturation level?
16	Question:	Is it ESPECIALLY important that the trend change is recognized properly?
17	Question:	Should the result be graphically displayed?
18	Question:	Do you want to open a new file?
23	Question:	Is the chosen model economically plausible?
24	Question:	Do you want to use the proposed model?
26	Question:	Which model would you like to see?
27	Question:	What is the minimal amount of values to be forecasted?
29	Question:	Do you want the expertise printed?
30	Question:	Are you dealing with monthly data?
32	Question:	In which period begins the time series?
34	Question:	In which period does the time series finish?
35	Question:	Do you think the growth of population in the FRG can influence the series to be explained?
36	Question:	In which areas is the growth of population relevant?
37	Question:	Of which sex is the relevant group?
38	Question:	Of which age is the relevant group?
39	Question:	Are there more groups whose growth could influence the series to be explained?
40	Question:	Are there any explaining factors?
41	Question:	What should happen to the results from the endogene series?
42	Question:	Which name should the series to be analysed have?
43	Question:	Which name should the model have?
44	Question:	Are the explaining factors yet in a file?
45	Question:	Which number should the explaining series have?
46	Question:	Which name should the explaining series have?
47	Question:	Are there any other explaining factors that are not stored in a file?
99	Question:	Which project do you want do work on?

Table 2: List of Questions

All answers are related to one another, but are not identical. There are slight differences which enable the Expert to act differently.

The first answer is the default. It forces the Expert to select a model, estimate parameters **and** produce a forecast. Thus it is the most comprehensive choice.

The second answer only concentrates on the influence which exogenous variables might have on the endogenous variable. Univariate models are not to be considered. We don't need a forecast and consequently we don't need the future values of the regressors. We are able to even process unlagged time series.

The third answer only asks for the best fit of the turning points, also neglecting the forecast. It forces the Expert to regard the prediction of ups and downs as being more important than any other quality measurement. Another question asked is for example:

```
"Is it possible that the growth of population influences the
series to be explained ?"
```

If this question is answered with 'yes' the Expert continues the user dialogue by asking for more details about the age group, sex and market area. It then accesses a database containing a large selection of time series concerning population and provides some for further analysis.

Once the process of asking the user questions about the problem and its economic background has finished, the Expert can start to produce further knowledge about the problem. This will be described in the next step.

3.2 Step 1.2: Produce Knowledge

In contrast to other systems which only judge externally provided information, the Expert is able to **produce** quantitative information about the problem **itself**. This means the Expert is able to start computation on the given set of variables. It decides which method has to be applied, triggers computation and determines further steps depending on the new situation.

As mentioned in the previous section the Expert uses the preset macros of the programming language. A sample of what kind of macros can be performed is listed in Tab. 3.

The following example shows the source code of the macro which applies the seasonal method of WINTERS to a series.

No.	Description
1	seasonal method of WINTERS
2	various sort of trends
3	statistical parameter about a variable
⋮	
7	forecast using moving average
8	exponential smoothing
⋮	
12	trend extrapolation
13	exponential function
14	logistic function
⋮	
18	regression analysis with trend and sine cycles
19	sine cycles with various frequency
20	regression analysis with exogenous variables
21	calculates autocorrelation coefficients
22	plots two series on screen
⋮	
24	shifts a series by n periods
25	erases a series from the project file
26	edits a series on screen
⋮	

Table 3: Available Macros

```
;-------------------------------------------------------------
;                         EXPERT01

REAL tprogh                         ;forecasting horizon

OPEN SESSION
OPEN  INPUT  FILE "??????????.BIN"
OPEN OUTPUT  FILE "??????????.BIN"
READ SERIES  R??? TO STORAGE S1
SET tprogh  = ???
SET S4 = S1

;--- Winters model with alpha=0.3 ---------------------------
SET S1 = S4
SET DEFAULT  INTERVAL    = STORAGE INTERVAL S1
SET BASIC    INTERVAL    = DEFAULT INTERVAL
SET FORECAST INTERVAL    = BASIC   INTERVAL + tprogh
SET S2 = FORECAST WINTERS  (S1,ybtp,0.3,0.3,0.3)
SET ybja = ybja +1
SET ybtpa= ybtpa-ybtp
```

```
TRUNCATE SERIES S1 TO S1

;------------ prepare forecast for further use --------------
INSERT VALUE ymocnt(6,0) INTO STRING yfac01(1:6)
SET $STRG1(1:6)  = $STRG2(1:6)
SET $NAM(1:6) S2 = $STRG1(1:6)
SET $NUM      S2 = 999
WRITE STORAGE S2                   ;save forecast

;------------ calculate quality measurements ----------------
DEFINE STORAGE INTERVAL (S3,1,1,0,1,10)

ADD WP (S1,S2) TO S3          ;Trend Change
WRITE STRING yfac04(1:067) TO FILE "exout.dba"
ADD MAD(S1,S2) TO S3          ;Mean absolute Deviation
ADD DW (S1,S2) TO S3          ;Durbin Watson
WRITE STRING yfac03(1:079) TO FILE "exout.dba"
ADD BM (S1,S2) TO S3          ;Coefficient of Determination
ADD SA (S1,S2) TO S3          ;Standarddeviation
ADD TK (S1,S2) TO S3          ;Theil's Coefficient
ADD KK (S1,S2) TO S3          ;Correlation Coefficient
WRITE STRING yfac02(1:111) TO FILE "exout.dba"

END SESSION
STOP PROGRAM
END
```

The macro opens the project file containing the data and reads the endogenous series to storage. It then adjusts the intervals according to the series and forecasting horizon and applies the method. The forecast is then compared with the true data and some quality measurements are derived. All information about this model is finally passed to the databases of the Expert. A comprehensive list of facts gathered during computation is given in Tab. 4.

The macros are only one type of possible actions. Beside the macros the Expert knows some other actions. Another set of very important actions are the already mentioned questions. A third type of action only serve job control purposes. They make sure that the Expert can detect errors during computation and thus keeps running without endless loops and utmost flexibility to the user. A complete list of different types of action is given in Tab. 5. The Expert has to define which action should be performed next. Therefore it consists of a set of rules which have to be applied to the facts already collected. The production rules are constructed as follows:

```
IF   (condition_1 .and.
      condition_2 .and.
      ...                ) THEN action_x
```

Each condition refers to certain facts in the knowledge database. Several conditions can be combined by the logical operator 'and'. Each single condition can be inverted using

exogene_faktoren	(number of factors, list of factors)
modell_guete	(model number, quality)
modell_guete_info_dw	(model number, quality measurement, quality measurement, quality measurement, quality measurement)
modell_guete_info_wp	(model number, integer, integer, integer, integer)
modell_guete_temp	(model number, quality)
modell_input_param	(model number, name of the method, list of model parameters)
modell_interval	(model number, interval)
modell_methode	(model number, name of the method)
modell_output_param	(model number, name of the method, list of model parameters)
modell_reihen	(model number, number of influencing series, list of the numbers of influencing series)
modell_reinam	(model number, number of influencing series, list of the names of influencing series)
modell_summe	(model number, quality measurement)
modell_summe_temp	(model number, quality measurement)
reihen	(series number, name of the series, interval, list of parameters)
reihen_definition	(series number, name of the series, comment, interval, format of the series data, file in which the series is stored)

Table 4: Data Base Facts Dealing With Information About Models

action	meaning of that action
frage	ask a question to the user
macro	perform a macro
plausi	test some facts for plausibility
reiles	convert facts about time series into the format the Expert can use and read them into the database
frage_loeschen	delete the answer to a question
interpret	perform a complex task interpreting the results of other actions
loeschen	delete some control facts
logik	write a fact into the database. This fact can be used in the conditions of other actions to represent all the conditions of that specific logic action
meldung	display some text

Table 5: List of Actions

the functor 'n(condition)'. The logical operator 'or' can be implemented by repeating the complete rule with a different condition in the if-clause. The internal representation of the production rules is as follows:

```
bedingungen_fuer_aktionen ( number   , action, [conditions], number )
keyword                     selector, action,  list of     , priority
                                               conditions    of action
                                               connected
                                               by logical
                                               AND
```

An example shall demonstrate its use:

```
bedingungen_fuer_aktion(35,frage, ,007)

                             [file_exist("bvg"),
                              sprache(1),
                              frage(40,antmenu(1)),
                              frage(05,antmenu(1))]

IF:

        the file of type "bvg" exists
.AND.   the selected language is "German"
.AND.   the first menu item ("yes")
        was selected as an answer to question 40:
        "Do you know any explaining factors?"
.AND.   the first menu item ("Yearly values")
        was selected as an answer to question 5:
        "What kind of values does the series contain?"

THEN:

Ask the question 35:  "Is it possible that the growth of
              population in the FRG has an influence on
              the time series to be explained?"
```

Some very important conditions refer to the user's answers. They are called 'question' and have to state the number of the question and the answer with which the condition should be verified. For example:

```
question(14,ansmenu(1))
```

This condition is true, if the question 14 ("whether data has already been stored in the project file") has been answered with the first choice of the menu, which is "yes". A simple rule using this condition could be:

```
IF (question(14,ansmenu(1))) THEN macro(1)
```

expressing that macro 1 should be processed if question 14 was answered with 'yes'. Extensive use of the facts collected in the database is provided by another group of conditions. They allow access to any parameter of the models calculated and variables involved. The condition:

```
"seriesdef(6,6,"in_file",001,12)"
```

for example checks, whether the series number 001 in the project file is defined as a monthly series with 12 values per year. The first two integers "6,6" refer to the database fact containing this definition. In the same way, the quality measurements of models calculated can be accessed. The condition

```
modqual_lt (3,7,expost,modbest,val_rea(1.0))"
```

checks whether the Theil's coefficient of the best model found is less then 1.000. If so the model can be classed as being better than the naive forecast. Beside the Theil's coefficient some other quality measurements are available. A selection of possible conditions is given below:

```
1.  conditions in relation to the status of the expert
      faktanzok
      frage_neu(integer)
2.  conditions in relation to the status of the system
      sprache(integer)
      file_exist(string)
3.  conditions monitoring facts about the series
      reihendef(integer,integer,interval_typ,
                db_reinum_spec,dbaval)
4.  conditions monitoring the results of performed actions
      frage(integer,antwort)
      logik(integer,char)
      plausi(integer,char)
5.  conditions monitoring performed actions
      interpret(integer)
      macro(integer)
6.  conditions in relation to results of performed macros
      modgue(integer,integer,guete_typ,db_modell_spec,dbaval)
      modmeth(integer,db_modell_spec,dbaval)
      modsum(integer,db_modell_spec,dbaval)
7.  other conditions
      n(bedingung)
```

The next very important problem is how to compare different models with each other and how to determine the best. For each model 7 different quality measurements are provided:

- Coefficient of Determination (CoD)
- Durbin-Watson Statistic (DW)
- Relative Mean Absolute Deviation

score	CoD	DW
5 (best)	0.990–1.000	1.90–2.10
4	0.900–0.990	
3	0.800–0.900	1.60–1.90 or 2.1–2.4
2	0.500–0.800	
1 (worst)	0.000–0.500	0.00–1.60 or 2.4–4.0

Table 6: Transformations of Quality Measurement

- Relative Standard Deviation
- Trend Change
- Correlation Coefficient
- Variance Quotient

These measurements are combined to a single fact

```
modqual("project",model,quality("type",value_CoD, ...,))
```

and stored in the database.

According to their actual values the measurements are transformed to scores between 1 and 5. The closer the value is at the optimal value the higher the scoring. Tab. 6 shows the upper and lower limits for the measurements Coefficient of Determination (CoD) and Durbin-Watson Coefficient (DW). The other measurements are treated in the same way.

With this transformation we achieve a standard scale for all different measurements varying only between 1 and 5. We can now weigh them with a factor which corresponds to the importance of the particular measurement. Finally the weighted scores are accumulated and the model with the maximum sum is regarded as the best. An example demonstrates this:

> Let us assume we gained a model with CoD = 0.79 and DW = 1.65. The CoD lies within the upper and lower limits of 0.5–0.8 and scores 2. The DW scores 3. The total scoring of the model is 5 if no weights are applied.

This method is generally applicable and leads to good results. However there are some exceptions which have to be dealt with. The multiple regression analysis normally produces better results when more variables are included into the model. This is even the case if the variable is not significant. In this case two solutions are proposed. Either further rules have to be introduced preventing that this model becomes the best or a modified CoD has to be calculated considering the number of variables.

Now we know the most important principles of the Expert and we should switch to an application.

4 Application

This case study demonstrates how the Expert solved a sales forecasting problem in the consumer goods industry. The case study comes from an actual application. The data and all related information was gained from an individual case and is presented here in general form.

4.1 The Economic Problem

A manufacturer of perishable consumer goods wants to forecast future sales at various levels as accurate as possible. His objective is to make sure that:

- as little goods as possible remain unsold
- few goods perish in store rooms
- production can be planned to match demand
- distribution to regional wholesalers is controlled individually
- materials can be ordered in time.

As achieving these aims increases turnover and market shares and saves considerable costs, solutions should be found for both the whole market and for parts of it.

4.2 The Solution

Data on past performance must be available for the analysis. In our case, sales data has been collected weekly. This data was collected and maintained in a DBASE database. From here the data could be transferred easily.

The sales department acquired a great deal of experience about the market reaction to certain measures they had taken. These internal influencing factors were the starting point in creating a model. The three most important factors were:

- the number of products supplied to the wholesalers,
- advertising campaigns,
- appearance of the product.

There is no clear evidence as to how sales are affected by external or environmental factors. One does however assume that changes in the environment influence sales to some extent. The clearly defined factors are:

- number of inhabitants on vacation,
- length of the sales period.

4.3 The Best Model

Once ideas about market reactions have been made concrete and the necessary data is available, the best model for showing these effects must be found.

First the Expert asks the user various questions about the economic background of the forecasting problem. The Expert then creates a variety of models independently and checks them for suitability. In doing so it double checks the user's answers and checks all data for plausibility. Contradictions are recognized and the Expert queries the user to resolve them. As a result the Expert informs the user of the most suitable model in form of a short interpretation.

```
Expertise:

The project is called: DISTRIBU.BIN
The goal is  'Estimate future development        '.

The series to be forecasted is:002  Sales
from file: D:\FOCAUSER\TEST\DISTRIBU.BIN
It is derived from 'Sales,Distribution,Marketing  '.
The series was observed between: 001' 087- 014 '089.
At least 001 and at most 003 values were prognosed.
The values represent ' weekly values           '.

The displayed model is No:    000564
The following factors are considered:
 - Series : 181  Saison 2      C:\FOCAUSER\TEST\DISTRIBU.BIN
 - Series : 180  Saison 1      C:\FOCAUSER\TEST\DISTRIBU.BIN
 - Series : 110  Advertisment  C:\FOCAUSER\TEST\DISTRIBU.BIN
 - Series : 001  Delivery      C:\FOCAUSER\TEST\DISTRIBU.BIN

  The method is called:  Multiple linear regression analysis
  The output parameters are :
     b1 = 0.0487 (Saison 2     )   without influence
     b2 = 0.0431 (Saison 1     )   without influence
     b3 = 0.2001 (Advertisment)    with high influence
     b4 = 0.8348 (Delivery     )   with very high influence
     c  = -0.447 (constant)        with high influence

  The quality of the model can be judged as follows:
  The model defines the deviations quite well.
  One can assume that a regular structure remained unexplained.
  The deviation of the forecast from the data is small.
  The trend change is forecasted moderately.
  The forecast is much better than the 'naive forecast'.
  The forecast is almost exactly the same as the real development.

  Conclusion: The model is well suitable.

                                                   to end press : F10
```

Figure 4: Expertise Produced by the Expert

Fig. 4 shows

- which method was used
- how good the model is and whether it is suitable
- which parameters have been estimated

The work of the Expert can—**but does not have to**—be augmented by analyzes of the user, which are also interpreted and judged. To do this the software provides a dialogue-oriented procedure which is graphically supported and clearly explained by a HELP function. Thus an optimal co-operation between the user and the Expert is achieved. The Expert deals with the labour and time intensive part of the analysis, identifying the most important information and preparing the result.

4.4 The Final Result

For the problem in this case study nearly all retailers found a highly significant and economically convincing model. The wholesaler XY has been chosen for this example (see Fig. 5). The development of the previous years could be explained to 90.1% accuracy. The average forecasting error was only 2.9% of the mean value and was more than halved in comparison with that in earlier years. Also, the turning point measurement leaves us

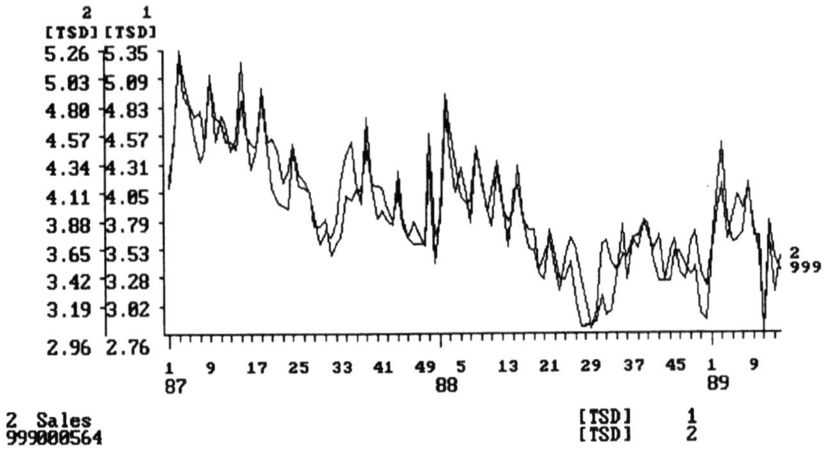

Figure 5: Sales and Forecast

no room for doubt about the suitability of the model. With a value of 0.576 it shows that the vast majority of the trend turning points have been correctly forecasted. This result is extremely important in practice. A wrong decision at this point is particularly serious. The forecasting error and the resulting costs increase considerably if a trend change is not recognized and this in turn is detrimental to the firm's success. Also the Durbin-Watson is satisfactory. The value 1.82 does not indicate any kind of autocorrelation of the residuals. Theil's coefficient proves the forecast to be much better than the naive.

5 Conclusion

As presented here we see that the system is able to handle a given forecasting problem independently. It selects a statistically best model and considers economic constraints simultaneously. The user does not need to be a mathematician or forecasting expert in order to achieve good and reliable results.

References

CHADWICK, M., and HANNAH, J.A. (1986), *Expert Systems for Personal Computers*, Sigma Press, Wilmslow.

FORD, N. (1988), *So denken Maschinen*, Oldenbourg, München Wien.

JACKSON, P. (1986), *Introduction to Expert Systems*, Addison-Wesley, Wokingham.

MICHIE, D. (1982), *Machine Intelligence and Related Topics*, Gordon and Breach, New York London.

NAYLOR, C. (1985), *Build your own expert system*, Halsted Press, New York.

PARTRIDGE, D. (1986), *Artificial Intelligence*, Ellis Horwood, New York Chichester Brisbane Toronto.

SAVORY, S.E. (1982), *Künstliche Intelligenz und Expertensysteme*, Oldenbourg, München Wien.

SCHEFE, P. (1986), *Künstliche Intelligenz—Überblick und Grundlagen*, Bibliographisches Institut, Mannheim Wien Zürich.

SIMONS, G.L. (1985), *Expert Systems and Micros*, NCC Publications, Manchester.

Expert Systems: A Database Perspective

Michael Kifer
Department of Computer Science
SUNY at Stony Brook, U.S.A.

Summary

In recent years rule-based and frame-based systems became popular tools for developing a wide range of knowledge intensive applications. Although these tools provide significant help to the application developer, building expert systems remains largely an ad hoc and a very labor-intensive job.

Recent progress in knowledge representation and database research made time ripe for attempting a systematic logic-based approach to expert systems. Our contention is that expert system programming can be made much more declarative by releaving the developer from the burden of specifying most of the nitty-gritty details of the search strategy underlying the language implementation. This burden should be taken over by the system which will use various optimization techniques to achieve desirable response time.

In this paper we survey our on-going research in which the database philosophy and technology is being applied in the field of expert systems, and then outline a knowledge representation language whose two major components were separately described in (Kifer and Li (1988); Kifer and Lausen (1989)). Being purely declarative, this language is more suitable for expert systems programming, and its use should result in shortening the development phase of knowledge-intensive applications, making them more reliable and extensible.

1 Introduction

Combined rule- and frame-based languages became popular tools for developing so called intelligent systems (Buchanan and Shortliffe (1984); Harmon, Maus and Morrissey (1988); Hayes-Roth (1985); Petrie, Russinoff and Steiner (1987)). By supporting the very concept of a rule, frame, certainty factors, etc., these languages provide a great help to the application developer. Despite that, building expert systems remains largely an ad hoc and a very labor-intensive job (Feigenbaum (1977); Hayes-Roth, Waterman and Lenat (1983); Hayes-Roth (1985); Parnas (1985)).

At present, the languages used for programming knowledge-intensive systems normally require the user to be aware of such low-level details of program control as backtracking, (Prolog-style) cuts, and even whether the rules are to be applied in a forward or backward chaining. Such systems have no declarative semantics, i.e., the user is almost entirely at the mercy of the algorithm underlying the language implementation; they inherit most of the notorious non-logical constructs of Prolog (Clocksin and Mellish (1981)), aggravating the situation even further by new features intended to cope with knowledge representation

NATO ASI Series, Vol. F 61
Knowledge, Data and Computer-Assisted Decisions
Edited by M. Schader and W. Gaul

idiosyncrasies. For instance, as in Prolog, queries to knowledge bases are not guaranteed to terminate and/or retrieve all answers, the notion of query/program optimization is virtually nonexistent, and the computational efficiency is almost solely a user's responsibility. All this renders expert system development a very time-consuming and error-prone task. At present, verifying correctness of expert systems is next to impossible, and their reliability is always in question (Parnas (1985)).

Our contention is that this situation can be improved dramatically by utilizing the recent achievements in the deductive database research (e.g., Beeri and Ramakrishnan (1987); Gardarin (1987); Kifer and Lozinskii (1986); Vieille (1986)). We believe that expert systems programming can be made more declarative, thereby releaving the developer from the burden of specifying most of the nitty-gritty details of control strategy. This burden should be taken over by a system which uses various query optimization techniques to achieve desirable response time. Unfortunately, none of the commercial or experimental expert system shells we are aware of attempts any serious query optimization. To compensate for this deficiency, they supply numerous ways of specifying control information, heavily relying on user's experience in the art of what became known as "knowledge engineering".

In many problem domains (medical, military, etc.) expert systems have to deal with pieces of knowledge which are uncertain or incomplete. A well known example of such system is MYCIN (Buchanan and Shortliffe (1984)). Not surprisingly, the aforesaid problems become only worse when users have to face uncertain data or imprecise reasoning.

In the recent work (Kifer and Li (1988)), we considered such systems, and made several steps towards our declared goal of rendering expert systems programming a less demanding enterprise. We proposed a declarative semantics for general rule-based systems which utilize certainty factors as a means of representing incomplete or imprecise knowledge. We would like to stress that the theory of evidential, probabilistic, or fuzzy reasoning is *not* our concern here. That is, we do not address the issue of how different evidences for the same fact can be combined together to yield a new (possibly stronger) evidence. Surveys of this field can be found in Buchanan and Shortliffe (1984), Frost (1986), Kanal and Lemmer (1986), Prade (1983). Instead, in Kifer and Li (1988) we proposed a model-theoretic semantics for quite a large class of theories of evidential reasoning that satisfy a number of general requirements to how strength of causal links is to be computed. In particular, all the theories considered in Prade (1983) fall under this category. Neither do we want to get into a discussion of the controversial issue of where do the certainty factors come from. These issues are orthogonal to the problem of logical deduction which we are trying to attack here. Our goal is providing formal grounds to a class of practical problems which so far has received only an ad hoc treatment.

Another popular knowledge engineering tool used in expert systems is the concept of a *frame* (Minsky (1981)). The well-known systems like ART or KEE offer its users the convenience of rules and frames in one language. Unfortunately, no solid semantics for frames underlies these implementations. Although Hayes (1979) has described a translation of the frame notation to predicate calculus, this translation provides only an indirect semantics, and leaves a number of important features of frames out[1].

In Kifer and Wu (1989), Kifer and Lausen (1989), we have developed a language, called F-logic (a logic for frames) which naturally combines frames with deduction of

[1] In fact, ART has adopted Hayes's approach.

the predicate calculus style. This logic is surveyed in Section 4. Then we show how uncertainty à la Kifer and Li (1988) can be combined with frames in a way that preserves semantic properties of both approaches.

The rest of this paper is organized as follows. In Section 2 we outline our vision of what a logic-based system for knowledge representation should look like, and in Section 3 we discuss the relevant work done by others. Sections 4 and 5 survey the results from Kifer and Li (1988), Kifer and Wu (1989), Kifer and Lausen (1989) regarding the semantics of logic programs with uncertainty and frames. In Section 6 we describe a logic language that combines frames with uncertainty and Section 7 discusses future research.

2 Our Vision

In this section we outline several (minimalistic, in our view) requirements to a knowledge representation language. Then, in the next section, we discuss several related works, and show where they fail to meet these requirements. In the subsequent sections we describe our ongoing research in the directions outlined below, and point to the areas where more research needs to be done.

In our opinion, logical foundations underlying expert systems must support at least the following:

1. reasoning in the presence of uncertain information;
2. tolerance to inconsistent data;
3. frame representation and property inheritance;
4. "logic programmability".

Reasoning with uncertainty is in the very nature of expert system applications, where even the experts in the respective domains do not have complete understanding of causal links between the events. Although much work has been done in this direction, most of the approaches are dealing with very restricted types of uncertainty. Furthermore, abundance of different theories and the lack of consensus as to which one should be preferred calls for a semantic framework general enough to accommodate several popular proposals. Actually, there seems to be a consensus that different theories have their own application domains, which emphasizes the need in a unifying framework. We propose just that: a framework which accommodates a number of different ways of handling uncertainty under the same roof.

When the information is uncertain or imprecise, inconsistency creeps in very naturally because evidences from different sources may contradict each other. Representing inconsistency in a semantically sound manner is thus very important. Unfortunately, in most cases this issue is either ignored or treated incorrectly. This criticism concerns most of the works on probabilistic reasoning and those using the Dempster-Shafer theory. The problem is that the probability-based theories assume that contradicting facts neutralize each other, and thus they are unable to distinguish a 'no information' from a 'contradiction'.

We claim that such distinction is important. Indeed, suppose that a system for medical diagnosis responds with a 'no information' answer. A normal reaction to this should be performing additional *new* tests since, apparently, the old ones have revealed too little information about the disease. In contrast, if the response is contradictory then, provided that the medical theory underlying the tests is consistent, we have an indication of an inaccurately performed test. The meaningful action should then be re-doing the *old* tests, rather than administering new ones.

As mentioned earlier, the concept of *frame* is among the favorite ones in knowledge representation and supplying logical foundation for it is extremely desirable. In fact, the recent 'object-oriented' trend in databases is nothing else but the adoption of frames as a major data modeling paradigm. 'Logic programmability' means the ability to specify and execute logic rules in a way similar to Prolog (Clocksin and Mellish (1981)), LDL (Beeri et al. (1987)), NAIL! (Morris et al. (1987)), etc. While frames represent a relatively static aspect of knowledge representation such as data clustering, class/subclass relationship, etc., rules represent implicit relationships between objects and also define objects which are not explicitly stored in the knowledge base. The semantics of computation in a knowledge base essentially amounts to finding these implicit objects. Because of the popularity of knowledge description by means of rules, we believe that logic programmability is an important requisite feature. Unfortunately, all previous implementations of rule-based systems heavily relied on the user-supplied information for controlling the search, and because of the lack of query optimization, these systems were completely inadequate for handling large amounts of data. However, the recent advances in query processing in deductive databases, e.g., Balbin, Port and Ramamohanarao (1987), Beeri and Ramakrishnan (1987), Beeri et al. (1987), Gardarin (1987), Cuntzer and Bayer (1987), Kifer and Lozinskii (1986), Kifer and Lozinskii (1990) have demonstrated that efficient implementations of logical languages are feasible, and LDL developed at MCC is an early example of such a system.

3 Review of the Related Work

3.1 Logics for Handling Uncertainty

In this section, we survey the relevant work on declarative semantics of logic programs with uncertainty, and highlight the differences with our approach. Lee (1972) describes a model-theoretic semantics and the resolution principle for one of the fuzzy logics, called *K-standard sequence logic* (Dubois and Prade (1980)). Essentially the same semantics is described in Rine (1986), although the latter relies on the formalism of Post algebras instead of the fuzzy logic.

Van Emden (1986) also deals with K-standard sequence logic, providing both model-theoretic and fixpoint semantics for a special case, which he calls *quantitative reasoning*. Shapiro (1983) considers a similar logic, but his framework for computing certainties is more general than that of van Emden (1986). He describes a model theoretic semantics and discusses some implementational issues, but his treatment is rather imprecise and lacks solid computational foundations.

Blair and Subrahmanian (1989), Subrahmanian (1987) extend the work of van Emden (1986) by allowing negative information to be represented explicitly. For instance, in this extended logic it is perfectly acceptable for both p and $\neg p$ to have some supporting evidences. However, in these works, each literal in a rule may have only a constant certainty factor, which is too restrictive. For instance, there is no way to say "If an evidence for A is z-strong and an evidence for B is y-strong then conclude that C is supported by an xy-strong evidence, where x, y are variables".

Work has also been reported on fuzzy relational calculus (Zemankova-Leech and Kandel (1984); Zvieli (1986)). These studies have also concentrated on the aforesaid K-standard sequence logic. In addition, fuzzy calculi do not allow recursion. Therefore, their expressiveness and logic programmability are very limited. It was demonstrated in Kifer and Li (1988) that some problems in image recognition require recursive rules, and the relatively complex certainty functions needed in that domain cannot be supported by the approaches described in Shapiro (1983), Subrahmanian (1987), van Emden (1986), Zemankova-Leech and Kandel (1984), Zvieli (1986).

We believe that the approaches based on K-standard fuzzy logic have the following fundamental weakness: In this logic, given a pair of evidences of strength α and β respectively, for the same fact p, the combined evidence for p is assumed to be of strength $\max(\alpha, \beta)$. This may be inappropriate in some problem domains. For instance, MYCIN (Buchanan and Shortliffe (1984)) uses so called *stochastic* logic (Dubois and Prade (1980)) in which the combined evidence would be $\alpha + \beta - \alpha \times \beta$.

All this makes the aforesaid theories of quantitative and fuzzy reasoning (although semantically sound) practically uninteresting, which calls for more general approaches. Our proposal is not restricted to any of the above logics. We only assume that evidences are combined subject to certain natural restrictions which are general enough to accommodate a number of popular methods. In this general situation, new difficult issues arise, which are mostly due to the problem of independence of different evidences supporting the same fact. To the best of our knowledge, this issue has not received semantically sound treatment, suitable for expert system logic programming. In existing systems, like MYCIN, evidential independence is handled in a pretty ad hoc way.

It is often argued that associating a single certainty factor with each fact in the database is not enough for many applications. For instance, in MYCIN each fact has a measure of belief and a measure of disbelief. This technique is often used to cope with contradictory information commonly arising in medical, military, and other domains. A promising approach utilizing this idea is based on, so called, belief/disbelief pairs. Recently several calculi for computing combined evidence in such logics have been described (Baldwin and Monk (1987); Baldwin (1987)). However, no semantics was proposed for such logics, and their implementations (Baldwin, Martin and Pilsworth (1987)) still share most of the drawbacks of the rule-based languages mentioned earlier. This lack of declarativeness prevents any systematic study of query optimization in such systems. A semantic approach to the problem is described in our recent work (Kifer and Li (1988)), and is sketched in Section 4.

Several other approaches also use belief/disbelief pairs to handle uncertainty (e.g., Driankov (1987); Ginsberg (1984); Hajek and Valdes (1987); Shafer (1976)). None of these deals with inconsistency or frames though, and some seem to be non-logic-programmable.

Recently, a number of works has been published on the so called probabilistic logics (Fagin, Halpern and Megiddo (1988); Nilsson (1986); Ruspini (1987); Tzvieli (1988)). Although these logics have a well defined semantics, we do not see how, for instance, (Fagin, Halpern and Megiddo (1988); Nilsson (1986); Ruspini (1987)) can be made into a logic programming system. Regarding PL (Tzvieli (1988)), the published results are very preliminary, but it appears that this logic can be easily accommodated within our framework. Besides, none of the aforesaid logics is able to handle inconsistency. We will not discuss or compare our work to a large number of proposals based on semantic and belief networks (e.g., Pearl (1986)) which we consider non-logic-programmable, as they deal with simple propositions rather than quantified rules.

3.2 Logics for Frames

The recent trend towards object-oriented languages in databases is very close in the spirit and contents to the thrust towards frame-based languages in AI. Marriage of frames with deduction has been a hit in AI for quite some time (e.g., Fikes and Kehler (1985)), but no semantically solid theory has been ever proposed. Frames are essentially scaled-down versions of complex objects (plus inheritance), and pointers used to refer to other frames are (logically) nothing else but object identities. Although Hayes has shown that certain features attributed to frames can be translated into predicate calculus (Hayes (1979)), this translation does not provide a direct semantics for frames and does not capture many aspects naturally enough. To our knowledge, Kifer and Wu (1989), Kifer and Lausen (1989) is the first comprehensive approach which directly marries frames and deduction with the blessing of a respectable logical theory.

This approach to frames is based on O-logic first proposed by Maier (1986) which, unfortunately, had numerous semantic problems. However, Maier's basic insight into the problem proved to be very fruitful, which allowed us to extend his work to a full-fledged logic with a sound and complete resolution-based proof procedure. Prior (and in parallel) to these works, there was a number of attempts (Abiteboul and Beeri (1987); Abiteboul and Grumbach (1987); Abiteboul and Kanellakis (1989); Bancilhon and Khoshafian (1986); Beeri et al. (1987); Beeri (1988); Beeri, Nasr and Tsur (1988); Chen and Warren (1989); Kuper and Vardi (1984); Kuper (1987); Roth, Korth and Silberschatz (1985); Rubinski (1987)) to provide logical foundations to various aspects of frame-based languages, which set up the stage for the recent developments. A more complete discussion of these works can be found in Kifer and Wu (1989).

4 Overview of the Logic for Reasoning With Uncertainties

In this section we sketch the semantics of logic programs with uncertainty, which is a modification of the one given in Kifer and Li (1988). We assume the knowledge of logic programming at the level of the first few chapters of Lloyd (1987) and deductive databases at the level of Ullman (1988).

Imprecise information is modeled by means of, so called, *certainty factors*, which are assumed to be ranging over a totally ordered interval, Λ, e.g. $[0,1]$, or, say, a discrete interval such as [*no-info, very-low-chance, low-chance, probably, likely, very-likely, certainly*]. Besides being ordered, we require Λ to have a symmetric inverse operator, denoted with the overbar (symmetric means that if $b = \bar{a}$ then $\bar{b} = a$). For instance, if $\Lambda = [0,1]$ then $\bar{\alpha} = 1 - \alpha$ and if $\Lambda = [\textit{no-info}, \ldots, \textit{certainly}]$ then the inverse would be a symmetric flip around the middle element '*probably*' (e.g. $\overline{\textit{no-info}} = \textit{certainly}, \overline{\textit{very-low-chance}} = \textit{very-likely}$). We denote the smallest element of Λ by $\bot$ and the largest by $\top$. Each fact,

p, has a *measure of belief*, MB, and a *measure of disbelief*, MD, both drawn from the same interval Λ. The latter is the measure of belief in $\neg p$. Thus, each fact, p, is assigned a *belief pair* $< MB_p, MD_p >$, which can be interpreted as saying that the strength of belief in p is somewhere between MB_p and $\overline{MD_p}$. The 'distance' between MB_p and $\overline{MD_p}$ is the *knowledge gap* about p. Literal $\neg p$ is then assigned the belief pair $< MD_p, MB_p >$. In other words, belief pairs are elements of $\Lambda \times \Lambda$, which hereafter will be denoted by Λ^2. This suggests a *negation* operator $\neg : \Lambda^2 \to \Lambda^2$ s.t. $\neg < \alpha, \beta > = < \beta, \alpha >$, which can be extended to literals by defining $\neg p : \gamma$ as $p : \neg\gamma$.

Literals in our logic are of the form $p : \alpha$, $\neg p : \alpha$, $p : f(\alpha_1, \ldots, \alpha_n)$, or $\neg f(\alpha_1, \ldots, \alpha_n)$, where p is a usual first-order atomic formula, f is a function $\Lambda^n \to \Lambda$, and $\alpha, \alpha_1, \ldots, \alpha_n$ are either variables over or elements of Λ^2. Rules are the statements of the form

$$p(\vec{x}) : f(\alpha, \beta, \ldots, \gamma) \leftarrow a(\vec{y}) : \alpha, b(\vec{z}) : \beta, \ldots, c(\vec{u}) : \gamma,$$

where $p(\vec{x})$, $a(\vec{y})$, $b(\vec{z})$, $c(\vec{u})$ are positive or negative (usual) first-order literals, $\alpha, \beta, \ldots, \gamma$ are either variables over or elements of Λ^2, and f is a certainty function *associated* with this rule. Certainty functions compute belief pairs for the rule head, given certainty information for the literals in the rule body. Note that negative literals may appear in rule bodies as well as in their heads. An *expert system* consists of a set of rules, **P** (the intensional component), and of data, **D** (the extensional component).

Belief pairs are organized in a lattice: $< \alpha, \beta > \preceq < \gamma, \delta >$ if $\alpha \leq_\Lambda \gamma$ and $\beta \leq_\Lambda \delta$, where $\leq_\Lambda$ is the total ordering on Λ. The idea here is that a $\preceq$-bigger belief pair means that stronger positive and negative evidences are available for the corresponding fact. It is easy to verify that $< \bot , \bot >$ and $< \top , \top >$ are the smallest and the largest elements in Λ^2, respectively.

If we view a literal $p :< \alpha, \beta >$ as a statement that the actual belief in p is somewhere between α and $\bar{\beta}$, then $< \alpha, \beta > \preceq < \gamma, \delta >$ can also be interpreted as saying that $p :< \gamma, \delta >$ represents less uncertainty regarding p than $p :< \alpha, \beta >$, since the interval $[\gamma, \bar{\delta}]$ representing the knowledge gap in the belief pair $< \gamma, \delta >$ is a subinterval of $[\alpha, \bar{\beta}]$, which represents the knowledge gap in $< \alpha, \beta >$. Under this latter interpretation, a statement $p :< \alpha, \beta >$ such that $\bar{\beta} \leq_\Lambda \alpha$ is considered 'overdefined', since there is no certainty factor which can possibly be the actual belief in p. We call such belief pairs *inconsistent*, and the corresponding literals are called *inconsistent literals* (or beliefs).

The Herbrand base of an expert system, $\mathbf{E} = \mathbf{P} \cup \mathbf{D}$ is a collection of all positive ground facts $p(\vec{a}) : \gamma$, where γ is a belief pair, p is a predicate symbol from **P**, and $\vec{a}$ is a vector of values from the domain $D_\mathbf{E}$ (the set of all ground terms). Interpretations are downward closed subsets of the Herbrand base. A set I is *downward closed* iff

1. $p : \alpha \in I$ and $\beta \preceq \alpha$ imply $p : \beta \in I$, and

2. $q :< \bot , \bot > \in I$ for every ground atom q.

As suggested by the form of the rules, certainty functions associated with the rules represent causal links between rules' premises and consequents. We impose certain natural restrictions on these functions, such as *monotonicity* (i.e., $f(x_1, \ldots, x_n) \preceq f(y_1, \ldots, y_n)$, if $x_i \preceq y_i$ for $i = 1, \ldots, n$; informally this means that higher certainty of premises should yield higher confidence in the consequent) and *continuity* w.r.t. $\preceq$ in each of the arguments.

In expert systems, evidences obtained from different sources all supporting the same fact are combined to determine strength of the overall support for the fact (or for its negation). In different problem domains and, perhaps, for different types of facts, combination methods may be different. Furthermore, different researchers may be fond of different theories of evidential reasoning. In order to be independent from any such theory, we postulate that associated with each predicate symbol, p, there is a unique *combination function*, F_p, used to calculate strength of combined evidences for p. Combination functions accept a single argument which is a multiset of belief pairs. This implies that the combined strength of evidences for a fact is independent from the order in which these evidences are obtained. We impose a number of natural restrictions on combination functions listed below:

1. *Monotonicity*: $S \trianglelefteq S'$, where S, S' are multisets of elements of Λ^2, implies $F(S) \trianglelefteq F(S')$. The order on multisets is defined as follows: $S \trianglelefteq S'$ if there is a 1-1 mapping $\tau : S \rightarrow S'$ s.t. for each $x \in S$, $x \trianglelefteq \tau(x)$. This condition ensures that stronger evidences yield stronger overall support.

2. *Associativity*: $F(S \cup S') = F(S \cup F(S'))$. That is, the order in which evidences are combined is immaterial, and to obtain the overall strength of support for a fact there is no need to wait until all evidences for that fact are collected.

3. *Correctness*: $F(S \cup \{< \bot\ , \bot >\}) = F(S)$ and $F(\{\alpha\}) = \alpha$. This means that the 'no information' evidence does not change the overall belief in anything, and that support provided by a single evidence of strength α is exactly α.

4. *Continuity*: F is continuous in its argument w.r.t. the order on multisets.

5. *Enhancement*: $\alpha \trianglelefteq F(S)$ for each $\alpha \in S$. This property follows from (1) and (3); it postulates that every new evidence is potentially useful, since it may increase the overall belief in the respective fact.

Certainty (resp. combination) functions map tuples (resp. multisets) of belief pairs into the lattice of all belief pairs Λ^2. A ground positive fact, $p : \gamma$, is true in an interpretation, I, iff $p : \gamma \in I$. A negative fact, $\neg p : \gamma$, is true in I iff $p : \neg\gamma$ is true in I (recall that $\neg < \alpha, \beta > = < \beta, \alpha >$). Satisfaction of rules by I is defined as follows. A ground rule $p(\vec{a}) : f(\alpha_1, \ldots, \alpha_k) \leftarrow q_1(\vec{e}_1) : \alpha_1, \ldots, q_k(\vec{e}_k) : \alpha_k$ is true in I iff whenever all the $q_i(\vec{e}_i) : \alpha_i$'s are true in I, the head of the rule, $p(\vec{a}) : f(\alpha_1, \ldots, \alpha_k)$, is also true in I. A (nonground) rule is true in I iff all its ground instances are true. In this framework, a ground rule with a true body can be viewed as an evidence supporting the fact in its head.

A program, $\mathbf{P}$, is true if all its rules are true *and*, in addition, the following *combination requirement* is satisfied:

For every set of *independent* (explained later) ground instances of the rules of $\mathbf{P}$ with the same head $p(\vec{a})$,

$$\begin{array}{lcl} p(\vec{a}) : f_1(\alpha_{11}, \ldots, \alpha_{k_1 1}) & \leftarrow & q_{11}(\vec{e}_{11}) : \alpha_{11}, \ldots, q_{k_1 1}(\vec{e}_{k_m m}) : \alpha_{k_1 1} \\ & \vdots & \\ p(\vec{a}) : f_m(\alpha_{1m}, \ldots, \alpha_{k_m m}) & \leftarrow & q_{1m}(\vec{e}_{1m}) : \alpha_{1m}, \ldots, q_{k_m m}(\vec{e}_{k_m m}) : \alpha_{k_m m} \end{array}$$

such that the premises of each individual rule are true in I, the literal $p(\vec{a}) : F_p(\{f_1(\alpha_{11}, \ldots, \alpha_{k_1 1}), \ldots, f_m(\alpha_{1m}, \ldots, \alpha_{k_m m})\})$ must be true in I.

The last definition expresses the fact that independently obtained evidences for the same fact are combined to obtain a possibly stronger evidence. An unusual consequence of this is that although each individual rule of a program might be true, the program itself may not be satisfied by the interpretation, because some of the facts may not be known with sufficient certainty to satisfy the combination requirement (since one of the requirements to F is that for all $\alpha \in S$, $\alpha \trianglelefteq F(S)$).

Another important point is that the combination requirement stated above implicitly depends on the assumption about what independent evidences are. Our semantics does not rely on the specifics of any of the variety of such assumptions, which makes it very general. The only requirement is that, to be combinable, supporting evidences should be independent form each other. Evidential independence may be defined differently for different predicates, which makes our framework even more flexible. In general terms, independence is a meta predicate defined on sets of ground instances of the rules in **P**. Some of the possible candidates are listed below.

Let $\rho_1 \equiv p : \alpha \leftarrow q_1 : \beta_1, \ldots, q_n : \beta_n$ and $\rho_2 \equiv p : \gamma \leftarrow r_1 : \delta_1, \ldots, r_m : \delta_m$ be a pair of ground rules. Then ρ_1 and ρ_2 *provide independent evidences* for the fact p if

Independence-1:
the sets $\{q_1, \ldots, q_n\}$ and $\{r_1, \ldots, r_m\}$ considered as sets of ground literals are different;
Independence-2:
the sets $\{q_1, \ldots, q_n\}$ and $\{r_1, \ldots, r_m\}$ are incomparable w.r.t. $\subseteq$;
Independence-3:
the sets $\{q_1, \ldots, q_n\}$ and $\{r_1, \ldots, r_m\}$ are disjoint.

Clearly, Independence-2 and 3 imply Independence-1. The latter appears to be the minimal requirement that must be satisfied by independent rules. However, it is too weak for most purposes. Its importance is in providing a basis for studying other, practically more interesting, independence requirements. Independence-2 and 3 are given as simple alternatives to the first notion. Developing additional syntactic notions of independence is an important research issue.

Rule independence is crucial for the semantics to make sense. Indeed, pulling together the support provided by dependent rules may yield bizarre results. For instance, in the degenerated case, one could repeat the same rule supporting, say, p, with a negligible positive evidence $\gamma =< 0, 0.0001 >$ many times over, raising the overall support for p to $F_p(\gamma, \gamma, \ldots)$. If F_p were the MYCIN function for combining beliefs (i.e. $F_p(\alpha, \beta) = \alpha + \beta - \alpha \times \beta$, where $+$ and $\times$ are applied to belief pairs component-wise), then it can be shown that the certainty of p necessarily would have to be $< 0, 1 >$, even though we have started with only a small positive evidence (which, in fact, can be arbitrarily small). This, of course, is unnatural and shows that combining dependent evidences is likely to lead to nonsensical results.

We say that I is a *model* of **E**=**P**$\cup$**D**, where **P** is a set of rules and **D** is a set of facts of the expert system **E**, iff **P** and each fact in **D** is true in I. We also write $\mathbf{E} \models p(\vec{q}) : \alpha$ if $p(\vec{q}) : \alpha$ is true in every model of **E**.

Notice that an interpretation containing inconsistent literals (e.g. $p :< \bot , \bot >$) may still be a model of an expert system. However, in our logic, inconsistent facts cannot cause much damage, since they can only affect the facts which are directly dependent on them. Thus, it is possible in our semantics to detect inconsistency and still proceed with other inferences without getting into deep troubles. This is particularly useful in analyzing business, medical, or intelligence information.

This type of inconsistency has been studied in Blair and Subrahmanian (1989), Kifer and Lozinskii (1989), and is related to inconsistency in multivalued logics (Belnap (1975); Belnap (1976); Fitting (1989); Ginsberg (1987)). More details on this approach can be found in Blair and Subrahmanian (1989), Kifer and Lozinskii (1989b).

In the logic outlined above, negation (either in the form of disbelief in positive literals, or in the form of belief in negated literals) is monotonic, meaning that any set of rules (even in the presence of negation) has a unique minimal model. This is unlike the situation in the standard logic programming, where rules with negated body literals may have multiple minimal models. Although, at the first sight, this may look like an advantage, it turns out that monotonicity of negation is not what we are looking for in expert systems. Expert systems are inherently non-monotonic, and the process of 'jumping' to logically unwarranted conclusions is very important. For similar reasons, nonmonotonic negation has been also adopted in most logic programming and deductive database systems (Beeri et al. (1987); Lloyd (1987); Przymusinski (1988)). Consider the following example:

Example: Suppose the database contains a single fact $bird(tweety) : < .7, .1 >$ and the following rule:

$$flies(X) : f(\eta, \mu) \leftarrow bird(X) : \eta, \neg abnormal(X) : \mu,$$

where $f(< \alpha, \beta >, < \gamma, \delta >) = < \min(\alpha, \gamma), \min(\beta, \delta) >$. Since nothing is known about *abnormal*, it means that we can only derive $abnormal(tweety) : < 0, 0 >$ and $\neg abnormal(tweety) : < 0, 0 >$ (no information). Applying the rule, we infer $flies(tweety) : < 0, 0 >$.

In this example, $flies(tweety) : < 0, 0 >$ is hardly an answer that we would expect from a common sense reasoner. Instead, such a reasoner will most likely conclude that, since most birds fly and nothing is said about Tweety's inability to fly, *abnormal*(*tweety*) can be assumed false, i.e. $abnormal(tweety) : < 0, 1 >$ (or, equivalently, $\neg abnormal(tweety) : < 1, 0 >$) should hold. Using this in the above rule yields $flies(tweety) : < .7, 0 >$, i.e., "Tweety almost certainly flies".

Note that the above conclusion is not logically warranted but, instead, is a result of jumping to a negative conclusion regarding Tweety's abnormality. Likewise, if we were told that $abnormal(tweety) : < .4, .3 >$ (or $\neg abnormal(tweety) : < .3, .4 >$) holds, i.e., Tweety *may* be abnormal, then we may want to jump to a negative conclusion by closing the knowledge gap about *abnormal*(*tweety*) and deriving (nonmonotonically) that $abnormal(tweety) : < .4, .6 >$ holds. Then the above rule will yield $flies(tweety) : < .6, .1 >$. Note that if we were using the usual logical implication instead of the nonmonotonic jump, we would have gotten $flies(tweety) : < .3, .1 >$. This type of reasoning was formalized in Kifer and Li (1988), generalizing the perfect model semantics of Przymusinski (1988) to the case of reasoning with uncertainties. Details can be found in Kifer and Li (1988).

It should be remarked that, in fact, the lattice Λ^2 used above is only needed to enable us to treat negation nonmonotonically. The rest of the theory goes through for arbitrary

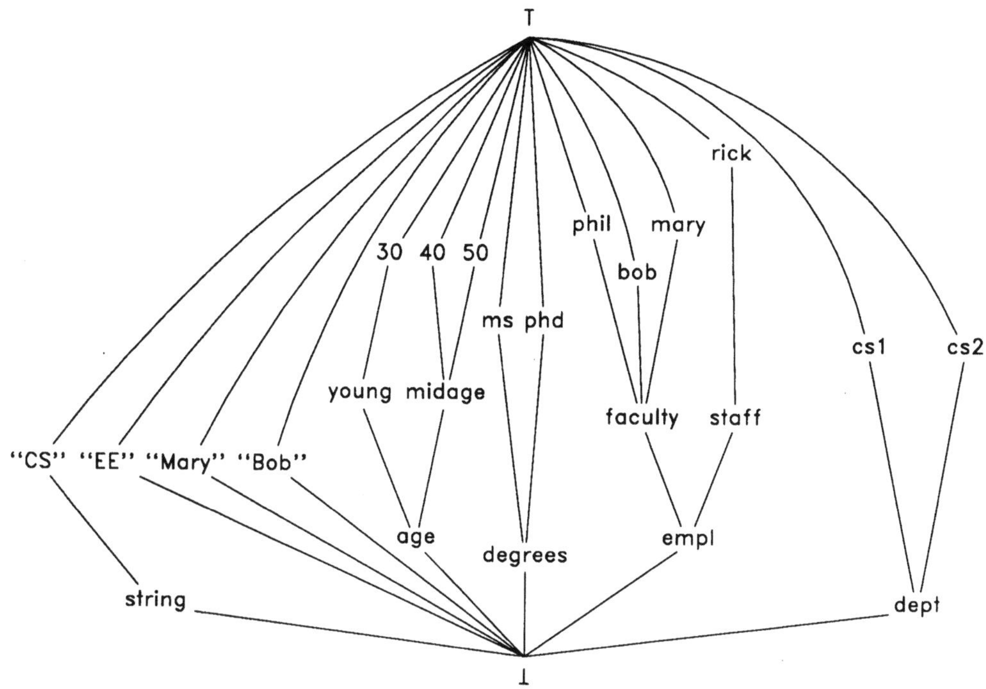

Figure 1: Part of the IS-A Hierarchy

lattices. The results about the negation can be further generalized from Λ^2 to, so called, interlaced bilattices with conflation (Fitting (1989)), but we will not dwell on this issue here.

In Kifer and Li (1988) a bottom-up proof procedure is described, which realizes the semantics outlined above. It generalizes the well-known semi-naive query evaluation algorithm (Balbin and Ramamohanarao (1987); Guntzer and Bayer (1987)) to handle inference in the presence of uncertainty. This can be further extended to include query optimization techniques, such as Magic Sets (Beeri and Ramakrishnan (1987)), to achieve an efficient implementation.

5 Overview of the Frame Logic

In this section we outline the, so called, F-logic developed in Kifer and Wu (1989), Kifer and Lausen (1989). This logic was designed to provide formal foundations for object-oriented and frame-based languages the same way as the standard predicate calculus provides foundations for logic programming and deductive databases.

5.1 Motivation

As mentioned earlier, the idea here is to try to capture in a direct and logically correct way the paradigm of knowledge representation by means of frame-based languages. Consider a scenario depicted in Fig. 1 and 2.

Facts:

$$faculty : bob[name \rightarrow "Bob", age \rightarrow 40,$$
$$works \rightarrow dept : cs_1[dname \rightarrow string : "CS", mngr \rightarrow empl : phil]]$$
$$faculty : mary[name \rightarrow "Mary", age \rightarrow 30, degree \rightarrow ms, friends \rightarrow \{bill, bob\}$$
$$works \rightarrow dept : cs_2[dname \rightarrow "CS"]]$$

General Class Info:

$$empl : faculty[degree \rightarrow phd, supervisor \rightarrow faculty]$$

Rule:

$$empl : E[supervisor \rightarrow M] \Leftarrow empl : E[works \rightarrow dept : D[mngr \rightarrow empl : M]]$$

Query:

$$faculty : X[supervisor \rightarrow Y, age \rightarrow midage : Z, degree \rightarrow V,$$
$$works \rightarrow D[dname \rightarrow "CS"]]?$$

Figure 2: Facts about Employees, Departments, etc.

Fig. 1 shows part of the IS-A hierarchy. All classes and individual objects as organized in an upper semilattice. Fig. 1 asserts that *faculty* and *staff* are subclasses of *empl* ; *bob*, *phil* and *mary* are faculty; "CS" and "Bob" are *strings*, age 30 is considered *young*, while ages 40 and 50 are classified as *midage*. Fig. 1 may look upside-down to those who are used to see superclasses higher in the hierarchy than their subclasses. This is because, in our framework, it is more natural to compare classes w.r.t. the amount of information they carry, rather than w.r.t. the size of their extensions. For instance, a statement *student : john* (John is a student) is considered more informative than *person : john* (John is a person), since *student*, being a subclass of *person*, gives a more precise information regarding *john*. In other words, we order classes and objects w.r.t. their 'knowledge content' (Ginsberg (1987)).

Fig. 2 presents facts about employees, departments, etc. The first clause says that the object *bob* is a faculty whose name is "Bob" (notice: *bob* is an id of the object, while "Bob" is a string representing *bob*'s name). In addition, this clause states that *bob* works in the department identified as cs_1 whose name is denoted by the string "*CS*" and is managed by the employee identified as *phil*. The second clause presents similar information about the frame *mary*. A point to note here is that the attribute *friends* in the second clause is *set-valued*, while the other attributes mentioned in the first two clauses are *functional*.

The third clause provides general information about the class *faculty*: a faculty is normally a Ph.D. whose supervisor is also a *faculty*. In addition, we have a rule stating that employee's supervisor should be the employee's department head. The query then asks for all middle aged faculty members who work in "CS" departments. It also requests the age and the supervisor of each such faculty.

The expected answer to this query is $bob[supervisor \rightarrow phil, degree \rightarrow phd, age \rightarrow 30, dept \rightarrow cs_i]$. Here supervisor and age are inferred directly from clause (1) and rule (4), while the degree is *inherited* from the superclass of *faculty* to which *bob* belongs. *Mary* is not included in the answer, since her age is 30, which is not *midage* according to the class lattice of Fig. 1.

However, if we remove the restriction *midage* : Z in the query, then $mary[supervisor \rightarrow faculty, age \rightarrow 30, degree \rightarrow \top, dept \rightarrow cs_2]$ will be also an answer. Since no supervisor is explicitly stated in the description of the object *mary*, her supervisor is inherited from class *faculty*. In other words, the best we can tell regarding mary's manager is that he is another faculty and not, say, a student. This is better than knowing that the manager is an *employee* or just a *person*, but not as good as knowing a specific person, as in the case of *bob*. Regarding the degree, we have contradictory information: Mary's frame shows that she has only an M.S. degree, but by virtue of being a faculty she should be a Ph.D. We conclude that our information about *mary*'s degree is contradictory, which is manifested by the value $\top$, where $\top$ is the least upper bound (abbr. lub) of *ms* and *phd* (see Fig. 1). Note that in this particular case lub(*ms,phd*) happens to be the maximal semilattice element, but this need not always be the case (e.g., we could postulate that $ms \leq phd$ in which case $\text{lub}(ms, phd) = phd$, i.e., the inherited value would suppress the one appearing in Mary's frame).

5.2 F-logic Syntax

Formally, the alphabet of F-logic consists of

1. a set O of *basic* objects and classes (of objects),

2. a set of *object/class constructors* **F**,

3. an infinite set of *object variables*, **V**, and

4. logical connectives and quantifiers $\vee, \wedge, \forall, \exists, \neg$, etc.

We assume that O, **F**, and **V** are disjoint.

Informally, 'objects' in F-logic are either complex objects in the usual sense, or classes of objects. Unlike many other proposals (especially in the database field) which treat classes and instances as inherently different entities, we do not emphasize the distinction. In F-logic, classes are similar to those in frame-based languages in AI because a class is viewed as an instance (rather than a subset) of a superclass. This feature enables F-logic to have a built-in inheritance mechanism as opposed to the algorithmically defined inheritance in most of the other approaches. Logically, object constructors are function symbols over O; they are used to construct new objects and classes.

Central in F-logic is the notion of an *F-term*. These play the role of atomic formulas in F-logic. For convenience, we first introduce id-terms, which are similar to terms in the classic predicate calculus. An *id-term* is a term composed of object constructors, base objects/classes from O and object variables in a usual way. The set of all ground (variable-free) id-terms, denoted by O^*, plays the role of Herbrand universe of F-logic. Conceptually id-terms should be perceived as objects themselves or as object abstractions which are commonly referred to as *object identity* (id) (Khoshafian and Copeland (1986)).

We will use names consisting entirely of lower-case letters to denote ground terms, and the names starting with capital letters to denote terms which may be nonground. An

F-term (Kifer and Lausen (1989)) is either a simple F-term of the form $P : Q$, where P and Q are id-terms, or a complex term of the form

$$Q : P[Lab_1 \rightarrow T_1, \ldots, Lab_m \rightarrow T_m, Lab_1{}' \rightarrow \{S_{11}, \ldots, S_{1k_1}\}, \ldots, Lab_l{}' \rightarrow \{S_{l1}, \ldots, S_{lk_l}\}], \quad (1)$$

where $m \geq 0$, $k \geq 0$, Lab_i, $Lab_j{}'$, P, Q are id-terms, and the T_i, S_j are F-terms.

In the above F-term, Lab_i, $Lab_j{}'$ are called *labels* or *attributes*; they play the role of attributes in databases, or frame slots in frame-based languages. Some or all of the labels may be omitted. In the latter case we will simply write $Q : P$. The terms Lab_i appear in the context which makes them *functional* labels, while $Lab_j{}'$ are set-valued labels, which is designated by the set constructor $\{\ldots\}$. The id-term P represents the object-identity of (1), while Q represents the class of this F-term.

Notice that in (1), P, Q, etc. may have variables, so this F-term represents not a single frame but a "template" for similar frames (compare this to nonground facts, e.g. $P(X, f(Y, a), c)$, in predicate calculus).

Elements of O^* are organized in an upper semilattice by means of the ordering $\leq_O$. We do not discuss here ways of specifying such an order, but only mention that the least upper bound, lub, must be decidable. The top element in O^* is denoted by $\top$, and we also assume the existence of the smallest element $\bot \in O^*$. The largest element, $\top$, should be viewed as a "meaningless" object, or as a class with no instances, while $\bot$ is the "undefined" object or the largest class.

The ordering on O^* is similar to the conceptual scheme of a database: it represents the transitive closure of the subclass-of and the instance-of relationships among classes, i.e. $p \leq_O q$ (e.g. $person \leq_O stud$ or $stud \leq_O john$) means that q is a (possibly indirect) subclass or an instance of p. In fact, we do not distinguish between objects and classes: any object, d, is treated as a class whose extension contains d and all objects/classes found above d in the lattice. Furthermore, any element $p \in O^*$ may appear in F-terms in the "object position", $q : p$, as well as in the "class position", $p : r$, which means that F-logic has a higher-order syntax. Accordingly, we will use the terms 'object' and 'class' interchangeably. A sample semilattice structure on O^* is depicted in Fig. 1. As follows from the syntactic form of F-terms, any id-term can also play a role of an attribute. In particular, variables may range over attributes. This is another higher-order aspect of F-logic, which allows certain level of metaprogramming (Kifer and Lausen (1989)).

Formulas are constructed out of F-terms in a way resembling predicate calculus: Every F-term is also an atomic *formula*. More complex formulae are constructed from simpler ones in the usual way, by means of logical connectives $\wedge$, $\vee$, $\neg$ and quantifiers $\forall$ and $\exists$.

5.3 Semantics of F-logic

To simplify the matters, we only consider Herbrand interpretations, which is usually enough for the needs of logic programming. More details can be found in Kifer and Lausen (1989).

Given a language **L** of F-logic, a Herbrand interpretation I is a tuple $< O^*, \leq_I, j_\#, j_* >$. Here O^* is the universe of I, i.e. the set of all ground id-terms in **L**, and $\leq_I$ is an upper semilattice order on O^* compatible with $\leq_O$ (upper semilattice is a partial order in which every pair of elements has a unique least upper bound). The mapping $j_\# : O^* \rightarrow$

$Mon(O^*, O^*)$ maps O^* to monotonic mappings on O^*; it interprets an object, $s \in O^*$, in its role as a functional attribute, by a mapping from objects to objects. For instance, in *bob* [*name* → *"Bob"*], *name* would be interpreted by a mapping that maps objects to strings which represent objects' names. Finally, $j_* : O^* \rightarrow Mon(O^*, 2^{O^*})$ interprets objects in their role as set-valued attributes by monotonic mappings from objects to sets of objects (the order on sets is the usual set inclusion). For instance, in $mary[friends \rightarrow \{bob, sally\}]$, friends plays the role of a set-valued label which maps each object (a person) to a set of other objects representing person's friends.

A variable assignment, ν, is a mapping from object variables, $\mathbf{V}$, to U. We extend it to id-terms in the usual way: $\nu(t) = t$, if $t \in O^*$ and $\nu(f(\ldots, T, \ldots)) = f(\ldots, \nu(T), \ldots)$.

Let I be an interpretation and ν a variable assignment. Intuitively, I satisfies an F-term $T = P : Q[\ldots]$ w.r.t. ν, denoted $I \models_\nu T$, iff in I the object $\nu(Q)$ is in the class $\nu(P)$ and has (at least) the properties specified in $\nu(T)$. For instance, $I \models_\nu$ $student : john[status \rightarrow freshman]$ iff in I *john* is a student (i.e. $student \leq_I john$) and he has status of a freshman (i.e. $freshman \leq_I j_\#\ (status)(john)$). Formally, given an F-term

$$T = P : Q[\ldots,\ Lab_i \rightarrow P_i : T_i[\ldots]\,, \ldots, Lab_j{}' \rightarrow \{\ldots,\ V_l : S_l[\ldots]\,, \ldots\}], \qquad (2)$$

we write $I \models_\nu T$ if the following three conditions are met:

1. $\nu(P) \leq_I \nu(Q)$;

2. for each single-valued label (e.g. Lab_i), $\nu(T_i) \leq_I j_\#(\nu(Lab_i))(\nu(Q))$ and $I \models_\nu P_i : T_i[\ldots]$;

3. for each set-valued label (e.g. $Lab_l{}'$, $\nu(S_l) \in j_*(\nu(Lab_l{}'))(\nu(Q))$ and $I \models_\nu V_l : S_l[\ldots]$.

Meaning of the formulae $\phi \vee \psi$, $\phi \wedge \psi$, and $\neg\phi$ is defined in the standard way. The meaning of quantifiers is also standard: $I \models_\nu \psi$, where $\psi = (\forall V)\phi$ (resp. $\psi = (\exists V)\phi$) iff for every (resp. some) variable assignment μ which agrees with ν everywhere except, possibly, on $V, I \models_\nu \psi$.

Clearly, for a closed formula, ψ, its meaning is independent from variable assignments, and we can simply write $I \models \psi$, if ψ is closed. An interpretation I is a *model* of ψ if $I \models_\nu \psi$.

5.4 Databases and Queries

A *database* is a set of formulas. If $\mathbf{S}$ is a set of formulas and ϕ a formula, we write $\mathbf{S} \models \phi$ (ϕ is logically *implied* or *entailed* by $\mathbf{S}$) if ϕ is true in every model of $\mathbf{S}$.

A *query* is a statement of the form $Q?$, where Q is an F-term. The *answer* to $Q?$ w.r.t. a database $\mathbf{D}$ is the smallest set closed under logical entailment containing all instances of Q logically entailed ($\models$) by $\mathbf{D}$.

5.5 Proof Theory

F-logic has a sound and complete proof procedure based on the resolution principle. Apart from the usual resolution and factorization, it needs additional derivation rules, called *reduction* and *elimination*, that are also used in other related logics (Kifer and Lozinskii

(1989b); Kifer and Wu (1989)). To give a flavor of these new inference rules, let us consider a pair of objects *john*[*status* $\rightarrow$ *student*] and *john*[*status* $\rightarrow$ *empl*]. If lub(*empl*, *student*) = *assistant* then *john*[*status* $\rightarrow$ *assistant*] logically follows from the above two statements. Indeed, according to our semantics, $j_{\#}(status)$ is a monotonic function. Thus, in order to make the first two statements about *john* true, it has to map *john* to an object which is above *student* and *empl*. Since lub(*empl*, *student*) = *assistant*, $j_{\#}(status)(john)$ has to be above *assistant* in the semilattice ordering, hence *john*[*status* $\rightarrow$ *assistant*] is logically entailed. The elimination rule is used to delete unsatisfiable literals, such as $\neg a[lab \rightarrow \perp]$, from clauses.

Most of the concepts from logic programming are also applicable to F-logic and can be ported with appropriate adjustments. Details of the proof theory will be given in the full version of Kifer and Lausen (1989)[2].

5.6 Discussion

One of the most interesting features of F-logic is the inheritance mechanism built into its semantics. Consider again the example of Fig. 2. It is easy to see that for every *faculty*, its supervisor is also a faculty, namely, $X[supervisor \rightarrow faculty] \Leftarrow faculty : X$. Since the *supervisor* attribute may not be present in every F-term for a faculty, this phenomenon can be rightfully attributed to the fact that each individual faculty inherits this attribute from its superclass.

To see how the value of the *supervisor* attribute is inherited, consider some faculty, *john*, (i.e. $faculty \leq_O john$). Since each label is a monotonic function, $j_{\#}(supervisor)$ $(faculty) \leq_I j_{\#}(supervisor)(john)$. However, the third clause in Fig. 2 states that $faculty$ $= j_{\#}(supervisor)(faculty)$, hence $faculty \leq_I j_{\#}(supervisor)(john)$, which means that *john* [*supervisor* $\rightarrow$ *faculty*] is true.

There has been a number of works on the semantics of inheritance. Cardelli (1984) considered inheritance in the framework of functional programming. He describes a type inference procedure which is sound w.r.t. the denotational semantics of his system. We consider inheritance in a different, logical, framework and provide a sound and *complete* proof procedure.

Ait-Kaci and Nasr (1986) incorporate inheritance into logic programming by introducing a new unification algorithm. Although intuitively appealing, their algorithm was not given any semantically sound justification. In addition, Maier (1986) has pointed out that their algorithm may be correct for type inferencing, but not for querying databases. Later, Smolka and Ait-Kaci (1987) presented a semantics for the aforementioned unification algorithm using the equational logic. However, it is not clear how to extend this semantics to a logic in which the corresponding resolution procedure (based on their unification) would be sound and complete. Besides, this still does not make LOGIN suitable for database querying.

There is also sample literature on, so called, *nonmonotonic* inheritance, e.g., Etherington and Reiter (1983), Touretzky (1986), Touretzky, Horty and Thomason (1987), which is different from the monotonic inheritance of F-logic. For instance, if in the above example it were known that *john*[*supervisor* $\rightarrow$ *staff*] is true, then in F-logic we could derive *john*[*supervisor* $\rightarrow \top$], since lub(*staff*, *faculty*) $= \top$ (i.e., both the inherited and the

[2] A closely related, but much simpler theory has been described in Kifer and Wu (1989).

explicit values are taken into account). In contrast, nonmonotonic inheritance sanctions only $john[supervisor \rightarrow staff]$, completely overriding the value *faculty* that *john* inherits from its superclass. Nonmonotonic inheritance can also be incorporated into F-logic, but we will not discuss this issue here.

Besides inheritance, F-logic can naturally support other aspects of frame based languages, such as procedural attachments (also known as *methods* in the object-oriented jargon). Consider the following example:

$$X[graduation\_date(I) \rightarrow Y] \Leftarrow university : I[alumni \rightarrow \{alumnus\_record : G[stud \rightarrow person : X, date \rightarrow year : Y]\}]$$

What we have defined here is the 'graduation_date' procedure: For each person, it is a function from *universities* to *years*. Thus, one can ask queries such as

$$X[graduation\_date(I) \rightarrow 1988]?$$

(retrieve all people graduated from anywhere in 1988) or

$$bob[graduation\_date(X) \rightarrow 1984]?$$

(which university did Bob graduate from in 1984?). We refer the reader to Kifer and Lausen (1989) for more examples on the uses of F-logic.

6 Combining Uncertainty and Frames

Given an F-term, $a : b\,[lab \rightarrow c, \ldots, set \rightarrow \{d, e\}]$, we can associate certainty information with the term itself or with its sub terms. In the first case we get[3] $a : b[lab \rightarrow c, \ldots, set \rightarrow \{d, e\}]@\alpha$, while in the second we obtain $a : b\,[lab \rightarrow c@\alpha, \ldots, set \rightarrow \{d@\beta, e@\gamma\}]$, where α, β, γ, etc. are either elements of or variables over Λ^2.

Among these two possibilities, the second one seems more promising, and the F-terms with certainty factors attached in this way will be called *fuzzy* F-terms. In the rest of this section we will briefly sketch semantics of the resulting language.

The only change is in the semantics of functional and set-valued attributes. Previously, functional attributes were interpreted by functions that map objects to other objects; the latter objects were considered to be the values of these attributes. In the presence of uncertainty, this interpretation is no longer adequate, since the 'exact' value of an attribute is unknown. Instead, every object can be a value of any attribute with some associated certainty factor. In fact, $a[lab \rightarrow b@ <\perp, \perp>]$ should be true for any a, b and *lab*, since $<\perp, \perp>$ means that there are no grounds to either believe or disbelieve $a\,[lab \rightarrow b]$.

This suggests that the interpretation of a label must be a function $O^* \rightarrow [O^* \rightarrow \Lambda^2]$ which assigns a belief pair to every possible value of the label. This is applicable to functional as well as set-valued labels, i.e.

$$j_{\#}, j_{*} : O^* \rightarrow [O^* \rightarrow \Lambda^2] \tag{3}$$

[3]From now on we will attach certainty factors by means of "@" instead of ":" (which is the symbol we used herefore) in order to avoid confusion with ":", which is now used to specify classes in F-logic.

It turns out that (3) suffices for modeling set-valued labels in the presence of uncertainty. However, this is not enough in order to generalize the semantics of functional attributes. First, let us note that for functional labels, $a\,[lab \rightarrow b]$ and $c \leq_O b$ implies $a\,[lab \rightarrow c]$. Therefore,

- for each $a, lab \in O^*, j_\#(lab)(a)$ must be a *downward closed* function $O^* \rightarrow \Lambda^2$. This means that for every $c, d \in O^*$ s.t. $c \leq_O d, j_\#(lab)(a)(d) \trianglelefteq j_\#(lab)(a)(c)$.

This ensures that, say, if *john*[*supervisor* $\rightarrow$ *bob*@ $< .6, .2 >$] holds then also *john* [*supervisor* $\rightarrow$ *faculty*@ $< .6, .2 >$] must hold, since *Bob* is a faculty. In addition, we need to capture the phenomenon exhibited by functional attributes according to which if $a\,[lab \rightarrow b]$ and $a\,[lab \rightarrow c]$ both are true then $a\,[lab \rightarrow \text{lub}(b, c)]$ holds as well. This is formalized as follows:

- Let $j_\#(lab)(a)(b) = \alpha$ and $j_\#(lab)(a)(c) = \beta$. Then $\text{glb}(\alpha, \beta) \leq_O j_\#(lab)(a)(\text{lub}(b, c))$,

where glb denotes the greatest lower bound operator on Λ^2. This means that if we know with confidence α that b is the value of a's attribute *lab* and with confidence β that this value is c, then we must be able to conclude, at least with confidence $\text{glb}(\alpha, \beta)$, that this value is $\text{lub}(b, c)$.

The notion of satisfaction of F-terms by interpretations needs only a slight change. Let I be an interpretation and ν a variable assignment. Here ν must assign values not only to object variables that range over O^*, but also to certainty variables that range over Λ^2. A fuzzy F-term

$$T = P : Q[\ldots\ Lab_i \rightarrow P_i : T_i[\ldots]@\alpha_i\ \ldots, Lab_j{}' \rightarrow \{\ldots\ V_l : S_l[\ldots]@\beta_l\ \ldots\}], \quad (4)$$

is satisfied by I w.r.t. ν, denoted $I \models_\nu T$, if the following three conditions are met:

1. $\nu(P) \leq_I \nu(Q)$;
2. for each single-valued label (e.g. Lab_i), $\nu(\alpha_i) \trianglelefteq j_\#(\nu(Lab_i))(\nu(Q))(\nu(T_i))$ and $I \models_\nu P_i : T_i[\ldots]$;
3. for each set-valued label (e.g. $Lab_l{}'$), $\nu(\beta_l) \trianglelefteq j_*(\nu(Lab_l{}'))(\nu(Q))(\nu(S_l))$ and $I \models_\nu V_l : S_l[\ldots]$.

This definition of satisfaction generalizes the one given in Section 5.3 in the following sense. We can embed the language of F-logic (without uncertainty) into the combined language by mapping each F-term, T, of the form (2) (see Section 5.3) into a fuzzy F-term, T_Λ, of the form (4), where α_i and β_l are all equal to $< \top\,, \bot >$ (which is the belief pair representing true beliefs). Likewise, each interpretation, I, of F-logic can be made into an interpretation I_Λ of the combined language by converting each function $f : O^* \rightarrow O^*$ and $f : O^* \rightarrow 2^{O^*}$ into a function $f_\Lambda : O^* \rightarrow [O^* \rightarrow \Lambda^2]$ as follows: If $b \in f(a)$ or $b = f(a)$ then put $f_\Lambda(a)(b) = < \top\,, \bot >$ (i.e. *true*); otherwise put $f_\Lambda(a)(b) = < \bot\,, \top >$ (which is the pair representing false beliefs). The reader can easily verify that $I \models_\nu T$ iff $I_\Lambda \models_\nu T_\Lambda$.

Expert system rules are similar to those in Section 4, except that instead of literals of the form $p : \alpha$ we use fuzzy F-terms. The definition of satisfaction of rules is the same as in Section 4.

It is not hard to see that the resulting language has all the properties of each of the formalisms described in Sections 4 and 5. In fact, we have obtained what can be dubbed as *fuzzy F-logic*. All the features of F-logic such as property inheritance, procedural attachments, etc. are preserved but get a "fuzzy flavor", because belief pairs are attached to each property.

7 Conclusions and Future Work

In this paper we sketched the semantic foundations of different aspects of expert systems proposed in Kifer and Li (1988), Kifer and Wu (1989), Kifer and Lausen (1989) and proposed a way to combine these previously disparate proposals in one language. The resulting language is much more general and expressive than the earlier works on these issues (e.g., Hayes (1979); Shapiro (1983); Subrahmanian (1987); van Emden (1986)).

To put uncertainty to work, we had to impose certain restrictions on certainty and combination functions, such as monotonicity. Although simple and intuitively appealing, this assumption may not be so natural when facts can be disbelieved. For instance, it may be desirable to assume that, as the belief in $\neg p$ increases, the belief in p decreases. The monotonicity assumption about certainty and combination functions rules this possibility out. Particularly, one of its deplorable casualties is the well-known Dempster-Shafer's combination rule (Shafer (1976)).

One way to overcome this difficulty is to try to extend our semantics to other important combination rules. However, a more promising and intriguing direction seems to be replacing Dempster-Shafer's rule with something more suitable. As we have remarked in Section 2 this rule does not treat contradictions correctly, since conflicting evidences neutralize each other. It would be interesting to attempt a revision of the foundations of Dempster-Shafer's theory to adapt it to our notion of inconsistency.

Additional cases of evidential independence need to be studied. The three independence criteria presented in Section 4 do not always produce the desired effect. For instance, under both criteria, combination of the rule $p : \alpha \leftarrow p : \alpha$ and the fact $p : .0001$ would lead us to conclude $p : 1$. This conclusion may not be the expected one in some situations. Likewise, given the following three rules: $p \leftarrow b$, $p \leftarrow a$ and $a \leftarrow p$, we may not want to view the first pair of rules as being independent (because of $a \leftarrow p$). Thus, additional syntactic independence conditions need further study.

Furthermore, the very concept of independence may be too restrictive. The problem is that we view rules as being either totally independent, or totally dependent on each other. In practice, however, one may want to think of a pair of rules $p \leftarrow a, b$ and $p \leftarrow a, c$ as only being *partially* dependent (because of the common premise a). This means that different evidences supplied by the two rules should not be combined to a full extent, as it would be in the case of totally independent rules.

There is also a host of theoretical and pragmatic issues related to the implementation of fuzzy F-logic described in Section 6. These include query optimization and efficient storage and retrieval of fuzzy F-terms.

References

ABITEBOUL, S., and BEERI, C. (1987), *On the Power of Languages for Manipulation of Complex Objects*, unpublished manuscript.

ABITEBOUL, S., and GRUMBACH, S. (1987), COL: A Logic-Based Language for Complex Objects, *Workshop on Database Programming Languages*, Roscoff, France, 253–276.

ABITEBOUL, S., and KANELLAKIS, P.C. (1989), Object Identity as a Query Language Primitive, *Proc. of the ACM-SIGMOD Intl. Conf. on Management of Data*, 159–173.

AIT-KACI, H., and NASR, R. (1986), LOGIN: A Logic Programming Language with Built-in Inheritance, *Journal of Logic Programming, 3, 1*, 185–215.

BALBIN, I., PORT, G.S., and RAMAMOHANARAO, K. (1987), *Magic Set Computation for Stratified Databases*, Tech. Rep. 87/3, Dept. of Computer Science, Univ. of Melbourne, Australia.

BALBIN, I., and RAMAMOHANARAO, K. (1987), A Generalization of the Differential Approach to Recursive Query Evaluation, *Journal of Logic Programming, 4*, 259–262.

BALDWIN, J.F. (1987), Evidential Support Logic Programming, *Fuzzy Sets and Systems, 24*, 1–26.

BALDWIN, J.F., MARTIN, T.P., and PILSWORTH, B.W. (1987), *FRIL Manual*, EQUIPU-AIR, Ltd., Bristol, UK.

BALDWIN, J.F., and MONK, M.R.M. (1987), *Evidence Theory, Fuzzy Logic and Logic Programming*, ITRC Tech. Rep. 109, University of Bristol, UK.

BANCILHON, F., and KHOSHAFIAN, S.N. (1986), *A Calculus of Complex Objects*, Proc. of the ACM SIGACT-SIGMOD Symp. on Prin. of Database Systems, 53–59.

BEERI, C. (1988), *Data Models and Languages for Databases*, 2nd Int. Conf. on Database Theory (ICDT), LNCS 326, Bruges, Belgium, 19–40.

BEERI, C., NAQVI, S., SHMUELI, O., and TSUR, S. (1987), *Sets and Negation in a Logic Database Language (LDL)*, MCC Report.

BEERI, C., NASR, R., and TSUR, S. (1988), *Embedding Ψ-Terms in a Horn-Clause Logic Language*, MCC Tech. Rep. ACA-ST-050-88.

BEERI, C., and RAMAKRISHNAN, R. (1987), *On the Power of Magic*, Proc. of the ACM SIGACT-SIGMOD Symp. on Prin. of Database Systems, 269–283.

BELNAP, N.D. (1975), A Useful Four-Valued Logic, in: *Modern Uses of Multiple-Valued Logic*, eds. J.M. Dunn and G. Epstein, D. Reidel Publishing Co., Dordrecht.

BELNAP, N.D. (1976), How a Computer Should Think, in: *Contemporary Aspects of Philosophy*, ed. G. Ryle, Oriel Press, 30–56.

BLAIR, H.A., and SUBRAHMANIAN, V.S. (1989), Paraconsistent Foundations for Logic Programming, *Journal of Non Classical Logic*, to appear.

BUCHANAN, B.G., and SHORTLIFFE, E.H. (1984), *Rule-Based Expert Systems*, Addison-Wesley, Reading, MA.

CARDELLI, L. (1984), *A Semantics of Multiple Inheritance*, Int. Symp. on Semantics of Data Types, LNCS 173, 51–67.

CHEN, W., and WARREN, D.S. (1989), *C-logic for Complex Objects*, Proc. of the ACM SIGACT-SIGMOD Symp. on Prin. of Database Systems, 369–378.

CLOCKSIN, W.F., and MELLISH, C.S. (1981), *Programming in Prolog*, Springer Verlag, Berlin Heidelberg New York.

DRIANKOV, D. (1987), A Many-Valued Logic for Belief/Disbelief Pairs, in: *Proc. of the 2nd Int. Symposium on Methodologies for Intelligent Systems*, eds. Z.W. Ras and M. Zemankova, North-Holland, Amsterdam, 25–32.

DUBOIS, D., and PRADE, H. (1980), *Fuzzy Sets and Systems: Theory and Applications*, Academic Press.

ETHERINGTON, D.W., and REITER, R. (1983), *On Inheritance Hierarchies with Exceptions*, AAAI-83, Washington D.C., 104–108.

FAGIN, R., HALPERN, J.Y., and MEGIDDO, N. (1988), *A Logic for Reasoning about Probabilities*, Proc. Conf. Logic in Computer Science, 410–421.

FEIGENBAUM, E.A. (1977), *The Art of Artificial Intelligence: 1. Themes and Case Studies of Knowledge Engineering*, IJCAI-77, 1014–1029.

FIKES, R., and KEHLER, T. (1985), The Role of Frame-Based Representation in Reasoning, *Comm. of ACM*, Sept., 904–920.

FITTING, M. (1989), Bilattices and the Semantics of Logic Programming, *Journal of Logic Programming*, to appear.

FROST, R. (1986), *Introduction to Knowledge Base Systems*, Macmillan Publishing Co.

GARDARIN, G. (1987), *Magic Functions: A Technique to Optimize Extended Datalog Recursive Programs*, Proc. of the ACM Intl. Conf. on Very Large Data Bases, 21–30.

GINSBERG, M.L. (1984), *Nonmonotonic Reasoning Using Dempster's Rule*, AAAI-84, Austin, TX, 126–129.

GINSBERG, M.L. (1987), Multivalued Logics, in: *Readings in Non-Monotonic Reasoning*, ed. M.L. Ginsberg, 251–255.

GUNTZER, U., KIESSLING, W., and BAYER, A.R. (1987), *On Evaluation of Recursion in Deductive Database Systems by Efficient Differential Fixpoint Iteration*, 3rd Int. Conf. on Data Engineering, 120–129.

HAJEK, P., and VALDES, J.J. (1987), *Algebraic Foundations of Uncertainty Processing in Rule-Based Systems*, Ceskoslovenska Akademie Ved (Matematicky Ustav).

HARMON, P., MAUS, R., and MORRISSEY, W. (1988), *Expert Systems Tools and Applications*, John Wiley and Sons, New York.

HAYES, P.J. (1979), The Logic of Frames, in: *Frame Conception and Text Understanding*, ed. D. Metzing, de Gruyter, Berlin New York, 46–61.

HAYES-ROTH, F. (1985), Rule-Based Systems, *Comm. ACM, 28, 9*, 921–932.

HAYES-ROTH, F., WATERMAN, D., and LENAT, D. (1983), *Building Expert Systems*, Addison-Wesley, Reading, MA.

KANAL, L.N., and LEMMER, J.F. (1986), *Uncertainty in Artificial Intelligence (Machine Intelligence and Pattern Recognition, 4)*, North Holland, Amsterdam.

KHOSHAFIAN, S.N., and COPELAND, G.P. (1986), *Object Identity*, OOPSLA-86, 406–416.

KIFER, M., and LAUSEN, G. (1989), *F-Logic: A Higher-Order Language for Reasoning about Objects, Inheritance, and Schema*, Proc. of the ACM-SIGMOD Intl. Conf. on Management of Data, 134–146.

KIFER, M., and LI, A. (1988), On the Semantics of Rule-Based Expert Systems with Uncertainty, in: *2nd Int. Conf. on Database Theory (LNCS 326)*, eds. M. Gyssens, J. Paredaens and D. Van Gucht, Springer Verlag, Berlin Heidelberg New York, 102–117.

KIFER, M., and LOZINSKII, E.L. (1986), *A Framework for an Efficient Implementation of Deductive Database Systems*, Proceedings of the 6th Advanced Database Symposium, Tokyo, Japan.

KIFER, M., and LOZINSKII, E.L. (1989), *RI: A Logic for Reasoning with Inconsistency*, Symposium on Logic in Computer Science (LICS), 253–262.

KIFER, M., and LOZINSKII, E.L. (1990), *On Compile-Time Query Optimization in Deductive Databases by Means of Static Filtering*, ACM Transactions on Database Systems, to appear.

KIFER, M., and WU, J. (1989), *A Logic for Object-Oriented Logic Programming (Maier's O-logic Revisited)*, Proc. of the ACM SIGACT-SIGMOD Symp. on Prin. of Database Systems, 379–393.

KUPER, G.M. (1987), *An Extension of LPS to Arbitrary Sets*, IBM Research Report.

KUPER, G.M., and VARDI, M.Y. (1984), *A New Approach to Database Logic*, Proc. of the ACM SIGACT-SIGMOD Symp. on Prin. of Database Systems.

LEE, R.C.T. (1972), Fuzzy Logic and the Resolution Principle, *Journal of the ACM*, 109–119.

LLOYD, J.W. (1987), *Foundations of Logic Programming*, Springer Verlag, New York.

MAIER, D. (1986), *A Logic for Objects*, Proc. of the Workshop on Foundations of Deductive Databases and Logic Programming, Washington D.C., 6–26.

MINSKY, M. (1981), A Framework for Representing Knowledge, in: *Mind Design*, ed. J. Haugeland, MIT Press, Cambridge, MA, 95–128.

MORRIS, K., NAUGHTON, J., SARAIYA, Y., ULLMAN, J., and VAN GELDER, A. (1987), *YAWN! (yet another window on NAIL!)*, unpublished manuscript.

NILSSON, N.J. (1986), Probabilistic Logic, *Int. J. Artificial Intelligence*, 71–87.

PARNAS, D.L. (1985), Software Aspects of Strategic Defence Systems, *American Scientist, 73*.

PEARL, J. (1986), Fusion, Propagation, and Structuring in Belief Networks, *Artificial Intelligence, 29*, 241–288.

PETRIE, C.J., RUSSINOFF, D.M., and STEINER, D.D. (1987), *Proteus 2: System Description*, MCC Tech. Rep. AI-136-87-Q.

PRADE, H. (1983), A Synthetic View of Approximate Reasoning Techniques, *IJCAI*, 130–136.

PRZYMUSINSKI, T.C. (1988), On the Declarative Semantics of Deductive Databases and Logic Programs, in: *Foundations of Deductive Databases and Logic Programming*, ed. J. Minker, Morgan-Kaufmann, Los Altos, CA, 193–216.

RINE, D.C. (1986), *Some Relationships between Logic Programming and Multiple-Valued Logic*, Symp. on Multiple-Valued Logic, 160–163.

ROTH, M.A., KORTH, H.F., and SILBERSCHATZ, A. (1985), *Extended Algebra and Calculus for ¬1NF Relational Databases*, Tech. Rep.-84-36, Dept. of Computer Science, Univ. of Texas, Austin.

RUBINSKI, H. (1987), On First-Order Databases, *ACM Trans. Database Systems, 12, 3*, 325–349.

RUSPINI, E.H. (1987), Epistemic Logics, Probability, and the Calculus of Evidence, *IJCAI, 87*, 924–931.

SHAFER, G. (1976), *A Mathematical Theory of Evidence*, Princeton University Press, Princeton.

SHAPIRO, E. (1983), Logic Programs with Uncertainties: A Tool for Implementing Rule-Based Systems, *IJCAI, 83*, 529–532.

SMOLKA, G., and AIT-KACI, H. (1987), *Inheritance Hierarchies: Semantics and Unification*, MCC Tech. Rep. AI-057-87.

SUBRAHMANIAN, V.S. (1987), *On the Semantics of Quantitative Logic Programs*, IEEE Symposium on Logic Programming, 173–182.

TOURETZKY, D.S. (1986), *The Mathematics of Inheritance Systems*, Morgan-Kaufmann, Los Altos, CA.

TOURETZKY, D.S., HORTY, J.F., and THOMASON, R.H. (1987), *A Skeptical Theory of Inheritance in Nonmonotonic Semantic Nets*, Proceedings of AAAI87.

TZVIELI, A. (1988), *PL — A Probabilistic Logic*, Proc. IEEE Data Engineering Conf., 462–469.

ULLMAN, J.D. (1988), *Principles of Database and Knowledge-Base Systems*, Computer Science Press, Rockville, MD.

VAN EMDEN, M.H. (1986), Quantitative Deduction and its Fixpoint Theory, *The Journal of Logic Programming*, 37–53.

VIEILLE, L. (1986), *Recursive Axioms in Deductive Databases: The Query-Subquery Approach*, Proc. of the 1st Conf. on Expert Database Systems, Charleston, SC, 179–196.

ZEMANKOVA-LEECH, M., and KANDEL, A. (1984), *Fuzzy Relational Databases — a Key to Expert Systems*, Verlag TÜV Rheinland, Köln.

ZVIELI, A. (1986), *A Fuzzy Relational Calculus*, Proc. of the 1st Int. Conf. of Expert Database Systems, Charleston, SC, 225–240.

Interpretation of Numbers as Search

Peter Latocha
Gesellschaft für Mathematik und Datenverarbeitung
Sankt Augustin, Germany

Summary

Most current statistical packages and expert systems lack an important feature: they provide numbers, but no interpretations. Interpretation of numbers presents a special class of problems. Usually, one thinks of an interpretation of the results of a statistical analysis as a translation from the technical language of mathematics and statistics into the language of the researcher's speciality. Building a knowledge-based system for domain-specific interpretation of data, we choose an utterly different approach. In this approach, interpretation is seen as a search process in proposition spaces.

1 Statistical Expert Systems

The term statistical expert system is rather vague. However, a statistical expert system should be able to do what statisticians usually do, and they generally perform the following functions:

- refine the research objectives and questions,
- choose appropriate statistical techniques to address the questions,
- apply the techniques,
- interpret the results.

We also know that the construction of statistical expert systems involves immense problems. This should make us realize that "building statistical expert systems we must start small". Therefore, "attention is often focussed on just one of the above four areas" (Hand (1986)). We focus on the fourth area, on which relatively little work has been done (cf. Hand (1986) and Gale and Pregibon (1985)).

2 Interpretation: An Example

If, for instance, an election researcher obtains new election results together with sociodemographic data, characteristics of political parties and other information, he, perhaps, would like to focus on the number of votes obtained by each political party. Possibly, he compares the new results with previous ones, investigates specific regions and the factors possibly determining those results, etc. In other words, he verifies which propositions of the following types are true:

NATO ASI Series, Vol. F 61
Knowledge, Data and Computer-Assisted Decisions
Edited by M. Schader and W. Gaul

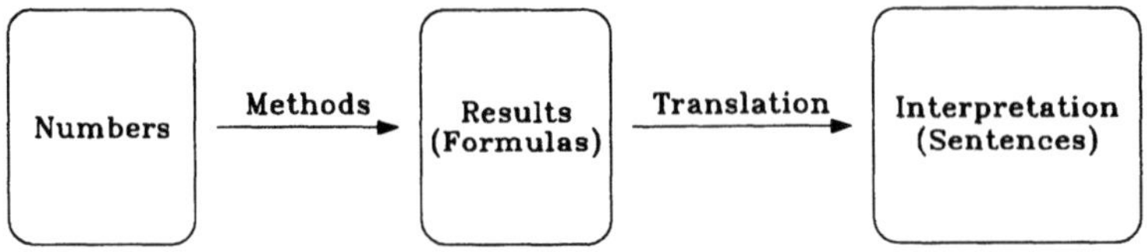

Figure 1: Interpretation of Numbers Described as a Translation Process

a. The <party> obtained ... % of the votes.

b. That means a ... % loss/increase of votes.

c. It is the worst result for the <party> since <year> and the greatest loss of votes since <year>.

d. ... % of the electoral districts in <region> belong to the 50 best districts.

e. ... % of the regions with <characteristic> are regions of a high percentage of votes for the <party>.

The result of the above analysis of an election researcher is a paper containing the most interesting findings. In other words, an appropriately ordered set of the most interesting propositions verified by the available data.

3 Interpretation of Numbers is no Translation Process

Usually an interpretation of numbers is described as a translation process (see Fig. 1) from the technical language of mathematics and statistics into an appropriate terminology[1].

However, if we choose to view the interpretation of numbers as a translation process, then the real problem appears to be finding adequate natural-language representations. Of course, this is not the case. If a statistical expert system were to apply statistical methods to data, thereby not considering that some results possibly are redundant and also failing to account for an orderly presentation of the propositions pertaining to the results, then this analysis could certainly not be accepted. Only a coherent, non-redundant and appropriately ordered set of propositions can be considered an interpretation.

The picture, therefore, is an inadequate description of the interpretation process. Furthermore, no statistician would proceed to evaluate any numbers by means of any methods and interpret them, thereby not being informed about the domain of data. An expert must also know what to look for—what problem to solve. Only with sufficient information about the data and the problem to be solved, he will be able to select adequate methods, to apply them and to interpret the results.

[1] "Interpretation of the results of a statistical analysis is a translation from the technical language of mathematics and statistics into the substantive language of the researcher's speciality" (Hand (1986)).

If the problem is known, the logical and natural-language form of possible findings is also known[2], so, there is no need for a translation. It would be more correct to say that a function of an expert is to verify the propositions of the given types (types (a)–(e) in our example) with respect to the data.

Constructing a system for the knowledge-based, content- and subject-oriented interpretation of data, we are pursuing the following approach: the interpretation is regarded as a search process in proposition spaces.

4 The Problem

The problem of our approach can be described as follows. In a domain $\mathcal{B}$, the data and the corresponding domain knowledge $\mathcal{D}$ are given. Let $\mathcal{A}$ be a set of meaningful propositions with respect to $\mathcal{B}$. Find the set of all true and interesting propositions from $\mathcal{A}$ which does not contain any redundant proposition. The search should, of course, be efficient.

As an example, let us assume that $\mathcal{B}$ be the domain of German Federal Elections and $\mathcal{D}$ the relevant election results, sociodemographic data, characteristics of political parties etc. In this example, the set $\mathcal{A}$ contains the following propositions:

- losses of votes for all large political parties in the last election;
- losses of votes for the governing political parties since 3 elections;
- significant losses of votes for the CDU in the last 3 elections in all electoral districts with a high percentage of blue-collar workers.

In this case, we would find a set of propositions that are interesting for the user and could be used for the elections analysis. The problem can be formulated in even more abstract and general terms:

GIVEN :

- data $\mathcal{D}$ (data + knowledge),
- a formal language $\mathcal{L}$ whose expressions can be evaluated based on the data,
- constraints $\mathcal{C}$.

FIND : The set of all expressions from $\mathcal{L}$ which

- possess desired characteristics concerning $\mathcal{D}$,
- satisfy constraints $\mathcal{C}$.

Of course, the constraints $\mathcal{C}$ pertain only to the expressions to be found. The particular form of the constraints is rather free, but they refer to the language or the data. For example, they can be requirements with respect to the form of the expressions to be found. By desired characteristics of expressions from $\mathcal{L}$ with respect to $\mathcal{D}$, we understand, for example, that they should be true with respect to the data.

[2]This shall not mean that its logical form is given by a simple formula and that its natural-language form is given by a simple textual framework or prefabricated text containing some few open passages to be completed by some elements. For example, for propositions of the record or series types, the logical and natural-language forms are not given by a simple formula or a prefabricated text, but rather by non-trivial programs.

5 Two Essential Differences Between Solutions

Many approaches to solve this problem and its special cases have already been developed (cf., for example, Hajek and Havranek (1977), Mitchell (1983) and Michalski (1984)). Although the formulation of basic principles in these approaches are very similar, the solutions often differ considerably (see Latocha (1989b)). The approaches were developed for different purposes (e.g., hypothesis generation, automatic formulation of theories, machine learning, tools for identifying interconnections in data), but the essential characteristics in which they differ are as follows:

- the types of the admissible data which can be evaluated in their framework, and
- the expressive power of the language used.

A general solution should of course be applicable to almost any data and should provide a powerful language (a language at least as powerful as the language of first order predicate logic).

6 The Overall Objectives

A general solution should at least have the following characteristics:

- applicability to all data occurring in relevant applications;
- the language used allows a natural representation of quite different types of propositions[3];
- the system is modular, easily extensible and appeals to intuition.

Of course, these characteristics are fairly vague and every point could most certainly be extensively discussed. The list, however, provides information about goals pursued by us. An essential part of our work is the attempt to find out how to attain these goals. The following is an outline of our solution. A detailed description can be found in Latocha (1989a).

7 The Solution: The Proposition Explorer

As already mentioned, the most important characteristics of a solution are the admissible data and the formal language in which the propositions to be found are expressed.

7.1 The Admissible Data

To support a great number of applications, there are no special requirements to be met by the structure of the data analyzed. Currently, structures common in statistics are used, i.e., tables and micro data files. A connection to available database systems is planned. For representing the domain knowledge we use an object-oriented formalism and the language of the system.

[3]In this context, we are only interested in the extensional propositions.

7.2 The Formal Language PL_ω

An adequate language selection is a most crucial point. In general, slightly modified versions of the language of first order predicate logic are selected. It is relatively uncomplicated and suitable for handling such aspects as the truth of propositions. Our language PL_ω, introduced in Latocha (1989a), is very similar to the language of predicate logic. Nonetheless, it shows analogies to natural languages. The most important syntactic, and also semantic, categories of our language are *object, operation, predicate* and *proposition*. Operations applied to objects generate new objects and predicates applied to objects generate propositions. The grammar of our language is lexically oriented. Therefore, the generated expressions are always semantically correct.

The language PL_ω was constructed in such a way that it allows one to use the same algorithms at different levels (atomic propositions, propositions with connectives and quantifiers etc.). It contains connectives and quantifiers from different logical systems. It is used not only for representing interesting propositions, but also for representing domain knowledge.

7.3 The Search Algorithm

A further component of the solution is a search algorithm based on the formalism of partially ordered sets. Our language represents a proposition as a list

$$(\text{predicate object}_1 \ldots \text{object}_n),$$

which consists of a predicate and a corresponding number of objects. Therefore a set of interesting propositions, a proposition space, can be represented as the cross product $P \times O_1 \times \ldots \times O_n$ where P is a set of 'homogeneous' predicates and $O_1, \ldots, O_n$ the corresponding argument sets. On all of these sets, specific partial orderings are defined, which induce a partial ordering to the cross product. The induced ordering, interpreted as "semantically more powerful", is the basis of the search algorithm. It searches for the semantically most powerful true propositions in this space and eliminates all propositions which are semantically more powerful (and therefore false) or weaker with respect to the found propositions. For examples, see Latocha (1989a).

7.4 Two Further Components of the Proposition Explorer

The proposition explorer searches the set of potential propositions for the true and most interesting propositions. Obviously, *interesting* means *interesting to the user* in this context. The user has to communicate to the system what is more interesting and what is less interesting to him. Accordingly, the system must provide the user with tools supporting his specification.

If all true and most interesting propositions are found, then these should be coherently ordered in accordance with the user's requests.

8 The Functional Model

Our approach can be represented as in Fig. 2. In the first phase (specification phase), the user should specify his interests:

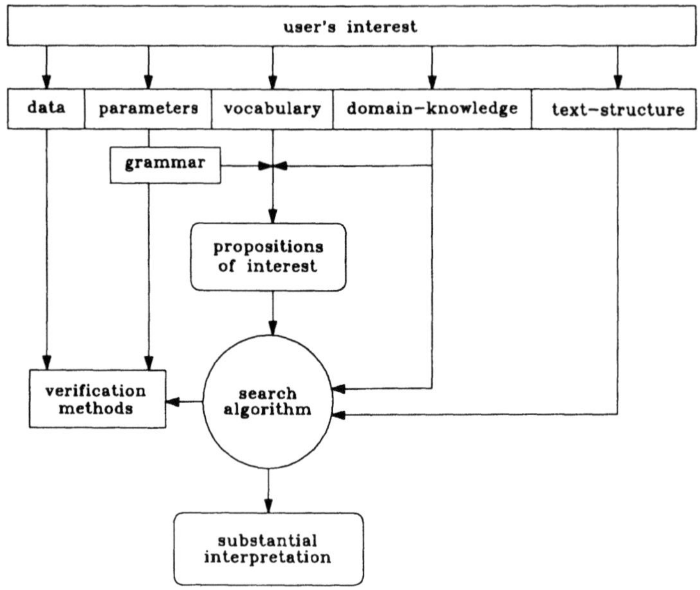

Figure 2: Overview of the Functional Model

- which data are to be evaluated,
- under which aspects (i.e., which types of propositions are interesting),
- for which groups of arguments the propositions are interesting,
- which parts of the domain knowledge should be considered,
- how to order the results etc.

In the second phase (main phase), the corresponding proposition spaces are generated. The search algorithm uses the semantic relations between arguments, predicates, propositions and proposition spaces to identify 'intelligently' (efficiently) the most interesting propositions which are verifiable by the data. Each proposition type is assigned a verification method which determines when a proposition of a given type is true. The verification methods may use a quite sophisticated repertoire of statistical methods.

9 The Knowledge-Intensive Nature of the Problem

Our system needs only to be provided with data and knowledge from some domain and then returns all interesting—and only interesting—findings in form of a natural-language text. In the ideal case, it is sufficient to provide the system with the data on elections and the corresponding knowledge for obtaining an expert analysis of the elections.

However, the problem of proposition exploration is very knowledge-intensive. To accomplish the task, the system needs a lot of knowledge from different domains and to provide such knowledge is rather difficult.

Our approach is a general solution to a very broad problem. General solutions have a disadvantage: they are almost never the optimal and most efficient solutions for special cases. Therefore, nobody should be surprised that this approach does not yield a (close to) optimal solution for a special application and that it is not so efficient as an approach tailored to the special case.

Acknowledgements

This research was done at the GMD in the EXPLORA project. A first prototypical implementation of this approach was presented in 1988 at the Hannover fair for information technology. An improved and extended version and some applications are currently implemented and run in Common Lisp and the Common Lisp Object System (cf. Bobrow et al. (1988)) on Symbolics LISP-Machines and Apple Macintosh II.

References

BOBROW, D.G. (1988), *Common Lisp Object System Specification*, X3J13 Committee Document, Stanford.

GALE, W.A., and PREGIBON, D. (1985), Artificial intelligence research in statistics, *The AI Magazine*, 72–75.

HAJEK, P., and HAVRANEK, T. (1977), On generation of inductive hypotheses, *Int. Journal Man-Machine Studies 9*, 415–438.

HAND, D.J. (1986), Expert systems in statistics, *The Knowledge Engineering Review 1(3)*, 2–10.

LATOCHA, P. (1989a), *Exploration von Aussagenräumen. Ein semantischer Ansatz (Exploration of proposition spaces. A semantical approach)*, Sankt Augustin, GMD-Studie 164.

LATOCHA, P. (1989b), *Der Aussagen-Explorator in einer Landschaft von Problemen und Ansätzen (The Proposition Explorer in a landscape of problems and approaches)*, Technical Report, GMD.

MICHALSKI, R.S. (1984), A theory and methodology of inductive learning, in: *Machine learning. An artificial intelligence approach*, eds. Michalski, Carbonell and Mitchell, Springer, Berlin Heidelberg New York, 83–134.

MITCHELL, T.M. (1983), Generalization as search, *Artificial Intelligence 18*, 203–226.

DSFINANCE —
Decision Support for Financial Planning

Hermann Locarek and Carl-M. Preuß
Faculty of Economics and Social Sciences,
University of Augsburg, Germany

Summary

Management of financial resources is one of the key managerial tasks of a company. Models used for planning in this application area must be of a high complexity, because corporate finance is influenced by many decisions in other corporate areas. This paper describes an ongoing project within the context of the faculty computer pool. The project integrates preplans from other corporate areas into a central decision support system to support the financial planner in his planning task. The prototype system under development provides a menu driven user interface on a personal computer, that makes use of decentralized information, sophisticated forecasting methods, and centralized knowledge about financial dependencies within the company. The system uses information that is either given by external sources, naive forecasting and explicit forecasts associated with every position in the company's accounting scheme. Financial indicators are generated either automatically or by request of the user. The indicators are displayed as numbers, various types of business graphics output or time series. Warning levels can be generated and measures of deviation applied to show financial indicators that are below their respective goal values. Scenario-oriented deterministic simulation is used to simulate the consequences of financial decisions. The hierarchic nature of the multiple dependencies allows "what if?"- and "how to achieve?"-questions answered by prolog-style forward- and backward-chaining mechanisms. Currently problems are found but not solved automatically via stochastic simulation or optimization. The system is written in Pascal and uses well known personal computer spreadsheets and databases, and the company's general ledger system as data source which may be distributed throughout the computer pool's local network.

1 Introduction

This paper describes an ongoing research and education project for the computer pool at the University of Augsburg Faculty of Economics and Social Sciences. The project is motivated by practical considerations and research interests in forecasting, decision support and financial modelling. It has been initiated in 1988 and the project proper has been started in 1989. This is the reason why we cannot describe a completed project with all its final results. Instead, in the first section we briefly introduce the framework of both the faculty computer pool and the theoretical background as well as the practical work done in the area of computer-aided financial planning in Germany. Section 2 gives a survey of the goals and dependencies of financial planning and its position in the company's

NATO ASI Series, Vol. F 61
Knowledge, Data and Computer-Assisted Decisions
Edited by M. Schader and W. Gaul

planning system. The description of the system DSFINANCE is started in section 3 and divided into two sections. First, we will discuss the structure of the available input data and the starting point of the planning process. Second, the necessary attributes of a system that can give decision support for financial planning are discussed. Again, we first look at the existing computer aided financial planning systems. Based on this analysis, the elements of DSFINANCE are described.

1.1 Faculty Computer Pool

The goal is to provide a system that is as simple as required for teaching financial models. On the other hand it should be applicable for a broad range of company types but not lack reality. Having this in mind, we chose the target companies to be small or medium sized corporate enterprises (GmbH). We hope to avoid problems with consolidation of daughter companies of large companies, and many different products or areas of operation. Of course, these problems may exist in smaller companies also. However, an extension of the system in this direction must be subject of further research. The remaining corporations are required to prepare an annual financial statement that is up to the standard of the German accounting law of 1986 (BilRiLiG (1986)). More than 300.000 companies with a total revenue that makes up more than 50% of the german industrial revenue, are covered by this law. Another assumption is made in respect of the type of the company under analysis. Like most textbooks, we assume a manufacturing enterprise with a narrow range of production. This seems necessary to give the students a chance of coping with the system quickly. The system DSFINANCE takes data directly from the financial accounting system of the company. The financial accounting system of the faculty computer pool is patterned after the industrial account classification of DATEV (1989).

1.2 Existing Systems for Computer Aided Financial Planning

A review of published work in the field of computer aided financial planning in Germany by Günther (1988) shows, that such tools exist in unsatisfactory number and quality. The review gives information about seven systems, most of which have been developed within doctoral dissertations. Only two of the systems, both by Gabele and Sahm (1986), run on personal computers and provide high quality graphics output. All other systems must be rated as outdated, because they were prototypes written for older mainframe- or minicomputers in Fortran, Cobol or APL. Some of them are even using batch mode. The system described by Busch (1983) shows to be the most complete, but is also only a prototype with one running system and more than 6 years old. The programs *FIBIP* and *LIQUIDAS* are state of the art in their user interfaces (Lotus 123). However, they lack some of the required features (see below, section 5) as well as an interface to external data sources. All data needed in the spreadsheets must be entered manually. None of the systems can be called an adequate decision support environment. Fig. 1 gives a condensed view of the seven systems mentioned by Günther (1988).

2 The Domain

The history of financial planning theory in Germany may be one of the reasons for the lack of decision support systems for financial planning. The axioms that have been given for

	Busch	Detlefsen FIPLA	Drünkler KUFIPLAN	Drünkler MIFIPLAS	Gabele/S. FIBIP	Gabele/S. LIQUIDAS	Gahse DYPOL
Language	APL(1)	Fortran IV	COBOL 74	COBOL 74	Lotus 123	Lotus 123	Fortran
Computer	main-frame	mini-computer	mini-computer	mini-computer	PC	PC	n/a
Processing	Dialog	Dialog/ Batch	Batch	Dialog	Dialog	Dialog	Batch
Graphics-quality	low	low	none	none	high	high	none
Inter-faces	avail.	avail.	avail.	avail.	n/a	n/a	n/a

Figure 1: Characteristics of Existing Financial Planning Systems

financial planning were patterned after the axioms for accounting (GoB): completeness, exactness, elasticity, to name only some of them. This leads to a total model of all financial activities of the company. In addition, all dependencies from other corporate planning areas (e.g., sales, production, capacity, investment) and all possible retroactive effects must be considered.

The solution for this problem was not found in simple linear optimization models, because the dependencies and input data are of stochastic nature. Today, considerations of practical applicability give way to sequential coordination of the company's plans. The coordination starts with the production plan, which is judged to be the bottleneck of the company in most cases (see Gutenberg (1979)). The financial- and liquidity plans are coordinated after most other plans. The other plans are called preplans to the financial plan. They must be replanned only, if the financial sector turns out to be the real bottleneck (see Steiner and Kölsch (1987)).

This sequential approach is used also in DSFINANCE (see Fig. 2). It is supported by the advantage that it has a clear structure, and the complexity is less compared to simultaneous approaches. However, it is necessary for this method to work properly, that the assumed dependency of the partial financial plans really exists or at least can be justified. This assumption is critical especially for long-term planning. The more the financial planning turns to strategic management of the balance-sheet structure, the more the need for simultaneous planning increases. Although DSFINANCE contains tools that allow tampering with the balance structure, it does not really support long term strategic planning. The system works best on the operational and the tactical level. The sequential approach does not mean that profit and liquidity could not be planned with an integrated approach. The opposite is true: the balance-sheet and the income statement are the platform for financial analysis and planning (see Chmielewicz (1972)) within the system. Some preplans are also based on these two statements.

3 Conceptual Design

As discussed above, the balance-sheet and the income statement of the company are the central resources of data for the system DSFINANCE. Although both have the primary

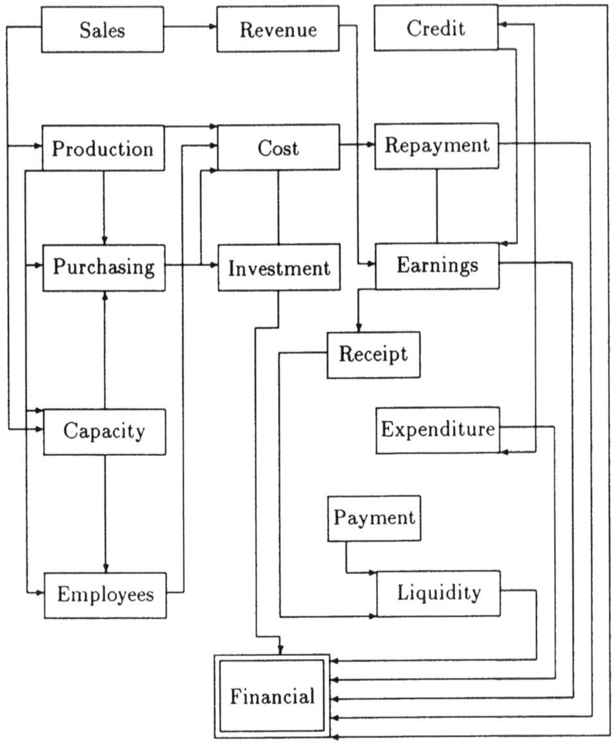

Figure 2: Preplans of the Financial Plan (taken from Schütt (1979))

purpose to show the profit, assets and liabilities of the company, liquidity indicators like cash flow can be extracted also. For external analysis, the balance-sheet will be condensed and rearranged in most cases. As the balance-sheet fits to a structure given by the BilRiLiG, this analysis can be done similarly unless special rules apply for given branches.

Most of the aggregation of balance-sheet items is done by simply adding them or subtracting them from others. Indicators are calculated by dividing simple items, aggregated items or indicators by each other. This simple scheme can be found in many applications of spreadsheet programs. A complete system for external financial analysis has been built in Augsburg with Lotus Symphony (see Dürr (1987)). Some liquidity indicators taken from this application are shown in Fig. 3. In this figure the indicators are numbered like the accounts in the account classification (column one). The formulas used for computing the indicators are given in the third column. Items beginning with a letter denote positions taken from the balance-sheet.

Putting indicators, condensed balance-sheet items and a condensed income statement to a screen image, gives a complete picture of the company on the highest level. The opening balance-sheet is taken as the starting point for the planning period. If no additional information is entered, it is assumed that all relevant numbers in the income statement will not change unless depending from items in the balance-sheet. For example, the interest payable on short term loans is computed using the average amount of short term

No.	Indicator	Formulas
⋮	⋮	⋮
2105	current assets	B
2109	liquid funds	B IV
2111	short term assets	B II[>1 year]+ B II.1[>1 year] + B III
2112	short term current assets	2109 + 2111
2211	short term liabilities	C[<1 year] + C4[>1 year]
2301	Working Capital	2112–2211
⋮	⋮	⋮
	Liquidity	
2320	- 1. Degree	2109/2211
2321	- 2. Degree	2112/2211
2322	- 3. Degree	(2112 + B I.1)/2211
2323	Working Capital Ratio	2301/2211
⋮	⋮	⋮
2401	Quick-Ratio	(2105-B I)/2211
2402	Current-Ratio	2105/2211
⋮	⋮	⋮

Figure 3: Financial Indicators

loans and a given interest rate. This is necessary, because the cash flow will change the working capital over time. The system compiles a closing balance that is a consequence of the company's activity as given in the aggregated income statement. All financing and investment resulting from changes in cash flow is done with short term liabilities and assets. Therefore even unchanged business activities will require decisions in the long run.

The financial planner can analyze the numbers and indicators on this level already. This can only be a raw analysis with "what if?"- and "how to achieve?"-questions answered by the system. Especially the last feature is a powerful instrument. The complete system has to be solved backwards for the (one) unknown variable. (see Fig. 4). This is possible, because the structure of the interrelations is explicitly modelled and not hardcoded within the system. If data or forecasted values from other plans are available, it is possible to enter them into the system manually. The values entered may be derived from a detailed preplan or an intuitive forecast as well. If no such values are available, then a starting value may be determined by simple spread sheet calculations. This allows effects from plan changes and explicit forecasts of the preplans to be taken into account.

There are several reasons, however, that make this type of raw analysis insufficient for internal short- and mid-term financial planning:

- The period of one financial year is too long if it is used as the only planning period.
- If the planning periods are divided into smaller subperiods, the seasonal structure can be used for better forecasts.
- On the other hand, accounts and items of the financial accounting system contain valuable information—e.g. exact payment data and regular payments —which can be used by the system.

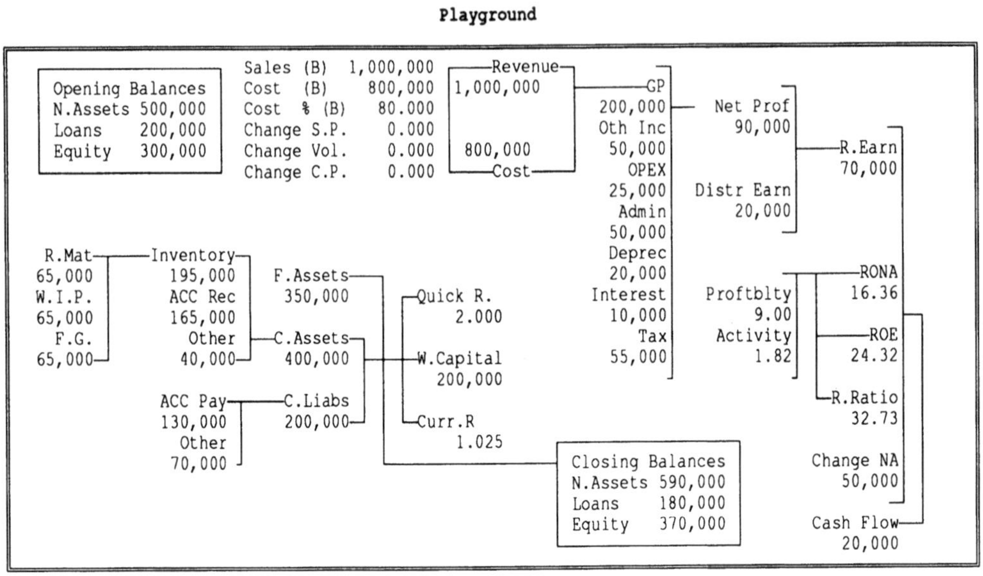

Figure 4: The Financial Manager's Playground

4 Modelling Data Structures and Domain Knowledge

First we take a look at the data model. At any given day within the planning period we can create a preliminary balance-sheet by performing the closing entries. In some positions, the balance-sheet depends on the valuation of some positions or the inclusion of inventory shortages. In most cases of financial analysis we can leave out these extraordinary items.

The positions of the account classification are allocated in detail to the positions of the balance. In addition, a new position for short term liabilities is inserted in the balance-sheet. To do this, the accounting system already contains split short and long term positions. Further aggregation is done between the balance positions and the shortened balance, within the income statement, and between the balance-sheet, the income statement and the indicators.

All these summaries have the same structure: the closing of an account is always the difference of debit and credit. The accounts are closed, depending on the type and the sign of the closing position, to the major debit or credit accounts. In the same way the balance positions and the positions of the income statement are closed. This simple structure makes a "what if?"-analysis easy. Also the question "how to achieve?" is easy to solve: the answer is the typical example for "backward-chaining". In the same way the "what if?"-question is answered by "forward-chaining". The Prolog unification-mechanism is the correct method for addressing this problem. The hierarchical relations of all data used can also be stored in Prolog data-structures. But not a pure standard Prolog-system is used. A tiny Prolog-interpreter within the system SIGMA (Locarek (1988)), written in Pascal is applied for this purpose (Klužniak and Szpakowicz (1985)). The SIGMA-system has been built within a doctoral dissertation. The advantage of this product is an unique

	Busch	Detlefsen FIPLA	Drünkler KUFIPL.	Drünkler MIFIPLAS	Gabele/S. FIBIP	Gabele/S. LIQUIDAS	Gahse DYPOL
Forecasting	yes	yes	yes	yes	yes	yes	yes
Optimizing	yes	yes	no	no	no	no	no
Simulation	yes	yes	no	yes	yes	no	no
Controlling	yes	no	no	no	yes	no	no
Sensitivity-analysis	alternative strategies	only recalc	only recalc	alternative strategies	alternative strategies	alternative strategies	only recalc
Stochastic elements	several methods	sales only	—	—	—	—	several methods

Figure 5: Configuration of Models

implementation of Pascal-programs together with Prolog data-structures and clauses.

5 Dynamic Financial Planning

A computer aided financial planning system should include the following elements in an appropriate quality:

- forecasting,
- deviation analysis (simulation, optimization),
- financial controlling.

The previously introduced computer aided financial planning systems contain these elements in varying number and quality. A review of the qualitative aspects bears some difficulties. Therefore, Fig. 5 (see Günther (1988)) gives only a yes/no discrimination for each entry. DSFINANCE currently contains and supports most of these features, but especially the last two rows are subject of further research.

5.1 Financial Forecasting

Up to now we only have looked upon DSFINANCE as a statical system that aggregates and analyzes the company's accounting and financial statements at one given moment in time. On the contrary, the requirements for a financial planning system state that it is necessary to forecast future payments with suitable procedures to guarantee the company's ability to meet the demands for payment. All cases that require frequent or one-time payment can be extracted directly from the matching accounting item. These cases include interest or amortization payments on loans, or rental payments. Other independent payments have to be forecasted with suitable procedures. The third group of payments depends directly or with a time lag from independent or fixed payments like sales revenues. In Fig. 6 (see Günther (1988)) the existing financial planning systems are classified by their forecasting efforts.

	Busch	Detlefsen FIPLA	Drünkler KUFIPL.	Drünkler MIFIPLAS	Gabele/S. FIBIP	Gabele/S. LIQUIDAS	Gahse DYPOL
Sales	several methods	data from sales	seasonal trend	input	input	input	several methods
Receipt	distri-bution	distri-bution	distri-bution	earnings= receipt	earnings= receipt	distri-bution	several methods
Payment	several methods	% of turnover	from past	input	expenditure= payment	distri-bution	several methods
Indep. payment	input	read from file	n/a	input	input	input	input

Figure 6: Comparison of Forecasting Methods

Method	Method
Projection with internal relations	Additive / multiplicative seasonal adjustment
Simple averages	Arithmetic or geometric extrapolation
Estimating with expected value	Multiple regression
1st order exponential smoothing	Weighted moving averages
2nd order exponential smoothing	Winters
Box-Jenkins	Adaptive filters
Lag distribution of sales revenue	

Figure 7: Forecasting Methods in PCPROG

Our system makes use of PCPROG, a software system for computer aided forecasting of univariate timeseries (see Wiedemann (1988)) developed at our institute. For the forecast of the required univariate time series values very powerful procedures are available. Within the scopes of the dissertation it showed that especially the forecast procedures considered problematic (e.g., Box and Jenkins) are not necessarily the most efficient. Adaptive filtering and 2nd order exponential smoothing proved to be good substitutes when their parameters were estimated good enough. For many procedures PCPROG provides features for automatic selection of parameters from past data, so the user doesn't have to deal with this task explicitly. These procedures can estimate trend and saisonal influences simultaneously. The table in Fig. 7 shows the implemented forecast procedures in DSFINANCE and PCPROG.

Payments that depend in a certain manner from others, will be forecasted in dependence of these. The required values can be estimated with forecast procedures. The

	Busch	Detlefsen FIPLA	Drünkler KUFIPL.	Drünkler MIFIPLAS	Gabele/S. FIBIP	Gabele/S. LIQUIDAS	Gahse DYPOL
Investment-payments	from file	from invest.plan	outside system	outside system	input	outside system	n/a
discount strategy	n/a	several strategies	% from past data	—	—	% from past data	n/a
consider changing prices	n/a	yes	only abs. amount	only abs. amount	only abs. amount	only abs. amount	yes
Finance strategies a) opt. funds b) investm.	 4 3	 6 5	 n/a n/a	 n/a	 12 19	 — —	 — —
Taxes	—	ESt,KSt, GewKSt.	GewSt, KfzSt	GewSt, KfzSt	KSt,GwSt, GSt,VSt	n/a	n/a
Value added tax	n/a	read from file	yes	yes	—	yes	n/a
Depreciation	—	—	—	—	degr./lin./ geom.	—	—

Figure 8: Comparison of Strategies

specific forecast procedure and its estimated parameter will be stored in the matching position of the data structure. With this approach we make sure that every new forecast uses the same procedure.

5.2 Strategies, Simulation and Optimization

For the adaptation of plans to given tasks in preplans the literature describes various methods. Currently, DSFINANCE is only able to offer "what if?"- and "how to achieve?"-analysis, also known as deterministic simulation models. Obviously, this is not satisfying and therefore this is subject of further research. These considerations also include stochastic optimization, like the one Dempster and Ireland (1988) introduced with their system MIDAS, and models using duration (see Alexander and Resnik (1985)) and real stochastic simulation.

5.3 Financial Controlling

The task of financial controlling includes the control of deviation, expressed by different measures, between actual and forecasted values. The most effective measure of error for symmetric deviations seems to be Theil's coefficient. But in certain time series, especially in financial planning, deviations in one direction can be more harmful than in the opposite direction. Suitable measures of error have not yet been implemented in PCPROG. Another way of financial control is the monitoring of various indicators computed from balance-sheets and income statements. For such indicators that can be defined by the user warning limits are available. If the limit is exceeded, the values are inserted into a list of problems. A preselection of some well known financial indicators is listed in the table shown in Fig. 9.

Description	Formula	Value	Warning
CURRENT RATIO	C.ASSETS / C.LIABS	2.0	<1
QUICK RATIO	(C.ASSETS-INV.) / C.LIABS	1.0	<0.8
TIMES INTEREST EARNED RATIO	E.B.I.T. / INTEREST	15.5	<10
FIXED COSTS TO EARNING RATIO	E.B.I.T. / (INTEREST + ADMIN)	6.6	<2
CASH FLOW TO O. LOANS %	CASH FLOW / O.LOANS	10.0	
CURRENT ASSETS TO TOTAL ASSETS %	C.ASSETS / TOTAL ASSETS	53.3	
CURRENT LIABS TO CURRENT LOANS %	C.LIABS / C.LOANS	110.0	>200

Figure 9: Liquidity Ratios

6 Conclusions

Looking at the existing computer aided financial planning systems, one must criticize the missing integration of preplans into the systems. DSFINANCE is designed to be a flexible, dynamical system to present information taken from the balance-sheet and income statement in a clear and structured manner. The core element is the hierarchical data-structure which is constructed by starting with the classification of accounts, closing to positions of the balance-sheet and calculating indicators. Many complex forecasting-methods supplement the projection of data into the future. Automatical selection of the needed parameters is essential. Several controlling-mechanisms can be defined by the user and will be managed by the system. The deviation analysis is implemented by "forward"- and "backward-chaining" and analyzing alternative scenario plans. Future research will include integration of stochastic optimization and duration analysis into the system.

References

ALEXANDER, G.J., and RESNICK B.G. (1985), Using Linear and Goal Programming to Immunize Bond Portfolios, *Journal of Banking and Finance 9*, North-Holland, Amsterdam, 35–54.

BRÜNA, M. (1986), *Liquiditätsplanung*, Oldenbourg, München Wien.

BUSCH, H.W. (1983), *ADV-gestützte Finanzplanung und Finanzkontrolle*, Peter Lang, Frankfurt Bern.

CHMIELEWICZ, K. (1972), *Integrierte Bilanz- und Erfolgsplanung*, Poeschel, Stuttgart.

CHMIELEWICZ, K. (1974), Fallstudie: Integrierte Finanz- und Erfolgsplanung, in: *WiSt Heft 10*, Gabler, Wiesbaden.

DATEV (1989), Kontenrahmen nach dem Bilanzrichtlinien-Gesetz SKR 03, Art.-Nr. 11177.

DEMPSTER, M.A.H., and IRELAND, A.M. (1988), MIDAS: An Expert Debt Management Advisory System, in: *Data, Expert Knowledge and Decisions*, eds. W. Gaul and M. Schader, Springer, Berlin Heidelberg New York.

DRÜNKLER, W. (1983), *Computergestützte Finanzplanung in Klein- und Mittelbetrieben dargestellt am Beispiel eines Großhandelsunternehmens*, Peter Lang, Frankfurt Bern.

DÜRR, M. (1987), *Vergleichende Bilanzanalyse mit Hilfe von Tabellenkalkulationsprogrammen*, Diplomarbeit Augsburg.

GAHSE, S. (1971), *Die neuen Techniken der Finanzplanung mit elektronischer Datenverarbeitung*, Moderne Industrie, München.

GÜNTHER, TH. (1988), Computergestützte Finanzplanung, *Die Betriebswirtschaft, Heft 1*, 109–129.

GUTENBERG, E. (1980), *Grundlagen der Betriebswirtschaftslehre, 3. Band: Die Finanzen*, 8. Aufl., Berlin Heidelberg New York.

HAFNER, S., and WIEDLING, H. (1986), *Liquiditätsplanung auf dem IBM PC*, Gabler, Wiesbaden.

IBM (1987), *Finanz-Informationssystem II, 5777-WAF*, Announcement Letter ZP86–2015, Stuttgart.

KLUŹNIAK, F., and SZPAKOWICZ, S. (1985), *Prolog for Programmers*, Academic Press, London.

LOCAREK, H. (1986), A Concept for Integrated Data Analysis on Microcomputers, in: *Classification as a Tool of Research*, eds. W. Gaul and M. Schader, North-Holland, Amsterdam.

LOCAREK, H. (1988), *Wissensbasierte Systeme zur Durchführung Statistischer Analysen*, Peter Lang, Frankfurt/Bern.

POGUE, G.A., and BUSSARD, R.N. (1971/1972), A linear programming model for short term financial planning under uncertainty, *Sloan Management review, Vol.13*, 69–99.

ROBICHEK, A.A., TEICHROEW, D., and JONES, J.M. (1965), Optimal short Term Financing Decision, *Management Science, Vol.12, No.1, 1–36.*

SCHEER, A.W. (1988), *Wirtschaftsinformatik*, 2. Aufl., Springer, Berlin.

SCHÜTT, W. (1979), *Finanzierung und Finanzplanung deutscher Industrieunternehmen*, Toecher-Mittler, Darmstadt.

STEINER, M., and KÖLSCH, K. (1987), Finanzplanungsrechnungen und -modelle, *Die Betriebswirtschaft, 47.Jg., Heft 4*, 749–763.

WIEDEMANN, R. (1988), *EDV-gestützte Prognoseerstellung für univariate Zeitreihen*, Dissertation, Augsburg.

Applying Data Analysis Techniques to Acquire Knowledge About Database Use and Contents

Rokia Missaoui
Département de mathématiques et d' informatique
Université du Québec à Montréal, Canada

Summary

This paper describes the application of data analysis techniques in the database field. First we present some results of applying this approach to objects such as users and queries in order to capture database usage patterns. Furthermore, we consider ways in which semantic constraints can be captured by applying data analysis techniques to the contents or views of a database. The knowledge acquired by means of this approach is integrated into a knowledge-based system allowing enhanced decision capability with regard to query optimization and database schema refinement.

1 Introduction

The problem of inferring rules from data has become popularly known as a machine learning (see Michalski, Carbonell and Mitchell (1983)). The objective of this paper is to briefly present some applications of data analysis techniques in the database field in order to capture knowledge about the usage patterns and semantics of data. Research in this area is just beginning. Borgida and Williamson (1985) used machine learning techniques to accommodate exceptional information that may occur in a database (e.g., in some special cases, a person may earn more than his/her supervisor), and to refine underlying conceptual schema so that the integrity constraints are consistent with exceptions. Missaoui (1987) applies correspondence (cf. Benzécri (1980)) and cluster analysis (cf. Jambu and Lebeaux (1978)) techniques to a set of database (DB) queries and shows how the knowledge acquired about the usage patterns is used within an expert system aimed at performance optimization and DB schema refinement purposes.

The motivation behind this research is the following:

1. DBs are generally large in size and the complete semantics may be difficult to capture using simple statistics. Moreover, the DB administrator (DBA) may not be aware of accurate and complete semantics of the real world application.

2. DB applications are frequently subject to evolution in their use and structure after the DB design step. Therefore, it is crucial that the DBA be aware of this evolution.

3. Usually DB's are addressed by various types of queries posed by numerous users whose profiles are interesting to determine. Moreover, the well-known rule 20–80 is often true when interacting with a database. So, it would be efficient to determine the relevant relations, attributes and tuples.

NATO ASI Series, Vol. F 61
Knowledge, Data and Computer-Assisted Decisions
Edited by M. Schader and W. Gaul

The paper is organized as follows. We start with a brief overview of the relational model and then we present in section 3 the application of some data analysis (DA) techniques to a set of queries in order to determine the database usage patterns. Section 4 deals with the use of this techniques for capturing the semantics of the database. In section 5, we briefly describe an expert system called ESPOIRS that incorporates pieces of knowledge for database performance optimization purposes. We finally give our conclusion and present some limitations of this approach.

2 Background

A relational database schema (see Maier (1983) and Ullman (1988)) is described by a couple (S, Σ) consisting of a collection of relation schemas $S = \{R_1, R_2, \ldots, R_m\}$ and a set Σ of inter-relational integrity constraints. A relation schema R_i is a pair (U_i, Σ_i) where $U_i = \{A_1, A_2, \ldots, A_j, \ldots, A_n\}$ is a finite set of attributes A_j whose values are taken from domain D_j and Σ_i is a set of data dependencies on U_i. A relation r_i relative to the schema R_i is said to be an instance or extension of R_i and consists of a finite set of mappings of U_i over the corresponding domains. Each mapping is represented by a tuple noted $t[A_1, \ldots, A_n]$. A key of a relation is a set of attributes whose values identify a unique tuple. A database extension is a set of relations extensions $r_1, r_2, \ldots, r_m$ which verify all the constraints of the set Σ. One of the most important and well-known integrity constraints is functional dependency introduced by Codd (1970).

A relation $R_i(A_1, \ldots, A_n)$ satisfies the functional dependency: $X \rightarrow Y$, where X and Y are subsets of $\{A_1, \ldots, A_n\}$, if for every pair of tuples t_1 and t_2 of r_i, $t_1[X] = t_2[X] \Longrightarrow t_1[Y] = t_2[Y]$. In other words, X determines Y if to each value of X corresponds a unique value of Y.

Query optimization in database systems consists of choosing a good execution strategy for processing a query (see Jarke and Koch (1984) for a survey). It remains a challenging and important research field. Much research has been conducted on various aspects of query optimization among which we cite the following: fast implementation of basic operations, especially the join operation; heuristics for efficient query processing, optimal selection of indexes (see Piatetsky-Shapiro (1983)), efficient physical organization of data such as records clustering (see Yu and Chen (1985)). Yet another aspect of query optimization deals with the semantic constraints of a database and consists into transforming a query into a semantically equivalent one which may be executed more efficiently (cf. King (1984), Jarke (1986), Shenoy and Ozsoyoglu (1987)).

For the purposes of illustration, a part of a medical database will be used. The underlined attributes represent the keys of relation.

- HOSPITAL (<u>HCODE</u>, HNAME, ADDRESS, HCAPACITY)
- UNIT(<u>HCODE</u>, <u>UCODE</u>, UNAME, UCAPACITY, PRCODE) where PRCODE is the code of the paramedic responsible for the care-unit
- DOCTOR (<u>DCODE</u>, DNAME, SPECIALIZATION, DSALARY), where DNAME, and DSALARY are respectively the name and the salary of the doctor
- PATIENT (<u>PCODE</u>, PNAME, BIRTH, SEX, ADMIT, HCODE, UCODE), where PNAME and ADMIT are respectively the name of the patient and his date of admission to the hospital.

- PARAMED (PRCODE, PRNAME, FUNCTION, PRSALARY, PBONUS, HCODE, UCODE), where PRNAME, PRSALARY and PBONUS are the name, the salary and the bonus of the paramedic.

3 Database Use Analysis

Our objective is to use DA techniques to capture the hidden structure of the relationships that may exist between objects such as queries, users, relations and attributes. These relationships may be useful for the DBA. For example, if the DBA learns that the two relations R_1 and R_2 are rarely involved in a same query, then he will discard the possibility to store the tuples of R_1 and R_2 within a same cluster.

In order to capture knowledge about the DB usage, we applied correspondence and cluster analysis techniques for a set of 50 retrieval queries formulated by 6 users of the medical DB described before. The relations scanned during the execution of queries are among the variables used in the analysis. More details can be found in Missaoui (1987).

For an easy understanding of the output, the identification of individuals is a four-characters code in which:

- the first character is the user's code (e.g. A or B, ...)
- the second one is the number of relations involved in the query (e.g., the value 3 means a join between three relations of the DB)
- the last two digits represent a query sequence number.

A subset of the output of the analysis (Fig. 1 and Fig. 2) is the following:

- It is scarce that the relations HOSPITAL and DOCTOR are together present in a query because Fig. 1 reflects two opposite positions for the corresponding variables (abbreviated as HOPI and MEDE).
- The relation UNIT is frequently joined with the relation HOSPITAL. This fact will be referenced further as F_1.
- The relation UNIT is always involved in queries that use more than one relation (e.g., join queries). This fact will be referenced further as F_2.
- User D frequently formulates unary queries (e.g., queries referencing one relation) while user B tends to express complex ones.
- Unary queries referencing the relation HOSPITAL are more frequently formulated by user D.
- There are five distinct classes of queries: 57, 95, 86, 93, and 94 (see Fig. 2). For example, the class 93 includes queries with a prevalence of the relation PATIENT and a rare occurrence of the relation DOCTOR.

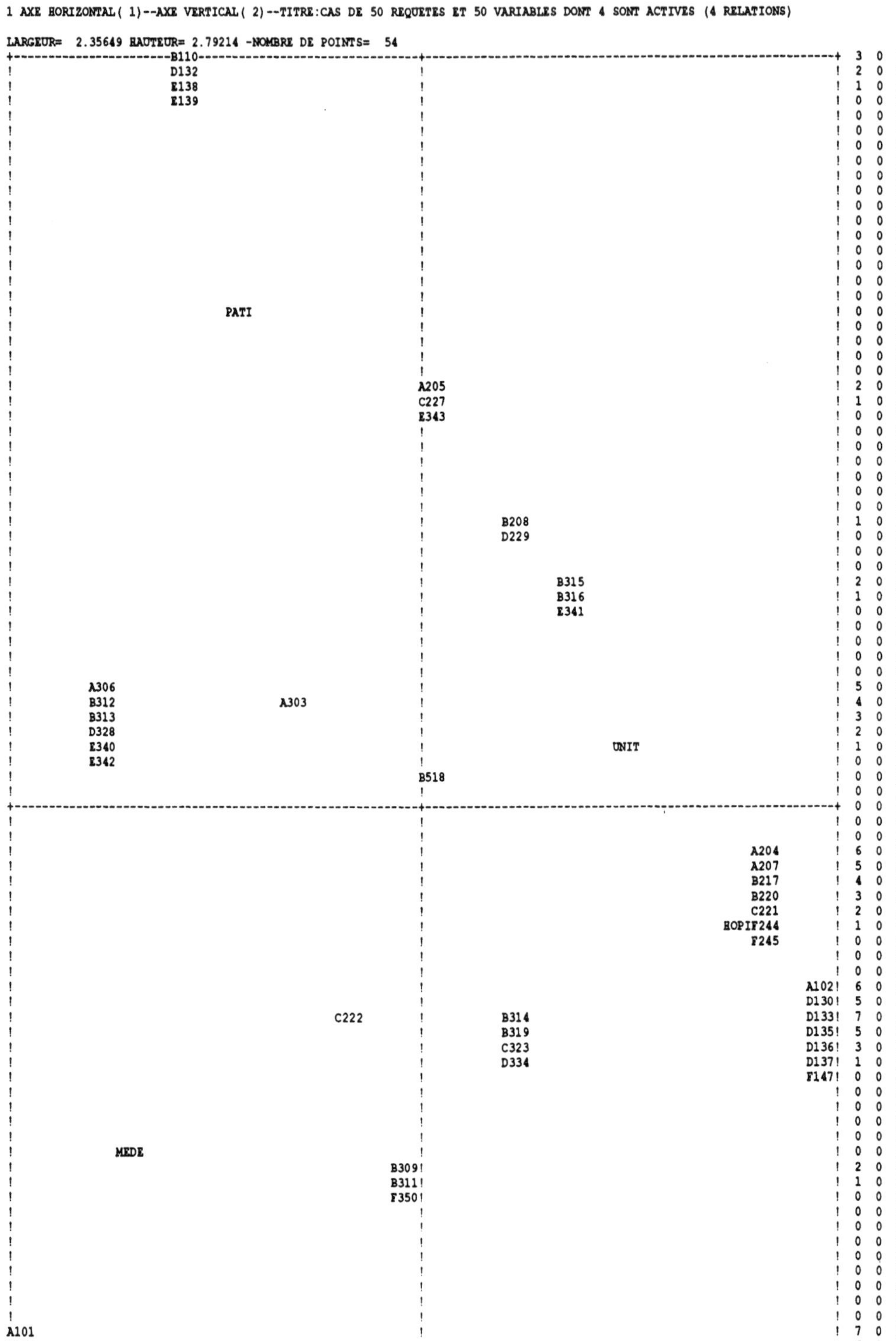

Figure 1: A Scatter Diagram Representing Queries and Relations

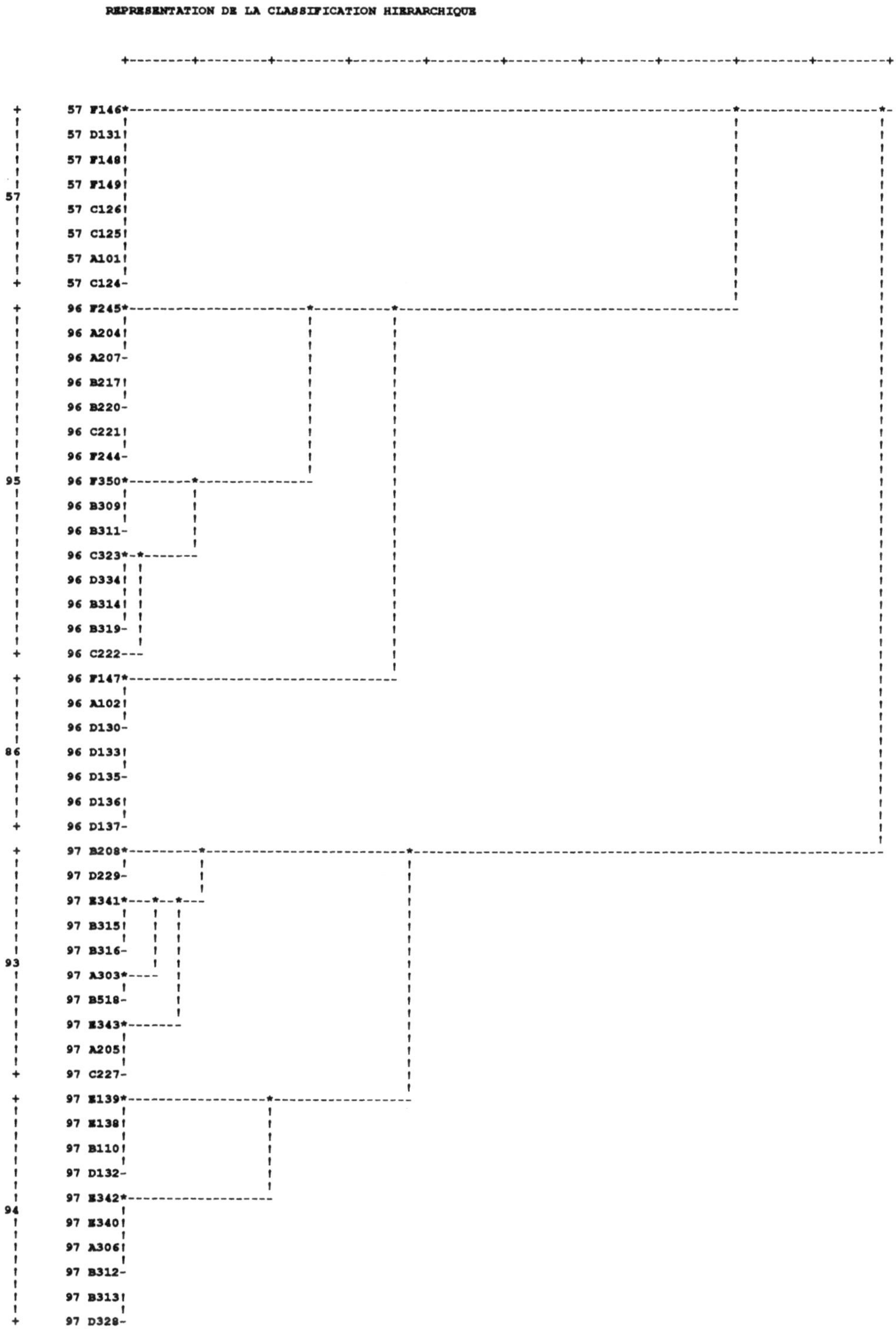

Figure 2: Classification of Queries According to the Relations Used

4 Database Structure Analysis

Semantic constraints are of growing importance in many DB research areas, including query optimization, integrity enforcement and database design. When a DB is being designed, the administrator is aware of many integrity constraints concerning the DB considered but he has not necessarily the knowledge about the whole semantics. Moreover, a DB schema may evolve in time so that it becomes necessary to refine the underlying schema in order to capture the accurate semantics. Our objective is to supply the DBA with tools for capturing some hidden semantics about the DB used and for checking if the existing DB schema accurately captures the real world the application dealt with.

Here we restrict our experiments to 280 individuals representing a view (of paramedics) which is obtained using the following SQL query:

```
SELECT PARAMED.PRCODE, FUNCTION, PBONUS, UNIT.HCODE, UCAPACITY,
       UNIT.PRCODE
FROM   PARAMED, UNIT
WHERE  PARAMED.HCODE = UNIT.HCODE
AND    PARAMED.UCODE = UNIT.UCODE.
```

Then, the structure of the resulting tuples includes the following variables:

- the identification of the paramedic
- his function (F)
- his bonus (B)
- the hospital in which he works (H)
- the care-unit where he is assigned (U)
- the capacity of the care-unit (C)
- the code of the responsible for the care-unit (R).

Each variable A_i of n modalities has been converted into n disjunctive variables A_{i1}, A_{i2}, ..., A_{ip}, ..., A_{in} (i.e., the variable A_{ip} is set to 1 if the modality p is true and 0 if not). For example, the variable F9 corresponds to the modality 9 of the function F.

For an easy understanding of the output, the identification of individuals (paramedics) is set to a four-character code in which:

- the first character is the hospital code where the considered employee works
- the second one is the unit code (within a hospital)
- the third one is the code of the function practised by the employee
- the last one is a sequence number within a same function of the same care-unit.

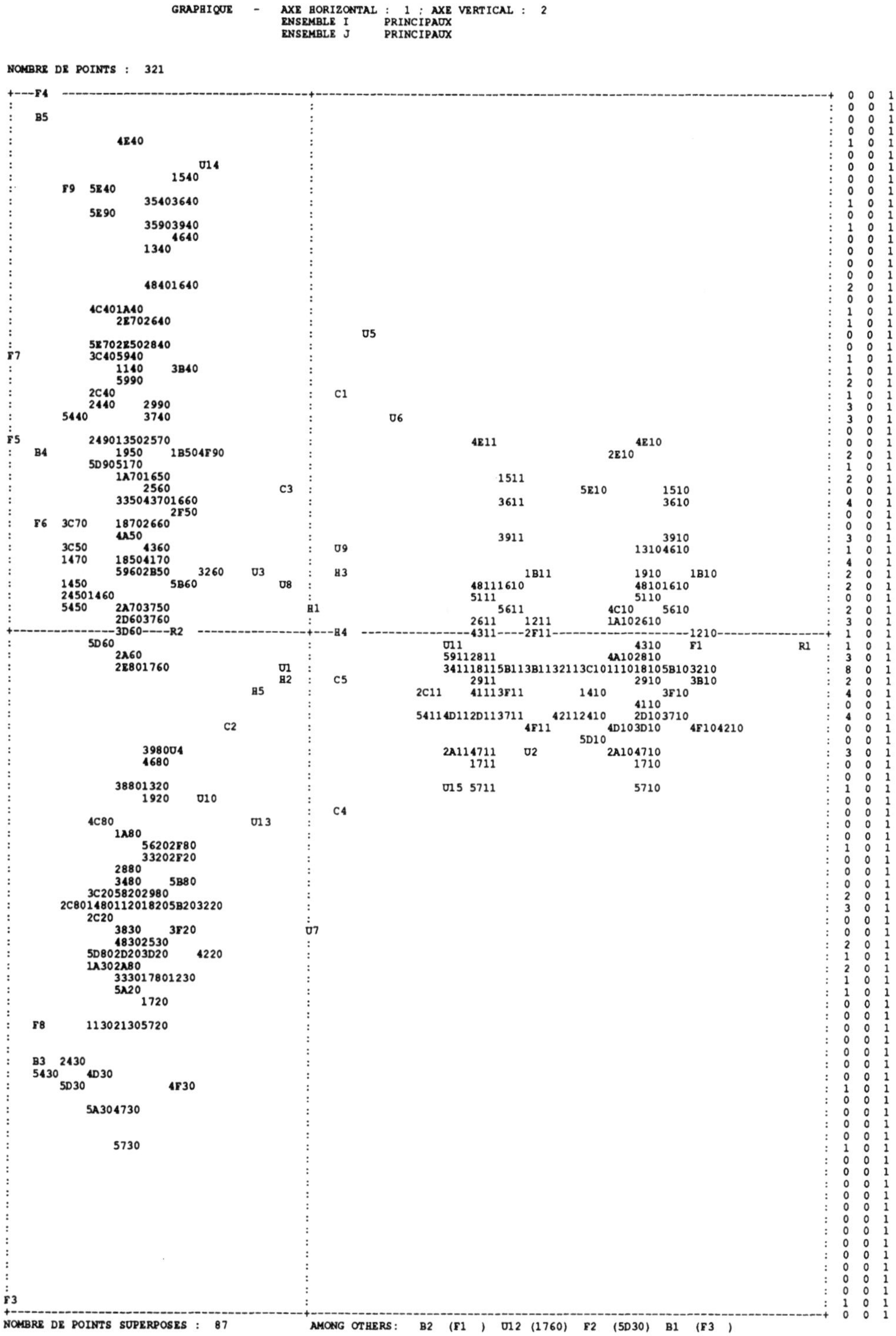

Figure 3a: A Scatter Diagram Representing Tuples and Attributes

Example:
The individual identified by the code 1780 represents the first encountered employee of the care-unit 7 of the hospital 8 who has the function 0.

In order to be partial and rigorous, the interpretation of the correspondence analysis output has been conducted by a specialist in data analysis techniques who has no knowledge about the use and semantics of the DB. The scatter diagram in Fig. 3a shows that the first axis reflects two groups within the paramedics population. At the right side we get the employees that are nurses (including male nurses) while at the opposite side we get the employees that practise other functions. The individuals exhibited in the right hand side are divided into two groups of employees: those who are close to the variable R1 (i.e., those having the property "responsible") and those who are not close to R1. We also notice that the variable F1 (i.e., nurses) is close to R1. This leads to the following rule:

Rule 1 If an employee is responsible for a care-unit then he/she is a nurse.

This integrity constraint (IC) called implication IC by Shenoy and Ozsoyoglu (1987) may be represented by a Horn clause as:

PARAMED.FUNCTION = 'NURSE' ← UNIT.PRCODE = PARAMED.PRCODE

The reverse of this statement (i.e., if an employee is a nurse, then he/she is responsible for a care-unit) is not true since the right side of the first axis exhibits two groups of individuals: those who have the properties F1 and R1 altogether and those who have the properties F1 and R2.

Moreover, Fig. 3b shows that the variables F_i are partioned into 5 subsets corresponding to the 5 variables B_j. This means that when we know a particular F_i (i.e., a particular value of the paramedic's function), then we know the corresponding value for B_j. This leads to the following IC:

Rule 2 PARAMEDIC.FUNCTION → PARAMED.PBONUS.

The converse of this statement is not true since there may be more than one F_i for a particular B_j.

It is important to notice that the knowledge captured using DA techniques reflects much more tendencies than exact rules. The ICs discovered can be useful for:

- query optimization purposes (see Kambayashi and Yoshikawa (1983), Missaoui (1987)). For example, the following query becomes trivial using the rule 1 above: "what are the distinct functions practised by the responsible for the care-units ?".

- schema refinement. For example, if the DBA had no knowledge about the rule 2, this newly captured functional dependency between F_i and B_j will force the DBA to revise the DB schema by applying the normalization process to the table PARAMED, leading to the two following tables:
  PARAMED (<u>PRCODE</u>, PRNAME, FUNCTION, PRSALARY, HCODE, UCODE)
  FUNCT_BONUS (<u>FUNCTION</u>, PBONUS)

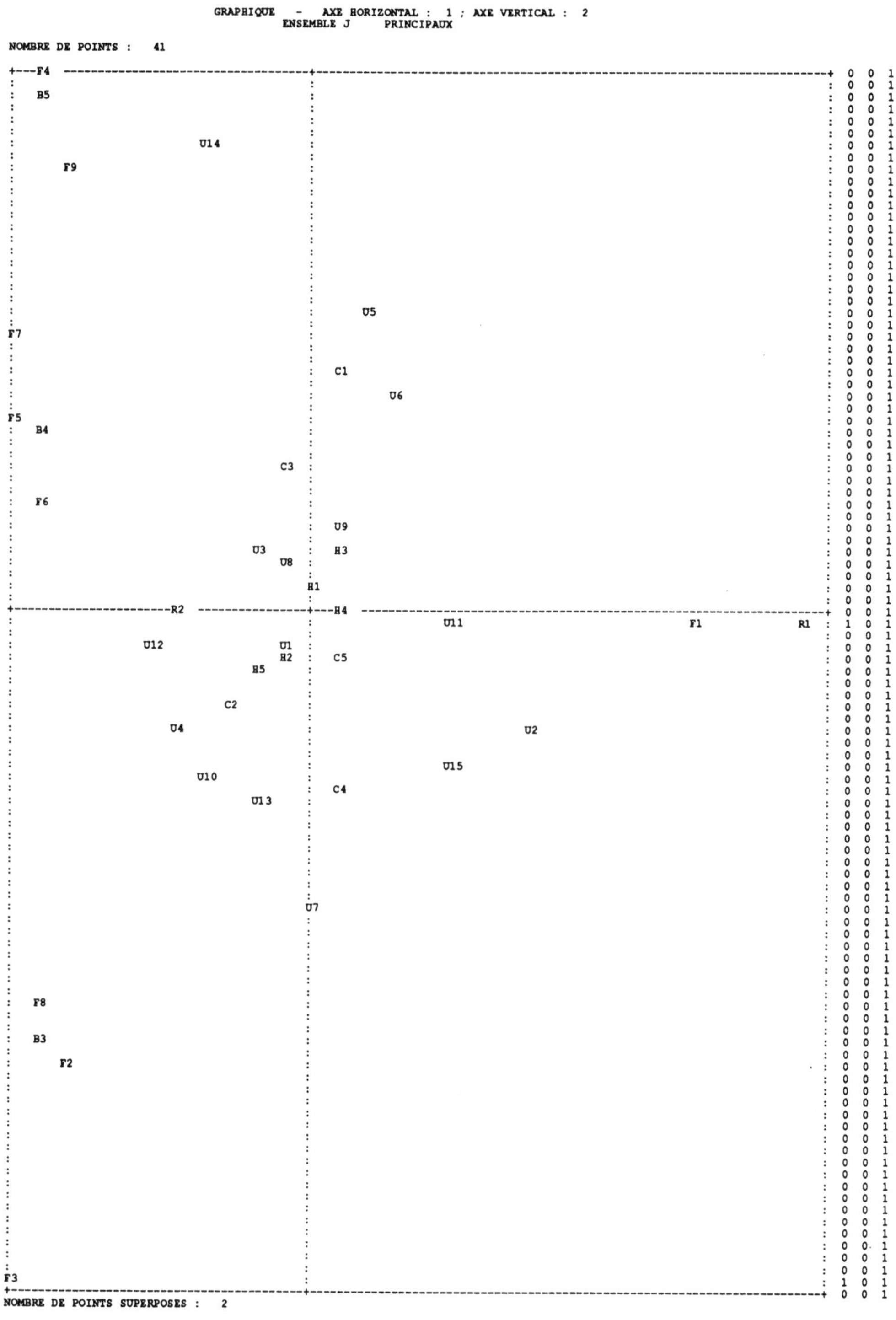

Figure 3b: A Scatter Diagram Representing Attributes

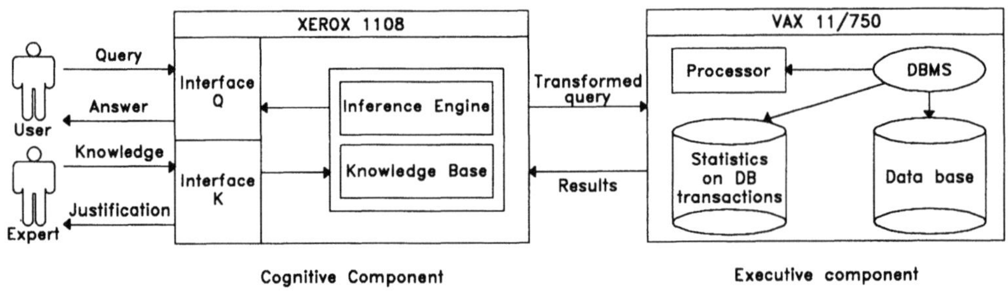

Figure 4: The Architecture of ESPOIRS

5 A Knowledge-Based System for DB Performance Optimization

The elements described before are integrated within the system ESPOIRS (an Expert System for Performance Optimization In a Relational System) currently implemented in LOOPS (see Bobrow and Stefik (1983)) on a Xerox workstation, and connected to a Vax 11/750 using the system Oracle (cf. Oracle (1986)). Fig. 4 shows the architecture of ESPOIRS (see Missaoui (1987)) which includes two components:

- A cognitive component that acts like a competent user. This component receives the user's query, parses it and transforms it into an equivalent one whose execution by the second component is likely to be more efficient. Moreover, it suggests efficient storage strategies and access methods and contributes to the enforcement of the DB integrity. The knowledge (K) base includes properties of the relational model, optimization rules for the DBMS considered as well as the physical, logical and transactional description of the DB used. Besides the knowledge base (KB), the cognitive component incorporates two interfaces Q and K helping in the manipulation of the DB and the KB respectively. The interface Q offers at the present time two ways to introduce a query: direct formulation in SQL language and an iconic menu which assists the user in introducing his query. Once formulated, the query is then converted into an intermediate formalism and is also represented by a query graph if it involves a join operation. The interface K allows the expert user (as opposed to the application user) acquire some meta-knowledge (e.g., information about the different classes of K, the meaning of some heuristics, the methods that reference a selected piece of knowledge).

- An executive component on a VAX 11/750 for the effective processing of queries. It includes the following elements: the DB management system (DBMS), the DB and the processor which interfaces between the expert system and the DBMS.
  The knowledge obtained from the data analysis techniques can be used by ESPOIRS to answer some queries without accessing the DB, and to help to enforce integrity constraints. Moreover, ESPOIRS may take advantage of this knowledge for suggesting to the DBA a physical reorganization of data or a refinement of the conceptual schema for the underlying DB.

Example:
Considering a physical DB reorganization the following facts and rules represent a subset of the knowledge base:

- F_1: the most frequent join is the one between the relations HOSPITAL and UNIT
- F_2: the relation UNIT is not involved in unary queries
- the size of the relation HOSPITAL is 19 pages of 2 K bytes
- the size of the relation UNIT is 107 pages of 2 K bytes.
- Heuristic: *If* two relations R_1 and R_2 are the most frequently joined ones *and* the less voluminous relation has a low probability to be scanned alone or together with another relation R_3 *then* it is performant to store R_1 and R_2 within a same cluster using the join attributes for clustering.

Using the above pieces of knowledge, the expert system will suggest a physical clustering of the records belonging to the two relations HOSPITAL and UNIT.

6 Conclusion and Further Research

By analyzing and acquiring knowledge about the use and the semantics of a database, and then integrating this knowledge within an expert system, we can ensure that this system is in tune with the needs of the users, reflects most of the semantics of the DB used and provides a more efficient tool for improving understandability and maintainability of complex DB application. This approach may be useful in discovering new rules (e.g., the rule 1 referenced in section 3) or temporary knowledge (e.g., at this moment, there is no physician whose specialization is pediatrics). The knowledge captured reflects much more tendencies than exact rules. However, it is our opinion that the application of data analysis techniques in the DB field presents some limitations:

- the complexity of a DB schema such as a large amount of attributes (variables) and a great number of possible modalities of the attributes, may force the analyst to decompose his task into a sequence of partial analysis steps, or to take a subject of the DB schema, or to consider a snapshot of the DB usage and contents, or to appeal to a preliminary time-consuming step of codification.
- it is less trivial to capture a dependency between composite attributes than one between elementary attributes. As an example, the functional dependency {HCODE, UCODE } $\rightarrow$ UCAPACITY was not detected by this approach because the determinant is a composite attribute.
- DA results are not easy to interpret by a novice. We are currently investigating the use of the symbolic analysis approach proposed by Diday (1988) to deal with imprecise queries and to establish a taxonomy of queries expressed as symbolic objects.

Acknowledgements

I am grateful to Robert Latour and Ameur Boujenoui (Ecole des Hautes Etudes Commerciales) for their helpful comments about applying data analysis techniques. This research has been supported by the Natural Sciences and Engineering Research Council of Canada under grant No OGP0041899.

References

BENZÉCRI, J.P., and BENZÉCRI, F. (1980), *Pratique de l' analyse des données. Analyse des correspondances, exposé élémentaire*, Dunod, Paris.

BOBROW, D.G., and STEFIK, M. (1983), *The LOOPS Manual*, Xerox, Palo Alto Research Center.

BORGIDA, A., and WILLIAMNON, K.E. (1985), Accommodating Exceptions in Databases, and Refining the Schema by Learning from them, *Proceedings of the Eleventh Conference on Very Large Data Bases*, Stockholm, 72–81.

CODD, E.F. (1970), A Relational model of data for large shared data banks, *Communication of ACM*, *13*, *6*, 377–387.

DIDAY, E. (1988), Introduction à l' analyse des données symboliques, in: *Symboliques—Numériques pour l' apprentissage des connaissances à partir des observations*, eds. E. Diday and Y. Kodratoff, Université Paris IX (Dauphine), CEREMADE.

JAMBU, M., and LEBEAUX, M.O. (1978), *Classification Automatique pour l' analyse des données*, Dunod, Paris.

JARKE, M. (1986), External Semantic Query Simplification: A Graph-Theoretic Approach and its Implementation in Prolog, in: *Expert Database Systems, proc. First International Workshop*, ed. N. Kerschberg, 675–692.

JARKE, M., and KOCH, J. (1984), Query Optimization in Relational Database Systems, *Computing Surveys, 16, 2*, 111–152.

KAMBAYASHI, Y., and YOSHIKAWA, M. (1983), Query Processing utilizing dependencies and horizontal decomposition, *ACM SIGMOD*, San Jose, 55–67.

KING, J.J. (1984), *Query optimization by semantic reasoning*. UMI Research Press.

MAIER, D. (1983), *The Theory of Relational Databases*, Computer Science Press.

MICHALSKI, R., CARBONELL, J., and MITCHELL, T. (1983), *Machine Learning: An Artificial Intelligence Approach*, Tioga Publishing Company.

MISSAOUI, R. (1987), *Optimisation des Performances d' un système expert*, thèse de doctorat, Université de Montréal.

ORACLE (1986), *Oracle Database Administrator's Guide*, version 5.1, Oracle Corp., Menlo Park.

PIATETSKY-SHAPIRO, G. (1983), The optimal selection of indexes is NP-complete, *ACM SIGMOD, 13, 2*, 72–75.

SHENOY, S.T., and OZSOYOGLU, Z.M. (1987), A System for Semantic Query Optimization, *ACM SIGMOD*, 181–195.

ULLMAN, J.D. (1988), *Principles of Database and Knowledge-Base Systems*, vol. 1, Computer Science Press, New York.

YU, C.T., and CHEN, C.H. (1985), Adaptive Information System Design One Query at a Time, *International Conference On Management of Data, ACM SIGMOD*, 280–290.

Knowledge Acquisition for a Diagnosis-Based Task

Daniel E. O'Leary and Paul R. Watkins
Graduate School of Business
University of Southern California, Los Angeles, U.S.A.

Summary

The basic research task discussed in this paper is the investigation of the relative effectiveness of alternative knowledge acquisition methodologies at eliciting different types of knowledge for a diagnosis task. In order to investigate this task, a field study was used.

The scope of the study was to elicit the knowledge required to build an expert system to solve a diagnosis task. The study was designed to solve a specific problem within a specific organization. However, because of the generic diagnosis nature of the task, the study and design of the system offers insights into knowledge acquisition in similar settings.

The study used four basic forms of knowledge acquisition and identified at least five different types of knowledge used in the solution of the diagnosis problem. Further, it was found that different forms of knowledge acquisition were more effective in the elicitation of the different types of knowledge. Finally, an entire portfolio of approaches was necessary to elicit the knowledge to construct the system.

1 Introduction

Recently, there has been dissatisfaction with the knowledge elicitation and acquisition literature. In particular, there has been concern over which knowledge acquisition approaches should be used. Researchers have responded with theoretical discussions of which types of approaches should be used. Unfortunately, for each approach that is suggested as plausible, alternative arguments can be presented to make other approaches equally as plausible. Researchers also have begun to employ experimental techniques in an effort to see which technique can be used to 'best' establish the knowledge base for an expert system (e.g., Burton et al. (1987)). Clearly, it is important to use appropriate methodologies to examine the problems of knowledge acquisition: purely logical or theoretical approaches are incomplete. However, it is also true that a single approach to knowledge acquisition rarely is used to build an expert system. In addition, the use of a single approach is likely to result in a single dimensional system. As a result, it is important to study the process of building expert systems and the employment of a portfolio of knowledge acquisition approaches.

As with previous experimental research, such an inquiry is likely to be specific to the generic type of system (e.g., diagnostic) and the domain (e.g., business). However, it is also important to not divorce the investigation too much from the setting and the resulting experiences in which the experts are based (e.g., Kolodner and Riesbeck (1986)). Thus, in order to capture the context, such systems could be developed in the particular firm or organization.

NATO ASI Series, Vol. F 61
Knowledge, Data and Computer-Assisted Decisions
Edited by M. Schader and W. Gaul

1.1 Field Study Research

Even though there appears to be a generic nature to particular tasks (e.g., Hayes-Roth et al. (1983)), the domain and the organizational setting of the task can play a critical aspect in the expertise, and thus, the knowledge acquisition, associated with the task. One way to study the issue of the effectiveness of alternative knowledge acquisition methods for such generic-like systems, yet still allow for context is to use a field study.

That is the methodology used in this paper. As discussed by Kaplan (1964), "Much of ... science is occupied with field studies, that is, with direct or indirect observation of behavior in the circumstances in which it occurs without any significant intervention on the part of the observer. ... Of course in his role as a consulting expert the ... scientist may be taking part in some part of an experiment. We should not overlook the opportunities for genuine and important scientific work afforded by this social role".

The field study approach to expert systems has been used in previous research. For example, Watkins and O'Leary (1987) present a paper that employs a field study approach to the study of the development of expert systems by consulting experts.

1.2 This Paper

This paper proceeds as follows. Section 1 has presented an introduction to the paper and the approach. Section 2 discusses diagnosis-based systems, in general, and for the particular application of this paper. Section 3 reviews the four basic knowledge acquisition approaches used to develop the system discussed in this paper. Section 4 discusses the findings. Section 5 provides a brief summary of the paper.

2 Diagnosis and Diagnosis Systems

Typically, in diagnosis, a situation is presented to an investigator. The investigator is then asked to determine what is wrong or how to remedy the situation. This requires eliciting data on the situation and then recognizing patterns of problems from that data. Based on the patterns recognized, possible solutions are suggested, as part of the diagnosis, to solve the problem in the situation. Thus, the quality of the diagnosis is based on the ability to solicit the appropriate situation information and to recognize the resulting patterns. One without the other is useless.

Expert systems designed to solve diagnosis problems have been developed for applications in medicine (e.g., Buchanan and Shortliffe (1985)), mining (e.g., Duda et al. (1979)), and business (Meservy (1985)). Hayes-Roth et al. (1983) describe diagnosis expert systems in the following manner: "Diagnosis systems infer system malfunctions from observables. ... Diagnosis systems typically relate observed behavioral irregularities with underlying causes ...".

Diagnosis tasks have been among the most successfully modeled activities using expert systems technology (Hayes-Roth et al. (1983)). As with human diagnosis, computer diagnosis is dependent on the ability of the system to solicit the appropriate information, from which patterns can be elicited.

2.1 Particular Diagnosis Task Used in the Field Study

Because of the widespread nature of such tasks, we choose a diagnosis situation to determine what knowledge acquisition approaches "worked best". The particular task was diagnosing communications problems for a large timesharing software company.

In particular, the company has a number of clients that use programs on a time sharing basis, via communications to the company's central computer. The users of those systems are not sophisticated computer users. As a result, the company employs a large base of technicians to assist these users with problems they may have using the software. Included in this base of problems that technicians must address are communications problems (modems, etc.).

The technicians are located at a central location to which users refer all questions on their use of the software. All questions are answered over the phone. Either the questions are solved while the user is on the initial call or the technician will call back with the information. Sometimes this is an iterative process, with the technician offering a solution, getting feedback from the user and then offering another solution.

Since the diagnosis is off-site, the information must be gathered by someone other than the person doing the diagnosis. This person typically is not a sophisticated communications expert.

Unfortunately, the 'technicians' often come into their role without adequate understanding of the technology. In addition, the underlying technology continually changes. Further, these technician positions experience rapid turnover. When they completely understand the technology, they are attractive to other departments or firms. As a result, the company must continually educate the technicians about communications and other problems. This education process takes the form of direct education and indirect apprenticeship-like learning.

In each case the training is facilitated by documentation, that also is useful in the assistance of technicians on a day-to-day basis. The documentation consisted of segments of manufacturer's documentation, additional documentation on internally developed software and 'tips' on recent problems. Typically, these 'tips' are developed by the more expert technicians in response to recent events that have the potential to affect a number of different clients, and thus, technicians.

2.2 Scope of This Paper

The scope of this paper is to investigate multiple forms of knowledge acquisition for the development of a system. This is in contrast to much of the formal investigation of alternative forms of knowledge acquisition (e.g., Burton et al. (1987)) which has examined tasks that may or may not ultimately lead to the development of an actual system.

3 Knowledge Acquisition for a Diagnosis System

As part of the construction of the system, knowledge acquisition was initiated. In that field study, a portfolio of four different approaches knowledge acquisition process were employed: Interview, Observation (watching technicians and listening to phone calls),

Phone Taps (with scripts) and Examination of Documentation (used for education of the technicians and reference by the technicians).

3.1 Interviews

The initial approach used was interviews. This took two primary forms:

- interviews with individuals and
- a meeting with a group of seven technicians of varying experience.

The interviews were unstructured. However, the focus of the interviews was on how experienced technicians identify and solve communications problems.

The interview approach led to the understanding that this was a complex diagnosis problem. Again and again, the technicians indicated that,

1. there were many different communications problems,
2. in some cases, the problems were difficult to identify over the phone and
3. that there were alternative ways to solve these different problems.

The group interview process suggested that some solution approaches were better than others. Further, more experienced technicians (and higher in the managerial hierarchy) kept indicating that there was a substantial difference in their understanding of communications problems, as compared to lower level personnel.

The interview process was employed with the understanding that the context of the firm, clients and experiences are critical (e.g., Kolodner and Riesbeck (1986)). As a result, the interviews were done on site at the firm and in the department. In addition, the interviews stressed the use of examples to illustrate discussions and facilitate further discussion of given points. Thus, interviewees would relate their experiences with particular clients to illustrate certain concepts.

3.2 Observation

Observation at the firm's location of the technicians took two primary forms.

1. The technicians were observed for their 'external' problem solving process. That is, what kinds of behavior did they use when they solved problems.
2. We were permitted to listen in on calls from clients that dealt with communications issues, in order to understand what processes were used by the technicians to identify and solve client problems.

The first approach was particularly fruitful in seeing what the technicians *physically* do when they solve diagnosis problems, in general. It also was useful in determining what knowledge they used to solve problems and the form in which that knowledge was stored. In order to assist them in the decision process the technicians would, for example, go over to a modem on-site in order to visualize the problem. Buttons would be pressed, directories would be entered and files would be run. Since the technicians were not on site, it was found that they needed to visualize what was happening at the client's operations.

The technicians also made extensive use of the documentation. In general, the most experienced analysts did not use the documentation, but they were able to refer other technicians to where in the documentation certain information could be found. Less experienced technicians typically made use of personal notes to find where they had previously found particular items in the documentation. The most inexperienced technicians found movement through the documentation difficult, since they did not understand many of the basic concepts and had no experience with much of its contents.

The second approach was less fruitful. Since communications calls occurred only seldom during the period of the study (which was purposely not during the 'rush' season), there were hours spent just waiting for a phone call to occur, only to find that it was not a communications problem after all.

Since it was unpredictable when communications calls would occur, we left tape recorders so that the technicians would be able to tape the appropriate phone calls. The tape recorders were left with multiple levels of technicians, ranging from relatively new technicians to the more experienced technicians. This was done so that alternative problem solving styles could be observed and summarized.

Strangely enough, whenever a communications call occurred either the technician 'forgot' to turn on the tape recorder or the technician could not get the tape recorder to 'work'. This led to an alternative approach to ensure that the calls would be recorded.

3.3 Phone Taps

Phone taps were made to further analyze the technician's solution of diagnosis problems. Skeleton scripts were prepared in conjunction with management, and given to another department that understood communications problems. The phone calls from the scripts were represented to the technicians as coming from legitimate clients. The scripts even went to the extent of providing legitimate client numbers so that it would appear that the calls were from clients. The technicians did not know that the calls were staged.

The same scripts were used to interrogate different technicians to determine the similarity of alternative solution generation processes. The scripts were developed to test the expected range of anticipated responses of the technicians. The scripts were developed to elicit both surface knowledge and deep knowledge about the application. Then the scripts were compared for differences used in problem solving.

The phone tap scripts had the advantage of having an external party record the calls. In addition, the use of the scripts also guaranteed the ability to have multiple responses to the same questions, from different technicians. This allowed the examination of the similarity of the technicians problem solving processes.

3.4 Examination of Documentation

The final form of knowledge acquisition had the best initial structure. It entailed a detailed examination of the existing documentation.

Since there is substantial turnover of personnel, the firm has been concerned with documenting the communications diagnosis process for educational and reference purposes. As a result, the documentation serves a purpose of providing reference material for the technicians, should they forget or not understand a particular process. Further, changes to the communications environment are constantly occurring and thus, need to be documented. The communications process documentation included both the original manufacture's documentation on, e.g., modems and the time-sharing vendors additional documentation.

The documentation took the form of checklists, to-do lists and straight summaries of information. Unfortunately, the knowledge was highly fragmented. Information on communications appeared in a number of places in the written documentation.

Since the documentation was detailed and designed to educate the technician about communications problems, it is also useful for 'educating a computer program'—not just a human technician. Further since it was designed for educating technicians, it was sufficiently detailed so that an understanding of the documentation yielded important understanding for the particular communications problem investigated.

4 Findings

The field study scope included the development of an expert system and the corresponding necessary knowledge acquisition to solve the diagnosis problem. The knowledge acquisition effort led to the determination of at least five different types of knowledge and the finding that different knowledge acquisition methods were more effective at identifying those different kinds of knowledge. The use of a single approach would have been impossible or yielded an ineffective system. After using all four of these knowledge acquisition methodologies we identified five primary findings.

4.1 Extent of Knowledge

The diagnosis process is, in part, a knowledge intensive process. Expertise is a function of knowledge about certain key characteristics. For example, the technician must be familiar with the particular types of modems. Lack of knowledge of a particular type of modem differentiates the 'more expert' from the 'less expert'. Thus, a critical issue in building this diagnosis system was obtaining enough relevant and timely knowledge for the system. For example, in order to 'make a difference' knowledge about each of the modems used by their clients must be in the system.

The interview process was helpful in identifying the extent of knowledge necessary to solve the problem. However, because there was such extensive documentation, the documentation established clearly the extent of knowledge required.

4.2 Integrative Knowledge

Even though the documentation in its entirety provides virtually all the relevant technical facts, it is highly fragmented. That fragmentation does not inhibit the more expert users, who have developed a familiarity with the fragmentation. However, that fragmentation does have an impact on the less experienced technicians, who have difficulty finding information. The system that was developed mitigated that difficulty in the communications area by providing a knowledge base that integrated that knowledge.

The need for integrative knowledge rapidly became apparent in the investigation of the documentation. Observation showed that the less experienced technicians had notes to facilitate the use of the documentation, while the most inexperienced had to continually consult the expert users. A reader of the documentation needed knowledge that integrated, e.g., modems and occurrences to modems, different types of modems, etc.

4.3 Data Solicitation Knowledge

One type of knowledge only used to a limited extent in the documentation was what we called 'data solicitation knowledge'. As noted above, a critical variable in the recognition of patterns of causation, is the extent to which the appropriate data has been solicited. This knowledge was referred to data solicitation knowledge. In the system discussed here that is particularly critical since the clients that call the technicians may know absolutely nothing about the communication process or equipment.

Much of the documentation was aimed at what solutions were to particular problems, rather than what questions should be asked to determine what knowledge was required. These questions were as simple as "what has happened since the last time you used the system?". This type of knowledge differentiated the 'more' expert from the 'less' expert. It is critical to assuring that the technician moves down the correct path. This knowledge primarily was identified from the scripts and from the interview process. This knowledge was manifested in the system, by the rules designed to ferret out this information.

4.4 Ordering of the Groups of Knowledge

The results from the different scripts and the interviews indicated that 'more expert' technicians and 'less expert' technicians sometimes differed in their solution approaches to different problems. One cause of such differences was their ordering of the information search process. Different orderings can result in substantially different decision trees being established. This was manifested in the system by the order of the rules.

4.5 Word and Picture-Based Knowledge

Finally, the technicians used more than just 'word-based' knowledge to solve the diagnosis problems. Observation and interview found that technicians often had to 'see' what was happening.

In order for the system to meet the behavioral needs of the technicians, this means that pictoral-based knowledge facilitates understanding of the problem. That is, pictures and the ability to do things to the pictures were found to be a critical issue in the successful representation of the knowledge for the solution of the diagnosis problems the technicians solved.

5 Summary

This paper discussed the knowledge acquisition required for the development of a system to diagnose communication problems for users of a large mainframe time sharing system. The investigation employed a field study approach in order to exploit the experiences and existing knowledge structures of the technicians. The paper finds that multiple forms of knowledge acquisition and representation were required for the development of the system. A portfolio of approaches was required.

No one form of knowledge acquisition was found to provide insight into each of the different types of knowledge that ultimately were used in the development of the system. Thus, this study suggests that individual task comparisons of different forms of knowledge acquisition may understate or misstate the problems of interest to developers of expert systems. Individual approaches each have their own strengths and weaknesses so that in a portfolio of approaches, weaknesses of one approach can be mitigated by strengths of other approaches.

References

BUCHANAN, B., and SHORTLIFFE, E. (1985), *Rule-based Expert Systems*, Addison-Wesley, Reading, MA.

BURTON, A., SHADBOLT, N., HEDGECOCK, A., and RUSS, R. (1987), *A Formal Evaluation of Knowledge Elicitation Techniques for Expert Systems*, Proceedings of the First European Workshop on Knowledge Acquisition for Knowledge-Based Systems, Reading University.

DUDA, R., GASCHNIG, J., and HART, P. (1979), Model Design in the Prospector Consultant System for Mineral Exploration, in: *Expert Systems for the Micro Electronic Age*, ed. D. Mitchie, Edinburgh University Press.

HAYES-ROTH, F., WATERMAN, D., and LENAT, D. (1983), *Building Expert Systems*, Addison-Wesley, Reading, MA.

KAPLAN, A. (1964), *The Conduct of Inquiry*, Chandler Publishing, San Francisco.

KOLODNER, J., and RIESBECK, C. (1986), *Experience, Memory and Reasoning*, LEA Hillsdale, NJ.

MESERVY, R. (1985), *Auditing Internal Controls: A Computational Model of the Review Process*, Unpublished Ph.D. Dissertation, University of Minnesota.

WATKINS, P., and O'LEARY, D. (1987), *Knowledge Acquisition for Small Scale Expert Systems from Consulting Experts: A Field Study Approach*, Proceedings of the First European Workshop on Knowledge Acquisition for Knowledge-Based Systems, Reading University.

A Simple Software System for Eliciting Structured Sets of Notions From a Group of Experts (Methods and Experiences)

Jan W. Owsiński
Systems Research Institute
Polish Academy of Sciences, Warszawa, Poland

Summary

A simple software system is presented, meant primarily for IBM-PC-like equipment, based mainly upon a relatively flexible application of three types of algorithms:

- aggregation of precedences,
- clustering and
- simple structural analysis.

This software is meant as a probe in a broader project of constructing a system which would enable effective conduct of expert sessions aiming at the establishment and analysis of a quasi-model related to a problem domain under consideration. With that respect the software refers to some extent on the one hand to the ideas of precedence aggregation and clustering as well as interpretive modelling or analysis, and on the other hand to the AI- and expert-system related applications dealing with knowledge acquisition. As mentioned, though, it is primarily oriented at gathering experience at the present stage, and this purpose is the reason for differences with other existing software products.

The system as of now supports an expert session conducted, in one place and in one time segment, by a session manager with the help of an assistant and a PC-operator. Main stages of the session are:

- notion elicitation, evaluation and ranking,
- establishment of a certain class of relations among notions,
- analysis of the thus obtained structural models.

The paper presents some results of experimental sessions.

1 Introduction

In many domains of human life, in which decisions of crucial importance for particular persons, societal groups or whole societies are made, the foundations of such decisions are uncertain and even often stem from emotions or convictions with low degree of rationality. A good example for such a domain is the question of choice of principles which should

NATO ASI Series, Vol. F 61
Knowledge, Data and Computer-Assisted Decisions
Edited by M. Schader and W. Gaul

regulate the functioning of the Polish national economy. It can be seen through the contents of statements pronounced and the manners of reasoning presented in discussions that there are troubles in reaching the rational and agreed upon core of the problem. Such a state of affairs, together with the growing capacities of computer equipment and software, has become a reason for the development of a range of methods, applied in management and planning, based mainly upon the aggregation of knowledge of experts on a concrete question, while assuming only quite general frames of proceeding, see e.g., Godet (1985) or Warfield (1984). Simultaneously, in many domains in which knowledge gathered, though not fully accurate, is adequate for the conduct of practical actions based to a high degree on the tested and agreed-upon rules of concluding and proceeding, the so called expert systems appeared. These systems, see e.g., Barton and Sviokla (1988), Blanning (1985), Hayes-Roth (1988) or Retour (1989), are composed of the "knowledge base" and the "reasoning (search) device". It appears that the crucial problem in these systems is at present the construction and implementation of knowledge bases. The importance of this problem results from the fact that knowledge within particular domains and also within particular schools of thought in the very same domain may be contained in completely differing structures. Such differences may also emerge among a group of experts (specialists) and among the particular fragments of the problem domain. Similar conclusions can be drawn for other types of artificial intelligence methods and applications, where very narrow knowledge and/or reasoning constructs dominate in practical applications, see e.g. Nilsson (1980) or Rich (1987).

The group at the Systems Research Institute of the Polish Academy of Sciences, working on methods of computerized decision-aiding, see e.g., Kacprzyk (1983), Kacprzyk, Fedrizzi and Zadrozny (1988), Owsiński (1982a), Owsiński and Zadrozny (1988b), and, at the same time, on their applications to definite domains of social and economic life, e.g., to agriculture, see Owsiński (1982b), Owsiński, Kacprzyk and Zadrozny (1986), encountered the problem mentioned before when trying to establish an expert system at the farm level, for a farm working in Polish conditions (high variety of products, high uncertainties stemming from various origins, lack of well defined objectives). It turned out quickly that no one-way approach could embrace within a manageable expert system even a portion of the agrotechnical and economic system of a farm. Existing forms of expert systems could at most be proper for very detailed few-objects decision making. Thus, two vistas could be envisaged: first – to start construction of an expert system shell allowing for a variety of methods and approaches (e.g., easy incorporation of simple mathematical programming problems and their solutions, or treatment of uncertainties of very different kinds), and second – to try to establish a system which, in a way, would stand before an expert system, allowing to elicitate the notions proper for a given problem and their relations, and only then to try to attach decision-oriented device to the thus formed system of notions. It was decided that the second approach was more appropriate. This would mean taking a step back from what is happening now in computer applications in this area and analyzing a broader perspective. Thus, the work here reported has a twofold goal:

1. to create a draft- or test-software system which would make it possible in a flexible way, to put a structure over a set of notions related to a concrete problem domain, considered by a group of experts during a working session with preservation of the time and space unity,

2. to conduct a number of experimental sessions with the test system aiming at determination, on the one hand, of the requirements as to the final version of the system, and on the other hand, of the ergonomy rules for the session itself.

2 Structure of the Session

It is assumed that the session shall have a working character, with the predetermined purpose and a framework of proceeding. A session is conducted on a definite SUBJECT, having the nature of a PROBLEM (say, "perspectives of the Polish economy", "hostages in the Middle East", "outlook for the firm X on the Y market", "technical and functional requirements on product V on market Z", "future of the W's couple"). This subject can be announced to the session participants at the start of the session, or a few days before—together with the appropriate information on the way and goal of proceeding.

The purpose of the session is first of all determination of the SET OF NOTIONS related to the session subject, to which the session participants all agree. These notions may have the nature of elements composing the whole of the problem status, or of factors influencing this status. Concrete meaning of the notions should get an explicit interpretation during the session. It is essential that the set of notions be EXHAUSTIVE in the opinion of session participants.

After the set of notions has been agreed upon the following stage would be to determine the STRUCTURE, meaning, most generally, establishment of mutual dependences and relations among notions (including also the session subject), with three kinds of relations strictly distinguished: AFFINITY, HIERARCHY and CAUSALITY. Naturally, these kinds shall often be confounded by the session participants and that is why treatment of appropriate results should be very careful.

The last stage of the session would be the construction—on the basis of the structure previously obtained—of a simplified STRUCTURAL MODEL, referring to the problem domain considered, and then, eventually, generation of (plausible) hypotheses as to the possible statuses of the session subject with the thus constructed model. This last stage is not seen as a necessary part of the procedure, since it may sometimes be sufficient—in view of the nature of the subject—to obtain the structure, and sometimes it may be impossible to obtain a workable model at all.

The above threefold goal of the session (NOTIONS, STRUCTURE, MODEL) can be obtained via various ways. For purposes of the project here described a certain concrete manner of proceeding was assumed, quite general, it seems. This generality and flexibility causes that at the start computer programs have a purely auxiliary, non-intervening role, and only gradually during the course of the session their significance and input increase. It is assumed that the whole of the session could be carried out if only one expert took part. This is important for testing purposes and in special applications. Of course, some results lose then their significance. As mentioned, the session is subject to certain organizational constraints, resulting from the way of proceeding adopted and within it from the requirements of ergonomy of a concrete session. This concerns first the number of experts taking part, and then the numbers of notions: given by particular experts and finally accepted. Two questions should here be especially taken into consideration: time devoted to discussions and consultations, and technical capabilities of experts in responding to questions of growing complexity. Thus, in accordance with the goals here given the main functions of the software system are, in temporal sequence:

- completion of the files of notions and their attributes for particular experts;
- ordering of the list of notions;
- formation of the matrices of affinities, hierarchical relations and causal relations;
- notion aggregation and analysis of hierarchy;
- structural analysis and projections.

3 Conduct of the Session and the Methods Used

Now the course of the session, problems related to its subsequent stages and methods implemented in the software shall be commented upon in more detail.

3.1 Formulation of Notions

At the very start of the session experts are given forms into which they will be writing their notions. At the top of the list of notions, bearing no. 1, is the subject of the session. Total maximum number of notions each expert is allowed to write in is decided by the session manager or discussed shortly and decided by the session participants. Notion names have limited length. Each notion is given two attributes by an expert: WEIGHT (IMPORTANCE) and LEVEL (DIRECTNESS). The first one is given in integer numbers from 1 to 10 (0 meaning no importance and therefore inconsequential nature of the notion), with 10 standing for decisive importance of this notion for the status of the subject. The second attribute is less obvious in its meaning for a participant. It takes values of 1, 2 or 3 and the value of 1 means that a given notion is directly related to (influencing, composing, ...) the subject status. Then, a value of 3 would mean quite indirect relation to the subject status (although this relation may be very strong, as shown through the value of weight). If necessary, the session manager may allow a short discussion as to whether the second attribute does also in fact indicate the level of a notion in terms of hierarchical structure. It is assumed by default that it does.

Participants are given definite time for writing in their set of notions together with the attributes, but not more than 2–3 minutes per notion. After that they are presenting their notions, one notion at a time, according to a random sequence of participants, generated ad hoc. Each notion thus generated is shortly discussed (5–15 minutes) in order to allow participants other than the presenting one to check whether they do not have identical (or: sufficiently similar) notions. Participants should be aware of consequences of notion overlapping, of their growing number, as well as lack of adequate discernibility. Non-presenting participants, who find that the notion currently spelled out is identical (sufficiently similar) with one of their own, signal this fact and all give their attributes to be put into the notions file. Such a procedure goes on until there is no more notion left written in by the participants.

3.2 Processing of the Notion List

Let us at this point introduce some notations: N stands for the number of experts, NU for the expert number, so that $NU = 1,\ldots,N$, the random number generator yields numbers $LK[NU]$ being sequential numbers of experts for notion presentation, M is the maximum admissible number of notions accepted, MP is the actual total number of notions presented, MK is the notion number, $W[MK,NU]$ are weights of notions MK with participants NU, analogously $P[MK,NU]$ for the levels, $NP[MK]$ stands for the number of experts announcing the notion MK, and $WN[MK]$, $PN[MK]$ are averages of weight and level, respectively, for the notion MK. These all are data directly resulting from the first stage of the session. Further processing contains two operations "hidden" from the experts in that they may not be fully aware of their contents, although they may be notified of the existence of such operations.

First is computation of the "participant weight". Namely, on the basis of all weights and levels given by a participant for all his/her notions a function value is calculated with the following rationale: if a participant assigned 10 as weight and 1 as level to all the notions elicitated and there were at least half the number of notions allowed on his/her list then this participant NU obtains the minimum weight $FW[NU]$, whose values are contained between 0 and 1. The value of $FW[NU]$ increases as the average weight of notions given by NU decreases and as the average level of notions given by him/her increases and as the number of notions given by this expert decreases, so that at a certain point ("sufficiently" low or diverse weights, "sufficiently" high level numbers and/or "sufficiently" low numbers of notions specified) the value of $FW[NU]$ attains 1. Parameters of the function defining $FW[NU]$ may be to some extent set by the operator, with special attention given to the minimum value of $FW[NU]$ which, for purely numerical reasons, corresponding here very well with the substantial ones, cannot fall below 2/3. The justification for the introduction of the weight function—which can also be omitted—is the danger of the bias introduced by some experts. Once $FW[NU]$ established the subsequent stage follows—that of ordering of notions. At this point notions are already implicitly ordered according to three variables: number of experts proposing a given notion, averages (along experts) of weights and levels for a given notion. Now these variables are recalculated using $FW[NU]$, and thus slightly different implicit orderings can be obtained. These implicit orderings are aggregated using the simple technique described in Owsiński and Zadrozny (1986, 1988a). Resulting are numbers $LP[MK]$ meaning rankings of MK in the aggregate ordering. Only notions with $LP[MK] \leq M$ can be accepted for further considerations, although this point could also be discussed at the end of the first stage of the session, especially in cases of indifferences in the resulting orderings.

3.3 Specification of Relations

As mentioned before, relations among notions are assumed to take three following forms: AFFINITY, HIERARCHY and CAUSALITY. Thus, experts are asked to fill in three matrices in the ways explained below. It is assumed that this task should not be made too heavy for participants, mainly by adequate trimming of the notion list, by simple nature of signs (numbers) entering the matrices, and by the requirement that only where an expert is certain as to existence of a relation he/she should put something else than void into the matrix.

The affinity matrix is a triangular matrix, denoted *SU[MK1,MK2,NU]* for an individual expert and *S[MK1,MK2]* for all experts, the latter obtained as a simple average. All entries are assumed 0 (void) by default. Everywhere where an expert is certain of it—writes in 1, 2 or 3, depending upon the strength of relation (3 meaning the highest affinity).

The hierarchy matrix is a square matrix, denoted *SBU[MK1,MK2,NU]* for an individual expert and *SB[MK1,MK2]* for all of them, the latter obtained as the average of the previous. Again, all entries are assumed 0 (void) by default. Wherever an expert is certain of it, number 1 is entered, meaning that notion *MK2* is subject in terms of a hierarchy to notion *MK1*. The particular nature of this relation should be clear in view of previous specifications of notions and their nature.

The causality matrix is a square matrix, denoted *AU[MK1,MK2,NU]* for an individual expert and *A[MK1,MK2]* for all experts, the latter obtained as an average of the previous. All entries are assumed 0 (void) by default. Experts introduce numbers: $-2, -1, +1$ or $+2$, meaning the direction and strength of influence. In addition to the causality matrix the experts may be asked to fill in the initial state vector *IU[MK,NU]* (*I[MK]* for all) in the very same units as the causality matrix.

The above three matrices, eventually together with the vector *I[MK]*, constitute the basis for a computerized analysis of structure and contents of the set of notions and of the hypothetical model resulting therefrom. With the three matrices given there are many paths of proceeding available to the session manager and to the participants.

3.4 Analysis of Structure

The simplest case of analysis based upon the three matrices specified by the experts is the following:

- structural analysis, using causality matrix is performed directly on the set of notions accepted at a predefined cutoff level for causality parameters; results of cluster analysis of the affinity matrix and of hierarchy analysis are treated only as additional information; this option is plausible or even advised when the number of notions is low (up to 10).

When the number of notions accepted exceeds 10, it is assumed—in view of the fact that all the results should be subject to meaningful discussion by the experts—that structural analysis should not be performed directly on the original notions. The second group of paths of utilization of the software could therefore be characterized as follows:

- structural analysis is performed on the clusters of notions and not directly on notions themselves; results of cluster analysis may or may not be discussed with the session participants; these results define the proxy aggregate notions used in structural analysis; hierarchy analysis is used only for information purposes.

The most complicated, and of course also the least reliable, option envisages consideration of hierarchy relations in addition to affinity in determination of the objects for structural analysis:

- structural analysis is performed in stages in which, consecutively, appear aggregate proxy notions first from the lower levels of hierarchy and then from the higher ones;

such an approach is meaningful only when the number of original accepted notions is high enough (at least about 20) or when an obvious affinity and hierarchy structure is detected.

It is of course possible to perform parallel computations based upon various options within their space outlined above. Again, however, in view of the postulated transparency and simplicity of results such a possibility should not be employed too lighthandedly.

Cluster analysis is conducted according to the method of Owsiński (1984, 1989), while structural analysis according to the procedure by Romanowicz (1983). Analysis of hierarchy relations is performed via a simple heuristic algorithm checking the weights ascribed to particular edges and finding tree-like substructures at consecutive cutoff levels from the maximum weight down, stopping whenever an overlapping is found. The whole of the procedure is described in more detail in Owsiński, Romanowicz and Zadrozny (1989).

4 Some Experimental Results

The examples of experimental results cited here come from a test session conducted on an academic subject entitled "Shall couple X stay together?". It was assumed that the participants of the session know both husband and wife on social and/or work place grounds, but that their acquaintance with both of them is not too close, so that the participants are not aware of many aspects of their purely private life. On the other hand as neighbors and job colleagues they are positively interested in the future of couple X. It was naturally assumed that the subject of the session arose because some difficulties within couple X had been observed. There were four participants of this experimental session, with the limitation of 10 notions maximum per participant, including the session subject, rephrased so as to accommodate the status evaluation further on in the session.

Participants were given 15 minutes for thinking of and writing down on special sheets their notions together with the attributes. Then, according to the procedure adopted, the notions were sequentially presented, discussed, agreed upon and input into the notion file of the software. An example of the list of notions and their attributes for one of the participants is shown below:

No.	Name of notion	Weight(1–10)	Level(1–3)
1	Firmness of couple X	10	1
2	Financial situation	6	1
3	Marital faithfulness	9	1
4	Number of children	5	1
5	Presence at home	7	2
6	Unity of interests and goals	8	1
7	Personal culture	8	1
8	Material aspirations	5	2
9	Sexual life	8	2

Presentation of notions and discussion lasted for one and half hour. Finally, altogether 18 notions were accepted for further considerations. These notions are listed also together with the number of participants who proposed this notion, average weights and levels, excluding, here the session subject:

MK	Name of notion	*NP[MK]*	*WN[MK]*	*PN[MK]*
1	Long absence	2	4.5	2
2	Domination	1	8	1
3	Number of children	1	5	1
4	Presence at home	1	7	2
5	External options	1	3	3
6	Sexual life	1	8	2
7	Religious beliefs	1	7	1
8	Environment	2	6	1.5
9	Stabilization	1	9	2
10	Financial situation	4	5.75	1.75
11	Character	1	8	1
12	Cultural traditions	2	7	2
13	Housing conditions	1	3	2
14	Marital faithfulness	2	9.5	1
15	Emotional links	2	9.5	1
16	Propensity to agree	2	6.5	2
17	Unity of goals	3	6.67	1.67

Naturally, during notion presentation and discussion some of the individual ones were modified so as to fit the common ones and some were altogether dropped. The subsequent stage consists in weighting by *FW[NU]* and ordering in order to then cut the list of notions down to manageable dimensions. The accepted list of notions is given below together with notion attributes used in the ordering.

LP[MK]	*MK*	Notion name	Weighted by *FW[NU]*:		
			NP[MK]	*WN[MK]*	*PN[MK]*
1	5	Marital faithfulness	1.86	8.84	1.21
2	4	Emotional links	1.82	8.63	1.27
3	15	Domination	0.88	7.04	1.36
4	16	Character	0.88	7.04	1.36
5	8	Unity of goals	2.80	6.24	1.82
6	6	Religious beliefs	0.88	6.16	1.36
7	3	Environment	1.83	5.46	1.70
8	2	Financial situation	3.68	5.30	1.93
9	7	Long absence	1.89	4.26	2.11
10	14	Propensity to agree	1.85	5.99	2.17
11	10	Cultural traditions	1.82	6.40	2.18

Then, participants were asked to provide the notion affinity data in the form of triangular matrices *SU[MK1,MK2,NU]*. These matrices were aggregated to *S[MK1,MK2]*, and the clustering procedure was applied yielding the following equivalent suboptimal partitions:

Partition 1: {1},{2,5},{3},{4,10},{6,7,11},{8},{9}

Partition 2: {1,9},{2,5},{3},{4,10},{6,7,11},{8}

where the numbers used are the *LP[MK]* from the previous table. Thereby the number of notions to be taken into account could be reduced to 7 or even mere 6, in accordance with the options presented before. Note that with such a low number of notions it becomes possible to show the results of further steps of the procedure, not illustrated here, in a visual display.

5 When Does a Session Fail?

A measure can be used for determining the "level of success" of a session, or, better, of each of the session stages. Such a measure is first of all oriented at the degree of agreement among experts as consecutive issues are addressed during the session. This measure can also be used to a certain extent in the management of a session. A good example is provided by the first stage of the session, where two extreme cases are: all experts give the same list of notions with identical weights and levels, and—all experts give different lists of notions so that *NP[MK]* = 1 for all *MK*. In the first case the value of the stage-proper measure is 1, in the second it is 0. For the cases in between, however, two values of the measure can be computed: before and after the trimming of the notion list. Certainly, the second value is not less than the first one, and it can be made—up to a limit—higher by cutting the notion list shorter. Similar applies, for instance, to notion clustering and the ordering itself, where the measure proposed by Owsiński and Zadrozny (1988b) can be used. The introduction of the success measure makes it possible, in case of sufficiently high disagreement, to pronounce the failure of a session.

6 Concluding Remarks

The system outlined is a link in a chain of ventures aiming at the elaboration of a broader approach encompassing an expert system and management software for handling situations where a priori structure of knowledge cannot be directly determined. Experiments performed show that the system can serve its purpose and can constitute, in its final form, an input package for the whole approach. With time, particular numerical and ergonomic problems encountered in practice shall be solved and appropriate solutions imbedded in the system, keeping, however, to the main idea of simplicity and flexibility.

References

BARTON, L., and SVIOKLA, J.-J. (1988), Putting expert systems to work, *Harvard Business Review, March–April*, 91–98.

BLANNING, R.W. (1985), Expert systems for management: research and applications, *Journal of Information Science, 9*, 153–162.

GODET, M. (1985), *Prospective et planification stratégique*, Economica, Paris.

HAYES-ROTH, F. (1988), Knowledge-based expert systems: the state of the art, in: *Management Expert Systems*, ed. C. Ernst, Addison-Wesley, Wokingham.

KACPRZYK, J. (1983), *Multistage Decision Making Under Fuzziness: Theory and Applications*, TÜV Rheinland Verlag, Cologne.

KACPRZYK, J., ZADROZNY, S., and FEDRIZZI, M. (1988), An interactive user-friendly decision support system for consensus reaching based on fuzzy logic with linguistic quantifiers, in: *Fuzzy Computing*, eds. M.M. Gupta and T. Yamakawa, Elsevier-North Holland, Amsterdam.

NILSSON, N. (1980), *Principles of Artificial Intelligence*, Tioga, Palo Alto.

OWSIŃSKI, J.W. (1982a), Normative application of clustering methods in location/allocation problems, in: *Integrated Rural/Spatial Development: Elements of Systems Analytic Approach*, eds. A. Straszak and J.W. Owsiński, Systems Research Institute of the Polish Academy of Sciences, Warsaw.

OWSIŃSKI, J.W. (1982b), Agriculture, population, environment and balanced regional development: a modelling project in Poland, *Agricultural Systems, 8*, 87–104.

OWSIŃSKI, J.W. (1984), On a quasi-objective global clustering method, in: *Data Analysis and Informatics III*, eds. E. Diday et al., Elsevier-North Holland, Amsterdam.

OWSIŃSKI, J.W. (1989), On a new naturally indexed quick clustering method with a global objective function. To appear in: *Applied Stochastic Models and Data Analysis.*

OWSIŃSKI, J.W., KACPRZYK, J., and ZADROZNY, S. (1986), Agricultural production planning via a fuzzy linear programming model, *Nonconventional Problems in Optimization*, ed. J. Kacprzyk, Prace IBS PAN, 136, 3, Systems Research Institute of the Polish Academy of Sciences, Warsaw.

OWSIŃSKI, J.W., ROMANOWICZ, T., and ZADROZNY, S. (1989), *A Testable Software Package of Data Analysis for Studying Problems With Weakly Identified Structure* (in Polish), internal report, Systems Research Institute of the Polish Academy of Sciences, Warsaw, in preparation.

OWSIŃSKI, J.W., and ZADROZNY, S. (1986), Structuring a regional problem: aggregation and clustering in orderings, *Applied Stochastic Models and Data Analysis, 2*, 83–95.

OWSIŃSKI, J.W., and ZADROZNY, S. (1988a), *Cluster-wise aggregation of relations: the case of paired comparisons of cognac ads.* Paper presented at the international conference on Applied Stochastic Models and Data Analysis: "The Ins and Outs of Solving Real Problems", Nancy, Dec., INRIA, Le Chesnay.

OWSIŃSKI, J.W., and ZADROZNY, S. (1988b), A flexible system of precedence coefficient aggregation and consensus measurement, Systems Analysis and Simulation 1988, eds. A. Sydow, S.G. Tzafestas and R. Vichnevetsky, *Mathematical Research, 47*, Akademie Vlg., Berlin.

RETOUR, D. (1989), L'évaluation des systèmes experts de gestion: proposition d'un cadre d'analyse, *Revue Française de Gestion, Jan.-Fev., 72*, 45–51.

RICH, E. (1987), *Intelligence artificielle*, Masson, Paris.

ROMANOWICZ, T. (1983), Structural sensitivity analysis in certain class of linear systems, IEEE SMC, *SMC-13, No. 3.*

WARFIELD, J.N. (1984), *Progress in interactive management*, Proc. of the 6th International Congress of Cybernetics and Systems, AFCET, Paris, XXIX–XXXIV.

Demand Forecasting for Strategic Decision Support

Hean L. Poh
Engineering-Economic Systems Department
Stanford University, U.S.A.

Summary

The purpose of this paper is to explore the role of demand forecasting in the strategic decision making process of managers. It begins with a demand model for the workstation[1] industry, which can also be adopted by any other industry, verified by an economic equilibrium model. This model can eventually be used in a demand forecasting system. This is then followed by a discussion of the various forecasting methods that are commonly used for this purpose. In particular, the pros and cons of quantitative vs judgmental forecasting are compared, since the demand model is a combination of both judgmental and quantitative forecasting techniques, using such methods as Analytic Hierarchy Process and Decision Calculus to capture experts' knowledge about the various factors affecting the demand of the products of a company. Finally, as a prelude to further research, the paper examines how demand forecasting information fits best into a strategic mangement framework of an organization.

1 Introduction

The success of a company depends on the ability of the manager to foresee the market situation in the future. This is especially true of a high-tech company, where the products are rapidly evolving due to the high rate of technology changes, and where the prices are dropping very fast, all of which lead to the uncertainty of the demand of the high-tech products. The future demand of a product of a company is essential in determining the strategies of a company with regard to production, inventory of the products and its parts, marketing effort (promotion, advertising etc.), price, the launching of new products and R & D efforts, and hence also the organizational change of the company. In other words, demand forecasting affects the marketing decisions and thus also the interactions of the relationship of strategies-environment-goal. It can be easily seen that, failure to predict correctly the demand of a product, either under-prediction or over-prediction might lead to the loss of competitive advantage of a company.

Given the importance of demand forecasting, it is not surprising that companies are serious about investing in it. Traditionally, subjective/qualitative forecasting has been the most popular method of demand forecasting due to the fact that it is easiest and most readily available, however this method is rather ad-hoc and might not lead to a good decision. On the other hand, quantitative methods based on historical data, though

[1] A workstation is at least a 32 bit machine with 1 MIPS, 5MB of RAM, 150MB of disk, multi-tasking operating system (UNIX), and with its CPU dedicated to a single user but with networking capabilities. Increasingly, workstation is a price definition, since it generally sells from $10,000 to $100,000 dollars.

NATO ASI Series, Vol. F 61
Knowledge, Data and Computer-Assisted Decisions
Edited by M. Schader and W. Gaul

providing a more objective view of the situation, is more susceptible to change in environment which is not reflected in the historical data. Thus, an ideal method would be to extract both the expert knowledge about the changing environment and the objective information about the market nature, which is what the proposed method is striving for.

To take this issue of demand forecasting for strategic management a step further, it is necessary to recognize the need for a decision support system incorporating demand forecasting. A decision support system as defined by Keen and Scott Morton (1978) would provide comprehensive information which might otherwise be left out easily and avail the managers with their own judgment and other expert judgments as well as system models that process the information, before any decision is made. Hence, the decision support system including demand forecasting as a subsystem will definitely enhance the quality of the managers' decision[2].

2 Demand Modeling

2.1 Workstation Industry

The demand of products of workstation industry is chosen as an example for the modeling of demand. The model should be applicable to other industries as well. The workstation industry is the most rapidly growing sector of the computer industry and also the most competitive one. The leader of the industry is now Hewlett Packard after the purchase of Apollo, the pioneer of the industry, followed by Sun Microsystems, Digital Equipment Corp. (DEC) and IBM. This industry is rapidly substituting the minicomputer market once dominated by DEC and IBM, and hence these big computer companies are entering the race with their huge resources for market share, which makes the forecast of demand for products by smaller companies such as Sun even more important. The demand for a certain workstation product is shaped by such factors as compatibility of hardware (microprocessor) and software (operating system and available application software), price and performance ratio, user-friendliness and others.

2.2 Demand Network for the Workstation Industry

A representation of the demand network (for a country) is provided below to capture the complicated relationship between suppliers of hardware/software and workstation manufacturers and that between the users and the manufacturers. The network divides the industry into 4 levels of production and marketing centers, starting from hardware and software suppliers to end-user markets. Between these two levels are markets for hardware and software products and manufacturers of workstations. Fig. 1 indicates only some of the major players of the industry and it is not meant to be exhaustive.

2.2.1 Arcs and Nodes

At each of the 4 levels as represented in the network, there are various products either on 'sale' at the markets or being produced by the plants. The end-user markets draw its

[2]It is noted that a good decision does not necessarily lead to a good outcome as it is not possible to predict the future with certainty. However, a good decision should increase the chance of a good outcome.

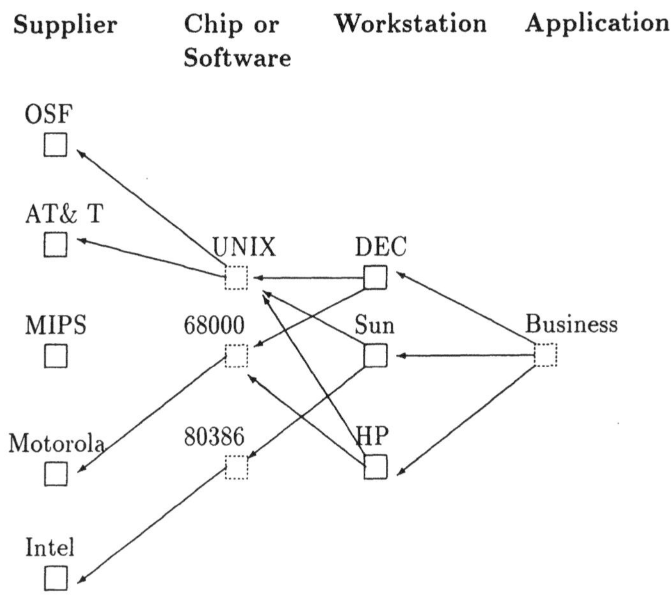

Figure 1: Demand Network for Workstation Industry

supply of workstations not necessarily from traditional workstation manufacturers[3]. This relationship between plants and markets or among themselves is represented by an **arc** and each of the markets and plants is represented by a **node**. An arc always originates from a demanding node and points towards a supplying node.

2.3 Models

To model a real world problem, it is advisable to set up a benchmark model using well established theory to counter-check on the validity and redundancy of the current model. This not only justifies the adoption of this model but also provides an insight into the tradeoffs associated with each model. It is also advisable to prove that the two models actually converge under certain conditions and tradeoffs.

In the following write-up, Model I is the current model under investigation. Model II is the benchmark model using economic equilibrium theory.

2.3.1 Model I

Assumptions and Demand Model

The model is set up to analyze the competing workstations of *different* manufacturers for a certain application such as business.

For simplicity, only two factors are considered to be affecting the demand of a certain type of workstation. One of them is the **growth of the economy** which leads to the

[3]In other words, traditional chip manufacturers like Motorola and Intel have entered or planned to enter the workstation business.

growth of the demand for workstations; the other is the **substitution** of workstations types among themselves and with other competing types of systems, such as personal computers on the low end of the market and minicomputers or even supercomputers on the high end of the market. These are called **intra-product substitution** and **inter-product substitution** respectively.

S-Curve

Substitution is represented in terms of the change of market share of the various workstation models from different manufacturers for a *particular application* area, such as business, education or engineering. It can be modeled in terms of a S-curve or a logistic curve (Luenberger (1979)) which depicts the change of market share over time, starting with relatively slow progress and moving with relatively fast progress after a certain time and eventually saturating at an ultimate level of market share. There are two parameters to be determined in a S-curve, namely the **ultimate level** of the curve and the **time constant** or **penetration rate** which indicates the inertia to the change in market share (i.e. the speed of change).

A S-curve is derived from the following differential equation which captures the form described above:

$$\dot{x}(t) = a\left(\frac{1 - x(t)}{c}\right)x(t)$$

which leads to a solution of

$$x(t) = \frac{c}{1 + be^{-at}}$$

where c denotes the ultimate market share MS since $x(\infty) = c$ and a denotes the time constant.[4] Hence, the rate of change of market share is given by:

$$\epsilon_{market-share} = \frac{x(t) - x(t-1)}{x(t-1)}$$

Suppose f_i denotes the initial market share of workstation type i, then from

$$x_i(0) = \frac{c_i}{1 + b_i} = f_i \quad \text{we have} \quad b_i = \frac{c_i}{f_i} - 1$$

AHP for S-Curve Parameters

The ultimate level and the time constant can be each determined by AHP (Syed (1988b) and Saaty (1980)). In AHP, a problem is decomposed into a hierarchy; each level consists of a few elements, and each element is, in turn, decomposed into a set of elements. In this case, there are two levels. Within each level, the relative importance or priorities of each element with respect to an element at a higher level is assessed by experts. Using a scale of 1 to 9, with 1 being equally important, and 9 being absolutely important, two elements of the same level are compared with respect to an element of a higher level. The results are entered in a $n \times n$ matrix, with n being the number of elements at that level. The matrix is a reciprocal matrix with diagonal elements equal to one. The dominant eigenvector is solved and normalized, which represents the relative importance of the elements at that level with respect to an element at a higher level.

[4]The bigger the time constant, the faster it approaches the ultimate level c.

The requirement level in the AHP tree for the ultimate level can be determined by **technology/performance, user-friendliness, social factors and price etc.** The alternative level of the AHP tree, which indicates the workstations used, depends on the end-user applications. For instance, in the case of office automation (business applications), the users has a choice of different types of workstations from different vendors, such as Sun SPARCstation 1, DECstation 2100, and HP 9000 series. In other words, the ultimate market share of each workstation manufacturer for a certain end-use application is determined by such factors as competition, pricing and technology.

The time constants can be established by another AHP, whereby the requirement level captures such factors as **fabrication capacity, capital availability, technological requirement and social issues, and pricing strategy.** In other words, these factors determine how fast the market share reaches a saturation level. (What happens after that, such as the commencement of decline is ignored here). The alternative level remains the same.

In the case of ultimate level, the technology (performance) requirement of the end-users applications affects the ultimate market share of Sun, DEC and HP workstations. The same applies to the aesthetic requirement, prices and other social factors. Suppose the relative importance of an element is denoted by w_j for the requirement level and w_i for the alternative level, then $\sum_j w_j = 1$. In this case, $w_{technology} + w_{user-friendliness} + w_{price} + w_{social-factor} = 1$. For a factor j in the requirement level, say technology, the relative importance of an alternative workstation type i, say Sun 386i, is given by w_{ij}. Hence, the ultimate market share of a workstation type i is given by:

$$MS_i = \sum_j w_j w_{ij}$$

where

$$\sum_j w_j \sum_{i=1}^{i=3} w_{ij} = 1$$

Similar consideration can be also done for the time constant, which is a relative term, using AHP. For instance, given one of the constraints such as capital availability, the relative 'dynamism' of the elements at the alternative level is estimated.

Decision Calculus

Hence, the AHP incorporates such factors as technology constraints, competition and pricing in a model depicting substitution. This justifies for the two-factor model for demand forecasting. After estimating the two factors, demand forecasting can be achieved using **decision calculus** as described in Little (1975). Thus, both the growth of the industry and the effect of substitution can be described in the following demand forecasting equation:

$$D_i(t) = D_i(t-1) \times \epsilon_g \times \epsilon_{ms}$$

where $\epsilon_g = 1 + \epsilon_{growth}$ and $\epsilon_{ms} = 1 + \epsilon_{market-share}$ and $D_i(t)$ is the demand of workstation i at time t in this case. Hence, the first factor on the R.H.S. accounts for the effect of industry growth rate which can be determined by quantitative methods, and the second factor for the effect of the rate of change of market share on the demand of a workstation i in a time period, which can be determined by AHP with input from experts.

2.3.2 Model II

In this model, a more general approach is taken to forecast the demand of *any* node based on its interaction with other nodes. Every node is thus an autonomous entity.

A simple formulation to represent the relationship between a supplying node i and its demanding nodes based on a product k is captured in the following optimization problem subject to some arc constraints:

Suppose the inputs necessary for the production of k are denoted by $1, 2, \ldots, l$, and node i can draw its input from a variety of sources, the distribution among which is another optimization problem not discussed here, then we have:

$$\min_p \sum_{j \neq i} d_{ij}^k(p) - f\left(\sum_{j \neq i} d_{ji}^1(p), \sum_{j \neq i} d_{ji}^2(p), \ldots, \sum_{j \neq i} d_{ji}^l(p) \ldots\right)$$

i.e. $\min_p \sum_j$ demand on i of product k by j $-$ supply of product k by i

s.t. substitution, capacity, technology and other constraints

where $\sum_j q_{ji}^l = 1$ and $q_{ji}^l c_l = d_{ji}^l$

Notations:

d_{ij}^k : amount of k-th product of node i demanded by node j (end-user)
d_{ji}^k : amount of k-th product of node j (supplier) demanded by node i
q_{ji}^k : proportion of input from j in the total input at node i to produce the product k
c_l : total input of l-th 'material' for producing product k

Specific Formulation

To facilitate comparison with the first model, the following formulation is adopted for a market node of hardware and software supplies, with the simplification that there is no inventory. Then, the following market material balance equations, which capture the node constraints, have to be satisfied: (using the notations above assuming that there is only one product at each node, i.e. $k = 1$)

- hardware and software supply market node i

$$\sum_{j \neq i} d_{ij} + d_{export} = \sum_{j \neq i} d_{ji} + d_{import}$$

i.e.

$$\sum_{j \neq i} d_{end-user_j} + d_{export} = \sum_{j \neq i} d_{vendor_j} + d_{import}$$

- workstation end-user market node i

$$d_i + d_{export} = \sum_j d_{ji} + d_{import}$$

where d_i is the total demand of node i.

Besides the market *node constraint*, the *arc constraints* have to be considered too. The arc originates from the end-user application node and points toward the workstation manufacturer node. The relationship between these two markets (nodes) is represented in the following optimization problem for an workstation node i given an end-user node j:

$$\min_{p} d_j(p) - \sum_{i} f_i(d_{li}(p))$$

$$\text{s.t. } b_i \leq f_i(d_{li}) \leq a_i$$

(capacity constraints of workstation manufacturers)

where a_i is the maximum capacity of i in producing the workstations and b_i is the minimum operating level, and f_i represents the production function of vendor i for producing workstation to satisfy the end-user application j. (Hereby l represents the supplier of hardware and software 'material' for the manufacturing of workstation for simplicity)

$$\text{s.t. } f_i(d_{li}) \leq c_{ij}$$

$$\text{in fact, } f_i(d_{li}(t)) = c_{ij}/(1 + b_{ij}e^{-\alpha_{ij}t})$$

(substitution and technology constraints)

where c_{ij} is the ultimate demand for i's product (e.g. Sun, DEC or HP's products) and α is the time constant as defined in Model I.

The above is equivalent to the minimization of excess demand to achieve Walrasian equilibrium (Varian (1978)). Associated with the minimization problem is the maximization of each workstation manufacturer node i's profit:

$$\max_{y_i} p_i y_i - c_i$$

where y_i is the output of node i and c_i is the cost of production.

Economic Equilibrium

The concept of economic equilibrium was applied to provide a framework for both models. The tradeoffs of each model can be then assessed (Weyant (1985)).

General Economic Equilibrium

In Luenberger (1988), equilibrium for a private ownership economy is defined as follows:

1. The market is cleared and the allocation is feasible (material balance). The excess demand[5] is zero in the long run.

2. Each consumer maximizes utility.

3. Each firm's plan maximizes profit.

[5]Excess demand is defined as the difference between demand and existing supply originating from the endowment and production. It could be positive, zero or negative.

However, in this case there are no consumers involved in the equilibrium. Thus, a framework is established to model the equilibrium associated with such an *industry supply-demand* network.

Industry Supply-Demand Equilibrium

This is achieved by each node (producer) maximizing its profit and the minimization of excess demand, which is given by the difference between the demand and the output of the supplying node. No consumer and hence no maximization of utility is considered here. Profit maximization is given by the following equation:

$$\max_{y_i} \pi$$

$$\text{where profit } \pi = p_i y_i - c_i$$

Differentiating the above w.r.t. y_i, we have

$$p_i = \frac{\partial c_i}{\partial y_i}$$

In this case, material balance cannot be achieved due to the various constraints such as capacity constraint and technology constraint. This is, however, replaced by the minimization of the excess demand subject to the constraints as described above.

2.3.3 Theorem

The industry supply-demand equilibrium implies general economic equilibrium as defined above.

Proof: Since no consumer is involved in the consideration, the second condition of the general equilibrium follows trivially. The first and third conditions are satisfied by the definition of the "industry supply-demand" equilibrium. (Feasibility and profit maximization). *q.e.d.*

Model I in Relation to Model II With Respect to Equilibrium

Model I applies decision calculus for estimating the demand/output of each of the workstation nodes without solving the equilibrium equations for demand/output and without referring to the equilibrium price. However, in the case of excess demand minimizations, one of the constraints, namely the substitution constraint in Model II is represented in terms of a S-curve which can be determined only by AHP, as in Model I. Hence, the two models unify in this respect.

With respect to the industry supply-demand equilibrium, the market clear condition is satisfied in Model I since market share is considered here. The excess demand is zero. However, profit maximization of each workstation node is not required explicitly in Model I. If this condition can be imposed on the model by including it as an additional requirement in the AHP tree, or by simply considering the equilibrium price as one of the requirements, then Model I is also a special case of the industry supply-demand equilibrium.

Advantages and Disadvantages of the two Models

The tradeoffs for not complying strictly with the equilibrium model are that in Model I, no separate submodels need be conceived for pricing, competition and substitution etc.

These are all incorporated in the AHP tree of substitution. The various factors relating to substitution are usually not easily formulated in closed mathematical form. In this case, expert heuristic knowledge is consulted. This can be easily incorporated in AHP which is the core of Model I. The factors are also easily adjustable to account for the change in situation. Besides, it takes time for any system to arrive at an equilibrium, thus Model I is able to model the dynamics of the system better than any derivation of an economic equilibrium model. This is essential for forecasting demand for a given industry, which is a dynamic factor.

The drawback is of course the subjectivity of the values assigned to the relative importance of the various factors influencing the demand level of the products. Some interesting real world examples on the influence of subjective views on forecasting are given in Brody (1988).

Validity of S-Curve

Both models rely heavily on S-curve to model the trend in technology and competition and thus substitution. Wheelwright (1985) provides a good insight into the suitability of S-curve. A S-curve implies a slow start, a steep growth, and then a plateau. This curve is characteristic of many technological developments and the sales of several products (market share). The main problem arises in the determination of the most suitable functional form for the S-curve, which is a problem typical of Model II. Hence expert judgment is used to find an approximation of the S-curve form. It is obvious that the curve chosen will influence the forecast significantly. This is typical of the problems faced by Model I. There are numerous papers that deal with judgmental forecasting and the use of expert knowledge given the inaccuracy and biases associated with it, such as those collected in Wright (1987). Tversky (1974) deals with the cognitive biases due to representativeness, availability, adjustment and anchoring in probability assessment. These cognitive biases based on judgmental heuristics are also prevalent in the determination of the relative importance of each requirement in an AHP tree and have to be reduced too.

Reliability and Generalizability of Model I's Result

Given the uncertainties and inconsistency associated with expert knowledge, it is not advisable to follow completely the result of the demand forecast or market share forecast provided by Model I. It is, however, advisable to apply the information provided by Model I in conjunction with decision analysis for strategic management. This will be an interesting research topic to pursue.

It is also worth mentioning that the model is generalizable to other industries with similar supply-demand manufacturing and market structure. A similar demand model was presented for the petrochemical industry in Poh (1988), which was derived in part from Syed (1988a).

3 Judgmental vs Quantitative Forecasting

3.1 Survey of Forecasting Methods

A survey of the commonly used forecasting methods is summarized in Ascher et al. (1983) and discussed in details in Wheelwright (1985). Forecasting methods can range from the most technical concerns of how to smooth data points into extrapolation, to the integration of forecasting and strategic decision making.

In judgmental forecasting, the final forecasts are made subjectively. This method is most commonly used in business and government organizations. Forecasts are based on individual judgments or group agreements. According to Rowe et al. (1986), qualitative techniques have two characteristics, namely the explicit incorporation of subjective assessment of individuals or groups and the recognition of the fact that *the decision maker has some influence on the future developments.* Under quantitative forecasting, there are three different methods of forecasting (Wheelwright (1985)). Time series methods focus on historical patterns and forecast using a time-based extrapolation of the patterns. Explanatory methods study the relationships that led to past events and use these relationships to forecast the future. Monitory methods seek to identify both the changes in patterns and relationships. Among these three methods, time series method is most widely used, and it forms the basis of comparison to judgmental forecasting.

The choice of a forecasting method or methods depends on the problem and also the information and knowledge of a forecaster. For instance, a forecaster who understands the system and situation poorly might be better off relying on some straight forward methods such as extrapolation which relies solely on historical data. An ill-founded theory about what is going to happen and how the various factors interact in a situation can lead to even worse prediction than simply relying on data.

3.2 Suitability of Each Forecasting Method

Judgmental forecasting is suitable for industries with rapidly changing technology and intense competition so that historical data do not necessarily reflect the future situation. In industries where competitive situations do not change frequently, time series forecasting can be useful. Such industries, however, are rather rare. A combination of both methods also provides a good solution. Using regression and other statistical techniques, one can find causes for changes in historical data. This provides some hints on the future trend of the data though the relationships driving the demand in the past would have changed in the future. Winkler (1987) suggested combining the opinions of several experts, either by mechanical methods or by some qualitative methods, such as consensus in a face to face meeting. This would also allow feedback to be incorporated in the readjustment of the forecast. Quantitative forecasts may also be included in this process.

4 Forecasting and Strategic Management

4.1 Introduction

Demand forecasting can be important to strategic decisions. The case of Xerox 9700 printing machine discussed in Oren et al. (1980) illustrates this point. In fact, as Rowe et al. (1986) pointed out, forecasting, if used strategically, can help the firm examine the implications of the change in strategic variables such as sales on strategies. Given the uncertainty involved in judgmental forecasting, the interesting question becomes how best the information provided by forecasting can be used for effective strategic management.

4.2 Definitions

Montgomery (1985) explains what the difference is between strategic and tactical planning. Strategic is long term, corporate oriented whereas tactical is short term and functionally oriented. While there is no consensus as to how the word *strategy* should be defined, it is easier to understand if it is compared to the word tactics. Schendel (1985) provides an overview of the definitions proposed by various people, most of these regard strategy as dealing with the setting of goals, allocation of resources and establishing of policies and course of actions for achieving these goals. Schendel considers strategy in terms of 5 components:

1. scope of operations,
2. resources availability and deployment,
3. competitive advantage,
4. operating policies,
5. administrative structure.

Strategy is typically needed in all three levels of a modern organization, namely corporate level, business level and functional area level. According to Schendel (1985), *strategic management* is concerned with the processes and techniques for developing and implementing a balance among the three elements, goals, strategy and environment which imposes a constraint on the strategy for achieving a goal. A detailed description of the various steps and methodologies leading to a strategic plan and its integration into the organizational structure can be found in Hax et al. (1984).

4.3 Role of Demand Forecasting in Strategic Management

Demand forecasting serves the purpose of marketing. Marketing is mainly involved in strategies making at the business level, which concerns about market position, competitors, market share, growth rates and product life cycles. Since marketing is by nature environmentally oriented, it plays an important role in strategic management. Effective marketing and hence effective strategic management leads to competitive advantage[6] which is a measure of the quality of strategy. Competitive advantage is necessary for a firm's survival.

In general, environmental forecasting and assumptions together with information about the existing situation are important in strategies formulation[7]. Good strategic management, which consists of good strategies that interact and respond well to the environment, will lead the firm to its goal-competitive advantage over other firms.

The role of a demand forecasting system (DFS) can be summarized by the following diagram (Fig. 2) which consists of five levels of interactions, covering information, tools, organization, strategic management and competitive advantage.

[6] Competitive advantage arises from the excess in value provided to the buyer vs the cost of creating such a value (Porter (1985)). It can be achieved by providing the same benefit at a lower price than the competitors (cost leadership) or providing a unique benefit which more than offsets the higher price (differentiation).

[7] This can be done using decision analysis. By examining all the alternatives, together with the use of the forecasting result that has only a certain chance of being accurate, a good strategy can be formulated.

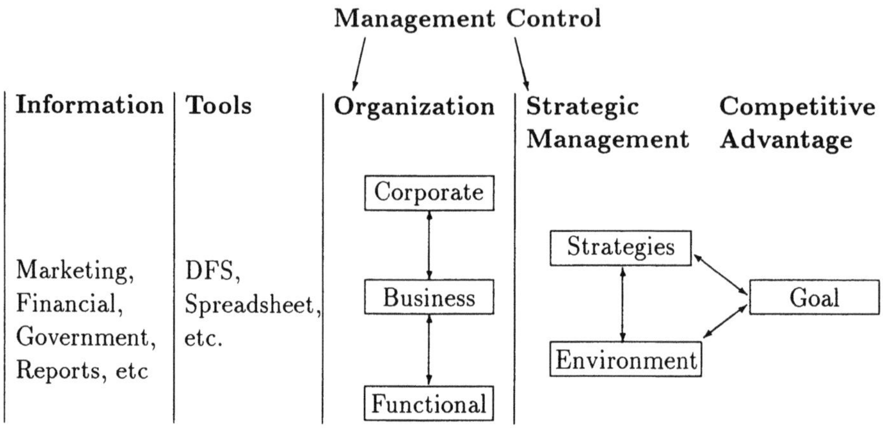

Figure 2: Five Levels of Interactions for Competitive Advantage

4.3.1 Information and Tools

Demand forecasting systems, like spreadsheets, serve as tools for the managers or decision makers in an organization to process the information from marketing reports, financial statements, and government reports etc. In fact, information is like raw materials, and the information processing systems such as the demand forecasting system are the machine tools. Intrinsic in a machine tool is a methodology for carrying out the processing. In this case, the underlying methodology is judgmental forecasting.

4.3.2 Organization

In general, a corporate is decomposed into several businesses, and these are again decomposed into several functional units or are linked to them in a matrix form. The decomposition is done to reap the benefits of increased autonomy and reduced bureaucracy, but it has to bear with the waste associated with inevitable resource duplication. The relationship between the corporate level and the business/functional level is as follows: The Company's Executive Officer (CEO) approves strategic and operational funds (long and short term). The business units impress the corporate level with the quality of its work; and this has some impacts on the decision made by the corporate CEO and the fellow business units. The CEO generally decides the resource allocation, growth-profitability tradeoffs and cash balancing etc. Demand forecasting is generally used at the corporate level. It can be also used by the individual business unit to ensure the congruence of corporate and business goals.

4.3.3 Strategic Management

As mentioned above, strategic management deals with the interactions among the strategies, environment and goal. Strategies can be adopted at every level of the organizational structure. Good strategies should

- lead to more market opportunities;

- neutralize adverse environmental impacts such as the reduction of the bargaining powers of suppliers and buyers;
- deal effectively with new entrants and substitutes.

All in all, good management control which oversees the interactions between organization and strategic management (including the interactions with the environment) should lead to competitive advantage, which should be the overall goal of the firm.

4.4 Impact of Demand Forecasting System

The impact of the demand forecasting system depends on

- the quality (timeliness, accuracy, extensiveness, importance/relevance etc.) of the information,
- the appropriateness of the methodology,
- the acceptance of the forecasting system in an organization,
- the quality of feedback by its users, and finally
- its interactions with the environment.

Hence, the demand forecasting system is not a static system. It is dynamic in the sense that it should be updated constantly as time goes by.

5 Conclusion and Future Research

The main result of this work was to establish a model for demand forecasting of industries competing in the market share of supplying workstations to end-user groups classified by applications. The justification for using this model is done by comparing it to a general equilibrium model, noting the differences and tradeoffs. The paper further attempted to explain the reasons for choosing judgmental forecasting, instead of the more popular quantitative forecasting. Forecasting is useful only if it is integrated into the whole strategic management process. Hence, future research in this context would not be "how to do forecasting" since there has been a lot of work on that, rather "what significance does forecasting have", and "what impact does forecasting have on strategic management" and "how to maximize the use of forecasting".

Acknowledgements

I would like to express my gratitude to Professor John P. Weyant of Engineering-Economic Systems Department, Stanford University, for his many fruitful comments and advice in the process of this research and the writing up of this paper. I am also thankful to Dr. Jaffer R. Syed and Dr. Chulho Park of Petrochemicals, Polymers and Energy Center, SRI International, for helping me in the initial stage of this research.

References

ASHER, W., and OVERHOLT W.H. (1983), *Strategic Planning and Forecasting*, A Wiley-Interscience Publication, John Wiley & Sons, New York.

BRODY, H. (1988), Sorry, Wrong Number, misprediction of the course of technology business, *High Technology Business, September.*

HAX, A., and MAJLUF, N.S. (1984), *Strategic Management, An Integrative Perspective*, Prentice Hall.

HOWARD, R.A. (1988), Decision Analysis: Practice and Promise, *Management Science, 34, 6.*

KEEN, P.G.W., and SCOTT MORTON, M.S. (1978), *Decision Support Systems: An Organizational Perspective*, Addison-Wesley, Reading.

LITTLE, J.D.C. (1975), Brandaid: A Marketing-Mix Model, *Operations Research, 23, 4.*

LUENBURGER, D.G. (1979), *Dynamic Systems*, John Wiley & Sons, New York.

LUENBURGER, D.G. (1988), *Economic Analysis*, Stanford University's EES Dept. Course Note, EES 212 A & B.

MONTGOMERY, D.B. (1985), Toward Decision Support Systems for Strategic Marketing, in: *Strategic Marketing and Management*, ed. by H. Thomas et al., John Wiley & Sons, New York.

POH, H.L. (1988), *Demand Forecasting and Strategic Management*, Tutorial Report, EES Department, Stanford University.

PORTER, M.E. (1985), *Competitive Advantage*, Free Press.

ROWE, A.J., MASON, R.O., and DICKEL, K.E. (1986), *Strategic Management and Business Policy—A Methodological Approach*, 2nd ed., Addison-Wesley, Reading.

SAATY, T.L. (1980), *The Analytic Hierarchy Process*, McGraw-Hill, New York.

SCHENDEL, D.E. (1985), Strategic Management and Strategic Marketing: What's strategic about either one?, *Strategic Marketing & Management*, ed. by H. Thomas and D. Gardner, John Wiley & Sons, New York.

SYED, J.R. (1988a), *An integrated Demand Forecasting System for Petrochemical Industry, report of SRI's Petrochemicals*, Polymers and Energy Center, Menlo Park, CA.

SYED, J.R. (1988b), *An Intermaterial Substitution Simulator, report of SRI's Petrochemicals*, Polymers and Energy Center, Menlo Park, CA.

TVERSKY, A., and KAHNEMAN, D. (1974), Judgment Under Uncertainty: Heuristics and Biases, *Science, 185*, 1124–1131.

VARIAN, H.R. (1978), *Microeconomic Analysis*, W.W. Norton & Company, New York.

WEYANT, J.P. (1985), General Economic Equilibrium As A Unifying Concept In Energy-Economic Modeling, *Management Science, 31, 5.*

WHEELWRIGHT, S.C. (1985), *Forecasting Methods For Management*, 4th ed., John Wiley & Sons, New York.

WINKLER, R.L. (1987), Judgmental and Bayesian Forecasting, in: *The Handbook of Forecasting*, ed. by S. Makridakis and S.C. Wheelwright, John Wiley & Sons, New York.

WRIGHT, G., and AYTON, P. (1987), *Judgmental Forecasting*, John Wiley & Sons, New York.

Model Management: The Core of Intelligent Decision Support

Franz-J. Radermacher
Forschungsinstitut für Anwendungsorientierte Wissensverarbeitung (FAW)
an der Universität Ulm, Germany

Summary

Supporting decision making in an intelligent way is a major topic in automated system design since many years. Scientific fields such as decision analysis, artificial intelligence, decision support systems and expert systems have contributed to this area. By now, main insights into the problems arising suggest that, in essence, the hard core of problems to be addressed deals with questions of modeling and model management. The idea herein is that relevant data concerning ongoing processes has to be transformed via appropriate models into insights that are then the basis of good decision making. Models employed range from classical approaches like differential equations, games, probability theory, decision analysis and others to modern frameworks in artificial intelligence, ranging from logic programming to all kinds of knowledge-based reasoning. Herein, the latter aspects particularly serve as a meta-knowledge specification tool that allows the representation of how human professionals use and employ all kinds of classical tools for problem solving. The present paper discusses these insights in some detail and interprets, how model management is related to phenomena such as intelligence, learning, adaption, insight and, at the highest level, consciousness as well. The paper also addresses the questions of adequately using model management approaches for different application areas and also includes an overview on projects of that type, presently dealt with at the FAW in Ulm.

1 Artificial Intelligence and Modeling

When talking about intelligent systems or artificial intelligence in general, there is an immediate connotation to notions like intelligence, learning, adaption, insight, and at a very high level pre-consciousness or consciousness as well. Of course, the question for the nature of intelligence and, similarly, for the potential of artificial intelligence is an old one, that finds many answers but will hardly be fully settled (Dreyfuss (1985), Hofstadter (1985), Hofstadter and Dennet (1982), Winograd and Flores (1986)). The traditional paradigm of artificial intelligence is that symbol manipulation is at the core of intelligent behavior. With the strong emphasis on neural nets in recent years this view is however changing. The present paper, therefore, takes a different perspective, already discussed in a number of publications (Applegate, Konsynski and Nunamaker (1986), Bartusch, Möhring and Radermacher (1989), Jarke and Radermacher (1988), Keeney, Möhring, Otway, Radermacher and Richter (1988, 1989), Radermacher (1988)), and sees modeling and the manipulation of models as the hard core of intelligent behavior. Herein, modeling is to be understood in a sense that surpasses symbol manipulation, e.g., with respect to

NATO ASI Series, Vol. F 61
Knowledge, Data and Computer-Assisted Decisions
Edited by M. Schader and W. Gaul

aspects inherent in pure geometric form or in the dynamic aspects of neural nets seen as a kind of black box modeling of the surrounding world. Even within the symbolic processing paradigm, the types of models that might be used go beyond models of logic nature or inheritance, or decomposition and constrained propagation mechanisms that presently dominate the approaches used in AI applications. So, other interesting models should come into view as, e.g., models from optimization theory, statistics, decision theory, stochastics, game theory, differential equations, theory of automata, data bases, and others (Jarke and Radermacher (1988)). In fact, there is a particular potential in employing the more recent frameworks from artificial intelligence as a meta representation scheme with which to integrate more classical modeling frameworks toward specific goals. Meta-level knowledge to be represented will in particular concern the ways of how human professionals use and employ all kinds of classical tools for problem solving. If symbolic manipulation is seen in such a broad context, it can be particularly helpful with regard to decision making and decision support, as is discussed later. We just mention that viewing intelligence as the ability to master a variety of models of the environment allows the easy integration of other concepts as well. E.g., the ability to modify and manipulate such models in response to experience can be seen as processes of learning and adaption; finding invariants, dependencies, connections, and so on within such models are forms of insight and the basis for future model variations and adaptions. Proceeding this way, hierarchies of Eigenmodels of systems might eventually be seen as forms of pre-consciousness of systems and as a very first step even towards consciousness of systems. Certainly, these are difficult subjects of a basic and philosophical nature that reach into the future. But certainly, though, the framework of model manipulation—when seen from a broad enough prospective—seems to offer an enormous potential to cope with phenomena that are encountered everywhere in real life. Consequently, the test bed for the modeling and model management approach to (artificial) intelligence should be real-life applications, where the essence is the ability to model relevant parts of the world in a meaningful way and to draw relevant conclusions (inferences) from such models as a basis for further actions. Herein, notions like "meaningful" have ultimately to be traced back to the evolutional principle of "relative fitness" or "survival" as the last interpretation of "successful behavior". Of course, reality may shrink to sub-worlds, if we restrict attention and performance requirements to very specific domains. Extreme specializations of this type are "toy worlds" such as the block worlds in special robotics applications or man-made "artificial worlds", if we deal with, e.g., simple games or specific mathematical theories. The more, however, we deal with real-life applications—and decision problems as discussed later are usually of this type—the more we have to deal with phenomena that man himself understands only to a certain extent. I.e., we deal with a reality for which we do not possess more than (maybe quite elaborate) models which are open to falsification in the course of progress of science; and as we know such—sometimes major—modifications have occurred several times in the history of science (Kuhn (1970), Popper (1974)). Given this emphasis on evolutional principals, the building in of such mechanisms into intelligent systems seems to be a very important point, and to some extent learning in essence seems to be of that nature. Considering the data situation, trying to find out what dependencies, connections, or hidden variables might be there, taking reasonable decisions on what to assume, staying to some extent with such decisions over time (a form of truth maintenance), monitoring the own performance, and then, on a higher level, trying to intermix different but partly successful approaches into always new generations of systems is the kind of genetic feedback cycle one should have in mind. This includes genetic algorithms and special variants of this like simulated annealing (Fogel, Owens and Walsh (1966), Grefenstette (1985)). In taking that position, evolution is seen as the meta-principle that naturally comes along with every evolved process of adaption, learning and reproduction. It allows to understand how higher levels of life eventually carry models of their environment. Models are very coarse in the beginning, reducing the whole world to, e.g., two states but become more involved over time in this evolutionary process driven by the ultimate criteria of survival. Basic to survival is often a higher degree of granularity in modeling, e.g., splitting given states into sub-cases can be an important achievement. The principles involved here can be characterized by processes of recombination and randomization. Recombination is a quite safe way to produce new solutions in an implicitly given solution space. Randomization is a smoothing device and a cautious way of extending the borderline of the implicitly defined solution spaces.

Driving force is the survival criterion that statistically gives a higher degree of influence on shaping the next generation to individuals that "behave" better. With sexual reproduction and group coherence, more weight is put on carrying latent information, spreading of information over group members, or even carrying mutually beneficial abilities over various cooperating group members.

Copying the evolutional process is the best hope for real "smart" systems which should eventually show really surprising and impressive behavior. There is a long scientific tradition in this respect, known as "evolution strategy" or "genetic algorithms" (Fogel, Owens and Walsh (1966), Grefenstette (1985)). Weaker versions of evolutionary strategies are statistical adaption, simulated annealing, and related approaches which in their easiest form mean that one favors actions successfully in earlier stages relative to other available actions by decreasing accordingly the probability of activating unsuccessful actions. This is a simple way of accumulating knowledge and system experience over time. This approach can be combined with the possible modification of the notion of "situation", (i.e., the basic entities) through simple set-theoretic or logic operators. Often, local optimization alone leads to locally good solutions or notions only. The annealing principle therefore to a certain extent prefers worse solutions to better ones in order to avoid local optimality traps. For stability reasons, the probability of accepting bad steps decreases over time, following basic properties of thermodynamic processes. Of course, all such "blind" adaption processes are only recommendable if deeper (human) insight is missing.

Also, the more vague and unintentional these "learning" or "adaption" processes become, the slower they work. There is often no way of using old collected data for training and acceleration of such an adaption process, as the interaction of the constantly modified system with this old data would be missing. Thus, adaption is slow; it is comparable to the adaption of living beings, thus limiting exaggerated expectations when seen for applications in typical sophisticated problem areas involving constant human-machine interaction.

2 Cognitive Aspects of Decision Making

The topic of this paper and of the workshop is on decision and on decision making. We just mention that making adequate decisions over long time periods in a changing environment and subject to incomplete information, misinformation, uncertainty, and changing preferences is one of the central and most sophisticated cognitive abilities of man (Jarke and Radermacher (1988), Radermacher (1988)). Understanding the determinants of good decision making resembles the understanding of intelligent behavior. The extreme degree of cognitive complexity of decision making is to some extent still overlooked in artificial intelligence. In fact, as was argued in a number of recent papers, the contributions of modern AI to the real hard topics in decision making, e.g., with respect to major industrial or political decisions, is comparatively small (Frank (1989), Radermacher (1989)). There is a number of reasons for that which can essentially be summarized as follows:

Hard decisions usually deal with processes over time. Major determinants of what will eventually happen are not controlled by the decision maker. Essential parts come from the general process of the development of the world which has an enormous degree of chaotic behavior and certainly allows only limited options of guaranteeing or controlling particular outcomes. The situation becomes even more complicated with other decision makers being involved, who partly may react independently, but partly also in form of feedback. In general, it is not clear what other people will do, how they will react to moves of oneself, how the general public will see certain things in the future, how general politics will evolve. Given this uncertainty on the state of the environment and the limited cause-effect relationships within the part of the system where there is at least some control by the decision maker, this situation for decision support is already hard. But on top of that come the difficult problems of varying preferences. Usually, whatever strategy is followed, there is an opportunity for different outcomes, and these different outcomes have a number of interesting aspects. Generally, there will be no strategy that gets dominating solutions in all respects to other strategies. So, generally, there will be a kind of trade-off or balancing of different aspects against each other, meaning there are preference modeling aspects involved for often quite nasty trade-off-situations. Usually, it will already be hard on the level of a single individual to formulate his preferences. Not to speak about the problems if different humans have to agree on one preference model. It might then even be that the indication of a personal preference will already influence the preference of others in one way or another. So, there are extremely involved problems, and the situation would be almost hopeless, if not the decision makers would have at least a certain influence on defining a posteriori what the outcome really is and how it is to be interpreted (Frank (1989)). Reviewing this very complicated and involved situation, there are hard limitations to what can be done. In fact, we are confronted with a quite weak form of modeling, i.e., with models of low predictive power in the sense that the statistical coincidence between conclusions from the models and the real outcome is loose at best. On top of that, as a society we often need humans to be responsible for the outcome, in particular if the outcome is bad. So, for a number of practical and psychological reasons (limited models, personal responsibility, human influence on defining a situation) we need humans to be involved in hard decision making. Involving humans with their personal risk also seems to be the best kind of insurance of the society against deliberate wrong-doing by people who are in charge. With this in mind, we have to look carefully for the kinds of models that might be used in decision making and in decision support systems.

Given huge data sets, all kinds of statistical tools and tools from data analysis, such as correlation or regression analysis, the identification of statistical dependencies or of hidden variables in a statistical sense are about the best to hope for in general settings. Concerning cause-effect relationships, statistical evidence is important, as long as no deeper models are already identified and (again statistically) validated. Of essential importance is certainly the preference modeling, i.e., trying to model (at least on the level of a single human) very carefully trade-offs between certain aims. In all these tasks, the available theory helps. Still, one will generally be confronted with the risk of a "bad" decision (seen ex post), whatever was decided ex ante. Good decisions can in general at best increase the probability for a good outcome, but cannot guarantee it. As mentioned already, the evaluation of an outcome is a question of preferences, where preferences may change over time; even if a decision yields the originally preferred solution, it may no longer be wanted when realized. Luckily, it may also be the other way round.

The very involved nature of these different intermixed aspects of preferences and uncertainty have somewhat limited the degree to which humans have a systematic and uniform ability to cope with difficult decision situations in a satisfactory way. It is known from cognitive psychology that there is a quite stable human reaction pattern only in relative simple decision situations. In more complicated situations, however, reactions may become instable, may possibly be revised after a thorough examination, and may often also contradict certain logical principles that the same person wants to follow. Research on such so-called Bias phenomena in behavioral sciences (Fischhoff, Slovic and Lichtenstein (1980), Hersey, Kunreuther and Shoemaker (1982)) constitutes an important help in the design of adequate user interfaces for advanced systems. The main underlying ideas in this area date back to the basic work and central representation theorem by von Neumann and Morgenstern (1976) that identifies good decision making as maximizing the expected utility over an action space with regard to (subjective) probabilities for world-states involved and with regard to a (multi-attribute) utility function for the evaluation of (vectors of) results (Fishburn (1977), Keeney and Raiffa (1976)).

This utility-theoretic framework is by now very rich and has successfully been applied in many applications. There exists by now also a number of software tools, e.g. for finding single or multi-attribute utility functions or for doing decomposition of such functions. Available are also quite general decision-theoretical framing systems, such as PREFCALC or MAUD. Similar tools are available in multi-person decision situations, especially of game-theoretic nature either in the cooperative or noncooperative framework. However, given the much greater complications with many people involved, the normative basis for solid inferences is of course much more limited.

Besides preference modeling probability theory is another basic normative ingredient to general model building in decision support. General principles like ergodicity, limit theorems, best statistical tests or, more recently, stochastic bounds are important contributions to the solution of practical problems. With general results and principles, probability theory partly overcomes data acquisition problems that it seems to cause in the first place, and this is done in a normatively correct fashion.

Note that such general theories and theorems, as present e.g. in decision theory, probability theory and statistics, form about the strongest inference mechanisms available in the area of vague data. For reasons of efficiency and consistency, their use is recommended over other forms of knowledge-processing, whenever they might be employed (Jarke and Radermacher (1988)). We just mention that in a number of interesting applications, the stochastic aspects are the dominating elements of modeling. So, in certain situations, good systems should do automatic stochastification and a subsequent sensitivity analysis if needed, and communicate certain risks to the user (who might be ignorant of the whole theory behind such system performance).

In this context, it should be pointed out that classical theories for the handling of preferences and probabilities, when properly employed, allow the handling of most problems recently addressed under the notion of fuzziness. Such treatment is based on hard scientific insight and corresponding theorems. Naturally, certain extensions of classical models such as the Shafer-Dempster theory of evidence (1976) have to be integrated with a solid theoretical foundation.

To summarize, decision making is identified as a particularly hard subject from a cognitive point of view. Additional support is particularly reasonable for decisions of sophisticated nature but limited social impact. The more responsibility-rich the nature of a decision, the more support will be limited to information collection and recommendations. In any case, the employment of the typical models for this area, that deal with notions of uncertainty and preference modeling, will be in order. There are classical tools around for this purpose, and there are new developments in work at some places, e.g., at the Artificial Intelligence Laboratory (FAW) in Ulm. Such basic research efforts should make the respective models better handable, better integrable, and thus bring them to a better use in decision support.

3 Model Management as Important Ingredient for a Number of Projects at the AI Laboratory (FAW) in Ulm

The FAW was founded in 1987 as a cooperative venture of the state of Baden-Württemberg and six major industrial partners, namely Daimler-Benz AG, Hewlett-Packard GmbH, IBM Deutschland GmbH, Mannesmann Kienzle GmbH, Nixdorf Computer AG, and Siemens AG and maintains close ties with the university of Ulm. At the institute, about 120 people, including about 40 full-time scientists as well as staff, scientific guests, students, and others, are working in 14 projects for the development of new ideas and solutions for applied knowledge-based systems in fields such as computer-integrated manufacturing, office automation, environmental information systems, assistance systems, and management of distributed resources. The institute recently acquired a new building with a variety of sophisticated technical installations to support its projects, including demonstration facilities, advanced communication networks, and a CIM mini-factory. The institute relies conceptionally on synergistic effects among industrial sponsors, state administration, and scientific support from industrial and university scientists, involving a great number of academic disciplines. An additional goal is to integrate AI tools and classical modeling methods, for example decision theory, statistics, and optimization. We just mention that among the 40 full-time scientists working at the FAW, 20 come directly from the sponsoring companies and institutions. From the FAW-employed scientists, five chief scientists are responsible for the research areas "Computer-integrated manufacturing", "Office automation", "Human-machine communication", "Fundamental concepts of knowledge processing", and "Infrastructure". Each of these chief scientists is at the same time responsible for one of the already mentioned application areas. In addition to the full-time scientists and about 60 students, one of the major ingredients is an average number of 10 visiting scientists from all over the world. Other synergistic effects result from the fact that these scientists come from about 8 academic disciplines, that they deal with the visiting scientists, and that there is a large program of short-term visitors, a lecture program, and a program of both theoretical and applied workshops in different fields. In all the work, the FAW is strongly oriented toward the kind of model-oriented AI approach that was described at the beginning of the text, and in doing so, the institute regards itself to be at the front of actual scientific progress in this field. As proved reasonable in many projects, the idea to use modern AI techniques as a meta-representation language to integrate a variety of classical models seems to be particularly fruitful. In the following, the FAW projects will shortly be described with some hints to modeling ideas involved. Note that the institute is presently working in 14 projects associated with the 5 mentioned application areas.

4 FAW Projects

4.1 Automated Production

(senior scientist: Dr. H.-J. Held)

In this application area, the classical CIM chain, including computer-aided design, computer-aided planning, computer-aided manufacturing, and computer-aided quality control, is of particular interest. Related FAW projects are described next:

CAD/KI: This pre-market project tries to enhance the potential of present CAD systems by feeding back information on productivity and cost aspects as early as possible to the engineer. An important feature is the extension of available knowledge in form of product models. Such models will contain more information than might eventually be obtained from geometry information via feature extraction. Such information may concern the fact that certain work processes have to precede others, that particular tools have to be used to do certain activities, and that the use of certain tools may cause certain times to do the respective tool-movements. Consequently, modeling relies strongly on relations, tables, functional dependencies, and so forth.

CAP (Nixdorf Computer AG): Information from product models can be a basis for computer-aided planning for the generation of e.g. NC-programs in a way that surpasses present day approaches using decision tables. In such applications, the FAW is also attempting to employ complex optimization algorithms to obtain work plans guaranteeing a special quality. This means that from a product or geometry model, it is possible to deduce via given relations an abstract mathematical model of the situation, which in certain applications is e.g. a travelling salesman model with precedence constraints. Here, available and involved optimization algorithms can be employed in a proper way to find the best movements of production tools which can then be translated into working plans. Such plans might then, for instance, be directly visualized in the CAD systems and can be used to feed back immediately time and cost aspects resulting from a particular layout. It should be mentioned that in this project, the FAW started a cooperation with the research group around Prof. Dr. M. Grötschel, University of Augsburg, that is among the world-wide leading groups in the field of combinatorial optimization with respect to travelling salesman problems.

KWEST: Computer-aided manufacturing is the topic of this project, which aims at a simultaneous production planning and control. This project is being conducted in co-operation with the IPA institute in Stuttgart and with industrial partners from small and medium enterprises and is partly sponsored by the state of Baden-Württemberg. It is this project where new solutions will be demonstrated via the CIM mini-factory at the FAW. In addition, computer-aided quality control will be included using, for example, image processing. In KWEST, emphasis will be given to the use of multi-attribute decision-making as a tool to model the different targets a user might want to follow. Also, insights from stochastic scheduling concerning the identification of appropriate strategies with view to the possibility of system-component break-down will be employed.

AIDA (Daimler-Benz AG, Hewlett Packard GmbH): The AIDA project is related to quality control and concerns the diagnosis of one of the most complex multiple die pressing production lines in the European automobile industry. This is a very involved project in the area of process control for technically involved processes. The FAW hopes to be pivotal in establishing an account of relevant cases for a classification of faults and introducing different kinds of database and statistical tools for identifying in a problem-dependent way particularly promising solutions. So, in particular, the essential modeling here is given via relations that indicate certain relationships between means and effects, where the transitions will include success with certain probability, causing certain cost. The nature of the used description is statistical. There is a great interest towards automatic learning, e.g., concerning the identification of certain hidden parameters. Some ideas from the field of markov chains seem to be useful, for instance, in finding good actions with a look-ahead policy over many steps as compared to a single-step horizon.

4.2 Office Automation

(senior scientist: Dr. D. Karagiannis)

The area of office automation bears a particularly high potential for increased efficiency due to effective decision support. This potential even seems to extend the one in the CIM area, where the degree of automation is already much higher. On the other hand, the office field contains particular problems, e.g., the strong human involvement, the importance of processes such as information sharing, bargaining and so forth. It is, therefore, an area in which the FAW has a great deal of interest, specifically concerning the integration of office automation and computer-integrated manufacturing. An important contribution is the introduction by Dr. Karagiannis of the idea of flexible office systems. Flexible office systems attempt to model the level of automation in flexible manufacturing systems in industrial environments, which has not yet been fully exploited in the field of office automation. In a number of projects, the FAW is presently trying to establish and promote this idea of flexible office systems.

OSSY: OSSY is a pre-market project on organizational support systems and is the main test bed for the idea of flexible office systems. Within OSSY, a process control system, an intelligent mailing system, and an intelligent retrieval system are integrated via a task management component as a basis for distributed office work support. The system will be employed at the FAW with a view to processing complicated text documents involving updates and contributions from many people and many aspects of cooperation and bargaining. Typical examples will include the FAW research reports, the annual budget plan, and software documentation. As already mentioned, OSSY is just one way for testing this idea of flexible office systems, and there is interest in finding project partners in other fields such as banking or technical offices support. In the banking field as in the office in general, the aspect of cooperation and bargaining sometimes is of major importance. The FAW in this field uses modeling tools that allow to understand certain bargaining situations as partly cooperative games between the involved participants, and at the moment uses simple game-theoretic strategies to find reasonable compromises. In doing so, organizational knowledge, e.g., knowledge concerning earlier situations of the same type, of burden on particular persons, and so forth, is employed as a way to determine the degree to which certain people are to be satisfied by compromise solutions, proposed by the system.

MHS (IBM Deutschland GmbH): Concerning technical office work, the FAW is concluding a project for IBM concerning the support of the design of material handling systems. This project is based on application knowledge for the field of factory layout planning for electronic devices. The emphasis is again on the integration of AI tools and classical modeling and optimization tools. The resulting system, developed with the expert system tool KEE, consists of an expert system for factory layout in which a wide variety of domain knowledge is incorporated as rules as well as via inheritance from frame-oriented representations, including certain constraints. On the other hand, given a system layout, classical tools from, e.g., queuing theory are used to infer performance parameters such as the steady handling of material, the size of buffers, the processing speed, and others. In addition to performance parameters, cost information is also deduced. This information exceeds directly quantifiable values and contains qualitative aspects in form of a rough multi-attributive cost modeling and integration.

4.3 Environmental Information System

(senior scientist: Dr. O. Günther)

The state of Baden-Württemberg is pioneering new concepts for the establishment of statewide environmental control systems. Representatives and experts from the Ministry for Environment, together with partners from designated state institutions and external consultants and partners from science, are working together in this field. The FAW appreciates being involved as a scientific partner in a number of activities and has mounted a number of projects in this field. Three major projects are described next. There is a close connection to an additional database project WINHEDA, discussed below. Also, presently in preparation is another joint FAW-project between the state of Baden-Württemberg and IBM Deutschland GmbH in the field of natural language access to distributed databases. This new project should begin in October 1989, and will be related to the three projects described next.

ZEUS: Zeus is a pre-market project that addresses fundamental research requirements for the construction of environmental information systems. ZEUS uses a top-down approach and is concerned with the representation of meta-knowledge. Emphasis is not on narrow specialization, but on the integration and presentation of knowledge from a broad context (in this case the water department area). The FAW effort will consider the meta-knowledge associated with available databases or data collection, administrative responsibilities, and competence (organized from a geographical and scenario-oriented viewpoint), as well as available scientific knowledge, including information on modeling and computation tools, their precision, time consumption, data dependencies, and compatibility. Major considerations are the formulation of relevant scenarios that cover the range from surface water, rivers, and lakes to underground water control, to the placement of water quality monitoring stations, to installations for water clearance, and so forth. We just mention that there are many kinds of models of importance in environmental systems which range from diffusion models in form of differential equations for the diffusion of underground water, to location problems and to decisions problems, e.g. where to build e.g. certain technical installations. The ZEUS project is closely coordinated with the two projects, described next.

RESEDA (state of Baden-Württemberg, Siemens AG): The FAW RESEDA project is jointly financed by the state of Baden-Württemberg and the Siemens AG and deals with the extraction of useful data from satellite and aircraft sensors. The methodological emphasis is to use knowledge about ground conditions, geographical aspects, etc., in order to facilitate the automatic interpretation of such images. The thematic emphasis will be on the reliable extraction of basic data from images in a regular way. This will form the basis for performing time series analysis as an example with the aim of detecting slow long-term changes as well as sudden rapid changes of the state of the environment. Informations of interest within the RESEDA project will (at least indirectly) be of relevance for the field of water analysis.

WANDA (state of Baden-Württemberg, Hewlett Packard GmbH): The WANDA project sponsored by the state of Baden-Württemberg and the Hewlett Packard GmbH, aims at the development of an expert system for water analysis to help in detecting (unexpected) dangerous contamination in water samples. Again, knowledge of related environmental parameters and information concerning the location of the contaminants will be used to ease combinatorial problems in resolving ambiguities in data interpretation. The data is acquired by means of chemical testing, e.g., high performance liquid gas chromatography. The modeling problems here are partly from the field of functional analysis and mean, e.g., the right kind of description of "distances" between chromatographic patterns. Other modeling aspects are combinatorially in nature and deal with the description of substances via reference values with regard to certain tests.

In all of its projects in the area of environmental information systems, the FAW relies heavily on the close contact with its administrative partners in Baden-Württemberg and with the scientific environment, including in particular the Ministery for Environment and corresponding institutions such as the LfU (Landesanstalt für Umweltschutz in Baden-Württemberg) in Karlsruhe.

4.4 Assistance Systems

(senior scientist: Dr. D. Rösner)

Assistance systems attempt to bridge the gap between involved technical applications and humans responsible for useful decision-making under severe conditions. Major problems concern the cooperative interface between automatic systems and humans.

IKARUS (Daimler-Benz AG, Mannesmann Kienzle GmbH): The interface question is the major topic in the FAW project IKARUS, financed by Daimler-Benz and Mannesmann Kienzle. The aim is to address the human-machine interface problems for the car of the future. The project aims at the development of a system that will simulate, test, and collect data concerning the effects of different ways of establishing the interface between human-machine communication and automated system behavior (e.g. automatic braking upon the detection of an obstacle in front of the vehicle without any reaction from the driver). As a consequence of the concluded phases of the project, the FAW will be concerned with a number of identified scenarios of typical and dangerous situations for which advanced system abilities might proof helpful. Mutually agreed upon aspects concern the kind and reliability of information available to the system. This last aspect has interesting consequences for modeling, particularly concerning the probability of mistakes of two kinds, namely the probability to identify correctly something that is there and the probability of identify the same thing, although it is not there. These and other aspects yield stochastic elements into the project that have to be properly taken into account in the simulation context.

PROMOTEX (Daimler-Benz AG): The FAW project PROMOTEX concerns a problem of engine diagnosis. The FAW is a subcontractor of Daimler-Benz, which itself is a partner of an ESPRIT project dealing with the validation of PROLOG III. The language PROLOG III is a major extension of earlier PROLOG dialogues developed by Prof. Colmerauer (Marseille) and the company PrologIA. The validation of the potential and expressiveness of this language is being performed by two German industrial partners, Daimler-Benz AG and Robert Bosch GmbH. These partners build a development environment and additional inference and explanatory facilities using this language, and test the system with industrial diagnosis problems. Particularly, PROMOTEX deals with the diagnosis of a car engine. One of the essential features is a deeper modeling of the engine by breaking it up hierarchically into components and by representing parts of the (sometimes nonlinear) functional dependencies between certain parameters involved (e.g., between gas use and power) in PROLOG III via piecewise linear functional approximations, and as logical expressions with additional integer constraints.

WINHEDA: The FAW pre-market project WINHEDA deals with accessing distributed knowledge sources, in particular databases, where the particularities of the special data sources and questions of physical access are hidden from the user, perhaps even to the extent that the user might be able to communicate with the system in natural language to some degree. Major aspects of present efforts in this project concern the representation of meta-knowledge concerning the available knowledge sources, the kind of information available in these sources and the physical access to these sources.

4.5 Distributed Resource Management

(senior scientist: Dr. D. Solte)

Distributed resource management is a topic of great importance for the FAW. The FAW uses distributed hardware and software facilities of great diversity, together with sophisticated internal and external communication, mailing, telephone, and telefax facilities. Such facilities are difficult to exploit in the most efficient way by the FAW staff, as they are for partners in industry in comparable environments. At present, knowledge-based components for handling these distributed systems seem to be the primary means for extracting the full benefit out of these investments. However, effective system solutions will have to include learning facilities to determine the most appropriate processors and tools for a specific task. A system should know how to handle and process certain wishes of users via a distributed environment, and, thereby, the system should make the best use of presently available hardware resources. The FAW is presently looking for project partners in these fields, while working already on some basic research projects.

SESAM: The FAW SESAM project is a pre-market activity and generally deals with decision support in the field of scheduling (Bartusch, Möhring and Radermacher (1989)). Scheduling was chosen as an application area where there is deep basic research knowledge available at the FAW. At the same time, scheduling plays a role in a number of FAW projects, particularly whenever time and resource consuming tasks have to be taken into account. Within this project, the FAW is also attempting to extend the present-day modeling abilities of AI tools. This concerns in particular the availability of representation schemes for multi-attribute utility functions and user preferences as part of user modeling as well as representation schemes for probability distributions or classes of distributions for the treatment of classical problems of uncertainty. In this respect, new inference mechanisms, in particular for the computation of stochastic bounds in monotonic systems (Bartusch, Möhring and Radermacher (1989), Klein-Haneveld (1986), Meilijson and Nadas (1979)), were realized jointly with Prof. Dr. H. Möhring and his group from the Technical University of Berlin and are now available at the FAW. Also, scheduling is used as a test-bed for the integrated use of hundreds of different algorithmic tools for the treatment of subtypes of difficult (NP-complete) problems in a coordinated way (Bartusch, Möhring, Radermacher (1989), Jarke and Radermacher (1988), Lawler, Lenstra and Rinnooy Kan (1982)). These include the use of heuristics, of approximation schemes, of upper and lower bounds, and so forth, where the emphasis is on learning via the observing of the potential of employed tools over time. Such internal knowledge should improve decisions concerning the appropriate tool use in a given situation, and should yield an effective test-bed for statistical learning components.

ALIAS: The pre-market project ALIAS at the FAW is being performed jointly with Prof. Dr. P. Bock from the George Washington University and three of his PhD students. The work is partially sponsored by the University of Ulm and by the Robert Bosch GmbH and employs a hierarchical distributed parallel-processing network architecture to simulate the signal processing of a very small section of the human cerebral cortex, applied to the problem of image understanding. The model of the cortical processes is very detailed from the point of view of information processing, information bandwidth, and feed-back control. Emphasis is on acquiring the statistical regularity of pixel distributions through unsupervised and supervised learning, instead of explicit pre-programmed world knowledge. During unsupervised learning, the system acquires an understanding of an equivalence class of images, which is revised and refined during supervised learning to include normal irregularities (e.g., roads in fields) and abnormal irregularities (e.g., buildings in deserts).

5 Concluding Remarks

To summarize this paper, it was tried to give an idea of where artificial intelligence should put emphasis on and where there are big opportunities to overcome some of the difficulties that AI applications to date have encountered many times in practical situations. The main aspect seems to be a concentration on modeling of the respective applications as the hard part of knowledge acquisition and knowledge engineering and the right use of available tools to handle such models. Certainly, the more recent AI contributions from the field of logic models including object-oriented programming, inheritance, splitting up of systems into components, and integrating these with constraint propagation and truth maintenance give strong and powerful tools at least for building meta-level descriptions of applications which allow the incorporation on a lower level of classical modeling insight that has proved to be fruitful in the respective application domains. This idea is followed consequently at the AI Laboratory in Ulm in almost all of the projects and in a number of workshops. To the extent statements are possible at this stage, this approach has proved fruitful and promising. From the given perspective, work in data analysis is certainly one of the basic ingredients that are available for good and intelligent system design. At a deep level, data analysis is at the very core of automatically identifying cause-effect relationships, new notions, stable behavior, and so forth, which, on higher levels of description, may lead to concepts such as analogy and adaptive model changes. Thus, data analysis is close to any attempt to automatically model insight into the world, as it becomes available over the time.

Acknowledgements

I would like to thank all my co-scientists at the FAW in Ulm who helped and supported me in developing project-specifically the ideas that were reported in this text.

References

APPLEGATE, L.M., KONSYNSKI, B.R., and NUNAMAKER, J.F. (1986), Model Management Systems, Design for Decision Support, in: *Decision Support Systems 2, 1*, 81–91.

BARTUSCH, M., MÖHRING, R.H., and RADERMACHER, F.J. (1989), Design Aspects of an Advanced Model-oriented DSS for Scheduling Problems in Civil Engineering, *to appear in: Decision Support Systems.*

DREYFUSS, H.L. (1985), *Die Grenzen Künstlicher Intelligenz*, Athenäum, Königstein.

FISCHHOFF, B., SLOVIC, P., and LICHTENSTEIN, S. (1980), Knowing What You Want, Measuring Labile Values, in: *Cognitive Processes in Choice and Decision Behaviour*, ed. T. Wallstein, Erlbaum, Hillsdales, NJ.

FISHBURN, P.C. (1977), *Utility Theory for Decision Making*, John Wiley, New York.

FOGEL, L.J., OWENS, A.J., and WALSH, M.J. (1966), *Artificial Intelligence through Simulated Evolution*, John Wiley, New York.

FRANK, U. (1989), Expertensysteme: Ein erfolgversprechender Ansatz zur Automatisierung dispositiver Fähigkeiten, *Die Betriebswirtschaft 1*, 19–36.

GREFENSTETTE, J.J. (1985), *Proc. Intern. Conf. on Genetic Algorithms and their Application*, The Robotics Institute, Carnegie-Mellon University.

HERSEY, P., KUNREUTHER, H., and SCHOEMAKER, P.J. (1982), Bias in Assessment Procedures for Utility Functions, *Management Science 28*, 936–954.

HOFSTADTER, D.R. (1985), *Gödel, Escher, Bach*, Klett-Cotta, Stuttgart.

HOFSTADTER, D.R., and DENNETT, D.C. (1982), *The mind's I*, Bantam Books, London.

JARKE, M., and RADERMACHER, F.J. (1988), The AI Potential of Model Management and Its Central Role in Decision Support, *Decision Support Systems 4*, 387–404.

KEENEY, R.L., MÖHRING, R.H., OTWAY, H., RADERMACHER, F.J., and RICHTER, M.M. (1989), Multi-Attribute Decision-Making via O.R.-Based Expert Systems, (eds.), *Special Issue of Annals of Operations Research*.

KEENEY, R.L., MÖHRING, R.H., OTWAY, H., RADERMACHER, F.J., and RICHTER, M.M. (1989), Design Aspects of Advanced Decision Support Systems, (eds.), *Special Issue of Decision Support Systems*.

KEENEY, R.L., and RAIFFA, H. (1976), *Decisions with Multiple Objectives*, John Wiley, New York.

KLEIN-HANEVELD, W.K (1986), Robustness Against Dependence in PERT, An Application of Duality and Distributions of Known Marginals, in: *Mathematical Programming Studies 27*, 153–182.

KUHN, T.S. (1970), *The Structure of Scientific Revolutions*, Chicago University Press.

LAWLER, E.L., LENSTRA, J.K, and RINNOOY KAN, A.H.G. (1982), Recent Developments in Deterministic Sequencing and Scheduling, A Survey, in: *Deterministic and Stochastic Scheduling*, eds. M.A.H. Dempster et al., Reidel, Dordrecht.

MEILIJSON, I., and NADAS, A. (1979), Convex Majorization with an Application to the Length of Critical Paths, in: *J. Appl. Prob. 16*, 671–677.

POPPER, K.R. (1974), *Objektive Erkenntnis. Ein evolutionärer Entwurf*, Hoffmann & Campe, Hamburg.

RADERMACHER, F.J. (1988), Entwicklungsperspektiven rechnergestützter Entscheidungsfindung, in: *Proceedings des IBM-Symposiums 'Entscheidungsunterstützende Systeme'*, ed. J. Wolff, Oldenbourg Verlag, München.

RADERMACHER, F.J. (1989), Dialogbeitrag zu der Arbeit von U. Frank "Expertensysteme: Ein erfolgversprechender Ansatz zur Automatisierung dispositiver Fätigkeiten?", *Die Betriebswirtschaft 2*, 393–396.

SHAFER, G. (1976), *A Mathematical Theory of Evidence*, Princeton University Press, Princeton.

VON NEUMANN, J., and MORGENSTERN, O. (1976), *Theory of Games and Economic Behaviour*, University Press, Princeton.

WINOGRAD, T., and FLORES, F., Understanding Computers and Cognition, A New Foundation for Design, Ablex Publ. Co., Norwood, NJ.

SAM: A Knowledge-Based System for Modeling an Economist

Jean Louis Roos
Institut National de la Statistique et des Etudes Economiques
CNIA, Les Milles, France

Summary

Econometric softwares (TSP, TROLL, SYMSYS, ...) are used for modelling economy. The results are econometric models that realize economic forecasting. SAM is an experimental knowledge based system that modelizes not the economy but the economist's behavior. It can be seen as an assistant that aids economists to write economic diagnosis. It is written in Common-Lisp and LCE and runs on MVS (IBM 30xx) at the French National Statistical Institute (INSEE). The aim of the system is to realize a complex diagnostic of an economic problem and write it in natural language (French), associated with the most interesting statistical tables, as well as a human economist could do.

1 Introduction

Thirty years ago, economists worked with little quantitative data. Economic analysis consisted only in reflexion and links between certain data and great economic theory. Computers changed all that. Quantitative information is present in all economic activities: planning, forecasting, surveys and so on. Statistics are the leading tool for helping economists to understand and treat complex and large quantities of data. In addition, econometry can be used to determine a structural causal model of economic activity using a large statistics-based information system. The results are econometric models that carry into effect economic forecasting. Furthermore, econometric forecasting models sometimes give disappointing results. So, more and more frequently, economists wish to analyze data as economists, not as statisticians. The shape of a series, the instantaneous (and not structural) relationship, or causal link, between a particular data item and others, are economic problems, not statistical ones, but due to the large data base used and its complexity economists need an 'assistant' to help them to determine what is important and what is not.

SAM is an experimental knowledge based system that modelizes not the economy but the economist's behavior. SAM is a non-human assistant written in Common-Lisp and LCE[1] that runs on MVS (IBM 30xx) at the French National Statistical Institute (Institut National de la Statistique et des Etudes Economiques—INSEE). The aim of the system is to work out a complex diagnosis of an economic problem and write it down in natural language (French), associated with the most interesting statistical tables, as well as any

[1]LCE: Language de Connaissance Economique is a functional software that includes a Common-Lisp dialect.

NATO ASI Series, Vol. F 61
Knowledge, Data and Computer-Assisted Decisions
Edited by M. Schader and W. Gaul

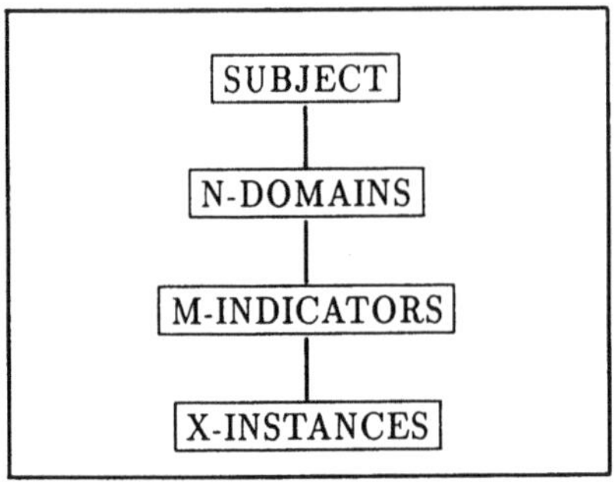

Figure 1: General Organization

human economist could do. SAM can work with any economic data base. The work of SAM is to provide a text that can be used to enlighten the economist in his work, or even be given as raw material outside the statistical institution.

2 A Frame Based Representation

SAM is shaped around a semantic knowledge base organized with hierarchical level and analogic process. We will discuss here the hierarchical organization and the knowledge base.

2.1 A Hierarchical Organization

SAM is organized in subject, domains and indicators. This organization is hierarchical: each subject has n domains and the domains possess indicators. Each indicator can have instances. In this case, the indicator is a class object and only some instance's attributes are set. The others are the same as the class attributes with an inheritance process (see Fig. 1). Each object: subject, domain, indicator is represented inside frames. The frame has 150 slots of information, most of them are arrays, vectors and lists. Any frame can inherit any part from an other with an analogic process. When the subject is a report of the current economic situation in France, the domains are: international economic situation, prices and wages, labor market, finances, consumption, international trade, etc.

In the domain "international situation" the indicators are the international growth rate, the prices, the US balance of payments, the interest rate in the U.S.A. and Federal Republic of Germany (two instances), ... and so forth. When the subject is a short term economic survey of enterprises the domains are the industrial sectors, in each domain we have the production, the demand, the stocks and the prices.

2.2 A Knowledge Base

SAM needs a knowledge base shaped by four elements: numeric data, representation of the world used, heuristics and model of discourse.

2.2.1 The Data

They are found in any database file (from e.g., ADABAS, SAS, TROLL, etc.) used at INSEE.

2.2.2 The Frames

The semantic knowledge is filled inside frames. The frames are forms permitting a changing complex world to be efficiently and adequately represented (Pylyshin (1988)). The frame contains all the semantics used by the system:

- text fragments associated with their appropriate grammar form (this is used in text generation). The fragments can be simple words like nouns, verbs, adjectives, but also sets of words and parts of sentences. The frame knows in each situation what fragment can be used. Most of them have at least three synonyms. Each fragment provides two informations: the syntactic rule to use and the main meaning (the focus);
- units and formats for representing quantitative data (e.g., "million dollars");
- definitions, titles and units for tables, period for statistical series and their name, etc;
- program and formula to calculate the values of the indicators and the changes;
- judgement tables;
- date of the last update of the frame;
- old values and judgement factors for the last 24 periods of analysis (usually the month).

Encoding the fragments and a frame is a tedious task that requires a considerable amount of time and effort since it must be generated by hand. Furthermore, an analogic tool with a question-answering process will be developed (probably an expert system).

2.2.3 The Rules

Different rule bases are present in SAM. 150 rules are used at this time.

- rules about the graphic shape of the series;
- economics rules to modify frames;
- economic rules to add information in the generation step.

All the rules are simple heuristics like:

"IF (list of conditions with AND & OR) THEN (list of actions)".

Economic rules can be set into economic paradigm bases (Keynesian, Neo-classical, ...).

2.2.4 The Schemata

SAM uses types of standard patterns of discourse structure named schemata as in TEXT (McKeown (1985)). A schema is a representation of a standard pattern of discourse structure which encodes the set of communicative techniques that a speaker can use for a particular discourse purpose. It defines a particular organization of future generated text and is used to guide the generation process.

The schemata will be used to decide what is said first, what next and so forth. To construct these a variety of economic texts were examined. We retain the most relevant forms but the base of schemata will grow. There are 20 schemata for indicators at this time. As an example we found level-indicator schema and changes schemata, for each one simple schemata, one contrasted, one compared and one enumerated. A simple level schemata has roughly this pattern:

> <level value and judgement about it> <number of periods with this judgement> <rule about the level> <value and judgement about the most important change> <rule about it> <complement value and judgement> <rule about it> <economic rule>

Such schemata can generate such texts:

> "U.S. current account deficit climbed to 15 billion dollars this month and 33 billion dollars in the last quarter. The deficit for the year is 150 billion dollars. Economists attribute the deficit increase to a credit-induced consumer boom that sucked in a huge volume of imports."
>
> "employment increase of 10,000 jobs in January compared to less than 5000 in the last quarter and 20,000 for the last twelve months."
>
> "oil price on the spot market increase for seven months (17.30 a barrel for May)."

More complex schemata like "contrast" or "enumerate and compare" can generate things like this:

> "interest rates are high in U.S. (7.5%) while they are low in West Germany (3%). However, they have both increased."
>
> "U.S. sales fell in February (0.4% drop). Much of this month's decline was caused by a large fall in car sales and nondurables like food and clothing. Other commercial sales increased."

The schemata information support is a lisp vector and the system uses a transition network during the generation phase. All schemata are recursive descriptions and may be embedded in other schemata.

3 The Action Steps

The SAM process consists of three components:

1. a diagnosis step,

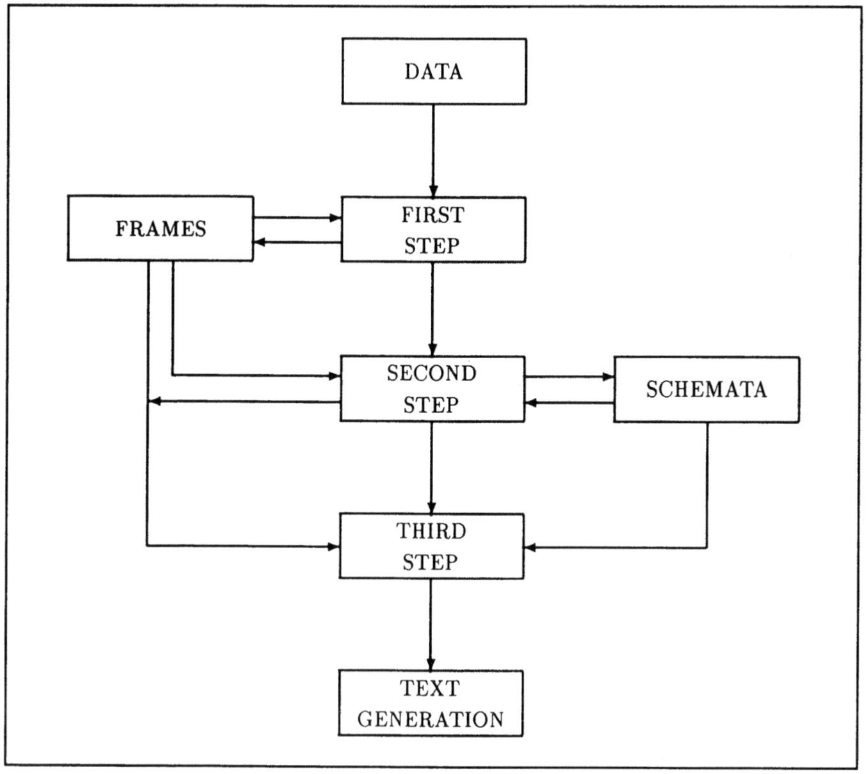

Figure 2: The Action Steps

2. a schemata step, and

3. a generation step.

Each step is done for each domain, and in each domain for each indicator.

3.1 The Diagnosis Step

The task of this process involves

- the search and the calculation of all the current period values for the indicator (level and changes); this is done using the data base and lambda function supported by the frame (Fig. 2),

- the determination of judgement factors about this value; this is carried out by applying values on judgement tables, the results are kept by the frame.

For an indicator the judgement tables are lists of 6 boundary values, from "very low" to "very high" (for the level and the changes of the indicator). The judgements factors are aggregated to determine a global judgement for each domain.

3.2 The Schemata Step

This second step may be broken down into a set of subprocesses:

1. select a schema among an accepted list possessed by the indicator. Each indicator possesses at least one main schema, and sometimes a secondary schema that can be selected in special situations of values or judgement,

2. fill the schema with the more relevant values and judgement factors and with the result of rules matched on the indicator. Sometimes the rule refers back to previous results,

3. infer on economic rules between indicators in different domains. The result fills the schema. For some indicators a link is generated between indicators,

4. determine the relative importance of each indicator. A sort orders the schemata, and in fact the future paragraphs.

3.3 The Generation Step

This third step consists of two phases: determining the pattern of what is to be said, and the natural language generation.

3.3.1 Determining the Textual Shape of What Is To Be Said

Each schemata determines an immediate focus on the future text. Each fragment can have a focus, it is a position in a focus network. Inserting new fragments in the schema can modify the current focus. The focus and the judgement factor are used to avoid repetition of words and to connect fragments and sentences in a coherent discourse. So the program will translate the schema into a deep structure representation of the generated sentence. Example (on a future text):

> <FOCUS: strength of Franc> "The french Franc held near its highest level in seven months against the Deutsche Mark in trading this month (3.39 Francs for one Mark)." but <change the focus> <FOCUS: weakness of Franc> "in one year the Franc loses 10% against the Mark" "this can be explained ..." <same focus>

3.3.2 The Grammar

SAM does not use a general grammar formalism. The fragments encapsulate in each frame the correct use of words, as an example, the concept of "big" involves these possibilities: "strong growth", "large deficit", "high interest rate". The fragments can also be Common Lisp formats and text can be inserted into. The advantages of such a system is a fast generation process and a correct place and correct use of words and sentences in the context of the indicator. The disadvantage is of course a weak flexibility. The fragments can be modified by the use of synonym dictionnaries, concord rules and conjugation of verbs.

3.3.3 Transforming This Message Into Natural Language

Fragments from the frame and from the dictionnaries are composed inside patterns. Dictionnaries are used for grammatical concord (gender, number), special processes handle synonyms to avoid repetition. The generated text is written with the usual printing rules: uppercase after full-stop, space after a punctuation character. The text is right adjusted. The user can choose the margin position and the line length. The titles are centered. Next versions will use all the possibilities of IBM-DCF (Document Composition Facility) and GDDM (Graphic Data Display Manager).

4 Conclusion and Future Directions

SAM is not an exceptionally sophisticated treatment of semantic problems. It provides a powerful computational process of a large quantity of data and knowledge. The system is used for experimentation but it is also in advanced development on a SUN work station.

4.1 The Applications Used

Two applications are being experimented with at this time:

4.1.1 A Sample Survey Output Analysis

The "enquête mensuelle dans l'industrie" (Monthly Enquiry on Industrial Activity) is a panel survey realized by the "Institut National de la Statistique et des Etudes Economiques—INSEE" (French National Statistical Institute, a direction of the French Ministry of Finance). This survey is an european enquiry; so it is realized in each of the 12 countries of the European Community. In France 4000 firms are interviewed every month and the result is a production of 250 values about the national activity, production and orders, stocks and forecasting trends.

In statistics there is a continuous automation in the production process but the computer assistance is limited to the production of data. For this survey (as for others) each month a 15 pages paper of analysis and comments is "hand written" by an economist. He analyzes the 250 new values and the last 12 months old (so about 3000 values). It is a tiring job because he must find the most interesting information. As an experiment SAM gives a similar result in half an hour CPU on IBM 3090 but not all the problems are solved, mainly the introduction of economic rules, memory place and introduction of fine graphics. The final objective is to send back, each month, to the firms that reply to the enquiry a diagnosis about the industrial sector it belongs to.

4.1.2 A Monthly Diagnosis of the French National Economic Situation

The "Banque de données macroéconomiques" (Macroeconomic database) is a very large macroeconomic data bank in use at INSEE and supported by ADABAS. It contains all the time-series dealing with different aspects of economic and social trends, national accounts, both for France and the international environment.

The experiment generates a text of six pages that gives each month a consolidated report on the current French economic situation. Other experiments are expected with

Eurostat and other statistical or economic national and international institutions to write automatic comments in French but also in other languages. In each case the idea is to give the economist the help of an "artificial" assistant, not very intelligent but one that can signal the most important events.

4.2 Possibility of Request for the User

SAM gives at this time a complete text in French (see Appendix). The user cannot ask any questions. One direction is to give an assistant that will provide on any subject it knows, more available information, definitions, explanations about the inference process.

4.3 Cost, Time and Price

The cost of developing the language that supports SAM was 20 man-months of a computer scientist (the language is used for other applications), SAM and the knowledge base for the running prototypes represent 30000 Lisp lines and 10 months work. A diagnosis costs half a CPU minute of time for one page of text on a IBM 3090. The size of the load module is 4 MB, but 8 MB will be needed in the future for a complete application.

Appendix: Sample output of the SAM system (French)

Sample 1: Report of the current economic situation

Avec une valeur limite en Janvier de 3.40 francs pour un mark, la position du franc reste, tout au long de ce dernier semestre, exessivement basse. Durant le dernier semestre, l'évolution du taux de change du franc est orientée dans la direction d'une forte baisse, la chute du franc approche 1%. La tendance est du même ordre pour les douze derniers mois. Le déficit de la balance des paiements américaine est, depuis plus de 12 mois, d'importance (-8.6 milliards de dollars ce mois-ci). Pour le dernier trimestre, le déficit cumulé américain est de l'ordre de 34.5 milliards de dollars et sur l'année écoulée, celui-ci est de 135.6 milliards de dollars. On note cependant une très légère amélioration, vers une réduction du déficit, avec le montant observé ce mois-ci, inférieur à 10 milliards de dollars. L'activité de l'économie de nos partenaires est stable. Sur le dernier trimestre, la progression de l'activité est légèrement inférieure 1%. L' augmentation se confirme depuis deux mois. En un an, la progression de l'activité atteint presque 6%.

Avec une augmentation mensuelle de 0.40%, le rythme de l'inflation chez nos principaux partenaires est, depuis plus de 12 mois consécutifs, très élevé. La tendance observée sur les 5 derniers mois est à une accélération de la hausse.

Le prix du baril de pétrole est à un niveau correct (17.0 dollars le baril en Janvier). Néanmoins, pour le semestre écoulée, l'évolution des prix du baril fait apparaitre une forte tendance à la hausse: l'augmentation du prix du pétrole est supérieure à 13%. Cette hausse est régulièrè depuis 3 mois.

L'indice précurseur aux Etats-unis progresse, depuis 2 mois consécutifs, sensiblement (0.5% ce mois-ci).

Enfin, les taux d'intérêt réels, aussi bien en Allemagne que aux Etats-unis, sont particuliérement forts.

En conclusion, il ressort une situation économique internationale plutot négative (position du franc) avec heureusement des facteurs positifs (indice précurseur aux Etats-unis) (cf. Tab. 1).

LES EVOLUTIONS NOMINALES

Avec une augmentation mensuelle de 0.40%, l'évolution des prix de détail reste, depuis plus de 12 mois, assez sensiblement inflationiste. Pour les douze derniers mois, l'augmentation des prix de détail est

l'environnement international					
	mois	francs pour un mark	balance des paiements	activité de nos partenaires	prix de nos partenaires
Février	1988	3.37	-15.68	106.00	101.68
Mars	1988	3.39	-12.30	107.00	101.98
Avril	1988	3.39	-11.00	106.00	102.32
Mai	1988	3.38	-8.99	107.00	102.58
Juin	1988	3.37	-13.74	108.00	102.87
Juillet	1988	3.37	-10.14	110.00	103.25
Aout	1988	3.38	-11.50	110.00	103.76
Septembre	1988	3.40	-10.60	107.00	104.05
Octobre	1988	3.41	-9.13	111.00	104.37
Novembre	1988	3.41	-11.41	107.00	104.68
Décembre	1988	3.41	-14.45	112.00	104.99
Janvier	1989	3.40	-8.68	112.00	105.45

Table 1: The International Environment

légèrement supérieure à 3%. Cette hausse est régulière et continue depuis un an.

L'augmentation des prix à la consommation, ce mois-ci, a été observé pour tous les secteurs d'activités.

Si l'on fait une analyse plus détaillée des secteurs d'activités on observe que, la variation des prix alimentaires reste, depuis 8 mois, assez nettement en augmentation (0.5% en Janvier). Durant les douze derniers mois, l'augmentation des prix de détail approche 3%. Cette hausse est régulière et continue depuis huit mois.

Avec une augmentation mensuelle de 0.40%, l'évolution des prix manufacturés marque, depuis 2 mois consécutifs, une très sensible progression. Sur l'ensemble des six derniers mois, l'augmentation des prix de détail atteint presque 1%, la tendance observée sur les 4 derniers mois est à une accélération de la hausse. Sur l'ensemble de l'année, la hausse des prix de détail atteint presque 3%. Pour finir, l'évolution des prix des services fait ressortir, depuis plus de 12 mois, une augmentation non négligeable (0.5% en Janvier). Cette hausse est régulière et continue depuis un an.

Les données sur les salaires horaires des ouvriers ne sont pas disponibles à cette périodicité.

En conclusion, il ressort une situation, dans le domaine des salaires et des prix, légèrement inquietante pour l'avenir (cf. Tab. 2).

Sample 2: Comment of a sample survey

Les chefs d'entreprise interrogés à l'enquête indiquent, depuis plus d'un an, que leur activité à connu une sensible augmentation. Au cours des douze derniers mois, la variation de la production est très fortement en progression. Cette hausse est régulirèe et continue depuis un an.

Les stocks de produits finis restent, pour le cinquième mois consécutif, un niveau légèrement inférieur à la normale. Néanmoins, pour les trois derniers mois, le niveau des stocks est faiblement en progression. Les carnets de commande globaux et étrangers se situent, depuis 11 mois, à un niveau relativement élevé. Durant les douze derniers mois, la variation des commande est faiblement en augmentation.

Le niveau relativement bien garnis des carnets, ce mois-ci, peut s'expliquer par le niveau bien garnis des carnets du secteur des biens intermédiaires, du secteur des équipements professionels et du secteur des automobile et transport terrestre. Les carnets de commande globaux et étrangers du secteur des biens de consommation ont joué au contraire en sens inverse.

les évolutions nominales			
	mois	indice des prix	indice des salaires
Février	1988	100.90	
Mars	1988	101.20	
Avril	1988	101.71	102.52
Mai	1988	101.91	
Juin	1988	102.22	
Juillet	1988	102.52	103.34
Aout	1988	102.83	
Septembre	1988	103.04	
Octobre	1988	103.24	104.27
Novembre	1988	103.35	
Décembre	1988	103.55	
Janvier	1989	103.97	

Table 2: The Nominal Developement

A travers une analyse plus fine, par secteurs d'activités, on montre que, les carnets de commande du secteur des biens intermédiaires restent, depuis plus de 12 mois consécutifs, plutôt bien garnis. Il faut cependant remarquer que, sur l'ensemble des trois derniers mois, l'évolution des commandes est très sensiblement en diminution. Les carnets de commande du secteur des équipements professionels restent, depuis un semestre, faiblement garnis. Sur l'ensemble de l'année, la variation des commande est assez sensiblement en augmentation. Les carnets de commande dans le secteur automobile et transport restent, pour le onzième mois consécutif, plutôt bien garnis. En un mois, l'évolution des commandes est faiblement en augmentation. Pour finir, les carnets du secteur des biens de consommation restent, depuis plus d'un an, à un niveau légèrement inférieur la normale. Il importe toutefois de noter que, au cours du mois écoulé, on constate une faible augmentation du niveau des commandes.

Les perspectives de prix, aussi bien selon les industriels interrogés que pour l'ensemble de l'industrie, sont en nette augmentation.

Pour finir, les perspectives de production, aussi bien selon les industriels interrogés que pour l'ensemble de l'industrie, font ressortir une progression non négligeable (cf. Tab. 3).

References

ABELSON, H., and SUSSMAN, G.J. (1985), *Structure and Interpretation of Computer Programs*, The MIT Press, Cambridge, MA.

DANLOS, L. (1985), *Génération automatique de textes en langues naturelles*, Masson, Paris.

MACKEOWN, K.R. (1988), *Text Generation*, Cambridge University Press.

NOGIER, J.F. (1988), Generation automatique de texte: survoi du problème, *Afcet Interfaces, no. 67.*

PYLYSHIN, Z.W. (1986), *The Robot's Dilemma*, Ablex publishing.

ROOS, J.L. (1986), *Logiciel de Connaissances Economiques, Manuel de référence*, Institut National de la Statisitique et des Etudes Economiques.

SIMONIN, N. (1987), *An Approach for Creating Structured Text*, Cap Sogeti, First European Workshop on Language Generation.

	ensemble de l'industrie					
	Nov 88	Déc 88	Jan 89	Fév 89	Mar 89	Avr 89
production	17	22	27	26	20	22
stocks	5	0	-8	-4	0	-1
carnets de commande globaux et étrang.	34	33	29	34	28	19
du secteur des biens intermédiaires	74	67	67	78	52	42
du secteur des équipements professio.	20	29	4	10	18	6
du secteur automobile et transport	41	21	36	37	27	30
du secteur des biens de consommatio.	-15	-13	-8	-15	-24	-12
perspectives de production						
selon les industriels interrogés	18	17	19	12	12	13
pour l'ensemble de l'industrie	18	20	34	24	28	22
perspectives de prix						
selon les industriels interrogés	31	35	25	28	18	25
pour l'ensemble de l'industrie	40	43	44	40	45	46

Table 3: The Industry as a Whole

Index

NATO ASI Series, Vol. F 61
Knowledge, Data and Computer-Assisted Decisions
Edited by M. Schader and W. Gaul

NATO ASI Series F

Including Special Programme on Sensory Systems for Robotic Control (ROB)

Vol. 1: Issues in Acoustic Signal – Image Processing and Recognition. Edited by C. H. Chen. VIII, 333 pages. 1983.

Vol. 2: Image Sequence Processing and Dynamic Scene Analysis. Edited by T. S. Huang. IX, 749 pages. 1983.

Vol. 3: Electronic Systems Effectiveness and Life Cycle Costing. Edited by J. K. Skwirzynski. XVII, 732 pages. 1983.

Vol. 4: Pictorial Data Analysis. Edited by R. M. Haralick. VIII, 468 pages. 1983.

Vol. 5: International Calibration Study of Traffic Conflict Techniques. Edited by E. Asmussen. VII, 229 pages. 1984.

Vol. 6: Information Technology and the Computer Network. Edited by K. G. Beauchamp. VIII, 271 pages. 1984.

Vol. 7: High-Speed Computation. Edited by J. S. Kowalik. IX, 441 pages. 1984.

Vol. 8: Program Transformation and Programming Environments. Report on a Workshop directed by F. L. Bauer and H. Remus. Edited by P. Pepper. XIV, 378 pages. 1984.

Vol. 9: Computer Aided Analysis and Optimization of Mechanical System Dynamics. Edited by E. J. Haug. XXII, 700 pages. 1984.

Vol. 10: Simulation and Model-Based Methodologies: An Integrative View. Edited by T. I. Ören, B. P. Zeigler, M. S. Elzas. XIII, 651 pages. 1984.

Vol. 11: Robotics and Artificial Intelligence. Edited by M. Brady, L. A. Gerhardt, H. F. Davidson. XVII, 693 pages. 1984.

Vol. 12: Combinatorial Algorithms on Words. Edited by A. Apostolico, Z. Galil. VIII, 361 pages. 1985.

Vol. 13: Logics and Models of Concurrent Systems. Edited by K. R. Apt. VIII, 498 pages. 1985.

Vol. 14: Control Flow and Data Flow: Concepts of Distributed Programming. Edited by M. Broy. VIII, 525 pages. 1985.

Vol. 15: Computational Mathematical Programming. Edited by K. Schittkowski. VIII, 451 pages. 1985.

Vol. 16: New Systems and Architectures for Automatic Speech Recognition and Synthesis. Edited by R. De Mori, C.Y. Suen. XIII, 630 pages. 1985.

Vol. 17: Fundamental Algorithms for Computer Graphics. Edited by R.A. Earnshaw. XVI, 1042 pages. 1985.

Vol. 18: Computer Architectures for Spatially Distributed Data. Edited by H. Freeman and G.G. Pieroni. VIII, 391 pages. 1985.

Vol. 19: Pictorial Information Systems in Medicine. Edited by K. H. Höhne. XII, 525 pages. 1986.

Vol. 20: Disordered Systems and Biological Organization. Edited by E. Bienenstock, F. Fogelman Soulié, G. Weisbuch. XXI, 405 pages. 1986.

Vol. 21: Intelligent Decision Support in Process Environments. Edited by E. Hollnagel, G. Mancini, D.D. Woods. XV, 524 pages. 1986.

NATO ASI Series F

Vol. 22: Software System Design Methods. The Challenge of Advanced Computing Technology. Edited by J.K. Skwirzynski. XIII, 747 pages. 1986.

Vol. 23: Designing Computer-Based Learning Materials. Edited by H. Weinstock and A. Bork. IX, 285 pages. 1986.

Vol. 24: Database Machines. Modern Trends and Applications. Edited by A.K. Sood and A.H. Qureshi. VIII, 570 pages. 1986.

Vol. 25: Pyramidal Systems for Computer Vision. Edited by V. Cantoni and S. Levialdi. VIII, 392 pages. 1986. *(ROB)*

Vol. 26: Modelling and Analysis in Arms Control. Edited by R. Avenhaus, R.K. Huber and J.D. Kettelle. VIII, 488 pages. 1986.

Vol. 27: Computer Aided Optimal Design: Structural and Mechanical Systems. Edited by C.A. Mota Soares. XIII, 1029 pages. 1987.

Vol. 28: Distributed Operating Systems. Theory und Practice. Edited by Y. Paker, J.-P. Banatre and M. Bozyiğit. X, 379 pages. 1987.

Vol. 29: Languages for Sensor-Based Control in Robotics. Edited by U. Rembold and K. Hörmann. IX, 625 pages. 1987. *(ROB)*

Vol. 30: Pattern Recognition Theory and Applications. Edited by P.A. Devijver and J. Kittler. XI, 543 pages. 1987.

Vol. 31: Decision Support Systems: Theory and Application. Edited by C.W. Holsapple and A.B. Whinston. X, 500 pages. 1987.

Vol. 32: Information Systems: Failure Analysis. Edited by J.A. Wise and A. Debons. XV, 338 pages. 1987.

Vol. 33: Machine Intelligence and Knowledge Engineering for Robotic Applications. Edited by A.K.C. Wong and A. Pugh. XIV, 486 pages. 1987. *(ROB)*

Vol. 34: Modelling, Robustness and Sensitivity Reduction in Control Systems. Edited by R.F. Curtain. IX, 492 pages. 1987.

Vol. 35: Expert Judgment and Expert Systems. Edited by J.L. Mumpower, L.D. Phillips, O. Renn and V.R.R. Uppuluri. VIII, 361 pages. 1987.

Vol. 36: Logic of Programming and Calculi of Discrete Design. Edited by M. Broy. VII, 415 pages. 1987.

Vol. 37: Dynamics of Infinite Dimensional Systems. Edited by S.-N. Chow and J.K. Hale. IX, 514 pages. 1987.

Vol. 38: Flow Control of Congested Networks. Edited by A.R. Odoni, L. Bianco and G. Szegö. XII, 355 pages. 1987.

Vol. 39: Mathematics and Computer Science in Medical Imaging. Edited by M.A. Viergever and A. Todd-Pokropek. VIII, 546 pages. 1988.

Vol. 40: Theoretical Foundations of Computer Graphics and CAD. Edited by R.A. Earnshaw. XX, 1246 pages. 1988.

Vol. 41: Neural Computers. Edited by R. Eckmiller and Ch. v. d. Malsburg. XIII, 566 pages. 1988.

NATO ASI Series F

Vol. 42: Real-Time Object Measurement and Classification. Edited by A. K. Jain. VIII, 407 pages. 1988. *(ROB)*

Vol. 43: Sensors and Sensory Systems for Advanced Robots. Edited by P. Dario. XI, 597 pages. 1988. *(ROB)*

Vol. 44: Signal Processing and Pattern Recognition in Nondestructive Evaluation of Materials. Edited by C. H. Chen. VIII, 344 pages. 1988. *(ROB)*

Vol. 45: Syntactic and Structural Pattern Recognition. Edited by G. Ferraté, T. Pavlidis, A. Sanfeliu and H. Bunke. XVI, 467 pages. 1988. *(ROB)*

Vol. 46: Recent Advances in Speech Understanding and Dialog Systems. Edited by H. Niemann, M. Lang and G. Sagerer. X, 521 pages. 1988.

Vol. 47: Advanced Computing Concepts and Techniques in Control Engineering. Edited by M. J. Denham and A. J. Laub. XI, 518 pages. 1988.

Vol. 48: Mathematical Models for Decision Support. Edited by G. Mitra. IX, 762 pages. 1988.

Vol. 49: Computer Integrated Manufacturing. Edited by I. B. Turksen. VIII, 568 pages. 1988.

Vol. 50: CAD Based Programming for Sensory Robots. Edited by B. Ravani. IX, 565 pages. 1988. *(ROB)*

Vol. 51: Algorithms and Model Formulations in Mathematical Programming. Edited by S. W. Wallace. IX, 190 pages. 1989.

Vol. 52: Sensor Devices and Systems for Robotics. Edited by A. Casals. IX, 362 pages. 1989. *(ROB)*

Vol. 53: Advanced Information Technologies for Industrial Material Flow Systems. Edited by S. Y. Nof and C. L. Moodie. IX, 710 pages. 1989.

Vol. 54: A Reappraisal of the Efficiency of Financial Markets. Edited by R. M. C. Guimarães, B. G. Kingsman and S. J. Taylor. X, 804 pages. 1989.

Vol. 55: Constructive Methods in Computing Science. Edited by M. Broy. VII, 478 pages. 1989.

Vol. 56: Multiple Criteria Decision Making and Risk Analysis Using Microcomputers. Edited by B. Karpak and S. Zionts. VII, 399 pages. 1989.

Vol. 57: Kinematics and Dynamic Issues in Sensor Based Control. Edited by G. E. Taylor. XI, 456 pages. 1990. *(ROB)*

Vol. 58: Highly Redundant Sensing in Robotic Systems. Edited by J. T. Tou and J. G. Balchen. X, 322 pages. 1990. *(ROB)*

Vol. 59: Superconducting Electronics. Edited by H. Weinstock and M. Nisenoff. X, 441 pages. 1989.

Vol. 60: 3D Imaging in Medicine. Algorithms, Systems, Applications. Edited by K. H. Höhne, H. Fuchs and S. M. Pizer. IX, 460 pages. 1990.

Vol. 61: Knowledge, Data and Computer-Assisted Decisions. Edited by M. Schader and W. Gaul. VIII, 421 pages. 1990.

Vol. 62: Supercomputing. Edited by J. S. Kowalik. X, 425 pages. 1990.

Vol. 63: Traditional and Non-Traditional Robotic Sensors. Edited by T. C. Henderson. VIII, 463 pages. 1990. *(ROB)*

Vol. 64: Sensory Robotics for the Handling of Limp Materials. Edited by P. M. Taylor. IX, 343 pages. 1990. *(ROB)*

Vol. 65: Mapping and Spatial Modelling for Navigation. Edited by L. F. Pau. VIII, 357 pages. 1990. *(ROB)*

MIX
Papier aus verantwortungsvollen Quellen
Paper from responsible sources
FSC® C105338

If you have any concerns about our products,
you can contact us on
ProductSafety@springernature.com

In case Publisher is established outside the EU,
the EU authorized representative is:
Springer Nature Customer Service Center GmbH
Europaplatz 3, 69115 Heidelberg, Germany

Printed by Libri Plureos GmbH
in Hamburg, Germany